HENRY II

The Seal of Henry II (reproduced from a cast in the British Museum; actual size). The seal is double-sided. Above is shown the obverse, portraying the king enthroned and bearing the orb and sceptre. The legend reads: + HENRICUS DEI GRATIA Rex ANGLORUM. Below is shown the reverse on which the king appears mounted and accoutred for war. The legend reads: + HENR(icus) DEI GRA(tia) DUX NORM(annorum et) AQUIT(anorum) ET COM(es) ANDEG(avorum).

Since the seal was double-sided, it could not be impressed upon the face of a document but had to be suspended from it, either on a cord or a parchment 'tag' let through slits in a fold at the bottom of the document, or on a 'tongue' made by not quite severing a strip of parchment from the document itself.

A double-sided seal was produced in a metal matrix of two parts. The attachment cord or parchment tongue was sandwiched between two lumps of sealing-wax (softened by warming), laid upon the engraved face of the lower (reverse) portion of the matrix. The upper (obverse) portion was then laid face down upon the wax and pressure applied.

The sealing-wax was made from two parts of beeswax to one of resin. In Henry II's time a seal might be coloured by coating it with tinted varnish, though it was more usual later to add pigment to the wax itself. Frequently, however, seals were left the natural colour of the wax.

Although it is customary to refer to this seal as a 'Great Seal', there were not, in Henry II's reign, any other smaller seals from which the large seal had to be distinguished. There were, however, two identical pairs of matrices, one held in the chancery that travelled with the king, and the other at the exchequer.

The portrayal of the ruler enthroned on one side of the Great Seal and equestrian on the other, had been the normal practice (with very few exceptions) from the Norman Conquest to the present day. This conventional treatment should not, however, be allowed to obscure the symbolic significance it must still have had in Henry II's day. The king appears in a dual capacity: both as a sovereign, bearing the insignia of royal authority, and in the accoutrements of knighthood, as a characteristic figure of a feudal society.

HENRY II

W. L. Warren

Reader in History at
The Queen's University of Belfast

ἄνδρα μοι ἔννπε, Μοῦςοα, πολύτροπον
Tell me, Muse, of the man of many wiles.
Homer, Odyssey, I, 1.

UNIVERSITY OF CALIFORNIA PRESS
BERKELEY AND LOS ANGELES
1973

UNIVERSITY OF CALIFORNIA PRESS
Berkeley and Los Angeles, California

ISBN: 0–520–02282–3
Library of Congress Catalog Card Number: 72–82220

FOR

Anne

CONTENTS

page

Part III · HENRY II AND THE CHURCH

Part IV · THE ANGEVIN COMMONWEALTH

ILLUSTRATIONS

Acknowledgement and thanks for permission to reproduce the photographs are due to Aerofilms Ltd for plates 2, 3, 4, 6, 8, and 10; to Archives Photographiques, Paris, for plates 5, 25 and 26; to the National Monuments Record, London, for plate 7; to Walters Art Gallery for plate 11; to the Radio Times Hulton Picture Library for plate 12; to the Friends of Canterbury Cathedral for plate 13; to Belzeaux-Zodiaque for plate 14; to the British Museum and Richard Du Cane for the frontispiece and plate 15; to the Public Record Office for plates 16, 17 and 18; to the Dean and Chapter of Westminster for plate 19; to the Dean and Chapter of Lincoln for plate 20; to Foto Marburg for plate 22; and to the British Museum for plate 23.

Plate 1 is from *Norman Britain* by Henry Loyn and Alan Sorrell and is reproduced here by courtesy of Alan Sorrell and Lutterworth Press; plate 9 is Crown Copyright and is reproduced by permission of the Controller of H.M.S.O.; plate 21 is from *The Life of Thomas Becket*, ed. George Greenaway; and plate 24 is from *Medieval Carvings in Exeter Cathedral* by C. J. P. Cave.

All the maps and diagrams were re-drawn from the author's originals by Maureen Verity.

MAPS

DIAGRAMS

ACKNOWLEDGEMENTS

This book has been more than ten years in the making, and I no longer feel confident of being able to identify each of the influences which have shaped my mind upon it. The extensive Bibliography will, I hope, be taken as a recognition of the contribution made by numerous scholars, both living and dead. There are, however, some debts which I must record specifically. To Michael Roberts, Professor of History at The Queen's University of Belfast, I acknowledge myself as a disciple to a master; his inspiration, encouragement, and pungent criticism, have been beyond price. To David Douglas, editor of the series, I am grateful for indulgence and wise advice. To Professor J. C. Holt I am obliged for allowing me to see his article on the texts of Henry II's Assizes before publication, and also for much stimulation in correspondence and discussion. To John Bright-Holmes of Eyre Methuen I owe the deeply valued privilege of personal friendship, as well as the encouragement of a considerate publisher. To others of the staff of Eyre Methuen I am grateful for meticulous assistance in preparing the typescript for the printer; and in particular to Ann Mansbridge for enthusiastic help with the illustrations. My children should receive acknowledgement, too, for bearing with equanimity the intrusion of Henry II into their household throughout their young lives. But the greatest debt is to my wife, Anne, to whom this book is dedicated, and without whom it could never have been written.

The Queen's University   W. L. W.
Belfast 1972

NOTE ON REFERENCES

Full details of all works cited are given in the Bibliography, and abbreviated references employed in the footnotes. Chronicles, and other contemporary works, are normally cited by the name of the author alone. Titles of chronicles and other contemporary works are given (in short form) only (a) if the work is anonymous, or (b) to distinguish different works by the same author. Books and articles by modern authors are normally cited by the surname of the author and short title. The titles of books are printed in italic. The titles of articles are not italicised, but are placed between inverted commas. Details of the journal in which an article is published may be ascertained by reference to the Bibliography under the name of the author.

NOTE ON TRANSLATIONS

Many of the quotations in this book are rather freely translated. Attempts at literal translation all too often result in prose which sounds stilted to the modern ear, and which may obscure the sense and quality of the original. I have, therefore, particularly in translations from narrative sources, endeavoured to convey the meaning and flavour of the original without attempting to reproduce the *ipsissima verba*. Documents are for the most part translated conservatively, though paraphrase has sometimes been employed to render technical or obsolete terms more readily intelligible. If the precise wording of the original is an important consideration, I have endeavoured to translate word for word; and if the interpretation is open to doubt, the Latin has been included within brackets.

PREFACE

No contemporary, it may be suspected, approached King Henry II without trepidation; and anyone who attempts his biography must suffer similar qualms. Nothing about Henry II was predictable, save for the overwhelming force of his formidable personality, and the thunderclaps of his anger when his will was flouted. And although his caustic jibes and wrathful exclamations have come booming down the centuries, no one was more secretive than he about his intentions and motives. He was an enigma in his own day, and has excited widely differing opinions among historians ever since.

Moreover, the tireless energy of Henry II in pursuit of several objectives at once, which continually astonished contemporaries, also presents his biographer with a perplexing variety of interwoven, but distinct themes. Henry's efforts to bring order and organisation to diverse dominions may be considered together with his relations with his overlord in France as one theme; but this is quite distinct from his relations with Wales, Scotland, and Ireland. The story of his dealings with England has a different character altogether, for its chief interest lies in the reconstruction of an English government which had unique traditions. And as for his relations with the Church, and his notorious quarrel with Thomas Becket, that is a tale which can be, and indeed often has been, told on its own.

This multiplicity of diverse themes presents the writer of a book about Henry II with a serious problem, for the several stories proceed not consecutively but concurrently, and are interrelated. If the historian, however, attempts to combine them into a single chronological narrative, he finds himself having to set aside one story in the middle to take up another, and in chasing many hares catches none. But if, alternatively, he attempts to separate the themes and pursue them one by one, he parts company with Henry II, the essence of whose problem was that he had to deal with them all at once.

These difficulties account for the somewhat unusual construction of this book. The first two chapters deal with the period before Henry of Anjou became king of England. The long chapter which follows is the narrative core of the book, in which are surveyed the major events of thirty years. The chief concern in this chapter is Henry's chief concern

– the integrity of his dominions and his pursuit of the rights of lordship – but into this story are woven the other main themes, briefly, and in their proper chronological order. These other themes are then taken up again in subsequent chapters, for separate and more detailed examination. Finally, in Part Four, the later years of the reign are considered, during which it was the activities of the king's sons, rather than Henry's own initiative, which largely determined the course of events. This plan makes some repetition unavoidable; but in this way, it is hoped, the relationship of events in time may be made plain, while allowing for the examination in depth of each of the major themes and the problems it presents.

Part I

POLITICS

Chapter 1

PROLOGUE

At twilight on 25 November 1120, Henry I, king of England and duke of Normandy, set out with all his household to cross the Channel from Barfleur. The last to embark were the younger members of the royal entourage, including the sons of the barons who, as was customary, were receiving instruction in chivalry at the court of their lord. They had at their disposal the swiftest vessel of the king's fleet, and believing that they would soon overtake the rest, they delayed putting to sea while they caroused on the shore. The crew too broached the wine, so that it was a merry if somewhat unsteady company which launched the vessel after dark. There was no more than a gentle breeze and a calm sea, so they might have sailed to England as safely as the king himself if the drunken helmsman had not put the ship's head hard upon a rock in the bay. Panic took charge. Attempts to push free with boathooks and oars made the situation worse, and the vessel began rapidly to fill with water. Some abandoned ship and rowed away in the dinghy, but put back to pick up one of the king's young illegitimate daughters, and so many other people tried to clamber aboard that it too sank. Only one man, clinging all night to the mast of the wreck, survived to tell the tale.[1] The loss of the *White Ship* caused as much consternation in the twelfth century as did the loss of the *Titanic* in the twentieth. It was even more calamitous, for, in addition to the bereavement of many noble families, the fortunes of both England and France were shaken in that shipwreck.

At the beginning of the twelfth century the future of the kingdom of France was uncertain. The descendants of Hugh Capet, who had taken the crown from the Carolingians in 987, called themselves kings of France, but in practice they controlled little more than the immediate neighbourhood of Orleans, Sens, and Paris. Monarchy itself was not despised, for it had its place in the order of things. Without it men would have been at a loss to know whence they derived the authority they

[1] William of Malmesbury, *De Gestis Regum Anglorum*, II, 496–7; Henry of Huntingdon, 242–3; Eadmer, *Historia Novorum*, 288–9; Orderic Vitalis, IV, 412–18.

themselves claimed – a feudal society needed a feudal suzerain. When necessary, and not too inconvenient, the great vassals would perform such services to their suzerain as custom required, if only to set a good example to their own vassals. The early Capetian kings, for their part, wisely did not make too many demands. They did not over-rate their own importance and realised that if they embarrassed their greater vassals they might have to suffer humiliation. They contented themselves with formal recognition and left their greater vassals alone. The greater vassals fought their own wars, made their own alliances, and tried to impose their will upon their provinces as if they were autonomous rulers. For a long time most of them were not very successful, for as with the Capetian kings, their real power did not measure up to the authority they claimed. Sometimes indeed power was so sub-divided that the only effective rulers appeared to be the local lords who controlled a castle and commanded the loyalty of a few knights and men-at-arms.

Appearances of anarchy are, however, deceptive; and by the end of the eleventh century a power structure was beginning to emerge which, if it did not yet promise stability, was at least soundly based on those economic, geographical, demographic, and military realities which may for a time be obscured, but which will always in the end shape political destinies. The Capetian kings, painstaking and thrifty, had for several generations devoted their attention to reducing to real subjection their immediate vassals of the Ile de France and the Orleanais, and had extended themselves to the east and south to become at last a power to be reckoned with. But their hopes of appearing as the effective overlords of the realm were inhibited by the emergence of powerful feudatories in the west.

The counts of Poitou had linked themselves to Bordeaux and had drawn together the old Carolingian provinces of Aquitaine and Gascony into a great duchy covering much of central and south-west France. But the duchy of Aquitaine, as they called it, though impressively large, was not in practice a major power. The counts of Poitou had neglected to build for themselves a secure enough base for their authority, and their grand duchy was in truth a somewhat shaky house of cards. Their claim to overlordship of the whole of the south was successfully resisted by the counts of Toulouse, who themselves managed to establish a precarious hegemony over all the Mediterranean estuaries of France. Moreover, although Aquitaine was culturally the foremost province of France, it was, in economic development, falling behind the more barbarous north.

Slowly but surely the balance of economic advantage was swinging in favour of the inhabitants of north-western Europe. Responsible for this at bottom were improvements in agricultural technique which enabled the northerners to take advantage of their richer soils and more evenly spread rainfall. The three-field system of crop-rotation, with spring as well as autumn sowings, and the heavier cropping of oats and barley, peas, beans, and lentils (with their invaluable addition of vegetable protein to the diet), promoted a rise in population. The evidence is too scanty from which to derive the shape of the demographic curve, but there can be no doubt that the developments which were to transform France into the most populous kingdom for its size in Europe were already well established by the twelfth century. It was this expansion of population which made possible, and encouraged, the opening up of the primaeval forest which still covered much of northern Europe. It was surplus population which made the northern Franks the mainstay of the crusading movement, filled the cathedral schools with scholars eager for self-advancement, promoted the development of communities of urban artisans, and made available men who would offer their services as mercenaries to anyone who could afford to hire them.[1]

The manorial economy which characterised much of northern France was, at the time, an efficient agency for the more intensive cultivation of the land and for the absorption of the forest into the productive area, bringing ever greater profits to the military caste which controlled it. The castles which sprang for the defence as well as the exploitation of the labouring peasants seemed for a time to imply the fragmentation of political authority, for the well-found castle could defy contemporary methods of assault. It was for this reason that eleventh-century France seemed anarchic. But private war was not, as it often appears, merely the indulgence of the warlike instincts of a warrior class; it was a means of making quick profits in an age which had yet barely learned how to make long-term ones, and it established a local pecking order out of which a more soundly based political order could grow.

The coalescing, absorption, or conquest of neighbouring fiefs provided some eight or nine growth points for what Professor Le Patourel

[1] For the background to the situation in France in the early twelfth century, *see* Beryl Smalley, 'Capetian France', in *France: Government and Society*, ed. Wallace-Hadrill and McManners, 61–82; Southern, *The Making of the Middle Ages*, esp. 81–95; Feuchère, 'Essai sur l'evolution territoriale des principaultés française'; Jarry, *Provinces et Pays de France*; Boussard, 'La vie en Anjou au xie et xiie siècles'; Latouche, *The Birth of Western Economy*, Pt IV, ch. 3; White, *Medieval Technology and Social Change*; Duby, *Rural Economy and Country Life in the Medieval West*.

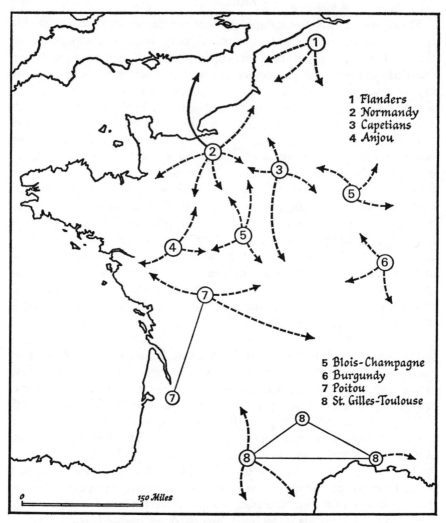

1 Flanders
2 Normandy
3 Capetians
4 Anjou

5 Blois-Champagne
6 Burgundy
7 Poitou
8 St. Gilles-Toulouse

0   150 Miles

I The growth points of feudal empires
Note: The arrows are general indications only

has aptly called 'feudal empires' in eleventh-century France.[1] Of these the most politically important were Blois, Anjou, and Normandy, and it was these which provided the direct obstacle to Capetian ascendancy. Blois for a long time appeared the most formidable, as its counts, closely linked by family ties with the counts of Champagne, who controlled the important commercial centre of Troyes, assembled fiefs which threatened to ring the royal demesne and curtail Capetian expansion. But although Blois appeared the most formidable, Anjou had even better prospects for development since it commanded the rich valleys of the tributaries of the Loire which met at Angers. Anjou, however, was repeatedly shaken by the determined resistance of its prosperous vassals to discipline, and by the vicissitudes of its counts. The duchy of Normandy, although rather better disciplined than the others, was probably poorer and certainly less well-placed for expansion, and it may well have seemed that the ambitions of its dukes could be contained by Anjou, Blois, and the Capetian royal house – until, that is, the whole power structure of northern France was drastically altered by that daring and astonishingly successful adventure, the Norman conquest of England.

The acquisition of the English throne probably made the Normans for the moment less dangerous to their neighbours. Their hold upon England was only slowly consolidated, and even in Henry I's day their influence was thinly spread north of the Humber, and could barely encompass control of Wales. But after 1066 no one in France could ignore the effect which the new-found wealth of the Normans could exert on the balance of power. The Angevins and the Capetians were the most affected. The Angevins had long disputed control of the county of Maine with the dukes of Normandy. For the counts of Anjou it was vital to hold the triangle formed by Angers, Le Mans, and Tours if they were to maintain effective control of the northern valleys of the Loire. To the Capetians the fact that the dukes of Normandy had obtained a crown was itself insupportable, and it spurred them to more active intervention in the politics of the provinces. The link between the duchy of Normandy and the kingdom of England was not, however, necessarily permanent. William the Conqueror had not intended it to be so, and at his death had divided his dominions between two of his three sons. But William Rufus and Henry had reversed their father's intention by wresting control of the duchy from their older brother, Robert Curthose, and denying the succession to his son, William Clito. It was only to be expected that the Capetians favoured separation and

[1] Le Patourel, 'The Plantagenet dominions'.

mustered all the help they could behind Robert and his son. Alone the Capetians were not formidable opponents, but in hostility to the Normans they could call on allies. The counts of Flanders were powerful allies, but capricious, for much of their prosperity rested on trading links with England. The counts of Anjou were more resolute, although primarily concerned for their own advantage.

Henry I achieved his ambition of firmly uniting the kingdom of England and the duchy of Normandy, but only with difficulty and after many years of campaigning against the partisans of his brother and nephew. The interventions of the Capetians and Angevins were repulsed; but defensive victories could not alone ensure the security of Normandy. There were two particularly vulnerable places in its defences. One was the marchland in the Seine valley, known as the Vexin, midway between the rival cities of Rouen and Paris. It was here that Normans and Capetians confronted one another, and that their hostility found expression in the struggle for control of a border castle or a bend in the river. It was here, therefore, that Henry I concentrated the most impressive of his many fortifications. The other danger zone was on the border with Maine. Here most of the ground was inhospitable watershed, but there was a gap which gave ready access to the valley of the Orne, to Falaise, and to the heartland of the duchy. The castle of Argentan guarded the northern end of this gap, whence the rivers flowed to the Channel; and the castle of Alençon guarded the southern end, whence the rivers flowed to the Loire. But Alençon was exposed and Henry's hold on it insecure, and its temporary loss or the defection of its custodian more than once jeopardised the security of Normandy. Henry could not be content until the approaches to it were in trustworthy hands – and that meant control of Maine or at least of Le Mans. It was here, however, that the Angevins triumphed. Count Fulk V of Anjou married the heiress of Maine and consolidated his hold on the county. It was this fact which determined Henry I's policy.

King Henry was not without an ally in the defence of Normandy. If the king of France could call with confidence upon the help of the count of Anjou, Henry could with equal confidence rely on the help of the count of Blois. Greater Blois (incorporating the Dunois and Chartres) was a buffer between Anjou and the royal demesne; but Blois had lost to Anjou in the struggle for control of Tours and its power was on the wane. In practice the help of Normandy was more useful to Blois than was the help of Blois to Normandy. Henry I, however, knew better than to depend on the help of allies. Bribery, intrigue, and the combination

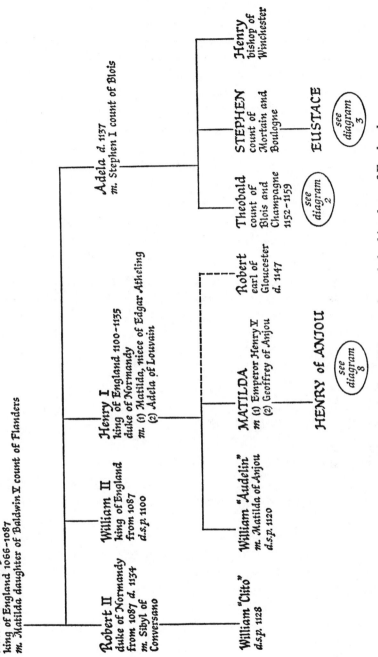

William I
duke of Normandy
king of England 1066–1087
m. Matilda daughter of Baldwin V count of Flanders

Robert II
duke of Normandy
from 1087 d. 1134
m. Sibyl of
Conversano

William II
king of England
from 1087
d.s.p. 1100

Henry I
king of England 1100–1135
duke of Normandy
m. (1) Matilda, niece of Edgar Atheling
(2) Adela of Louvain

Adela d. 1137
m. Stephen I count of Blois

William "Clito"
d.s.p. 1128

William "Audelin"
m. Matilda of Anjou
d.s.p. 1120

MATILDA
m (1) Emperor Henry V
(2) Geoffrey of Anjou

Robert
earl of
Gloucester
d. 1147

Theobald
count of
Blois and
Champagne
1152–1159

STEPHEN
count of
Mortain and
Boulogne

Henry
bishop of
Winchester

HENRY of ANJOU

see
diagram
8

see
diagram
2

EUSTACE

see
diagram
3

1. Contenders for the duchy of Normandy and the kingdom of England

of the two known as diplomacy, were his preferred weapons. In a lifetime of diplomatic manœuvring he achieved two spectacular *coups*. One was to persuade Pope Calixtus II to abandon the just claims of William Clito; the other was to detach Anjou from its Capetian alliance. In June 1119 Henry married his only legitimate son and heir presumptive, William Audelin, to the daughter of Count Fulk V of Anjou. Maine was to be the dowry of the bride. The marriage alliance had

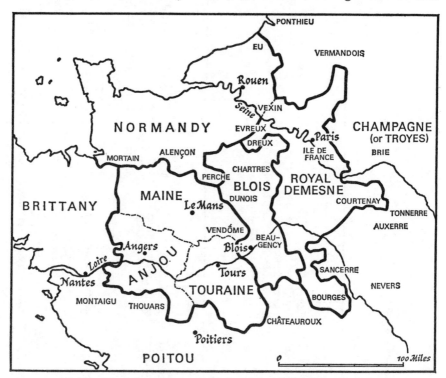

II The feudal empires of the Loire and the Seine, c. 1135

been mooted as early as 1113, but Count Fulk had vacillated. Like Henry, Fulk had to struggle with recalcitrant barons, but unlike Henry he felt the lure of the Holy Land. While Maine remained a bone of contention with his Norman neighbours, he did not feel free to depart; but whether his interests were best served by an alliance with the Capetians or an alliance with the Normans was an open question. Tradition pulled him one way, Henry's growing ascendancy the other. In 1119 he made up his mind, married his daughter to the heir of Normandy, and departed on crusade. For Henry I, self-made king of England and self-made duke of Normandy, this was a moment of triumph. The struggle for Normandy was still not quite won, but the future seemed assured: Anjou was neutralised, Maine secured by a satisfactory compromise, his dynasty established. In January 1120, William Audelin was formally presented to the Norman barons as their future overlord and received their homage. In November he was drowned in the wreck of the *White Ship*.

Henry I spent much of the rest of his life scheming to rebuild his grand design. Although he had sired numerous bastards, his only surviving legitimate offspring was his daughter Matilda, who in 1114 had been married to Emperor Henry V of Germany. He himself was a widower; and though he married again, the marriage was childless. Fortunately for King Henry, the emperor died in time to save his desire to be succeeded by his own legitimate blood. In September 1126 he recalled his widowed daughter from Germany, against her wishes, and despite, it is said, appeals from the princes of the Empire. In January 1127 he publicly recognised her as his successor, and required his barons to swear fealty to her. A few months later he retrieved the Angevin alliance by having her marry Count Fulk's son and heir, Geoffrey Plantagenet. As a marriage alliance this was, however, of an entirely different character from the earlier match, for whereas that merely settled the future of Maine, this implied that Anjou and Normandy were to be united under the rule of the heir of Anjou. The Anglo-Norman barons were hostile to the marriage; and the bride herself was reluctant, for she was twenty-five and the widow of an emperor, while her new husband was fourteen and the son of a count. They were an ill-assorted pair and the marriage seems never to have developed deeper roots than those of political convenience. Nevertheless they did what their parents expected of them. On 4 March 1133 at Le Mans, Matilda gave birth to a son. He was christened Henry.[1] Subsequently, she was safely delivered of two more sons: Geoffrey, born in June 1134, and William, born in August 1136. When an inheritance was at stake it was desirable to have a quiverful of sons, for infant mortality was high and the afflictions of adolescence frequently fatal. In this case, however, the precaution was unnecessary. Henry, the firstborn, survived to manhood, and to become duke of Normandy, count of Anjou, duke of Aquitaine – and king of England. His birth was the contrivance of his grandfather and namesake; but whether he would be allowed to fulfil his grandfather's intentions was to remain for twenty years in doubt.

[1] *Actus Pontificum Cenomannis in Urbe Degentium*, ch. 36; Orderic Vitalis, IV, 9; Robert de Torigny, 123.

Chapter 2

THE PURSUIT OF AN INHERITANCE
(1135–54)

Henry I, king of England and duke of Normandy, died on 1 December
1135. His throne was taken not, as he had planned, by his daughter
Matilda, but by his nephew, Stephen of Blois. It was the will of the
most influential of the barons that it should be so, despite the promises
King Henry had extracted from them to recognise Matilda as his
successor.

There were several reasons why the barons should have wished to set
Matilda aside. She was a stranger to most of them, almost a foreigner,
and what little was known of her endeared her to no one. She had been
taken to the imperial court when barely eight years old and groomed as
a future empress, speaking only German and learning the punctilios
of a rigid court etiquette which was alien to Norman tradition. She
was a strikingly handsome woman, but haughty and domineering,
expecting devotion as her due instead of trying to earn it – the very
archetype of a *belle dame sans merci*. But her greatest handicap was simply
that she was a woman. There was no precedent known to the Normans
for the rule of a woman. Their family law and land law taught them to
expect that all her property and rights would be at the disposal of her
husband.[1] Matilda's marriage to Geoffrey of Anjou was repugnant.
To judge from their chroniclers, Normans were brought up to believe
that the Angevins were barbarians who desecrated churches, slew
priests, looted indiscriminately, and ate like beasts.[2] Henry I's policy
of neutralising the threat from Anjou by a marriage alliance was not
widely understood: he was a wilful man and had not, it seems, taken
any pains to justify it to his barons.[3] Nor had he sought their consent to
the match: he thrust it at them as a *fait accompli* and demanded their
oaths of acceptance. As the author of *Gesta Stephani* relates, King Henry
had 'in that thunderous voice which none could resist rather compelled than invited men to take the oath'.[4] It is indeed unlikely that

---

[1] Cf. *Glanvill*, VI. 3, 60.   [2] Cf. Orderic Vitalis, V, 69, 73.
[3] Cf. William of Malmesbury, *Historia Novella*, 2.
[4] *Gesta Stephani*, 7; William of Malmesbury, *Historia Novella*, 5.

Henry I could have obtained free consent to the Angevin marriage, for those who had grown rich and powerful in King Henry's service must have had grave misgivings as to Count Geoffrey's attitude towards them. They had grown rich and powerful on the forfeiture of those who had sided with William Clito, whose cause the Angevins had espoused. The 'disinherited' would expect their reward when the count of Anjou controlled the lands which had once been theirs.[1] Geoffrey was apparently under no illusion as to the reluctance of the Norman barons to observe their oaths to his wife, and demanded from his father-in-law custody of strategic castles in Normandy. This Henry was reluctant to grant, and Count Geoffrey was making war on Normandy to try to gain possession of the castles he desired at the very time of the old king's unexpected death.[2]

Much more acceptable as candidates for the throne than Matilda and her husband were the surviving grandsons of William the Conqueror. One of them was Henry I's bastard son, Robert earl of Gloucester. The others were sons of Henry I's sister, Adela, who had been married in 1081 to the count of Blois. It was this marriage which formed the bond in the alliance of Blois with Normandy for survival against the Capetians and Angevins. Adela's husband had been killed at the battle of Ramleh on the First Crusade, and it was her influence which for many years guided the destiny of Blois and the policy of the young Count Theobald. Her younger sons, Henry and Stephen, were recommended to the patronage of their uncle, the king of England. Henry, trained as a monk at the great abbey of Cluny, the nursery of influential churchmen, was in 1126 made abbot of Glastonbury, and three years later given the bishopric of Winchester. Stephen was brought up at King Henry's court, and as he grew to manhood was endowed by his uncle with lands forfeited by rebels: the county of Mortain on the border with Brittany, the honors of Eye and Lancaster in England, and the towns of Alençon and Séez in the marcherlands of Maine. In 1125 his uncle arranged for him to marry the only daughter and heiress of the count of Boulogne, who besides being descended from Charlemagne and closely related to the crusader kings of Jerusalem, controlled the important Channel port of Wissant, and held extensive lands in England.[3] In his standing at King Henry's court, Count Stephen had only one peer, and that was

[1] This is a point made by Davis, *King Stephen*, 14.
[2] Orderic Vitalis, V, 45; Robert de Torigny, 125, 128.
[3] She brought him also a connection with the ancient royal house of England, for her grandmother was Margaret, sister of Edgar Atheling and wife to King Malcolm III of Scotland, *see* Diagram 10, p. 176.

Robert earl of Gloucester. When the barons came to take the oath to Matilda in 1126 the two had disputed as to which of them should swear next after the bishops and King David of Scotland. Robert's power had indeed been built up as a counterpoise to Stephen's, and he had been endowed with lordships of almost equal value principally in the west country in England, and in Normandy.[1] Stephen was successful in pressing his claim to precedence in 1126, but his influence later waned as the alliance with Anjou came to supplant the alliance with Blois in the old king's mind.

Hesitating to decide between closely matched rivals, such as Count Stephen and Earl Robert, many barons seemed to have favoured the claims of Count Theobald of Blois; but Stephen surprised everyone by taking decisive action. As soon as he heard of the death of King Henry he swiftly crossed the Channel to England, secured the support of the leading citizens of London, took possession of the royal treasury at Winchester, and presented himself for coronation before the archbishop of Canterbury. The archbishop's hesitation to break his oath to Matilda was overborne by the timely arrival of Hugh Bigod, a powerful baron of East Anglia and one of the stewards of the old king's household, who publicly swore that on his deathbed King Henry had released the barons from their oath and designated Stephen as his successor. Stephen was anointed king on 22 December 1135, a mere three weeks after King Henry's death.[2] Meanwhile the barons of Normandy had been deliberating about their choice of an alternative to Matilda, and had proclaimed Count Theobald as their duke; but no sooner had they done so than news arrived of the coronation in England. The barons wavered, for they had no wish to jeopardise their English estates by a divided allegiance.[3] Theobald was affronted by his brother's presumption but allowed himself to be placated and withdrew.

Stephen's *coup d'état* routed all his rivals. The swiftness and efficiency with which it was carried out strongly suggests that it was planned in advance of the old king's death; and there can be little doubt that the chief agent, and probably inspirer of it, was Stephen's brother Henry, the bishop of Winchester.[4] Winchester was at the time the administra-

[1] For the value of Robert's lands, *see* Patterson, 'William of Malmesbury's Robert of Gloucester', 994 n.1, and for Stephen's, Davis, *King Stephen*, 8–9 and 14 n.2. For the erection of Robert as a counterpoise to Stephen, *see* Southern, 'The place of Henry I in English history', 135 n.1.

[2] William of Malmesbury, *Historia Novella*, 14–16; *Gesta Stephani*, 2–4; Henry of Huntingdon, 256, 270; Gervase of Canterbury, I, 94–5; John of Salisbury, *Historia Pontificalis*, 84.   [3] Orderic Vitalis, V, 56; Robert de Torigny, 128–9.

[4] William of Malmesbury, *Historia Novella*, 15.

tive centre of the realm, and Henry had won over not only the custodian of the royal castle and treasury there, but also the man who was the lynchpin of the government of England, Roger bishop of Salisbury. 'He was second only to the king' wrote Henry of Huntingdon.[1] During Henry I's frequent absences abroad Roger's name alone was sufficient to authenticate royal writs. Several of the principal officers of govern-

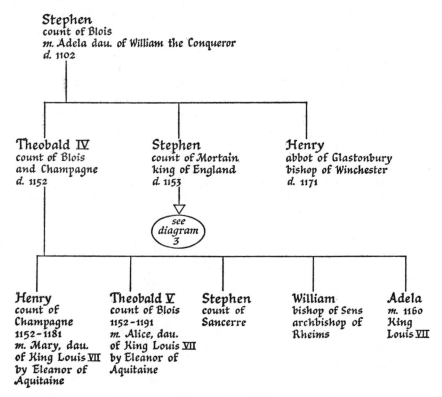

2. The house of Blois

ment were his kinsmen; most of its local agents, the sheriffs, were his nominees, and many of them his protégés. His reasons for allowing himself to be won to the cause of Stephen are unknown, but it may be surmised that he expected that the administrative class fostered by Henry I, able, ruthless, powerful, but for the most part lowly-born, would not survive Matilda's Germanic notions of aristocracy nor stand against the revenge of the 'disinherited', whom Geoffrey might be

[1] Anglo-Saxon Chronicle, 251 (AD 1122); Henry of Huntingdon, 245; cf. William of Newburgh, I, 36, and West, *The Justiciarship in England*, 16ff.

expected to favour. King Henry's servants had ruthlessly engineered the downfall of those suspected of conspiracy against their master, and had picked over the spoils of their forfeitures. The Angevin marriage alliance had, Bishop Roger claimed, been none of his making; as William of Malmesbury, a contemporary chronicler, reports, 'I myself have often heard Roger bishop of Salisbury say that he was released from the oath he had taken to the empress because he had sworn only on condition that the king should not give his daughter in marriage to anyone outside the kingdom without consulting himself and the other chief men, and that no one had recommended that marriage or been aware that it would take place except Robert earl of Gloucester, and Brian FitzCount, and the bishop of Lisieux.'[1] Stephen, on the other hand, was a man who had himself profited by the ruination of those whom the old king feared, and could be expected to preserve the new order from any attempt at a *revanche* by the old. Secondly, Henry of Blois persuaded the leaders of the clergy that his brother's accession would be for the good of the Church, and he himself went surety for Stephen's promise to restore and maintain the Church's liberty.[2] It must have seemed, indeed, a golden opportunity to put into practice the notion, assiduously fostered by the abbey of Cluny, of the Christian commonwealth managed by pious laymen under the guidance and inspiration of Cluniac monk-bishops. The brothers of Blois, the bishop and the king, were a ready-made vehicle of such a conception.[3] Cluniac influence ran strongly in the family of Blois, for not only was Bishop Henry himself a Cluniac monk but their mother, Adela, had ended her days as a Cluniac nun.

The support of the Londoners is to be explained by the sympathetic attitude Stephen displayed towards commercial interests. This was unusual in a baron of the day, but Stephen had gained exceptional experience of the value of trade as Count of Boulogne. The port of Wissant gave Boulogne much of its strategic and economic importance and was the chief port of entry for English wool en route for the weaving towns of Flanders.[4]

None of this, of course, won for Stephen the allegiance of the barons of England, but it put him in a commanding position. Moreover, his coronation, though hastily arranged and attended by only a handful of

---

[1] William of Malmesbury, *Historia Novella*, 5.

[2] *Ibid.*, 15.

[3] Cf. Davis, *King Stephen*, 18–20.

[4] Cf. *ibid.*, 10–12. Davis points out that Boulogne was then relatively more important than it is now, for sandbanks blocked what were later to be the rival ports of Calais, Dunkirk, and Ostend.

nobles, made him the Lord's anointed, and put rebellion or resistance under the taint of treason. It nullified too any lingering anxiety men may have felt about the oaths they had taken to recognise Matilda. At first hesitantly, but then hastily, the barons accepted a *fait accompli* and tendered their fealty and homage. One of the last to do so was Robert earl of Gloucester.

Fate was unkind to Robert of Gloucester. If he had not had the wrong mother he would have been unquestioned king of England on his father's death, and the claims of Matilda and the pretensions of Stephen would have been unknown to history. By all the evidence he was well fitted to rule. He was a man of honour, generosity, and dignity. He was cultured and sagacious. His grandfather, William the Conqueror, was a bastard too; but William the Conqueror had lived in an age before the Church had taken up a moral crusade. Society still treated high-born bastards with sympathy, but it no longer accorded them rights. It seems that fundamentally Robert of Gloucester was loyal to his half-sister and loyal to his oath – he was later to endure much on her behalf when he might better have protected his own interests; but in April 1136 he did what then seemed unavoidable: he accepted Stephen as king. He submitted conditionally, 'that is to say,' wrote William of Malmesbury, 'for as long as the king maintained his rank unimpaired and kept the agreement, since having long observed the king's disposition he foresaw that he would be likely to break his word'.[1] That he submitted at all, however, and maintained his allegiance to Stephen for three years, was to Matilda a source of grievance and disappointment; but it is also an indication of the weakness of her cause.

It is somewhat surprising that Henry I had done so little to entrench his daughter and her husband in power before his death, and it may indicate his repentance of the match. King Henry desired an Angevin alliance to thwart his enemies, but he showed no more enthusiasm for Geoffrey of Anjou than did his barons, and little more for his daughter. Geoffrey was gay and dashing, the hero of many early tales of chivalry, and a man who won his way through constant difficulties by his cleverness, charm, and courage. But the charm was shallow, the cleverness devoted to selfish ends.[2] He made no secret of the fact that he valued his marriage to a widow eleven years his senior for no other reason than it would enable him to gain control of Normandy. He made no secret either of his impatience for King Henry's death. Henry's refusal to

[1] William of Malmesbury, *Historia Novella*, 18.
[2] Cf., e.g., John de Marmoutier, Historia Gaufredi, 183–99; Kate Norgate, *England under the Angevin Kings*, I, 260–5.

allow Geoffrey custody of the castles in Normandy, which had in fact been promised at the time of the marriage, was probably more than mere resentment, or the cantankerousness of a selfish old man, for it seems likely that he hoped to defer the ambitions of Geoffrey until his grandson and namesake was old enough to receive the bestowal of the duchy and the kingdom.[1] But death overtook him too soon. All that he did for his daughter was to require the barons to take oaths to her. It should be recognised, however, that the oaths were of more force than the barons cared to admit. The king had required them to swear three times: in 1126, shortly after Matilda's return from Germany, in 1131 after her marriage to Geoffrey of Anjou, and in 1133 after the birth of her first son.[2] The argument which William of Malmesbury attributes to Roger of Salisbury, that the marriage had abrogated the oath of 1126, was therefore worthless. The alternative argument that the oaths had been given under duress was captious: that men went in fear of King Henry's displeasure was doubtless true, but that does not amount to compulsion. Decisive in the acceptance and coronation of Stephen by the archbishop of Canterbury was the testimony of Hugh Bigod that on his deathbed the king had released the barons from their oath to Matilda; but it was testimony which failed to stand up to investigation. Matilda appealed to the pope against the coronation, and her advocates alleged that Hugh Bigod had not even been present at the time. The allegation was never, so far as is known, effectively rebutted, and no witness who was undeniably at the deathbed of Henry I was ever brought forward to corroborate Bigod's testimony. Stephen's advocates, indeed, were reduced to the dubious argument that Matilda was in any case unworthy of consideration since she was the offspring of an incestuous union and that her mother was a professed nun. This was hardly an argument which could survive a reminder that Henry I's marriage had been solemnised by the saintly Archbishop Anselm.[3]

The oaths were crucial for Matilda. She later claimed hereditary right, but this was because the oaths failed her. In charters she com-

---

[1] Cf. Kate Norgate, *op. cit.*, 269–70.

[2] William of Malmesbury, *Historia Novella*, 3–5; Roger of Howden, *Chronica*, I, 187.

[3] The date of the hearing before the papal curia is uncertain. Round argued for 1136 in his *Geoffrey de Mandeville*, Appendix B, Poole for 1139 in his edition of the *Historia Pontificalis* of John of Salisbury, Appendix VI. It is possible that there was more than one hearing. Detailed but somewhat differing reports of the arguments advanced are provided by John of Salisbury, *op. cit.*, 83ff., and by Gilbert Foliot, *Letters and Charters*, No. 26, 60–6 (cf. Davis, 'Henry of Blois and Brian FitzCount'). These reports are analysed by Cronne, *The Reign of Stephen*, 89–93, and Chartrou, *L' Anjou de 1109 à 1151*, 42ff.

monly described herself as *regis Henrici filia*, and her son, before he became king, styled himself 'Henry son of the daughter of King Henry and right heir of England and Normandy'.[1] In reality there was no ground for claiming that the English crown should descend by right to the nearest blood relative. Kinship with the royal family was undoubtedly a factor in influencing the choice of successor, but an element of choice remained. The principle of primogeniture was not yet fully established in feudal law, and questions of precedence of blood could still arouse sharp disagreements. It is true that in the succession to the French throne the eldest surviving son had followed father since 987, but luck, the indifference of the barons, and the prudence of French kings in having their sons crowned in their own lifetime all played a part in this, and it is doubtful if it could be said that an inflexible principle had thereby been established. In Germany attempts to establish an hereditary monarchy had made little headway against an elective principle which paid scant attention to blood relationship. English history could offer examples of both hereditary and elective succession, but recent history lent no support to primogeniture. On such a principle Robert Curthose, and after him William Clito, would have been kings of England and dukes of Normandy, not Henry I. Nevertheless, the upheavals in the tenure of fiefs which had attended the history of many families since the Norman conquest of England inclined the barons to favour clearer and stricter rules of hereditary succession, and it became increasingly hard for them to deny in the case of the Crown the sort of principles which would satisfy their own ambitions to establish dynasties.

The insistence of Matilda and her eldest son on their right by primogeniture was therefore well-judged, and the attempt of Stephen's advocates to cast aspersions on Matilda's legitimacy reveals uneasiness on this score.[2] The papacy, however, had no reason to be disposed in favour of hereditary succession and resisted it steadfastly in the case of the Empire. Perjury was the charge that weighed most in the deliberations of the papal curia on Matilda's appeal; but no pope could lightly set aside the verdict of a papal legate, the archbishop of Canterbury. Perhaps it had been made in error on the double perjury of Hugh Bigod, but the point was almost incapable of proof. The papacy prudently declined to pronounce upon the appeal, but continued to recognise Stephen as king. It could not do otherwise: however suspect Stephen's ascent to the throne, he had undeniably been anointed, and

[1] *Recueil des Actes de Henri II*, I, 6ff.
[2] Cf. Davis, 'What happened in Stephen's reign'.

that beyond question made him a king. Yet though Stephen survived the appeal, his position was undermined by his failure to remove the suspicion of perjury. His kingship was tainted. As an anointed king he could not readily be set aside, but there was no reason to accord to his heirs the claim which he denied to Matilda and her son. If a wrong had been done, the time to set it right was at Stephen's death. A prudent man might hesitate to break his allegiance to King Stephen, but he would not choose to incur, if he could avoid it, the disfavour of young Henry of Anjou. Time ran against Stephen of Blois.

Although few but the most ardent partisans of Matilda ever sought to deny Stephen the title of king, it soon became apparent that he would not be an effective king. It is doubtful if anyone expected him to be. His seizure of the throne had been promoted or supported not because of his innate qualities, but because leaders of faction thought he could be made to serve their interests. He was promoted by a coalition of factions which had no common bond except a distrust of Matilda's husband. Stephen, however, was not a nonentity. The well-known comments of the Peterborough Chronicle that he was 'a mild man, soft and good, who did no justice', and of Walter Map that 'he was adept at the martial arts but in other respects little more than a simpleton', are pardonable exaggerations, but exaggerations none the less.[1] Ordinary men are often no less complex than geniuses, and Stephen was certainly both ordinary and complex. There was a streak of shifty cunning in him to set beside the affability and undoubted kindness; and he displayed, when hard pressed, a dogged courage which belied his apparent softness. William of Malmesbury, who sided with the Angevin cause, generously allowed that 'if he had legitimately acquired the kingdom and had administered it without lending trusting ears to the whispers of malevolent men, he would have lacked little which adorns the royal character'.[2] But chivalry and generosity, though virtues admired in aristocratic circles, were not enough for a king of England. Stephen proved incapable of foreseeing the further consequences of his actions. He was prone to attempt brisk, simple solutions to dangerous problems, but to abandon his purpose as soon as he encountered difficulties. He vacillated, and his word, though generously given, could not be trusted. His cardinal error, springing from the depths of his character, was his failure to impose himself from the first upon his barons.[3] In his dealings with those who resisted or flouted his authority he showed himself an appeaser. The consequence was a

---

[1] Anglo-Saxon Chronicle, 263 (AD 1137); Walter Map, 236.
[2] William of Malmesbury, *Historia Novella*, 20.   [3] Cf. Davis, *King Stephen*, 24–6.

struggle between groups and factions to safeguard their own interests in which increasingly little heed was paid to the king himself.

The inadequacies of Stephen's personality might have counted for little if he had been sensibly guided by a character stronger than himself. He was disposed to lean on strong men. Undoubtedly Henry of Blois expected to be able to use his brother to establish himself as the power in both Church and State, and the history of the reign would have been very different had he done so; but Stephen, though prone to lean, leant on arms of his own choosing, and he framed his policy on the advice not of his older, domineering brother, but of his personal friends, the twin brothers of Beaumont, Waleran and Robert le Bossu.

The Beaumont family was of considerable prestige and dignity. The twins' mother was the granddaughter of a King of France. Their father, seigneur of Beaumont in the heart of Normandy, count of Meulan in the Vexin, and earl of Leicester in England, had been a close adviser of Henry I until his death in 1118. From the age of fourteen the twins had been educated at King Henry's court. They were intelligent and had a reputation for learned cleverness. They were also ambitious. Their intention was to make themselves the controlling influence in England and Normandy, their method was to weave a web of family connections about the centre of power, their instrument was to be King Stephen, the companion of their youth and close friend. At the beginning of the reign Waleran was count of Meulan, and Robert, earl of Leicester, their half brother William de Warenne was earl of Surrey, and their cousin Roger de Beaumont was earl of Warwick. Rapidly the net of their influence spread wider: Waleran was made earl of Worcester, a younger brother, Hugh, was made earl of Bedford, a brother-in-law, Gilbert de Clare, became earl of Pembroke, and a cousin acquired the bishopric of Evreux.[1]

It was convenient for Stephen to have his friends among the barons firmly planted in the Midlands and in the most sensitive regions of Normandy; but the ambition of the Beaumonts, pursuing an undivided control of Stephen, led them to break apart the fragile coalition upon which his acceptance as king rested. Henry of Blois was brusquely elbowed aside: the archbishopric of Canterbury, which he expected for himself after the death of William of Corbeil, was conferred instead, in December 1138, upon the worthy but little known Theobald, abbot of Bec. The abbey was in the patronage of the count of Meulan.[2] Six

[1] Cf. White, 'The career of Waleran, count of Meulan and earl of Worcester'; Cronne, *The Reign of Stephen*, 165ff.
[2] Saltman, *Archbishop Theobald*, 7–13; Davis, *King Stephen*, 29.

months later Roger of Salisbury found himself the victim of a plot: at a meeting of the king's court members of his household were deliberately embroiled in a *fracas*; the king demanded satisfaction for the disturbance of his peace, and required as security the castles held by Bishop Roger and by his nephews in the service of the Crown, Alexander bishop of Lincoln, and Nigel bishop of Ely. Bishop Roger's son, Roger le Poer, was arrested and replaced as chancellor by a protégé of Count Waleran. The royal seal was changed to mark the introduction of a new dispensation.[1]

It was a cardinal error. The imprisonment of bishops (even of curial bishops) and the seizure of property on ecclesiastical estates destroyed confidence in Stephen's promises to respect the liberties of the Church. More immediately serious: the administrative system upon which Henry I had relied for the exercise of his authority was rocked to its foundations. Historians no longer believe, as they once did, that the system was wrecked – undoubtedly it continued to function outwardly as before; but the secret of its efficient operation was lost, for it remained locked away in the experience of the men whom Stephen dismissed.[2] Moreover the local agents of the system could no longer feel secure from the revenge of those they had despoiled, in the interests of themselves as well as the Crown; and with their discomfiture the network which provided the central government with information and secret intelligence was disrupted.[3] It seems probable that Stephen, besides a lack of understanding of administrative processes, shared with the Beaumont brothers an aristocratic distaste for the lowly-born careerists to whom Henry I had entrusted the executive offices of local and central government. It had been a major element of Henry I's policy to divest the great landed families of that share in the exercise of royal government which feudal lords were accustomed to expect as their due. Stephen reversed the policy and put the shires under the control of military governors drawn from the landed aristocracy. They were dignified with the continental title of *comes* – count, though it is customary to call them by the English name of earl. Between 1138 and 1140 a score of new earldoms were created.[4] The shire came to be thought of as a 'county', and the sheriff – under the continental title of *vice-*

---

[1] William of Malmesbury, *Historia Novella*, 26–8; Davis, *King Stephen*, 31–2.

[2] Cf. below, pp. 258ff.

[3] Orderic Vitalis, IV, 239, says of Henry I: 'He penetrated everyone's secrets and clandestine operations, so that the people concerned were at a loss to understand how the king obtained his knowledge.'

[4] Davis, *King Stephen*, 33 and Appendix I. Round's argument in *Geoffrey de Mandeville*, 267–77, that the earldoms were merely 'fiscal' cannot be sustained.

comes – was the earl's subordinate and as much his man as the king's. Putting the provinces into the hands of men who commanded their own forces of knightly vassals may have seemed to Stephen at the time a realistic and economical policy for mastering the uncertain loyalty of Henry I's 'new men'; but it created more problems than it solved. The elevation of some families to titles of dignity and positions of provincial power sharpened local rivalries, and intensified family feuds at the same time as it dismembered and decentralised royal authority. Since the new earls were, by and large, friends of the Beaumonts, the king came to be identified with the faction they represented, and the disappointed were thrust into disloyalty.

The break-up of the coalition which had given Stephen the throne, and the discontent of the disappointed, emboldened Robert of Gloucester to promote the fortunes of his half-sister the empress (as everyone continued to call her). Hitherto her hopes of displacing Stephen rested entirely on her husband's attempts to invade Normandy from Anjou. Earl Robert had for long maintained a cautious neutrality, remaining quietly on his estates in central Normandy, unwilling it seems to commit himself either to the hated Angevin invaders or to the open defence of Stephen's interests as duke. It was not until Geoffrey began to make real headway with the conquest of Normandy that Robert, in June 1138, renounced his allegiance to Stephen and submitted Caen and Bayeux to the invader.[1] Even then he delayed for more than a year before campaigning personally for Matilda's cause. He has in consequence been accused of negligent procrastination; and certainly his lingering in Normandy prevented him uniting his forces with those of Matilda's uncle, King David of Scotland, who mounted an invasion of the north of England in the summer of 1138. He did not even bring succour to those of his vassals in England who were hard pressed by Stephen's men. Had Earl Robert taken the field immediately after his renunciation of homage, it is possible that he could have prevented the rout of the Scots at the Battle of the Standard in August 1138, and also the loss of several of his own strongholds in the west country. It is probable, however, that Earl Robert regarded the Scots' invasion as an undesirable intervention and an unlooked for complication, and that his inactivity was a deliberate attempt to dissociate himself – and Matilda's cause – from the efforts of outsiders such as David of Scotland and Geoffrey of Anjou to promote their own interests. The enthusiastic mustering of northerners of all classes at the call of Archbishop Thurstan of York, parading behind crosses and saints' relics, showed, indeed,

---

[1] William of Malmesbury, *Historia Novella*, 23.

that the dynastic question could all too easily be submerged under patriotism and the spontaneous defence of hearth and home.[1] The respectable support which was necessary to secure the throne for Matilda could come only from men of position and power in England who despaired of Stephen. By the summer of 1139 – after Stephen had alienated the English bishops, disrupted the administration, and involved himself in the feuds of faction – the time seemed ripe, and in September Earl Robert crossed to England with Matilda and set up headquarters for her at his stronghold of Bristol.

If Earl Robert expected a spontaneous rally of great men to Matilda's banner he was grievously disappointed. It was not so much that there was genuine loyalty to Stephen as that too many men had too much to lose by a premature commitment to an uncertain cause, which in any case offered no readily acceptable alternative. The most eager recruits for rebellion were those whose hopes had been disappointed by Stephen, but this very fact involved Matilda's cause with local faction struggles, and made the interests of those who had been entrusted with power indistinguishable, for the time being at least, from the king's. The convenience, for Stephen, of entrusting the provinces to military governors was demonstrated in the speedy suppression of insurrections. There were only two notable defectors to Matilda, and they were barons of the second rank, Brian FitzCount and Miles of Gloucester. Brian was the bastard son of a count of Brittany, who had been befriended by Henry I, and who felt a debt of gratitude as well as personal devotion to the old king's daughter. His importance to Matilda was that he held the honor and castle of Wallingford, a major stronghold on the upper reaches of the Thames, astride the main lines of communication in the south of England.[2] Miles was one of Henry I's 'new men', elevated by marriage to a barony in the Welsh march, constable of Gloucester castle, sheriff of both Gloucestershire and Staffordshire, and the holder of other royal offices which made him, in effect, governor of the west midlands.[3] His local interests conflicted with those of Earl Robert of Gloucester, but he evidently judged that his future was precarious under Stephen. His adherence consolidated Earl Robert's hold on the lands of the Severn valley. Even so, the empress's party could not be said to be anything more than a faction, locally strong in the Cotswolds and the southern March of Wales, but without major influence in the rest of the

[1] Cf. Kate Norgate, op. cit., I, 289–92; Ritchie, The Normans in Scotland, 259–68.

[2] Cf. Davis, 'Henry of Blois and Brian FitzCount', 298–9.

[3] Cf. Cronne, The Reign of King Stephen, 156–9; Walker, 'Miles of Gloucester, earl of Hereford'.

country, and unlikely on its own account to topple Stephen's throne. Her cause failed to gather momentum.

The balance of power lay very much with King Stephen, and he was confident in the size of the forces he was able to muster; yet he failed signally to snuff out the dimly flickering light of his rival's challenge. Miles of Gloucester showed the way to exploit Stephen's military ineptitude and nullify the effect of superior forces. His tactic was to avoid a direct encounter with the king's main army, and instead to make diversionary attacks on royalist-held strongholds, retreating if Stephen came up and attacking somewhere else. As Stephen swivelled indecisively this way and that he dissipated his efforts and lost the military initiative. The empress's forces were thus able to survive, but moved no nearer to victory.

The major threat to Stephen's position came not from the empress's inadequate forces, but from his own mishandling of his greater vassals, and in particular of the earl of Chester. In the extent of the lands he held and the number of his vassals, Earl Ranulf de Gernons eclipsed all the other barons of the realm. The marcher lordship of Cheshire was only one element, and not the most important, in an honor which embraced wide estates throughout the midlands, major holdings in Yorkshire and Lincolnshire, and manors scattered over most of the southern counties. In addition he held important lordships and hereditary fiefs which made him a dominating influence in western Normandy as far as the confines of Brittany. Stephen might have done well to cultivate the support of Earl Ranulf; but he chose instead to build up the power of his friends the Beaumonts, who vied with the earl of Chester for paramount influence in the midlands. Earl Ranulf found himself slighted, not merely in the creation of new earldoms in the east midlands, but also in Stephen's attempts to buy peace from the king of Scots. As part of the price of peace Stephen granted King David possession of Carlisle. Unfortunately Earl Ranulf coveted Carlisle, rightly so in his own estimation, for it had been held by his father until Henry I deprived him of it in 1120. No feudal baron readily reconciled himself to the loss of part of his patrimony, whatever its value. It is surprising that Earl Ranulf did not throw in his lot with the empress, especially since his wife was the daughter of Earl Robert of Gloucester. That he did not do so is probably another indication of the frailty of her pretensions.[1] Of course the widespread estates which gave Earl Ranulf his political importance also made him vulnerable to forfeiture by the king; but considerations such as these cannot have weighed

[1] Cf. William of Malmesbury, *Historia Novella*, 47, and Orderic Vitalis, V, 126.

heavily with him in declining to declare for Matilda, since they did not
prevent him taking action on his own account against King Stephen.
Together with his devoted half-brother, William of Roumare, who
aspired to the earldom of Lincoln, he seized possession of the castle of
Lincoln from its royal garrison late in 1140. Stephen was persuaded to
admit that Earl Ranulf had a justifiable grievance and made extensive
concessions to him as compensation. But a few weeks later King Stephen
recklessly broke the peace he had just concluded and attempted to take
Earl Ranulf prisoner by a lightning attack on Lincoln. Ranulf eluded
him and appealed for the help of his father-in-law, Earl Robert of
Gloucester.[1] Quickly they brought up to Lincoln all the forces they
could muster and found the king still besieging the castle. Stephen was
taken by surprise; his siege forces were inadequate to fight a pitched
battle, but he disregarded advice to retreat and stood his ground. The
battle was fought on 2 February 1141. It was a disaster for King
Stephen: his troops were overwhelmed and he himself made captive.

The realm of England did not, however, fall at the feet of Empress
Matilda. The slowness with which she moved towards coronation is an
indication of the necessity of negotiating and bargaining her way to the
throne. Stephen's defeat at Lincoln was attributable in large measure
to the desertion of many of the greater magnates at the critical moment;
but though they deserted the king they did not rally to the empress.
Their chief concern was with their local interests, and in the turmoil
which followed the king's capture most of them maintained a cautious
neutrality. Henry of Blois, bishop of Winchester and papal legate,
hoped by sponsoring Matilda as queen to gain the influence which his
brother had denied him; but though he used his legatine authority to
promote it, even the bishops were reluctant to change their allegiance
until Stephen himself gave them permission to 'move with the times'.[2]
The fact was that the future was still very uncertain, and the empress's
party could not be sure of gaining control of the whole of the country.
Stephen's queen, another Matilda, proclaimed a courageous defiance,
sending a chaplain to the church council which Henry of Blois summoned to demand the honouring of oaths of allegiance and the release
of her husband.[3] Her defiance was no mere bravado for she had behind

---

[1] For the earldom of Chester and Earl Ranulf's relations with King Stephen, *see*
Barraclough, *The Earldom and County Palatine of Chester*; Round, 'Stephen and the earl
of Chester'; Cronne, 'Ranulf de Gernons, earl of Chester'; Davis, 'King Stephen and
the earl of Chester, revised'; Davis, *King Stephen*, 49ff.; Cronne, *The Reign of Stephen*,
174ff.

[2] William of Malmesbury, *Historia Novella*, 50–1.

[3] *Ibid.*, 55.

her considerable resources in men and money. She was in her own right countess of Boulogne, and held the English vassals of the honor of Boulogne to their allegiance. From the estates of the honor in Essex she could keep open communication by sea with Boulogne itself.[1] Moreover Stephen's captain of mercenaries, the high-born but illegitimate William of Ypres, remained faithful and held Kent with a host of Flemish soldiers of fortune. His control of the southern ports enabled him to bring in as many more mercenaries as could be paid for. The parallel with the empress's own previous situation was indeed very close. The major difference was that the sympathies of the Londoners were with the underdog, and until the empress could gain control of London and Westminster she could not be crowned. The policy she adopted was similar to that of Stephen in the creation of military governorships – exploiting the local ambitions of prominent barons in order to keep her opponents in check. She created fresh earldoms and granted new powers to those of Stephen's earls whose support was buyable. To Geoffrey de Mandeville, in particular, whom Stephen had made earl of Essex in 1140, she granted complete jurisdiction over Essex, London, and Middlesex, with the prospect of acquiring estates from the honor of Boulogne if he could eject the queen from Colchester.[2] It was with his help that she at last gained entry to the city of London in the summer of 1141.

By this time, however, Empress Matilda had already justified the fears of those who had been reluctant to have her as queen in the first place. Her behaviour was headstrong, overbearing, and unbelievably tactless. Ever since the bishops had agreed to accept her as queen-designate, her haughtiness had been intolerable. Men noted with dismay that she was arrogant even with her kinsmen Earl Robert of Gloucester and King David of Scotland.[3] She made no attempt to reassure the hesitant, treating those who hesitated too long with abusive contempt. Henry of Blois was soon driven to regret bitterly his efforts to have Matilda accepted: she rebuffed his requests that the hereditary lands of the House of Blois should be settled on his nephew, Eustace, Stephen's son, and what was worse she broke her undertaking to follow his advice in church affairs. Indeed, the intervention she threatened in matters ecclesiastical would have been thought grossly

---

[1] For the long-standing connection between Boulogne and England, see Round, 'The counts of Boulogne as English lords', *Studies in Peerage and Family History*, 147–80.

[2] Davis, *King Stephen*, 59–60.

[3] *Gesta Stephani*, 79; William of Malmesbury, *Historia Novella*, 57–8; Henry of Huntingdon, 275; John of Hexham, II, 309; William of Newburgh, I, 41.

improper even in Germany. The last straw was her imperious demand for an exorbitant sum of money from the Londoners. In desperation they made a pact with the queen to try to restore King Stephen, and set upon the empress as she was sitting down to a banquet at Westminster on 24 June.[1]

Still uncrowned, the empress fled the capital to the greater safety of Oxford. The papal legate, Henry of Blois, smarting from the treatment he had received, raised the sentences of excommunication laid on those who had refused to abandon King Stephen. The empress went to Winchester to chastise him, and Bishop Henry appealed urgently for the help of his sister-in-law, the queen. Her commander, William of Ypres, moved his forces down from London so swiftly and deployed them with such professional skill that the empress's contingent was taken by surprise and very nearly encircled. Earl Robert fought a desperate rearguard action to enable his half-sister to escape. With a tiny escort she reached the safety of Gloucester, but Earl Robert, attempting to follow her, was captured. Without her half-brother, the only man who could give any semblance of respectability to her cause, Matilda was helpless. She had no option but to release King Stephen in exchange for him.

Even with Earl Robert restored to her, Matilda's plight at the end of 1141 was serious. Her supporters were demoralised by her failure to secure coronation in the thirty-two weeks of her triumph, and by the rout at Winchester. Many of her men had been taken prisoner, and most of those who escaped had done so only by casting aside their weapons and armour, and abandoning even their war-horses in an attempt to disguise their identity from ransom-seekers.[2] Those who had professed their allegiance only after the battle of Lincoln had of course fallen away; some, such as Geoffrey de Mandeville, in time to ride the wave of the queen's victory. For the old hands among the empress's supporters, facing the prospect of defeat and disinheritance by a king back on his throne, the immediate problem was simply survival. Urgent appeals for help were sent to Matilda's husband. Geoffrey replied, after three months, that he did not know what credence to place in the messages he had received, but 'if the earl of Gloucester would cross the sea and come to him he would do his best to meet his wishes; but for anyone else to make the journey would be a waste of time'.[3] Count Geoffrey had no intention, in fact, of being distracted by his wife's

---

[1] Davis, *King Stephen*, 60–2.
[2] *Gesta Stephani*, 88.
[3] William of Malmesbury, *Historia Novella*, 71.

misadventures in England from his own objective of conquering Normandy. His purpose in seeking the presence of Earl Robert was to smother the Normans' instinctive resistance to Angevin attack with a cloak of respectability.[1] Earl Robert stifled his impatience with Geoffrey's excuses for delay for more than two months and helped him take several castles – until news arrived that King Stephen had surrounded the empress at Oxford and was closely besieging her in the castle. Earl Robert returned at once with a force of more than three hundred knights, without Geoffrey, who refused to abandon his self-appointed task, but bringing with him his nephew, Matilda's eldest son, Henry. At the age of nine, at the end of November 1142, Henry of Anjou first set foot in England – perilously, for the earl had to force a landing at Wareham. Nothing could justify subjecting the heir of Anjou to the peril of a winter crossing of the Channel, the dangers of a forced landing, and hazards of warfare in England, save that the Angevin cause needed a new figurehead to replace the discredited Matilda. It was a baptism of fire.[2]

A march to rescue young Henry's mother at Oxford was unnecessary, for Matilda escaped from the beleagured castle by daringly walking through Stephen's lines in the dead of a snowy night, making her way on foot to Abingdon and thence on horseback to Wallingford. With his fresh troops, Earl Robert was able to halt Stephen's offensive and win control of vital castles in Somerset and Dorset, which gave him secure lines of communication to the English Channel and established the authority of the empress's men in the south-west. 'This lordship of his,' writes the anonymous author of the *Gesta Stephani*, 'the earl very greatly adorned by restoring peace and quietness everywhere, except that in building his castles he exacted forced labour from all and, whenever he had to fight the enemy, demanding everyone's help either by sending knights or paying money in lieu. And there was indeed in those regions a shadow of peace but not yet complete peace, because nothing more grievously vexed the people of the country than working for others and in some sort increasing by their own efforts the causes of strife and war.'[3] Forced labour and military service could not alone, however, provide for fully garrisoning and equipping all his castles against the continual danger of attack. Earl Robert found that his revenues were strained, and that it was necessary to husband his resources.[4] He did not, after 1143, mount any major new offensive. He had to be ready to

---

[1] *Ibid.*, 72–3.   [2] *Ibid.*, 73, 74–5.   [3] *Gesta Stephani*, 99.
[4] Cf. *ibid.*, 137, '. . . brooding like a usurer over his money bags . . . to meet his own requirements'.

bring help to any of his supporters who were threatened, or to seize a
local advantage from Stephen's men; but his basic policy seems to have
been to hold tight to what he had until the young Henry was old
enough to take over the leadership. To try again to place the discredited
Matilda on the throne would be futile; the only hope rested in her son.
In the meantime Henry was returned to the greater security of his
father's dominions.[1]

A holding policy was all the more sensible in that Geoffrey of Anjou
was in the final stages of the conquest of Normandy. It was in the duchy
that Henry could be established as a ruler of Normans, and there that
he might recruit the forces necessary to prosecute his claim upon the
throne of England. Hence the importance of holding Dorset and the
Channel port of Wareham: this was to be the bridgehead for a new
Norman invasion of England.[2]

Count Geoffrey's conquest of the duchy was a tremendous victory
which changed the course of King Stephen's fortunes decisively. The
details of it are little known: Angevin chroniclers were unequal to the
task, and chroniclers of Norman origin seem to have found the story
too shaming to tell. It had been Count Geoffrey's objective from the
moment of King Henry's death. The back door to the duchy had been
opened to him by officers of the old king, who, in acknowledgement of
Matilda, handed over the southern fortresses of Alençon, Domfront,
Séez, Argentan and Exmes; but Geoffrey at first found it hard to exploit
the opening effectively. He was as yet insecure in Anjou and suffered the
distraction of baronial revolts whenever he tried to concentrate his
attention on Normandy. The effects of his intermittent campaigns in
Normandy were ephemeral, for they became, in effect, little more than
plundering raids which confirmed the Normans in their instinctive
hostility to the Angevins. There were some who declared for Matilda
but not many, and usually for a special reason, such as a debt of
gratitude to Henry I or a grudge against Stephen. Gradually, however,
the Norman will to resist was sapped from within, as the duchy was left
without effective leadership. Old sores from King Henry's reign were
reopened after years of uneasy peace. Men who had suffered the consequences of having backed the losing side in the struggle between
Henry I and William Clito now saw a chance for recovery. Some joined

---

[1] Gervase of Canterbury, a later writer, believed that Henry remained in England
for four years (I, 124–5); Poole, however, has shown that Henry was in Angers late in
1143 or early in 1144, 'Henry Plantagenet's early visits to England'.

[2] For Earl Robert's determination to hold Wareham and the king's efforts to
dislodge him, see William of Malmesbury, Historia Novella, 73–6; Gesta Stephani, 95–6.

forces with Geoffrey, but others sought a speedier remedy by waging private war. Preoccupied with the military situation, Stephen's agents virtually abandoned any attempt to administer the duchy. Stephen himself had crossed to Normandy in the spring of 1137, fifteen months after he became king of England; but such success as he then achieved in establishing order was fleeting. Indeed, his efforts crippled his reputation, for the depredations of his unruly mercenaries were resented as much as those of Count Geoffrey's men. Surrounded by quarrelling barons, and troubled by the then still dubious loyalty of Earl Robert, Stephen found it impossible to mount an effective counter-attack against Geoffrey and was reduced to concluding a truce. He retired to England in November 1137, never to return; and after the civil war began there some of his ablest captains were called over to join him. Law and order disintegrated. Pillage and private war, ambushes, sieges, and sacrilege darken the last pages of the chronicle of Orderic Vitalis, who brought his great work to a close, without hope, in 1141.[1]

It was in the same year, 1141, that King Stephen was made prisoner at Lincoln; and it was at this very time that Geoffrey, freed for a while from trouble in Anjou, was able to abandon raids in favour of a systematic campaign. Although Stephen's captivity proved to be short-lived, he was never thereafter to be a factor in the history of Normandy. For most of the Normans all confidence in him had gone. A few remained loyal, but it was a loyalty without hope. The response to Stephen's imprisonment was a desperate appeal to Theobald of Blois to assume the ducal title. In the hope of salvaging something from the wreck of his brother's ambitions, Theobald at first tried to negotiate with Geoffrey, but when his overtures were rebuffed he prudently withdrew. Even some of the barons who still upheld Stephen's cause against Matilda in England now abandoned resistance to Geoffrey in Normandy. Half the duchy surrendered at once. To persuade the rest, Geoffrey deployed his forces in well planned and doggedly executed campaigns. Piece by piece he gained control. By the time of young Henry's first visit to England, some of the more important clergy of Normandy were already addressing his father as 'duke', although Geoffrey himself did not presume to adopt the title until after the surrender of the castle at Rouen in 1144. The castle of Arques held out longest, but that too submitted in 1145.[2] Even before Arques fell, the king of France accepted the inevitable and recognised Geoffrey as duke, though doubtless with a reluctance which was only partly assuaged by

---

[1] Cf. Chartrou, op. cit., ch. 3; Ilsa Wolff, Heinrich II, 83; Haskins, Norman Institutions, 127–8.　　[2] Chartrou, op. cit., 65–6.

Geoffrey's concession to him of the key fortress of Gisors in the long-disputed Vexin.[1]

Count Geoffrey's control of Normandy posed a cruel dilemma for the barons who held estates on both sides of the Channel. The completeness of the conquest, and the improbability that Stephen could ever recover the duchy, forced them to weigh their interests and reconsider their attitude to the dynastic question. Those whose English interests would not allow them to break their allegiance to King Stephen, could acquiesce only temporarily in the loss of their Norman estates. The long-term solution to the problem was the reuniting of England and Normandy after Stephen's death. Their obligation to Stephen as crowned king did not extend to accepting his eldest son, Eustace, as his successor. The answer to the problem, already becoming clear, was to recognise Henry as heir. If, as must have seemed to many, the disasters of the reign were a consequence of breaking their oaths to Matilda, the acceptance of her son as next king was a way of putting wrongs right. Those whose Norman interests were paramount had to declare themselves without delay if they were not to see the lands from which they derived title and dignity pass, perhaps beyond recall, into other hands. The dilemma is well illustrated by the behaviour of the twin brothers of Beaumont. Robert, who inherited the family's English lands, had been Stephen's lieutenant in Normandy; while Waleran, who inherited the Norman estates, had been Stephen's right hand in England. After Stephen's capture, Waleran had joined the queen, but the imminent loss of his patrimony of Meulan must have unnerved him. Robert secured a truce from Geoffrey that he might go to England to confer with his brother. Their decision was that Robert should transfer to England while Waleran went to Normandy to make his peace with its effective ruler. Waleran did homage to Geoffrey and helped him besiege Rouen; but escaped as soon as he decently could from the torment of a divided allegiance by going on crusade.[2]

Geoffrey perceived the drift of baronial thinking, and cleverly exploited it. He let it be known that as soon as his son, Henry, was old enough to take charge of the duchy, he himself would step aside. He advertised his purpose by sometimes issuing charters 'with the advice and consent of Henry my son', or in both their names jointly.[3]

[1] How much of the Vexin was conceded by Geoffrey and how much by Henry in 1151 is not clear from the sources; see Lemarignier, *Recherches sur L'Hommage en Marche*, 45 and n.53.

[2] White, 'The career of Waleran, count of Meulan and earl of Worcester'; Davis, *King Stephen*, 67–8. His men in England continued to support the king: *Gesta Stephani*, 151.

[3] Haskins, *op. cit.*, 131, and nn. 29 and 31; *Recueil des Actes de Henri II*, I, 13.

Henry, however, seems to have been young enough and high-spirited enough to prefer immediate action to distant prospects. After his father's victory had brought peace to Normandy, he ventured forth on what seems to have been a private escapade. In 1147 he gathered a few companions and a small party of mercenaries, hired on credit, and set sail for England. He was fourteen at the time. Rumour said that he

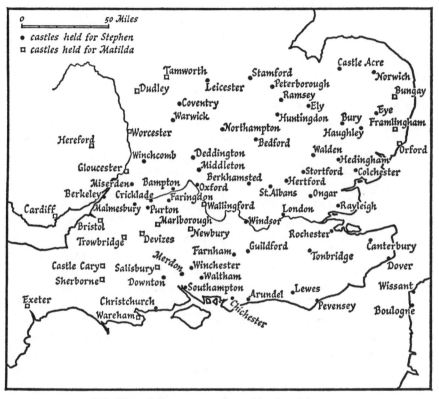

III The civil war: southern England in 1147

came at the head of a large army, and panic spread among the king's men. Henry tried to take advantage of the panic by a bold attempt to seize the castles held for the king at Cricklade and Purton; but boldness was no substitute for experience or proper siege equipment, and he was beaten off. When the real size of his force became known, the king's men pressed him hard. His companions began to desert for fear, and his mercenaries for lack of plunder to reward them. In dismay at the ignominy of being unable to maintain his men, young Henry appealed for help to his mother and Earl Robert. They refused; either, as the *Gesta Stephani* alleges, from parsimony, or, more probably, because they disapproved of such foolhardy escapades, and wished to oblige him to return forthwith to the security of Normandy. He then, cheekily, applied to his other uncle, King Stephen, who sent him some money, so that he might pay off his mercenaries and go home.[1]

It is possible that Stephen's action was motivated not simply by quixotic generosity, but by a prudent desire to show that he at least was unperturbed by the one influence which could threaten his attempts to stabilise his position in England. King Stephen changed his policy after his release from captivity. Though never entirely relaxing his pressure against the adherents of the empress, he placed above it the re-establishment of his authority as king in the rest of the country. He abandoned the reliance he had earlier placed on members of the military aristocracy, and leant instead on his own 'new men': professional soldiers such as William of Ypres, and professional administrators such as Richard de Lucy, William Martel, and Gervase of Cornhill – men whose worth had been demonstrated by their loyalty in adversity. The influence of the Beaumonts had been virtually extinguished by the defection of Waleran, and Stephen paid more heed to the sager advice of his courageous wife and of his worldly-wise brother, the bishop of Winchester. The advice that Stephen accepted was to make his authority as king in England impregnable.[2] Only in this way could men be brought to reconcile themselves to the loss of Normandy, and accept that their best interests lay in cooperation with him in England. Only in this way could men be brought to acquiesce in the succession of his son and the establishment of a dynasty. The practical expression of the policy was to be the mastery of the earls, the reconstruction of the kind of administration which had made Henry I strong, and (following the example of the Capetian kings of France) the coronation of his successor in the present king's own lifetime. When these were achieved the Angevin party would wilt and die.

Earl Robert's decision to concentrate on defence gave Stephen the respite to try to consolidate his kingship. Mastering the earls was not easy, for Stephen was obliged to make concessions to compensate for

[1] *Gesta Stephani*, 135–6. Round, *Feudal England*, 373–6, dismissed the story as a fabrication, relying on the statement of Gervase of Canterbury that Henry came to England in 1142, stayed for about four years, and was then absent for over two years, and returned in the spring of 1149. Poole, 'Henry Plantagenet's early visits to England', has, however, shown that Gervase is wrong, and that there is no reason for rejecting the story told in the *Gesta Stephani*.

[2] Davis, *King Stephen*, 69ff.

losses in Normandy. But he was not without successes. The two earls whose self-interest had caused him most trouble, Geoffrey de Mandeville and Ranulf of Chester, were both humbled and forced to surrender strategic castles. In 1146 Stephen triumphantly held his Christmas court at Lincoln, to efface the shame of his defeat there when trying to take the castle from the earl of Chester in 1141. The castle of Faringdon,

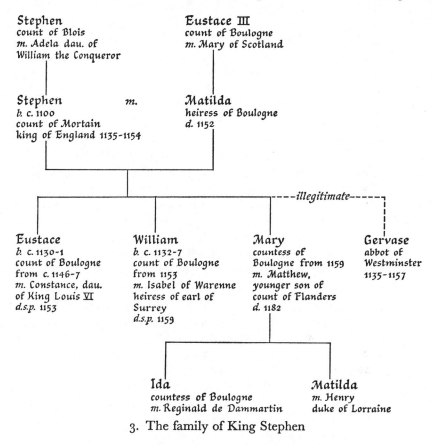

3. The family of King Stephen

specially built by Earl Robert of Gloucester to impede the king's communications with his enclave at Malmesbury, fell in 1146 to a determined assault by Stephen's men. Its fall was followed by the defection of Earl Robert's own son Philip, who 'seeing that at that time the king had the upper hand, entered into a pact of peace and concord with him, and after being lavishly endowed with castles and lands, he gave hostages and paid him homage'.[1] Eventually he, like many others who

[1] *Gesta Stephani*, 123.

had been involved for years in the atrocities of war, went off to expiate his sins on the Second Crusade. The empress's party seemed to be breaking up. On 31 October 1147 Earl Robert himself died, and Matilda, at the beginning of 1148, retired to Normandy. The king's courts in 1148 were better attended than at any time since his captivity – a sure sign that Stephen had once more become a factor to be reckoned with in the lives of the great feudatories.

That the Angevin party did not disintegrate altogether is probably attributable in large measure to Stephen's treatment of the earls of Essex and Chester. He had lulled them into a false security, confirming them in their acquisitions and heaping fresh dignities upon them, but then suddenly arrested them when they were in attendance at his court and under his peace and protection, and clapped them in irons until they consented to relinquish their castles. Stephen may have thought that he was consolidating his authority, but he was hardly likely to win the confidence of those who owed title and lands to the empress.[1] Even so the Angevin party needed encouragement if it were to hold together as an effective basis for Henry's eventual challenge for the throne. Henry himself provided the encouragement by a visit in 1149. His ostensible purpose was to seek knighthood from the most eminent of his kinsmen, King David of Scotland. The ceremony was performed at Carlisle on Whit Sunday 1149.[2] The festivities, however, were also a cover for a rally of the opposition to Stephen. The successor of Miles of Hereford, his son Roger, was knighted at the same time. Henry Murdac, abbot of Fountains, whom Stephen refused to accept as archbishop of York, also attended – a representative of the growing opposition among churchmen to the ecclesiastical policy of both the king and his brother, Henry of Blois.[3] More important was the attendance of Earl Ranulf of Chester. The treacherous treatment he had received from Stephen overcame even his hostility to King David's acquisition of lands he coveted in the north. In his father's old castle at Carlisle he came to terms with his rival. He recognised David as lord of Carlisle and did him homage. In return King David released to him all his claims upon Lancashire north of the Ribble.[4] Together they planned to seize York. The intention was to deprive Stephen of effective control of the whole of the country north of Humber and Trent, under cover of a righteous campaign to install the papally-approved Henry Murdac in the

[1] For Stephen's treatment of the earls and its consequences for his reputation, see Davis, 'What happened in Stephen's reign', and King Stephen, 80–2, 93–6.

[2] Gesta Stephani, 142; Gervase of Canterbury, I, 141.

[3] John of Hexham, 322.

[4] Ibid., 323. For Scottish claims upon the north-east, see below, ch. 4.

archbishopric of York. King David already controlled Northumberland and Cumberland; the bishop of Durham, ruler of the vast Liberty of St Cuthbert, was sympathetic; Ranulf could dominate Lancashire, Cheshire and north Staffordshire, and with his northern flank secure, could hope to recover his former strength in Lincolnshire. King David moved south from Carlisle, and Ranulf brought up forces to Lancaster, intending to strike from there across the Pennines. Unfortunately Stephen received early news of what was afoot from loyal supporters in York, and hurried north with a strong force of knights. The enterprise, which could achieve success only by surprise, was abandoned, and the allies dispersed.[1]

Stephen's principal objective then became the elimination of Henry. Search parties of knights were sent out to waylay him as he retreated from Lancaster. The king's son, Eustace, was alerted in the south, and penetrated between the enemy strongholds in Gloucestershire to set ambushes. But Henry eluded them all, slipping through the net at night and travelling by devious routes until he reached the safety of Bristol.[2] Stephen brought his main forces down from the north towards the end of September, and joined with Eustace in a concentrated effort to smash the resistance of his enemies, and corner Henry. 'They took and plundered everything they came upon,' says the Gesta Stephani, 'set fire to houses and churches, and, what was more cruel and inhuman to behold, fired the crops which had been reaped and stooked all over the fields, and consumed or destroyed everything edible they found.'[3] Clearly perceiving that the intention was to force Henry to a decisive and perhaps fatal battle, his friends elsewhere created diversions. Earl Ranulf launched a major attack across country to Lincolnshire, obliging the king to hurry to the defence of Lincoln. Payn de Beauchamp created a diversion at Bedford, and Hugh Bigod, who for years had maintained a lonely independence in Norfolk, created a diversion in East Anglia, which forced Eustace to abandon for a time the devastation of Wiltshire. Henry occupied himself in smoking out the king's supporters in Devon and Dorset to consolidate his control of the south-west, and when Eustace returned to mount a surprise attack on Devizes, he beat him off. Henry's advisers recommended him to return to Normandy; while he stayed he would be the focus of continuous attack, and reinforcements were needed if he were to take the offensive and save his supporters from ruin.[4]

[1] Gesta Stephani, 142–3; John of Hexham, 323.
[2] Gesta Stephani, 143–4.
[3] Ibid., 145.   [4] Ibid., 145–8.

Henry may have been disappointed by his lack of major success in 1149, but he had shown himself resourceful, courageous, and resolute – even at the age of sixteen a worthy leader of those who staked all on opposition to King Stephen. The savagery of the onslaught by Stephen and Eustace shows that they recognised it as a critical moment in their fortunes, and their failure either to destroy Henry or to overwhelm his supporters was a serious blow to their hopes. Stephen's plan to make his dynasty impregnable was thoroughly undermined by the events of 1149. Not only had the opposition been given fresh heart; more serious was Earl Ranulf's unequivocal commitment to the Angevin cause. No longer would the barons he hoped to humble feel it necessary to submit to the king's demands. Most serious of all there was now a clearly viable alternative to his son as next king. Even those upon whose loyalty he had been able to rely would begin to think of safeguarding their future.

Henry's emergence as a man of destiny was widely appreciated in Normandy, where, says the *Gesta Stephani*, he was 'magnificently welcomed by all who flocked together from every quarter on hearing of his arrival'.[1] His father chose this moment to make over to him the duchy and invest him with the ducal title.[2] The knighting of Henry at the age of sixteen, and his installation as duke of Normandy before his seventeenth birthday, marked the end of his formal training. There are signs that pains had been taken with his education. It would have been difficult, in any case, to find better places for instruction in the martial and courtly arts than the households of Geoffrey of Anjou and Robert of Gloucester; but both of them were also acknowledged by contemporaries to be patrons of book learning.[3] It was said of Geoffrey that, much as he loved hunting, it took second place to reading among his recreations; and the story was told that when the castle of Montreuil-Bellay had defied him for an unconscionable time, he discovered the way to capture it from reading the *De Re Militari* of Vegetius Renatus.[4]

The young Henry was first put to school with Peter of Saintes, a noted

---

[1] *Gesta Stephani*, 148.

[2] The precise date is uncertain. Haskins, *op. cit.*, 130 n.26, and Z. N. and C. N. L. Brooke, 'Henry II, duke of Normandy and Aquitaine', demonstrate that his installation must fall between November 1149 and March 1150. Gervase of Canterbury, I, 142, gives January as the month of Henry's return from England, and this receives support from the most recent edition of the *Gesta Stephani*, which gives additional material illustrating Henry's activity in England late in 1149.

[3] Cf. John de Marmoutier, *op. cit.*, and the preface to William of Malmesbury's *Historia Novella*, which was not only dedicated to but apparently commissioned by Earl Robert.

[4] The story from the Historia Gaufredi, 218, is related in Kate Norgate, *op. cit.*, I, 386–7.

grammarian of the day; and while under his uncle's care at Bristol he had been tutored 'in letters and manners' by a certain Master Matthew. On his return to Normandy he had studied with the foremost Norman scholar, William of Conches, who dedicated to the young Henry a treatise on moral philosophy, the *De Honesto et Utili*.[1] Henry was to retain throughout his life a love of reading and he derived pleasure as well as instruction from constant discussion with the learned.[2]

By 1150 King Stephen could no longer exercise much influence on the course of English affairs. Even the barons who respected their allegiance to him were disinclined to wage war on the adherents of Duke Henry, even in their own interest. If Henry were to succeed by force of arms, they stood to lose all they might gain in the interval to his victorious supporters. The best they could hope for was an arrangement which would enable them to serve Stephen until his death and Henry after him – a negotiated peace in which rival claims could be settled by compromise.

Moreover, many of the barons were becoming anxious to see a speedy end to the state of hostilities – the *tempus werre* as chroniclers called it. It was not so much that they were weary of fighting itself as that they were alarmed at the consequences of turmoil. The devastation which war caused – the plundering, pillaging, and destruction of crops – was not confined to the principal battlegrounds of the war between King Stephen and his opponents. Private war affected many parts of the country remote from the main theatre of operations. Wherever it occurred, and whether it was between the adherents of rivals for the throne or the personal quarrel of neighbours, warfare tended to the devastation of the countryside. The defensive reliance on castles was largely responsible for this. Contemporary siege techniques were not equal to the easy reduction of castles, and if a surprise assault failed to take a castle by storm, the attackers would settle down to starve it out, living, meanwhile, off the neighbouring countryside. If they were obliged to abandon the siege they would destroy the remaining food supplies to deny them to the defenders. The decay of the royal power to control castle-building led to the erection of many unlicensed castles – estimated in 1153 to exceed 1,115.[3] Most of these must have been simple structures – a mound of earth with a watchtower on top,

---

[1] Gervase of Canterbury, I, 125; William FitzStephen, III, 103; Haskins, 'Adelard of Bath and Henry Plantagenet', 516, *Norman Institutions*, 131 and n.28. William of Conches dedicated his Dragmaticon to Count Geoffrey, and in the introduction praised his care for the education of young princes, cf. Poole, *Illustrations of the History of Medieval Thought and Learning*, 347ff.

[2] *See* below, ch. 5, p. 208.

[3] Robert de Torigny, 177.

surrounded by a timber palisade, with a ditch as the outer defence – but sufficient to provide a place of refuge and proof against all but the most persistent attackers or an army with a well-equipped siege train. All had, however, to be garrisoned and supplied with provisions from the vicinity; and even when there was no warfare, the depredations of the 'castlemen' were notorious. Even lords who were insensitive to the miseries of their peasants could not for long remain indifferent to the diminution of revenues. More serious than this to the greater barons was that their vassals tended to get out of hand, asserting an independence, denying their due services, or transferring their allegiance. Castles erected for the vassal's defence of his lord's property could just as easily be used against the lord himself. When, twelve years after the death of King Stephen, a royal inquiry was made into the vassal service owed to the great lords, many instances came to light of services which had been lost to the lord and still not recovered.[1] If the barons were unenthusiastic about the kind of strong government Henry I had provided, they regretted even more the 'anarchy' of Stephen's reign. The memory of Henry I's oppressions had helped Stephen to the throne; the memory of Henry I's peace helped his grandson.

Attempts were made by several of the barons to chain the dogs of war by elaborating a network of private treaties among themselves. From the first, solemn pacts had been necessary between those with conflicting interests who found themselves for political reasons on the same side in the civil war. Earl Robert of Gloucester concluded a *confederatio amoris* with Miles of Gloucester (whom the empress made earl of Hereford in 1141). Earl Robert's successor, William, swore another with Miles's successor, Roger.[2] It is significant, however, that in the later years of the reign pacts were made which cut across the lines of party. Robert de Beaumont, earl of Leicester, not only came to an arrangement with Simon de Senlis, earl of Northampton, on his own side, but also made pacts with Roger, earl of Hereford, and Ranulf, earl of Chester, on the other side. With Earl Ranulf he agreed that if they were obliged to follow their respective liege-lords against each other, they would do so with no more than twenty knights, and that any chattels captured should subsequently be restored. They agreed to limit castle-building in the districts where their estates marched together, and undertook to restrain their allies and vassals from injuries to the other. This agreement (*conventio*) was sworn before the bishop of

---

[1] e.g., *Red Book of the Exchequer*, I, 237, 250, 251, 394, 415.

[2] The documents are printed in Davis, 'Treaty between William earl of Gloucester and Roger earl of Hereford'.

Lincoln; no reference was made to the king.[1] Earl Robert was contracting out of the civil war and arranging insurance for the future.

Stephen was also handicapped in his efforts to establish his dynasty by a change in the attitude of the clergy. His disregard of his early promises to respect the liberty of the Church opened a breach with the bishops which never healed. His reconciliation after 1141 with his brother, Bishop Henry of Winchester, availed him little, for Henry had lost much of the influence he had once wielded in ecclesiastical affairs. The prestige of Cluniac monks came to be eclipsed as the Cistercian order swept to popularity in England in the 1140s, as it had already done in much of western Europe. To St Bernard of Clairvaux, the persuasive spokesman of the Cistercians, Henry of Blois was, as a prince-bishop, the very epitome of all that was most deplorable in a worldly and unrighteous Church. The two were pitted against each other in their efforts to influence the appointment of an archbishop to York, and Henry lost. His commission as papal legate was not renewed after 1143. Archbishop Theobald of Canterbury had always resented Bishop Henry's legatine power as an injury to the prestige and authority of Canterbury, and as Henry's star waned, he worked patiently and with a large measure of success to restore archiepiscopal control of ecclesiastical affairs. King Stephen, in his later years, vacillated between attempts to placate and attempts to coerce the bishops. Theobald, however, had a hold over Stephen which he was careful not to relinquish to either blandishments or bullying: only he, as archbishop of Canterbury, could secure the succession for the king's son Eustace by anointing and crowning him.[2]

For everyone in England, after 1149, what King Stephen did mattered less than what Duke Henry proposed to do. He kept them in suspense for longer than either he or they could have expected, for events on the continent repeatedly delayed his return to England. The first obstacle was the hostility of King Louis VII of France. King Louis had been absent from his realm for over two years on the Second Crusade. On his return at the end of 1149 he was startled at the prospect of the reunion in one pair of hands of the duchy of Normandy and the kingdom of England – a possibility which had seemed remote at his

---

[1] Davis, *King Stephen*, 111–14; Cronne, *The Reign of Stephen*, 178–80. The treaty between the earls of Chester and Leicester is printed and discussed in Stenton, *The First Century of English Feudalism*, 250–6, 286–8. About 1150 Earl Robert married his daughter to William, earl of Gloucester, the son of the empress's champion, *Complete Peerage*, V, 688.

[2] Davis, *King Stephen*, 98ff.; Saltman, *Archbishop Theobald*, 36ff.; and below, ch. 11, p. 426.

departure in June 1147. His response was to refuse to recognise Henry as duke and to summon his sister's husband, Stephen's son Eustace, to help him deprive Henry of the duchy. But whether they attacked from Boulogne, the Capetian royal demesne, or Blois, they could not rupture the defences of the Norman frontier. St Bernard exerted himself as a peacemaker, and Count Geoffrey advised his son to barter the Norman Vexin for recognition as duke. Peace was made at Paris at the end of August 1151: Henry did homage to King Louis and was formally invested with the duchy.[1]

Henry immediately began to make preparations for an expedition to England; but they were overtaken by the sudden death of his father at the age of thirty-nine, on 7 September. Henry had to go into Anjou to take possession of his inheritance and assure himself of the fidelity of its vassals. His supporters in England were becoming impatient, and in March 1152 they sent over Earl Reginald of Cornwall to implore him to delay no longer.[2] A council of barons was summoned to Lisieux on 6 April to make arrangements for the invasion. But by then Henry was involved in another matter, at the time highly secret, which came startlingly to light when on 18 May 1152 he married Eleanor, daughter and heiress of William X, duke of Aquitaine, and cast-off wife of King Louis VII of France. The marriage took place barely eight weeks after a council of the French clergy had fallen in with the king's wish to be parted from his wife. Henry had probably met her only once before – at the peace talks at Paris the previous summer (though scandal said she knew his father better than she should have done).[3] Gervase of Canterbury speaks of a love match, but was writing much later and seems to be embroidering a doubtful tale.[4] The contemporary Norman chronicler, Robert de Torigny, was uncertain whether Henry married her 'on an impulse or by premeditated design'.[5] But although everyone seems to have been taken by surprise, it is difficult to believe that their union had not been prearranged. It had been clear for some months that King Louis wished to have his marriage annulled, and already at Christmas 1151 he had withdrawn his garrisons from Aquitaine.[6]

Louis VII has often been criticised for political folly in repudiating his wife. The criticism is misplaced. It is true that as duchess of Aquitaine in her own right she took from him direct control of nearly half of

---

[1] Robert de Torigny, 160–3. For the intervention of St Bernard see *Patrologia Latina*, clxxxv, 329.   [2] Robert de Torigny, 164.   [3] Gerald of Wales, VIII, 300.

[4] Gervase of Canterbury, I, 149. Gerald of Wales, VIII, 300–1, passes on a rumour that they had been lovers before the marriage.

[5] Robert de Torigny, 165: 'sive repentino sive praemeditato concilio'.

[6] *Recueil des Chroniques de Touraine*, 135. Cf. Geoffrey de Vigeois, II, 307.

France and transferred it to a vassal whose growing power already
looked dangerous; but Louis did not set aside his wife lightly. It was
said that he loved beyond reason the black-eyed beauty whom he had

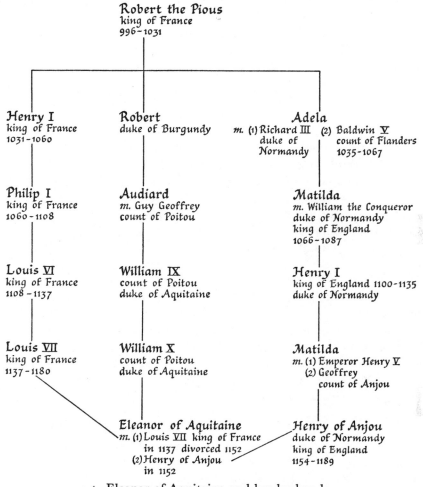

4. Eleanor of Aquitaine and her husbands

married in 1137 when she was fifteen, shortly before he himself ascended
the throne. Henry of Anjou was four years old at the time. It is possible
that they had become incompatible, for King Louis developed into a
devout ascetic, while she, lively, headstrong, and worldly, preferred
amorous dalliance, and had been less than discreet in her flirtations
when she accompanied her husband to the east on the Second Crusade.[1]

[1] John of Salisbury, *Historia Pontificalis*, 52–3, cf. Richard of Devizes, 25–6. The

But Louis did not set her aside for this reason. The technical ground for the annulment was consanguinity, but the real reason was that in fourteen years of married life she had borne only two children and both of them daughters. King Louis had to try again with a new wife, for the secret of the Capetians' survival lay in always having a son to succeed peacefully. Beside this, the right to exercise direct authority over Aquitaine was of little account, for King Louis had insufficient resources to be able to master the unruly vassals of the duchy who divided real power there among themselves. There could be no thought of merely holding it in trust for his successors: Eleanor's father had insisted that her marriage to the heir of the French throne should not lead to the incorporation of the duchy in the royal demesne.[1] Louis's mistake did not lie in divorcing Eleanor; it lay in failing to prevent her marrying Henry of Anjou. As the heiress of a fief of the French Crown she should not, by feudal custom, have remarried without the king's consent. The unauthorised marriage was a slight on the royal dignity, besides being a personal insult, for Eleanor was as closely related by blood to Henry as she was to Louis himself.[2] And what was worse, she might now bear a son who would automatically disinherit her two daughters by her first marriage, and hence exclude from Aquitaine the husbands which the king destined for them.[3]

Henry's marriage was a gamble, politically as well as personally. Besides incurring the hostility of his overlord, it saddled him with a province which most men would have thought ungovernable. But Eleanor's marriage to anyone else could have been dangerous. The county of Poitou was the stronghold of ducal power, and Poitou marched with Anjou south of the river Loire. Some of the most strategically important castles of the Angevin dominions lay in territories for which the counts of Anjou were technically vassals of the lords of Poitou.[4] Louis's repudiation of his wife was a blessing, for it removed Capetian influence from Anjou's borders, but real security could be found only by marrying Eleanor himself. Having appraised the situation, Henry acted with the unhesitating resolution which was soon to

---

date of Eleanor's birth is not precisely known but she was at least thirteen and probably fifteen when she married Louis on 25 July 1137. Her father had died the previous April. Cf. Labande, 'Pour une image véridique d'Aliénor d'Aquitaine'.

[1] *Histoire des Institutions Françaises*, ed. Lot and Fawtier, II, 247.

[2] *See* Diagram 4, p. 43.

[3] Robert de Torigny, 165, makes this point; cf. *Gesta Stephani*, 149.

[4] These included the castles of Loudun and Mirebeau in the lands between the rivers Le Touet and La Vienne; cf. Boussard, *Le Comté d'Anjou*, ch. 1 and 2, and map facing p. 64.

be seen as typical of him. Eleanor could no doubt have had her pick of the bachelors and widowers who were prepared to flout King Louis's right as feudal overlord to find a husband for her. Henry was eleven years her junior; but of all the eligible bachelors he, as duke of Normandy, count of Anjou, Maine, and Touraine, and moreover with a strong claim upon the throne of England, came nearest to being a worthy partner for a discarded queen. It is typical of her too that she acted to make herself mistress of the situation before she became its victim. As soon as the conclave of complaisant French prelates at Beaugency on the Tuesday before Palm Sunday declared her marriage to be within the prohibited degrees of kinship, she hastened away from the French court, eluded an attempt by the count of Blois to waylay her, escaped narrowly from an ambush laid by Henry's younger brother Geoffrey, and reached the safety of Poitou. There Henry joined her and they were married at Poitiers on Whit Sunday 1152.[1]

A month later Henry was at Barfleur on the Normandy coast completing his preparations for an invasion of England.[2] Again he was forced to postpone it, this time because King Louis, furious at being outwitted by his ex-wife, and refusing to accept Henry as duke of Aquitaine, had launched an attack across the Norman frontier. The king had some hope of success for he had allies among those whose ambitions were threatened by Henry of Anjou. One of these allies was Henry count of Champagne, a nephew of King Stephen, who was betrothed to Louis's eldest daughter by Eleanor, and who saw his prospects of acquiring Aquitaine in her name slipping away. Another ally was King Stephen's eldest son Eustace. He had been invested by his father with part of the family's fiefs, the county of Boulogne, but was denied the county of Mortain in Normandy and threatened with being denied the throne of England. He rightly judged that his best hope of being crowned king of England lay in defeating his rival on the continent. The third ally, and in some ways the most troublesome, was Henry's own brother Geoffrey. He was disappointed at the inheritance he had received from his father, and had been thwarted of his ambition to cut a figure in the world by marrying Eleanor himself.

Precisely what Count Geoffrey bequeathed to his younger sons is uncertain, for he conveyed his intentions to those who attended his deathbed by word of mouth. According to the Norman chronicler Robert de Torigny, Count Geoffrey bequeathed to his second son and

---

[1] *Recueil des Chroniques de Touraine*, 135; Gervase of Canterbury, I, 149; Robert de Torigny, 165. Cf. Boussard, *Le Government d'Henri II*, 9, 10, and *Le Comté d'Anjou*, 69.

[2] Robert de Torigny, 165; he had been preparing since Easter, *ibid.*, 164.

namesake four castles. He does not name them, but they almost certainly included the castles of Chinon, Loudun, and Mirebeau. These were the key strongholds controlling the territories which the counts of Anjou had acquired from the counts of Poitou, and there is reason for believing that they were traditionally regarded as the appanage of a younger son of the house of Anjou.[1] Geoffrey, however, asserted that his proper inheritance was Anjou itself. The story was told – either then, or more probably later – that Count Geoffrey intended Henry to have possession of Anjou and Maine only until he recovered the whole of his mother's inheritance. When he had gained England he was to release his paternal inheritance to his brother Geoffrey. In the meantime Geoffrey's right was to be safeguarded by the custody of the castles. Since, as the story went, Henry did not arrive before his father's death, Count Geoffrey made the bishops and barons swear that his body would not be laid to rest until Henry had taken an oath to observe his father's will, before being told what it was. Henry, it is said, was reluctant, but, implored by those who wished to see the dead count given decent burial, took the required oath at the funeral at Le Mans, and was dismayed by what was then revealed. The story appears in contemporary sources only in a minor chronicle written at Tours.[2] The English chronicler, William of Newburgh, who repeats it much later, believed that Henry secured release from his oath from the pope on the valid ground that an oath sworn in ignorance of its obligations could not be upheld.[3] Many historians have accepted the story on Newburgh's authority, but it is improbable. It is unlikely that Count Geoffrey would have believed it possible to hold his son to an oath sworn in such circumstances. Even as a moral obligation, the proposed division would have seemed improper to contemporaries. It is true that a division of territories between sons was quite customary, but it was usual for the eldest son to receive the patrimony, the second son to receive the lands which the father had acquired by marriage or conquest. It was in accordance with this principle that William the Conqueror bequeathed Normandy to his eldest son, and the kingdom of England to his second son. Moreover, if the story were true, it would have been in young Geoffrey's interests to help his brother to acquire England in 1152, not to impede him. Almost certainly the story was spread to justify young Geoffrey's second rebellion against his brother in 1156. It never seems to have

---

[1] These castles are named in *Recueil des Chroniques de Touraine*, 136, and Geoffrey's possession of them is demonstrated in the sequel. It was with these castles that Henry II later proposed to endow his son John: Roger of Howden, *Gesta*, I, 41.

[2] *Recueil des Chroniques de Touraine*, 136; Boussard, *Le Comté d'Anjou*, 68.

[3] William of Newburgh, I, 112–13.

recommended itself to anyone of importance, and significantly, not even to King Louis VII, who would have been glad to use it if it had a basis in fact.[1] The real basis for Geoffrey's insurrection was that the barons of Anjou would welcome a rival for the countship. They had only recently, and reluctantly, been brought to respect the authority of Count Geoffrey; and a disputed succession would give them an opportunity to reassert their autonomy, or at the very least extort concessions for their support.

The coalition was formidable, but Henry dealt with it with the determination and despatch which were soon to become the hallmarks of his defensive military operations. He was never one to be distracted by a multiplicity of threats into dissipating his efforts. He selected a target for counter-attack, concentrated his forces against it, and outwitted his opponents by the rapidity of his movements. In the summer of 1152 he moved his army so swiftly from Barfleur to the threatened regions of the Norman frontier, that, it is said, several horses fell dead on the road.[2] He did not engage King Louis's forces directly but counter-attacked elsewhere, ravaging the Vexin and distracting the king by invading the lands of his ally, the count of Dreux. Having thus reminded his opponents that it was dangerous to play with fire, and having assured himself that his frontier defences were adequately manned, he then suddenly swung his counter-attack against the supporters of Geoffrey. He first undermined his brother's position by persuading the castellans of Chinon, Loudun, and Mirebeau to surrender their charges to himself, and next directed the whole weight of his forces into a siege of Montsoreau where the major rebels were ensconced. It was captured; most of the rebels fell into his hands, and Geoffrey submitted. King

[1] To judge from contemporary lawbooks there seems to have been some uncertainty as to whether the general principle that a younger son might be given his father's acquisitions could properly be applied if the acquisitions were larger than the patrimony. It should be observed however, that Count Geoffrey had already decided this issue when in 1149 he handed over Normandy to Henry, who was then installed as duke. In 1151, therefore, the only question was the destiny of the patrimony. It would have been unusual but not unreasonable if Count Geoffrey had on his deathbed willed his second son to have Anjou; nothing, however, could justify a proposal that Henry should be invested with the county of Anjou but forfeit it if he acquired the kingdom of England, thereby disinheriting his own heirs. The impropriety of the alleged proposal is not, however, the only reason for dismissing the story as a fabrication. John of Salisbury was either ignorant of it or gave it no credit: writing, as Archbishop Theobald's secretary, to the bishop of Norwich in 1156 to excuse the king's demands for money to put down his brother's second rebellion, he remarks that 'justice is on our side', *Letters*, I, 21–2. There is no mention of the pope having absolved Henry from an oath to deliver up Anjou to his brother.

[2] Robert de Torigny, 169–70; Gervase of Canterbury, I, 149–50.

Louis, thwarted of success even in Henry's absence, and falling sick of a fever, sought a truce.[1]

Duke Henry's reputation had no doubt been enhanced by his brisk defence of his patrimony, but necessity had denied him the opportunity to mount a summer campaign in England, and it was quite likely that by the time suitable weather returned for safely ferrying an army across the Channel, his position there would have been seriously eroded. This was Stephen's strategy; while his son Eustace had joined King Louis to harass Henry in Normandy, incessant attacks were mounted on the duke's supporters in England, wearing them down piecemeal, in a determined effort to destroy the bridgehead for Henry's invasion.[2] Against the numerous mercenary troops whom Stephen imported to wage war in many places at once, the duke's adherents were hard put to defend themselves, and were prevented from mounting a concerted counter-attack. The main weight of Stephen's effort was directed against Wallingford, the stronghold of Brian FitzCount on the Upper Thames, which ever since the banner of the empress had been raised had been a finger poking defiance at the heart of Stephen's kingdom. It should have fallen after the king's capture of Faringdon in 1145 had disrupted its communications with the Angevin bases in the west, but it had survived with the help of courageous defence and a trickle of supplies and reinforcements across the bridge over the Thames – a persistent mockery of Stephen's attempts to establish his authority. Its strategic importance after the rout of the empress had not been great, but Stephen rightly fastened upon it in 1152 as a symbol of his opponents' refusal to submit and put an end to the civil war. If he could capture Wallingford while Duke Henry was preoccupied with his interests on the continent, it would very probably demoralise the duke's adherents in England and persuade them to save themselves by coming to terms, instead of waiting in the hope, so many times frustrated already, of the succour of an army from Normandy.

The siege of Wallingford was pursued with determination and with the persistence which the use of well-paid mercenaries made possible. Two castles were built over against Wallingford to ensure the besiegers an adequate store of supplies and protection against sallies by the defenders or relieving forces, so that they might at all seasons harass the defence and cut off provisions. Attempts by Earl Roger of Hereford to bring help or to divert Stephen's attention to Worcester met with little success. By the winter of 1152 the bridge over the river was securely in

---

[1] Robert de Torigny, 171; Gervase of Canterbury, I, 149–50; Boussard, *Le Comté d'Anjou*, 69–70.　　　　　　　　[2] *Gesta Stephani*, 150.

the hands of the king's men and all access denied to both town and castle. The defenders took the only course still open to them: they notified their lord, Duke Henry, of their peril, and informed the king that they were ready to surrender if their lord could not bring them help.[1] No ignominy was attached to a beleagured garrison which sought terms for surrender if its position were hopeless, and besiegers were usually ready to agree for it saved them from the hazards of direct assault. No help could really be expected from Duke Henry. The invasion forces he had mustered had been deployed for the defence of the Normandy border, and no reliance could be placed on the fragile truce, for King Louis was almost certain to renew his offensive in the spring.[2] Eustace remained on the continent, presumably with the intention of keeping Henry in fear of a threat in Normandy while his father crushed the remaining opposition in England. They had mistaken their man: Henry of Anjou never allowed himself to become a victim of circumstances – he moulded situations to his will. A fortnight after Christmas he embarked for England and crossed the Channel despite a severe mid-winter gale.[3] He took with him a force composed almost entirely of mercenaries hired, in all probability, with borrowed money. William of Newburgh puts it at 140 knights and 3,000 foot soldiers, and Robert de Torigny reports that it was transported in thirty-six vessels – a smaller number of ships than Earl Robert of Gloucester had needed for the reinforcements he brought over in 1142.[4] It was hardly a massive invasion; but the decisive fact was that Henry disconcerted his enemies and heartened his friends by a bold and unexpected move. Eustace hastily followed him across the Channel.[5]

Although doubtless disturbed by Henry's arrival, King Stephen may well have thought that the military initiative remained in his hands. To relieve Wallingford Henry would have to march far from his bases at Devizes and Bristol, to a neighbourhood denuded of provisions, and with transport made difficult by winter rains. But Henry's grasp of

[1] *Ibid.*, 150ff.; Henry of Huntingdon, 284; Gervase of Canterbury, I, 153.

[2] According to Robert de Torigny, 171, 172, King Louis repudiated the truce, and in April fired Vernon.

[3] Henry of Huntingdon, 285; *Gesta Stephani*, 150. Gervase of Canterbury, I, 151, says that he arrived on 6 January, Robert de Torigny, 171, says 'within the octave of Epiphany'.

[4] William of Newburgh, I, 88; Robert de Torigny, 171. Earl Robert had employed fifty-two vessels: William of Malmesbury, *Historia Novella*, 74. The *Gesta Stephani*, 152, says that Henry landed 'cum immenso militum et pedestrium agmine', but Henry of Huntingdon, 285, confirms that it was a small force. That Henry was relying on loans is suggested by the extent of his debt repayments after becoming king, cf. Richardson, 'The chamber under Henry II', 605ff.   [5] *Gesta Stephani*, 152.

strategy was equal to such a problem. He did not go to King Stephen, he obliged Stephen to come to him – and hence raise the pressure on Wallingford. Henry coolly turned the tables by mounting a surprise attack on Malmesbury, the royalist equivalent of Wallingford at the head of a salient thrust within the triangle formed by the Angevin strongholds of Bristol, Gloucester, and Devizes. By the time the king arrived with his army the town had fallen and the castle was closely besieged. The two forces faced each other across a river Avon swollen with flood waters. The winter was bitter, and there was famine in those parts. A biting rain beat down on the faces of the king's men, who were so numb they could barely hold their weapons. Stephen, moreover, was uncertain of the loyalty of some of his barons. They had discharged their allegiance by answering his call to arms, but, as the *Gesta Stephani* says, 'were very slack and negligent in their services and had sent envoys secretly to make their peace with the duke'.[1] Stephen was obliged to offer a truce. Henry, whose troops were also suffering privations, agreed. The terms are not known for certain, but it seems that Stephen was to be allowed to withdraw his garrison safely from the castle at Malmesbury and to destroy its fortifications, while Wallingford was to have a respite for six months.[2]

At this point Earl Robert of Leicester openly changed sides and negotiated Duke Henry's acceptance of his homage.[3] His submission put thirty castles into Henry's hands, and opened the way to control of the midlands. Henry moved next to make sure of it, leading his army through Worcestershire, Warwickshire, Northamptonshire, and Bedfordshire. At Tutbury he forced Earl Robert de Ferrers to submit; Warwick castle was surrendered to him by the countess of Warwick; Bedford was besieged and captured.[4] At the end of July or the beginning of August he turned to the relief of Wallingford, and set about trying to break down Stephen's fortifications at the approaches. Stephen brought up what is described as an 'inexpressibly large army from every part of his kingdom', and was attended by 'many earls and

[1] *Gesta Stephani*, 154.

[2] Henry's delay in going to Wallingford until the summer is explicable only in these terms. The *Gesta Stephani*, 154, relates that Stephen and Henry agreed to the demolition of Malmesbury castle, but that the man sent in by the king to supervise the work handed it over intact to the duke. Cf. Gervase of Canterbury, I, 152–3, Henry of Huntingdon, 286–7.

[3] *Regesta Regum Anglo-Normannorum*, III, 165–6; *Recueil des Actes de Henri II*, I, 52–3; he appears as a witness to Henry's charters, *ibid.*, I, 59, 70.

[4] Henry's itinerary is difficult to reconstruct; *see* Poole's introduction to the *Gesta Stephani*, xxiii–xxix; Z. N. and C. N. L. Brooke, 'Henry II duke of Normandy and Aquitaine', 86–8; Davis, *King Stephen*, 119.

countless barons'.[1] His intention was to settle the issue in a pitched battle, but again he was thwarted by the reluctance of the barons. As the author of the *Gesta Stephani* writes, 'The leading men on both sides and those of deeper judgement, shrank from a conflict which was not merely between fellow countrymen, but meant the desolation of the whole kingdom'.[2] Few, it seems, were prepared to consign to the uncertain outcome of battle a problem which was susceptible to a negotiated settlement. Even among those who had faithfully supported the king and still deemed it their duty to follow him, there was a widespread conviction that Henry should be recognised as legitimate heir.[3] They obliged Stephen to agree to another truce and to open negotiations. The two armies which had again confronted each other across a river, once more drew apart. The archbishop of Canterbury and the bishop of Winchester worked as mediators, though without at first much apparent success. Duke Henry and King Stephen both sought to strengthen their bargaining positions, but seem to have carefully avoided each other. Henry resumed his progress through the midlands, in the course of which he captured Stamford and sacked Nottingham. Stephen chastised Hugh Bigod, an old enemy who had long escaped retribution, by seizing his castle at Ipswich. Eustace, furious at the avoidance of a decisive encounter, tried to bring his rival to battle by rampaging through Cambridgeshire, spreading wanton destruction. On 17 August, however, he suddenly died, struck down, some said, by divine vengeance for the damage he had done to the property of St Edmund's abbey.[4] Few had much good to say of Eustace, but he was a determined and courageous warrior, and it was probably he who had stiffened his father in his last dogged resistance and refusal to negotiate. Stephen had a younger son, William, but the death of Eustace seems to have robbed him of resolution.

The mediators now began to make real headway. The king and the duke were persuaded to meet on 6 November 1153 at Winchester for a reconciliation. According to Robert de Torigny peace was made on these terms:

The king first acknowledged before the assembled barons, earls and other magnates, the hereditary right which the duke had in the kingdom of England. And the duke generously conceded that the king should hold

---

[1] *Gesta Stephani*, 157; cf. Gervase of Canterbury, I, 153; Henry of Huntingdon, 287.
[2] *Gesta Stephani*, 157.
[3] Gervase of Canterbury, I, 154. Even the author of the *Gesta Stephani*, a supporter of the king, referred to Henry as 'the lawful heir to England', 142, 148.
[4] Robert de Torigny, 176; Gervase of Canterbury, I, 155; *Gesta Stephani*, 158.

the kingdom for the rest of his life, if he wished, provided, however, that the king himself, the bishops and other magnates should bind themselves by an oath that the duke, if he survived, should succeed to the kingdom, peacefully and without denial. It was also sworn that lands which had fallen to intruders should be restored to their former and legitimate possessors who had held them in the time of the excellent King Henry; and that castles which had been erected since the death of that king should be destroyed.[1]

This however, was merely the basis for a settlement. The precise terms took longer to arrange. They were announced by Stephen in a charter addressed 'to all his liegemen of England' from Westminster at Christmas. In it the king declared that he had adopted Duke Henry as his 'son and heir', and that the duke had done homage to him and sworn to be his liegeman as long as he should live. The duke had confirmed to the king's son William all the honors which the king had himself conferred on his son, the properties which came to him by marriage to the daughter of the earl of Warenne, and had agreed to restore to him the castles belonging to the honor of Mortain in Normandy. The duke's vassals, including, it was specially noted, 'those who keep the castle of Wallingford', had done homage to the king, and the king's men had done homage to the duke, saving only the fealty they owed to the king as long as he should live. The key castles of the Tower of London, Windsor, Oxford, Lincoln, and Winchester, and the 'fortification' of Southampton were entrusted to custodians acceptable to both parties, and were to be handed over to the duke at the king's death. If the custodian of any other royal castle should be rebellious, 'then the duke and I making common cause shall wage war upon him until he had been compelled to give satisfaction to both of us'. In conclusion the king declared that 'in all the business of the kingdom I will act with the advice of the duke', but claimed as the prerogative of the crown the right to exercise royal justice throughout the realm.[2]

The other aspects of the basis for settlement agreed at Winchester presented greater difficulties. The implications of the agreement on the restoration of the dispossessed to disputed properties were to dog Henry II for the whole of his reign, for rival claims could not easily or always be disentangled.[3] The agreement to destroy 'adulterine' castles

---

[1] Robert de Torigny, 177.

[2] *Regesta Regum Anglo-Normannorum*, III, 272; *Recueil des Actes de Henri II*, I, 62–5, translated in *English Historical Documents*, II, 404–7.

[3] *See* Davis, *King Stephen*, 124–6, for illustrations of the difficulties and the kind of compromises which were arranged.

was already, by January 1154, producing strains in the relations between duke and king, the former complaining that the latter was not
so resolute as himself in proceeding with the work. It was only to be
expected, of course, that some men would not take kindly to the sacri-
fices demanded of them personally in the interests of peace. There were
even rumours of plots to ensure that the duke did not survive the king.[1]
Henry deemed it prudent to retire to Normandy and took his leave
before Easter 1154.

Henry was still in Normandy, besieging a troublesome vassal in the
castle of Torigny, when news reached him that King Stephen had died
on 25 October. He did not hurry to England: the reduction of the castle
was completed first and his affairs in Normandy set in order, while
contrary winds blew themselves out in the Channel. For six weeks
England was kingless but at peace – 'for love or fear of the king to
come' as Henry of Huntingdon remarks. On 7 December 1154 Henry
of Anjou and his wife, Eleanor of Aquitaine, crossed from Barfleur; on
19 December they were crowned together at Westminster Abbey by
Archbishop Theobald of Canterbury.[2] The new king was twenty-one
years of age.

[1] Henry of Huntingdon, 290; Gervase of Canterbury, I, 158.
[2] Henry of Huntingdon, 290–1; Robert de Torigny, 180–1; Gervase of Canterbury,
I, 159; William of Newburgh, I, 95–6.

Chapter 3

KING, DUKE, AND COUNT:
A CHRONOLOGICAL SURVEY,
1154–c. 1182

(1) *Pacification* (1154–8)

Henry II began his reign with three advantages. In the first place he was undisputed successor to the throne. It was not necessary for him to make concessions to win friends and buy support. The charter which he issued to his subjects immediately after his coronation was brief and inexplicit. He confirmed all concessions, grants, liberties, and free customs which King Henry his grandfather had granted and conceded; and he foreswore in the name of himself and his heirs all those evil customs which his grandfather had abolished. It was a proclamation of respect for good law, but at the same time it implicitly made void all the concessions and grants of King Stephen.

The second advantage which the new king enjoyed was the lapse of a year between the treaty of Winchester and the death of King Stephen. Had Henry of Anjou been called upon to assume the throne at short notice, his small acquaintance with England would have told against him. He might have been obliged to lean too heavily upon the advice of those who had served in his household as duke of Normandy. Archbishop Theobald privately expressed the liveliest apprehensions about companions of the young duke who were known for their anti-clericalism.[1] That Henry was able to allay such anxieties and appoint as chief ministers in England men who were neither friends nor partisans is a clear indication that the period when he was heir presumptive had been used profitably in stocktaking and consultation. Immediately after his coronation Henry appointed to high office three men drawn from each of the three elements which were crucial in control of the realm: the baronage, the clergy, and the administrative service of King Stephen.

From among the late king's servants, Henry selected to be in charge of the royal administration a man who had recently fought against him

[1] William of Canterbury I, 4–5; Roger of Pontigny, IV, 11; John of Salisbury, Vita Sancti Thomae, 304.

at Oxford – Richard de Lucy. His social background was that of the knightly class, but he was already, by making himself useful both to the Crown and to members of the baronage, quietly collecting fiefs which would eventually make him a man of substance. His precise status under Stephen is uncertain; but he was undoubtedly in the later years of the reign sheriff and royal justice in Essex and held custody of the Tower of London and of Windsor castle, which imply that he had taken charge in the king's name of the extensive authority forfeited by Earl Geoffrey de Mandeville. Whether he was also, as has been suggested, already in charge of the exchequer and supervisor of all the king's officers, with the title of justiciar, is more doubtful; but he was certainly one of the most experienced and trusted of Stephen's servants.[1]

It was, of course, sensible to entrust control of the English administration to a man already intimately familiar with its workings; but Henry II was wary of creating another Roger of Salisbury. He recognised that to place royal authority in the hands of a non-noble servant, as his grandfather had done, ran the risk of alienating the greater baronage. To offset this possibility Richard de Lucy was given a colleague: as co-justiciar Henry appointed Robert de Beaumont, earl of Leicester, who, since the death of Earl Ranulf of Chester in 1153, was probably the most powerful baron in England. The influence of Earl Robert and of his twin brother Waleran, count of Meulan, upon King Stephen in the early years of the reign had been unfortunate, and they had slipped from favour after the king's captivity. It seems, however, that Robert was always the more sober and practical of the two, and as he matured he began to reveal more statesmanlike qualities than the rest of the barons. He soon came to realise that the barons had as much to lose as the Crown by the continuance of anarchy, and tried to mitigate the effects of private war in the midlands by concluding treaties and marriage alliances which cut across political allegiances. He did not try to barter his allegiance as others did, but in quest of a lasting solution to the dynastic conflict he gave his support to Duke Henry in the spring of 1153 – late enough to have allowed King Stephen a reasonable opportunity of winning the war, but soon enough to avoid the accusation of being simply a political turncoat backing a certainty.[2] He was well educated for a layman. He had received schooling as a boy at the

---

[1] Robert de Torigny, 174; West, *The Justiciarship*, 37ff.; *Regesta Regum Anglo-Normannorum* III, nos. 543, 546–50, 552, 559; Richardson and Sayles, *The Governance of Medieval England*, 166; Cronne, *The Reign of Stephen*, 188, 256; *Recueil des Actes de Henri II*, Introduction, 434ff.

[2] *See* above, ch. 2, pp. 40–1, 50; Davis, *King Stephen*, 111–14, 118; charters to him by Duke Henry, *Regesta Regum Anglo-Normannorum*, III, nos 438, 439.

abbey of Abingdon, and training for knighthood at the court of Henry I. He is said to have astonished the college of cardinals with his precocious learning when in 1119 he accompanied the king to meet the pope at Gisors; and John of Salisbury wrote with respect of his views on kingship. As co-justiciar he was noted for his prudence and discretion.[1] Since, until his death in 1168, he is more frequently mentioned as justiciar than Richard de Lucy, it has been assumed that he overshadowed his colleague; but the records of the period are too sparse for any such judgement to be made. Earl Robert's social position ensured him prominence as well as precedence, and it was probably deliberate policy that he should appear publicly as the king's deputy. Whether there was any formal division of function between them is equally hard to say; though it would not be surprising if Richard de Lucy provided professional expertise to the partnership and directed the operations of the administration, while the earl contributed political judgement, dealt with the barons, and presided at public sessions of the king's court in Henry's absence.[2] There is no sign whatever of discord between them.

Henry II's third major appointment was to the office of chancellor. The chancellor was master of the royal chapel and head of the royal secretariat. It was a post which made him not only the king's confidant, but also responsible for translating the royal will into charters, letters, and writs. The office, although vital, had not hitherto been one of great prestige. Henry might have been expected to appoint to it one of his own chaplains; but astutely he consulted Archbishop Theobald and accepted his recommendation, appointing the archbishop's own favourite clerk, Thomas Becket, archdeacon of Canterbury. Although later fiction sometimes spoke of Becket as an Englishman, he came, in fact, from a humble if respectable Norman family. His father, Gilbert Becket, born in Rouen, had become a prosperous merchant in London and served a term as one of the two sheriffs of the city. Thomas himself, after education at Merton priory and Paris, had been for a time clerk and accountant to the sheriffs of London, before entering the household of Archbishop Theobald.[3] The fact of his new chancellor's close con-

---

[1] *Chronicon Monasterii de Abingdon*, II, 229; John of Salisbury, *Policraticus*, II, 74; *Dialogus de Scaccario*, 57.

[2] Cf. West, *The Justiciarship*, 35ff. The *Dialogus de Scaccario*, 58, it is true, mentions the earl presiding at the exchequer and not Richard de Lucy, but the treasurer's references to the higher officers of the *curia regis* are infrequent; and it may be significant that the account in which the reference to the earl occurs, reveals his unfamiliarity with exchequer procedure.

[3] William FitzStephen, III, 14–18; Herbert of Bosham, III, 167–73; William of

nections with the ruling oligarchy of London may have helped Henry II's relations with the city, which had always been suspicious of the Angevins and consistently loyal to Stephen. But the main advantage of the appointment, besides giving Henry a very able chancellor, was that it gave him the confidence of Archbishop Theobald, and through him the support of the English Church. It also – although this was unexpected and in the end nearly disastrous – gave Henry a companion with whom he developed the closest friendship.

The third advantage which Henry of Anjou enjoyed at his accession was weariness with the *tempus werre*. The widespread desire for an end to disorder enabled Henry II to take bold decisions for the restoration of royal authority which at any time were unpalatable and which at any other time would have been insupportable.

Nevertheless, despite the advantages which he enjoyed, the problems facing the young king were formidable. Much of the country was demoralised by disorder and the struggle to survive: crimes of violence by those who set themselves beyond the law, brigandage by mercenary troops, the tyranny of the 'castle-men', were all symptoms of a situation in which, as the chronicler of Battle Abbey wrote, 'he who was strongest got most'.[1] Stephen, in his last months, paraded himself, writes William of Newburgh, 'as if he were a new king', and made some show of putting down robber barons; but he never, after his abortive attempts in 1143–6, engaged in a trial of strength with any of the earls.[2] Even his undisputed authority in his last days was hollow, for he was king by grace and favour of the greater barons who divided effective control of the realm between them. The civil war was at an end, but the country was not disarmed, and strife might readily break out again if the reconciliation of rivals and the settlement of conflicting claims were mismanaged. No man would willingly lay down his arms and demolish his strongholds unless his neighbours did likewise, or at least until there was an authority in the land which could ensure the preservation of public order. Stephen had the will but not the power, and it is likely that his commands were obeyed only when it suited the convenience of great lords to enforce them. Determined efforts seem to have been made by King Stephen after his release from captivity in November 1141 to

---

Canterbury, I, 3–5; Edward Grim, II, 356–63; Roger of Pontigny, IV, 3–12; Anonymous of Lambeth, IV, 81–4.

[1] *Chronicon Monasterii de Bello*, 106; cf. *Chronicon Abbatiae Rameseiensis*, 334: 'The whole island was ruled by force rather than reason.'

[2] William of Newburgh, I, 94.

restore the crumbling structure of royal government, and he recruited the services of men whose worth was to be recognised by Henry II; but they struggled with only a modicum of success against the stranglehold of the magnates on local government. Royal writs and royal officers had for many years been denied access to those areas of the country dominated by adherents of the empress, and it was unlikely that they would be welcomed again merely because Duke Henry made a treaty to secure his succession to the throne. Even in those areas of the country controlled by men loyal to Stephen the efficient functioning of the royal administration could not be guaranteed. The strife of rivals hindered sheriffs and royal justices, and impoverished those liable to contribute to the royal revenue even in shires which did not become battlegrounds for the armies of the king and the empress.[1] That the royal exchequer functioned at all and garnered what revenue it could is a tribute to the resilience of the institution fashioned by Henry I, and an indication of Stephen's belated recognition of its importance; but it never, in Stephen's reign, entirely recovered from the dislocation caused by the downfall of Henry I's ministers, and was unable even to check properly either the honesty or the efficiency of the sheriffs who answered its summons.[2] Stephen had been saved from financial disaster by subsidies from sympathetic towns and by his wife's revenues from Boulogne. Henry of Anjou had no such resources: the revenues of Normandy were barely adequate for its defence, and he began his reign heavily burdened with debt from his campaign of 1153.[3]

Many of those problems could not be solved overnight, and at Henry's accession it must have seemed to many doubtful if they could be solved at all. If Stephen, devoting all his attention to it, had tried in vain to establish his authority, what chance had the young Henry of Anjou, who was saddled besides with provinces stretching from the Channel to the Pyrenees, and threatened both by the ambition of his brother Geoffrey and the hostility of King Louis of France? The general expectation was probably that Henry would acquiesce in the dispersion of effective power among the great barons, and rely on their cooperation in holding the kingdom at peace while he busied himself on the continent. Indeed it may well have been this calculation which prompted many of the barons to accept Duke Henry as Stephen's heir.

[1] The evidence for this is the allowances for 'waste' in the Danegeld assessments for many countries in the early pipe rolls of Henry II; cf. Davis, 'The anarchy of Stephen's reign', and the comments of Cronne, *The Reign of Stephen*, 224–5.

[2] Cronne, *op. cit.*, ch. 8; cf. below, pp. 258–9, 266.

[3] Cf. Jenkinson, 'William Cade, a financier of the twelfth century', 215ff.; Richardson, 'The chamber under Henry II', 605ff.

They were to be rudely disillusioned: Henry was determined to be not merely king, but just such a king as his grandfather had been. He did not, however, make his mother's mistake of behaving like an autocrat while real power lay elsewhere: he manœuvred himself into a position of dominance, extending his control one step at a time, cleverly exploiting the general desire for a restoration of order, and acting only after consultation with his barons in frequent meetings of the great council, so that his decisions might seem to be their own and his actions the proper outcome of 'advice and consent'. From the first Henry II displayed a power of persuasion which few could equal and none could resist, and which his enemies could counter only by abusing it as the cunning of a fox.

Henry's immediate purpose was, in the words of Gervase of Canterbury, 'to root out all causes for renewal of warfare and to clear away all inducements to distrust'.[1] He perceived that the essential requirement was to restore confidence in the determination of the government to maintain impartial law and order; and one of his first acts was to set a time limit for the demolition of all remaining strongholds, and for the departure from England of the Flemish mercenaries who had been the mainstay of Stephen's kingship in his later years. These were the two most obvious symbols of the still prevailing uncertainty and insecurity. The dismissal of the late king's mercenaries, however, undoubtedly weakened the new king's military strength, and it is probable that he simply could not afford to retain them; but the effect on public opinion was adequate compensation. To all the chief chroniclers the expulsion of the Flemings was the most striking and gratifying sign that peace had been restored.[2] Even in the next generation, William of Newburgh recorded what was still a lively memory when he wrote that 'the Flemings slipped quickly away like a phantom which is here one moment and gone the next, so that everyone marvelled at their sudden disappearance'.[3] More important, however, was the king's command that the barons must relinquish custody of castles which belonged to the Crown. This was a bold and challenging move, for it struck at the roots of baronial control of the provinces. It was also a gamble, for it is doubtful if Henry could have enforced his demand if there had been concerted resistance. He seems to have relied on exploiting the rivalries of the barons, and on the anxiety of many of them – particularly among

---

[1] Gervase of Canterbury, I, 161.

[2] e.g., Robert de Torigny, 183, Gervase of Canterbury, I, 161, William Fitz-Stephen, III, 18-19.

[3] William of Newburgh, I, 101-2.

Stephen's adherents – to stand well with their new king, in ensuring sufficient support to coerce the recalcitrant.

William le Gros, count of Aumale, was openly defiant. He had been created earl of York by Stephen in 1138, and in the region of the Humber he was, wrote William of Newburgh, 'more truly a king than his master'. Henry marched against him within a month of his coronation. Prompt action against open defiance was ever to be the partner of persuasion in Henry II's dealings with his vassals. In this case the demonstration of Henry's determination was sufficient: when the king reached York, William prudently (though, it is said, with extreme reluctance) submitted, and gave up the royal properties which had for long been in his custody, including the reputedly impregnable fortress on the craggy peninsula at Scarborough.[1] Rebuilt by Henry at considerable expense it was thereafter a bastion of royal authority in the north. The earldom of York was allowed to lapse.

Any suspicion that William le Gros had been singled out for attack as an old and prominent opponent of the house of Anjou was, however, overtaken by Henry's insistence on the resumption of Crown properties from his partisans. Roger, earl of Hereford, and Hugh Mortimer, lord of Cleobury and Wigmore, were indignant at the demand and prepared to resist by force. Earl Roger had particular reason to feel that he deserved well of Henry. He was the son of Miles of Gloucester, whose support had been crucial to Matilda in the early days of her challenge to Stephen. He himself had sustained the Angevin cause in its darkest days after Matilda's withdrawal from England in 1148. Long practised at guerilla warfare and the defence of hard-pressed strongholds, he was a formidable opponent, and it was fortunate for Henry that after his anger had cooled he allowed himself to be persuaded by his kinsman, Bishop Foliot, to submit and hand over his castles at Gloucester and Hereford. When he died later in the year the earldom of Hereford was allowed to lapse. Hugh Mortimer was more obdurate, and Henry had to resort to force. Hugh's three castles – his own castles of Cleobury and Wigmore and the royal castle he held at Bridgnorth – were invested simultaneously. One by one they fell, and Hugh surrendered. His formal sub-

1 William of Newburgh, I, 103–4, cf. *Early Yorkshire Charters*, I, 284. It is possible that the king's bargaining counter with William le Gros was the restoration of the county of Aumale and the family properties in Normandy, which, as a supporter of Stephen, he had presumably forfeited when Geoffrey of Anjou overran the duchy. William was related to the king of France, and by marriage to the royal house of Scotland, cf. Boussard, *Le Gouvernement d'Henri II*, 37–8. The pipe rolls record considerable expenditure on the castle of Scarborough for several years from 1158, cf. Brown, 'Royal castle building, 1154–1216', 379.

mission was received by the king before a full assembly of the archbishops, bishops, earls and barons, summoned to meet at Bridgnorth on 7 July.[1]

Two others of the greater barons shied away from a confrontation with Henry. As the king returned from York via Nottingham, William Peverel, lord of the honor of Peverel of Nottingham, fled the country, fearing retribution, according to the chroniclers, for having procured the death of his rival, Earl Ranulf of Chester, by poison.[2] His honor was forfeit to the Crown.[3] Later in the year, probably after the submission of Hugh Mortimer, Henry of Blois, bishop of Winchester, the princely brother of the late king, who had virtually been earl of Hampshire, retired abroad to the abbey of Cluny without seeking King Henry's leave. Doubtless he could not stomach the humiliation of surrender. His castles were demolished.[4]

Henry II had mastered the barons. There could have been no clearer demonstration of this than the enforcement of his will against leading representatives of each of the three factions which had disputed control of the realm in the previous reign: Stephen's earl of York, Matilda's earl of Hereford, and the prince-bishop of Winchester. The contrast with King Stephen's lackadaisical response to defiance, and his failure to impose his will from the first upon his barons, was inescapable. Henry's ascendancy opened the way for his ministers to pursue fearlessly a policy for the restoration of the royal demesne to its pristine state. According to the chronicler of St Albans, the policy was enunciated in a royal edict that 'all lands throughout Britain which should be identified as having formed part of the demesne of his predecessors as kings of England, no matter who had been in occupation of them in the meantime, should be surrendered without quibble, to remain for the future in his demesne and that of his successors'.[5] The execution of the policy was not quite so drastic as it sounds: those who had received grants of demesne lands might have the grants confirmed or renewed by Henry II, and even those who had usurped or encroached upon

---

[1] Gervase of Canterbury, I, 161–2; William of Newburgh, I, 105; *Chronicon Monasterii de Bello*, 75.

[2] Gervase of Canterbury, I, 155, 161; *Gesta Stephani*, 156; Robert de Torigny, 183.

[3] The pipe rolls reveal that the honor of Peverel was in the king's hands throughout the reign. On the family of Peverel of Nottingham *see Complete Peerage*, IV, 761ff.

[4] Ralph of Diceto, I, 301; Robert de Torigny, 186; cf. Pipe Roll 2 Henry II, 54. The length of his self-imposed exile is uncertain; he seems to have been reconciled to the king by 1158, cf. John of Salisbury, *Letters*, I, 37–69; Voss, *Heinrich von Blois*; Patricia Barnes, 'The Anstey Case', 17.

[5] *Gesta Abbatum Monasterii Sancti Albani*, I, 123; cf. William of Newburgh, I, 103, and the charter of St Peter's church, Northampton (c. 1155–8), printed in Stenton, 'Acta episcoporum', 4.

lands which the king claimed as his, might often be allowed to retain them on payment of a fine and rent.[1] Moreover, recoveries were not made by the arbitrary decision of royal officers but by a sworn inquest of local men, and mistakes could be rectified by appeal to the king.[2] Nevertheless some undoubtedly suffered forfeiture, and for those who continued to enjoy possession of Crown properties it was clearly to be understood that they did so as a royal favour and on terms which were precisely defined.

If law-abiding subjects felt a grievance at the resumption of royal demesne, it was to some extent at least offset by a greater hope of recovering properties usurped by other people. Justice had been a major casualty of the years of anarchy, and one of the crucial elements in the agreement for establishing peace at Winchester in November 1153 was, in the words of the *Gesta Stephani*, that 'the disinherited should be restored to their own and laws and enactments made binding on all as they used to be'.[3] The judicial processes for recovery pass largely without record, but there can be no doubt that the hearing of plaints was a prime concern of the young king and occupied much of his time. William of Newburgh relates that 'In the early years he gave serious attention to public order and strove to revive the vigour of the laws of England which had seemed under King Stephen to be dead and buried.' From the chronicle of the abbey of Battle it appears that the king was pursued even to the siege of Bridgnorth by an abbot anxious to have a plea heard without delay.[4] Many of the numerous charters granted by the king as he travelled through his realm may conceal in their phraseology of confirmation the recovery of lost rights. The adjudication of claims cannot have been easy. According to Robert de Torigny, the principle enunciated at Winchester was that 'those landed possessions which had fallen into the hands of intruders should be restored to the ancient and lawful possessors who had them in the time of King Henry I'.[5] This principle had the merit of cutting through the thicket of appropriations and of partisan adjudications during the period of civil war, and was important in establishing hereditary right as the basis of succession; but it by no means resolved all the problems. It was itself vague about what constituted 'lawful possession' in the time of

---

[1] For the execution of the policy see below, ch. 7, p. 274.

[2] For example, St Albans recovered the vill of Luton on appeal: *Gesta Abbatum*, I, 123–4. For the procedure of recovery see *Glanvill*, IX. 11–13.

[3] *Gesta Stephani*, 158, with the amendment of the text proposed by Davis, *King Stephen*, 123, n.25; cf. Robert de Torigny, 177.

[4] William of Newburgh, I, 102; *Chronicon Monasterii de Bello*, 75–6.

[5] Robert de Torigny, 177, following the translation of Davis, *op. cit.*, 122.

King Henry I, and did not specify which period in the long reign of
Henry I was to be taken as the datum line. There was good reason for
this: the ill-defined rules of succession had often in the past been
manipulated by the Crown or overriden in arbitrary forfeitures and
regrants. Many of the rivalries of the years of anarchy were between the
'lawful possessors' of the beginning of Henry I's reign against the 'lawful
possessors' of the end of the reign. To have overturned wholesale the
'recoveries' made in Stephen's day would have been to precipitate a
renewal of war. Furthermore, it would have been politically impractic-
able to have applied the principle dogmatically and to have required
the greater barons to surrender all gains made during the civil war and
confirmed by charters of Stephen or Matilda; it might be possible to
whittle them down, and desirable to compensate or placate those
deprived, but to have expropriated them wholesale would have been
a certain recipe for rebellion. The problem for Henry II, then, was to
balance justice, equity, and expediency in establishing settlements
which claimants could regard as reasonable. The general practice
seems to have been to take the situation at the death of Henry I as
establishing a strong presumption of right, but to allow latitude for
other considerations to be taken into account. Rival claimants were
permitted, and probably encouraged, to settle their differences by
compromise. But arbitrary decisions had sometimes to be made by the
king: political expediency might dictate that the situation as it existed
at his own coronation rather than at his grandfather's death be taken
as the limit of legal memory, or a compromise might have to be imposed on rival claimants who could not reach an amicable settlement.
The scope for the exercise of royal discretion was considerable, and
there were some who in later years would claim that Henry II had 'dispossessed' them; but the general acceptance of the settlement, and the
rarity of subsequent attempts to challenge it, testifies to the judicious
way in which peace was established after the chaos of civil war. The
young king deserved the soubriquet of 'Henry the Peacemaker' which
the chronicler of Battle Abbey bestowed upon him.[1]

---

[1] *Chronicon Monasterii de Bello*, 113: 'Rege Stephano decedente, et pacifico rege
Henrico secundo succedente, hostilitas expellitur, pax jampridem expulsa revocatur.'
Cf. *Chronicon Abbatiae Ramesiensis*, 336: 'Et sic Regis Stephani tediosam transegit potes-
tatem vel tempestatum. Quo defuncto successit ei Henricus Secundus, regni solio jure
sublimatus.' The political and juridical problems involved are further discussed
below, ch. 9, pp. 332ff, cf. also Davis, *King Stephen*, 122–6. For an example of political
expediency, see the charter by which Henry II revokes the forfeiture of Pontefract
made against Robert de Lacy by Henry I, restoring it to Hugh de Lacy and pardoning
him his adherence to Stephen during the civil war, *Early Yorkshire Charters*, II, 147–9.

By the end of 1155 Henry's authority was probably more secure in England than it was in his continental dominions. There Henry was menaced by the resentment of his brother Geoffrey at the smallness of his inheritance, and by the refusal of King Louis to recognise him as duke of Aquitaine. Separately their hostility was not serious, for Henry had already shown that he could defend himself against them, but in alliance they could be troublesome. It is likely that the barons both of Anjou and Aquitaine viewed with the deepest misgiving Henry's acquisition of the throne of England, for it confronted them with the unaccustomed prospect of being saddled with a ruler whose authority was buttressed with massive resources. Geoffrey fostered a story that he was rightfully ruler of Anjou since his father had intended that Henry should hold it only until he had gained the kingdom of England.[1] It was a story which many would doubtless have wished to believe. The castles which Geoffrey held as his inheritance lay in the marchlands between Anjou and Poitou, and it is probable that he had recruited allies on both sides of the border.[2] If King Louis had chosen to accept the story, had recognised Geoffrey as count of Anjou, and had pressed his own claim still to be duke of Aquitaine, Henry could have been confronted with the necessity of enforcing his lordship over half his dominions by the sword. Henry's estimation of the seriousness of the situation is demonstrated by his efforts to raise considerable sums of money in England for the hire of mercenaries, by levies upon his barons, and by what were euphemistically known as 'gifts'.[3] On the other hand there were signs that King Louis was reconsidering his policy. He had abandoned the kind of attacks he made on Normandy in 1154 and sold back two castles he had taken on the border; and though he received Geoffrey in audience, he had not publicly recognised him, and, moreover, he had given up using the title of duke of Aquitaine. It is probable that Louis's active hostility since 1152 had been an aberration, an expression of his resentment of Henry's *coup* in marrying Eleanor. It ran counter to the policy laid down by Abbot Suger, for long the power behind the throne at Paris and the architect of the reconstruction of the French monarchy. He had argued that the military inferiority of the French Crown made cooperation with powerful vassals the only sensible course to follow; the king might in this way establish his authority as

---

[1] *See* above, ch. 2, p. 46.

[2] Possibly with both the viscount of Thouars and the count of Blois, who remained hostile to Henry until 1158, cf. Robert de Torigny, 198, *Chroniques des Eglises d'Anjou*, 39. That Geoffrey visited King Louis is reported by John of Salisbury, *Letters*, I, 21–2.

[3] John of Salisbury, *loc. cit.*, cf. Round, *Feudal England*, 217.

feudal suzerain by securing the voluntary homage of vassals he could not hope to reduce to submission.[1] Louis had followed this advice in seeking accord with both Count Geoffrey and the young Henry as dukes of Normandy. It had brought him their homage and control of the Norman Vexin.[2] His subsequent hostility, however, had denied him the homage of Henry as count of Anjou. The signs that he was prepared to revert to his former policy encouraged Henry to resort to diplomacy. Though nothing is known from contemporary sources it is likely that while he was occupied in England he had sent envoys to Paris to propose mutual recognition, for within a few days of crossing the Channel, he met King Louis at the border of Normandy on 5 February 1156 and there did him homage for Normandy, Anjou, and Aquitaine.[3]

A few days later Henry met his brother Geoffrey in conference at Rouen, but without success. Geoffrey, however, had been isolated by King Louis's formal recognition of all the titles claimed by Henry, and few of his allies rose to join him when he fortified his castles at Chinon, Mirebeau, and Loudun. In the summer of 1156 Henry laid siege to them and forced his brother to submission, depriving him of his castles and giving him instead an annuity.[4]

In the autumn Queen Eleanor crossed from England to join Henry, and together they made a progress of Aquitaine, receiving homages and hostages and exercising the prerogatives of feudal lordship.[5] In the course of it Henry ejected the viscount of Thouars from his lands in north-west Poitou and destroyed his castle, ostensibly for having aided Geoffrey in rebellion, but rather, suggests a local chronicle, because Eleanor had found him a troublesome vassal.[6] The appearance of a new power in the region encouraged the citizens of Nantes to throw off the unwelcome lordship of their ruler, Count Hoël, and to appeal for Henry's help. He offered them his brother Geoffrey as their count.[7]

[1] Cf. Pacaut, *Louis VII et son Royaume*, 180ff.   [2] *See* above, ch. 2, pp. 31–2, 42.

[3] Robert de Torigny, 180, 186; Roger of Howden, *Chronica*, I, 215. For Henry's use of the title of duke of Aquitaine *see* Z. N. and C. N. L. Brooke, 'Henry II, duke of Normandy and Aquitaine', 86–8.

[4] The evidence is marshalled by Boussard, *Le Comté d'Anjou*, 72–3. According to some authorities Geoffrey was suffered to retain Loudun. The annuity amounted to £1,500–a considerable but not a princely sum, cf. Boussard, *Le Gouvernement d'Henri II*, 408 n.2.

[5] Gervase of Canterbury, I, 162; Eyton, *Itinerary of Henry II*, 19–20, and the dating clauses of the charters in *Recueil des Actes de Henri II*, I, 114–17, Richard, *Comtes de Poitou*, II, 122–3.   [6] Cf. Boussard, *Le Comté d'Anjou*, 74.

[7] Robert de Torigny, 187; William of Newburgh, I, 114; Pocquet du Haut-Jussé, 'Les Plantagenêts et la Bretagne', 4; Boussard *Le Gouvernement d'Henri II*, 409–10.

Nantes was the great seaport of Brittany and control of it had long been the ambition of counts of Anjou, for it commanded the mouth of the great river of Anjou and Touraine – the Loire. In 1156 it passed under Angevin control without Henry having to fight for it.

Henry II returned to England in April 1157 and promptly addressed himself to three awkward problems simultaneously. One of these was the final, and most delicate, problem of pacification, involving two of the most powerful barons in the land, Hugh Bigod and William of Blois, son of King Stephen. The circumstances are unfortunately veiled in obscurity, for no contemporary chronicler discusses them, but may be tentatively reconstructed, at least in outline, from scraps of information.

Hugh Bigod had repudiated Stephen after the battle of Lincoln, and for twelve years had defied the king in East Anglia. The foundation of the Bigod family's fortunes had been the grant of the honor of Framlingham in Suffolk to Hugh's father, and to this had been added numerous and extensive holdings mainly in the eastern counties which placed Hugh Bigod, if not quite in the front rank of the barons of England, at least very close to it.[1] His break with Stephen in 1141 is commonly held to place him in the Angevin camp, but it is doubtful if Hugh Bigod was ever deeply concerned about any interests other than those of Hugh Bigod. And on the other hand it is unlikely that the Angevin party regarded him with any enthusiasm, for it was his perjured testimony as to Henry I's deathbed wishes which had cleared the way for Stephen's coronation. The empress nevertheless tried to encourage his adherence by granting him an earldom.[2] 'Earl of Norfolk' is the title by which he is commonly known, but in fact the earldom embraced both Norfolk and Suffolk, and was anciently known as the 'earldom of East Anglia'.[3] Bigod's ambition seems to have been to make himself the sole power in East Anglia, but in this he was thwarted by the king's men. Stephen himself was a major landholder in Suffolk, for Henry I had given him the honor of Eye; and his castles of Eye, Haughley, and Bury St Edmunds, effectively prevented Bigod gaining control of west Suffolk. The struggle became concentrated instead on control of Norfolk, where the king had few bases except for the royal castle at Norwich. Stephen, however, tipped the balance of power in Norfolk by marrying his younger son William to Isabella de Warenne in 1148. The vast honor of Warenne, of which she was the heiress,

[1] To the enquiry of 1166 into enfeoffments, Hugh Bigod replied that 125 knights' fees had been created on his estates before the death of Henry I, and 35¼ knights' fees since then: *Red Book of the Exchequer*, I, 395–7.

[2] Cf. Davis, *King Stephen*, 141–2.

[3] Henry of Huntingdon, 273; cf. Round, *Geoffrey de Mandeville*, 191.

embraced estates in most counties of England but was particularly strong in Norfolk. After the marriage, King Stephen bestowed on his son 'the castle and town of Norwich and the whole county of Norfolk', and the clear implication was that William was to be earl of Norfolk as well as earl of Surrey in right of his wife, as her father had been.[1] The very last campaign which Stephen waged in the civil war was directed against Hugh Bigod and deprived him of control of Ipswich.[2] What the balance of power was in East Anglia at the end of the war is not clear, and the treaty between king Stephen and Duke Henry left Bigod's position ambiguous. Stephen's proclamation of the terms of the treaty specified that his son William was to hold all that his father had held before he became King (including of course the honor of Eye), together with the 'increment' which his father had bestowed on him, including 'the castle and town of Norwich ... and the whole county of Norfolk, except what pertains to churches and prelates and abbots and earls, and excluding particularly the third penny which pertains to Hugh Bigod as earl'.[3] That some attempt at compromise had been made is suggested by Stephen's recognition of Bigod as an earl with the right to the 'third penny' of the profits of justice, which was the usual prerogative of an earl, but the fact that Bigod is not accorded a title, and that William was to have 'the whole county' suggests that it was an unsatisfactory compromise. When Henry became king he did something to clear up the ambiguity in a charter (probably of 1155) to Hugh Bigod, confirming him in his possessions and recognising him as earl of Norfolk; but Henry did not upset the treaty by insisting that William surrender the castle of Norwich, even though it had once been a royal castle.[4] It can hardly be doubted that tension persisted between Hugh Bigod and William of Blois, even to the extent of threatening the peace of the realm, for it engaged Henry's attention immediately on his return from France in the spring of 1157. The great council of the realm was summoned to meet at Bury St Edmunds in Suffolk on 19 May, and there Henry took drastic action, requiring Hugh Bigod and William of Blois to surrender all their castles.[5] This went far beyond his

---

[1] Davis, *King Stephen*, 141. No reference to William as earl of Norfolk survives, but this is not surprising since men who held more than one earldom were normally referred to by the title of only one of them. In fact, William was not called 'earl of Surrey' either, for he followed the practice of his wife's ancestors and called himself Earl William de Warenne. [2] *See* above, p. 51.

[3] *Regesta Regum Anglo-Normannorum*, III, 272.

[4] The charter is printed in *Foedera*, I, Pt I, 42, and the date discussed by Round, *Geoffrey de Mandeville*, 288.

[5] Robert de Torigny, 192–3. The meeting of the council at Bury St Edmunds is

previous demand for the surrender of royal castles held by baronial custodians: in effect they were disarmed. The silence of the chroniclers does not allow the situation to be penetrated more deeply than this; but the possibility that others were involved besides Earls Hugh and William, and that the whole of the eastern counties had teetered on the brink of upheaval during Henry's absence, is suggested by the record on the exchequer accounts for this same year of a payment for the demolition of the castles of Earl Geoffrey of Essex at the king's command.[1] Earl William (or 'Count William' as he is usually called from his inheritance of the county of Boulogne) subsequently maintained cordial relations with King Henry until his death in 1159; Earl Geoffrey of Essex was a loyal servant until his death in 1166; but Earl Hugh harboured a grudge until his death, at the advanced age of about eighty-three, in 1177.

Henry's masterful action is indicative of the dominance he had achieved, but the situation itself reveals something of the difficulties of reconciling old enemies and the precariousness of order in the realm. A guarantee of peace in England was necessary for Henry in 1157, for he was about to tackle two further problems which might involve him in war with his neighbours. These were the problems presented by the Scots and the Welsh, and the serious distortion of their relationship with the English Crown since the death of Henry I.

King David of Scotland did not live to see the triumph of the Angevin cause which he had espoused: he died on 24 May 1153 and was succeeded by his grandson Malcolm IV. A few months later died Simon de Senlis who had always disputed David's right to be earl of Huntingdon, and who had been granted the earldom by King Stephen from about 1141. Although Simon left a son, Henry II kept the earldom vacant, presumably in anticipation of restoring it to the royal family of Scotland.[2] He delayed doing so, however, for he had another matter to settle first. King David's invasions of England in the previous reign had not done much to help his niece, the empress, but they had wrung from King Stephen important concessions: Cumberland, Westmorland,

---

recorded by *Chronicon Monasterii de Bello*, 85. The pipe rolls record payments for the provisioning of castles in Norfolk and for the payment of castle-guard at Norwich, Pipe Roll 3 Henry II, 75, Pipe Roll 4 Henry II, 126. Bigod's castles of Framlingham and Bungay remained in the king's hand probably until 1165, and Walton for longer, cf. Brown, 'Framlingham castle and Bigod', 130–1.

[1] Pipe Roll 4 Henry II, 132.

[2] Cf. Davis, *King Stephen*, 134, 135; *Complete Peerage*, VI, 643–4. The lands seem to have been held in the meantime by Henry II's younger brother, William, *Bedfordshire Historical Record Society*, xiii, 272.

and Northumberland had passed under the control of the king of Scots. Henry had sworn to King David, when he was knighted by him at Carlisle in 1149, that if he became king of England he would uphold these concessions; but when he did become king he was not minded to allow this to prevent him restoring the situation to what it had been in the days of his grandfather. King Malcolm journeyed south at King Henry's invitation in May 1157 and Henry put it to him bluntly that he could not be expected to tolerate the diminution of his kingdom, and Malcolm 'prudently considering', as William of Newburgh put it, 'that the king of England had the better of the argument by reason of his greater power', acquiesced.[1] He was then granted the earldom of Huntingdon and did homage.

The Welsh princes were less tractable. Their relationship to the king of England in the time of Henry I is not altogether clear; but there can be little doubt that Henry I had established a measure of royal control over the Norman colonists in Wales, and that the leaders of the Welsh had acknowledged his overlordship. Nothing of this royal authority survived Stephen's reign. The marches of southern Wales had all been in the hands of adherents of the Angevin cause, and so too had the northern marches in the days when Earl Ranulf of Chester had been at odds with the king. The marcher barons, preoccupied in England, had been unable to defend their Welsh interests effectively; and the Welsh, better organised than before under able leaders, had ejected most of the colonists from their deeper penetration of the Welsh valleys. Only the ruler of Powys in central Wales, impressed perhaps by Henry's resolute action against Hugh Mortimer, was prepared to acknowledge that there was a new authority in the land; and it became clear that the Welsh of Gwynedd in north-west Wales and the Welsh of Deheubarth in the south would have to be coerced. At a meeting with his barons at Northampton on 17 July 1157 Henry secured approval for a campaign against Owain, prince of Gwynedd.[2] It is not immediately obvious why Henry should have resolved upon an expedition to the north: the south was not only more accessible, but of more immediate concern to former supporters of the Angevin cause. There were probably three reasons. First, Owain's brother Cadwaladr was a suppliant at Henry's court, claiming that he had been deprived of his rightful inheritance; and it is likely that it suited Henry's purpose to assert the overlordship he claimed in defence of a Welshman's rights rather than in support of

---

[1] William of Newburgh, I, 105–6; *see* below, ch. 4, pp. 181–2.
[2] For the situation in Wales and Henry's expedition of 1157 see Lloyd, *History of Wales*, II, 462ff., and below, ch. 4, pp. 159ff.

dispossessed settlers. Secondly, Owain of Gwynedd was the most powerful as well as the most truculent of the Welsh rulers, and his submission was more likely to influence the rest of them than their submission would have influenced him. Thirdly, the fact that the heir to the earldom of Chester was a minor in royal wardship, gave the king a rare opportunity to assert his authority in a region which had far too long been regarded by the earls of Chester as their preserve.

The expedition was intelligently planned. A well-equipped force consisting of a third of the knight service owed by the barons was mustered on the saltings south of Chester, and from there struck up the coast of the Dee estuary into the district which had long been disputed between the princes of Gwynedd and the earls of Chester. In addition a naval contingent operated off shore. Part of its purpose, no doubt, was to provision the king's army, but its main task seems to have been to harass Owain's rear, and prevent his retreat to Anglesey. This interesting experiment in combined operations nearly ended, however, in disaster. The naval contingent was badly mauled while attempting a raid on Anglesey; and the king, advancing, as Gervase of Canterbury says, with 'more dash than prudence', was trapped in a well-prepared ambush near Flint. Several barons were killed, and Henry of Essex, the hereditary bearer of the royal standard, believing that the king too was dead, cast aside his banner and fled, carrying panic to the rest of the army which was following behind.[1] Only the sudden appearance of the king, who had fought his way out of the ambush, averted a disorderly retreat. Thereafter the army proceeded more cautiously, and Henry set his men to hack paths through the woods. His determination to persist persuaded Owain to sue for peace. He performed homage to Henry, handed over hostages, and reinstated his brother. Henry left garrisons in the castles at Rhuddlan and Basingwerk – indications that not only had he come to stay, but that bounds had been set to the future expansion of the earldom of Chester. Shortly afterwards Prince Rhys of Deheubarth tendered his homage.[2]

Robert de Torigny wrote that Henry had 'subjected the Welsh to his will'.[3] He exaggerates. It is true that Henry had secured acknowledgement of his suzerainty, and this was probably in 1157 his principal purpose; but the implications of the oaths which had been sworn were a matter upon which differing views could be held, and, as later events

[1] Henry of Essex was subsequently adjudged guilty of treason and expropriated, Gervase of Canterbury, I, 165; Jocelin of Brakelond, 68–71.

[2] Annals of Tewkesbury, 48.

[3] Robert de Torigny, 195.

were to show, the Welsh rulers could, if pressed too hard, become obstinately defiant. Nevertheless Henry's run of success in recovering his hereditary rights and subduing his opponents was remarkable.

There were rights to be pursued on the continent also, and Henry returned there in August 1158 to pursue them. King Louis of France was, like the king of Scots, holding territories which had been held by Henry's grandfather; and the Bretons, like the Welsh, were withholding an acknowledgement of the lordship which tradition conveyed to him.

The settlement of the Normans in the valleys of the lower Seine in the tenth century had led to a partitioning of the old county of the Vexin along a tributary of the Seine, the river Epte. The northern portion of the Vexin became part of the duchy of Normandy, while the southern or 'French' half, as it was called, eventually became part of the demesne lands of the Capetian kings of France. But in the ten years before Henry of Anjou became king of England, King Louis VII had added the northern, or 'Norman', portion of the Vexin to his demesne. He acquired part of it as the price of recognising Henry's father as duke of Normandy in 1144, and the rest of it in 1151 as the price of recognising Henry himself as duke.[1] But Henry of Anjou could no more countenance as permanent the surrender of the northern portion of the Vexin to the king of the Franks than he could the surrender of the northern counties of England to the king of the Scots. It is likely that since Henry's performance of homage in February 1156, King Louis had been made aware that the restoration of the Norman Vexin was a precondition of harmonious relations. Negotiations for a resolution of the problem culminated in a magnificent embassy by Chancellor Becket to Paris in the summer of 1158. One of his biographers, William FitzStephen, writes in detail of the extravagant size of his retinue and the splendour of his equipage. Two hundred and fifty footmen led the van, filling the width of the road and singing as they went. Behind them the chancellor's hounds and greyhounds were led on leash by their keepers. Following them came eight great waggons, each drawn by five horses the size of chargers, laden with the impedimenta of the chancellor's household, and two with the finest English beer. Each waggon was guarded by a chained mastiff, and each horse carried a monkey on its back. Behind the waggons came twenty-eight packhorses carrying gold and silver plate, clothes, money, books, and the ornaments of his chapel. Some way behind came the chancellor's retinue, two hundred of them: squires carrying the shields and leading the horses of the mounted knights, then the falconers with hawks on their wrists, the

[1] Lemarignier, *op. cit.*, 33ff., 45 and n.53.

sons of barons who were in the chancellor's care, his clerks, stewards, and lesser servants, riding two by two; and last of all Thomas Becket himself with a few of his intimate friends. Frenchmen hurried out of their houses, writes William FitzStephen, to see the cavalcade pass, and said to each other, 'What a magnificent man the king of England must be if his chancellor travels in such great state.' It was, of course, intended as an ostentatious display of the wealth of England, and much that was carried in the waggons and panniers – including the chancellor's twenty-four changes of raiment – were to be disbursed as gifts to anyone who was influential at Paris.[1] The purpose was revealed when the two kings met on the border of Normandy, shortly after Henry crossed the sea in August 1158, and announced their intention of forming a marriage alliance. Margaret, the daughter of the king of France by his second marriage to Constance of Castille, was betrothed to Henry the Younger, the eldest son and heir of the king of England. The Norman Vexin was to be the dowry of the bride.[2] Since King Henry's son was not yet four years of age, and his intended bride barely out of the cradle, there could be no prospect of an early marriage, and until it took place King Louis was to retain control of the Vexin. The infant Margaret was, however, to be handed over to her future father-in-law as a pledge of good faith. If the young Henry were to die before the marriage, Margaret was to marry another of the sons of the king of England. Henry II was thus assured that the whole of the rights enjoyed by his grandfather in Normandy would one day be restored to his family. Of more immediate consequence, however, was another aspect of his agreement with King Louis – the latter's assurance that he might have a free hand in settling the affairs of Brittany. This had become an urgent problem for Henry II with the early death of his brother Geoffrey, count of Nantes, in July 1158.

Brittany was very like Wales, and not merely in terms of its racial composition and language. In both, an inhospitable heartland hindered political unification; both were penetrated to the east and south by Frankish elements, and were adjusting themselves, slowly, to the way of life of their neighbours. Brittany had apparently taken on more of the characteristics of a feudal society than Wales, though perhaps only superficially, for the use of feudal terminology could mask the persistence of customs and attitudes of a pre-feudal age.[3] Both had been drawn into the political orbit of their better organised neighbours, but

[1] William FitzStephen, III, 29–33.
[2] Continuatio Beccensis, 318–19; Robert de Torigny, 196; Annals of Osney, 30–1.
[3] Cf. Stenton, *English Feudalism*, 27–8.

had resisted absorption. Brittany, in fact, had never yet been properly incorporated in the kingdom of France. Although it had from Carolingian times admitted a dependent status, its relationship to the French Crown remained ill-defined and unstable. The French chancery referred to it as a county, but its rulers often styled themselves 'prince'

IV Brittany

or 'duke'. Although it had sometimes been dominated by a strong personality, no effective framework of government had been created, or even a stable hierarchy of lordship. The chief centres of political power lay in the more feudalised regions of the east, and it was on control of the river ports of Rennes and Nantes that those who called themselves 'counts' or 'dukes' of Brittany built a precarious ascendancy. But these lowland, French-speaking regions of eastern Brittany tended to be drawn into involvement with neighbouring Normandy, Maine, and Anjou. Many Bretons took service with William the Conqueror in the invasion and settlement of England.[1] Duke Alan Fergant (1084–1112), who triumphed over dynastic rivals to achieve a measure of supremacy in Brittany, was married first to a daughter of William the Conqueror, and secondly to a daughter of Count Fulk of Anjou. He joined the First Crusade as part of the Norman contingent; and his arrival with a force of Bretons at the critical battle of Tinchebrai in 1106 decided the issue in favour of his brother-in-law, Henry I.

There are grounds for supposing that Henry II believed that Brittany had become a dependency of Normandy in the distant past, and that Alan Fergant intervened at Tinchebrai as a vassal of Henry I.[2] When in 1113 King Louis VI of France concluded a treaty with Henry I it was reported by a contemporary chronicler that he acknowledged Brittany to be a dependency of Normandy.[3] But even if this report is true, it is very doubtful if a political affiliation became well-established. There is no evidence that Alan Fergant's successor, Conan III (1112–48), did homage; and though he was married to an illegitimate daughter of Henry I, it seems likely that he took advantage of Stephen's troubles to detach himself from involvement with the Anglo-Norman kingdom. On the other hand several prominent Bretons had close personal ties with England in Stephen's reign through their holding of land. Brian FitzCount, the devoted admirer of Empress Matilda and valiant defender of Wallingford, was an illegitimate son of Alan Fergant.[4] Geoffrey Boterel II, lord of Penthièvre in Brittany and a member of the cadet branch of the ruling family, was also an adherent of the empress and rendered her notable service at the siege of Winchester in 1141.[5] His brother Alan, however, was a staunch supporter of King Stephen and instrumental in the downfall of Bishop Roger of Salisbury in 1138.[6] He inherited what later came to be known as the honor of Richmond from Breton ancestors who had held it since the Conquest, and acquired the title of earl of Richmond from King Stephen early in the reign. Stephen also made him earl of Cornwall in 1140, but he was displaced there by a nominee of the empress. Earl Alan's importance was enhanced by his marriage to Bertha, daughter and heiress of Duke

---

[1] Cf. Stenton, *English Feudalism*, 24ff.; Clay, introduction to *Early Yorkshire Charters*, IV, ix.

[2] The evidence is reviewed by Lemarignier, *op. cit.*, pp. 115–21.

[3] Orderic Vitalis, IV, 307.

[4] Cf. Davis, 'Henry of Blois and Brian FitzCount', 298–9.

[5] John of Hexham, 310.   [6] William of Malmesbury, *Historia Novorum*, 26–7.

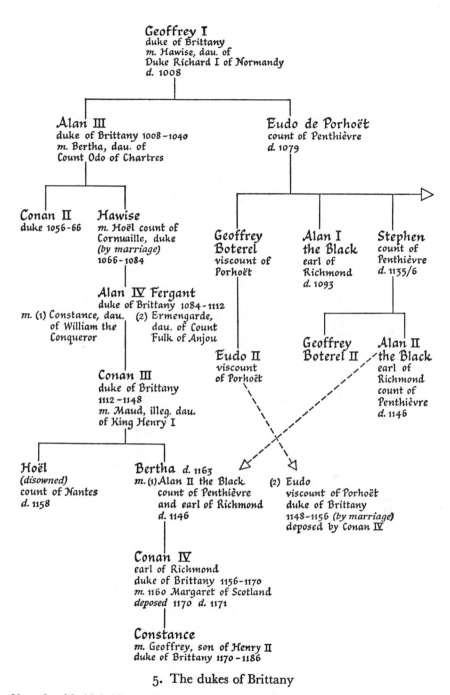

5. The dukes of Brittany

Note: the title 'duke' is used for convenience; some of the earlier rulers were known by other titles.

Conan III of Brittany. They had a son, also named Conan; but Earl Alan died in 1146, two years before his father-in-law, and Bertha subsequently married Eudo, viscount of Porhoët.[1] After the death of Duke Conan III in 1148, Eudo was generally recognised as duke of Brittany in right of his wife, but his position was not beyond dispute, for Bertha had a brother, Hoël, who had been disowned by his father. Hoël seized control of Nantes and made himself its count. It was this same Count Hoël whom the citizens of Nantes expelled in 1156; but since they had no wish to subject themselves to the rule of Duke Eudo and their rivals of Rennes, they appealed for the help of Henry II, and accepted his brother Geoffrey as their count. There was, however, another rival to Eudo in Conan, son of Bertha and Earl Alan. He was living in England, and was recognised as earl of Richmond by Henry II from the beginning of his reign. In September 1156 Earl Conan crossed to Brittany, besieged and took Rennes, expelled his stepfather, and took his place as duke.[2] Thereafter it was as *dux Brittaniae et comes Richemundiae* that he styled himself in charters.

It is improbable that Conan's return to Brittany and his assumption of the ducal title were made without Henry II's approval; indeed, it is more likely that Henry II gave the venture his full support. With his brother installed in Nantes and his vassal earl of Richmond installed in Rennes, he could feel confident that Brittany would lie within the orbit of his influence, and the navigation of the Loire, upon which both Angers and Tours depended, be free from interference. Unfortunately this convenient arrangement was upset when his brother Geoffrey died on 26 July 1158 at the age of twenty-four. Conan took possession of the county of Nantes, denying Henry II's claim to acquire it as his brother's heir. It was sensible in a duke of Brittany to wish to control both Rennes and Nantes; but it was foolish in a vassal of Henry II to defy his lord.

This was the situation when Henry crossed from England about three weeks after his brother's death to meet King Louis for the ratification of the marriage alliance. It is possible that Henry would have taken action against Conan even without King Louis's approval, relying on ancient homages to press a claim to overlordship of Brittany; but to have done so might have jeopardised his new-found amity with the king of France who might dispute with him the homage of Brittany, so it was prudent to consult him. King Louis also had no wish to jeopardise their good relations, but neither did he wish to prejudice the rights of the

[1] *Early Yorkshire Charters*, IV, 89–91.
[2] *Ibid.*, IV, 92.

French Crown by admitting the subordination of Brittany to the duke of Normandy. A convenient formula was found to circumvent the difficulty. King Louis resurrected for Henry the ancient but by this date largely honorific dignity of seneschal of France, and in this capacity charged him to pacify the quarrelsome Bretons and resolve the rival claims to the ducal title as he saw fit.[1] Armed with this commission, Henry summoned the knight service of Normandy to muster at Avranches at Michaelmas. On the appointed day Conan too arrived at Avranches and proffered his submission. He ceded Nantes to Henry and was recognised as duke.[2]

The accord of King Henry and King Louis was publicly demonstrated by state visits. In the interval between the summons and muster of his forces against Conan, Henry went to Paris, in September 1158, to collect his future daughter-in-law. In contrast with Becket's splendid embassy, he conducted himself modestly, travelling with only a small retinue, and declining the lavish hospitality which was offered him. He was nevertheless received with extravagant honour by King Louis and the barons of France, and, according to Robert de Torigny, the Parisians danced with joy 'both at the good relations of the two kings and at the visit of so notable a guest'.[3] In November King Louis was taken by Henry on a tour of Normandy as far as Mont Saint-Michel on the confines of Brittany. When they stayed overnight at the abbey of Bec, King Louis was heard to remark that there was no one he esteemed so highly as the king of England. 'Wonders never cease,' commented the chronicler.[4]

In December King Louis used his good offices to reconcile Henry and Count Theobald of Blois, and to secure the restoration of some border fortresses.[5] It was a fitting culmination to the first phase of Henry II's reign: in four years he had recovered all the territories and rights of lordship which his grandfather had held. His inheritance was complete.

*   *   *

[1] Gervase of Canterbury, I, 166. On the seneschalship of France *see* Kate Norgate, *England under the Angevin Kings*, I, 450 n.4; Luchaire, *Histoire des Institutions Monarchiques de la France*, I, 173–81, Luchaire, 'Hughes de Clers et le *De Sonescalia Franciae*'.

[2] Robert de Torigny, 197; William of Newburgh, I, 114, notes that Henry's first move was to seize the honor of Richmond.

[3] Robert de Torigny, 196–7; Continuatio Beccensis, 319; Gervase of Canterbury, I, 166.

[4] 'Mirabile dictu', Continuatio Beccensis, 320; Robert de Torigny, 198; Gervase of Canterbury, I, 166.

[5] Robert de Torigny, 198–9; Continuatio Beccensis, 320; cf. *Recueil des Actes de Henri II*, I, 195.

Henry, at the age of twenty-five, had every reason to congratulate himself. He had not only established his authority and won respect for his kingship, but also had sons to succeed him. Queen Eleanor conceived with remarkable regularity. Their first child was a son, William, born in August 1153, fifteen months after their marriage. He died at the age of three, but they had by then two other children: Henry, born in February 1155, and Matilda, born in 1156. Two further sons followed, born at intervals of a year – Richard in September 1157 and Geoffrey in September 1158. They had two further children born at appreciably longer intervals (with possibly some still-births in between): Eleanor in 1161 and John in December 1167.[1]

It is unfortunate that the early years of Henry II's reign are poorly served by contemporary chroniclers. The middle years of Stephen's reign had been caught in the crossed searchlights of the incomparable William of Malmesbury and the conscientious author of the *Gesta Stephani*, and were additionally illuminated here and there by the harsh flares of Henry of Huntingdon; but there is only the intermittent light of flickering torches to show the way young Henry of Anjou trod in the years when he set about putting his world to rights. Honest annalists there were, recording, though meagrely, the bare facts of what seemed to them the newsworthy events of their day; but Henry, even when he occupies their pages, is no more than a name. Even those, such as Robert de Torigny, who encountered him personally, vouchsafe no description and give no help in divining his personality. His character has, in consequence, to be read largely from his actions. Largely but not entirely, for there are some other sources – the correspondence of John of Salisbury, the biographies of Thomas Becket, and of contemporary abbots – in which the young King Henry occasionally bursts into view, masterful, quick-tempered, and decisive.

It is remarkable that he inherited none of the well-known characteristics of his parents. He had neither his mother's haughty dignity, nor his father's dashing charm. All the signs are that he was indifferent to rank and impatient of pomp, careless of his appearance, and disdaining the trappings of monarchy. He did not even have the booming authority of his grandfather's awful presence. He was stocky, freckled, restless,

---

1 Eleanor had two other children, both daughters, born of her former marriage to King Louis VII. Her eldest daughter Mary had once, ironically, been intended as a bride for the young Henry of Anjou, St Bernard, Epistolae, ccclxxxi. She was subsequently betrothed to Henry count of Champagne, and her sister Alice to Count Henry's brother, Theobald count of Blois. Henry is known to have had two illegitimate sons, Geoffrey and William, who were probably both born before his marriage to Eleanor.

and unkempt. Yet the force of his personality was unmistakable. Great men, be they barons or bishops, quailed before his sudden surges of anger, and ran for harbour like fishing smacks before a storm. Archbishop Theobald of Canterbury, an elder statesman who had outmanœuvred Henry of Blois, defied King Stephen, and turned the wrath of a pope, treated Henry of Anjou with respectful deference.[1] Bishop Hilary of Chichester, when pleading a case against the abbot of Battle in the king's court, was reduced to quivering prevarication when his agents were accused of acting against the dignity of the Crown, and King Henry thunderously demanded to know the truth of the matter.[2] The abbot of St Albans, a man accustomed to exercising dictatorial authority, behaved like a schoolboy who had stolen apples when the young king asked to see the charters and bulls of privilege which the abbey claimed.[3] Such examples make it easier to understand why those who had dominated the realm in Stephen's day were so quickly reduced to insignificance. Beside Henry of Anjou, even the young Henry of Anjou, everyone else seemed small. The only man who ever dared to pit his will against Henry's was Archbishop Becket, and even he soon lost his nerve and fled across the sea to fight the king from a safer distance.

Some of the biographers of Thomas Becket have given the impression that their hero, as royal chancellor from 1154 to 1162, was the mastermind and impresario of the achievements of Henry II's early years. William FitzStephen writes:

> All things were entrusted to Thomas, while the king gave himself up to youthful pursuits. . . . Only in name did he differ from the king, and he governed the whole realm according to his will. The nobles and magnates were subject to his orders, knowing for certain that only what Thomas judged expedient would be pleasing to the king. . . . It was difficult at that time for any step to be taken which Thomas had not first approved. . . . The house and table of the chancellor were thrown open to all men of whatever rank who came to the king's court and were in need of hospitality, no matter whether they were really honourable or only seemed so. He hardly ever dined without the company of sundry earls and barons whom he himself had invited. He ordered his hall to be strewn every day with fresh straw or hay in winter and with green rushes or leaves in summer, so that the host of knights who could not find room on the

---

[1] Cf. e.g., John of Salisbury, *Letters*, nos 104, 120, 125; *Gesta Abbatum Monasterii Sancti Albani*, I, 163.

[2] *Chronicon Monasterii de Bello*, 101ff.

[3] *Gesta Abbatum*, I, 137–54; *see* also below, p. 440.

benches might sit on a clean and wholesome floor without soiling their precious clothes and fine underwear. His board was resplendent with gold and silver vessels and abounded in dainty dishes and precious wines, so that whatever food or drink was commended by its rarity, no price was too high to deter his agents from purchasing it. [1]

Undoubtedly Becket had the manner of a grand vizier. Undoubtedly, too, he enjoyed both the confidence and intimacy of the king, and was entrusted with matters of state beyond the customary duties of a chancellor. But it may be doubted if he ever eclipsed the king in the way that FitzStephen would have us believe. In no sources other than the biographies of Becket does the chancellor appear as of any greater consequence than Earl Robert of Leicester, Richard de Lucy, or Richard du Hommet, the constable of Normandy, and all appear as very much the servants of a young master who was completely in command of every situation. It seems likely indeed that Henry shifted on to Becket's shoulders those aspects of kingship which irked or bored him: the necessity of keeping up a splendid court, of extending hospitality to visiting magnates, however dull, of impressing the envoys of foreign rulers, and of providing the monarchy with trappings of pomp and ceremony.[2] It is significant that on their separate visits to Paris in 1157 about the business of the marriage alliance, Chancellor Becket travelled with a retinue of oriental magnificence and overwhelmed Paris by the prodigality of his hospitality, while King Henry travelled with a small escort and declined any pomp and show. Thomas Becket was always to display the eagerness of a self-made man for marks of status and the privilege of rank; and it seems that Henry, in the days of their friendship, found it a source of fond mockery. This at least is the implication of the story which William FitzStephen tells of the poor man and the cloak:

> One day they were riding together through the streets of London. It was a hard winter and the king noticed an old man coming towards them, poor and clad in a thin and ragged coat. 'Do you see that man?' said the king. 'Yes, I see him,' replied the chancellor. 'How poor he is, how frail, and how scantily clad!' said the king. 'Would it not be an act of charity to give him a thick warm cloak?' 'It would indeed; and right that you should attend to it, my king.' Meanwhile the poor man drew near; the king stopped, and the chancellor with him. The king greeted him pleasantly and asked if he would like a good cloak. The poor man, who did now know who they were, thought this was a jest and not to be taken

[1] William FitzStephen, III, 18–21.
[2] The chancellor's reception of envoys from Norway is noted *ibid.*, III, 26.

seriously. Said the king to the chancellor, 'You shall have the credit for this act of charity,' and laying hands on the chancellor's hood tried to pull off his cape, a new and very good one of scarlet and grey, which he was loth to part with. A great din and commotion then arose, and the knights and great men of their retinue hurried up wondering what was the cause of this sudden strife. But it was a mystery; both of them had their hands fully occupied, and more than once seemed likely to fall off their horses. At last the chancellor reluctantly allowed the king to overcome him, and suffered him to pull the cape from his shoulder and give it to the poor man. The king then explained what had happened to his attendants. They all laughed loudly, and some of them offered their own capes and cloaks to the chancellor. The poor old man walked off with the chancellor's cape, joyful and rich beyond expectation, and giving thanks to God.[1]

There is a hint of gentle mockery, too, in Henry's habit, when he returned from hunting, of riding his horse right into the chancellor's hall as he sat at dinner, leaping over the table, sitting himself down in his hunting gear amid the courtiers in their finery, and asking to be fed.[2]

But although Henry did not share his chancellor's sense of dignity and grand style, it is probable that his policy was strongly influenced in the early years of his reign by another of his friend's characteristics. As archbishop of Canterbury, Becket was to display an uncompromising determination to let slip no tittle of the rights of lordship which history, or God, conveyed to the office he held. It was to him as a sacred duty; and it seems likely that he imparted to Henry a similar sense of mission in discharge of the duties of kingship, to which Henry was already conditioned by the circumstances of his early life and upbringing.[3] Henry's mother almost certainly reinforced such a conception of duty. The empress lived until 1167, in retirement near Rouen, given to pious works, somewhat mellowed and much wiser, and exercising until the end a strong influence on her son.[4] It is not surprising that Henry, having recovered his inheritance from the usurper, should immediately have set about gathering up the rights of lordship which had slipped through Stephen's fumbling fingers; but only a sense of mission superimposed on a sense of duty, and perhaps an arrogant confidence born of success, can explain his pursuit of a tenuous claim which fell to him as duke of Aquitaine in right of his wife to the lordship of Toulouse – against the entreaties of King Louis and to the jeopardy of their alliance.

[1] *Ibid.*, 24–5.   [2] *Ibid.*, 25.
[3] *See* below, pp. 457ff.
[4] Stephen of Rouen, 780; cf. Robert de Torigny, 186, and Walter Map, 238.
H—D

(ii) *The expedition to Toulouse and its consequences* (1159–61)

The Toulousain was a distinct region, physically isolated from northern France by the mountains of the Massif Central. Its political allegiance to the Capetian kings had long been nominal. Indeed, whether it would remain a part of the kingdom was, in the twelfth century, very much in doubt. The political interests of the counts of Toulouse were directed south to the Mediterranean, and to the recreation of what had once been the Roman province of Septimana. It drew them into involvement with the affairs of Provence, which lay within the bounds of the German empire, and of Barcelona in the march of Spain. More than once in the twelfth century it seemed that an amalgamation might be effected which would split southern France horizontally and create a new state stretching from the Pyrenees to the Alps.[1] At the beginning of the twelfth century it had seemed possible that the family of St Gilles, which controlled Toulouse, might make itself a power to be reckoned with in the Mediterranean: Raymond of St Gilles, a hero of the First Crusade, was, until his death in 1105, not merely count of Toulouse and through his wife lord of half Provence, but also count of Tripoli in the Holy Land. The possibility did not materialise: the hold of his successors on some of the major vassals of Toulouse was insecure, and the counts of Barcelona competed strongly for influence in Provence. Nevertheless the outcome remained for long in doubt and the rulers of Paris were confronted with the possibility that the Toulousain might break away from the kingdom into a new political grouping at the same time as it seemed that Normandy might break away and be absorbed into the kingdom of England. The far south of France was not to be fully integrated into the Capetian kingdom until after the blood-bath of the Albigensian crusade in the early years of the thirteenth century, but its political isolation from the north was first breached by King Louis VII. On the Second Crusade he struck up a friendship with Count Raymond V of Toulouse, and friendship developed into an alliance. In 1154 the count married the king's sister, Constance, widow of Stephen's son, Eustace. She gave the count three sons in as many years, and for a long time they remained the only male children of the Capetian royal line.[2]

[1] Cf. Higounet, 'La rivalité des maisons de Toulouse et de Barcelone'.

[2] King Louis VI was survived by five sons and one daughter, Constance. Of the five sons, two were churchmen. His eldest son, King Louis VII, married three times. His first two marriages each produced two daughters. It was not until 1165 that he had a son, Philip, by his third wife. His brother Robert eventually had a family of three sons and two daughters, but again only as a result of a third marriage. His

Unfortunately for King Louis, Henry of Anjou acquired an interest in Toulouse with his marriage to Eleanor. Historically there were good grounds for arguing that Toulouse should be a part of the duchy of Aquitaine, for it had once been a major city in the Carolingian kingdom

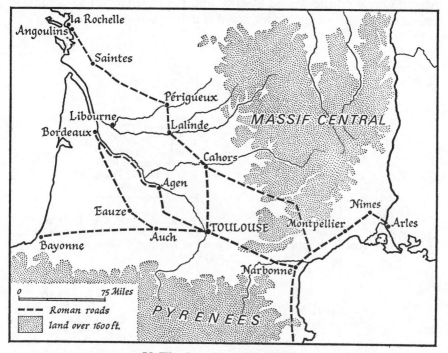

V The location of Toulouse

of Aquitania. The counts of Toulouse and the counts of Poitiers were in fact rivals for several generations in an attempt to forge a 'feudal empire' in south-west France out of the fragments into which Aquitania had disintegrated. The issue was decided when, in the eleventh century, the counts of Poitiers established themselves in Gascony and assumed the ducal title. The counts of Toulouse had then concentrated their attention on their neighbours to the south-east and forged their political fortunes in Narbonne and Carcassone. But though the counts of Toulouse

---

youngest brother, Peter, had one son by his marriage to Isabella de Courtenay, but it is unlikely that he was born before 1159. King Louis VII's concern with the political problems of southern France and northern Spain is reflected in his second marriage to Constance of Castille at the same time as the marriage of his sister Constance to Count Raymond V. Castille was a counter-balance to Barcelona and Aragon. For a brief account of Louis VII's policy see Pacaut, *Louis VII et son Royaume*, 185ff.

turned their backs on the political future of Aquitaine they remained
of vital concern to the Poitevin lords of Bordeaux, for they dominated
the network of trade routes in south-east France. The city of Toulouse
was the crucial link in the passage from the Mediterranean to the
Atlantic between the Massif Central and the Pyrenees. It stood at the
upper end of the navigable waters of the river Garonne which emptied

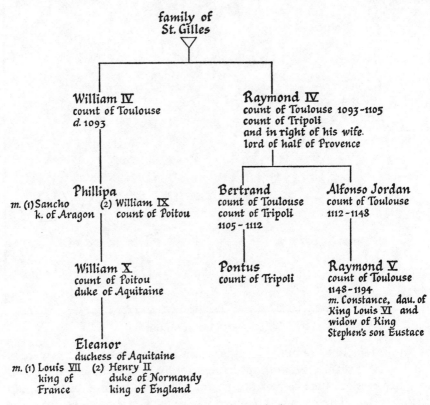

6. Toulouse and Aquitaine

into the Atlantic at Bordeaux, and it was the focus of the Roman road
system which linked Bayonne, Bordeaux, and La Rochelle on the
eastern seaboard with Narbonne and the commerce of the Mediterranean.[1] Control of Toulouse was, indeed, of as much concern to the
feudal empire builders of Aquitaine as control of Tours and Nantes
had been to the rulers of Anjou. Without it the Poitevin lordship of
Aquitaine was both incomplete and fatally weakened.

[1] Cf. Renouard, 'Les voies de communication entre pays de la Méditerranée et
pays de l'Atlantique'. See Map V.

The dukes of Aquitaine were unable to prevent the defection of Toulouse, but they had some hope of gaining control of it by hereditary right. The countship of Toulouse had for various but perfectly proper reasons not descended in the direct line of the family of St Gilles. Count William IV of Toulouse, who died in 1093, left an only daughter, and the countship passed to his brother Raymond – the hero of the First Crusade – and subsequently to Count Raymond's second son. But Duke William IX of Aquitaine (Eleanor's grandfather) had married the daughter of Count William IV after her father's death, and in virtue of this the dukes of Aquitaine claimed that Toulouse should belong to them and not to the descendants of Count Raymond.[1] It was not the kind of claim which carried much weight in the south of France; but to such a man as Henry of Anjou it was compellingly persuasive.

Henry began his attempt to secure Eleanor's inheritance by forming an alliance with Count Raymond-Berengar of Barcelona, who was already at war with the count of Toulouse and in league with some of his rebellious vassals.[2] When this failed to induce the count of Toulouse to seek terms, Henry summoned his forces to assemble at Poitiers at midsummer 1159. But neither did the threat of war persuade Count Raymond V to submit, for he relied on his alliance with King Louis. Henry talked with King Louis about it at the beginning of June, reminding him of their marriage alliance, and trying to persuade him to bring pressure upon his brother-in-law. The meeting lasted for three days and was inconclusive.[3] King Louis was in a dilemma. He could not contest Henry's claim, for he had himself pressed it when he was Eleanor's husband, leading an abortive expedition to Toulouse in 1141; but he could not allow Henry to succeed because of his sister and nephews.[4] It was not simply a question of homage, for Eleanor's claim to Toulouse by right of inheritance implied dispossession of Count Raymond and his family.

Since his diplomacy was unsuccessful, Henry was driven to wage a

---

[1] This is a bare outline of a complicated family history; for the details see Devic and Vaissète, *Histoire de Languedoc*, III, 808ff. Some of the ramifications may be discerned from Diagram 6.

[2] Robert de Torigny, 200. The situation in the south since 1150 is summarised by Pacaut, *Louis VII et son Royaume*, 184–5. Henry promised to the count of Barcelona a marriage between his son Richard and the count's daughter, with the reversion of the duchy.

[3] Continuatio Beccensis, 321–2; Robert de Torigny, 201.

[4] Cf. Richard, *Les Comtes de Poitou*, II, 74–5. Louis's concern over his nephews is emphasised by Continuatio Beccensis, 322, and Ralph of Diceto, I, 303.

military campaign. The preparations were prodigious. Robert de
Torigny credits Henry with 'not wishing to vex the country knights
[*agrarii milites*] with the length and difficulty of the journey', and says
that he took money from them in lieu of service (a payment known as
scutage).[1] The towns, the Jews, and the moneyers were obliged to contribute to the funds for the campaign, and so too, much to their consternation and indignation, were the clergy.[2] Mercenaries were hired
in such large numbers as to suggest that a major new rôle was being
found for them.[3] The lay barons, however, were expected to serve in
person and gathered together from all parts of Henry's dominions.
King Malcolm IV came from Scotland, with a retinue which required
forty-five vessels for transport across the Channel, to join the barons of
England, Normandy, Anjou, Brittany and Aquitaine at Poitiers. Even
an unnamed Welsh prince came.[4] It was a grand parade of Henry's
vassals. In addition came the count of Barcelona (who, as William of
Newburgh remarks, was the equal of kings, for his wife was queen of
Aragon), together with some of the disaffected vassals of the lordship
of Toulouse – Raymond Trencavel, viscount of Béziers and Carcassone,
and William of Montpellier.[5] Nothing like such an army can have been
seen save on a major crusade.

The grand army made a fairly leisurely progress through Périgord
to Quercy, control of which had long been denied to the dukes of
Aquitaine by the counts of Toulouse. Some time was spent in taking
possession of its principal city of Cahors, while Raymond Trencavel
successfully raised rebellion in the eastern Toulousain. The intention
still seems to have been to persuade Count Raymond to submit without
the necessity of engaging him in battle, much as Conan of Brittany had
submitted when Henry mustered his forces against him. In the first
week of July, as the army approached Toulouse, King Louis came to

---

[1] Robert de Torigny, 202. It has been assumed from this that Henry replaced his
feudal host with mercenaries. Round, *Feudal England*, 221–2, has pointed out, however, that the amount of scutage recorded on the English pipe rolls was comparatively
small, suggesting that the knights owed in service by the tenants-in-chief actually
served. The argument, though persuasive, is not conclusive: the pipe rolls record
scutage collected by the sheriffs only, and it is possible that much of the scutage was
collected by the barons and paid directly into the royal chamber.

[2] Round, *op. cit.*, 219–21. For the levy on the clergy, cf. Gerald of Wales, III, 357,
and for some of their complaints, *Materials for the History of Becket*, V, 378–9, 525–6,
Saltman, *Archbishop Theobald*, 44–5.

[3] Cf. Boussard, 'Les mercenaires au xiie siècle', 198–200.

[4] Continuatio Beccensis, 323; Anderson, *Early Sources of Scottish History*, 240–3; the
Bretons are mentioned by William FitzStephen, III, 33, the Welsh prince by Gervase
of Canterbury, I, 167.   [5] William of Newburgh, I, 125.

talk with Henry, apparently in the role of mediator.[1] Nothing is reported in the chronicles of the nature of the talks, but, according to Robert de Torigny, Henry was persuaded that he could count on Louis's help.[2] King Louis, however, apparently formed the impression that Henry was intractable and was using their *entente* only for his own convenience, for he went straight to the city of Toulouse and put himself in charge of its defence. Henry baulked at mounting a direct attack on his overlord, for, besides being a bad example to his own followers, it would, if successful, have left him with the awkward problem of having his king as his prisoner. Instead he tried to escape from the dilemma in two ways: he set his army to take castles in the neighbourhood of Toulouse, to seize important towns, and devastate the region in the hope of persuading Count Raymond of the futility of resistance, and he gave orders for raids on the Captain royal demesne in the hope of persuading Louis to depart. But King Louis remained where he was, guarding his sister, says Robert de Torigny, by day and night.[3] Henry persisted until the autumn, but as time went on the threat which his army posed diminished, for it was ravaged by sickness.[4] At the end of September he withdrew, abandoning his conquests in the neighbourhood of Toulouse, but leaving garrisons in Quercy. The recovery of the county of Quercy for the duchy of Aquitaine was the one substantial achievement of the great campaign.

When Henry returned to Normandy he found that the diversionary attacks he had ordered against the royal demesne had been countered by raids on Normandy led by King Louis's brothers, Henry, bishop of Beauvais, and Robert, count of Dreux. Henry flung himself into the fray, devastated Beauvais and forced the count of Evreux to do him

---

[1] Continuatio Beccensis, 323: 'rex Francorum cum rege Anglorum colloquium habuit, de obtinenda pace cum comite'.   [2] Robert de Torigny, 203.

[3] *Ibid.*, 203; Continuatio Beccensis, 323. Henry's reluctance to attack his overlord is emphasised also by William of Newburgh, I, 125, Stephen of Rouen, II, 609, Geoffrey de Vigeois, II, 310, Ralph of Diceto, I, 303, William FitzStephen, III, 33. Some historians have questioned Henry's sincerity on the ground that he was not always so scrupulous; and it may be that many of the barons were more reluctant than Henry himself to attack their liege lord. But it should be noted that although Henry did on other occasions wage war against the king of France, he did so only after he himself had been attacked. Gervase of Canterbury, I, 167, gives the totally false impression that Henry invested Toulouse and sat fruitlessly before its walls for months. All the English chroniclers are very vague about the progress of the campaign. The attempt to reconstruct its chronology by Ramsay, *The Angevin Empire*, 21, is unacceptable; see Boussard, *Le Gouvernement d'Henri II*, 419 n.5.

[4] *Chronicon Angliae Petriburgense*, 97; Roger of Howden, *Chronica*, II, 217. Among the deaths were King Stephen's son, William count of Boulogne.

homage and hand over castles which effectively cut the royal demesne
in two. Since Henry could not expect to hold such an exposed position
without enormous difficulty, it seems likely that he was merely indulging
in a bitter reprisal for his discomfiture at Toulouse. The fighting died
down with the close of the campaigning season, and a truce was
arranged to last until the feast of Pentecost, the following May.

By the time the truce expired, tempers had cooled and peace was
made. Henry gave up his acquisitions in Evreux and remitted the
homage of its count. Louis confirmed to Henry 'all the rights and tenements' which his grandfather had held on the day of his death, with the
exception of the Vexin. About the Vexin elaborate arrangements were
made. Fiefs in the Vexin held by the archbishop of Rouen, the earl of
Leicester and the count of Evreux were to be restored to Henry's
lordship; but the future of the rest of the Vexin was to be dependent
upon the marriage of the young Henry and Margaret. If they were
married within three years 'with the consent of Holy Church', Louis
would hand over the rest of the Vexin and its castles to the king of
England for the benefit of his son. In the meantime the Vexin would
remain in Louis's lordship, but its castles would be entrusted to Knights
Templar, who would act as guarantors of the treaty. As for the southern
problem, Louis formally confirmed to Henry 'all the rights and tenements of the counts of Poitou, with the exception of Toulouse'; and
Henry was to concede to Count Raymond a truce to last for one year.[1]

Although the marriage – convenient to both sides – had been salvaged, there was no return to the *status quo ante bellum* implied in this
peace. The policy of *entente*, so briefly pursued, was at an end. A
judicious chronicler of the next generation, William of Newburgh, was
of the opinion that the expedition to Toulouse marked the beginning of
forty years of war, and other chroniclers seem to have felt the same.[2]

That King Louis was reformulating his policy became clear in the
autumn of 1160. His second wife, Constance of Castille, died in child-
birth, and with unseemly haste Louis married the sister of the brothers
of Blois, Theobald count of Blois, and Henry count of Champagne. It
amounted to a reversion to the policy which Louis had pursued in the
days when the Angevins had been challenging King Stephen: the king
of France had then cemented an alliance with Blois by betrothing his

---

[1] Contemporary chroniclers do not record the terms upon which peace was made;
but by a rare chance a copy of the text of the agreement survives, and is printed in
Recueil des Actes de Henri II, I, 251–3.

[2] William of Newburgh, II, 491; cf. Ralph of Diceto, I, 303, Gervase of Canterbury,
I, 167.

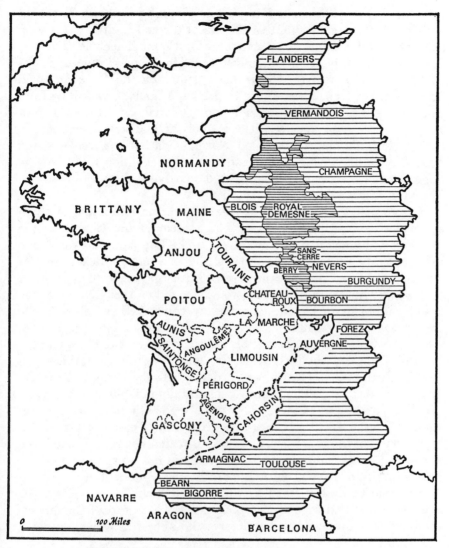

FLANDERS

VERMANDOIS

NORMANDY

CHAMPAGNE

BRITTANY

MAINE

BLOIS

ROYAL
DEMESNE

ANJOU

TOURAINE

SANS-
CERRE

BERRY

NEVERS

BURGUNDY

CHATEAU-
ROUX

BOURBON

POITOU

LA MARCHE

FOREZ

AUNIS

AUVERGNE

SAINTONGE

ANGOULÊME

LIMOUSIN

PÉRIGORD

AGENOIS

CAHORSIN

GASCONY

ARMAGNAC

TOULOUSE

BEARN

BIGORRE

NAVARRE

ARAGON

BARCELONA

0   100 Miles

VI Henry II's continental dominions, c. 1160

Uncertain or disputed boundaries are shown by a broken line. The extent of ducal authority over the Auvergne and Armagnac is particularly doubtful.

two daughters by Eleanor to King Stephen's young nephews, Theobald and Henry. The renewal of this alliance at the end of 1160 was a *volte-face* not only for King Louis, but also for Count Theobald. For two years he had cultivated the friendship of King Henry; indeed, it was he who had mounted the diversionary attack on the Capetian royal demesne when Henry was trying to persuade Louis to withdraw from Toulouse, and he had actually done homage to Henry in the autumn of 1159.[1] Louis's marriage to Adela of Blois at one stroke produced a realignment of political forces on Normandy's borders, renewed the possibility of his having a son, and created a coalition hostile to the hopes Henry reposed in the projected marriage of his eldest son to Margaret of France.

Henry retaliated by having the two children married immediately so as to gain control of the Vexin. The consent of the Church to the marriage of minors was obtained by a trick. Two cardinals were then in Normandy to canvas support for the new pope, Alexander III, against the claims of an imperial puppet. Henry gave them to understand that his recognition of Alexander would depend on their consent to the match, although in fact he was already committed privately to the recognition of Alexander.[2] They were married on 2 November 1160, a few days before Louis effected his marriage to Adela of Blois, and the Knights Templar, who held the castles of the Vexin in trust, thereupon handed them over to Henry in accordance with the terms of the treaty of the previous May. King Louis was naturally indignant, and so were his brothers-in-law. Count Theobald made threatening gestures against Touraine and reinforced his great border castle of Chaumont on the bank of the Loire. It was rash to threaten Henry of Anjou, even at the end of the campaigning season. He did not wait to bring up the knight service of Anjou, but fell upon the castle suddenly with a force of mercenaries, and stormed it within a few days. In an age when a brilliantly executed siege was a talking point, the capture of Chaumont-sur-Loire was quite a famous victory: the abbess of Ronceray dated a charter by it.[3]

---

[1] Robert de Torigny, 203; Continuatio Beccensis, 324. For the betrothal of the brothers of Blois to Louis's daughters by Eleanor, *see* Kate Norgate, *England under the Angevin Kings*, 445 n.11; and for the marriage of Louis to Adela of Blois, Ralph of Diceto, I, 303, Robert de Torigny, 207, 208 (they were married on 13 November 1160).

[2] Arnulf of Lisieux, *Letters*, no. 24; cf. Barlow, 'The English, Norman and French councils called to deal with the papal schism of 1159'.

[3] Robert de Torigny, 208–9; Ralph of Diceto, I, 303–4; *Recueil des Actes de Henri II*, I, 337.

In the spring of 1161 Henry and Louis were mustering troops against each other on the border of Normandy. Their objectives are obscure, and it seems likely that their confrontation was simply an expression of the deep hostility bred over the past two years.[1] But saner counsels prevailed and a truce was arranged which matured into a peace arranged at Fréteval in October. Its terms have not survived. Ralph of Diceto says that the two kings 'were made friends'; but he is presumably speaking figuratively, for it is doubtful if the peace was anything more than an agreement to stop fighting – for the present.[2]

(iii) The consolidation of authority (1161–8)

The expedition to Toulouse was Henry II's first serious reverse, and in some respects a turning point in his reign. He tried hard for the rest of his life to recover the confidence of the king of France, but never quite succeeded; and despite his remarkable achievements, his failure in this respect was to be a fatal flaw in his political designs. Furthermore, it was probably from the time of the expedition to Toulouse that the influence of Thomas Becket began to wane. What advice Henry received about the campaign cannot be wholly recovered; but there can be no doubt that Becket was one of its strongest advocates and most belligerent supporters. He played a major part in organising it, and personally led, it is said, a force of seven hundred knights which he had raised at his own expense – a strange rôle for the king's chancellor.[3] One of his biographers reveals that, 'If the chancellor's advice had been taken, the king's army would have assaulted and captured the city of Toulouse, and with it the king of France in person . . . for the chancellor argued that the French king had forfeited his position as overlord by engaging in hostilities against the English king in defiance of existing treaties.'[4] After the withdrawal from Toulouse Becket was given charge of the captured castles of Quercy, and reduced the whole county to submission by brutal methods.[5] Henry had followed other advice in the decision not to besiege Toulouse, and it is likely that, as he came to realise that the whole enterprise had been not merely a miscalculation but a serious mistake, he also came to see that his friend was a man of defective judgement. This was probably one of the factors which

---

[1] Cf. William of Newburgh, I, 130–1.
[2] Ralph of Diceto, I, 305; Robert de Torigny, 210–11.
[3] William FitzStephen, III, 33–4, 53–4; Herbert of Bosham, III, 175–6.
[4] William FitzStephen, III, 33–4.
[5] Robert de Torigny, 205; Continuatio Beccensis, 323; William FitzStephen, III, 34; Edward Grim, II, 365; Herbert of Bosham, III, 176.

prompted Henry, after the death of Archbishop Theobald on 18 April
1161, to press his chancellor upon the electors of Canterbury. He was
warned against it, and seems himself to have had some hesitation; but
Henry was loyal to his friends and Canterbury was an appropriate
reward for a man who had been trained in the household of the
previous and much respected incumbent.

Nevertheless, it was probably Becket's chagrin at being removed
from the inner counsels of the royal court, and his determination to cut
a figure as archbishop even more splendidly than he had done as
chancellor, which prompted him into provocative and ill-judged actions
which soured the king's affection. The notorious quarrel which followed
soon after Thomas Becket's elevation to Canterbury in May 1162
dominates the pages of most of the chroniclers to such an extent that it
might be supposed that Henry, too, was preoccupied with it for the best
part of eight years. But this is far from the truth. The quarrel was for
a long time a nuisance and a distraction; but after Becket's precipitate
flight abroad in November 1164, Henry pushed it to one side and
occupied himself with other great business – at least until 1170. Becket,
however, strove hard to keep his sufferings, in what he regarded as the
cause of righteousness, before the world; and few chroniclers could
bring themselves to admit, after his martyrdom, that his activities had
been for most people at the time only an irritant.[1]

The one major chronicler to reduce the quarrel to something like the
proper proportions was Robert de Torigny, who was abbot of Mont
Saint-Michel in the western extremity of Normandy. His chronicle was
written up from year to year, and not, as with most other chronicles of
Henry's reign, after the murder of Becket had worked a distorting
influence. Unfortunately, Robert de Torigny is not the most helpful of
chroniclers. He was assiduous in noting down events, but the facts he
records are often both brief and bald. Under the year 1165, for example, he notes: 'Henry king of the English crossed to Normandy in
Lent and spoke with the king of the French at Gisors. Returning thence
he royally received his cousin the count of Flanders at Rouen.'[2] The
purpose of the meetings passes without mention. Yet were it not for
Robert de Torigny's note, the meetings would not be known at all. The
lack of adequate chronicles – before Roger of Howden began his
massively detailed *Gesta Regis Henrici Secundi* in 1170 – is all the more to
be regretted because there are indications that the late 1160s were a

[1] *See* below, ch. 13.
[2] Robert de Torigny, 224. Henry II and Philip of Flanders were distant cousins:
they had a common ancestor in Baldwin V, count of Flanders (1035–67).

period of major shifts in policy and of seminal changes in administrative methods. For lack of sufficient information, their nature has to be read from later developments. Nevertheless, Robert de Torigny provides a useful corrective to the impression that the story of the 1160s was largely the story of Henry's conflict with the Church. With Torigny's help it is possible to see that Henry II's attempt to define the relationship of Church and State was simply one aspect of an attempt to clarify and define his relations with all of his vassals. The story of the 1160s is the story of Henry II's attempt to consolidate his authority as a ruler. Out of it, eventually, sprang beneficial developments in the strength of monarchy and in the quality and effectiveness of government; but the beginnings were fraught with conflict as powerful vassals saw their autonomy, their privileges, and their freedoms threatened. The reaction was all the more violent because of Henry's dogmatic definition of his rights as overlord, and his relentless pugnacity in pursuing them. The 1160s were a time of troubles; but Henry intelligently learned from them, and in the fires of conflict refined his methods and tempered his instruments of government.

Of the decade which elapsed between the expedition to Toulouse and the attempt to achieve a lasting peace with the king of France at the conference of Montmirail in January 1169, Henry II spent all but three years on the continent. It should not be supposed, however, that while in one part of his vast dominions the king was out of touch with the rest. The coming and going of messengers was constant. Information flowed to the king's court from all quarters, and much ingenuity was applied to devising administrative procedures for gathering information. Even the names of outlaws were conveyed to the king twice yearly by the English exchequer.[1] Intimate counsellors – men known as the king's *familiares* – travelled here and there on the king's business, and were frequently employed on special commissions to investigate local problems.[2] If important decisions had to be taken, Richard de Lucy or Earl Robert of Leicester might cross the Channel to attend the king in person. Persons with private problems to lay before the king made astonishing journeys to find him. The abbey of St Albans, seeking royal intervention in its litigation with a powerful neighbour, sent a monk to the king, 'who was then with his army before Toulouse'.[3] The

---

[1] Assize of Northampton (1176), clause 13.

[2] *See* below, ch. 8, pp. 305ff.

[3] *Gesta Abbatum Monasterii Sancti Albani*, I, 163. Richard of Anstey, in the course of a protracted suit, found the king at Auvillar on the river Garonne on his way to the siege of Toulouse: Patricia Barnes, 'The Anstey case', 18.

king of Scotland and the bishop of Man, coming to confer with Henry in the autumn of 1166 about the Western Isles, found him returning from an expedition to Brittany at Mont Saint-Michel.[1] An Irish king, King Dermot of Leinster, looking for Henry II to offer himself as a vassal in 1166, travelled as far south as 'the remote parts of Aquitaine'.[2] Henry II rarely stayed for more than a few weeks in one place – and often for only a few days. Personal visitation was an essential part of his method of government. 'He was ever on his travels,' writes Walter Map, 'covering distances like a courier and showing no mercy to his household.'[3] 'He does not linger in his palaces like other kings,' wrote Peter of Blois, 'but hunts through the provinces inquiring into everyone's doing, and especially judges those whom he has made judges of others.'[4]

The kind of malversation with which Henry II had to deal is well illustrated in a remarkable confession of about 1161 by Stephen de Marcay, seneschal of Anjou, when, on Henry's orders, he gave judgement in a suit brought by the abbey of Marmoutier against Hamelin d'Athenaise. In a charter declaring the finding of his court on the perquisites of the abbey, the seneschal explains that Hamelin had erected a wine press at Boire to the hurt of the monks, who for forty years had enjoyed a monopoly of pressing wine there. He continues:

> The monks, deeply disturbed, complained to the lord Henry, king of the English, who ordered me that I should ensure that they were not deprived of their right, but should compel Hamelin to stand trial, and should bring to a just conclusion the dispute between him and the monks by due process of law. Accordingly, I cited Hamelin to appear before me to answer to the monks, but he neither came nor sent reply. And when he ignored numerous citations, I let the matter drop on account of his noble status, doing less than justice to the monks. Whereupon the monks told the lord king that for justice I could never be found, but for injustice was always available. Learning this the king became extremely angry with me and did not hestitate to make the most violent threats. I left him in fear and summoned Hamelin. . . .[5]

But although Henry II was perpetually itinerant, he did quite frequently confine his perambulations for many months to one region of his 'empire', as if to master fully its particular problems. For three

[1] Robert de Torigny, 228–9.
[2] Gerald of Wales, V, 227.   [3] Walter Map, 237.
[4] Peter of Blois, letter to the archbishop of Palermo, *Materials for the History of Becket*, VII, 572–3.
[5] *Recueil des Actes de Henri II*, I, 335.

years after his return from Toulouse he was very largely concerned with the affairs of Normandy. Indeed it seems that he took direct charge of the government of the duchy, for after the retirement of Robert de Neubourg as seneschal in August 1159, no successor appears to have been appointed until the king departed for England at the beginning of 1163.[1] Information about his activities is sparse, but it would appear that one of his chief concerns was to establish the sort of ascendancy over the barons of Normandy which he had achieved in England in 1155, for Robert de Torigny records that early in 1161 the count of Meulan and other barons of the duchy were required to hand over castles of which they had custody to Henry's nominees.[2] Moreover, in January 1162, he obliged Geoffrey de Mayenne, the most powerful baron of Maine, to give up the castles of Gorron, Ambrières, and Châtillon-sur-Colmont which his family had held for thirty years. These strongholds all lay in the borderlands of Maine and Normandy, and their acquisition by Henry is an early sign of a persistent policy of reducing the power of marcher barons. Their military strength, justified in the days when they guarded frontiers, had become a dangerous anachronism now that the frontiers were no more than administrative boundaries within Henry's dominions.[3]

In addition, Robert de Torigny mentions two administrative measures. What he says about them is distressingly cryptic; but they are worth noting as indications of Henry's general policy in the '60s and the workings of his mind. In February 1162 Henry held a council at Rouen, at which he is said to have 'criticised the bishops, their agents, and his *vicomtes*, and ordered that the decrees of the council of Lillebonne be observed'. No more than this is revealed, but a clue to the nature of Henry's criticism is provided by the reference to the decrees of the council of Lillebonne. At Lillebonne in 1080, William the Conqueror had presided over a council of prelates and barons which, having defined some of the jurisdictional rights and perquisites of bishops, ruled that bishops should not lay claim to any other jurisdictional rights without the approval of the ducal court. These decrees had been reissued under the seal of Henry I.[4] The development of canon law since then

---

[1] After Robert de Neubourg, who had been seneschal of Normandy since Count Geoffrey's day, retired from office in 1159 to enter a monastery, Henry did not replace him until he sailed for England in 1163: he had no need of a lieutenant while he himself was able to take control, cf. Boussard, *Le Gouvernement d'Henri II*, 421–3. There was a similar delay in the appointment of a successor after the retirement of Richard de Lucy as justiciar of England in 1178, cf. West, *The Justiciarship*, 53.

[2] Robert de Torigny, 209.   [3] *Ibid.*, 211–12, and below, pp. 235–6.

[4] Robert de Torigny, 212; cf. Haskins, *Norman Institutions*, 30–5, 170.

had rendered them obsolete; but Henry II clearly regarded the council of Lillebonne as establishing the criterion of sound practice, and seems to have been complaining that the ecclesiastical courts had been expanding their jurisdiction without challenge from his own local officers, the *vicomtes*. This attitude that established precedent should determine current practice is also reflected in Henry's appointment in 1162 of two commissioners 'to inquire by sworn testimony into the respective rights of the king and the barons to revenues and customary dues in Normandy'.[1] There are hints in both these measures of what later appears clearly as a fundamental trait of Henry II: a dislike of ambiguity and a determination to quell the disorder which uncertainty provoked. Henry was eventually to learn to be flexible in the interpretation of precedent; but in the '60s a rather rigid insistence on the practice of his grandfather's day as the basis of good order brought much trouble on his head.

In January 1163 Henry crossed to England to quell a threat to good order in south Wales. Prince Rhys of Deheubarth had temporised when he submitted to Henry after the campaign against Prince Owain in the north, and had never allowed his supposed allegiance to deter him from harassing the king's subjects in the Norman colonies of the south. In 1162 he committed the insupportable insult of seizing the royal castle at Llandovery. Henry marched into Carmarthen in the spring of 1163, bearded Rhys in his lair of Cantref Mawr, and brought him back to England as his prisoner. Henry, however, seems to have been dissatisfied not only with Prince Rhys but with the equivocal nature of client status generally, for he summoned all the leaders of the Welsh together with the king of Scots to attend his court at Woodstock on 1 July, and required them to perform homage as his vassals. They apparently found the experience humiliating, for thereafter King Malcolm's relations with Henry became frigid, and the Welsh immediately broke into a massive uprising against Anglo-Norman occupation. Even the hitherto docile province of Powys declared its defiance. It was not, however, only the Welsh who were troublesome. At the same council of Woodstock Archbishop Becket publicly unfurled the banner of defiance, loudly condemning a not unreasonable proposal by the king to divert a larger proportion of sheriffs' profits into the royal treasury. The issue was not of major importance and Becket seems simply to have been seizing an opportunity to declare to the world that he was no

[1] Robert de Torigny, 217. To these administrative measures may be added an edict made at Falaise at Christmas 1159, noted only in the Continuatio Beccensis, 327; cf. below, ch. 12, p. 434 and n. 4.

longer the king's lackey. In October 1163 he found a more worthy cause for opposition, and one on which he could unite the clergy behind him.

Henry was at the time seriously concerned about lawlessness in his realm, and some of the most important, though ill-documented consequences to the three years he spent in England between 1163 and 1166 were the measures he took for the more rigorous enforcement of law and for better standards of public order.[1] One lesser but awkward aspect of the problem was the prevalence of crime committed by members of the clergy. The Church claimed jurisdiction over all clerks but had not yet developed adequate means for dealing with those accused of violent crimes. Henry proposed, at a council meeting held at Westminster in October 1163, that the Church should disown guilty clerks who could then be subjected to the full rigours of secular law. Archbishop Becket was not insensitive to the problem, but in the name of the Church's liberty, he steadfastly opposed the proposal on the ground of the clergy's immunity from all secular jurisdiction. From the point of view of canon law it was unsafe ground to stand on, but the bishops, fearing to admit a loophole in the clergy's defence, unanimously supported him. Henry angrily reminded them that clerks had been subject to secular jurisdiction in his grandfather's day, demanded to know whether they were prepared to accord him the same royal authority which his predecessors had enjoyed, and declared himself dissatisfied with the equivocating nature of their replies.

Faced with what seemed to him to be a conspiracy of resistance to the lawful authority of the Crown, Henry, at Clarendon in January 1164, confronted the bishops with a document setting out in unequivocal terms 'the customs and privileges of the realm' in respect of the exercise of royal authority over ecclesiastical affairs, and demanded that they take an oath to observe them. The bishops admitted that these 'Constitutions of Clarendon' did represent traditional practice, though it was not quite so unambiguous as the king claimed; but they resisted taking an oath which would compromise their adherence to the dictates of canon law. There were stormy scenes as Henry tried to browbeat the bishops into submission. Suddenly Becket capitulated and bade his suffragans do as the king wished; and then just as suddenly he recanted

[1] The scanty evidence poses serious problems of interpretation, and is reserved for discussion below, ch. 7. Lawlessness was a feature of medieval life, but it seems that England was at the time experiencing an unprecedented crime wave. The Continuatio Beccensis, 322, makes special mention under the year 1159 of a novel and widespread form of highway robbery: robbers disguised themselves as monks, attached themselves to unsuspecting parties of travellers, and led them into ambush.

and imposed a penance on himself. Incensed at what he took to be a betrayal of friendship, Henry determined to get rid of Becket as archbishop. Henry well knew his former chancellor's weakness of vanity and pride, and with the intention of humiliating him into resigning had him arraigned at Northampton in October 1164 on trumpery but plausible charges of contempt of court and malfeasance. Becket bore himself with courage, but did not help matters by insisting that his dignity as archbishop put him beyond the reach of the king's authority. It was, however, in his capacity not as archbishop but as a baron that he had been charged, and Henry demanded judgement on such a treasonable obstinacy. The bishops, torn between their duty to their primate and their growing conviction that Becket was an unstable and dangerously provocative leader, persuaded Henry to take the safer course of prompting the pope to depose him. Becket fled abroad, and cleverly using the Constitutions of Clarendon as a shield against the arguments of the king's envoys, convinced the pope that he was the harassed victim of a deliberate attempt to destroy the authority of the Church in England.[1]

Henry had been betrayed less by his former friend than by his own intemperate arrogance. His high-handed treatment of the bishops at Clarendon had converted a serious but resolvable problem in the relations of Church and State into a major dispute between Crown and Papacy. His persecution of Becket ensured that the restoration of the archbishop became inextricably linked with any attempt at compromise. By astute diplomacy he managed to avoid an open breach with the Papacy; but it was a situation from which Henry could not easily extricate himself without injury to the dignity of the Crown. For a time, however, it meant little more in practice than a vexatious complication in the conduct of ecclesiastical affairs. Becket's fulminations of excommunication against his ministers could be ignored, and the pope was hesitant to drive Henry into the arms of the emperor of Germany and his anti-pope. But what the world would not ignore was Thomas Becket's lonely defiance, and his brave demonstration that the mighty Henry of Anjou was neither irresistible nor invulnerable.

Henry could well have wished that no encouragement be given to defiance, for resistance to his authority was mounting in several quarters. Throughout the months of the quarrel with Becket the Welsh situation gave increasing cause for anxiety.[2] King Malcolm of Scotland was in treasonable correspondence with the king of France, and his death in December 1165 did not ease the situation, for his brother, who

[1] This is a brief résumé of a topic discussed more fully below, ch. 13.
[2] e.g., *Materials for the History of Becket*, III, 70; V, 174.

succeeded him as King William I, was even more openly hostile.[1] There was a dangerous conspiracy in the marches of Brittany against Henry's lordship, and resistance to the expansion of ducal authority in Poitou.[2]

VII The heartland of Henry II's continental dominions

[1] *Recueil des Historiens des Gaules et de la France*, XVI, 117; *Materials for the History of Becket*, VI, 72.

[2] Cf. Robert de Torigny, 223; Ralph of Diceto, I, 329; William of Newburgh, I, 146; letter of John bishop of Poitiers to Archbishop Becket, *Materials for the History of Becket*, V, 37–41. Henry crossed to the continent in February 1165 and stayed for three months, leaving Queen Eleanor in charge at Angers on his return to England, cf. Eyton, *Itinerary of Henry II*, 77–9.

Henry's response to overt defiance by the Welsh and the Bretons was, as in the case of Archbishop Becket, a policy of heavy-handed reprisals. In July 1165 he invaded Wales at the head of a large army. He had been making intensive preparations for it since October 1164. Forces were brought over from the continental dominions, mercenaries hired from Flanders and vessels from the Norse colony of Dublin. It was an irresistible force which Henry led out from his supply base at Shrewsbury, through Powys, for an assault on the heartland of Gwynedd. But the Welsh were saved by the weather and the terrain. It was the foulest summer in living memory. The mountain passes dissolved into rivers of mud, the supply system broke down, and with his vast army of foot soldiers on the verge of starvation, Henry was obliged to retreat. He seems for a few weeks to have intended to renew the assault from Chester, but by September all thought of continuing the campaign had been abandoned. Instead the marcher castles were strongly fortified.[1]

The winter months of 1165–6 were distinguished by important measures which Henry took for improving law enforcement and the revenues of the Crown. They are unrecorded by contemporary chroniclers and their nature can be recovered only with difficulty from surviving documents.[2] Henry did not remain in England to see how his measures worked out in practice for he sailed from Southampton in March 1166, and found himself beset by increasing difficulties in keeping control of his continental vassals and by a renewal of war by King Louis. He was not to set foot in his kingdom again for four years.

In the summer of 1166 Henry gave his attention to Brittany. He had long been concerned about the preservation of order in the border lands where Brittany marched with Normandy, Maine, Anjou, and Poitou, for these were regions where his predecessors had possessed few demesne lands and castles. Over the years he had gradually strengthened his hold. In 1156 he had made war on the powerful and troublesome viscount of Thouars, and truncated his vast fief.[3] In 1158 he had gained control of Nantes, and captured the reputedly impregnable castle of Thouars in three days.[4] In the northern marches he had had a new castle erected at Pontorson, pacing out the site himself and giving detailed instructions to his masons.[5] In January 1162 he had taken

---

[1] Cf. Eyton, *op. cit.*, 83; Robert de Torigny, 226; for the expedition to Wales *see* below, ch. 4, p. 163.

[2] *See* below, ch. 7, pp. 275ff.

[3] Cf. Richard, *Les Comtes de Poitou*, II, 125–6; Boussard, *Le Comté d'Anjou*, 74.

[4] Robert de Torigny, 198; Continuatio Beccensis, 319–20; Gervase of Canterbury, I, 166.

[5] Robert de Torigny, 197.

three castles from Geoffrey de Mayenne, and when John of Dol died in July of that year, leaving his heiress and estates to the guardianship of Ralph de Fougères, Henry had intervened to take possession of the stronghold of Dol.[1] But the region remained restless and lawless, and something of the difficulty Henry had even with his own castellans is revealed by serious complaints of extortion made by the inhabitants of the *châtellanie* of Pontorson in 1162. Henry had to relieve Evelin de Fours of his charge, and entrusted the castle temporarily to Robert de Torigny, the chronicler from whom much of our information for these years derives.[2] While Henry was in England a league had been formed among the border barons of Brittany and Maine, led by Ralph de Fougères, to resist his lordship. In August 1164, while Henry was occupied in his quarrel with Archbishop Becket, the constable of Normandy had to muster forces from both Normandy and Brittany against the confederates, and took the castle of Combourg from Ralph de Fougères. But even this was unsuccessful, for Queen Eleanor, who had been left in charge of the region while Henry was mounting his campaign against the Welsh, found her orders treated with contempt.[3] When he returned to the continent in 1166 Henry asserted his authority. Early in July 1166 he laid siege to the castle of Fougères with an army gathered, it is said, from all his continental dominions, and having captured it, levelled it to the ground. But a show of military force was not Henry's only purpose, for he had decided on a more drastic solution to the problem of Brittany and the insecurity of the marchlands. He seems to have held Duke Conan responsible for failing to keep order, and indeed the intervention of the constable of Normandy in August 1164 suggests that Conan was either unwilling to discipline his vassals or incapable of subduing them.[4] Henry deposed him: his heiress, the infant Constance, was betrothed to Henry's seven-year-old son Geoffrey, and Conan retired to his ancestral county of Guingamp. Henry went to Rennes, which had been the seat of Conan's government, and formally took possession of the duchy in the name of his son. In the autumn he received the homages of the barons of Brittany at Thouars.[5]

After Brittany it was the turn of Aquitaine. To many in the south the

---

[1] *Ibid.*, 211–12, 214.

[2] *Ibid.*, 212.

[3] *Ibid.*, 223, 228; cf. William of Newburgh, I, 146–7, Ralph of Diceto, I, 329.

[4] Conan of Brittany was a witness to the Constitutions of Clarendon in January 1164, and may have been summoned to England to discuss the situation.

[5] Robert de Torigny, 228, significantly uses the word *saisire* to describe Henry taking charge of the duchy: *seisin* was a technical term of feudal law indicating legitimate possession but not, necessarily, proprietary right; cf. below ch. 9, pp. 348–9.

overlordship of the duke of Aquitaine was acceptable only so long as it was ineffective. For as long as anyone could remember it had been ineffective, for the dukes lacked revenues commensurate with the task of government, and their military strength rested largely on the uncertain services of vassals. Outside Poitou and the district of Bordeaux there were vast regions where the dukes had neither estates nor strongholds. The allegiance of counts and viscounts could be counted on only when a common interest was involved, and declarations of independence were averted only because of the difficulty such men had in controlling their own vassals. All too often, and even in parts of Poitou, effective authority rested in the hands of castle-holders, whose word was law to men of the neighbourhood.[1] It was doubtful if the remote and mountainous Auvergne in the eastern extremity could be said to belong to the duchy at all, and no one could have traced the boundaries of the duke's lordship in the foothills of the Pyrenees. Even in the heart of Aquitaine there was little sense of belonging to a political entity. To the men of Gascony the Poitevins were foreigners. To the men of the ancient city of Limoges, Poitiers itself was an upstart capital.[2] When Louis, the young heir to the French throne, married Eleanor, the heiress to the duchy, the count of Angoulême absented himself from the ceremony. And when Louis had journeyed through the duchy for his installation as duke he went as if on a campaign, with an escort which was virtually an army. Even so, the castellan of Talmot attempted to hold him for ransom by shutting the gates of his castle when the vanguard had entered. The attempt was foiled; but the trick had been successfully practised on the entourage of a previous duke.[3] It was, then, inevitable that Eleanor would seek a strong protector when Louis divorced her, and inevitable too that there would be rebellious discontent in Aquitaine as soon as Henry attempted to introduce Norman and English conceptions of the rights and functions of an overlord.

The only occasion on which Henry is known to have been in Aquitaine between his return from Toulouse and 1167, was in the summer of 1161, when, according to Robert de Torigny, 'among other vigorous deeds, he laid siege to Castillon-sur-Agen, a castle well-fortified by both nature and artifice, and took it within a week, to the wonder and terror of the Gascons'.[4] The chronicle record is, however, too thin, and

---

[1] For the power and virtual autonomy of local lords in Poitou see Painter, 'Castellans of the plain of Poitou' and 'The lords of Lusignan', and Beech, *The Gâtine of Poitou.*

[2] Richard, *Les Comtes de Poitou,* II, 151–3.

[3] *Ibid.,* 60.   [4] Robert de Torigny, 211.

the documents too few, for any certain assessment of Henry's policy towards Aquitaine and the activities of his agents to be attempted; but there are scraps of evidence which strongly suggest that Henry was, from the beginning, trying to break down local particularism and import Anglo-Norman conceptions of centralised government. Eleanor is said to have reposed complete trust in her uncle Ralph de Faye, who was seneschal of Saintonge and seems to have been regarded as her deputy in Aquitaine.[1] But Henry had less confidence, and pursued a policy of appointing foreigners to important posts.[2] In 1156 he exercised the feudal right of wardship over the young heir to the viscounty of Limoges, and entrusted its government to two Normans who are said to have preserved peace there for three years. Northerners were nominated to the episcopal sees of Périgueux and Bordeaux in 1160, and to Poitiers in 1162.[3] And about 1163 Henry appointed Patrick earl of Salisbury to command his military forces in Aquitaine.[4]

Despite the lack of evidence as to the activities of Henry's agents, the complaints they provoked speak clearly of the increasing encroachment of ducal government on the traditional autonomy of the barons of Aquitaine. Gervase of Canterbury reports that 'the Poitevins withdrew from their allegiance to the king of the English because of his pruning of their liberties'.[5] And in a move almost of desperation they tried to dissolve the marriage between Henry and their duchess by laying a genealogical table demonstrating their affinity before cardinal legates who had come to confer about Archbishop Becket.[6] Henry went into Aquitaine soon after receiving the homages of the Bretons, and travelled the length and breadth of it, apparently curbing incipient rebellion.[7] But before he could complete the work he found himself distracted by the increasingly open hostility of King Louis of France.

As opposition built up against Henry's rule, King Louis began to cherish the hope of the disintegration of the Angevin 'empire'. The cautious attitude he had adopted to Henry since the peace of Fréteval

---

[1] Materials for the History of Becket, V, 197; Recueil des Actes de Henri II, Introduction 416; Boussard, Le Gouvernement d'Henri II, 354 and nn. 3 and 5.

[2] Cf. Boissonade, 'Administrateurs anglo-normands en Poitou'.

[3] Richard, Les Comtes de Poitou, II, 122, 130, 131, 134. Similarly in Brittany, one of Henry's chaplains was made bishop of Rennes in 1168: Robert de Torigny, 234.

[4] Recueil des Actes de Henri II, Introduction, 416; Ralph of Diceto, I, 331, calls Earl Patrick 'in Aquitania princeps militiae regis Anglorum'.

[5] Gervase of Canterbury, I, 205.

[6] Materials for the History of Becket, VI, 266.

[7] Cf. Eyton, Itinerary of Henry II, 103–6, Recueil des Historiens des Gaules et de la France, XII, 442.

in October 1161 had been changed by the birth of a son to his third wife on 22 August 1165. It diminished the importance of the marriage of his daughter to Henry's heir, and at the same time enlarged in his mind the fear that Henry might succeed in consolidating his rule over half of France, and leave his son, Philip, with a truncated kingdom. Conscious of his own military inferiority he reposed his hope in rebellion against Henry's brusque assertions of authority, and did his best to fan the flames of discontent. In November 1166 he offered Thomas Becket asylum at Sens, where he could with safety pursue his harassment of King Henry with sentences of excommunication on his ministers and demands to the pope for an interdict on England.[1] He made contact with the king of Scots, encouraged the rebellion of the Welsh, and offered the Bretons advice, and more rashly, help.[2] Henry countered with vigorous diplomacy: he lobbied the papal curia against Becket, threatened to transfer his allegiance to the anti-pope, negotiated with the count of Flanders and the count of Boulogne, offered marriage alliances to the marquis of Montferrat, the duke of Saxony, and Emperor Frederick Barbarossa, and tried to buy the neutrality of Count Theobald of Blois with an annuity of £500.[3] But there was more menace than real threat in these moves, and little came of them save the marriage of his daughter Matilda to Henry duke of Saxony early n 1168. Henry's real problem was not any need for allies but his failure to deal decisively with resistance to his authority, despite the

[1] Becket had been staying at the Cistercian abbey of Pontigny, but after he had on Whitsunday 1166 pronounced sentences of excommunication against Henry's chief advisers, the king threatened the Cistercians with reprisals against the property of the Order in England if the monks of Pontigny continued to shelter the archbishop, *Materials for the History of Becket*, VI, 48ff. The archbishop of Sens (where Becket found a new refuge) was king Louis's brother-in-law, William of Blois. In 1166 he wrote provocatively to the pope: 'The whole world is waiting to see what you will do for the exiled archbishop. . . . The king of England is doing his best not merely to cripple the church of Canterbury, but to destroy her, and with her all ecclesiastical liberty, so that the authority of the apostolic see will be excluded from his borders and he alone become all-powerful in his dominions. Unless his audacity is checked it may be feared that other kings and lords will do likewise, for men think lawful whatever goes unpunished . . .', *ibid.*, V, 373–5.

[2] *Recueil des Historiens des Gaules et de la France*, XVI, 117; *Materials for the History of Becket*, VI, 458; Ralph of Diceto, I, 329.

[3] For Henry's diplomacy against Archbishop Becket *see* below, ch. 13. For the negotiations with the counts of Flanders and Boulogne in 1166, *Materials for the History of Becket*, VI, 73; for the proposed marriage alliance with the count of Montferrat (who was apparently offering help in having Becket deposed), *ibid.*, VI, 68; for the negotiations for German marriages, Robert de Torigny, 224, Ralph of Diceto, I, 318, 330; for the negotiations with Theobald of Blois, *Materials for the History of Becket* VI, 74.

hard blows he had struck. Indeed the hard blows had produced a dangerous reaction. Archbishop Becket had escaped attempts to have him deposed, and was crying for vengeance. The Welsh were slowly but successfully besieging the royal castles which were supposed to contain them.[1] The Bretons were incensed at the deposition of Duke Conan, and rallied behind Eudo viscount of Porhoët, who had once been Conan's rival for the lordship of Brittany.[2] In Aquitaine a powerful confederation had been formed to resist Henry's authority, led by the count of Angoulême and the count of La Marche. They were threatening to break away from the duchy and offer their allegiance direct to the king of France.[3]

The worsening relations between King Henry and King Louis were publicly revealed in April 1167 when they quarrelled openly over an apparently minor point of prestige. They had previously agreed to the collection of money for the Holy Land throughout France, but while Henry intended to send the contributions from his dominions by his own messengers, Louis was insisting that all should be remitted through him. Hence, says Robert de Torigny, arose a 'magna discordia'.[4] But there were in fact deeper reasons for an open breach, of the same kind as had brought them to war in 1159. During Lent 1167, writes Robert de Torigny, 'the king of England spoke with the count of Toulouse at Grandmont'.[5] No more is revealed, but Count Raymond had recently divorced his wife, Louis's sister, and was presumably seeking a new ally.[6] And just as seriously, Henry was intervening in the Auvergne, where Louis had for years been patiently infiltrating his influence by offering protection to the local clergy. Henry had protested in 1164 that Louis's interference was a breach of his promise in their treaty of May 1160 to respect the integrity of the duchy of Aquitaine; and when in 1167 the young count of Auvergne was ousted by his uncle, Henry demanded that the usurper stand trial in his court. He refused and appealed to the king of France; whereupon Henry, in April 1167,

[1] Rhys demolished Cardigan in 1166, and Owain took Basingwerk and Rhuddlan in 1167, *see* below ch. 4, p. 164.

[2] Cf. Robert de Torigny, 236, *Materials for the History of Becket*, VI, 455. Eudo de Porhoët was the second husband of Bertha, the heiress of Count Conan IV. She died in 1163.

[3] Robert de Torigny, 237-8; Gervase of Canterbury, I, 205; *Materials for the History of Becket*, VI, 458.

[4] Robert de Torigny, 230.

[5] *Ibid.*, 229. Gervase of Canterbury, I, 205, writes that the main reason for the breach between Louis and Henry was 'propter Tolosam civitatem'.

[6] *Recueil des Historiens des Gaules et de la France*, XVI, 126, cf. Devic and Vaissète, *Histoire Générale du Languedoc*, VI, 7-8, 22-3.

marched into Auvergne and laid waste his lands.[1] Louis had acknowledged the justice of Henry's protest in 1164, but in 1167 he attempted
to distract Henry from invading Auvergne, by raiding the Vexin.[2] It
had the desired effect of persuading Henry to withdraw from Auvergne,
but brought him storming up to Normandy to demand reparation.
Robert de Torigny says that Louis was weak-kneed, but, urged to take
courage by his counsellors, refused to talk, and Henry, irritated, sacked
King Louis's arsenal at Chaumont-sur-Epte.[3] It was a brilliantly
executed operation against one of the most strongly fortified towns in
France, Henry sending some of his mercenaries to break in secretly by
swimming up the river while he tempted the defenders to sally out
against him. While they fought a brisk and losing engagement outside
the walls, the town and all King Louis's stores went up in flames behind
them.[4] Louis revenged himself by sacking towns in the Norman
Vexin, including Andely.

Stephen of Rouen tells a remarkable story about the sack of Andely:
Henry, he says, was advised by the count of Flanders and by his
mother, Empress Matilda, that in the interests of restoring peace it was
necessary to allow King Louis to recover the loss of face he had sustained at the sack of Chaumont, by allowing him to wreak his vengeance,
and that Andely was deliberately evacuated for the purpose.[5] Certainly,
Henry was not eager to embark on a serious war for he had yet to quell
the rebels of Brittany and Aquitaine, and a truce was arranged with
King Louis in August 1167 to last until the following Easter.[6]

As soon as the truce was concluded Henry marched against the
Bretons and caused terror by sacking castles far and wide, including
those of the viscount of Léon, Eudo's son-in-law, in the furthest
extremity of Brittany, which was usually safe from attack; but before
the work was complete he was recalled to Normandy by news of the
death of his mother on 10 September at Rouen.[7]

It was then the turn of Becket, for a papal delegation of two cardinals
attended Henry's court at Argentan from 29 November to 5 December,
and heard so powerful a case made out on the king's behalf by English

[1] *Recueil des Actes de Henri II*, I, 387–8; Robert de Torigny, 229–30.
[2] *Recueil des Actes de Henri II*, I, 388; Gervase of Canterbury, I, 203.
[3] Robert de Torigny, 231.
[4] Stephen of Rouen, 684–6.
[5] *Ibid.*, 688–90, and the preface by Howlett, lxxvi and n.3; Roger of Howden,
Chronica, I, 282. Ralph of Diceto, I, 330–1, on the other hand, says that Louis sustained very heavy losses in his attacks; cf. Robert de Torigny, 232.
[6] Robert de Torigny, 232.
[7] *Ibid.*, 232–3.

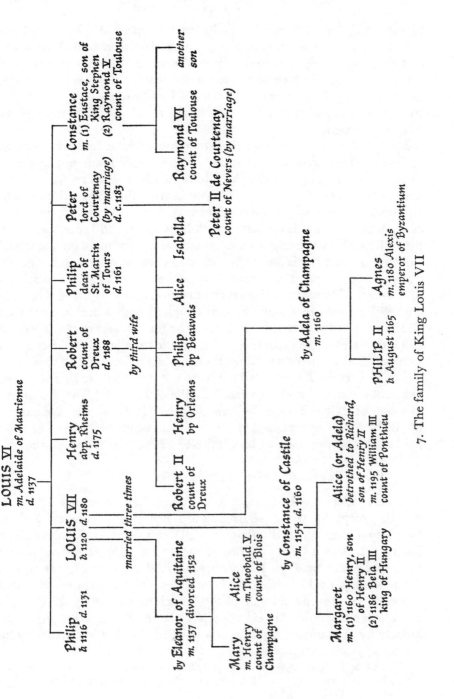

7. The family of King Louis VII

bishops that Becket feared he might yet be deposed.[1] After Christmas it was the turn of the rebels of Aquitaine: Henry marched upon the castle of Lusignan, captured it and devastated the neighbourhood.[2] He went to meet the king of France at the expiry of their truce in April, but distrusting Louis's sincerity, returned to Brittany and spread destruction by fire and sword through the lands of all the rebels throughout May and June.[3]

Mediators brought the two kings together again at La Ferté Bernard in July, but the rebels, in despair, pleaded with Louis not to desert them by making peace, and offered him their homage. Envoys from the king of Scots and the prince of Gwynedd were there too, offering help and tendering hostages as proof of their solidarity. Henry refused to discuss peace while Louis consorted with his vassals, and Louis, caught in the toils of his own intrigue, had no option but to break off the talks.[4]

Realising that Louis had to be forced to come to terms, Henry began a systematic campaign of devastation in the lands of Louis's vassals on the borders of Normandy. He set fire to more than forty villages belonging to the count of Ponthieu. Louis replied with a feeble attack on Chênebrun and suffered severe losses as he retired. Henry destroyed the castle of Hugh de Neufchâteau, then ravaged the lands of the count of Perche. 'And many other things the king of England did in this war,' writes Robert de Torigny, 'which have not come to our ears; or if we heard of them we have forgotten.'[5] By the end of 1168 King Louis was as weary of trying to wage the war as Robert de Torigny was of narrating it. He made approaches to Henry for a lasting peace in talks to be held at the border town of Montmirail in Maine in January 1169.

(iv) *The dynastic settlement and the great war* (1169–74)

The chroniclers record little, if anything, of the conference at Montmirail, except in so far as Archbishop Becket was concerned. It is tolerably clear, however, that the efforts made there to reconcile Henry and Becket were only one element in a comprehensive attempt to restore peace between Henry, his overlord the king of France, and the rebels against his authority. Henry seems to have appreciated that Louis feared the emasculation of the French monarchy by the creation of an over-powerful Angevin 'empire', and he sought to allay the anxiety by announcing his intention to divide his dominions among his

---

[1] *Materials for the History of Becket*, VI, 269–74.
[2] Robert de Torigny, 235–6.   [3] Cf. Eyton, *Itinerary of Henry II*, 113.
[4] Robert de Torigny, 237–8; *Materials for the History of Becket*, III, 418–19; VI, 458.
[5] Robert de Torigny, 238–9.

sons. His eldest son, Henry the Younger, was to receive his own inheritance of England, Normandy, and Anjou. Richard was to receive his mother's inheritance of Aquitaine. Geoffrey was to have Brittany. Geoffrey was to hold his duchy as a vassal of Henry the Younger, but Richard was to hold Aquitaine directly of the French Crown. King Henry also proposed that Richard should be betrothed to King Louis's daughter Alice, the sister of Margaret, who was already married to Henry the Younger. He was in fact offering Louis the prospect that his son Philip would one day be able to preside over a family consortium controlling the major part of the kingdom, for Louis's other two daughters (by his marriage to Eleanor) had been married in 1162 to the count of Blois and the count of Champagne. Louis readily agreed to the betrothal of Alice to Richard, and accepted the homage of Henry the Younger for Brittany – thereby admitting Henry II's claim to lordship of the duchy. And for the restoration of normal relations, he strove to reconcile to Henry those who had sought his protection against Henry's authority – the rebels of Brittany and Aquitaine, and the archbishop of Canterbury. Becket, however, was somewhat reluctant to have his own grievances submerged in the euphoria of a general peace settlement in which he had little interest. King Henry offered to reinstate the archbishop provided he would withdraw his denunciation of the Constitutions of Clarendon as 'heretical depravities'. The ancient customs of the realm had, after all, Henry pointed out, been accepted by Becket's saintly predecessors, and he was quite prepared to allow his own archbishop of Canterbury as much liberty as they had enjoyed. This seemed an eminently reasonable attitude to King Louis, and mediators laboured with Becket to persuade him to recover Henry's favour by a generous and unconditional acceptance of his offer. At length Becket, with a touching show of humility, abased himself before King Henry and entreated the royal mercy on the English Church which was committed to so unworthy a sinner as himself. As for the whole matter of the dispute between them, he placed himself at the king's pleasure – and then, to the consternation of the whole assembly, he added a rider which nullified the concession. No one could persuade him to retract it, for he insisted that it did not become a priest to submit himself to the will of laymen. The assembly broke up in despair with everyone reviling the archbishop for his obstinacy.[1]

King Louis himself lost patience with the archbishop at Montmirail; but his indignation did not persist for long. Becket justified himself to

---

[1] *Ibid.*, 240; Gervase of Canterbury, I, 207–8; Herbert of Bosham, III, 418–28; Ralph of Diceto, I, 336–7.

the French king by the argument that Henry was not to be trusted: he
had the cunning of a fox and the guile of a Proteus. He had offered only
promises at Montmirail and would keep faith no longer than suited his
convenience. King Louis began to believe that Becket was right when
he heard that Henry was dealing severely with the former rebels to
whom he had supposedly been reconciled at Montmirail.[1] It undermined his confidence in Henry's assurances about the future of the
Angevin 'empire'.

Henry certainly had no intention of allowing King Louis to dictate
his dealings with his vassals. He demolished the remaining castles of the
rebels in Brittany, put Eudo de Porhoët on trial and confiscated his
estates. He destroyed fortifications in Aquitaine, imprisoned Robert de
Silly, and, as Robert de Torigny puts it, 'pacified the count of Angoulême, the count of La Marche, and many lesser men'.[2] He behaved as
if he were preparing for a renewal of war: he had a great ditch dug on
the frontier of the Vexin, he constructed a splendid new castle at
Beauvoir near Mamers in the border district of Maine, and he bought
from Hervé de Gien the redoubtable castle of Montmirail which the
count of Blois coveted and claimed as his.[3]

On the other hand, Henry was perfectly sincere in declaring his intention to divide his dominions among his sons. If proof is required it
may be found in the will he made when he was struck down by a
serious illness in August 1170, which brought him close to death. In it
he fully confirmed the territorial dispositions he had announced at
Montmirail.[4] But even before this he had sought to have his sons' future
lordships recognised by the barons who were to be their vassals.
Geoffrey received the homage of the barons of Brittany at Rennes in May
1169.[5] In the same year Richard was proclaimed count of Poitou, and in
1170 was recognised as the future lord of Aquitaine in assemblies at
Niort and Limoges.[6] As for his eldest son, King Henry imitated the

---

[1] Herbert of Bosham, III, 438–9; Gervase of Canterbury, I, 210–11.

[2] Robert de Torigny, 241–2; Herbert of Bosham, III, 438; Roger of Howden,
Gesta, I, 3, *Chronica*, II, 3.

[3] Robert de Torigny, 242–3.

[4] Roger of Howden, *Gesta*, I, 6–7. Henry fell sick at Domfront about 10 August
1170, and rumour ran round France that he had in fact died. He recovered at the end
of September and made a pilgrimage to the remote monastery of Rocamadour in
Quercy. Cf. Robert de Torigny, 247, 248.

[5] Robert de Torigny, 242.

[6] Richard, *Les Comtes de Poitou*, II, 150, follows Geoffrey de Vigeois and Gervase of
Canterbury in saying that Richard was proclaimed duke at this time; but Ralph of
Diceto says that the duchy was not formally conferred upon him until 1179, and is
supported by Boissonade, 'Les comtes d'Angoulême', 275 and n.1.

practice of the Capetians and had him crowned king of England in his own lifetime. The ceremony was performed at Westminster Abbey on 24 May 1170.

The coronation of Henry the Younger presented a peculiar difficulty: by ancient tradition the coronation of kings of England was the privilege of the archbishops of Canterbury, and had been performed by someone else only in the most exceptional circumstances. Henry II had the ceremony performed by the archbishop of York. He knew full well that by doing so he was putting himself indisputably in the wrong and offending not only against tradition but also the express prohibition of the pope. Indeed, the ports had to be closely watched to prevent letters of prohibition reaching the English bishops. But guarding the ports could not prevent excommunication of the king or interdict upon his dominions. It seems, however, that Henry was taking a calculated risk, for he was ready with a counter-move to turn aside papal wrath. He calculated, correctly, that for Thomas Becket the insult to the rights of Canterbury would be insupportable, and that he would be ready to make any concessions to have the wrong put right. Henry announced that he was ready to make peace with the archbishop and met him near Fréteval on 22 July 1170. Henry offered Becket a peaceful return to Canterbury – and the opportunity to re-crown Henry the Younger. Becket accepted. Nothing was said about the Constitutions of Clarendon.[1]

That Henry intended all along that his son should be crowned again is confirmed by the fact that his wife, Margaret, had not been crowned with him. The reticent Robert de Torigny says simply that she arrived too late; but other sources reveal that she was deliberately delayed at Caen.[2] The implication is that Henry was contriving an insult to her father, the king of France, in order to deter him from attempting to dissuade Becket from accepting his offer. Henry the Younger was crowned again, with his wife beside him, at Winchester in August 1172 – but not by Thomas Becket, for Becket by then was dead.[3]

Henry had not been able to supervise personally the return of Thomas Becket to Canterbury. The sickness which induced him to make his will came upon him less than three weeks after the meeting at Fréteval on 22 July and left him incapacitated until the end of September. He then

---

[1] Roger of Howden, *Gesta*, I, 5–6, *Chronica*, II, 4–5; Robert de Torigny, 245; Gervase of Canterbury, I, 219–20. For a full discussion *see* below, ch. 13, pp. 500ff.

[2] Robert de Torigny, 245; *Materials for the History of Becket*, VII, 309, 316–17.

[3] Annals of Worcester, 60; Roger of Howden, *Gesta*, I, 31. The ceremony was performed by the archbishop of Rouen.

found himself confronted with warlike demonstrations by the outwitted King Louis. Henry wrote to Becket to explain that he could not keep their appointment to meet at Rouen to cross to England together because 'friends of mine in France have warned me that the king of France is preparing to take action against my vassals in Auvergne, and the men of Auvergne also have notified me of it and begged my help'.[1] Nothing more is known of the incident; but at the end of November there was an acute threat of war in neighbouring Berry. Henry claimed that the archbishopric of Bourges belonged by ancient tradition to the duchy of Aquitaine, and following the death of Archbishop Peter (who had admitted the claim) he went to Berry to take possession of the temporalities of the see. It was, however, a sensitive region where the Capetian royal demesne met and mingled with fiefs of the duchy of Aquitaine in an indeterminate frontier, and when he arrived there Henry found himself confronted by King Louis with an army, blocking the road to Bourges. Negotiations could not resolve the dispute, but in view of the season of Advent they agreed to a truce to last over Christmas.[2] Henry was at Bures in Normandy on Christmas day when he heard that Becket was behaving high-handedly in England. The reports spoke of the archbishop parading like a victor and refusing absolution to those he had excommunicated. Whether or not Henry ever uttered the words, 'Will no one rid me of this turbulent priest' – which have been attributed to him on no good authority – he did admit later to having uttered words in anger which prompted four knights of his household to slip away unobserved, wishing, as Roger of Howden says, 'to avenge him'. They murdered the archbishop in his cathedral on 29 December 1170.[3]

When he heard the news at Argentan on 1 January, Henry was overcome with grief and remorse. He shut himself away for three days, so that his friends feared for his sanity and even his life.[4] The murder brought on Henry's head the contumely of Christendom, and from the court of France attempts to turn the situation to political advantage. King Louis himself wrote to the pope:

> The man who commits violence against his mother [i.e., Holy Church] revolts against humanity. . . . Such unprecedented cruelty demands unprecedented retribution. Let the sword of St Peter be unleashed to avenge the martyr of Canterbury.[5]

1 *Materials for the History of Becket*, VII, 400.
2 Roger of Howden, *Gesta*, I, 10–11, *Chronica*, II, 13–14.
3 Roger of Howden, *Gesta*, I, 11. For the full story *see* below, ch. 13, pp. 508ff.
4 Arnulf of Lisieux, *Letters*, 122–3, quoted below, ch. 14, p. 520.
5 Roger of Howden, *Gesta*, I, 14–15, *Chronica*, II, 18.

His brothers-in-law were not far behind. Theobald count of Blois wrote to the pope:

> These dogs of the court, these retainers and intimates of the king of England have shown themselves true ministers of his will, and have grievously shed innocent blood. The detestable circumstances of this horrible crime I would give you in detail, did I not fear that you might think me prejudiced; but the bearers of these letters will disclose the details more fully and openly. . . . To you the blood of that righteous man cries out for revenge. . . . May Almighty God grant you the will to avenge him and the means of achieving it, so that the Church, distraught at the magnitude of so unparalleled a crime, may have reason to rejoice at the punishment of it.[1]

Count Theobald's brother, William, who was archbishop of Sens, wrote:

> I have no doubt that the cry of the whole world has already filled your ears of how the king of the English, that enemy to the angels and the whole body of Christ, has wrought his spite on that holy one. Arise thou man of God, and put on the strength of the successors of Peter; smite, thou son of smiters. . . . For of all the crimes we have ever read or heard of, this easily takes first place – exceeding all the wickedness of Nero, the perfidy of Julian, and even the sacriligeous treachery of Judas. . . .[2]

The archbishop of Sens had been commissioned by the pope, together with the archbishop of Rouen, to support as might be necessary with ecclesiastical censures the settlement at Fréteval. He used this authority to proclaim an interdict, despite the protests of his co-commissioner, and prayed the pope to ratify it, 'That God's honour and yours may be preserved.'[3]

The attempt to sweep Henry II away on a wave of revulsion failed. Pope Alexander III could not bring himself even to speak with an Englishman for a week; but when he had recovered his composure he behaved with judicious restraint. He did not lay an interdict on England or excommunicate the king personally, but simply prohibited Henry from entering a church until his guilt had been discharged. It was, of course, impossible for anyone to admit to a sense of relief at Becket's departure from the world, but it did in fact mean the removal of an obstacle to a sensible compromise over the ancient customs of the realm of England in matters ecclesiastical. And whatever Alexander III may

---

[1] Roger of Howden, *Gesta*, I, 15–16, *Chronica*, II, 20–2.
[2] Roger of Howden, *Chronica*, II, 22–5; *Materials for the History of Becket*, VII, 429–433.   [3] *Loc. cit.*

have felt personally about the murder of the archbishop and the conduct of King Henry, he was too much of a statesman not to realise that the long-term interests of the Church were best served by negotiating with Henry over the Constitutions of Clarendon while he was still eager to recover the Church's goodwill. Propriety would not allow of immediate talks (and it was only with some difficulty that the pope could be persuaded to write to Henry); but he announced that legates would be despatched 'to see whether the king were truly humbled', and they departed from Rome in the autumn of 1171.[1]

By then Henry was incommunicado. He had gone to Ireland to settle a problem which had reached the proportions of a crisis in the spring of 1170. Dermot king of Leinster had come to him in 1167 to ask for help against those who were trying to deprive him of his kingdom. Henry had not been very enthusiastic about Dermot's offers of homage, but had given him money and a generally worded permission to recruit freelances. Dermot at first had little success in persuading any of Henry's subjects to seek their fortunes in Ireland; but from 1169 he began to receive a trickle of recruits from among the Norman settlers in south Wales. They were prompted to go by a growing suspicion that King Henry did not intend to renew his offensive against the Welsh, but was instead seeking an accommodation with the Welsh leaders. In August 1170 – as Henry lay sick in France – the situation in Ireland changed dramatically with the arrival of one of the most powerful of the Norman barons of Wales with a strong force of knights. He was Richard de Clare (commonly known as 'Strongbow'), lord of Strigoil and Pembroke, and Dermot had recruited his services by promising him his daughter in marriage and the reversion of his kingdom. When Dermot died in May 1171, Richard de Clare fought off attempts by other Irish rulers to dislodge him and made himself master of Leinster. It was from just such small beginnings as these that the Norman kingdom of Sicily had risen to be a thorn in the side of the Holy Roman Empire and a powerful influence in the Mediterranean. It was an awful warning, and Henry II was determined not to allow any of his barons to establish an independent kingdom in Ireland. Since the Irish did not appear to be able to control the situation, he fitted out an expedition to take control himself, and sailed from Milford Haven on 16 October 1171. Henry's intervention was not resisted. Richard de Clare surrendered Leinster to hold it as a fief of the king. Several Irish rulers came to pay their respects and proffer their fidelity. The man who claimed to be high-king of Ireland, Rory king of Connaught, held aloof – it was not

[1] *Materials for the History of Becket*, VII, 476–7; *see* below, ch. 14, pp. 519ff.

until 1175 that he formally acknowledged the overlordship of the king of England – but he did not attempt resistance and a campaign against him was unnecessary. Most of the Irish bishops welcomed Henry's intervention: for a generation they had been struggling with little success against local custom to establish the kind of ecclesiastical government which was regarded as normal in England. Henry summoned a council of bishops at Cashel in November 1171 to reform Irish church law; and the bishops wrote to the pope expressing their confidence that at long last the Irish Church would be brought into conformity with Roman practice. Henry could not have found a better advertisement of the value to the Church of a strong secular authority.[1]

Strong winds hindered communication with Ireland throughout the winter of 1171–2. It was not until February that Henry learned of the arrival in Normandy of the papal legates who had been sent to negotiate his absolution; and it was not until the middle of April that he was able to cross from Wexford to St David's. By 17 May he was in conference with the legates at Savigny, and five days later, at Avranches, he was formerly absolved from complicity in the murder of Archbishop Becket and restored to the bosom of the Church. Henry had bargained astutely with the legates. He was required to release the bishops from their oath of the Constitutions of Clarendon, but he salvaged the principle that the Crown had a right to protect its interests if these were threatened in any way by the processes of ecclesiastical government. The agreement, known as the Compromise of Avranches, did little more than suggest the lines on which a concordat between Church and State could be arranged; it was enough for both the pope and for Henry to agree that a concordat was possible, and to leave to subsequent negotiation over particular problems the elaboration of detailed arrangements for avoiding open conflict.[2]

The Compromise of Avranches marks not so much a defeat for Henry as a change in his policy. He was not thereafter, in his dealings with the clergy or anyone else, to insist brusquely and obstinately on the letter of his rights as king, according to his own interpretation of past relationships. Instead he revealed a wholly pragmatic approach to problems, which enabled him to placate those who felt challenged, without sacrificing anything of the principles upon which his authority rested. It may be suspected that the removal of both his mother and Thomas Becket from the scene allowed him the more readily to retreat

[1] For a fuller discussion of Henry II's intervention in Ireland, and the sources upon which this paragraph is based, see below, ch. 4, pp. 192ff.

[2] See below, ch. 14, pp. 530ff.

from the dogmatic stance of earlier years. A more flexible approach to solving problems was not only to bring Henry II astonishing political success but was also to change the face of monarchy. Henry the pacifier became Henry the innovator.

In the spring of 1172, however, it probably seemed to contemporaries that Henry II had been humbled. His success in composing his differences with the Church passed largely unnoticed by contemporaries, who were more struck by the public aspects of the reconciliation at Avranches – the formal ceremony by which Henry put himself at the mercy of the Church and received absolution. Moreover, Henry might salvage his authority by patient negotiation and ingenious compromises, but there was little he could do to demolish the burgeoning myth of Thomas the Martyr. Visions and miracles proclaimed the murdered archbishop a saint, and his ultimate triumph became an article of faith among his partisans. There were those indeed who would contend that the persecutor of their hero had been broken to the will of the Church by his steadfast courage, whatever the evidence to the contrary. St Thomas was a much more powerful symbol of defiance than ever Archbishop Becket had been: he demonstrated Henry's unrighteousness, and the story of his refusal to bow to the king's will not only revealed that Henry was not omnipotent, but lent a cloak of virtue to rebellion. The defeated rebels of 1168 took new heart, and others prepared to join them.

In the months after his absolution at Avranches Henry gave his attention to the problem of Aquitaine. The vagueness of its boundaries, the confusion of history about its political structure, and the imprecision of tradition about ducal authority, were just the kind of uncertainties to trouble his tidy mind. In particular he was anxious to resolve the uncertain status of Toulouse. Although Norman and English chroniclers have little to say on the subject, Henry had not in fact ignored it since the abortive expedition of 1159. In 1162 and 1164 the citizens of Toulouse had been moved to appeal for King Louis's help against the menaces from Aquitaine.[1] Henry's interventions in Auvergne were at least partly designed to sever King Louis's connections with Toulouse. The count of Toulouse and the ruler of the united states of Aragon and Barcelona had meanwhile struggled for the allegiance of Béziers, Carcassone, and Narbonne. They had also competed for control of Provence beyond the boundaries of France and involved Emperor Frederick Barbarossa in their rivalries. Count Raymond transferred his allegiance to the emperor's anti-pope and secured from him the annul-

[1] Devic and Vaissète, *Histoire Générale de Languedoc*, VI, 11–12.

ment of his marriage in 1166. When King Louis had married his sister to Count Raymond in 1154 he had at the same time arranged an alliance with Castille (symbolised by his own marriage to Constance of Castille) in the hope that it would counterbalance the hostility of Aragon–Barcelona to the count of Toulouse. In 1170 Henry cut off the possibility of a renewal of Louis's influence there by himself forming an alliance with Castille and betrothing his daughter Eleanor to the young King Alphonso.[1] In 1172 he sought to contain the other end of the confused southern problem by seeking an alliance with a powerful neighbour of Provence – Count Humbert of Maurienne. The alliance was to be sealed by a marriage between Henry's youngest son John, and the count's daughter and heiress. The king of Aragon–Barcelona and the count of Toulouse both seem to have realised that Henry II was making himself master of their destinies: they both went to talk with Henry when in January 1173 he met Count Humbert at Montferrat in the Auvergne to arrange the details of the marriage settlement. They accompanied him to Limoges; and there at the end of February, before the assembled barons of Aquitaine, Henry publicly made peace between them and Count Raymond did homage for Toulouse.[2]

This moment of triumph was, however, marred for Henry by the outbreak of a dispute with his eldest son, which was soon to develop into the most serious crisis of his reign. The marriage settlement with Maurienne had specified in detail the fiefs that John was to receive as the husband of the count's daughter, even if the count subsequently had a son. At the conclusion of the agreement Count Humbert asked what John would receive of his father's lands, and Henry replied that he would have the traditional appanage of a cadet of the house of Anjou – Chinon, Loudun, and Mirebeau. Henry the Younger protested at this, saying that he had no wish to grant his brother these properties, and that his father had no right to dispose of them without his approval. As they quarrelled the reason for Henry the Younger's discontent emerged: he was a crowned king and had received the homages of England, Normandy, and Anjou, yet his father had not assigned him any lands from which he might maintain himself and his queen in proper estate. He had just celebrated his eighteenth birthday, and was already two

---

[1] Robert de Torigny, 247. For a survey of the situation in the south of France since 1159 see Pacaut, *Louis VII et son Royaume*, 191ff.

[2] Roger of Howden, *Gesta*, I, 35–41, *Chronica*, II, 41–5; Robert de Torigny, 255; Ralph of Diceto, I, 353. The marriage settlement arranged with the count of Maurienne is given by Howden and printed in *Recueil des Actes de Henri II*, II, 1–4; cf. Previté Orton, *The Early History of the House of Savoy*, 337–41.

years older than his father had been when Geoffrey of Anjou handed over to him the duchy of Normandy. His father even chose the members of his household and kept him short of money. He demanded that his father give him Normandy, England or Anjou. Henry had no intention of agreeing, for his eldest son was a charming, vain, idle spendthrift; but the quarrel took on a more serious aspect when Henry the Younger insisted that his father-in-law, the king of France, wished it, and so did the barons of England and Normandy. The suspicion that King Louis had been turning his son against him was reinforced by the warnings of Count Raymond of Toulouse that a plot was being hatched, in which all his family were implicated, to depose him. His desire to ensure the peaceful succession of his sons by having them recognised in the lordships they were to inherit was being used against him. King Henry II was in danger of becoming a King Lear.[1]

Henry hastily saw to the security of his castles in Aquitaine, and set off for Normandy taking his son with him. But when they were at Chinon Henry the Younger slipped away during the night and fled to Paris. His brothers, Richard (then fifteen) and Geoffrey (then fourteen), fled after him; and Queen Eleanor was apprehended by her husband's officers as she attempted to follow them disguised as a man. Henry sent envoys to Paris to reason with his heir. They found him in the company of King Louis, and when they requested him to return, King Louis intervened to inquire, 'Who asks?' 'The king of England,' they said. 'What nonsense,' he replied, 'the king of England is here; his father may still pose as king, but that will soon be remedied, for as all the world knows he has resigned the kingdom to his son.'[2] It was tantamount to a declaration of war.

The tables had been cleverly turned on Henry II; although perhaps not so neatly as the conspirators intended, for it seems likely that Henry the Younger had foolishly precipitated the crisis before the conspiracy was fully matured. King Louis's involvement needs no explanation, but it is not so easy to account for Queen Eleanor's betrayal of her husband.

[1] Roger of Howden, *Gesta*, I, 41, *Chronica*, II, 41-5; Gervase of Canterbury, I, 242, William of Newburgh, I, 169-70, Geoffrey de Vigeois, II, 319. Robert de Torigny, 255-6, attributes the origins of the quarrel to Henry II's removal of a member of his son's household. Roger of Howden, *Gesta*, I, 34, *Chronica*, I, 32, says that Henry the Younger had visited his father-in-law in the autumn of 1172, who then advised him to demand a share of his father's dominions. For the character of Henry the Younger *see* below, ch. 15, pp. 580ff.

[2] William of Newburgh, I, 170-2; Gervase of Canterbury, I, 242-3; Roger of Howden, *Gesta*, I, 41-3, *Chronica*, II, 46; Peter of Blois, *Opera Omnia*, II, 93; Robert de Torigny, 256; Ralph of Diceto, I, 355.

No chronicler gives any explanation, unless one can accept the opinion of Gerald of Wales that it was contrived by God to punish Henry for having married another man's wife.[1] It may be supposed that Eleanor had been alienated by her husband's adulteries, but there is very little evidence to support such an assumption. Henry undoubtedly had two bastards – Geoffrey 'Plantagenet', and William 'Longsword' – but both were almost certainly born before his marriage. Both were publicly acknowledged and generously treated. Geoffrey in particular was a prominent figure: he was bishop-elect of Lincoln in 1173 and subsequently royal chancellor. That these two were well-known and that no others are suggests that there were no more. It is true that Henry was alleged to be concupiscent, and was even said to have been accused by Eudo de Porhoët of having seduced his daughter while she was his hostage; but it is impossible in these stories to separate fact from malicious gossip.[2] And even if Henry were unfaithful it need not be supposed that Eleanor was unduly distressed. She had herself been imprudent in her younger days, and scandal spoke of liaisons with her uncle, Count Raymond of Tripoli, and with Henry's father, Geoffrey of Anjou.[3] William of Newburgh says that Henry lapsed into adultery only after his wife was beyond child-bearing.[4] Her last child, John, was born in December 1167. In 1173 Henry II was forty, and Eleanor over fifty. It is possible that Henry had already begun a liaison with Rosamund Clifford which was to last until her death about 1176. Undoubtedly she was the great love of his life – he had a shrine erected to her in the nunnery at Godstow. Tales were told of Queen Eleanor's jealousy of 'Fair Rosamund' and of how she had poisoned her; but since the tales relate to a period when Eleanor was in fact a closely guarded prisoner it is difficult to believe that they are anything more than romantic fantasies.[5] Nothing, indeed, can be recovered for certain about Henry's relations with his wife until their obvious estrangement in 1173, and although lack of information does not preclude the

[1] Gerald of Wales, VIII, 300, 302–3.

[2] e.g., *ibid.*, 165; William FitzStephen, III, 43; Ralph Niger, 168; *Materials for the History of Becket*, VI, 456. The Chronicle of Meaux, I, 256, says that Henry had a daughter by Alice, the betrothed of his son Richard, 'who did not survive'. For Henry's alleged seduction of Alice *see* below, ch. 16, p. 611.

[3] John of Salisbury, *Historia Pontificalis*, 52–3, cf. Richard of Devizes, 402, Walter Map, 237, Gerald of Wales, VIII, 300.

[4] William of Newburgh, I, 280; for a review of peripheral evidence *see* Morey and Brooke, *Gilbert Foliot and his Letters*, 173 n.1.

[5] Gerald of Wales, VIII, 165–6; Roger of Howden, *Chronica*, III, 167–8; cf. Archer, 'Rosamond Clifford', Chambers, 'Some legends concerning Eleanor of Aquitaine'.

possibility of her jealousy, it is probable that the explanation lies in another quarter entirely.

To judge from the chroniclers, the most striking fact about Eleanor is her utter insignificance in Henry II's reign. The chroniclers say nothing about her except occasionally to mention that she was present with the king here or there. And what makes this all the more remarkable is that her dominating personality is so marked a feature of the reigns of her

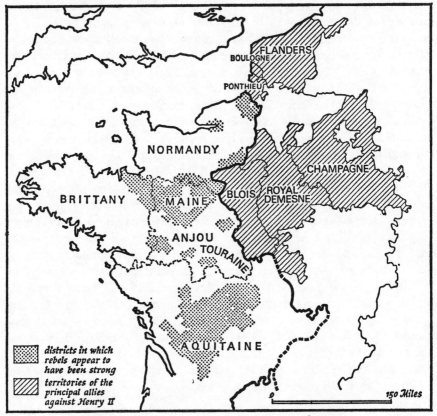

VIIIa   France: to illustrate the war of 1173–4

sons until her death in 1204. Moreover, her liveliness as the wife of King Louis VII suggests that she was far from being a nonentity even before she became a matriarch.[1] Gervase of Canterbury describes her as 'an exceedingly shrewd woman, sprung from noble stock, but fickle'.[2]

[1] For Eleanor's life *see* Labande, 'Pour une image véridique d'Aliénor d'Aquitaine', Pernoud, *Aliénor d'Aquitaine*.

[2] Gervase of Canterbury, I, 242–3: 'Erat prudens femina valde, nobilibus orta natalibus, sed instabilis'.

Yet for over thirty-five years she was almost totally eclipsed. Her scheming against her husband in 1173 and her arrest disguised as a man are the only notable events recorded of her in Henry II's reign. She is a figure of legend and romance, but not of history. It may well be that her political marriage to Henry of Anjou brought her neither the power nor the influence she – a duchess in her own right, and a queen before she married Henry – thought to be her due. She had to contend not merely with the dominating personality of her husband, but also, until 1167, with the influence of an even more proud and strong-willed woman than herself – his mother, Empress Matilda.[1] There were brief periods when Queen Eleanor acted as regent in her husband's absence, but she seems to have lent little more than the authority of her name to the actions of his ministers. The power which Eleanor had lost through her marriage to Henry she sought to regain through her sons. Her opportunity seemed to have come when her beloved son Richard was installed as count of Poitou and future lord of Aquitaine in 1170. This was when her separation from Henry began. She set up a regency council for Richard and seems to have expected to govern her duchy in his name.[2] Yet the real power remained with Henry. In late 1170 and again at the beginning of 1173 he was conducting the affairs of Aquitaine personally, and it is notable that when in 1171 the burgesses of Souterraine defied the prévot, it was to Henry that the prévot appealed for help, and Henry who sent in troops.[3] Urged on by Aquitainean lords who had always baulked at Angevin authority (and especially by her uncle, Ralph de Faye), Eleanor sought to turn the dynastic settlement of 1169 into a present reality by forcing Henry to divide the substance of power.[4] Her vain and feckless eldest son was a pliable instrument, and King Louis a willing ally. Her capture made her Henry's prisoner for sixteen years.

A great council of French barons was summoned at Paris to pledge support to the Young King (as he was sometimes called), and he in turn swore to seek no peace without their consent. A seal was cut for him by order of King Louis, and he used it to authenticate charters to purchase the support of allies. Matthew, count of Boulogne, who had married King Stephen's daughter, sought the estates of her family, and was promised the county of Mortain, the honor of Hay, and the soke of Kirton in Lindsey. His elder brother, Count Philip of Flanders, was

---

[1] For the empress's influence on Henry see Stephen of Rouen, 780, Robert de Torigny, 186, Walter Map, 238.

[2] Cf. Richard, *Les Comtes de Poitou*, II, 161ff.   [3] *Ibid.*, 158.

[4] Roger of Howden, *Gesta*, I, 42; Gervase of Canterbury, I, 242; Gerald of Wales, V, 304; cf. *Materials for the History of Becket*, V, 197.

promised what William of Ypres had virtually attained in King Stephen's day: the whole county of Kent with the castles of Dover and Rochester, and a thousand pounds in annual revenue in England. Count Theobald of Blois was promised what he had long coveted: the castle of Amboise and the jurisdiction he claimed in Touraine, together with two hundred pounds annual revenue in Anjou. William king of Scots was to have what Henry had promised his father in 1149, and taken from his brother in 1157: possession of all Northumbria as far south as the Tyne.[1]

This was a formidable coalition of enemies, and it was reinforced by many defectors from within Henry II's dominions. In England four earls declared openly for the Young King: Hugh Bigod earl of Norfolk, Robert Blanchemains earl of Leicester (the son of Earl Robert II of Leicester who had been justiciar until his death in 1168), Hugh earl of Chester, and Earl William de Ferrers of Derby. They were all men with large territorial ambitions. Earl Hugh Bigod had been as firmly denied control of East Anglia by Henry II as he had been by Stephen. Earl Robert of Leicester was old enough to remember the days when the Beaumont family dominated the Midlands. Earl Hugh of Chester was too young to remember the civil war (he had been in the wardship of the Crown until 1162), but he knew of the extensive grants which Henry had made to his father, Earl Ranulf, in 1153 when he was bidding for the throne, but had denied to the honor of Chester after he became king. Earl Ferrers believed he should have inherited the lands of Peverel of the Peak through his mother, but Henry II had confiscated them in 1155 when William Peverel fled the country. These earls had numerous vassals, many of high standing, and could also count on the active support of several other tenants-in-chief. In Normandy the principal defectors were to be found among the border barons, whose power Henry II had whittled down. In Brittany the defectors were those whose wings had been clipped since Henry took control of the duchy in 1166, led by his inveterate enemy, Ralph de Fougères. In the county of Anjou there were only half a dozen rebels named by the chroniclers, and about the same number in the county of Touraine; but there were many in the county of Maine, particularly in the valleys of the Mayenne, the Sarthe, and Huisne where Henry had been trimming the power of ancient lordships. In Aquitaine it was the castellans of the plain of Poitou and the count of Angoulême who once again raised their banners against Henry II.[2] Generally speaking, those who openly rebelled were

[1] Roger of Howden, *Gesta*, I, 43–5.

[2] For lists of defectors *see* Boussard, *Le Gouvernement d'Henri II*, 477ff., Kate Norgate, *England under the Angevin Kings*, II, 136ff.

the political irreconcilables, marcher barons whose independence and status had declined, and those who felt they had gained less than their due from Henry II.

There are no surprises among those who declared for the Young King, and Henry II could no doubt have predicted them. They were not overwhelmingly numerous, and the roll call of those who offered their lives in Henry II's service is almost as long.[1] Nevertheless the situation was alarming. For once all parts of Henry's dominions were disturbed at the same time, and the rebels were sufficiently widespread to undermine his authority and disrupt his government. Moreover, Henry could not be sure of the loyalty even of those who did not openly declare for his son. Lively suspicions were entertained of Hugh du Puiset, bishop of Durham, and of the king's cousin, Earl William of Gloucester, who, like the rebel earls, had received less than he might have expected from past services. Richard de Clare, lord of Leinster, is numbered among the king's supporters because he answered a summons to Normandy; but it seems likely that Henry wished to ensure that Ireland would not become a haven for rebels. After the war began there were further desertions among waverers: the defence of Aumale by its count, for example, was so perfunctory as to be treasonable. The chroniclers give the impression of a much wider revolt than can actually be identified. Gervase of Canterbury, Ralph of Diceto, and Gerald of Wales all speak of the desertion of Henry II by his friends, although they do not name any, and the only one of his intimate counsellors who is known to have betrayed his trust was Arnulf, bishop of Lisieux.[2] Roger of Howden, who listed the names of active rebels and knew very well that they represented only a fraction of Henry II's vassals, could nevertheless comment that 'nearly all the earls and barons of England, Normandy, Aquitaine, Anjou, and Brittany arose against the king of England the father'.[3] The explanation for this apparent inconsistency is presumably that those who were not actively in support of Henry II could be assumed to be against him. That Henry took a similar view is suggested by the fact that although open rebellion in England was concentrated largely in the Midlands, over forty royal castles were put in a state of readiness throughout the length and breadth of the realm.[4]

[1] Roger of Howden, *Gesta*, I, 51 n.4.

[2] Gervase of Canterbury, I, 248; Ralph of Diceto, I, 374; Gerald of Wales, VIII, 163–4.

[3] Roger of Howden, *Chronica*, II, 47.

[4] Cf. Pipe Roll 19 Henry II: there are forty-one castles listed in the index under *castellum sive turris*, and to these should be added the castles of Chichester (cf. p. 31), Newcastle-under-Lyme (cf. p. 58), and Wallingford (cf. p. 77).

Henry II had good cause to feel apprehensive about the loyalty of his vassals in England and Normandy, for his government had borne heavily upon them in recent years. The Assize of Clarendon of 1166 authorised sheriffs to override baronial franchises in their pursuit of felons, and threatened lords with the loss of their profits of justice if they did not speedily bring criminals to judgement. In the same year the king had demanded to be informed by his tenants-in-chief of the names of all their vassals who held by military service, and their returns had been made the basis for the levy of financial dues, although in 1168 the barons had made a concerted resistance and had agreed to pay only on the basis of the knight-service they traditionally owed to the Crown. In 1170 the king had launched a penetrating inquiry into the misdeeds of sheriffs, which was extended to the activities of the bailiffs of private landlords. The whole financial transactions between lords and their tenants, both legitimate and illegitimate, for several years back were laid bare.[1] In 1171 Henry, in the words of Robert de Torigny, 'caused an investigation to be made throughout Normandy as to the lands which King Henry his grandfather had held on the day of his death; and inquiry was also made into what lands, woods, and other property had been occupied by barons and other men since the death of King Henry his grandfather; and by this means he doubled his income.[2] In 1172 he required his barons of Normandy to inform him of their tenants by military service, as he had done in England in 1166.[3] The chronicler Ralph of Diceto, commenting on the defectors, writes of 'those men . . . who joined the party of the son, not because they regarded his as the juster cause, but because the father . . . was trampling upon the necks of the proud and haughty, was dismantling or appropriating the castles of the country, and was requiring, even compelling those who occupied properties which should have contributed to his treasury, to be content with their own patrimony'.[4]

The waging of war was therefore unusually difficult for Henry II. He could not afford even to appear to be losing, for he might then be swept away in the rush to desert. William of Newburgh says of the critical

---

[1] *See* below, ch. 7, pp. 275ff.

[2] Robert de Torigny, 251, cf. Haskins, *Norman Institutions,* 160–1.

[3] Cf. Boussard, 'L'enquête de 1172 sur les fiefs de chevalier en Normandie'. The detailed return made by Robert de Torigny as abbot of Mont St-Michel is given in *Chronicles of the Reigns of Stephen, Henry II, and Richard I,* 349–53, and the return of the bishop of Bayeux in *Mémoires de la Société des Antiquaires de Normandie,* VIII, 425–31, and *Recueil des Historiens des Gaules et de la France,* XXIII, 699–702. Cf. Powicke, 'The honor of Mortain in the Norman *infeudationes militum* of 1172'.

[4] Ralph of Diceto, I, 371.

situation in 1174 that 'there were only a few barons at that time in England who were not wavering in their allegiance to the king and ready to defect'.[1] It was probably for this reason that Henry II remained for long periods on the defensive, taking no risks. Instead of his usual tactic of bold and devastating attacks to crush his enemies at a stroke, he waited to catch them at a disadvantage.

As it is described by the chroniclers the war appears to have consisted of a number of unrelated sieges, and of several quite separate campaigns. Their accounts, indeed, give the impression that it was a haphazard, chaotic affair. This is misleading. The precise coordination of so great a war was, of course, beyond the possibilities of the time; but the elements of sound strategy are discernible on both sides. The rebellion in Aquitaine was virtually ignored by the main contestants (although young Richard tried to make something of it on his own in the later stages). The war was to be won and lost in the territories which the Young King claimed, and above all in Normandy and England. This was sensible: the loss of either would have crippled Henry II's power. England might well have been the prime focus of the struggle: rebel strongholds in the Midlands virtually cut the realm in two, and a simultaneous invasion from Scotland and Flanders would have brought King Henry to the brink of disaster. To guard against it the king's men tried hard to prevent the consolidation of the rebels' hold on the Midlands, and kept a naval force off Sandwich to challenge a sea-borne invasion.[2] It soon became apparent, however, that Normandy was to be the primary theatre of operations. Rebels made their way there from England: Earl Hugh of Chester (who was also hereditary viscount of Avranches) joined his forces with the Bretons on the western frontier; Earl Robert of Leicester and William de Tancarville joined King Louis on the eastern frontier.[3]

The fighting began in May 1173 with an assault on Pacy between the Seine and the Eure, and with the investment of the castle of Gournay by the Young King.[4] But these seem to have been probing attacks or feints, for the allies made no further attempt upon the Vexin, the scene of so much previous fighting. The route through the Vexin up the Seine valley was, indeed, the shortest distance to Rouen, but it was also the most strongly guarded. The capture of Rouen remained the allies' main objective but they adopted the novel plan of mounting a double

[1] William of Newburgh, I, 181.

[2] The chroniclers do not speak of a naval force, but it is clearly revealed in Pipe Roll 19 Henry II, 2, 13, 43, 117, 133, 134.

[3] Ralph of Diceto, I, 371. [4] *Ibid.*, 367, 369.

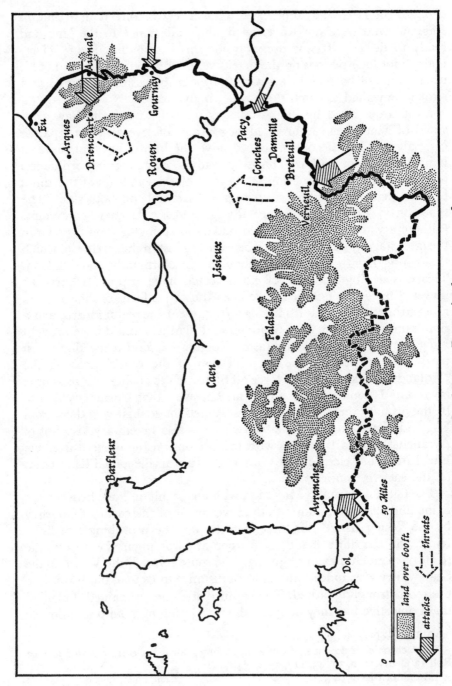

VIIIb France: the threat to Rouen in the summer of 1173

attack from the flanks of the Seine basin. Philip of Flanders crossed the Norman frontier at Aumale, which he took easily, and marched on to Driencourt, while King Louis launched an assault south-east of Rouen, crossing the Norman border from the county of Blois and laying siege to Verneuil.[1] The invasion points were well chosen: Philip of Flanders had the rebel count of Eu to protect his flank, while Louis at Verneuil could rely on the support of the neighbouring castle of Breteuil which belonged to the earl of Leicester, and that of Damville which belonged to another rebel, Gilbert de Tillières. There was a good prospect, therefore, of a double breakthrough, threatening Rouen from two directions at once, and by-passing the numerous defensive fortifications of the Seine valley. At the same time the Bretons caused a diversion in the west by attacking towards Avranches.

As soon as his enemies had committed themselves to a line of attack, and it was clear that the prime target was to be Normandy, King Henry slipped over to England to review the situation there and to draw off supplies. He went in secrecy and stayed for only a few days.[2] In England an attack was launched by the king's men on the rebel stronghold of Leicester; but in Normandy Henry remained content to trust to his defences until the right moment arrived to intervene with his field army. It came at the end of August. The advance of the count of Flanders faltered shortly after he had taken Driencourt, for Count Matthew of Boulogne was seriously injured by a bolt from a sniper's crossbow. He was not only Count Philip's brother but also his heir, and when he died from his injury, the count, overcome by the misfortune, called off the advance.[3] Henry was now free to concentrate his forces against King Louis. He mustered all available men, marched through Conches, seized and destroyed the rebel castle of Breteuil and advanced in battle order upon Verneuil. He was almost too late. Verneuil was well fortified and resolutely defended, but had suffered severely. The town surrounding the castle was divided into three 'burghs', each walled off from the other. The defenders of one of these, known as the 'great burgh', bore the brunt of the French assault, and were by the beginning of August running short of supplies. By the custom of contemporary

---

[1] Roger of Howden, *Gesta*, I, 47, 49.

[2] His visit to England is not mentioned by the chroniclers, but is revealed by Pipe Roll 19 Henry II, 33. The royal vessel, the *Esnecca*, made at least four trips across the Channel carrying treasure under escort from England before the end of September, *ibid.*, 54–5.

[3] Ralph of Diceto, I, 373; Gervase of Canterbury, I, 246; Roger of Howden, *Gesta*, I, 49; William of Newburgh, I, 173–4; cf. Kate Norgate, *England under the Angevin Kings*, II, 147 n.3.

warfare this was the point at which negotiations were started with the besiegers. A truce was concluded to last for three days during which the defenders were to ascertain if help was close at hand; if not, they were at the end of the three days to surrender without further resistance. On the third day, 9 August, King Henry's army ascended the hill overlooking the town. The citadel was intact, but a pall of smoke hung over the great burgh, for King Louis had broken the truce. His army was in retreat over the border, and King Henry's men fell upon the rearguard, massacring it as darkness fell. The chronicler Roger of Howden under-lines the ignominy of it: 'In order that these events may be kept in memory, it is as well to know that this flight of the king of France took place on the fifth day of the week, upon the vigil of St Laurence, to the praise and glory of our Lord Jesus Christ, who by punishing the crime of perfidy so speedily avenged the indignity done to his martyr.'[1]

It was indeed speedily avenged. Henry completed the work of sealing off this vulnerable section of the frontier by capturing Damville from the rebels.[2] Then as he retired towards Rouen he despatched a detach-ment of mercenaries across Normandy to harass the western rebels. The Bretons had not expected to be challenged, and hastily retreated, suffering heavy casualties, to the safety of the castle of Dol. As soon as news was brought to Rouen, Henry set off with his main army, travel-ling by forced marches. He reached Dol in less than two days. The defenders were astonished at his arrival, for they believed he was pinned down in eastern Normandy. They knew full well from 1167 and 1168 what he was capable of on a punitive expedition. In alarm they surrendered. Earl Hugh and Ralph de Fougères were made prisoner.[3]

With his enemies on the continent in disarray Henry tried to tempt them to abandon the struggle by offering generous terms to his sons. Talks were held at Gisors, but soon broken off.[4] That talks were held at all shows that there were misgivings at the French court, but there were militants enough to fire the courage of the waverers. Earl Robert of Leicester, in particular, was adamant that no terms from Henry were acceptable, and in an attempt to recover the initiative for the allies he embarked a force of Flemings and shipped them over to England. His destination was Suffolk, where he could rely on Earl Hugh Bigod to

[1] Roger of Howden, *Gesta*, I, 49–55, *Chronica*, II, 49–50; Ralph of Diceto, I, 374–375; Robert de Torigny, 257–8; William of Newburgh, I, 174–5.

[2] Roger of Howden, *Gesta*, I, 56.

[3] Robert de Torigny, 259–60; Ralph of Diceto, I, 378; Roger of Howden, *Gesta*, I, 56–7; William of Newburgh, I, 176.

[4] Roger of Howden, *Gesta*, I, 59–60.

VIIIc England: to illustrate the war of 1173–4

give him a safe landing. They joined forces at Framlingham at the end of September.[1]

In England, meanwhile, the king's men had kept the rebels in check by taking the offensive, but had not secured a decisive victory. Since the beginning of July the king's deputy, Richard de Lucy, had bent his efforts on the capture of Leicester, the principal rebel stronghold in the Midlands. By the end of July he had captured the town but not the

[1] Roger of Howden, *Gesta*, I, 60–1; Ralph of Diceto, I, 377.

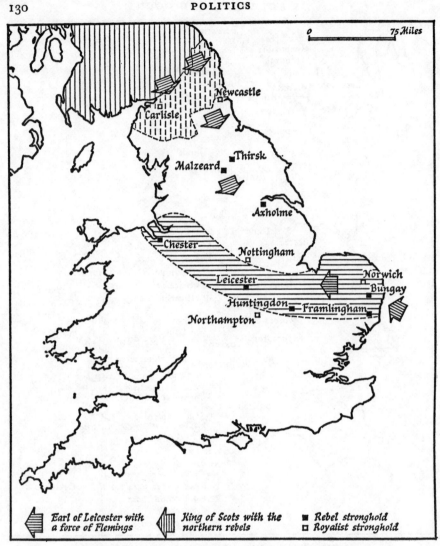

VIIId England: the rebels' probable intention in 1173

castle, and he had then to rest content with a temporary truce because
the king of Scots was raiding the north as far south as Yorkshire.
Richard de Lucy had some success against the Scots: he drove them
back over the border, and was about to retaliate by devastating
Lothian when he heard of the landing of Earl Robert in East Anglia,
and was obliged to break off the engagement. Earl Robert helped Earl
Hugh to capture the king's castle at Haughley, and then set off to bring
help to his men beleaguered at Leicester. The loyalists were waiting for

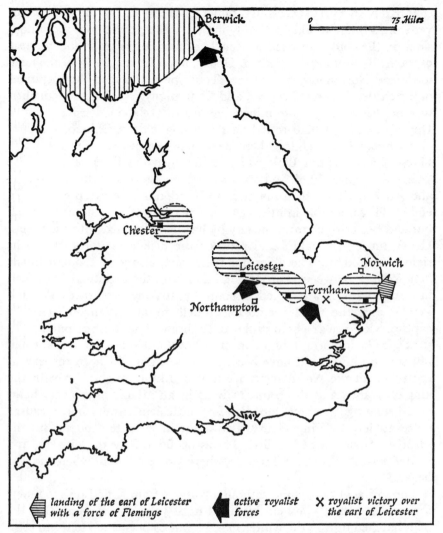

VIIIe England: the disruption of the rebels' plans in 1173

him in the marshes at Fornham near Bury St Edmunds. Ralph of
Diceto puts the odds at four to one against the king's men; but the
earl's knights were routed, and as his Flemish mercenaries scattered
they were set upon by local people and drowned in the bogs. Earl
Robert was captured, and with him his amazonian wife, Petronilla.[1]

[1] Roger of Howden, *Gesta*, I, 58, 60–2, *Chronica*, II, 54–5; Ralph of Diceto, I, 376–8;
Gervase of Canterbury, I, 246; William of Newburgh, I, 179; William of Canterbury,
I, 485–7.

It had been a very successful summer for Henry II, but the war was not yet won. Winter would inevitably impose truces; but before it did both sides on the continent tried to secure their positions ready for the start of the next campaigning season. Henry, freed for a time from the need to defend Normandy, moved into Touraine and forced the surrender of the castles at Haye, Preuilly, and Champigny. While these remained in rebel hands they undermined the security of the defensive pivot of Henry's empire, which rested on the strongholds of Chinon, Loudun, and Châtellerault. Unless these were made secure there was a possibility of attack from Blois which could turn the flank of the major defensive stronghold of Amboise on the river Loire and threaten Tours and Angers. Henry then marched to Vendôme to secure the northern end of this vulnerable frontier region. The count of Vendôme was loyal, but had been driven from the city by his son who sided with the rebels. Henry turned the tables and restored the defence of the castle to its rightful custodian. The allies, for their part, also gave thought to the long frontier between Henry's dominions and the county of Blois, and in January 1174 attempted a coup by striking westwards through Perche and the rebel territories of Bellême and Alençon to try to capture Séez. It was a bold stroke and a shrewd one: Séez commanded a strategically important junction of valleys and roads in the Norman hill country and could have become a base from which, in the spring, the rebels of the Norman border and of Maine might join with the king of France and the count of Blois in an attack on the very heart of Normandy. A threat to Falaise or Lisieux would have caused more anxiety to King Henry than a threat even to Rouen. But the surprise attack on Séez failed. It was beaten off by the citizens, and winter set in with the allies everywhere worse off than when the war began.[1]

The spring of 1174 came without any move from King Louis to renew the attack. Indeed, he held his hand until July, and it seems that the plan hatched during the winter months was to persuade Henry to cross the Channel, and to attack Normandy in his absence. Only a major threat to his position in England would induce Henry to go, and the task of providing it fell to William king of Scots, with the help of the northern rebels led by Roger de Mowbray, and with the cooperation, or at least the connivance, of the bishop of Durham. The king of Scots attacked shortly after Easter. He blockaded the royal fortresses at Wark and Carlisle while he sought to subdue the lesser castles which he could

[1] Roger of Howden, *Gesta*, I, 62–3; Ralph of Diceto, I, 379.

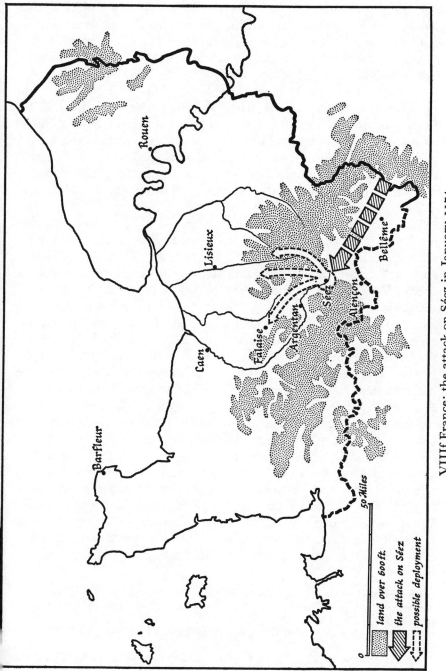

Rouen

Barfleur

Caen

Lisieux

Falaise

Argentan

Séez

Alençon

Bellême

50 Miles

land over 600 ft.

the attack on Séez

possible deployment

VIIIf France: the attack on Séez in January 1174.

not safely leave untaken in his rear. Liddell, Burgh, Appleby, Harbottle, and Warkworth fell to him. His brother David went south to reinforce the still defiant garrison of Leicester. The king's men, balked of the capture of Leicester castle, attempted to break the rebel chain of strongholds at two other points—Huntingdon and Tutbury. Huntingdon was doubtless selected to tempt David out of Leicester, for it was the administrative centre of the fief which had long been held of the English Crown by the ruling family of Scotland. Earl Simon of Northampton had a claim upon Huntingdon, and King Henry is said to have told him that he could have it if he captured it. The rebels, however, were not to be outwitted: their reply was a successful raid at Northampton; and they followed it by capturing Nottingham, which Richard de Lucy held in custody.[1]

Henry, however, remained unperturbed. He left Normandy in May, not for England but for Maine and Anjou. He reassured himself of the security of Le Mans, Poitiers, and Saintes, and established a base at Ancenis from which his lieutenant, Maurice de Craon, could harass the rebels of the west.[2] Meanwhile the rebel attack in the north of England, which was supposed to force him across the Channel, was losing momentum. King William failed to capture Carlisle and Wark, and even one of the lesser castles, Prudhoe, held by Odelin de Umfraville, successfully defied him in Northumberland. While he lingered, his ally in the north-east, Roger de Mowbray, suffered a crushing reverse. King Henry's bastard son, Geoffrey Plantagenet, besieged him at Axholme until the garrison began to run short of water. Mowbray slipped out, intending to go to Leicester to bring up a relieving force, but he was made prisoner by peasants in Derbyshire. Geoffrey pressed the assault on Axholme, secured its surrender, and went on to capture another of Mowbray's castles at Malzeard. Thirsk presented a more serious problem, but it was neutralised by the erection of a fort nearby at Topcliffe.[3] The allies' plan of campaign was in danger of collapse. There was only one way to revive it – an invasion of England. Count Philip of Flanders undertook this hazardous enterprise, and swore on a holy relic that he would put to sea within fifteen days of the feast of St

---

[1] Roger of Howden, *Gesta*, I, 64–6, 68, 70–1; Ralph of Diceto, I, 379. William of Newburgh, I, 180–2, has confused some of the events of 1174 with those of the previous year.

[2] Roger of Howden, *Gesta*, I, 71; Ralph of Diceto, I, 379–80; cf. Boussard, *Le Comté d'Anjou*, 28 n.6.

[3] Roger of Howden, *Gesta*, I, 65–6; cf. William of Newburgh, I, 181–2, and Pipe Roll 21 Henry II, 165.

John (24 June). An advance party of Flemings landed at Whitsand on 15 May and helped Earl Hugh Bigod to capture Norwich.[1]

In alarm the king's lieutenants in England despatched one of Henry's most trusted counsellors, Richard of Ilchester, to beg the king to come to their aid. Henry was persuaded that he would have to go, but he did not hurry: he carefully checked the defences of Normandy before embarking at Barfleur on 7 July. There was a fierce wind in the Channel and the sailors were fearful, but Henry ordered them to put to sea, saying that if God wished him to restore peace to his realm He would bring him safely to port; but if He had turned against him, he might as well die this way as any other. By nightfall he was in Southampton. His departure was what the allies had been hoping for. There was no need now to proceed with the invasion of England. Instead Philip of Flanders joined with King Louis in an immediate attack on Normandy from the breach in the eastern defences which had been made the previous year. By 22 July they had drawn up their forces before Rouen.[2]

On his arrival in England King Henry went to the tomb of Thomas Becket at Canterbury, and barefoot and fasting submitted to a public scourging for the rash words which had caused the martyr's death. It was very unusual, and indeed out of character, for Henry II to make such a dramatic gesture as this; but it was the best way to separate St Thomas from the rebels' cause. The sign of St Thomas's forgiveness – or so it appeared – followed swiftly. On 17 July, Henry was awakened from sleep to hear exciting news from the north. The local landowners of Yorkshire had made up a force, under the king's sheriff, to go to the relief of Prudhoe. When they arrived there they discovered that the king of Scots had moved on to Alnwick. The next morning, 13 July, they followed him. A mist thickened around them, and it was only after earnest debate that they decided to go on. Suddenly the mist lifted and they found themselves confronted by a party of Scottish knights taking their ease in a meadow before Alnwick castle. They fell upon them, and the Scots fought valiantly until every one of them had been either killed or captured. Among the captives was King William himself.[3] This virtually marked the end of the war in England. Henry

[1] Gervase of Canterbury, I, 247–8; Ralph of Diceto, I, 381.

[2] Ralph of Diceto, I, 381–2, 386; Robert de Torigny, 263–4; Gervase of Canterbury, I, 249.

[3] Ralph of Diceto, I, 383–4; Robert de Torigny, 264; Gervase of Canterbury, I, 248–9; Roger of Howden, *Gesta*, I, 72, *Chronica*, II, 61–3; William of Newburgh, I, 183–9; Edward Grim, II, 447; Herbert of Bosham, III, 544–8; Jordan Fantosme, lines 1711ff.

marched to the siege of Huntingdon; it surrendered. He marched to Northampton; and there everyone else came to surrender.

On 8 August Henry was back at Barfleur, a month after he had left. King Louis and his allies had meanwhile made little progress with the siege of Rouen. They had not even completely invested it, for its western gates were still open to traffic from the river Seine. On 10 August a general truce was proclaimed to celebrate the feast of St Laurence; but King Louis broke it in a desperate attempt to take possession of the city before Henry arrived. While the citizens made merry and the knights were holding a tournament on the river bank, two clerks, admiring the view from a lofty tower, noticed clandestine activity in the French camp and sounded the alarm. The garrison rushed to its posts just in time to prevent the Frenchmen scaling the walls. The next day King Henry entered the city with a large force of mercenaries, and immediately set about carrying the fight to the enemy. His skirmishers slipped out into the woods in the rear of the French and wrought destruction on a waggon train bringing up supplies. A ditch between the city walls and the French camp was filled in so that knights two hundred abreast could sally out. It was enough. King Louis fled, and before the end of September sued for peace.[1]

(v) *Henry triumphant* (1174–c. 1182)

'So the mighty learned that to wrest the club from the hand of Hercules was no easy task,' crowed Henry II's treasurer.[2] For those who had stood by the king in the dark days when so many deserted, the discomfiture of his enemies was sweet indeed. There were some who attributed the unparalleled victory to the intervention of God at the mediation of St Thomas of Canterbury; but this too was sweet to King Henry's friends, for it effaced the stigma of the martyr's death.

Henry II was not vindictive in victory. In the negotiations concluded at Montlouis on 30 September 1174, he was content to make peace on the basis of the *status quo ante bellum*. In the words of the official announcement, 'Our lord the king and all his liegemen and barons are to receive possession of all their lands and castles which they held fifteen days before his sons withdrew from him; and in like manner his liegemen and barons who withdrew from him and followed his sons are to receive possession of their lands which they held fifteen days

---

[1] William of Newburgh, I, 190–6; Ralph of Diceto, I, 385–7; Robert de Torigny, 265; Gervase of Canterbury, I, 249–50; Roger of Howden, *Gesta*, I, 74–6, *Chronica*, II, 65–6.

[2] *Dialogus de Scaccario*, 76.

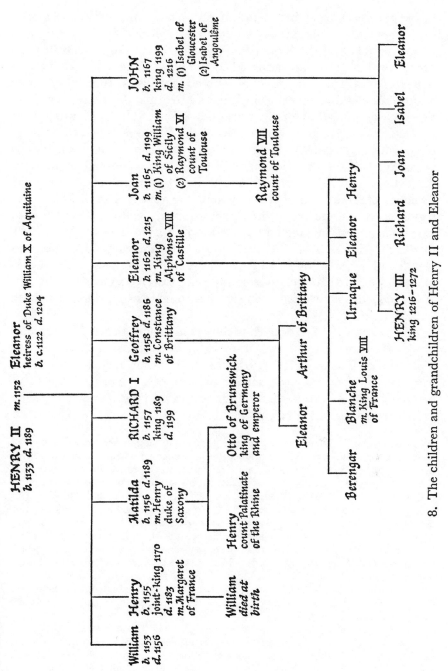

HENRY II m. 1152 Eleanor
b. 1133 d. 1189   heiress of Duke William X of Aquitaine
                         b. c. 1122 d. 1204

William   Henry   Matilda   RICHARD I   Geoffrey   Eleanor   Joan   JOHN
b. 1153   b. 1155   b. 1156 d. 1189   b. 1157   b. 1158 d. 1186 b. 1162 d. 1215 b. 1165 d. 1199 b. 1167
d. 1156   joint-king 1170 m. Henry   king 1189   m. Constance   m. King   m. (1) King William king 1199
               d. 1183   duke of   d. 1199   of Brittany   Alphonso VIII   of Sicily   d. 1216
               m. Margaret   Saxony   of Castile   (2) Raymond VI   m. (1) Isabel of
               of France   count of   Gloucester
                                                                                                 Toulouse   (2) Isabel of
               William   Henry   Angoulême
               died at   count Palatinate   Otto of Brunswick
               birth   of the Rhine   king of Germany   Raymond VII
                                                  and emperor   count of Toulouse

                                                  Eleanor   Arthur of Brittany

                              Berengar   Blanche   Urraque   Eleanor   Henry   HENRY III
                                         m. King Louis VIII   king 1216–1272
                                         of France
                                                                                      Richard   Joan   Isabel   Eleanor

8. The children and grandchildren of Henry II and Eleanor

before they withdrew from him.' The sworn alliance between Henry's sons and the rebel barons was of course formally dissolved, and both Henry II and the Young King declared that they would bear no ill-will to those who had adhered to the other. The Young King was required to accept that provision be made for his brother John by the grant of castles and revenues in England, Normandy, and Anjou, and thereby was obliged to forswear his *casus belli*; but Henry II at the same time acknowledged the justification for the Young King's deeper sense of grievance by assigning revenues to his sons. Henry the Younger was to receive two castles in Normandy and fifteen thousand pounds (in Angevin money), Richard was to receive two residences and half the revenues of Poitou, and Geoffrey half the revenues of Brittany. All prisoners were to be released on giving security, with the exception of four upon whom the king had pronounced judgement before peace was made; the king of Scots, the earl of Leicester, the earl of Chester, and Ralph de Fougères.[1] About Queen Eleanor nothing was said. She remained Henry's captive, courteously but closely watched for the rest of his life; although after 1183 she was sometimes allowed to appear publicly with him.[2]

The heaviest burden of defeat fell on the king of Scots. The price of his release from captivity was embodied in what is known as the Treaty of Falaise of December 1174, by which he acknowledged himself 'the liegeman of the lord king Henry against every man in respect of Scotland and all his other lands'. He was required to perform a public ceremony of submission at York and to surrender five castles in Scotland

---

[1] Negotiations for a truce were opened by the archbishop of Sens and the count of Blois when King Louis was still encamped before Rouen, and were reopened after his flight. A conference was arranged for 8 September at Gisors but no truce was concluded because Richard was still active against his father in Poitou. Another conference was arranged for Michaelmas at Montlouis (between Tours and Amboise) and King Louis and Henry the Younger agreed to disavow Richard and to make a truce excluding him from its benefits. Henry then immediately took an army to Poitou and enforced Richard's submission. The conference at Montlouis was resumed and Henry formally reconciled to his sons. A charter embodying the terms of the peace for his sons and the rebels was sealed by Henry at Falaise, probably about the beginning of October, Roger of Howden, *Gesta*, I, 75–9, *Chronica*, II, 66–9; *Recueil des Actes de Henri II*, II, 19–21; *Foedera*, I, Pt I, 30. Letters patent were also issued, announcing the terms of the peace to the king's subjects, Ralph of Diceto, I, 394–5; *Recueil des Actes de Henri II*, II, 21–3.

[2] Roger of Howden, *Gesta*, I, 305, 313, 333, 334, 337. Gervase of Canterbury, I, 326, says that she was set at liberty in 1185 at the instance of Archbishop Baldwin, but he later records that she was released by King Richard on his father's death in 1189 (I, 453–4). He also reports, I, 257, that Henry contemplated divorcing her in 1175.

to the custody of Henry's nominees. Yet Henry did not press the rights of overlordship implicit in William's homage, nor did he intervene in Scottish affairs, save occasionally to arbitrate in disputes between King William and his subjects. The earls of Chester and Leicester remained prisoners until January 1177, but then had their estates restored to them.[1] The fate of Ralph de Fougères escapes the attention of the chroniclers, but it seems that he too had recovered control of his property by 1177; indeed he subsequently became seneschal of Brittany, and lived to betray Henry II yet again.[2]

There were some who thought that Henry II was too lenient with his opponents, and that he allowed the French and Flemings to escape the crushing defeat they so richly deserved. Ralph of Diceto, dean of St Pauls, felt it necessary to enter a defence of Henry's pacific policy in his *Ymagines Historiarum*: the king, he says, accepted peace as best for his sons, but also because he believed it to be his duty to rescue his subjects from the turmoils, the bloodshed, the oppressions, and the retreat from law and order, which were inseparable from war.[3] Henry II's distaste for war was real enough. Gerald of Wales, who was no friend, says that 'he dreaded the doubtful arbitrament of war ... and grieved more than any prince for those lost in battle, mourning them with a grief far greater than the love he bore the living'.[4] Yet it may be suspected that Henry II's desire to terminate the great war as speedily as possible was prompted at least as much by its deleterious effects on government as by the waste of effort and loss of life involved. The continued functioning of shire government and the collection of revenues in all but the worst affected areas of England is a remarkable testimony to the strength of administrative institutions; but the regular visitation of royal justices had to be abandoned, and the enforcement of the forest laws temporarily suspended. In 1176, at the start of a renewed visitation of royal justices, the Assize of Clarendon of ten years previously was reissued and considerably strengthened, with savage punishments for those adjudged guilty or even reasonably suspected of serious crime.[5] And the king

---

[1] Roger of Howden, *Gesta*, I, 134, 135, *Chronica*, II, 118. The king retained in his hands Earl Hugh's castle of Chester and Earl Robert's castles at Mountsorrel in England and Pacy in Normandy. *See* also below, ch. 10, p. 366.

[2] The item 'De blado de Osmundestona Radulfi de Filgerius vendito', which appears on Pipe Roll 20 Henry II, 46, and subsequent rolls, has disappeared by 23 Henry II; *Recueil des Actes de Henri II*, Introduction, 417; Roger of Howden, *Gesta*, I, 357; II, 72.

[3] Ralph of Diceto, I, 393–4. Richard FitzNigel says that Henry deemed it punishment enough that his enemies should see his kingdom prosper, *Dialogus de Scaccario*, 76–7.   [4] Gerald of Wales, V, 303.   [5] *See* below, ch. 9, p. 355.

abandoned all hope of popularity by insisting on the retrospective punishment of offences against the forest law, even by barons and members of the clergy, despite the protest of Richard de Lucy, that he had expressly relaxed the laws during time of war. Many of the barons offered lump sums to avoid judgement; and Robert de Torigny, who was not given to using harsh language about Henry II, says that he 'defrauded them of a large amount of silver'.[1] Doubtless it was a speedy way of replenishing the depleted royal coffers, and this may well have been its main purpose; but it was also an impressive way of demonstrating the reassertion of royal authority. That it was deliberately conceived as such is suggested by the words of Roger of Howden, who reveals that as soon as Henry returned to England from the continent after the end of the war 'he impleaded all the earls and barons of England concerning the forests and the taking of venison, and put all at his mercy'.[2] Moreover, as he toured the country he repeated his impeachments locally: at York after the public ceremony of submission by the king of Scots, 'the lord king sued the earls and barons and also the clergy of Yorkshire, and even the clergy of the church of St Peter at York, concerning his forests and the taking of venison'.[3] Clearly there was something more involved here than the mere commissioning of a pertinacious inquiry into forest offences, which is all that Ralph of Diceto records.

King Henry kept his word over the treatment of rebels. Even during the war he had been remarkably lenient: there were no executions and no forfeitures, and, as Ralph of Diceto remarks, in contrast to his son he did not levy ransoms for those taken in battle.[4] The terms of peace provided that rebels would not be held to account for 'the chattels which they carried away' on going to join the Young King, and should be brought to justice for any crimes committed only by the normal processes of the law. Before Earl Hugh Bigod died, at over eighty years of age, in 1177, the king pardoned him the remaining 500 marks of a fine of 1,000 marks which he had been owing since at least 1166.[5] But there was one respect in which the rebel barons did not escape scot free: within a year of the end of the war their castles were, on the king's orders, systematically destroyed.[6] The justices itinerant appointed in

---

[1] Robert de Torigny, 267; Ralph of Diceto, I, 402; Roger of Howden, *Gesta*, I, 94, *Chronica*, II, 79.

[2] Roger of Howden, *Gesta*, I, 92.   [3] *Ibid.*, 97.

[4] Ralph of Diceto, I, 395.

[5] Pipe Roll 22 Henry II, 62, cf. Pipe Roll 21 Henry II, 19, and intervening rolls.

[6] Ralph of Diceto, I, 398, 404; Roger of Howden, *Gesta*, I, 126–7.

1176 were instructed 'to ensure that the castles which have been destroyed are utterly demolished, and those which are due for destruction
are razed to the ground'.[1] This was more than an act of reprisal or even
of security. A castle was a symbol of authority, as well as the centre of
government of a great fief. Its enforced destruction was a public
demonstration of the frailty of his power, and the mound denuded of its
fortification became a symbol of the rebel's humiliation. Ruins were
eloquent testimony to the folly of rebellion against Henry II. Even a
generation later, the biographer of William Marshal noted that re-
minders of the great war were to be seen in ruined castles throughout
England, Normandy, and Anjou, and he remarks, 'so passes the glory
of the world'.[2]

Royal authority was, however, undermined in time of civil war by
much more than the breakdown of law and order, and by what Ralph
of Diceto calls the 'insolence of rebel fortifications'.[3] In bringing the war
to an end as soon as possible, Henry II seems to have been just as much
concerned with the entrenchment of local influence by lords who were
not themselves directly involved in hostilities – as had only too seriously
happened during the anarchy of Stephen's reign. It is impossible to
penetrate behind the chronicles of events to the actual condition of the
realm during the war, but a hint of the pursuit of local ambitions is
supplied by the report of Roger of Howden that in 1175 'the king impleaded the earl of Gloucester, in that during the hostilities he had
expelled the royal custodian from Bristol castle, and had kept it in his
own hands throughout the war'.[4] Moreover the king's concern with the
entrenchment of local influence by powerful barons can be seen in his
treatment of baronial castles throughout the realm, even of those which
were held by loyalists. According to Roger of Howden the king in 1176
'took every castle in England into his hand, and removing the castellans
of the earls and barons, put in his own custodians; he did not even
spare his intimate counsellor, Richard de Lucy, the justiciar of England
but took from him his castle of Ongar'.[5] And furthermore, the custodians of castles in the king's hands were in 1177 changed around: the
archbishop of York was, for instance, deprived of custody of Roxburgh
castle, but was given Scarborough castle to hold instead, and Roger de
Coyners was given custody of Durham castle, but had to hand over
Norham to William de Neville.[6] Clearly, there were two elements in

---

[1] Assize of Northampton (1176), clause 8.
[2] *Histoire de Guillaume le Maréschal*, III, 33.
[3] Ralph of Diceto, I, 398.
[4] Roger of Howden, *Gesta*, I, 92.   [5] *Ibid.*, 127.   [6] *Ibid.*, 160–1.

Henry II's policy: first to establish the principle that all castles were at the king's disposal, and secondly, to ensure that custodians did not become too closely identified with the castles they held. It was the culmination of Henry II's attempts since the beginning of his reign to loosen the hold of the barons on fortifications which symbolised their military and territorial power. Ever since the days of William the Conqueror kings had insisted, with some success, that all castles should be licensed; but the implicit theory that all castles were at the disposal of the Crown had struggled vainly with the possessory instincts of baronial builders.[1] Henry II, at the end of the great war, put the principle beyond doubt – though not beyond resentment.

In Aquitaine, the task of destroying castles fortified by rebels during the war was entrusted by King Henry to his son Richard, as count of Poitou and future lord of the duchy.[2] The fact that Richard had himself been, at least nominally, their leader in rebellion was a piquant touch of irony. Richard had a difficult task, for the castles of the rebels were fortified against him. Aquitaine had not been drawn into the great contest of the kings, and Henry, apart from ensuring the security of Poitiers and helping the loyalists of Saintonge, had largely ignored the defiance of the major rebels of the duchy. In consequence they had not had the chastening experience of the English, Norman, Angevin, and Breton rebels in seeing their defences prised open and their defiance made a mockery. Richard therefore had to wage what was, in effect, a further campaign in the war. He did not find it easy, and was obliged to call on his father for help in men and money; but the task was completed when in the summer of 1176 he forced the surrender of the fortified city of Angoulême and made most of the rebel leaders prisoner. William count of Angoulême was sent to England in September 1176 to beg the forgiveness of Henry II upon his knees.[3]

By the end of 1176 Henry II, 'by the grace of God', as he styled himself in charters, 'king of the English, duke of the Normans, duke of the Aquitainians, and count of the Angevins', must have appeared to justify thoroughly the encomium of Richard FitzNigel that he was 'the greatest of the illustrious rulers of the world'.[4] The humiliation of King Louis of France in the great war, and the defeat of the Emperor Barbarossa by the Lombard League in May 1176, certainly left him

---

[1] The theory is expressed in the Consuetudines et Justiciae of the late eleventh century, printed in Haskins, *Norman Institutions*, 282, para 4. Cf. Powicke, *The Loss of Normandy*, 180–3, and Painter, 'English castles in the early middle ages: their number, location, and legal position'.

[2] Roger of Howden, *Gesta*, I, 81.

[3] For a more detailed account *see* below, ch. 15, pp. 564–7.   [4] *Dialogus de Scaccario*, 2.

without a rival in Europe. In November 1176 his court at Westminster entertained envoys from Emperor Manuel Comnenus of Constantinople, from the Holy Roman Emperor, from the archbishop of Rheims, from the duke of Savoy, and from the count of Flanders.[1] Emperor Manuel, addressing Henry as 'his most dear friend', wrote at length of the great battle with the Turks at Iconium. The king of Sicily sought the hand of Henry's youngest daughter Joan in marriage. The kings of Castille and Navarre asked his arbitration in disputes which plagued their relations, and swore to abide by any award that he might make.[2] Never before had all Europe paid court like this to the throne of England.

In the years immediately following the great war Henry II seems to have been particularly concerned to clear up all the uncertainties which plagued the fringes of his dominions. By the Treaty of Falaise of 1174 he had defined in unequivocal terms a feudal relationship with the king of Scots. By the Treaty of Windsor of 1175 with Rory king of Connaught he established clearly the nature of his overlordship of Ireland. And in a treaty worked out in talks at Geddington in May 1177 he reached an amicable understanding with the leading Welsh princes. The outstanding feature of all these was the recognition of the overlordship of the king of England, but at the same time the agreements confirmed the status and authority of the native rulers, and, tacitly at least, set aside any attempt at complete absorption into the kingdom of England.[3]

In addition there were two outstanding uncertainties in France. One was the vagueness of the authority of the duke of Aquitaine in Berry and Auvergne. The other was the equivocal nature of Henry II's relations with the king of France ever since King Louis's attempt to have him deposed in 1173.

The peace terms of September 1174 had been couched in the form of an agreement purely between Henry II and his sons, for it was easier to stop the war quickly by pretending that the Young King was the principal party involved. King Louis was not mentioned at all.[4] The

---

[1] Ralph of Diceto, I, 416.

[2] Roger of Howden, *Gesta*, I, 115–17, 128–30, 139–43, *Chronica*, II, 94–5, 102–4, 120–31; Ralph of Diceto, I, 408, 415–16, 418–20; Gervase of Canterbury, I, 260, 261. Henry sent gifts of hounds to Emperor Manuel, Pipe Roll 24 Henry II, 19. The Sicilian marriage made a deep impression on the chroniclers, who record in detail the negotiations, the journey to Palermo, and the marriage settlement. Even Robert de Torigny, 278, usually sparing of detail, transcribed a précis of the marriage settlement. Henry's judicious award in the dispute between the kings of Castille and Navarre was made in March 1177, Roger of Howden, *Gesta*, I, 151–4.

[3] *See* below, ch. 4.

[4] The peace terms are given the heading by Roger of Howden, *Gesta*, I, 77: 'Haec est concordia quae facta est inter regum et filios suos.'

two problems were closely related, for the king of France had a close interest in the vassal relationships of the lords of Berry and Auvergne and was apprehensive of possible encroachment by the duke of Aquitaine. Both were of considerable political and economic importance. Communications between Paris and the deep south of France depended on safe passage of Auvergne; and prosperous Berry was the junction of some of the most important trade routes traversing the country by the old Roman roads. With the development of large armies of mercenary foot soldiers the road system became just as important as it had been to the Roman legions. It was for this reason, indeed, that in later years Berry rather than the Vexin became the main focus of hostility between the Capetians and the Angevins. The Capetian kings had established themselves in eastern Berry at the beginning of the twelfth century when Philip I purchased the viscounty of Bourges from its lord, who was eager to raise money to go on crusade; but it was only in the reign of King Louis VII that royal power had become really effective in the region. With the threat that this posed of easy invasion by road into Touraine and Poitou, Henry II naturally became anxious about the loyalty of his vassals there, for the duke of Aquitaine had no demesne lands in Berry on which to build castles of his own.[1] He was sharply reminded of his tenuous hold on western Berry in 1176–7, for on the death of Ralph de Déols, lord of Châteauroux, and the most powerful baron of the district, his heiress was spirited away, and Henry's lawful claim to the wardship of the heiress and her estates was resisted. Similarly, when Odo, lord of Issoudun, died leaving an infant son as heir, Henry was denied guardianship, and the heir disappeared into Burgundy.[2] Whether King Louis had been meddling is not clear, though it seems probable; but in any case Henry was only too well aware from bitter experience that any attempt by him to assert his authority in either Berry or Auvergne had drawn warlike demonstrations from King Louis. Indeed the wars which had followed his previous interventions had distracted him from properly establishing his authority there over those he could rightly claim as his vassals. In the spring of 1177, therefore, Henry decided to take the initiative in forcing King Louis to have serious talks with him and to come to some sensible agreement before he intervened to assert his authority in these sensitive regions. In June 1177 he sent envoys to King Louis to present a provocative demand. Let the king of France, they said, honour the agree-

---

[1] For the feudal lordships of Berry see Boussard, Le Gouvernement d'Henri II, 128–32, and for Louis's policy, Pacaut, Louis VII et son Royaume.

[2] Robert de Torigny, 274; Roger of Howden, Gesta, I, 132.

ments he had made over the marriage of his daughter Margaret to Henry the Younger, and the intended marriage of his daughter Alice to Richard. The agreements, Henry claimed, were that the king of France would endow Margaret with the whole of the Vexin (and not simply the Norman Vexin), and that he would endow Alice with the city of Bourges and its dependencies in Berry. At the same time Henry summoned his barons in England to prepare the military forces they owed him in service to sail to Normandy.[1] There is not a shred of evidence that Henry's demands had any justification whatsoever, and his moves can only be construed as designed to embarrass and intimidate King Louis.[2] Henry may have hoped that Louis would be frightened into making concessions; but there is not much sign that he really intended to wage war. Indeed Henry allowed himself to be talked rather easily into drawing up a non-aggression pact with Louis – which was probably his real objective in the first place.[3] It was the unfinished business of 1174.

The negotiations were managed by a papal legate, who had been sent to persuade the kings to compose their difference and unite to relieve the Holy Land from the terrible menace of Saladin. The pact concluded at Ivry on the border of Normandy in September 1177 therefore takes the form of an agreement to prepare a joint crusade, but the heart of the matter was a solemn oath to respect each other's rights, and to put the awkward questions of the homage of local lords in Berry and Auvergne to arbitration. They declared that:

We wish all men to know that we are now and intend henceforth to be friends [amici], and that each of us will to the best of his ability defend the other in life and limb and in worldly honour against all men. And if anyone shall presume to do either of us harm, I Henry will aid my lord Louis,

[1] Roger of Howden, Gesta, I, 138, 168.

[2] That a king of France should ever have contemplated surrendering Bourges is unthinkable. According to John of Salisbury in a letter of 1169, Alice was dowerless, Materials for the History of Becket, VI, 513. It has been assumed that Henry's challenge to Louis in 1177 was a gratuitous piece of naked aggression: 'un acte de flagrante mauvaise foi', 'un simple et cynique prétexte à une aggression préméditée', Boussard, op. cit., 523, 524, followed by Pacaut, op. cit., 213. But the reason for Henry's action is revealed both in the sequel and in King Louis's admission that the source of the trouble, 'as to which dispute arose between us' lay in Auvergne, the fief of Châteauroux, and other fiefs in Berry, Recueil des Actes de Henri II, II, 61.

[3] King Louis countered Henry's challenge rather adroitly by appealing to the papacy against Henry's delay in having Richard and Alice married. A papal legate, at Rouen in September 1177, threatened to lay Henry's dominions under threat of interdict if the marriage was not speedily solemnised, Roger of Howden, Gesta, I, 190; Gervase of Canterbury, I, 271.

king of the French, against all men to the best of my ability, and I Louis will aid Henry, king of the English, as my vassal and liegeman [*sicut hominem et fidelem meum*]. . . . And to the end that henceforth all occasion for discord shall be removed, we mutually agree that henceforth neither of us will make demands upon each other's lands and possessions and rights as they now stand. . . .[1]

From this last clause an exception was made in respect of 'Auvergne, the fief of Châteauroux, and other small fiefs and portions of land in Berry', and detailed arrangements were made for arbitration about them. Roger of Howden reports a meeting of the kings at Graçay in November 1177 to hear the award of the arbitrators on the homage of Auvergne. Although six of the twelve arbitrators were nominated by King Louis from among his staunchest supporters, they are said to have declared unanimously that all of the Auvergne had always belonged to the lordship of the dukes of Aquitaine, with the exception of the bishop-ric of Clermont which was in the gift of the king of France. Louis was understandably disquieted, and demanded a commission of inquiry, to which Henry readily agreed.[2] Whether the matters in dispute were ever resolved is not known and seems doubtful.[3] Henry's complaisance at Graçay is, however, significant, for he had already secured what he wanted: assured by the non-aggression pact that King Louis would not seek to obstruct him, he had immediately taken steps to consolidate his hold on this vulnerable frontier region. Using the forces he had mustered to intimidate Louis, he marched on Châteauroux, took possession of the lands and castles of the late Ralph de Déols and forced those who had abducted the heiress to give her up.[4] And by a diplo-matic coup of startling boldness he arranged with the childless Count Adalbert of La Marche to purchase the whole of his lands and rights in the sprawling county which bordered both Berry and Auvergne, as well as Poitou and the Limousin.[5]

Henry's acquisition of the direct lordship of La Marche threatened to transform the whole power structure of eastern Aquitaine, and besides discomfiting King Louis, alarmed the restless barons of Angoulême, Poitou, and Limoges, who saw themselves being hemmed in by a more

[1] Roger of Howden, *Gesta*, I, 191–4, *Chronica*, II, 144–6; Gervase of Canterbury, I, 272–3; *Recueil des Actes de Henri II*, II, 60–2; cf. Ralph of Diceto, I, 421–2.

[2] Roger of Howden, *Gesta*, I, 196.

[3] The provisions for arbitration in the treaty of Ivry were repeated in precisely the same words in the treaty between Henry and King Philip in June 1180, *ibid.*, 247–8.

[4] *Ibid.*, 195–6.

[5] *Ibid.*, 197; Ralph of Diceto, I, 425. The count had lost his only son and proposed to go on pilgrimage.

effective ducal government. But if any of them thought they could count on the support of the king of France in resisting it, they were quickly disillusioned, for Henry had mastered King Louis. As if to emphasise the point, he obtained from the king of France, early in 1178, an explicit statement of the implications of the Treaty of Ivry. Roger of Howden transcribed into his chronicle a copy of the letters patent which Louis issued.

> Louis, king of France, to all to whom these present letters shall come, greeting.
> You should know that we have taken into our protection all the land of Henry, king of England, our most dear brother, situated on this side of the sea, in the event of his crossing over to England or undertaking a journey. And to the extent that his officers from beyond the sea shall require of us, we will in good faith and without evil intent, render them help for the defence and protection of those lands.[1]

Whether this agreement to live in peace would be lasting, however, was to depend less on Louis than upon his son Philip.

King Louis was growing old and his son was approaching the age at which Henry of Anjou had begun to work for his inheritance. Louis planned to have Philip crowned as co-king on his fourteenth birthday in August 1179, and he became seriously alarmed when a few weeks before the ceremony was due, his son fell sick of a malady so serious that the coronation had to be cancelled, and hope that he would live began to fade. King Louis was advised in a dream to seek the help of St Thomas of Canterbury and journeyed to England at the end of August, being graciously received by his 'most dear brother' King Henry and staying for five days.[2] Philip recovered and was crowned at Rheims on 1 November 1179, but his father was unable to attend the ceremony, for he had suffered a stroke on the return journey from Canterbury, and though he lingered in life until 18 September 1180, he ceased for all practical purposes to be king.[3] His retirement was followed by an unseemly wrangle at the French court for control of the young Philip, in which the count of Flanders pitted himself against the family of Blois, which included the queen, the count of Blois, the count of Champagne, and the archbishop of Rheims. Count Philip of Flanders was never quite sure whether his best interest was served by cultivating his connection with England or his connection with France. Since 1173

---

[1] Roger of Howden, *Gesta*, I, 198.
[2] *Ibid.*, 240–2; Gervase of Canterbury, I, 293; Ralph of Diceto, I, 432–3.
[3] Roger of Howden, *Gesta*, I, 243, 250; Ralph of Diceto, II, 4, 6, 7.

he had exercised a powerful influence over Henry the Younger, and for several years in the late '70s the two were almost inseparable companions; but at the end of 1179 he threw over the young king of England for the young king of France.[1] He succeeded in detaching Philip from his mother and arranged for him to marry his own niece, Isabella of Hainault. The family of Blois was reduced to the desperate expedient of appealing for help to Henry II, the man whose rule they had for nearly twenty years conspired to undermine. Henry intervened twice in person: once to reconcile King Philip to his mother, and later, at the request of King Philip, to persuade the count of Flanders that he would be well advised not to try to impose himself by force.[2] The spectacle of Henry of Anjou coming to the aid of his overlord, and of his sons ranging themselves beside the king of France to defy the rebellious vassal of Flanders, would have gladdened the heart of Abbot Suger, but it must have astonished those who witnessed it. Between Henry II and Philip II there seemed to be perfect understanding, and as a demonstration of their complete accord they renewed the Treaty of Ivry.[3]

On 22 February 1182 Henry II drew up his will. It specified in detail the bequests to be made to the Knights Templar, the Knights Hospitaller, to the religious houses of the Holy Land, of England, Normandy, and Anjou, to the order of Grandmont, to the Cistercians, to the Carthusians, to the monasteries of Cluny, Marmoutier, and Marcilli, to the Premonstratensians, to the Arroaisians, and finally – it was the only secular bequest he made – to provide marriage portions for impoverished maidens.[4] He was then nearly forty-nine years old, and in good health, though suffering periodically from an injured leg.

It might have been better for Henry's peace of mind if, like King Louis, he had died shortly after making his will; but he was to live for seven years more, and to find them embittered by the perfidy of his sons and the treachery of King Philip. But since he attempted no new venture, it may be said that, politically speaking, his reign was over by 1182. Whether he had accomplished all he intended is beyond

---

[1] Philip d'Alsace, count of Flanders, was a distant cousin of Henry II and had married a niece of Queen Eleanor. For his association with Henry the Younger, see Moore, *The Young King Henry Plantagenet*, ch. 1.

[2] Roger of Howden, *Gesta*, I, 244, 245–6, 277, 283–4, 285–6; Ralph of Diceto, II, 5, 6, 8–9, 11; Gervase of Canterbury, I, 294, 297; *Recueil des Actes de Henri II*, II, 230–1.

[3] Roger of Howden, *Gesta*, I, 247–8; Ralph of Diceto, II, 6.

[4] Gervase of Canterbury, I, 298–300; Ralph of Diceto, II, 10; *Recueil des Actes de Henri II*, II, 219–21; *Foedera*, I, Pt I, 47.

knowing; but his achievements spoke for themselves. He had enforced the rights which fell to him by birth and marriage; he had broken the back of rebellious independence; he had brought his overlord, the king of France, to guarantee the integrity of his continental lands.[1] The outer reaches of Henry's dominions, beyond the confines of England, Normandy, and Anjou, were still turbulent and still needed to be broken to the bit of political discipline; but from the time that peace was made after the great war, Henry seems to have judged this to be the work of his successors. He delegated much in the last fifteen years of his life. His governors in England, Normandy, and Anjou, hitherto merely the agents of Henry's will, came to be entrusted with powers more nearly approaching those of a viceroy. To some extent this was itself a consequence of the great war: Henry had then been obliged to rely as never before on the initiative, loyalty, and ability of his officers, and none of them betrayed him. But the change was not simply the result of confidence and convenience: it was the culmination of a long process of development in the methods and structure of government. There were two principal elements in this. One was the creation of a self-regulating administrative machine, with methods of accounting and control which meant that no official, however exalted, could entirely escape the surveillance of his colleagues and the king. The other was the perfection of administrative and judicial procedures which had the effect of reducing to routine much that had previously required the king's personal attention. It made possible a great increase in the scope of administrative activity without thereby increasing the personal power of the officials who discharged it. In short, if the governors of provinces became viceroys who no longer had to have Henry's express permission for everything they did, they were viceroys only to the extent that they could operate on their own initiative the administrative machine which Henry II devised. His greatest achievement, indeed, was not that he created a vast dominion, nor even that he held on to it and largely tamed it, but that he introduced to it the art of government.

[1] Before he died, King Louis even acknowledged Henry's overlordship of Toulouse, cf. Roger of Howden, *Gesta*, I, 198–9.

Chapter 4

THE LORDSHIP OF THE
BRITISH ISLES

In the preceding chapter the story of Henry II's relations with Wales, Scotland, and Ireland has been told only as an incidental counterpoint to the story of his political life in France and England. This, no doubt, would have seemed to him its proper status in his biography. He was in Wales four times in the thirty-five years of his reign. Three times he mounted a punitive expedition that lasted for three or four weeks at the most. On the fourth occasion, journeying through south Wales on his way to Ireland and delayed by contrary winds, he remained for about five weeks. He visited Ireland once for a period of six months. He never, so far as we know, set foot in Scotland at all (unless we count Carlisle as part of Scotland in 1149): his business with the Scots was conducted on the soil of England or of Normandy. Yet this is no reason in itself for relegating his dealings with the 'Celtic' periphery to the margin of his story. What was of lesser importance to him achieved an enduring place in history; and it is one of the ironies of his reign that those parts of his dominions to which he devoted least time and attention were those which remained for longest a concern of the English Crown – Gascony, Wales, Ireland and, in a somewhat different way, Scotland. Moreover, the very fact that Henry II's energies were chiefly consumed in France gives a peculiar interest to the story of his dealings with the outer reaches of the British Isles: he was obliged in the latter to seek short cuts to his objectives, and the variety of the methods he used there casts a clearer light on the inner purposes of his political policy than does the more straightforward conquer, subdue, and rule operation on the continent.

It is, however, a story which requires careful analysis, for it does not yield its secrets easily. The problems are numerous. For one thing, the factual evidence is often too fragmentary, too full of holes, to yield an intelligible narrative.[1] And even when the facts are tolerably well

[1] Lloyd's *History of Wales from the ancient times to the Edwardian Conquest*, first published in 1911 (3rd edn 1939), needs revision in detail and in some of its assumptions,

known, their interpretation is not always obvious and has too often been darkened by the anachronisms of nationalist sentiment. Fundamental problems remain unresolved. Whether these societies can properly be described as 'Celtic' is an open question, for the word has a more linguistic than cultural significance. The sociology of Celtic society has not yet received the scholarly attention it requires, and the true nature of its undoubted distinctiveness eludes us. We can attempt only a tentative evaluation.[1]

At first sight Celtic society displays institutions and traits that are perfectly familiar to the student of other regions of western Europe. Yet any attempt to expound the history of Celtic lands in the categories of thought which west European historiography is accustomed to use fails, and will always fail, to explain some of its most characteristic features. Institutions (such as kingship) which look at first sight familiar were in fact differently put together and informed by different traditions and habits. We are so accustomed to seeing social institutions closely integrated with political institutions, and states and societies developing within a readily definable political framework, that it is difficult to comprehend the development of a far from primitive and reasonably stable society in which political institutions were of comparatively minor importance. Yet such, it seems, was the situation in those western fringes of Europe which Carolingian influences had not greatly touched. Therein there was little impetus towards the creation of centralised political and administrative institutions because society had little need of them. The society's strength and stability lay in a generally diffused body of social customs and laws enforced entirely within the context of closely integrated neighbourhood units. Political power was something detached from this, something grounded not in social institutions, but in tribal loyalties, in charismatic qualities of

---

but it remains a monumental work of synthesis and the starting-point for any study of medieval Welsh history. As the most convenient guide to the interpretation of the sources, it is frequently cited in the footnotes which follow. The comparable book for Ireland, Curtis's *History of Medieval Ireland*, first published in 1923, is marred by misinterpretations, and the second edition was already out of date when it appeared in 1938; cf. Richardson, 'English institutions in medieval Ireland', and Moody, 'The writings of Edmund Curtis'. Jocelyn Otway-Ruthven has recently provided a useful revision of Curtis in her *History of Medieval Ireland* (1968), but it does not offer so comprehensive a guide to the sources. The lack of a similar synthesis for Scotland is compensated by useful collections of annotated source material edited by Anderson, *Early Sources of Scottish History*, and *Scottish Annals from English Chroniclers*.

[1] Cf. De Beer, 'Genetics and prehistory'.

leadership, and in military skill. With his security resting on social institutions, the Celt could the more readily indulge in political *laissez-faire*. The better known history of the successor states of Carolingian Europe might suggest that the Celt's acceptance of warfare simply as a fact of life condemned him to live in anarchy.[1] It was to become axiomatic in western Europe generally that peace and order were inseparable. Political order was in fact there made the groundwork of social stability and progress. But this pattern was not inevitable. The Celtic world found an alternative to political peace as the basis for an ordered social life. At the same time it should be recognised that this particular kind of security and this particular kind of indulgence were bought at a price. Since the social order was the sole source of security, to touch it meant chaos. The political order which other western states achieved was in fact a liberating factor for long denied to the Celts. The Celts tamed the effects of warfare not by the disciplining forces of political authority, but by reducing political ambition in importance; in so doing they achieved an equilibrium that could find little room for progress. A stable, static society can endure for centuries; but a stable, static society can survive only so long as it remains untouched by a society which accepts change as an inevitable ingredient of life. Once the energy and expansionism of Europe's *francigenae* and the revolutionary implications of the Hildebrandine reform movement in church government began to collide with Celtic conservatism something had to give way, either Celtic society had to change itself, radically, or it had to surrender to alien overlords who knew the secrets of ordered change.

Scotland, Wales, and Ireland were already deeply involved in the painful processes of change when Henry II encountered them. In Lowland Scotland a Europeanised monarchy had emerged which, recruiting its power by encouraging *sassenach* immigration, was slowly beginning the absorption of the conservative Highlands. But as a monarchy it was as yet too young to feel secure, and the kings of Scots seem to have believed that their resources would be more ample to their needs if the frontier of Scotland lay closer to the historic boundary of Hadrian's Wall than on the Tweed and the Solway. It was a belief which clashed with Henry's determination to abate no inch of the political rights he had inherited from his grandfather. In Ireland the

[1] This is the assumption which Orpen made in *Ireland under the Normans,* and it vitiates his strictures on Irish society before the Norman invasion; cf. Binchy, 'Secular institutions', *Early Irish Society,* 61–2.

forces of change encountered a more deeply entrenched conservatism, and the clash engendered a power struggle into which Henry II was drawn willy-nilly. In Wales the situation had been confused for the best part of a century by piecemeal Norman invasion and it was still an open question whether change would be generated from within or imposed from without. On the whole it seemed, in 1154, as if Norman intruders had acted as a catalyst in Welsh society, prompting it to a political cohesion never before known. What would be the consequence for the historic claims of the kings of England to lordship of Wales was a matter of considerable doubt.

(i) *Wales*

The history of Wales in the twelfth century has sometimes been represented as a struggle for Welsh freedom: the threat of Norman conquest, it has been suggested, engendered a 'national revival' which pushed the invaders back. But such an interpretation bears the misleading marks of nineteenth-century nationalism, and falsifies a complex situation. For a start, Welsh 'independence' was far from absolute even before the coming of the Normans. As early as King Alfred's day the Danish menace had driven the Welsh princes into the protecting arms of the West Saxon monarchy, and an English overlordship was established which found expression not only in the payment of tribute but also in the attendance of Welsh princes at the English court. Hywel Dda, whom tradition commemorates as the reformer of Welsh law, witnessed several surviving charters of King Athelstan (924–39).[1] Too much, however, should not be read into such evidence. Wales was never incorporated into the Old English state. The overlordship that existed was a fitful and personal relationship between individual Welsh princes and English kings, and to the end it smacked more of the old-fashioned *Bretwaldaship* of early English rulers than of the institutionalised monarchy of King Alfred's successors. The English ascendancy in Wales stretched only so far as the native rulers would allow or the English kings by force of arms could insist. Domesday Book could speak clearly of an inherited right to tribute from Wales, but William the Conqueror had to thank for the effectiveness of that right the victorious campaign that Harold Godwinsson waged against Gruffydd ap Llywelyn in 1063.

Such voluntary or enforced submission to the overlordship of a powerful neighbour was, however, only a part of the situation. Political

[1] Cf. Roderick, 'The feudal relations between the English Crown and the Welsh princes', 202–3; Lloyd, *History of Wales*, I, 353.

dependence was supported, indeed perhaps promoted, by a geographical and economic dependence. The boundary which the Mercians had staked out by the eighth century deprived the Welsh of easy communication within the lands that they themselves controlled. Mountains sundered the country, and then as now Welsh highways led to Shrews-

IX Wales

bury and to Hereford. Moreover, the Welsh pastoral economy was but precariously self-sufficient, if indeed it was self-sufficient at all. William of Newburgh, writing in the late twelfth century, says that Wales was 'incapable of supplying its inhabitants with food without importation from the adjacent counties of England; and since it cannot command this without the liberality or express permission of the king of England, it is necessarily subject to his power'.[1]

The situation of Wales then, it may be said, was not one of independence, nor yet was it one of complete dependence; rather it was a case of uneasy involvement.

Apart from asserting his inherited claims to tribute, William the Conqueror does not seem to have bothered much with Wales: it offered him little danger and less enticement. He established a 'march' of well-endowed border baronies to maintain the existing boundaries, and to protect the lands which owed him taxes from the Welsh pastime of cattle-raiding, and left it at that. But the border barons did not. Wales was a land of opportunity for the land-hungry, and within a few years of the Conquest Norman adventurers were beginning to carve out private lordships for themselves in Welsh territory.[2] Wales was a land of opportunity for the venturesome because of its lack of political unity and internal cohesion. Geography was a factor in this. The mountainous heart of Wales, its dense forests, and its marshes, impeded political unity and fostered the development of three distinct tribal groupings, each under the dominance of a powerful family that commanded a nucleus of fertile territory. These dynastic overlordships went by the names of Gwynedd in the north, Deheubarth in the south, and Powys in the valleys of the east – separated by small communities or loose federations of lesser princes who could maintain some kind of independence or separate identity in mountain or forest fastness. But geography was not the only factor: the very nature of Celtic society made it resistant to political unification. That is not to say, however, that Celtic Wales lacked any kind of unity. Welshmen were conscious of a 'oneness', of belonging to a comprehensible and distinctive community. They had a word for it: *Cymry*. It is highly significant that this word has a legal origin: the *cymro* was a free landed proprietor with a well-defined legal status. In time the word *Cymry* came to displace *Brythones* or

[1] William of Newburgh, I, 107.

[2] Cf. Douglas, *William the Conqueror*, 241; Nelson, *The Normans in South Wales*.

[3] Cf. Lloyd, *op. cit.*, I, 191–2. The same word came to be used of the predominantly Brythonic region of north-west England, and is the fundamental element in the names *Cumbria* and *Cumberland*.

Brittones as a general term for the men who lived in Wales, but it could not shake off the connotations of its origin, for these were firmly embedded in the general body of Welsh law. In fact Wales was not so much a *nation* as an *association*: an *association* of free landed proprietors, whose sense of belonging to one community was fostered by cultural traditions, social customs, and common laws. Within this all-embracing cultural 'association' there had developed well-defined and apparently very stable social cells – neighbourhood units with an internal structure that seems to have been common throughout the country. When they are met with in the twelfth century these neighbourhood social units had a territorial formulation that went by the name of the *commote*. It was within the commote, or over a group of commotes, that lordship was exercised.

The Wales which the Norman advance guard of post-Carolingian Europe encountered was a land of lordships, of lordships great and small, of lordships ascendant and of lordships subordinate, but of lordships that (however small and subordinate) were internally sovereign. It was a world in which political ambition was given free play, a world in which military enterprise was recognised in law, its heroism applauded in song, and its victories rewarded in plunder. It was a world, in short, of political competition, in which the military entrepreneur had the same respectable status as the commercial entrepreneur in the commercially competitive world of the nineteenth century. To the Norman on the border it may have seemed a somewhat alien world, but it was one for which his military training equipped him. To pursue the analogy with nineteenth-century commerce, we may say that with the arrival of the Normans in Wales, a hitherto isolated home market encountered a new element of cut-throat foreign competition. The analogy is useful if it deflects us from other and more misleading analogies, the analogy of a conflict of nation states, for instance, or that of colonial exploitation. The Normans were exploiters, but they exploited on the same terms and in the same way as the Welsh lords. Nor was the foreign invasion of the Welsh home market a combined or planned one. The Norman competitors were freelances, and they competed as fiercely between themselves as with the Welsh. The object of exploitation was the basic unit of Welsh social organisation: the *commote*. This was the 'business' for which both Norman and Welsh lords were making take-over bids. The acquisition of a *commote* by a Norman baron meant that he instead of a Welsh lord exploited the assets and collected the revenues—but it does not seem that fundamentally it meant much more than that. The law and customs that the Normans administered in their Welsh acquisitions came to be known as 'Marcher law', but it seems to have been no other than Welsh law seen through Norman eyes.

That is not to say that the Normans brought no great change. Welsh law seen through Norman eyes no doubt differed considerably from Welsh law seen through Welsh eyes. The Normans (to judge by their behaviour elsewhere in Europe) were very likely more ruthless exploiters than native lords, and they were no doubt less inhibited by traditional restraints and social sanctions. It is unlikely, for instance, that the assembly of *uchelwrs* (or heads of households) exercised as much influence over a Norman lord as over a native prince. It must be allowed, too, that the native Welsh were likely to tolerate with better grace the traditional exploitation of their own dynasts than of alien interlopers: for one thing there was not the same pride to be taken in his military exploits – especially when his minstrels sang in an alien tongue. All of which can readily account for the polarisation of the exploiting lords into native and alien, and explain the passionate desire expressed in Welsh chronicles 'to cast off the Norman yoke', without having to resort to the language and presuppositions of modern nationalist sentiment. The evidence, sometimes adduced, of a Welsh national struggle is too slight to be convincing. Political competition among the Welsh was rarely suspended for a common endeavour: the Welsh resistance to Norman penetration, though fierce and unremitting, was for the most part local and dynastic, not national and patriotic. National sentiment among the Welsh was much more a product of resistance to a foreign intruder than the cause of it. And if we speak of a polarisation of native and foreign exploiters, of a Norman Wales and a Welsh Wales, we should nevertheless be careful not to exaggerate it. Free competition can produce strange alliances and stranger mergers: frequent were the occasions when Normans and Welsh together fought Welsh or Normans, and not unknown were those when marriage vows cemented a condominium. Moreover, as the commercial analogy reminds us, cut-throat competition does not preclude, and may indeed promote mutual respect and admiration. Twelfth-century competitors, unlike those of the nineteenth century, had an heroic language in which to express it. 'It is to me,' said Rhys of Deheubarth when he encountered at Henry II's court the old Norman foes who had once despoiled him of the inheritance he had since recovered, 'It is to me no small source of pleasure that I once lost lands to no mean or laggard clan, but to a family of rare fame and distinction'; and his erstwhile foe replied that if lands captured from the Welsh had to be lost they could be lost to no one so acceptably as to the noble and valiant prince who now enjoyed them.[1] Norman respect extended also to the prowess and peculiar skills of the ordinary Welsh fighting man. The Welshman, trained to fight in the forests and mountains, excelled in skirmishing, the ambush, and archery, and could provide a welcome complement to the cavalry skill of the Norman knights and the tactics of the spear-bearing footmen. The earl of Chester brought a great host of the men of Powys to the battle of Lincoln in 1141; and their skills were so highly regarded by Henry II that he recruited Welshmen in large numbers for his wars on the continent.[2] Fighting men from the Welsh mountains were, indeed, the Gurkhas of the twelfth century.

Wales was, however, always much more important to the Welsh and to the marcher barons than it was to the English Crown. The policy of Henry II's Norman predecessors had rarely if ever been more than that of trying to ensure that Wales should be kept from becoming a problem to the English government. It was a policy that failed. Failure was probably inevitable, for Wales constituted a problem of a peculiarly intractable kind: it was a country which could not, without enormous effort, be conquered; it presented a long frontier which could not easily be securely defended; and it lacked an internal government with which treaty relations could be concluded. Anglo-Saxon kings had accepted, at least since the end of the eighth century, the impracticability of the conquest and assimilation of Wales, and while asserting a sovereignty over it, had in practice been content to stake out a border and ensure its integrity by local defensive measures and an occasional punitive expedition.

William the Conqueror seems to have agreed with his predecessors' appraisal. It is sometimes suggested that William, eschewing a campaign of conquest, looked to the marcher barons to secure the piecemeal acquisition of Welsh territory, and hence the gradual absorption of the country to the realm of England. It is true that he raised no objection to the acquisition of Welsh territory by his barons; but two facts militate against assuming that this was part of a deliberately formulated policy of absorption. In the first place no arrangements were made for the extension of the institutions of English government into the newly conquered territories. On the contrary the invaders were allowed to treat their acquisitions as private property and preserved within them

---

[1] Gerald of Wales, I, 57–8.
[2] Henry of Huntingdon, 268, 273; Orderic Vitalis, V, 126–7; Roger of Howden, *Gesta*, II, 40, 46, 50, *Chronica*, I, 282.

the traditional forms of Welsh social organisation, and, naturally, the rights and privileges of the Welsh lords they displaced. Secondly, William was prepared to accept the fealty both of the Norman settlers and of Welsh princes (when it was offered to him) on the easiest of terms, which contrasts strongly with the strict conditions of tenure applied in England, and which suggests that he had no aspirations to exercising a real authority in Wales.[1]

William's rather off-hand attitude had unfortunate consequences. Wales was not to feel the impress of a royal policy until it was too late to provide it with the kind of government it needed. The Norman adventurers were both too successful and not successful enough. They speedily overran the whole of the southern lowlands and much of the northern coastal plateau, and in so doing built private empires which in rebellious hands could seriously threaten the stability of the English throne itself. On the other hand they failed to learn how to defeat the Welsh in the highlands where their customary methods of warfare were unsuited to the terrain. Wales was exploited but not conquered. The Welsh princes, no longer able to place confidence in a policy of co-existence with the English Crown, were left in their mountain retreats to cultivate their independence and dream of recovering the valleys. Their habit of continual warfare, hitherto devoted to feuding and raiding, was given a new focus in the prosperous Norman settlements. Once they themselves learned the techniques of siegecraft and castle-building there could be no hope that the Norman intruders could live in peace. Already by the beginning of the twelfth century the permanence of the Norman conquests in Wales was in serious doubt. King Henry I set himself to do something about it.

No one was held in such awe by the Welsh princes as Henry I;[2] no king before or for many years afterwards could boast of such successful Welsh expeditions; yet despite the impression of a recovery of Norman initiative, the object of Henry I's intervention in Wales was much less its Normalisation than its stabilisation. And in seeking stabilisation Henry looked as much to the Welsh princes as to the Norman barons. His expedition into north Wales in 1141 stopped in its tracks the steady advance of Gruffydd prince of Gwynedd against the earlier conquests of the earl of Chester; but having secured Gruffydd's submission, Henry refrained from demanding territorial concessions or the recovery by the Normans of the Menai straits.[3] The forfeiture of the extensive

---

[1] Cf. Edwards, 'The Normans and the Welsh march'.
[2] Cf. the attitude of Gruffyd ap Cynan of Gwynedd, Lloyd, *op. cit.*, II, 464.
[3] *Ibid.*, 434–5.

Welsh lands of Robert de Bellême, earl of Shrewsbury, and of his brother Arnulf, lord of Pembroke, for treason, was followed by the restoration of several Welsh princes.[1] And even when Henry did not indulge the Welsh, he was at pains to break up, when he could, the previous invariable pattern of private Norman lordships. Thus Pembroke, forfeited by Arnulf of Montgomery, was entrusted to a castellan of the former owner, but the king had its internal economy transformed by the deliberate introduction of Flemish colonists, and obliged it to render dues to the English exchequer through a sheriff. Similarly, Carmarthen was retained in the king's hand and administered like an English shire.[2]

That Henry I's intervention in Wales secured a measure of equilibrium cannot be doubted; but his control was neither complete nor secure. The equilibrium had a shaky base. His policy seems to have rested on the notion of a partnership between king, Welsh princes, and Norman barons; but such a policy stood a chance of success only if the marcher barons were forcibly restrained from renewed penetration into *pura Wallia*. They were not. No doubt, given the previous history of the March of Wales, to restrain them was outside the realm of practical possibility for a Norman king; but without it the Welsh lacked that sense of security which was necessary to acquiescence in the sort of condominium that Henry I seems to have had in mind. For the Welsh, indeed, it must have seemed that real security could come only from such victories over the foreigner as would deter him from aggression. Quite apart from any question of the rise of a 'national spirit' (which may or may not have been a factor in the situation) a Welsh *revanche* was only to be expected if the royal deterrent to open warfare ever faltered in its effectiveness. In the event it not merely faltered, it disappeared. King Stephen soon showed himself incapable of inspiring the awe which had been the principal element in Henry I's success; and the marcher barons themselves soon became embroiled in the English civil war. By the time Henry of Anjou became king of England, Welsh leaders such as Owain of Gwynedd and Rhys of Deheubarth

---

[1] Hywel ap Gronw, for example, was made lord of Ystrad Tywi, Gower, and Kidwelly, Lloyd, *op. cit.*, II, 415. Even Owain of Powys, after years spent in exile, gained the favour of Henry I, was knighted by him and died in his service; and this was all the more remarkable, for it was the same Owain who was a hero of Welsh defiance for his exploit of burrowing into a castle held by Gerald of Windsor and abducting his wife, the beautiful Nest, erstwhile mistress of the king; but though he died in the king's service, it was the servants of the wrathful Gerald who slew him, *ibid.*, 417–22.

[2] Pipe Roll 31 Henry I, 89–90, 133, 136; Lloyd, *op. cit.*, II, 423–4.

had made themselves heroes of legend, and the Norman colony had been shattered into fragments.

The story of Henry II's relations with Wales seems, at first sight, to divide itself into two contrasting phases. During the first decade of his reign he mounted large military expeditions against the independent Welsh, with small return for the effort and cost involved. But this phase was then followed by a *rapprochement* between Henry and the Welsh princes, the establishment of a working relationship between them, and an honoured place for Welsh leaders at the royal court. It looks indeed as if Henry changed his policy. But on closer examination the change seems more apparent than real – and to have been a change of tactics rather than a change of policy. It is difficult to believe that Henry II at any time intended the conquest of Wales and its assimilation to the English state. The military expeditions of the early years were dictated by the need to restore order to a war-torn Wales, and to promote respect for the Crown's authority; they were, indeed, but one aspect of Henry's wider programme of pacification and the consolidation of his régime. The Welsh had to be taught that the hay-making days of King Stephen's reign were over, and that there was again in the land an authority that was intolerant of disorder.

His first expedition against Owain of Gwynedd in 1157 was conducted in a way well calculated to allay suspicions that the king might intend the complete Normanisation of Wales. It was provided with a justification in the appeal of Owain's brother Cadwaladr for help in securing the just inheritance which he claimed was being denied him.[1] It would be naïve to believe that the promotion of peace and justice between Welshmen was the sole or primary object of the expedition; but it was a useful earnest of royal policy to set beside the more obvious intention of a demonstration of power and an assertion of authority. The intention nearly foundered in disaster. While the main army marched along the coast, a royal party cut inland through the forest and was ambushed, the king himself barely escaping with his life. Moreover, a naval contingent, which it was proposed should sail from Pembroke to take Owain in the rear, put into Anglesey for plunder and suffered crippling casualties.[2] These two misfortunes, however, while no doubt instructing Henry in the perils of Welsh campaigning, did not hinder the progress of the main army. Owain recognised it as too formidable to engage in open battle and shortly came to terms. He had to restore his brother to his inheritance, and retire from his most recent

---

[1] Lloyd, *op. cit.*, II, 490–1.
[2] *Ibid.*, 497, 498–9; cf. Jocelin of Brakelond, 70.

conquests of Norman marcher positions in the neighbourhood of Rhuddlan; but that was all – his lordship of Gwynedd was recognised and his homage accepted.[1] In the reassertion of the king of England's overriding authority in north Wales the expedition of 1157 was successful. For several years Owain behaved with scrupulous rectitude. When, for instance, in 1160 a princely disturber of the peace in central Wales fell into his hands he promptly passed him on to Henry as his overlord.[2]

Rhys of Deheubarth, the other principal leader of *pura Wallia*, was less pliant. At the time of Henry's expedition to north Wales in 1157, Rhys had contemplated defiance, but then thought better of it and crossed the border to volunteer his submission. The price of his recognition was stiff. Much more of south Wales than north had suffered Norman penetration, and from most of Ceredigion the Normans had been ejected; but King Henry, deeply indebted to the southern marcher barons for the support of their Angevin cause against Stephen, felt bound to seek their restoration. Rhys accepted for the moment the confinement of his independent lordship to little more than the Cantref Mawr, but hated to see the Normans returning to garrison the castles he had so lately held. It took a show of force by King Henry to persuade him to keep the peace.[3] It was a precarious peace. While Owain in the north gave no cause for reproach, Rhys bucked and chafed at the ties of his allegiance. In 1162 he cast them off and seized the strategically important castle of Llandovery.[4] Henry II was abroad, preoccupied with continental problems since August 1158, but very shortly after his return early in 1163 he marched into Deheubarth at the head of an army. Rhys retreated to Pencader in his lair of Cantref Mawr; but when Henry forced his way in he surrendered and returned with him a prisoner to England.[5]

What was to be done with Rhys seems to have troubled the king for some weeks, and it was a real test of Henry's intentions towards the Welsh. In the end it was decided to reinstate him; but it seems that reinstatement was to be on redefined terms of allegiance which were to be a part of a reformulation of Henry's relations with the Welsh princes and with the king of Scots. They were all summoned to Woodstock in July 1163, and there, relates Ralph of Diceto, 'Malcolm king of the Scots, Rhys prince of the southern Welsh, Owain of the northern, and five of the greater men of Wales did homage to the king of England and

---

[1] Lloyd, *op cit.*, II, 499–500.
[2] *Ibid.*, 511.   [3] *Ibid.*, 506–7.
[4] *Ibid.*, 511 and n.3.   [5] *Ibid.*, 511–13.

to Henry his son'.[1] Robert de Torigny, the only other chronicler to mention it, says that King Malcolm had to surrender his younger brother David as hostage for the preservation of peace.[2] It is a pity that they are not more precise, for the council at Woodstock seems to have been of peculiar importance in the relations of the king of England with the Welsh and Scots. Scottish historians have inferred from other evidence that King Malcolm was in fact required to accept a status of dependent vassalage much more circumscribed than that of his predecessors. If we may suppose that the Welsh princes too were required to demean themselves by accepting instead of their previous client status that of dependent vassalage, we have a convincing explanation for what happened next: the immediate and simultaneous uprising of all the native Welsh. As the chronicler of St David's puts it, 'all the Welsh of Gwynedd, Deheubarth, and Powys with one accord cast off the Norman yoke'.[3]

Henry's response was a major campaign. It was prepared with surpassing thoroughness. At a council at Northampton in October 1164 the barons promised to furnish large numbers of infantry – for hill fighting dissipated the advantages of mounted knights. More troops were brought in from the continent. The sheriffs of London spent large sums fitting out mercenaries from the Low Countries. Shrewsbury became an arms dump. A fleet was hired from the Norsemen of Dublin. Henry, it seems, intended to settle the Welsh problem once and for all.

Gathering together a large army and equipping it was one problem; moving it into Wales, feeding it, and bringing it to grips with the enemy was another – and much more baffling. The army marched from Shrewsbury in July for Oswestry and the mountains by the route, known for generations as 'the English Road', which leads to the strategically important confluence of valleys and routes at Corwen. Difficulty piled on difficulty. The army was harassed by skirmishers; it had to cut back the undergrowth from the line of march as it made its way slowly through the forests of the Ceirog valley and up the foothills of the Berwyn range to the boggy moors that separated it from the valley of the upper Dee. In summer the mountain moors were readily passable, and Henry had evidently timed his expedition with care; but the weather was unseasonable in the extreme. Torrential rain was

---

[1] Ralph of Diceto, I, 311.   [2] Robert de Torigny, 218.

[3] *Annales Cambriae*, 50. Lloyd's explanation, *op. cit.*, II, 514–15, that the developing quarrel between Henry and Becket meant that the king 'had no longer the support of a united people' and that this persuaded the Welsh princes that 'the decisive hour had come in the struggle for Welsh independence', is very implausible.

whipped by a biting wind, and the army bogged down. Victuals ran low, the elements were implacable, and the army retreated the way it had come. Frustrated of his foe, Henry had twenty-two Welsh hostages mutilated and hanged.[1]

In March 1166 Henry II sailed for the continent, not to return to England for four years. With the abandonment of his attempt to enforce the submission of the Welsh princes they pressed with renewed confidence their attack on the possessions of the marcher barons. There was no general collapse of the Norman position, but Rhys and Owain gained signal successes. Within a few months Rhys had captured the territory he surrendered in 1157, crowning his efforts with the demolition of Cardigan castle.[2] Owain in the north proceeded more cautiously. Pushing west again across the river Clywd he took Basingwerk and beat off a relieving force. In 1167 he took the royal castle at Rhuddlan after three months' siege, and so brought under his control all the territories his family had long disputed with the earls of Chester. To the end of his life in November 1170 he maintained an imperious independence, defying Archbishop Becket over an election to the see of Bangor, defying the pope over his marriage to his first cousin, and proclaiming his defiance of Henry II by sending envoys in 1168 to King Louis of France offering help against the man who claimed to be his overlord.[3]

Never again did Henry II attempt to crush the Welsh by force. By the time he returned from the continent in 1171 he was ready for a new kind of understanding with the Welsh princes. During the weeks he had to wait in Pembroke for a fair wind to carry him to Ireland he struck up friendly relations with Rhys of Deheubarth. Amicable relations with the successor of Owain of Gwynedd and the lesser princes quickly followed. It has been suggested that Henry's change of front was prompted by his need for a secure route through Wales in order to reach Ireland. What brought him back from the continent in 1171 was the unwelcome success of Norman adventurers at carving out private empires for themselves in Ireland, and he was bent on bringing them under control. Effective control required good lines of communication with Ireland, and one of the best led through Milford Haven in Pembroke. But Milford Haven was not the only port for Ireland, and

---

[1] Annals of Waverley, 338–9; *Annales Cambriae*, 50; Chronicle of Melrose, 79. Gerald of Wales, VI, 143, says that Henry was turned back 'subita et inopinata pluvialium aquarum mundatione'; William of Newburgh, I, 145, refers to 'inextricabiles locorum difficultates'.

[2] Lloyd, *op. cit.*, II, 518–19.

[3] *Ibid.*, 519–22; *Materials for the History of Becket*, VI, 458.

the fact that Henry chose to use it in 1171 suggests that a *détente* had in fact already taken place in his relations with the Welsh. The chroniclers are too unhelpful for certainty, but it seems likely that Henry began rethinking his attitude to the Welsh soon after the débâcle of 1165. Indeed the action of some of the marcher barons in seeking new fields for their enterprise in Ireland after 1168 suggests that they had by then abandoned hope that Henry II would help them any more to recover lands they had lost in Wales. The basis of the *rapprochement* with the Welsh princes was indeed the abandonment of marcher interests and the acceptance of the existing boundaries of native Welsh rule as a *fait accompli*. Two things delayed a general reconciliation: Henry's preoccupation with the situation in France and the implacable hostility of Owain of Gwynedd. The truce of Montmirail in 1169 and the death of Owain in 1170 helped to clear both obstacles. But with other Welsh princes tension seems to have relaxed before this: while Owain was offering to send help to King Louis in 1168, a large force of Welsh mercenaries was helping Henry at the seige of Chaumont.[1]

It is quite probable that Henry had never been happy about attempting to restore the position of the Norman barons in Wales. The measures he was to take in Ireland speak clearly of his determination not to allow the reproduction there of the kind of tenures the marchers had created in Wales. That he had ever supported the desire of the marcher barons for reinstatement in the lands they had lost may be attributed to two things: his general desire to restore every situation to what it had been at the time of his grandfather's death, and a debt of gratitude owed to many of the marchers for their support of the Angevin cause in Stephen's day. Henry had, however, it seems, come to realise that the basic mistake of his initial Welsh policy lay in too crude an interpretation of what the situation had really been in Henry I's day, and hence in too great a commitment to marcher interests. Henry I's apparent mastery of the Welsh problem, and the extensive area then under marcher control, probably masked the real subtlety of his policy, which rested not on approval of the marcher dominance but on support for a measure of self-government by the unconquered Welsh, reinforced by an overseeing royal presence, as a defence against the creation of a baronial free enterprise monopoly. His grandson had been obliged to restore to equilibrium a balance of power that had tipped alarmingly in the direction of Welsh independence; but while Henry I had simply acquiesced in marcher power with reassurances for the Welsh, Henry II had allowed his policy to take the form of reinstatement for the marchers

[1] Stephen of Rouen, lines 684–6; Roger of Howden, *Chronica*, I, 282.

with humiliation for the Welsh. By 1171, however, the military situation in Wales had achieved a new kind of balance on its own, and the marchers were in disfavour. It was an excellent opportunity for Henry to readjust the emphasis of his Welsh policy, and he was ready to take it.

Whether a more liberal attitude to native rule in Wales would succeed in promoting peace there depended, of course, on whether the Welsh princes were prepared to cooperate. They were. To some extent this rested on fortuitous factors such as the death of Owain of Gwynedd. To some extent it rested on the growing statesmanship, prudence, and leadership of Rhys of Deheubarth. But to a great extent also it rested upon a realistic appraisal by the major Welsh princes of their position. Powys had produced no leader of note after 1160 and had become the scene of an indecisive struggle for power between the sons of Madog ap Maredudd. Their adhesion to the revolt of 1163 was something of an aberration, for geography linked Powys more to England than to the rest of Wales, and made it more vulnerable to reprisal. Their support of the revolt is indeed clear testimony to the brusque rigidity of Henry's attitude in 1163. The wilting of that attitude permitted them, already by the late 1160s, to re-establish cross-border ties, and Owain Cyfeiliog, for one, soon became a welcome visitor to the royal court and famous for his ready wit.[1] For Rhys the acquisition of Ceredigion was essential to the creation of a viable lordship. The fastnesses of Cantref Mawr gave him a secure refuge from attack but made him lord only of impenetrable forest and mountain tops. Ceredigion gave him meadows and men; but Ceredigion was vulnerable. The army brought by Henry to Milford Haven for Ireland could just as easily have been turned against Cardigan; and if Henry chose to be determinedly hostile there would be nothing for Rhys but Cantref Mawr. Rhys's profitable gains of recent years, in fact, impelled him to prudence, for his best hope lay in persuading Henry to accept what had been accomplished. Dafydd son of Owain in Gwynedd was better placed strategically, for the cornfields of Anglesey lay well to the rear of his defences in the mountains; but the conquests of Owain east of the river Clwyd that had crowned his career were both open to attack and a standing *casus belli*, unless King Henry could be persuaded to assent to their acquisition. Such considerations would not have weighed heavily if the Welsh princes had been hotly engaged with acquisitive marcher barons, and if the king had still pinned his hopes of stability in Wales upon marcher success; but the departure of the militants for Ireland had both eased the pressure of marcher encroachment and modified the attitude of the king.

[1] Gerald of Wales, II, 12; Lloyd, *op. cit.*, 520–53.

Henry's *rapprochement* with Rhys of Deheubarth in October 1171, while he waited to cross to Ireland, was no mere gesture of friendship. Henry showed his real intentions by recognising Rhys's right to the lands he had conquered, notwithstanding any Norman claims; and Rhys in return promised tribute in acknowledgement of Henry's overlordship.[1] As an earnest of goodwill Henry released to Rhys his son Hywel, who had for many years been held as a hostage. On his return from Ireland in 1172 Henry went further and appointed Rhys to be 'justice of south Wales'. Just what was implied in this remarkable title we have no means of knowing; but it seems to have involved jurisdiction over some of the lesser native princes, and to have made of Rhys a sort of royal pro-consul in the south.[2]

Gwynedd at this time was racked by succession quarrels among the sons of Owain, but by 1173 Dafydd was emerging as its leader. He was ready to follow Rhys's lead in seeking an accommodation with the king of England. When the great war broke out Dafydd of Gwynedd was to be found numbered among King Henry's staunchest supporters.[3] The war, indeed, gave the Welsh princes an opportunity which they readily seized to respond to Henry's liberality with loyalty. As soon as he heard of the rebellion Rhys sent his son Hwyel to join the king in Normandy. In 1174 he himself led a large force to the royalist siege of Tutbury, and later put a thousand men at the king's disposal in France.[4]

When the war was over Henry held a council in June 1175, at Gloucester, devoted principally to Welsh affairs. It was attended by a large gathering of native princes led by Rhys of Deheubarth, and by marcher barons headed by the earl of Gloucester and William de Briouze, lord of Builth. Information about the meeting is meagre, but it seems to have concluded with a solemnly sworn mutual assistance pact for the preservation of peace and order in Wales.[5] It still remained, however, to formulate a constitutional relationship between the king of England and the Welsh princes to take the place of that repudiated

---

[1] A hint that Henry sometimes compensated Norman followers for their loss is given by Pipe Roll 20 Henry II, 89: Odo, the eldest son of William FitzGerald, received twenty librates of land in Devon 'in escambium castelli et terrae de Emelin quamdiu Resus filius Griffini ea habuerit'.

[2] Lloyd, *op. cit.*, II, 541–2.

[3] *Ibid.*, 549ff.; Roger of Howden, *Gesta*, I, 55 n.4. Owain Cyfeiliog of Powys was numbered among Henry's supporters too. Henry rewarded Dafydd by giving him in marriage his half-sister Emma, natural daughter of Geoffrey of Anjou, Ralph of Diceto, I, 397–8; Pipe Roll 20 Henry II, 9, 16, 94.

[4] *Brut y Tywysogion*, 222; Brut y Saesson, 681; Ralph of Diceto, I, 384; Pipe Roll 20 Henry II, 21, 77, 121; Roger of Howden, *Gesta*, I, 74; Lloyd, *op. cit.*, II, 544 n.39.

[5] Roger of Howden, *Gesta*, I, 92.

in 1163. Henry seems to have moved cautiously. There was no repetition of his previously dictatorial attitude. It was 1177 before both sides were ready to reach a definitive settlement. In May of that year the king held a preliminary conference at Geddington, which was then adjourned to a full council meeting at Oxford in August. Royal writs summoned every Welshman of consequence to attend. And there, says Roger of Howden:

> the king of the English, Henry FitzEmpress, made over the land of Ellesmere to David king of north Wales; and David swore fealty and liege homage to his lord the king of the English, and swore to keep peace with the kingdom of the English. And likewise the king of the English gave the land of Merioneth to Rhys king of south Wales, and he too swore fealty and liege homage and promised to keep the peace.[1]

The constitutional relationship that emerges is clear. Henry II is formally accepted as overlord: the Welsh leaders swear oaths to him and the king exercises his right as overlord by bestowing fresh lands on Dafydd and Rhys. All the Welsh who attended had sworn fealty and promised to keep peace with Henry and his kingdom; but Dafydd and Rhys did more than this, significantly more: they swore not only fealty but liege homage too, and are referred to by the chronicler with the title of 'king'.[2] The implication is that they, and they alone, became the vassals of the English Crown, and that outside their own territories they exercised jurisdiction over the lesser native rulers.[3] The marcher barons, of course, would continue to owe allegiance to Henry. It was a curious situation, but not unparalleled: it was rather like India in the days of the British Raj.

It could not be expected that Wales itself would become a haven of peace: warfare as an instrument of dynastic ambition and economic advantage, or simply as an outlet for high spirits, was too deeply embedded in the social structure; but the preservation of peace with England – a feature of the oaths of 1177 – was observed for the rest of Henry's reign. It was not easy: there were alarms and excursions that could readily have led to bitterness and hostility. There was a serious incident in 1184 when the Welshmen of Gwent, seeking vengeance for a long remembered massacre, slew Ranulf Poer, who at the time was sheriff of Herefordshire. The justiciar, Ranulf Glanville, had to intervene to restore order. But Henry and the Welsh leaders remained calm

[1] Roger of Howden, *Gesta*, 159, 162; Lloyd, *op. cit.*, II, 552–3.

[2] Roger of Howden, *Gesta*, I, 162, *Chronica*, II, 134.

[3] For a further comment, and a comparison with the relationship between Henry II and the high-king of Ireland, *see* below, p.202 n.2.

and kept faith with each other. In 1179, for instance, a kinsman of Rhys who ruled in Maelienydd was murdered by followers of the heir to the Mortimer estates; but King Henry punished the perpetrators with severity.[1] As Rhys's sons grew to manhood they troubled with the ebullience of youth the delicate balance of their father's good relations with the king; but Rhys took care to come to Henry to apologise and to explain the difficulty he had in controlling them.[2]

Henry II's relations with the leaders of the Welsh were marked for eighteen years by good sense and goodwill. Wales, both native and marcher, was an acknowledged dependency of the English Crown. Henry II asked for no more. It was not in fact very much. Peace with England rested upon personalities, and the ties could easily be broken: within a few months of Henry's death Richard I's stupid mishandling of Rhys put the whole position in south Wales in jeopardy. There is little sign that the notion that the leading Welsh princes had become tenants-in-chief of the English Crown had really taken hold in Wales: no Welsh chronicler mentions the oaths of homage in 1177. Henry II had forged a link, but a frail one. He had really done no more than restore the kind of ascendancy his grandfather had had in Wales; but then, that was probably all that he wanted in the first place. Henry II had not solved the Welsh problem; he had shelved it. But if he built nothing enduring in Wales, to have recovered from the mistake of 1163 and to have held in check the dogs of war was no mean achievement.

(ii) *Scotland*

Malcolmus Dei gracia rex Scott, episcopis, abbatibus, comitibus, baronibus, iusticiis, viccomitibus, prepositis, ministris, omnibusque suis probis hominibus, Francis, Anglis, Scottis, salutem.[3] So reads the salutation clause of a charter from the first year of the reign of King Malcolm IV of Scotland (1153–65). It opens a window on to a rather different world from contemporary Wales or Ireland. Scotland had, by the grace of God, a king who united under his rule *Scotti*, the Picts and Scots of the predominantly Gaelic northern highlands, *Angli*, the Englishmen of Lothian – what had once been the Deiran province of the kingdom of Northumbria – and *Franci*, the Normans (or rather, men of north French origin) who within living memory had come to settle in the kingdom under the patronage of Scottish kings. The *Franci* stand first in the

---

[1] Lloyd, *op. cit.*, II, 567; Ralph of Diceto, I, 437–8; Pipe Roll 25 Henry II, 39.
[2] Lloyd, *op. cit.*, II, 568–9; Roger of Howden, *Gesta*, I, 314–17.
[3] *Regesta Regum Scottorum*, I, 175, no. 105.

order of greeting, for though as yet far from numerous they were dominant in the counsels of the king, in his administration, and in the cathedrals and abbeys of his kingdom. Had the salutation been more particular (as later ones sometimes were) it might have cited other peoples. Cumbria, a great swathe of country from the Clyde to the Lake District, still bore the impress of a British people, Brythonic Celts long cut off from their cousins in Wales, and penetrated somewhat, though slightly, by Northumbrians and Vikings. To the west of them was Galloway, the land of 'the foreign Gaels', Irishmen for the most part, but with a stiffening of Norse colonists. Scotland, in short, was a kingdom of diverse peoples and diverse cultural traditions, merging but not yet merged. Its unity was precarious: in particular Galloway was dissident and separatist, the far north distant and reactionary. 'Firm peace did not as yet sufficiently flourish in the kingdom,' said the chronicler of Melrose Abbey, writing an obituary of Malcolm IV; but the dynasty of Kenneth McAlpin had provided the one ruling house for the best part of a century and, though challenged and sometimes divided within itself, it was never to be overthrown.

Malcolm's salutation tells us more. It tells of a social élite of earls and barons, it professes an administrative organisation of justices, sheriffs, *praepositi* and *ministri*. We might be in Norman England. The impression is, however, something of an illusion. The titles of earl and baron sat incongruously on the shoulders of Gaelic *mormaer* and *tasech* and there were many places where the king's ministers, had they come with the king's writ, would have received short shrift. The kingship encompassed in the formulae of Malcolm's charters was, indeed, more of an intention than a fact; but it was an intention firmly planted by Malcolm's grandfather and predecessor on the throne, King David I (1124–53), and with every decade that passed the reality more nearly conformed.[1]

The Scots kings' patronage of Normans was no mere quirk of fashion: they knew Norman customs and Norman ways at first hand, and fashioned their monarchy on the model of Henry I's. Malcolm IV's father and his grandfather had held in their day the great midland earldom of Huntingdon, and had fought beside the best exponents of Norman warfare. Malcolm IV was rich in Norman blood: his mother was a Norman, his father's mother was granddaughter of the Conqueror's sister. All this was of great benefit to Henry II. It meant that

---

[1] Barrow, in his introduction to *Regesta Regum Scottorum*, I, 25, 89, warns against the assumption that an efficient chancery betokens an effective government, but adds that 'if it does not imply a strong king, it does imply a monarchy that meant business'.

when he negotiated with the ruler of Scotland he did not have to adjust himself to an alien tradition. It meant that Scotland was no disorderly region offering opportunities for private empire-building by adventurous Normans. It meant that those Normans who did seek their fortune there were settled in an orderly way, on landholding terms with

X Scotland

Note: The kingdom of Scotland is bounded by the heavy line which they were familiar, and without provocative disturbance to the native population. In all these respects Scotland offered a notable contrast to contemporary Wales, and even more so to contemporary Ireland; and in consequence Henry was never brought, as he was in Wales and Ireland, to the harsh necessity of personal intervention in the country's internal affairs.

Scotland did, however, present one problem, and a serious one. It is tempting to describe it as a border problem, but to do so would be misleading – at least if 'border' is made synonymous with 'frontier'. In this sense there was no demarcated border between England and Scotland until the sixteenth century.[1] Instead there was a very broad border area in which rights merged and jurisdiction overlapped. This came about because the Normans inherited from Anglo-Saxon kings a situation in the north that was curiously ill-defined. The familiar border from the Solway to the Tweed had no meaning for the Anglo-Saxons. Delvers into a fabled past could claim for kings of England an authority for a monarchy of all Britain.[2] More soberly the kings of Wessex who came to style themselves *Rex Anglorum* could claim jurisdiction over all Anglo-Saxons, and since there were Angles in plenty between the Tweed and the Forth, this would have set their authority at least to the foothills of the Highlands. But these kings' real power fell short even of the Tweed. Their power to control Northumbria, even southern Northumbria, was fitful and restricted. The old English state, in fact, was never successfully rounded off; it simply faded away north of the Humber in the east, and became lost beyond the Ribble in the west. *De facto* control of the ancient kingdom of Northumbria was disputed between the Danes who had pushed north from their stronghold at York, and the Scottish rulers of Strathclyde, who were eventually to draw into their hands the kingdom of all Scotland. The Scottish victory at Carham in 1018 proved decisive in this struggle and set a line of division between 'English Northumbria' (Northumberland) and 'Scottish Northumbria' (Lothian) at the lower reaches of the river Tweed, though inland the border petered out vaguely in the wilderness of Teviotdale. On the west the rulers of Strathclyde claimed authority over Cumbria. In the eleventh century the shires of Cumberland,

[1] Barrow has argued persuasively, in 'The Anglo-Scottish border', against the views that before 1237 the frontier fluctuated or was too vague to be called a frontier. It seems clear, indeed, that in the twelfth century it was possible to determine in practice a line of demarcation between the jurisdictions of the king of the English and the king of Scots; but this is not the same as saying that the frontier was fixed. Where it was in practice and where kings thought it ought to be could be two different things.

[2] Cf. Southern, *St Anselm and his Biographer*, 129–30.

Westmorland, and Lancashire did not exist, and the region known as Cumbria stretched south to Windermere and east to the 'Rere Cross' on Stainmore Common.[1] But it is extremely unlikely that Scottish kings exercised control over all of this; indeed it is unlikely that their influence was felt very far south of Carlisle. Here was a no-man's-land tamed only slowly in the course of the twelfth century. English kings made the best of the situation: they jibbed at Northumbrian independence but learned to tolerate its virtual self-government. They declined to abdicate their superior right to Lothian and Cumbria, and sometimes mounted compaigns, but accepted political facts and recognised the Scottish kings' standing there in return for an acknowledgement of their lordship.[2]

The Norman kings too had difficulty in controlling the north of England. The Domesday commissioners went no further than a line drawn, roughly, from the River Tees in the east to the River Esk in the Lake District, and that was probably about as far as consistently effective royal government went. The Conqueror's New Castle on the Tyne, founded in 1080, was very much an outpost of administration in an area that knew no firm peace. But royal influence was pushing forward, and in the days of King William Rufus the outposts were at Carlisle castle on the Solway and Norham castle on the Tweed.

These castles were built to command important river crossings on the only two practicable routes for an army passing from Scotland to England. Defence was necessary to guard against the kind of raids which King Malcolm Canmore (1058–93) had been accustomed to mount against English Northumbria. King Malcolm's espousal of the cause of Edgar Atheling gave his raids a political slant, but in fact he raided after the Norman seizure of the English throne much as he had raided before it, and his primary object was economic – the capture of peasants and livestock. There was hardly a homestead in Scotland, be it ever so humble, wrote Symeon of Durham, that had not a captive English handmaiden.[3]

No frontier was staked out clearly between Carlisle and Norham, but a frontier of sorts did nevertheless come to exist along the watershed

[1] Kirkby, 'Strathclyde and Cumbria', 91.
[2] Anderson, 'Anglo-Scottish relations', 2–10.
[3] Symeon of Durham, I, 192. Cf. Ritchie, *The Normans in Scotland*, 27–8: 'In the beggar my neighbour tactics the Scots had the less to lose and stood to gain, on balance, by seizure of livestock and transference of population for cheap labour. In Scotland there was land to spare for all. But land without cattle to stock it and labour to work it was valueless.'

of the Cheviots, if only because the Norman kings did not seek to enfeoff their men with land beyond it. It did not mark the limit of their aspirations to overlordship, but this line was in practice as far as they were prepared to attempt direct control. The reasons for this were probably military and logistic. In an effort to cow King Malcolm, William the Conqueror marched to Scotland in 1072 and learned on the way the difficulty of campaigning in the country and the impossibility of conquering it. Malcolm adopted the policy of retiring to the Highlands and drew his adversary as far as Abernethy on the river Tay before agreeing to compromise. It was a long march far from any secure base and William ran short both of time and supplies. It was a dangerous march too, with the impenetrable Highlands ever before him and the southern uplands crowding in to threaten his rear.[1] Carlisle and Norham were outposts of the known, and Norman kings prudently sought to know no more.

Nevertheless this extension of English government was something which Scottish kings were understandably reluctant to accept. For one thing, though the Tweed marked the limit of previous Scottish penetration of Northumbria, it did not mark the limit of their hopes. The dales of Northumberland were sparsely inhabited by English standards, and its moors inhospitable, but to a king who ruled too much mountain with the resources of too little lowland, its coastal plain seemed a Promised Land. History and the economics of power urged the Scots on to Hadrian's Wall. Nevertheless, political convenience obliged them for many years to accept the limits imposed by the Normans. Malcolm Canmore had to give thought to the precariousness of his monarchy. Possession of the Highlands was the key to the kingdom of Scotland; but possession had to be secured, and Malcolm's greatest source of power was Lothian. But Lothian lay within the claim to overlordship that the Normans inherited from Anglo-Saxon kings; they might not wish a campaign or a conquest, but the Conqueror's march to Abernethy showed what they were capable of if pressed. Rather than risk a direct challenge Malcolm preferred an arrangement that would leave him in undisputed possession of the lands that were necessary to his authority: so 'King Malcolm came and made peace with King William, and gave hostages, and was his man'.[2]

The succession struggle which followed Malcolm Canmore's death

---

[1] Ritchie, *op. cit.*, 29–34. Cf. the remarks of Richard of Hexham, 155, on King Stephen's invasion of Lothian in 1138: Stephen, he says, retired without giving battle, partly 'because his army lacked for food'.

[2] Anglo-Saxon Chronicle, 208 (AD 1072), cf. *ibid.*, 226–7 (AD 1091).

in 1093 provided a new basis for Norman influence in Scotland, for the right of sons to succeed to the father's inheritance was established there with Norman aid against the grain of Scottish tradition. The aid was repaid by homage, and by the open hand of welcome for Norman priests, Norman monks, and Norman knights. Ties of friendship were strengthened by Norman wives, and by the marriage of King Henry I of

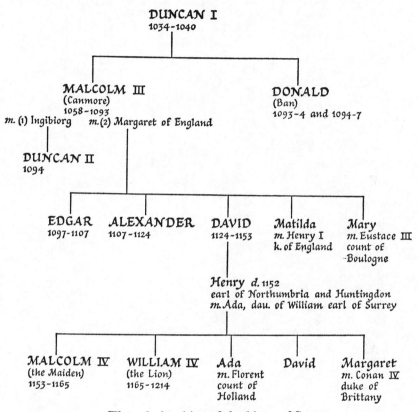

9. The relationships of the kings of Scots

England to Matilda, daughter of one Scottish king and sister to three others. For much of the earlier half of the twelfth century, indeed, the rulers of England and Scotland were members of an intimate family circle.[1]

Relations were made yet more harmonious by the Normanising policy and peculiar standing in England of King David (1124–53), the man who more than any other entrenched the monarchy of Scotland

[1] See Diagram 10; the relationships are analysed by Ritchie, *op. cit.*

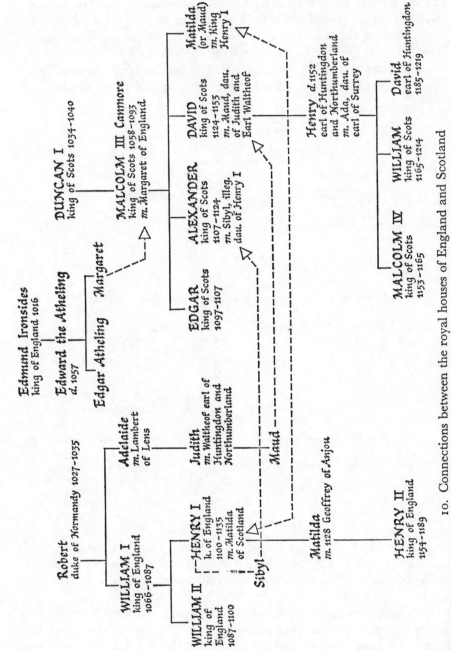

10. Connections between the royal houses of England and Scotland

and fashioned its government after the best European models. Before he became king, David was a man of power and authority both in Scotland and England. With Norman support he persuaded his brother King Alexander (1107–24) to allow him Cumbria and parts of Lothian as an appanage, and began the work, under the guidance of Norman counsellors, of colonising it with Norman settlers.[1] In 1113 King Henry I found for David, his brother-in-law, a wife in the widow of Simon de Senlis who brought him not only kinship with the family of the Conqueror (who was her grandmother's brother), and with the pre-eminent old English family of Earl Waltheof (her father), but also her inheritance of the splendid, sprawling Midland earldom and honor of Huntingdon. King Henry sealed for David a charter which confirmed him in possession of lands and rights in ten shires with liberties of surpassing privilege.[2] It was as David *comes* that [he began his Scottish charters before he became king, and as David *Dei gracia rex Scottorum* that he began his English charters after he became king.[3] And it was both as vassal king and premier earl that he held a place of honour at the court of King Henry I and was the first among laymen to take the oath to Empress Matilda as heiress to the throne of England in 1127.[4]

Yet close as was his intimacy with King David and close as were the links between King David's Normans and his own, King Henry would allow no trespass on his jurisdiction in the north: when a bishop of Glasgow took all Cumbria for his diocese and dedicated churches south of the Solway, Henry showed his displeasure by forcing through the creation of a bishopric at Carlisle.[5]

Few subjects have been so closely argued yet remained so dark as the precise nature and scope of the vassal relationship of the kings of Scotland to the kings of England. The only evidence is that of chroniclers; and the chronicle evidence is incomplete, imprecise, and not altogether trustworthy.[6] Shortly after Henry II had secured the

[1] Ailred of Rievaulx, Relatio de Standardo, 193; Ritchie, *op. cit.*, 125ff.

[2] Farrer, *Honours and Knights' Fees*, II, 296ff.; Barrow, introduction to *Regesta Regum Scottorum*, I, 99–100; cf. Richard I's confirmation of Henry I's charter, *Foedera*, I, Pt I, 48.

[3] *Early Scottish Charters*, e.g. no. xxxv; *Regesta Regum Scottorum*, I, 155, no. 37.

[4] William of Malmesbury, *Historia Novella*, 4–5; Symeon of Durham, II, 281–2. For further examples of King David's standing at the court of England *see* Anglo-Saxon Chronicle, 256.

[5] *Early Scottish Charters*, 269; cf. Robert de Torigny, 123; Henry of Huntingdon, 253. Symeon of Durham remarks, II, 277–8, that 'the river Tweed separates Northumbria and Lothian'.

[6] As an example compare the vague and divergent accounts of the relationship of Henry I and Alexander I. Anglo-Saxon Chronicle, 241 (AD 1107): 'In this year died

throne of England, in 1157 to be precise, Malcolm IV of Scotland, we are told, 'came to the king of England at Chester, and became his man, in such fashion as his grandfather had been the man of the older King Henry, saving all his dignities'.[1] In what fashion, then, was David the vassal of Henry I? We do not know; there is no direct evidence, and the interpretation of such indirect evidence as survives is complicated beyond unravelling by David's status as earl of Huntingdon. And what is meant by 'saving all his dignities'? We cannot be sure; but it is at least possible that the saving clause was intended to weaken the force of the oath of homage Malcolm made and to impart a deliberate quality of vagueness to the vassal relationship.[2] Oaths were sacred and words were dangerous and it behoved a man of property when swearing an oath not to pervert the past or prejudice posterity. The vassal status of the kings of Scotland was rooted, it seems, in ambiguity. We should not wonder at it. Medieval man frequently displayed, as Marc Bloch has reminded us, 'an admirable indifference to ambiguity'. 'Saving all his dignities' may be interpreted to mean 'with the exclusion of all those obligations commonly taken to be implicit in an oath of homage, but contrary to precedent in the relations of the kings of Scotland and England and derogatory to the dignity of a king'. And if this deprived the homage of most of its content, was that any great matter? Homage had been required and tendered in the first place to enable kings of England to save face and conserve their 'rights' in the matter of un-enforceable claims to territory, and to enable Scottish kings, who in fact held it, to do so in peace. There is nothing strange in this: feudal relationships were first instituted with the very similar purpose of regularising Charles Martel's sequestration of church lands for the sustenance of his mounted troops. Vassalage lacked precision until later medieval lawyers got to work codifying, systematising, and fossil-ising it; before then it meant what the parties were prepared to take it to mean. Its significance and implications would be determined by custom and precedent, by the nature of the personal relationship

King Edgar in Scotland . . . and Alexander his brother succeeded to the kingdom as King Henry granted him.' William of Malmesbury, *De Gestis Regum Anglorum*, II, 476: 'When King Edgar succumbed to his destined fate Henry allied himself to his successor, Alexander, giving him his illegitimate daughter in marriage.' The evidence is collected and discussed by Anderson, 'Anglo-Scottish relations'.

[1] Roger of Howden, *Chronica*, I, 216; Chronicle of Melrose, 76.

[2] The saving clause is discussed by Barrow, introduction to *Regesta Regum Scottorum*, I, 9–10, who holds that it was 'deliberately vague and undefined', and by Anderson, 'Anglo-Scottish relations', who suggests that the 'dignities' were 'the special privileges accorded to the Scottish king on his visits to England'.

between the parties, and by the practical considerations of what the lord could exact and the vassal bring himself to concede.

William Rufus is said to have tried to oblige Malcolm Canmore 'to do him justice in his own court, according to the judgement of his own barons alone; but Malcolm would in no way do this, unless upon the borders of their realms, where the kings of Scots were wont to do right by the kings of the English, and according to the decision of the chief men of both kingdoms'.[1] Here the lord is seen pushing a particular interpretation of vassalage, and the vassal resisting. Whether Malcolm Canmore's successors were constrained to greater subjection must remain an open question; but it seems likely that they went only as far as to concede an obligation to attend the overlord in war. King Alexander I led an army into Wales in 1114; King David joined the empress at the siege of Winchester in 1141; and Malcolm IV went with Henry II to Toulouse in 1159 and to Wales in 1165.[2]

It looks indeed very much as though the vassal relationship of the king of Scotland to the king of England was analogous to the vassal relationship of the kings of England to the kings of France. Kings of England who were dukes of Normandy did homage to the kings of France, they rendered military aid on occasion, but refused to pay relief (before the reign of John) and in case of dispute would meet the French court only at the Norman border – most commonly under an elm tree at Gisors. If the analogy can be pressed it would mean that the kings of Scotland were independent and sovereign within their kingdom but owed homage for additional lands they held of the English king. Though it is difficult to speak with certainty, something of the kind does seem to have been the situation: when the Scots kings did homage they did it for Cumbria and Lothian alone, not for Galloway, or for the kingdom of Scotland (*Scotia*) which was clearly understood in the twelfth century to be north of the Firth of Forth.[3] The kings of Scotland, in other words, were independent sovereigns in *Scotia* and

[1] Florence of Worcester, II, 31.

[2] *Brut y Tywysogion*, 292–3; Henry of Huntingdon, 275; Chronicle of Melrose, 76; *Annales Cambriae*, 50.

[3] Anderson, *Scottish Annals from English Chronicles*, 215 and n.3. Cf. the evidence from the reign of Malcolm IV collected by Barrow, introduction to *Regesta Regum Scottorum*, I, 39–40. Barrow suggests that Malcolm did homage only for land held south of the Tweed, i.e., for Huntingdon; but this seems improbable. Roger of Howden, for example, notes of the homage of William the Lion after the Treaty of Falaise of 1175, that the king of Scots became the vassal of Henry II for all the land he held, 'and expressly for Scotland and Galloway', *Gesta*, I, 95 – the clear implication being that these two regions alone (and not Lothian) had previously been excluded from oaths of homage. Cf. also Gerald of Wales, VIII, 156–7.

overlords without superior in the distinct region of Galloway, but held
Lothian and Cumbria by formal concession of the kings of England
as freely and with such dignity as the kings of England held Normandy
of the kings of France.

Unfortunately this sane and realistic arrangement was compromised
by King David during the disordered reign of Stephen. King David's
policy towards England during these years has been described by a
Scottish historian as 'purely selfish'.[1] This seems a little harsh. David
was steadfast in his oath to Matilda and in his refusal to accept Stephen
as lawful king, even though this jeopardised the honor of Huntingdon.
He gave direct help to the Angevin cause on two occasions: in 1141 he
personally joined Matilda and escaped only with difficulty from the
débâcle at Winchester; and in 1149 he gave hospitality to the young
Henry of Anjou, knighted him, and joined him in an abortive campaign against York. But quite independently of the empress and her
son, David mounted three major invasions of northern England, one
in 1136 and two in 1138, and it is beyond reasonable doubt that their
sole purpose was the acquisition of lands the Scots had long coveted.[2]
David's first invasion took place before the arrival of the empress and
the beginning of civil war. He declined to give battle whenever Stephen
offered it, and suffered a serious reverse at the hands of local defence
forces at the so-called Battle of the Standard in 1138; but his invasions
showed what destruction he was capable of bringing to the north.
Indeed the depredations of his army, particularly of the wild men of
Galloway, struck a chord of deep horror in contemporary choniclers.
The defence of the north was a problem Stephen would perhaps have
preferred to avoid, had it not been that some of his firmest supporters
were there. After trying unsuccessfully to come to grips with the
Scots, he was ready to make a compromise to secure peace. David drove
hard bargains. He was allowed in 1136 to retain Carlisle, and subsequently strengthened the castle there and used it as a base for the control
of Cumberland.[3] His conscience would not allow him to do homage to

---

[1] Hume Brown, *History of Scotland*, I, 87.

[2] David's first invasion took place before the empress landed in England. The
invasions of 1138 were probably preceded by a call to arms (*Gesta Stephani*, 35–6) but
would probably have been launched even without an appeal from the empress for
they were intended to oblige Stephen to honour his earlier promise to make over
Northumbria to the Scots, *see* Richard of Hexham, 150–1. David's proclamation of
support for Matilda may have been intended to win over those of his Norman friends
and vassals who were reluctant to wage war in England; but if so, he did not succeed
with all of them, cf. Ailred of Rievaulx, Relatio de Standardo, pp. 192–5.

[3] Richard of Hexham, 146; Chronicle of the Canons of Huntingdon in *Early Sources
of Scottish History*, II, 201; John of Hexham, 306. David also disputed with the earl of

Stephen, but his conscience raised no objection to allowing his son Henry to do homage, so Stephen was induced in 1136 to revive for him the long dormant earldom of Northumbria.[1] Henry of Scotland was thereafter in attendance at Stephen's court – until 1141, that is, when his father broke the terms of the treaty by joining the empress in war, and the earldom of Huntingdon was forfeited.[2]

David clearly came to regard Northumbria as subject to himself and intervened in it to confirm charters there: 'David by the grace of God king of Scots,' he writes from Newcastle, 'to his justices and sheriffs and all his barons French, English, and Northumbrian, greeting.'[3] When in 1152 Earl Henry died, David promoted his grandson to succeed: 'and he brought William to Newcastle, and took hostages from the chief men of Northumbria, making them all subject to the dominion of that child'.[4]

David's self-assurance in giving Northumbria to his grandson was no doubt strengthened by a promise he had extracted – and extracted is probably the right word – from Henry FitzEmpress in 1149 just before he knighted him. 'Now that Henry son of Empress Matilda was sixteen and in the care of the court of David, king of Scots and his maternal uncle,' writes Roger of Howden, 'he was knighted by King David at Carlisle, having first sworn on oath that should he become king of England he would hand over Newcastle and the whole of Northumbria to him, and allow him and his to possess in peace and without challenge for ever all the land that lies between the River Tweed and the River Tyne.'[5]

Chester control of the honor of Lancaster, and exercised some control there from *c.* 1141–9, Cronne, 'The honour of Lancaster in Stephen's reign'; Barrow, 'King David I and the honor of Lancaster'; John of Hexham, 322–3.

[1] Henry of Huntingdon, 259; Richard of Hexham, 177–8. Stephen, however, according to Richard of Hexham, retained the towns of Newcastle and Bamburgh, and allowed Henry no jurisdiction over the lands of St Cuthbert of Durham or St Andrew of Hexham; cf. Barrow, introduction to *Regesta Regum Scottorum*, I, 109–10.

[2] Richard of Hexham, 178; Henry of Huntingdon, 265. Stephen had not the power, however, to sequestrate Northumbria, and Henry continued to call himelf *comes* or *comes Northumbriorum* until his death in 1152, *Early Scottish Charters*, nos cxc, ccxlvi, cclvii. But if Henry were nominally earl, the real power belonged to King David, and William of Newburgh spoke of realities when he wrote, I, 70, that 'the northern districts as far as the river Tees remained in peace through that king's efforts'. That king's efforts, however, extended to protracted but ultimately unsuccessful attempts to gain control of the lands of St Cuthbert by intruding his chancellor, William Cumin, into the bishopric of Durham, Symeon of Durham, I, 143–4, 161–4.

[3] *Regesta Regum Scottorum*, I, no. 30, and p. 109.   [4] John of Hexham, 327.

[5] Roger of Howden, *Chronica*, I, 211. The story was not, apparently, widely known, for it is reported in no other chronicle save that of William of Newburgh, I, 70, who

When he became king, Henry was thus faced with a disagreeable choice: he had either to break his oath or abandon his principle that the realm should stand as it had stood in his grandfather's day. He chose to break his oath. David died in 1153 and when King Malcolm IV appeared before Henry to do homage at Chester in 1157 it was put to him that 'the king of England ought not to be defrauded of so large a part of his kingdom, nor could he suffer to be deprived of it'. Malcolm was then sixteen or seventeen years of age and sat yet insecurely on the throne; and so 'prudently considering that the king of England had the better of the argument by reason of his much greater power' he submitted. Cumberland, Westmorland and Northumbria were restored to the English Crown.[1] Malcolm was then given the earldom of Huntingdon, as his grandfather had held it from the older Henry, but his brother William was reduced to the lordship of Tynedale.[2]

Though he may well have considered it a great achievement, King David had made a serious mistake in departing from the treaty arrangements of 1139 and treating Northumbria as dependent on the Scottish Crown in the same way as Cumbria and Lothian were. There might have been a greater chance of retaining a foothold south of the Tweed if he had offered to hold Northumbria and the district of Carlisle as a vassal of Henry FitzEmpress on the same terms as the honor of Huntingdon had been held. But if David can be accused of over-reaching himself, King Henry can be accused of too dogmatic an insistence on the restoration of the kingdom to what it had been on the day of his grandfather's death. Prudence, charity, conscience even, should have prompted him to enfeoff William with the earldom of Northumbria, even if he had first demanded its surrender. But there had been no earl there in his grandfather's day, only a sheriff, and Henry Fitz-Empress would have his sheriff. Henry indeed made the same mistake in regard to Scotland as he made in regard to Wales in the first decade or so of his reign. Restoration, simple restoration on the basis of patent facts of the past, was the sum of his policy, with too little sensitivity to the inner subtleties of his grandfather's attitude. Woven into the

---

speaks of it as hearsay: 'Having first, it is said, given security that he would never deprive David's heirs of any portion of the lands which had passed from England to the dominion of that king.'

[1] William of Newburgh, I, 105–6; Chronicle of Holyrood, 32; *Early Sources of Scottish History*, II, 235 n.2.

[2] For Huntingdon in this period *see* Barrow, introduction to *Regesta Regum Scottorum*, I, 10, 105ff.; for Tynedale see *ibid.*, I, 10, 111, and Anderson, *Early Sources of Scottish History*, II, 235 n.2. Simon de Senlis, to whom Stephen granted Huntingdon after Earl Henry's forfeiture, died conveniently in 1153.

fabric of Anglo-Scottish relations in Henry I's day were friendship, mutual respect, generosity, family ties and the loyalties of intimacy. All these were lacking in Henry II's relations with Malcolm IV and his brother William. When the two kings met again at Carlisle in 1158, Henry declined to make Malcolm a knight – something on which he had set his heart; Malcolm could not with decency ask anyone else for the coveted honour, and he was made to wait two years for it.[1] How far good relations had decayed is revealed in 1163 when King Malcolm was summoned to attend King Henry at Woodstock, together with the Welsh princes, and was required not only to renew his homage but to surrender hostages, including his youngest brother David, 'that peace might be preserved'.[2] A. O. Anderson has suggested that this fortified oath was demanded because Malcom was in ill-health and Henry was taking precautions against the succession of his brother William.[3] But it is conceivable that Henry was alarmed at signs of alienation on Malcolm's part, reflected in the promotion of foreign marriage alliances – between his sister Margaret and Duke Conan of Brittany in 1160, and his sister Ada and the Count of Holland in 1162.[4]

However this may be, Anderson seems to be right in suggesting antipathy between Henry II and William of Scotland. Malcolm died childless – indeed unmarried – in 1165 and William succeeded to the Scottish throne; and within a year the two kings were at loggerheads – about what is not known. Indeed nothing at all would be known of the quarrel – such is the frailty of the evidence – were it not for a revealing passage in a piece of private correspondence. In a letter attributable to 1166 someone – it was probably John of Salisbury – wrote to Archbishop Becket:

> ... I heard that when the king was at Caen and was vigorously debating the matter of the king of Scotland, he broke out in abusive language against Richard du Hommet for seeming to speak somewhat in the king of Scotland's favour, calling him a manifest traitor. And the king, flying into his usual temper, flung his cap from his head, pulled off his belt, threw off his cloak and clothes, grabbed the silken coverlet off the couch, and sitting as it might be on a dung heap started chewing pieces of straw.[5]

---

[1] Cf. Barrow, introduction to *Regesta Regum Scottorum*, I, 10, 12, and Ritchie, *The Normans in Scotland*, 350 n.2.

[2] Robert de Torigny, 218; cf. Chronicle of Holyrood, 40, Ralph of Diceto, I, 311.

[3] Anderson, 'Anglo-Scottish relations', 17; the implication presumably being that William smarted with resentment at the loss of the earldom of Northumbria.

[4] Cf. Barrow, *op. cit.*, I, 13, and Ritchie, *op. cit.*, 353.

[5] *Materials for the History of Becket*, VI, 72.

Whatever the excess of Henry's passion, it seems to have had some justification, for in 1168 we catch another glimpse of King William in John of Salisbury's correspondence, proposing an alliance with King Louis of France.[1] Only the reconciliation of Louis and Henry in January 1169, it seems, averted it.

Yet there are signs that by 1170 Henry was moderating his attitude to the king of Scots as he was softening and reframing his policy towards the Welsh princes. King William and David his brother attended the coronation of the Young King at Easter that year, and Henry took them on to Windsor where at Pentecost he knighted David.[2] Small evidence, perhaps, yet clearly Henry blew less fiercely. The Welsh princes, it will be recalled, used the outbreak of the great war in 1173 to demonstrate a warm response; but not King William. Perhaps he had less need than they, but certainly he had a grievance yet to settle. Let the king, he said, restore to him 'the province of the Northumbrians'. Ralph of Diceto who tells the tale reports that William 'met with a refusal'.[3] The Young Henry, in eager rebellion, more readily consented, bartering for William's aid 'the whole of Northumbria as far as the Tyne'.[4] But William was unlucky. Not only had he backed a loser, he had taken up arms against the man whom St Thomas of Canterbury himself was prepared to forgive and protect. Or so it seemed. On the very day that Henry II did penance at the martyr's tomb, William was captured by a small party of loyalists who emerged from a mist to find him sporting on horseback in a field before Alnwick.[5] He was led, with his feet tied beneath the belly of his horse, to King Henry at Northampton, and carried to captivity in Normandy.

With the war won, Henry dictated to William the terms of a harsh peace. His release from prison was secured by a treaty made at Falaise and ratified at York in 1175:

This is the agreement and treaty which William, king of Scots, made with his lord king Henry, the son of Matilda the empress. William, king of Scots, has become the liegeman of the lord king Henry against every man in respect of Scotland and in respect of all his other lands; and he has done

---

[1] *Materials for the History of Becket*, VI, 458.
[2] Roger of Howden, *Gesta*, I, 4; Chronicle of Melrose, 81–2.
[3] Ralph of Diceto, I, 376.
[4] Roger of Howden, *Gesta*, I, 45, *Chronica*, II, 47.
[5] William of Newburgh, I, 183–5; Roger of Howden, *Gesta*, I, 67, *Chronica*, II, 63–4; Jordan Fantosme, 350–2. For the intervention of St Thomas *see* e.g. Edward Grim, II, 447, Roger of Howden, *Gesta*, I, 72, *Early Sources of Scottish History*, II, 284–91, Ritchie, *op. cit.*, 350 n.1.

fealty to him as his liege lord, as all the other men of the lord king are wont to do. . . .

And all the bishops and abbots and clergy of the king of Scots and their successors shall do fealty to the lord king Henry as their liege lord, in the same way as the lord's other bishops are wont to do. . . . And the king of Scots, and David his brother, and his barons and other men, have granted to the lord king Henry that the Scottish church shall make submission to the English church as it ought to do, and as it was wont to do in the time of the lord king's predecessors . . . .

The earls also and barons, and such other men holding land from the king of Scots as the lord king Henry may select, shall do homage to the lord king Henry as against all men, and shall swear fealty to him as their liege lord, in the same way as his other men are wont to do. . . . In order that this treaty and pact may be faithfully kept by the king of Scots and his heirs, the king of Scots has delivered to the lord king Henry the castle of Roxburgh, and the castle of Berwick, and the castle of Jedburgh, and the castle of Edinburgh, and the castle of Stirling, to be held by the lord king Henry at his pleasure. And the king of Scots shall pay for the garrison of these castles out of his own revenue at the pleasure of the lord king Henry. . . .

Furthermore, the bishops, earls, and barons have covenanted with the lord king Henry . . . that if the king of Scots shall by any mischance default in his fealty to the lord king Henry, and shall thus break the aforesaid agreement, then they will hold to the lord king Henry as their liege lord, against the king of Scots and against all men hostile to the lord king Henry. And the bishops shall place the land of the king of Scots under interdict until he returns to the fealty of the lord king Henry. . . .[1]

Yet harsh as was the tone of the treaty and rigid as were its stipulations, Henry did not in practice bear down hard on King William and his kingdom. The Treaty of Falaise – or more especially its formal ratification in the cathedral church of York – seems rather to have been a public penance, a political humiliation, than the opening of a new chapter in Anglo-Scottish relations. Hardest to bear, perhaps, was Henry's hold on the key castles of Lothian; but apart from this Henry did not press the rights that the treaty gave him. The intended subjection of the Scottish church was allowed to become lost in argument over the meaning of the phrase that it should make such submission 'as it ought to do, and as it was wont to do in the time of the lord king's predecessors'. So far as is known he intervened only three times as

[1] Roger of Howden, *Gesta*, I, 96–9; *Anglo-Scottish Relations, 1174–1328*, 1–5.

overlord in Scotland's internal affairs and each time probably by invitation: once to repulse the offer of dissident Glaswegians that 'he should receive them in his hand and remove them from the servitude of the king of Scotland'; once to issue a writ of protection, no doubt at the request of the monks, for Dunfermline Abbey; and once to arbitrate in a dispute between King William and two of his bishops.[1]

William behaved correctly and Henry relented. From the chronicles it appears that William was frequently in attendance at the English court and that better relations developed. In 1185 King Henry restored to him the honor of Huntingdon 'as honourably and fully as he had had it before the war', and this despite the fact that there were many who badgered Henry with their claims to the earldom.[2] And William came to Henry and sought of him the hand in marriage of his granddaughter Maud, who had Henry the Lion of Saxony for her father, 'And the king of England replied that, God willing, the matter would go well, but that the pope must be consulted; and with his consent the matter should be concluded most gladly'.[3] The consent of the Church was necessary because young Maud was William's niece. It was not forthcoming; but King Henry found for William another bride less consanguineous in Ermengard, daughter of the viscount of Beaumont and great granddaughter of King Henry I by one of that monarch's beloved illegitimate children. Troth was plighted amid expressions of benediction and friendship on Henry's part, and the nuptials were celebrated under his auspices and in his chapel at Woodstock by the archbishop of Canterbury. He released Maiden's Castle to William that he might bestow it in dower upon his wife, and then retired discreetly to another residence, while William and his bride were feasted at Woodstock at his expense.[4] Finally, in 1188, King William made so bold as to offer his overlord 4,000 marks for the release of the castles which remained in his hand and King Henry expressed himself well disposed to consider it if William would contribute a tithe from his kingdom for the Holy Land. William pressed his barons to agree, but they were adamant in refusing 'even if the king of England and their lord the king of Scotland swore that they would have it'.[5] And so the matter stood, but not for long, for within the year Henry lay dead, and William purchased release from all the treaty obligations from Henry's improvident son Richard.

---

[1] Roger of Howden, *Gesta*, I, 67–8, 79–80, 276–7, *Chronica*, II, 63; Barrow, 'A writ of Henry II for Dunfermline abbey'.

[2] Chronicle of Melrose, 93–4; Roger of Howden, *Gesta*, I, 357.

[3] Roger of Howden, *Gesta*, I, 313–14.   [4] *Ibid.*, I, 347–8, 350–1.

[5] *Ibid.*, II, 44–5.

It would probably be a mistake to regard the Treaty of Falaise as representing Henry's basic intentions towards the Scots. In practice he sought to gain no real advantage from it. It was the ransom price for William the Lion's release from captivity; in selling it back to him all that Richard I did was to realise the asset. If we remove the treaty from consideration as merely the temporary consequence of William's invasion, it becomes clear that the chief interest of Henry II's Scottish policy is that it was extremely limited. It seems clear indeed that his attitude towards the Scots was entirely determined by their attitude towards him. There were only two positive elements in his policy. One of these was simply to remove the Scots from the territory they had occupied in Stephen's reign, and to keep them off. In this respect the Treaty of Falaise was merely a guarantee of good behaviour. The other positive element in his policy was closely linked to the first: it was to achieve formal recognition of what Henry took to be the historic rights of the kings of England. It may be that the form of allegiance which Henry demanded from Malcolm IV in 1163 was unprecedented; but that is not to say that Henry was attempting to expand or develop his inherited rights by covert means: he was simply trying to put a defini-tion on an ambiguity. Dislike of ambiguity and an impatient insistence on clarification were characteristic of Henry II in his earlier years; only a more mature flexibility enabled him to escape from the trouble it almost always provoked.

(iii) *Ireland*

William of Newburgh remarks, in the course of his *Historia Rerum Anglicarum*, that politically speaking Ireland at the time of the Norman invasion was very like Britain in days of old.[1] It is an acute observation. The Irish *ard ri* (or 'high-king') was indeed very like an old English *Bretwalda* ('Britain-ruler') in the days of the Heptarchy. Ireland, it could be said, had stuck at this stage of political development: it had produced no one comparable to the West Saxon kings who had trans-formed the old *Bretwaldaship* into a monarchy of England. But what, understandably, William of Newburgh failed to see, was that the differences were more important than the similarities between the two situations.

Ireland exhibited to an unusual degree the Celtic characteristic of social conservatism. This was perhaps the product of its prehistory. Archaeology may one day tell us more than we know at present about

[1] William of Newburgh, I, 167.

the settlement of the Celts in Ireland; but subsequent history suggests
that they were not numerous enough entirely to displace, either gene-
tically or in influence, the existing non-Indo-European population.[1]
It may be that the fusion of the two peoples was finally accomplished
only on the basis of elaborate compromises, compromises that long
continued to affect the social structure, *mores*, and in particular the
laws of Irish society. Twelfth-century popes were to denounce the
Irish as an 'ignorant and barbarous people' who needed to have true
Christian doctrine expounded to them; as an 'undisciplined' and 'untamed' people who practised things which put their souls in peril.[2]
They did so in the face of a past history of cultural achievement and
missionary zeal second to none in the Dark Ages, and of a recent history
of flourishing monastic reform under the aegis of St Malachy and the
Cistercians. But papal horror is easily explained by Irish laws which,
for example, accepted eight forms of marriage and sanctioned easy
divorce and concubinage.[3] The reluctance to adapt the ancient laws
to Christian teaching, the reluctance indeed to admit any change in
the law save by tortuous 'interpretation', testifies to its essential place
as the basis of the social order. It was the necessary corollary to the
fragmentation of political authority so characteristic of the Celtic
polity.

In the early years of the twelfth century, however, there were signs
that political authority in Ireland might be transformed by escaping
altogether from the trammels of Irish law. Though it is hard to descry
its features it seems that the province kingship was becoming something
more than a tribal kingship writ large, and that a monarchy of all
Ireland might emerge that transcended the narrow bounds of the old
high-kingship with its primacy that was little more than one of honour
symbolised by the payment of tribute. There was an attempt, certainly,
to follow the Anglo-Saxons in the transformation of kingship from
military leadership into monarchical authority, but the difficulties
were almost insuperable. In the development of monarchical authority
the Anglo-Saxon king had two advantages denied to his Irish counterpart: he had the active assistance of an ecclesiastical hierarchy and he
was master of the law which his courts enforced. Anglo-Saxon law was
always cruder than Irish law; even in its most developed state it never
achieved the sophistication of Irish law, it never had glossators, it was
never professionalised with a corps of learned interpreters. In theory

[1] De Beer, 'Genetics and prehistory'.
[2] *See* below, p. 197.
[3] Binchy, 'The linguistic and historical value of the Irish law tracts', esp. 218–20.

Anglo-Saxon customary law was as immutable as the Irish; but it remained in the more malleable form of collective memory. The so-called laws of the Anglo-Saxon kings were strictly speaking nothing more than royal ordinances of human origin and temporary application; but in practice, from the earliest days of the written record, Anglo-Saxon kings were able to manipulate law so as to shape and transform the communities they ruled. Of course, the law-making of Anglo-Saxon kings was frequently inhibited by the restraining influence of the council of the elders (the *witan*), or by practical possibilities in the matter of enforcing law; but an Anglo-Saxon king had no competitors in the application of law to social problems as an Irish king did in the professional law-minders (*brehons*). Since Celtic law was the bedrock of a society that knew no other form of security, the immutability of law became an article of faith among its exponents. It was even given a spurious religious sanction: 'This then is Patrick's law,' says the introduction to the collection of laws known as the *Senchas Mar*, 'and no mortal jurist among the Irish is competent to rescind anything he shall find in it.'[1]

The Romanised English Church helped the Anglo-Saxon monarchy in several ways: it tended to favour a strong kingship as the guarantee of peace and order; it tended to favour a unified government because it facilitated church government; it cut across and tended to diminish provincial exclusiveness; and its ceremony of coronation helped to minimise the dangers of competing contenders for power. By contrast the Irish Church had been tribalised, and jurisdictional authority resided not in the bishops (who possessed only the power to bless and consecrate) but in the abbots (frequently hereditary) of the tribal monasteries.

Thus an Irish king was seriously handicapped by a three-fold division of authority within the community he supposedly ruled. He was without peer (though he probably had rivals) in his control over the politico-military aspects of the community's life; but its religious life was exclusively controlled by the abbots, while the *brehons*, through their guardianship of the law, controlled its social and economic structure. That Irish communities were in practice ruled not by monarchies but by triarchies is to be inferred from the equal status accorded in the laws to king, abbot, and chief *brehon*. It meant that an Irish king who aspired to the creation of a European-type monarchy had to contend not merely with rivals and political opponents, but with a fundamental social conservatism defended by deeply entrenched vested interests.

[1] *Ibid.*, 209.

Where the inspiration for change came from in early twelfth-century Ireland is difficult to say for certain, but it can probably be attributed to some of the Irish bishops. The creation of European-type monarchies was the best chance they had for the creation of European-type bishoprics. Their lack of jurisdictional authority had long been odd; in the

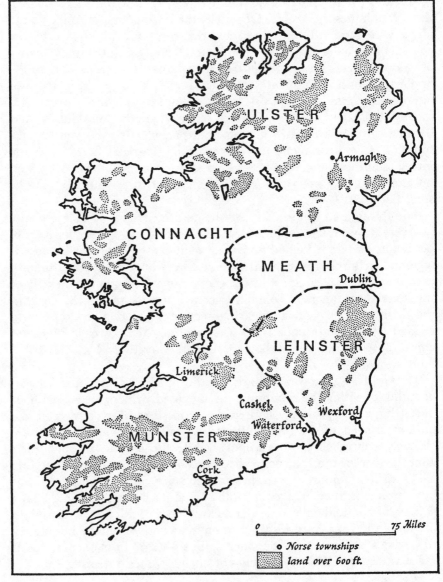

XI Ireland

post-Hildebrandine church of Rome it was incredible. There were a few bishops in Ireland, however, who were emancipated from Irish custom – the bishops of the Norse settlements in Dublin, Wexford, Waterford, Cork, and Limerick. Ever since the church reform movement in Europe had exalted the notion of sacramental grace, these bishops had been in the habit of slipping over to England for consecration by the archbishop of Canterbury, for Canterbury was the nearest place they could be sure of having it done properly. It is highly significant that King Murchetach O'Brien, who came nearest to establishing an all-Ireland monarchy early in the twelfth century, chose to form an alliance with such bishops.[1] He himself sent men over to England for consecration, and even brought back Irishmen who had taken service abroad to be bishops in Ireland. [He rescued the chief religious centre at Armagh from monastic control, and summoned synods to attempt the reorganisation of the Irish Church.[2] Unfortunately these attempts failed. The reforms proposed, laudable enough in themselves, did not take hold. The papacy tried to help in 1152 and sent a legate to hold a synod at Kells, but this failed too. Demarcating dioceses and propounding canon law did not by itself suffice to dissolve a centuries-old habit of mind.[3] The native attempts at ecclesiastical reform failed for lack of a strong monarchy to break the power of vested interests in the *status quo*. Murchetach O'Brien's promising attempt collapsed with his death in 1119. It was not, however, the last. Indeed the bitterness of the struggle for power in the twelfth century – a bitterness wholly foreign to Irish tradition – is best explained as the reflection of a struggle between modernisers and traditionalists. The kings of Munster and Leinster (those most in touch with the outside

---

[1] In the spelling of Irish names I follow the practice of Curtis, *A History of Medieval Ireland*.

[2] For example, it was he who nominated Samuel Oh-Aingli to be bishop of Dublin and sent him over to England to be consecrated by Archbishop Anselm in 1096. It was he who asked Anselm to consecrate as bishop of Waterford a man of Irish birth who had taken service with the bishop of Winchester. It was with his support that Armagh passed under the control of a man who was episcopally ordained. It was under his aegis (and, indeed, under his presidency) that the synod of Cashel was held in 1101, and that of Rathbreasail in 1111. *See* Gwynn, 'The first bishops of Dublin', 17–18, and 'The first synod of Cashel', 82.

[3] Eighteen years after Rathbreasail an obituary of Archbishop Celsus of Armagh describes him as having died 'after ordaining bishops and priests and persons of every grade, and after the consecration of many churches and cemeteries', and in these words reveals the persistence of the notion that a bishop's function was to bless rather than to rule a diocese; cf. Gwynn, 'The first bishops of Dublin', 24, and 'The centenary of the synod of Kells', 250–1.

world) were prominent among the modernisers, while the kings of Connacht found themselves leading the forces of reaction. This is doubtless why the annals are so prejudiced against kings such as Murchetach MacLochlainn of Munster and Dermot MacMurrough of Leinster: they were trying to change things, and the annals were written by those arch-apostles of conservatism – monks.

The collapse of Murchetach MacLochlainn's power in 1161 left his ally King Dermot militarily as well as politically vulnerable, and eventually the king of Connacht drove him out of Dublin. Dermot's response was to seek help from England. There were two precedents for this. One was the example of Scotland. In Scotland, too, at the beginning of the century, there had been a struggle between 'modernisers' and 'traditionalists'. It had expressed itself in a struggle for the succession to King Malcolm Canmore between the sons of Malcolm and their uncle Donaldbane. The conservatives under Donaldbane had briefly triumphed; but the sons of Malcolm had returned from exile to recover the throne, sustained and strengthened by help from the Normans of England. The second precedent was provided by King Murchetach O'Brien himself. He had allied himself with the Normans in Wales by marrying his daughter to Arnulf of Montgomery, lord of Pembroke. Unfortunately King Murchetach's Norman friends became involved in a conspiracy against King Henry I and King Murchetach himself became so suspect to King Henry that Archbishop Anselm had to mediate a reconciliation.[1] King Dermot was more tactful: he sought the king of England's approval first.

Dermot found Henry II in Aquitaine early in 1167.[2] Armed with letters patent from Henry giving him permission to recruit freelances, he set himself up in Bristol where he could catch the news from Ireland, and spent a few months touting for help among the barons of the Welsh March. By the summer of 1167 he was back in Ireland with a bodyguard of Flemish mercenaries and some promises of aid. Those who subsequently went to join him in Ireland were surprisingly few in number. First went Robert FitzStephen, son of the Norman castellan of Cilgerran and of Nest, daughter of Rhys ap Tewdwr, former mistress of King Henry I, as promiscuous as she was reputedly beautiful, and

---

[1] Gwynn, 'The origins of St Mary's abbey, Dublin', 119–21; Nelson, *The Normans in South Wales*, 118–21.

[2] Or possibly at Christmas 1166. Henry was then at Poitiers and subsequently went into Gascony. Gerald of Wales says, V, 227, that Dermot found him 'in remotis et transmarinis Aquitannicae Galliae partibus'; cf. *The Song of Dermot and the Earl*, lines 268–9.

mother of a vast progeny of Norman-Welsh half-breeds. He was a captive of Rhys of Deheubarth when news of Dermot's appeal was spread abroad, but begged his freedom with a promise to leave the country. He gathered together a small group which was virtually a family party of Nest's descendants: his half-brother Maurice FitzGerald, with his sons and nephews, the Barry brothers and the Cogans, and his brother-in-law Hervey de Montmaurice, 'a man of broken fortunes, without equipment or money'.[1] They went over in 1169, and were joined a year or so later by a more notable figure from the Welsh March – Richard son of Gilbert de Clare, first earl of Pembroke. Richard FitzGilbert was down on his luck. His father had helped Henry I to the throne, had held extensive lands in Kent and Sussex, had been made earl of Pembroke by King Stephen in 1138, and inherited the lordship of Strigoil from an uncle. But Richard (who succeeded his father in 1148) had been one of the few marcher barons to persist in support of Stephen after the empress raised her banner at Bristol. This mistake, and the Welsh *revanche* of those years, had cost him dearly. He probably lost the title of earl of Pembroke after Henry II gained the throne: his contemporaries called him 'earl of Strigoil', or, more familiarly, 'Strongbow'. As Gerald of Wales put it, 'his pedigree was longer than his purse', and it was in the hope of recouping his dwindled fortunes that he gave an ear to King Dermot's pleas for help.[2] He was fearful, however, of making another mistake, and went to Ireland only on the understanding that Dermot would give him his daughter in marriage and the reversion of his kingdom.

Though few in number Dermot's allies had the advantage of military techniques that baffled or terrified his Irish opponents – the continental device of the motte-and-bailey fort, and the combination, learned in the Welsh March, of skirmishing archers, disciplined footmen, and mounted knights.

It was enough to swing the balance – just. Dermot suppressed his rebellious subjects, drove his rivals out of Leinster, and began to aspire to the high-kingship.[3] But in 1171 Dermot died. He had given his daughter to Strongbow as he promised, and Strongbow claimed

[1] Gerald of Wales, V, 230. Gerald was himself a grandson of Nest, and one of the Barry brothers: see the genealogical tables in *English Historical Documents*, II, 996, and Barnard, *Strongbow's Conquest of Ireland*, 193.

[2] Gerald of Wales, V, 228, 246–7. Richard FitzGilbert was a cousin of King Malcolm IV and King William I of Scotland: his mother was their aunt, Anderson, *Early Sources of Scottish History*, II, 269.

[3] For the details of the Norman invasion *see* Orpen, *Ireland under the Normans*, I, 141ff.

Leinster as his heir. It was a claim which had no force in Irish law; but what was Irish law to men whose fortunes rested on the points of their lances? It was an awkward moment, however, for the Normans: they found themselves virtually alone, pinned to the coastal ports, and with Strongbow besieged in Dublin by Rory O'Connor, king of Connacht. Strongbow was prudent: he offered to submit if King Rory would allow him to hold Leinster as his vassal; but Rory would allow him only the Norse townships of Dublin, Waterford, and Wexford. In desperation the small band of Normans sallied forth from the fort at Dublin and routed King Rory's army on the banks of the Liffey. A few weeks later, on 18 October 1171, King Henry II landed at Waterford and demanded everyone's submission.

Henry's motives in going to Ireland are not easy to divine. Most contemporary chroniclers knew little about Ireland, and wrote less. Gervase of Canterbury offers an explanation. Henry, he says, was invited both by the Irish and by Strongbow. The Irish 'finding it impossible to prevail over soldiers who, although fewer in number than themselves, were braver and more skilful, sent envoys to the king of the English begging him to come to Ireland, and by taking over the lordship of the country preserve them from the ruthlessness of Earl Richard'. Strongbow, fearing that the king's hostility might persuade him to accept, also sent messengers proffering his submission if the king would allow him to hold what he had won, as his vassal. Henry, Gervase adds, was susceptible to the invitations since he was anxious to stave off the sentence of interdict that threatened because of the murder of Archbishop Becket.[1]

The modern view was established by G. H. Orpen who saw Henry's expedition of 1171 as the culmination of a long-cherished ambition: 'He had long cast hungry eyes towards Ireland': shortly after coming to the English throne he had proposed an expedition and gone so far as to obtain sanction for the invasion from Pope Adrian IV, but he had other preoccupations and the ambition was postponed; the arrival, however, of King Dermot seeking help and offering to become the king of England's man, 'suited Henry's ambitious projects too well to be ignored'; he was unable at that moment to mount an expedition himself because his attention was engaged in the struggle with Becket, but 'he did what he could in the circumstances to secure Dermot's allegiance and keep the opportunity open for carrying out his own designs later on'; by 1171 the success of Strongbow meant that 'the time was opportune for Henry to make his long meditated expedition'.[2]

[1] Gervase of Canterbury, I, 234–5.   [2] Orpen, *op. cit.*, I, 81, 82, 83, 84, 249.

Orpen's well-integrated thesis rests, however, on fragile evidence: a brief reference in the chronicle of Robert de Torigny (not the most reliable witness to events outside northern France) to a council meeting at Winchester in 1155, and the papal bull *Laudabiliter* of about the same date. English chroniclers of the time are silent about both. Torigny relates that a year after becoming king of England, Henry held a council at Winchester 'at which he deliberated with his barons about the conquest of Ireland and the grant of it to his brother William, but since his mother the empress opposed it the expedition was for the time being set aside'.[1] Torigny may well have written the last sentence with the knowledge of Henry's later expedition in mind. It does not really seem very probable that Henry himself would have promoted such a scheme in 1155: he had just deprived his brother Geoffrey of an appanage and was hardly likely to create a larger one for his younger brother William. Henry II never did much for his brothers. It is more likely that the scheme was put up by someone else and turned down by Henry; and one does not have to look further for a promoter than to Archbishop Theobald of Canterbury, by then a revered elder statesman whose suggestions would in courtesy have to be considered even if they were unwelcome. Archbishop Theobald had a powerful motive: the lapse since 1140 of Canterbury's jurisdiction over the bishops of the Norse townships in Ireland.[2] It was a by-product of the reform movement in the Irish Church. John of Salisbury tells us that it was he himself who successfully requested Pope Adrian IV to approve the incorporation of Ireland into the English realm.[3] John of Salisbury was Theobald's secretary. Pope Adrian's letter of approval is probably to be identified with the papal bull *Laudabiliter* which Gerald of Wales, some twenty years later, transcribed into his *Expugnatio Hibernica*:

> Adrian the bishop, servant of the servants of God, to his most dearly beloved son in Christ, the illustrious king of the English, greeting and apostolic benediction.
>
> Laudably and profitably does your magnificence contemplate extending your glorious name on earth and laying up a reward of eternal happiness in heaven, inasmuch as you endeavour like a catholic prince to enlarge the boundaries of the Church, to expound the truth of the Christian faith to ignorant and barbarous peoples, and to root out the seeds of vice from the lord's field; and for the better execution of this, you seek the advice and favour of the apostolic see. In which work the more lofty the counsel

---

[1] Robert de Torigny, 186.
[2] Saltman, *Archbishop Theobald*, 95.
[3] John of Salisbury, *Metalogicon*, I, 216.

and the greater the discretion with which you proceed, so much the more do we trust that by God's help your progress may be fortunate therein, in that those things which have their beginning in ardent faith and love of religion always tend to work out to a happy end. . . .

We, therefore, supporting with due fervour your pious and praiseworthy desire, and granting our generous assent to your petition, are well pleased to agree that, for the extension of the boundaries of the Church, for the restraint of vice, for the correction of morals and for the implanting of virtues, and for the increase of the Christian religion, you may enter that island and perform therein the things that have regard to the honour of God and the salvation of that land. . . . If, therefore, you deem fit to carry through what you have in mind, strive to imbue that nation with good morals . . . that the Christian religion may be implanted and made to grow, and the things which pertain to the honour of God and the salvation of souls may be so ordered that you may deserve to obtain from God the crown of everlasting reward and on earth a name glorious throughout the ages.[1]

It hardly sounds as if Henry had sent to the pope with a definite purpose in mind: it reads more like an attempt to encourage a hesitant king.

If it is correct to suppose that the whole notion was clerically inspired it would nevertheless be a mistake to see it solely as a piece of empire-building by Canterbury: the defence of rights once established was a duty any archbishop of Canterbury owed to God and St Augustine, and the monks of Canterbury would not have been slow to remind Archbishop Theobald of it.[2] The consolidation of episcopal jurisdiction was a feature of the age, and the claims of Canterbury in Ireland were certainly better grounded than the contemporary claims of the archbishop of Lyons to authority over Rouen and Sens, or the claim of the archbishop of Trèves to jurisdiction over Rheims.[3] That Pope Adrian was ready to support such a move by Canterbury is not surprising: besides being an Englishman, he was the pope who revived the high-Gregorian programme for the reform of church government after half a century of doubt and muddle at Rome.[4] The revolutionary effect of this programme was to dethrone monasticism as the pace-setter of Christendom and to give the bishop of Rome real powers for the direc-

---

[1] Gerald of Wales, V, 316; also given by Ralph of Diceto, I, 300–1, under the year 1154. The authenticity of the text, much disputed, is put beyond doubt by O'Doherty, 'Rome and the Anglo-Norman invasion of Ireland', 131–41.

[2] Cf. Southern, St Anselm and his Biographer, 127ff.

[3] John of Salisbury, Historia Pontificalis, 4–6.

[4] Ullmann, 'The pontificate of Adrian IV'.

tion and control of the Church's life-powers which were to be exercised, in the first instance, through the local bishops. It is no wonder that *Laudabiliter* should so pointedly ignore the work of St Malachy and the Cistercians in 'implanting the Christian religion in Ireland': from the point of view of popes like Adrian IV and, after him, Alexander III this was the wrong kind of reform.[1] What the papacy wanted was effective bishops not influential Cistercian abbots. Pope Eugenius III had intervened in the Irish reform movement by sending a legate to the synod of Kells in 1152; but the effect of this had probably been to convince the papacy that the cause of reform was hopeless without the support of a strong secular authority.[2] Pope Alexander III welcomed Henry II's intervention of 1171 with enthusiasm. He wrote to the Irish bishops, to the Irish 'kings and princes' and to Henry himself hailing it as the will of God. To the Irish bishops he wrote that he had heard from several of them

> how great are the enormities of vice with which the people of Ireland are infected, and how they have departed from the fear of God and the established practice of the Christian faith, so that souls have been placed in peril. We have further learned from your letters that Henry, the noble king of the English, our dearest son in Christ, moved by inspiration from God and summoning all his strength, has subjugated this barbarous and uncouth race which is ignorant of divine law; and through his power those forbidden things which used to be practised in your lands, now begin to diminish. We have been filled with great joy about this . . . and we earnestly pray that through the vigilance and care of the king, and by your cooperation with him, this undisciplined and untamed people may in every way be led to respect the divine law and the practice of the Christian faith, and that thereby you and all the men of the church may be brought to rejoice in honour and peace. In order that this work, so well begun, may continue, it is fitting that you should show it favour and respect. Therefore we order and command . . . that you zealously and powerfully assist the aforesaid king (who is a man of majesty and a devoted son of the Church) to maintain and keep that land. . . .

To the Irish laity he similarly enjoined obedience to 'that majestic king who is a devoted son of the Church'. To King Henry II he wrote with heartfelt thanksgiving and hopes for the future: 'We beg your royal excellency, nay, as you value the remission of your sins, we exhort you in the Lord – to continue in that which you have so laudably begun. We bid you to strengthen and renew your purpose to bring

[1] White, 'The Gregorian ideal and St Bernard of Clairvaux', 321–43.
[2] *See* above, p. 191.

this people to the worship of Christ and by your royal power to keep them in it.'[1] To ears still attuned to denunciation of Henry II for the murder of Archbishop Becket, the pope's reference to Henry as 'our dearest son in Christ', 'a devoted son of the Church', 'this catholic and most Christian king,' must have sounded oddly. His reference to Henry's respect for the rights of the Church must have been greeted with astonishment if not cynicism by those who read Becket's correspondence; but the papacy was realistic: the dictatorship of the monarchy was the necessary prelude to the clerical millennium.

These letters were no doubt welcome to Henry as manifestoes of papal approval; but they had little effect on his policy. Though he promoted a church synod during his visit to reform Irish canon law, he made no attempt to abolish the *brehon* law which moral reformers found so objectionable. In the time of his great-grandson, over a century later, Irish bishops were still trying to persuade the king of England to make English law compulsory for the Irish.[2] Nor did Henry revive Canterbury's dormant jurisdiction: the Irish Church was to retain the independence it had already asserted. But though Henry was to disappoint their hopes, there were clearly good reasons why churchmen both at Canterbury and Rome should have tried to push Henry II into an Irish commitment at the beginning of his reign. Whether he showed any real interest in the proposal at the council of Winchester in 1155, or merely feigned it from politic politeness (and put the blame for voting against it on to his mother) we shall probably never know; but certainly it does not seem that the passing years endeared the project to him. His response to Dermot's appeal and proffer of allegiance in 1167 was no more than lukewarm. Even Gerald of Wales (who had brothers among the Norman adventurers and was inevitably a propagandist for the Irish connection) says merely that Henry welcomed Dermot 'with his customary courtesy and affability', but in loading him with gifts gave him more hope than assistance.[3] The letters patent which Henry granted to Dermot bear him out:

> Henry king of the English, duke of the Normans and Aquitanians, and count of the Angevins, to all his liegemen, English, Norman, Welsh, and Scots, and to all nations subject to his authority, greeting.
> Know by these letters that we have received Dermot prince of the men of

---

[1] *Liber Niger de Scaccario*, I, 42–8.

[2] *See* the documents printed by Jocelyn Otway-Ruthven, 'The request of the Irish for English law, 1277–80', 167–8. For the synod of Cashel *see* Gerald of Wales, V, 280ff., and Roger of Howden, *Gesta*, I, 28, *Chronica*, II, 31.

[3] Gerald of Wales, V, 227.

Leinster into our grace and favour; wherefore whosoever within our frontiers shall be willing to aid him as our vassal and liegeman in recovering his dominion, let him be assured of our favour and permission for it.[1]

With such slight encouragement as this it is hardly surprising that even the Normans of Wales, despairing of making their fortunes at home, delayed for over a year in following Dermot to Leinster, nor that it was 1170 before Richard de Clare made up his mind to go.[2] It cannot be supposed that Henry was a party to the agreement by which King Dermot bought the services of Strongbow by making him his son-in-law and heir. When he did hear of it his reaction was to order Strongbow home, put an embargo on supplies to the adventurers, and punish anyone else who went to Ireland without his licence.[3] The point was clearly this: Henry had no objection to Dermot emulating the sons of Malcolm Canmore in Scotland and recruiting Normans into his service 'for the recovery of his dominion'.[4] It would help to ease the perennial feudal problem of what to do with landless younger sons, and provide an alternative to the Holy Land as an outlet for the restless and ambitious, particularly those who resented his policy of trying to reach an understanding with the Welsh. Ireland might thus become another Scotland, and the oath that King Henry took from Dermot was in line with his relations with the king of Scots. But it was quite another matter to have prominent barons – and a disgraced earl no less – establishing a position of private power beyond his jurisdiction and control. What sent Henry II across the Irish Sea was not 'a long cherished ambition' but a sequence of unforeseen events: the fact that Dermot gave his daughter to Strongbow, that he made him his heir, and that after Dermot's death Strongbow achieved the impossible by routing the army of the high-king, Rory O'Connor.[5] In short, Ireland, instead of becoming another Scotland, looked like becoming another Sicily.

It would have been impolitic of Henry simply to have ejected the adventurers from Ireland. For one thing the problem would merely

---

[1] *Ibid.*, V, 227–8.   [2] Cf. Nelson, *The Normans in South Wales*, 133ff.

[3] Pipe Roll 16 Henry, 78, 17 Henry II, 17, 92; Gerald of Wales, V, 259; William of Newburgh, I, 168. The continuing royal control over passage to Ireland is illustrated in *Calendar of Documents relating to Ireland*, I, 10, 12, 32.

[4] King William II authorised Duncan to recruit volunteers to help him secure the throne of Scotland, Ritchie, *The Normans in Scotland*, 61.

[5] William of Newburgh, I, 167–8, says that Henry was obliged to go to Ireland by the effrontery of Strongbow in being so successful against the king's disapproval. The point of view argued above was first suggested by J. F. O'Doherty in a doctoral thesis, *Laurentius von Dublin und das irische Normannentum* (1933), the main elements of which were reproduced in a series of articles in the *Irish Ecclesiastical Record* (*see* Bibliography).

have been deferred: Ireland was now advertised as a land of opportunity for anyone who thought to try his luck. But even more seriously,
it was a fundamental rule of feudal society that a man acquired a
proprietary right to what he had won by force of arms. Though
William always claimed to hold England as King Edward's rightful
successor, everyone knew that he held it by right of conquest and called
him the Conqueror. Strongbow gambled on the fact that Henry would
make trouble for himself if he tried to deprive him of what he had won.
Henry was just ruthless enough to try it, but might hesitate if there were
an alternative. Strongbow offered him one: he would surrender his
acquisitions freely into the king's hands if Henry would then grant him
Leinster as a fief.[1] He himself went over to see Henry as he made his
preparations for the expedition and put his offer personally. Henry
showed him his anger, but was brought at length to accept it on the
understanding that Strongbow would surrender without reservation
the key ports and all the castles.[2] Nevertheless the king went on with his
preparations and crossed to Ireland with an army laden with siege
equipment.[3] It is a significant pointer to his intentions: he was determined to prevent the Irish situation getting out of hand, and no opposition from the Normans there was going to stop him. Their conquests
were to be turned into fiefs held directly or indirectly of the Crown;
and a royal administration was to be set up in a royal enclave at
Dublin to see that they kept the rules.

Henry's show of force achieved the desired effect: there was no
fighting, no overt resistance. Normans and Irish alike came in to offer
their submission – all save Rory O'Connor (who, though he offered no
opposition, was reluctant to compromise his claim to be high-king) and
the kings of the far north who ignored now, as they did on so many
other occasions, what was happening in the rest of Ireland.[4] Henry let
them be: his main concern, for the moment, was with the Norman
colonists. Strongbow was confirmed in the lordship of Leinster as
agreed, but without control of the Norse kingdom of Dublin or the
townships of Waterford and Wexford. To these the king appointed his
own constable and garrisons. Moreover, to counterbalance Strongbow
and the 'race of Nest' in Leinster, he gave the former kingdom of

---

[1] Gerald of Wales, V, 259; Gervase of Canterbury, I, 235.

[2] Gerald of Wales, V, 273.

[3] Pipe Rolls 17 and 18 Henry II, contain much information about the equipping
and provisioning of the Irish expedition.

[4] Gervase of Canterbury, I, 235; Roger of Howden, *Gesta*, I, 25, *Chronica*, II, 30;
Ralph of Diceto, I, 348; Gerald of Wales, V, 277-9.

Meath as a fief to Hugh de Lacy, who had come over to Ireland for the first time with Henry's expedition. Hugh de Lacy, leader of the Herefordshire branch of the powerful Lacy family, was the equal in pedigree of the Clares, one of the major barons of the Welsh March and as familiar as Strongbow with the peculiarities of Celtic custom. He was given Meath on the same terms as Strongbow held Leinster, made constable of Dublin, and, it seems, given the powers of a viceroy.[1]

What kind of relationship Henry intended to establish with the native Irish is a question of some difficulty. It has often been assumed that when the Irish kings came in to make their submission they were required to take an oath of homage. If they had done so they too would have become the vassals of the king of England; but it is very doubtful if they did. The chronicles are somewhat ambiguous, but the weight of the evidence is against their having been asked for an oath of *homage* (which would have affected the terms on which they held their land) and suggests instead what they were asked for was an oath of *fealty* (which was simply a matter of personal allegiance).[2] Much the same is true of Rory O'Connor, the high-king. Though he declined to submit while Henry was in Ireland he eventually thought better of it. The terms of his allegiance – as defined in the Treaty of Windsor of 1175 – were not rigorous. He became the king of England's 'man' (*ligius homo*) which put him under a personal obligation; but there is no suggestion in the treaty that he was to hold his land as the feudal vassal of the king of England. As the treaty puts it, he was to hold his land 'as fully and peacefully as he did *before* the lord king entered Ireland'.[3] He was to owe personal service and render a tribute collected from the

---

[1] It is not known for certain by what title Hugh de Lacy was known in his capacity as king's representative. He was called 'justiciar' only by Roger of Howden in the revised version of his chronicle. Gerald of Wales refers to him by the vague title of 'procurator'. For the Lacy family *see* Wightman, *The Lacy Family in England and Normandy*. The charter of grant is printed in Orpen, *Ireland under the Normans*, I, 285–6. Henry's right to dispose of Meath in this way has been questioned. It is significant that by the terms of the charter Hugh was to hold it 'as freely as Murchad O'Melaghlin'. King Murchad of Meath had died nearly twenty years previously, and since then his kingdom had been disputed between rivals. Dermot MacMurrough invaded it, and probably reckoned himself overlord of Meath at the time of his death.

[2] Gervase of Canterbury, I, 235, speaks only of fealty. So does Roger of Howden, *Chronica*, II, 30, although in the *Gesta*, I, 25, he is more ambiguous. Gerald of Wales, V, 277, 278–9, speaks of fealty. Only Ralph of Diceto, I, 348, explicitly mentions homage. It may be worthy of remark that Ralph of Diceto was at the time in Italy on a mission to the pope, Eyton, *Itinerary of Henry II*, 165.

[3] Roger of Howden, *Gesta*, I, 102–3, *Chronica*, II, 84–5; 'et quod terram suam teneat ita bene et in pace, sicut tenuit antequam dominus res Angliae intraret Hiberniam, reddendo ei tributum'.

lesser kings, but his authority as high-king was recognised over all of Ireland outside the territories of Henry and his barons.[1]

It seems clear that Henry II's attitude to the native Irish was influenced by his dealings with the Welsh. He had learned from the consequences of his attempt to impose the obligations of feudal homage on the Welsh princes in 1163. At the time of his intervention in Ireland he was moving cautiously towards a less rigorous relationship with the Welsh that took final shape at the council of Oxford in 1177. Though we have no text of the treaty with the Welsh, the terms as described by the chroniclers are very similar to the terms of the Treaty of Windsor concluded two years previously with Rory O'Connor. Dafydd and Rhys were recognised as overlords ('kings', says Roger of Howden) of North and South Wales respectively; they alone swore homage and promised to keep peace with the king of England, while the lesser rulers who were recognised as subject to them did simple fealty to King Henry[2].

Despite the inevitable friction between the Welsh and the Normans

[1] The most striking feature, indeed, of the Treaty of Windsor, is the pains that were taken to avoid the terminology of a typical feudal charter. 'The king of the English,' says the treaty of Windsor, 'grants [concedit] to Rory his liegeman, king of Connacht, as long as he shall faithfully serve him, that he shall be king under him. And he shall hold his land as fully and peacefully as he did before the lord king entered Ireland, rendering him tribute.' By contrast, the charter granting Meath to Hugh Lacy clearly established a feudal relationship: 'Know that I have given and granted [dedisse et concessisse] and by this my charter confirmed to Hugh Lacy for his service the land of Meath with all its appurtenances, to be held by him and his heirs for the service of fifty knights, to have and to hold from me and my heirs as fully as Murchad O'Melaghlin held it.' Certainly the Treaty of Windsor was far less rigorous than the explicitly feudal Treaty of Falaise, concluded ten months previously, by which Henry II defined his relations with the king of Scots. The latter treaty minces no words: King William became the liegeman of King Henry 'in respect of Scotland and in respect of all his other lands', see above, pp. 184–5. If further proof is needed that Rory O'Connor did not become a fief-holding vassal of the king of England, it will be found in the arrangements that his successor, Cathal Crovderg O'Connor, made with King John. By the terms of an agreement made in 1205 John was to exercise a feudal lordship over one third of Connacht, which was to be granted to Cathal as a barony; for the remaining two-thirds Cathal was simply to render an annual tribute of 300 marks; see Dudley Edwards, 'Anglo-Norman relations with Connacht'. If a third of Connacht was made a fief in 1205, it is impossible that all of it could have been previously.

[2] There was, however, a difference. Dafydd and Rhys were the vassals of Henry II in a way which Rory was not. They were fief-holding vassals in respect of additional lands which Henry conferred upon them in 1177. They could thus freely admit to being Henry's vassals while being spared the ignominy of having to admit that they held their ancestral lands as vassals – which was probably what Henry II tried to make them do in 1163. In this devious way honour was preserved to both sides.

at the local level, the arrangement with the Welsh princes was astonishingly successful for the rest of Henry II's reign. The Irish arrangement was a failure. Henry's recognition of Rory O'Connor as high-king presumed too much upon the *political* maturity of Ireland: the king of Connacht proved incapable in practice of exercising the kind of control over the lesser rulers by which Rhys of Deheubarth and Dafydd of Gwynedd ensured the stability of Wales. There are signs that some attempt at least was made to carry out Henry's policy: Rory was able to call for the help of the king's men in Dublin as the treaty provided, the king's justiciar tried to rein in the Norman conquistadors, and several Norman expeditions were obliged to retire with their tails between their legs; but the situation rapidly got out of control, largely because of the reluctance of many of the Irish to accept the overlordship of the king of Connacht. The temptation to recruit Norman help in the internal struggle for power proved irresistible, thus reviving the very situation that Henry had gone to Ireland to suppress in 1171. When Rory O'Connor withdrew from any attempt to control Munster, Henry was driven in 1177 to the drastic step of dividing it up into fiefs before the Normans could take advantage of the confused political situation there to carve out private empires for themselves. In this way, at least, the principle behind the Treaty of Windsor could be preserved.[1]

That Henry regarded this as no more than a *pis aller* is shown by his quest for an alternative. Henry had begun (when King Dermot came to him in 1167) by thinking of Ireland in terms of Scotland; he had changed (when Strongbow forced his hand) to thinking of it in terms of Wales: he moved finally (when Rory O'Connor failed him) to frame his policy on an analogy with Brittany. His solution to the problem of pacifying that anarchic province had been to hand it over to his son Geoffrey and create for him the nucleus of a ducal administration. Ireland, too, was for Henry basically a problem in pacification, and when events forced him to intervene in Munster he began thinking of

[1] Henry II has been much criticised for this move; but O'Doherty has argued that 'the violations of the Treaty of Windsor in 1177 are explained, though not of course excused, not on the theory of Mr Orpen that the time had come to tear up the treaty, but on the theory that these annexations were necessary to safeguard the treaty position as a whole', 'St Laurence O'Toole and the Anglo-Norman invasion', Pt V, 136–8. It is significant that in the enfeoffments of 1177 no account was taken of John de Courcy's venture into Ulster. The circumstances there were different: there was less political anarchy in the north, and it could still be hoped that there the Irish would deal effectively with Norman invaders; and, indeed, although de Courcy's exploits were of heroic proportions, the Irish did manage to keep him pinned east of Lough Neagh and to inflict serious defeats upon him. It was only when the local situation became uncontrollable in any other way that Henry II intervened.

handing over the problem to his youngest son, John.[1] Like Brittany, Ireland presented the sort of problem that could not be adequately dealt with by a king with more pressing cares that took him to distant places: it needed a man on the spot, a man who had a personal stake in the country's future. Unfortunately John was, in 1177, only nine years old. The proposal had to be shelved. It was drawn out again in 1185 when John was seventeen. At that age Henry himself had been striving to gain the kingdom of England, and had been knighted by David king of Scots. In March 1185 Henry knighted John and sent him over to Ireland with an army and a corps of experienced administrators.[2] It was a mistake. John completely misjudged the situation and its need. He was young for his years, impatient of advice, and prone to folly. His first taste of power went to his head. The old hands among the Norman settlers were spurned, the Irish who sought to pay their respects were insulted, the army was mishandled and the mercenaries deserted.[3] After nine months (in December 1185) John retreated back to England, blaming his failure on the hostility and intrigues of Hugh de Lacy, who until his coming had been the royal justiciar.[4]

Hugh de Lacy had been something of a success, both as lord of Meath and during the periods he was allowed to act as justiciar or viceroy in Ireland. Henry might have been well advised to give Hugh more authority than he did. But though Hugh demonstrated his loyalty to Henry during the great war, his reputation as an ambitious man attracted suspicion, and the trust that Henry reposed in him fluctuated sharply. For several years indeed he had been replaced as

[1] It is worthy of note that a charter of the bishop of Coutance in 1172 is described as having been drawn up in the year in which Henry II was 'pacifying Ireland', *Recueil des Actes de Henri II*, I, 583. Roger of Howden, *Gesta*, I, 61, says that Henry made John king of Ireland in 1177. This is improbable. Howden's account is seriously blundered: he has mistaken Earl Hugh of Chester for Hugh de Lacy, earl of Meath, and seems to have confused some of the events of 1172 with those of 1177. Little credence can therefore be placed on information which he gives that is unsupported by other chroniclers. But that Henry at least expressed an intention in 1177 of making John king of Ireland is suggested by some words of Gerald of Wales, V, 359, who in describing the events of 1184 says: 'The king of the English now determined to carry into effect a design he had long entertained, namely to transfer the overlordship of Ireland to his son John.'

[2] Roger of Howden, *Gesta*, I, 339, *Chronica*, II, 303, 304–5. The administrators did not include, as is sometimes stated, Ranulf de Glanvill, cf. *Annals of the Four Masters, sub anno* 1185.

[3] Gerald of Wales, V, 388ff., 395. Gerald spoke as an eye-witness since he accompanied John to Ireland, *ibid.*, 381–2. *See* also Roger of Howden, *Gesta*, I, 339, *Chronica*, II, 305.

[4] *Annals of the Four Masters, sub anno* 1185.

viceroy by Strongbow.[1] This was unfortunate because Hugh de Lacy's policy in Ireland was the only one that held out any real prospect of bringing peace and reconciliation to Normans and native Irish. Though he naturally made provision for his Norman vassals by enfeoffing them with land and built numerous castles, he displaced the existing Irish lords only when necessity dictated. He took pains to encourage the Irish peasants to return to lands from which they had fled in fear. As Gerald of Wales reports:

> He made it his first care to restore peace and order, reinstating the peasants who, after they had submitted to the conquerors, had been violently expelled. . . . And having won the confidence of the Irish by the leniency of his government and by his strict regard for treaties, his next care was to reduce the inhabitants of the towns to order and respect for law.[2]

This was in line with royal policy: the Treaty of Windsor provided for the peaceful return of the Irish who had fled from lands seized by the Normans; but Hugh went further and advertised his attitude by marrying (in 1180) a daughter of Rory O'Connor. Not unnaturally it reminded Henry of Strongbow's marriage to King Dermot's daughter – especially since Hugh omitted to seek royal permission first. It cost him the justiciarship for a while.[3] It was probably Hugh's enlightened policy of combining firm rule, fair dealing, and respect for the Irish (when they did not menace his security) that brought him into conflict with John; for foolhardy John used his authority to make numerous grants to his cronies in complete disregard of all other considerations.[4]

In sending John to Ireland it was Henry's intention that he should become king of the whole country, combining under his rule the two distinct communities of Norman barons and native Irish. This would have been difficult but not impossible: the king of Scots was making

---

[1] For a description of Hugh de Lacy see Gerald of Wales, V, 353–4. A list of the 'chief governors' of Ireland is supplied by Orpen, *Ireland under the Normans*, I, 15, and by Richardson and Sayles, *The Administration of Ireland*, 73–4. From these it appears that Hugh was viceroy from 1172 until Henry summoned him to Normandy at the outbreak of the great war in April 1173. He was viceroy again from May 1177 until John's appointment in 1184 (with a short break while he was under suspicion in 1181). For most of the time between 1173 and 1177 Strongbow acted as viceroy. It seems that Henry, having given Meath to Hugh de Lacy to counterbalance Strongbow, came to feel that Strongbow was needed to counterbalance Lacy. But it was while Hugh was out of office that the Irish situation deteriorated rapidly. His reappointment in May 1177 coincides with Henry's attempt to stabilize the situation again.

[2] Gerald of Wales, V, 353.

[3] Roger of Howden, *Gesta*, I, 270; cf. Gerald of Wales, V, 355, 356.

[4] Cf. Gerald of Wales, V, 390ff.

some success of the same kind of problem, combining under his lordship the Normanised lowlands and the 'Pictish' highlands. But John gave up the task entrusted to him by his father even before papal approval for his coronation had been received from Rome.[1] The insufficiency of his son forced Henry to shelve his plan for divesting himself of the problem of Ireland by erecting it as a separate kingdom. It was still on the shelf when King Henry died four years later.[2]

Henry II's Irish policy can, then, only be accounted a failure. It was perhaps his one major failure, and certainly the one with the most serious consequences. But the policy itself was, given the circumstances at the time, quite reasonable. It failed partly for lack of satisfactory agents, but basically because Henry was unable or unwilling to give it the attention (and money) it required. The practice of relying on, while at the same time distrusting, men such as Hugh de Lacy and Richard de Clare for discharging royal policy was certainly economical, but it courted disaster. The partition policy that went with it – the division of Ireland into Norman Ireland and Irish Ireland, with an attempt to keep the two separate – prevented the unification of the country either on the Anglo-Norman model or the Scotto-Norman model. The Norman adventurers were restrained from conquering the whole country when it was still conceivably possible, while, on the other hand, fiefs having once been created under the English Crown, no English king could subsequently contemplate with equanimity their extinction in any Irish *revanche*. Henry knew that the partition policy was unsatisfactory: his proposal to unify the country under his son is proof enough of that; but with John's failure he was obliged to revert to it. The preoccupations of his successors perpetuated the pattern. At least it may be said, however, that the history of Henry II's dealings with Ireland, when properly understood, absolves him from the charge of acquisitive ambition. Ireland was a commitment that Henry entered upon reluctantly, tried to discharge cheaply, and hoped to get rid of.

[1] It was conveyed by papal legates, together with a crown of peacock feathers in 1186, Roger of Howden, *Gesta*, II, 3–4, *Chronica*, II, 306–7.

[2] It was thus more by accident than design that Ireland remained attached to the English Crown – a consequence of the fact that in 1199 John become king of England. As king of England he retained the title *dominus Hiberniae* – the title he had used in Ireland in 1185 in anticipation of becoming *rex Hiberniae* when properly crowned. Compare the parallel use of the title *dominus Angliae* by English kings before their coronation, and of the title *Anglorum domina* used by Empress Matilda, Poole, *Domesday Book to Magna Carta*, 3 n.1.

Chapter 5

HENRY II AND HIS EMPIRE

In appearance, Henry FitzEmpress might easily have been mistaken for one of his own huntsmen.[1] Although highly conscious of the dignity of kingship, he gave no hint of it in bearing or manner. He dressed simply and most often in clothes suitable for riding or hunting. He looked like a man who led a strenuous outdoor life: his complexion was ruddy, and his hands were rough and horny for he wore gloves only to carry a hawk. He walked, in later life, with the gait of a man who has spent long hours in the saddle, spurring on refractory horses. He spoke with the cracked voice of one more accustomed to shouting from horseback than to making fair speeches. But although he may not have looked very regal, there was something about him which compelled attention: his countenance, says Walter Map, was one upon which a man might gaze a thousand times, yet still feel drawn to return to gaze again. Moreover, his powerful personality found physical expression in his stature. He was a big man, somewhat above average height, with broad shoulders, a square chest, and a large, thrusting, leonine head. His legs were sturdy, his arms powerful, and no one, it was said, could match him in feats of strength and endurance. In anger his blue-grey eyes became fiery and bloodshot. His energy was overwhelming. 'He was impatient of repose,' writes Walter Map, 'and did not hesitate to disturb almost half Christendom.' Herbert of Bosham likened him to a human chariot, drawing all after him.[2] Gerald of Wales, who, like Walter Map, was for many years a member of his household, gives a similar impression:

> He was addicted to hunting beyond measure: at crack of dawn he was off on horseback, traversing wastelands, penetrating forests and climbing the

[1] General descriptions of Henry II are given by three members of his household: Gerald of Wales in his Expugnatio Hibernica, Opera, V, 302–6, part of which was incorporated in his De Principis Instructione, Opera, VI, 213–15; Walter Map, De Nugiis Curialium, 237–42; Peter of Blois in a letter to the archbishop of Palermo, written about 1177, printed in Materials for the History of Becket, VII, 570ff., Petri Blesensis Archidiaconi Opera Omnia, ed. Giles, I, 193ff., and Patrologia Latina, CCVII, 197ff. These passages are cited in the footnotes to this chapter by the name of the author followed by 'loc. cit.'.

[2] Herbert of Bosham, Liber Melorum, Patrologia Latina, CXC, 1322.

mountain tops, and so he passed his restless days. At evening on his return home he was rarely seen to sit down either before or after supper. And despite such tremendous exertions he would wear out the whole court by remaining on his feet.

It was, says Gerald, as if he were constantly at war with his body, fighting a tendency to corpulence by relentless exercise.[1]

The impression of a stocky, strong, restless, energetic, passionate man is inescapable in all contemporary descriptions of him; but his character is not easily sketched, for he was a complex man, of contradictory qualities. Despite his surges of anger and bloodshot eyes, he was not normally fiery or overbearing: Walter Map describes him as modest and unassuming, never insolent, unfailingly courteous, infinitely patient, and, despite his faults, 'exceedingly good and lovable'. Gerald of Wales says that he was 'readily approachable, condescending, and second to none in politeness'. Despite his hoarse voice he was a good talker, witty in conversation, and eloquent in argument.[2] Although he was so often engaged in military campaigns, he despised violence and hated war.[3] And despite his appearance as a weatherbeaten man of action, and his passion for hunting, his mind was of a decidedly intellectual bent. Tournaments and troubadours held no charms for him: 'with the king of England,' writes Peter of Blois, 'it is school every day, constant conversation with the best scholars and discussion of intellectual problems'.[4] He liked to retire to his chamber with a book, and was well-read for a layman – to the extent at least, says Walter Map, as was seemly and profitable. Gerald of Wales describes him as 'remarkably polished in letters'.[5] He had an astonishing memory: he never forgot a face, and could call to mind anything that he had ever heard that was worth remembering, 'so that he had at his finger tips an almost complete knowledge of history, and a great store of practical wisdom'.[6] He was conversant, it is said, with all the languages 'from the coast of France to the river Jordan', though he customarily made use himself of French or Latin.[7]

[1] Walter Map, *loc. cit.*, also attributes Henry's physical exertions to his fear of growing too plump. Peter of Blois, *loc. cit.*, confirming his love of hunting, says that he was never without a bow, sword, hunting spear, or arrows in his hand.

[2] Gerald of Wales, *loc. cit.*

[3] Peter of Blois and Gerald of Wales, *loc. cit.*, William of Newburgh, I, 282.

[4] Peter of Blois, *loc. cit.*, Henry II is praised for his love of learning by William of Canterbury, I, 137; cf. Haskins, 'Henry II as a patron of learning'.

[5] Cf. also Peter of Blois, *loc. cit.*

[6] Gerald of Wales, *loc. cit.*, and *Opera*, IV, 47, 51. Henry advised the monks of Glastonbury where to look for the bones of King Arthur, *ibid.*, VIII, 128.

[7] Walter Map, *loc. cit.*

ILLUSTRATIONS

Section I

NOTE ON CASTLES

The most common type of *castellum* in the early years of the twelfth century was a stronghold of earthworks and stout timber. A deep ditch was dug, and the earth thrown up into a mound, roughly conical, but with a flat top, known as a *motte*. Linked to the motte and surrounded by a ditch and rampart was a level enclosure known as the *bailey*. The perimeter was further defended with a stockade of stout timber. On the mound was erected a timber tower, also surrounded by a stockade. The mound served as a redoubt if the outer defences were breached. In the bailey were erected timber buildings to provide accommodation for the garrison, storerooms, and stabling. The tower on the mound may have been a simple scaffolding to support a look-out; but usually, and particularly if the lord used the castle as a residence, a tower-house of several stories would be constructed. (See Plate 1.)

The defensive strength of such apparently simple fortifications should not be underestimated. They were at the time proof against any but a determined enemy equipped with siege engines (as, indeed, the continued use of stockaded forts into modern times, in the colonies, or by the United States Cavalry in Indian territory, clearly demonstrates). Even in time of peace, in the middle ages, a motte-and-bailey castle was useful as a secure place where a lord might store his valuables, and as a symbol of his authority to overawe his tenants. It commonly served, too, as the administrative centre of an estate.

Many hundreds of motte-and-bailey fortifications were erected in England, with royal encouragement, in the years immediately following the Norman Conquest. As the country became settled, the Crown was less disposed to favour local strongholds in private hands, and many may have fallen into decay. There can be little doubt, however, that very many of the 'castles' of Stephen's reign were of this type, either re-occupied and re-fortified, or newly constructed. The earthworks associated with such castles remain in large numbers throughout the British Isles. (See Plates 2 and 10.)

Earth and timber strongholds were, however, obsolescent in England by the later years of the twelfth century. Some, but only a small proportion, were, with royal permission, strengthened with stone. The more primitive form continued, however, to be erected in large numbers by the settlers in Ireland. (A particularly fine example, at Dromore in County Down, is shown below, Plate 10.) They had the great advantage that they could be constructed quickly and cheaply, with readily available materials, and without the necessity of skilled labour.

Motte-and-bailey castles of earth and timber were not, however, even from the earliest days of the Conquest, the only form of fortification. The alternative was a rectangular tower of stone, resisting assault by the massiveness of its smooth-faced walls – known as a 'donjon' in French and as a 'tower' or 'keep' in English. Their construction required not only skilled labour and dressed stone in huge quantities, but also the services of an architect, or 'engineer' (*inginator*) as he was known at the time. They were therefore vastly more expensive, but also vastly more imposing – a suitable symbol of authority for the greatest of lords. The donjon at Falaise (Plate 5) and what is known as the White Tower at the Tower of London dates from the time of William the Conqueror. Other examples may be seen at Colchester and Castle Hedingham.

Less expensive was the strengthening of motte-and-bailey fortifications with stone. The simplest way of doing this was to replace the timber stockade with a stone curtain wall. Rebuilding the tower on the motte in stone was not always possible: a man-made mound might not be sufficiently stable to support the weight, and all that could be done was to replace the stockade on top of the mound with a circular stone wall (commonly called a 'shell-keep', see Plate 3). Sometimes, however, the motte had been sited so as to take advantage of natural features such as a hillock or outcrop of rock, and foundations for a stone tower could then be found by digging down. The alternative was to erect a stone keep in the bailey. (See, e.g. Plates 4 and 6.)

Throughout his reign, Henry II devoted much attention, and considerable sums of money, to the strengthening of many royal castles (see pp. 234ff and caption to Plate 2). Much of the new work was in stone. Massive rectangular keeps were erected at Scarborough, New-castle-upon-Tyne (Plate 7), the Peak, Bamburgh, Appleby, Brough, Bridgenorth, Dover (Plate 8, the most imposing of all), and probably also at Canterbury. Most, if not all of these, were on sites where there were already fortifications of some kind. A castle on a new site was erected at Orford in Suffolk, with a keep of an unusual polygonal design (Plate 9).

Though several of Henry II's castles were subsequently modified, and some have fallen into decay, enough of his work survives to justify his contemporary reputation as a great builder.

1 An artist's reconstruction of a typical motte-and-bailey castle of earthworks and timber.

2 *opposite* Berkhamsted. The surviving earthworks of a large motte-and-bailey castle are well illustrated here. Land at Berkhamsted was granted by William the Conqueror to Robert count of Mortain, who was probably responsible for the earliest fortifications on the site. The castle subsequently passed into the hands of the Crown, and Henry II placed it in the custody of Thomas Becket when he was chancellor. Extensive renovations and improvements were carried out under Becket's supervision, including the construction of accommodation suitable for the king in the bailey. At some time a circular tower was erected on the mound. William of Windsor took over from Becket in 1165, and considerable expenditure was incurred in fitting out on the eve of the great war. From 1174 to the end of the reign it was apparently leased to William de Mandeville, earl of Essex. The stone buildings are now reduced to a few ruins, but the massive earthworks remain as a testimony to the durability of such structures.

3 Trematon castle, Cornwall, on the estuary of the river Tamar, illustrates an
economical method of strengthening a motte-and-bailey fort by replacing the timber
pallisades with a stone curtain wall, and with a 'shell keep' on the mound. (The square
gatehouse and the mansion are of much later date.)

4 Norham castle, Northumberland. A border castle for defence against the Scots, it formed part of the vast estates of the bishopric of Durham. The first castle here was built by Ranulf Flambard, bishop of Durham 1099–1128 – the able, if highly unpopular, chief-minister of King William Rufus. It was destroyed by David, king of Scots, in 1138, in the course of his invasion of King Stephen's realm, supposedly in support of Empress Matilda (see above, p. 180). A new castle with a stone keep (a small portion only of which remains) was erected by Bishop Hugh du Puiset in the early years of Henry II's reign. Bishop Hugh, however, was believed by King Henry to have betrayed his trust in the great war of 1173–4: Norham offered no resistance to invasion by King William the Lion in 1174. The bishop was deprived of Norham by Henry II, together with his other castles at Durham and Northallerton; but it was too important to be destroyed, as were so many other baronial castles after the great war. It was returned to the bishop after a few years, but was taken into royal control again in 1185, when Henry II had renewed reason to mistrust the loyalty of those who had been against him earlier.

5 The donjon of Falaise, in the heart of Normandy. The alternative to motte-and-bailey fortifications was the massive stone *donjon* or *keep*. It was an expensive alternative, but dramatically symbolic of the prestige and resources of a great ruler. This squat, square tower was built by William the Conqueror, and had several parallels in England, including the oldest structure still surviving at the Tower of London. The basic design of such keeps did not change much for a century after the Conquest. Some of Henry II's most important castles on the continent were of this type (e.g., Loches, Loudun, Montrichard), built by his predecessors and requiring little modification.

6 *opposite* Castle Rising, Norfolk. An excellent surviving example of the stone keep of the Falaise type was built by one of the wealthiest of Henry II's earls, William d'Aubigny, earl of Arundel from c. 1141 to 1176, on his estates in Norfolk. The keep was erected within the ramparts of an earlier fortification, but had to be built at ground level for sufficiently secure foundations for its enormous weight. In the absence of a roof, the cross-wall – a characteristic feature of square keeps – can clearly be seen.

7 Newcastle-upon-Tyne, Northumberland. The construction of stone keeps to reinforce earlier fortifications was Henry II's major contribution to royal castle-building in England. That at Newcastle was constructed between 1172 and 1177 at a cost approaching £1,000. The walls are so massive that chambers are incorporated within their thickness. In outward appearance it has changed little from Henry II's day, apart from the addition of stone battlements, and the blackening of the honey-coloured stone by smoke from the nearby railway. The photograph shows well the elaborate structure against the east wall, protecting the entrance, which was at third-storey level. Though the architecture is in the main conventional, the masonry is unusual – instead of the stones being square-faced, they are long and narrow. This kind of masonry was to become common later.

8 *opposite* Dover castle, Kent. Henry II's keep at Dover still stands within the extensive additional fortifications erected at later dates. It was one of the strongest of all the square keeps, and also by far the most expensive. It was constructed between 1180 and 1190 at a cost probably not far short of £4,000. Like the earlier keep at Newcastle, it is somewhat loftier than those of the Norman period, but is still within the tradition represented by Falaise and the Tower of London.

9   Orford castle, Suffolk: the keep. The massive stone tower was proof against all missiles which could be hurled against it at the time, and also against fire. The square keep, however, had a weakness which could be exploited by improved siege techniques: the area at the base which the defenders could least effectively cover with missiles from above was the corner formed by the straight sides, and this also offered the best purchase for the picks of beseigers. Extra protection could be incorporated at the base in the form of a sloping revetment (as can be seen on the keeps at Newcastle and Dover); but the better solution was to enable the defenders to cover all parts of the walls with equal effectiveness. At the same time as building the last and most magnificent of the traditional square keeps, Henry II was experimenting with novel designs. One of the most impressive of these to survive is the polygonal keep erected at Orford between 1166 and 1172. For the strategic importance of Orford, see pp. 234–5.

10 Dromore, County Down, Northern Ireland. The splendour of royal castles should
not be allowed to obscure the continuing importance of motte-and-bailey fortifications.
In terms of 'cost-effectiveness' they still had much to recommend them; and it was only
against superior lords with well-equipped military forces that their owners need feel
insecure. Their value was clearly appreciated by the settlers in Ireland. Dromore dates
from the last quarter of the twelfth century, and was erected by the followers of John
de Courcy in Ulster. In plan it is indistinguishable from the motte-and-bailey forts
erected in England a century earlier.

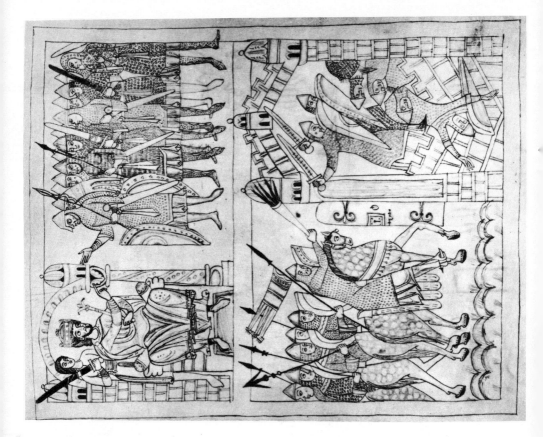

11 Arms and armour: the typical armour and weapons of the twelfth-century knight. The most expensive item of the knight's equipment was his *hauberk* of mail (consisting of interlocking iron rings). Apart from his war horse, it was the possession of a hauberk which chiefly distinguished the knightly warrior from the common foot soldiers. The latter might wear abbreviated mail armour, but usually had to rely on the less adequate protection of leather or quilted linen. Hauberks were handed down from father to son, and simpler types continued in use even after refinements had been introduced. Here, most of the knights are wearing hauberks with three-quarter-length, loose sleeves, but one has a close-fitting sleeve to the wrist – which had to be well wrought if it were not to curtail movement of the forearm. Hauberks were worn over a longer linen garment to protect against chafing. The back of the neck and part of the face were protected by a mail *coif* which extended over the head (as can be seen on the figure at the extreme top right). Helmets were conical, often beaten from a single piece of iron, and sometimes with a nose-piece attached. Some of the knights above are shown with mail laced to the leg (known as *chausses*). The kite-shaped shield was developed from the earlier round or oval shield especially for use by horsemen: its shape fitted the horse's flank and protected the rider's thigh on the side on which he was less readily able to defend himself. The knights' lance was an elongated spear (not the counter-balanced, tapering weapon of the later middle ages), and could be thrown like a javelin, or used for thrusting, as well as clamped into the side on a charge. If the lance had been thrown, or was broken, or for close combat, the knight used his sword – commonly rather a short, broad-bladed weapon used more for hacking than thrusting, though a longer, slimmer sword was coming into use in the twelfth century.

12—*caption overleaf*

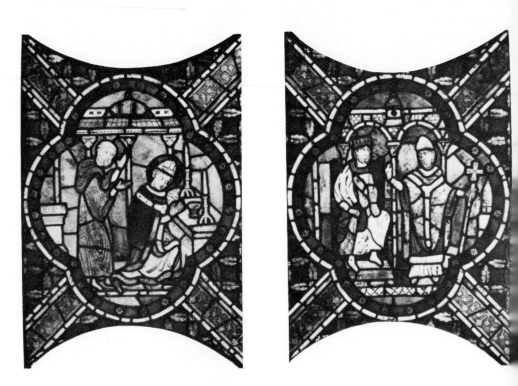

13 Thomas Becket as archbishop. The two scenes here are depicted in thirteenth-century stained glass in the Trinity Chapel at Canterbury Cathedral. On the left, the archbishop is shown celebrating Mass, and on the right, arguing with King Henry.

12 Henry II's father, Count Geoffrey of Anjou. A memorial plaque of enamel inlay, now in the Municipal Museum at Le Mans. The inscription may be translated: 'The host of robbers flees thy sword, O Prince; the churches, peace restored, are unmolested.' The original measures 63 cm × 32 cm.

Although he was sparing of food and drink, dressed simply, and was thrifty in private, he was, says Gerald of Wales, 'expansive towards strangers and prodigal in public'. He gave alms generously, though frequently in secret, according to Walter Map, and Peter of Blois commends his liberality towards his servants.[1] 'I was with him,' writes Walter Map, 'when we recently crossed the Channel with a fleet of twenty-five ships, which were provided as a service by the Cinque Ports without cost to the Crown. A storm scattered the fleet and dashed the ships on rocks or drove them on to a lee shore, all save the king's vessel which by God's grace was brought safely to port. The next morning the king sent for the seamen and made good the losses which each had sustained, although he was not obliged to do so, and the cost was high.'[2] Ralph of Diceto records that in 1176, when famine struck in Anjou and Maine, Henry emptied his private barns, cellars, and storehouses to relieve distress among the poor.[3] His concern for ordinary people is reflected too in an ordinance recorded by William of Newburgh: 'At the beginning of his reign he changed the ancient and inhuman custom with regard to those shipwrecked, and ordained that those who were rescued from the sea should be treated according to the dictates of humanity, and prescribed heavy penalties for anyone who molested them or plundered their goods.'[4]

Unlike his grandfather Henry I, who was a creature of habit, Henry II 'shunned regular hours'.[5] He worked as need dictated or the mood took him – well into the night sometimes.[6] It made a mockery of planned schedules and taxed the patience of his household officers. Peter of Blois, at one time his secretary, penned a rueful sketch of what life was like with the unpredictable Henry FitzEmpress:

> If the king has said he will remain in a place for a day – and particularly if he has announced his intention publicly by the mouth of a herald – he is sure to upset all the arrangements by departing early in the morning. And you then see men dashing around as if they were mad, beating pack-horses, running carts into one another – in short, giving a lively imitation of Hell. If, on the other hand, the king orders an early start, he is sure to change his mind, and you can take it for granted that he will sleep until

[1] Cf. Gerald of Wales, *Opera*, V, 304, who says that he was 'without equal in almsgiving.'

[2] Walter Map, 242.

[3] Ralph of Diceto, I, 406–7.

[4] William of Newburgh, I, 282.

[5] Ralph Niger, 169.

[6] Walter Map, *loc. cit.*, cf. Bracton, *De Legibus et Consuetudinibus Angliae*, IV. 4 (ed. Twiss, III, 38).

midday. Then you will see the packhorses loaded and waiting, the carts prepared, the courtiers dozing, traders fretting, and everyone grumbling. People go to ask the maids and doorkeepers what the king's plans are, for they are the only ones likely to know the secrets of the court. Many a time when the king was sleeping, a message would be passed from his chamber about a city or town he intended to go to, and though there was nothing certain about it, we would be comforted by the prospect of good lodgings. This would produce such a clatter of horse and foot that all Hell seemed let loose. But when our courtiers had gone ahead almost the whole day's ride, the king would turn aside to some other place where he had, it might be, just a single dwelling with accommodation for himself and no one else. I hardly dare say it, but I believe that in truth he took a delight in seeing what a fix he put us in. After wandering some three or four miles in an unknown wood, and often in the dark, we thought ourselves lucky if we stumbled upon some filthy hovel. There were often a sharp and bitter argument about a mere hut, and swords were drawn for possession of lodgings which pigs would have shunned.[1]

Henry himself never grumbled about the discomforts of constant travel, even in the heat and dust of summer or the cold and mud of winter. For a man reputedly so restless and volatile, he could be extraordinarily patient. Whenever he walked out into a crowd of people he would be confronted by jostling suitors, shouting to catch his ear and elbowing for position, and sometimes he would be swept off his feet and dragged from one side to the other; yet he never lost his temper and somehow managed to give each one a hearing.[2] In moments of crisis too his calmness was astonishing. There was never any sign of panic: when he saw what needed to be done he acted swiftly, but when the situation was inscrutable he bided his time until his enemies showed their hand.[3] In the early months of the great war, when it seemed that his whole empire was crumbling about his ears, he waited calmly at Rouen for his enemies to make a move, and passed the time in hunting.[4] He even had hawks and hounds shipped over to him from England.[5]

But although he could preserve his equanimity in hardship and danger, he could not abide that his will be flouted, his authority impugned, or his trust abused. His fits of rage against 'traitors' were notorious, and if the gossip of Becket's correspondents is to be believed,

[1] Peter of Blois, letter 14, *Patrologia Latina*, CCVII, 48–9; cf. Walter Map, *loc. cit.*
[2] Walter Map, *loc. cit.*
[3] Peter of Blois, *loc. cit.*: 'securior in periculis, in prosperis timidior, constantior in adversis'.
[4] Ralph of Diceto, I, 373–4; Jordan Fantosme, 213, lines 118–19.
[5] Pipe Roll 19 Henry II, 55.

he flung off his clothes and chewed the straw of the floor in his fury when the constable of Normandy had the temerity to speak in favour of his enemy, the king of Scots.[1] Gerald of Wales says that Henry was slow to abandon either a dislike or an affection once conceived, but also remarks that he was so charitably lenient towards rebels that he brought more trouble upon himself in consequence.[2] This was yet another of his seemingly paradoxical qualities. The explanation seems to be that he understood opposition and bore it no grudge, but that he could not abide betrayal – or what he took to be betrayal. There were bishops who opposed him as resolutely as Becket, yet never incurred the hostility he showed to his former friend.[3] Similarly the earls who opposed him in the great war were all received back into favour; but Arnulf bishop of Lisieux, a trusted counsellor who was suspected of private dealings with the other side, was so harassed and persecuted by the king's officers that he was driven to resign his see.[4]

It is not easy to assess Henry II's attitude to religion. Walter Map thought him pious; but Gerald of Wales could see no sign of personal devotion in him: 'would that he gave as much time to meditation as he did to the chase'. He would scarce spend an hour at mass; and even then, adds Ralph Niger, he would pass the time in whispered conversation or doodling.[5] The views of clerical chroniclers on the subject are perhaps, however, an unsafe guide, for they were understandably prejudiced by his disrespect for the clergy, of which his treatment of Archbishop Becket was only one sign. William of Newburgh, who on the whole thought well of Henry II, singled out for criticism his treatment of vacant bishoprics: he would delay approving an appointment so that the revenues of the see could be drawn into the royal exchequer. The king, he says, blandly justified this by arguing that it was surely better that the wealth of the Church should be spent to the benefit of the realm than on the pleasures of bishops. This was doubtless merely one of Henry II's characteristically caustic remarks, but William of Newburgh thought it a shocking sign of his irreverence.[6] On the other hand, Peter of Blois claims in Henry's favour that in making ecclesiastical appointments he avoided simony, and even Gerald of Wales admits that he nominated some good bishops.[7]

---

[1] *See* above, ch. 4, p. 183.

[2] Gerald of Wales, *loc. cit.*; cf. Peter of Blois, *loc. cit.*, and *Dialogus de Scaccario*, 76.

[3] *See* below, ch. 13.

[4] Cf. Barlow, introduction to *The Letters of Arnulf of Lisieux*, l–lix.

[5] Ralph Niger, 169: 'Oratorium ingressus, picturae aut susurro vacabat'.

[6] William of Newburgh, I, 280–1.

[7] Peter of Blois, *loc. cit.*; Gerald of Wales, IV, 345.

His attitude to religious orders is treated cursorily by the chroniclers, although it is worthy of more than a passing mention. Part of his penance for the death of Archbishop Becket was to build three monasteries, but he discharged it, said his critics, with ill grace and parsimony.[1] Their criticism is justified; but it is perhaps more an indication of his attitude to his penance than his attitude to monks, for he was lavish towards the abbey of Reading in England, to Grandmont in the Limousin, and to Fontevrault in Anjou.[2] The bequests he made in his last testament went almost exclusively to religious orders, and he expressed a wish to be buried at Grandmont, though in fact he came to rest at Fontevrault.[3] He frequently visited and took counsel with the austere monks of Grandmont, particularly during the controversy with Becket.[4] And though he joked with Walter Map about the Cistercians, there is little sign that he shared the genuine hostility that lay behind much of the secular clergy's ridicule of their righteousness.[5] Adam of Eynsham, the biographer of St Hugh of Lincoln, was convinced that Henry II had a deep regard for holy men, and his personal attachment to the austere Grandmontians and the even stricter Carthusians seems to confirm it.[6] As part of his penance for the death of Becket Henry II introduced the Carthusians to England and established them on a site at Witham in Somerset. That Henry was remiss in properly providing for the monks, as his critics alleged, is true; but the full story, as told by Adam of Eynsham, speaks more of the king's preoccupations than of parsimony. The new foundation languished at first partly from insufficient funds, partly because of the inadequacy of the first two priors, and partly because the foreign monks who came to start it found the local food inedible and their neighbours hostile. It might have foundered altogether if King Henry had not brought in as a new prior Hugh of Avalon, a monk from Grand Chartreuse recommended to him by a nobleman of Maurienne. The king promised Hugh everything he needed, but little was forthcoming:

> When the more important buildings had been erected, the king, absorbed in political matters, took little interest in the completion of the remainder.

[1] Gerald of Wales, VIII, 170; Ralph Niger, 168.

[2] Cf. *The History of the King's Works*, ed. Colvin, I, 49ff.; *Materials for the History of Becket*, VI, 386; Richard, *Les Comtes de Poitou*, II, 252 n.1. Many examples of Henry II's patronage are to be found in the *Recueil des Actes de Henri II*.

[3] *Recueil des Actes de Henri II*, II, 219–21; *Foedera*, I, Pt I, 47; Roger of Howden *Gesta*, I, 7.

[4] Cf. Kate Norgate, *England under the Angevin Kings*, II, 436 n.1.

[5] Cf. Knowles, *The Monastic Order in England*, 675–6.

[6] Adam of Eynsham, I, 70; cf. William of Newburgh, I, 282.

The masons became indignant when there was no money to pay them and abused the prior and brethren. The prior sent some of the monks to the king to tell him of the arrears and of what more was required. He promised that he would soon give the matter his attention and send what was needed. So the envoys returned merely with empty promises, and as the king did not fulfil his undertakings the building operations stopped altogether. The prior took the view that they should not protest, but should allow the king the opportunity, of his own accord, to take an interest in doing what was necessary. But as he failed to do so, other envoys were sent to him, after the lapse of a considerable time, who as before received empty promises and no gifts. . . . Some of the brethren became indignant with the prior, and reproached him with laziness and indifference because he had not gone himself to the king on such important business, even though he were far away.

One of the brothers named Gerard, a monk of rather harsh temperament though a good monk, whose words had considerable force with kings and magnates, spoke out, saying, 'How long, lord prior, do you intend to go on humouring this hard man, instead of bluntly telling him that either he must quickly finish the buildings which are essential to our way of life, or else, if he goes on procrastinating, you will take your leave of him and return home with us as soon as possible. Can't you see that his obvious neglect of us is bringing discredit upon our order, and that our being here for such a long time without being able to put roofs on our poor huts is making us the laughing stock of the whole neighbourhood? If your natural shyness prevents you giving this man a piece of your mind, let us go to him together, and you shall hear what I have to say to him.' The brethren all met to discuss the matter, and it was unanimously decided that Gerard should go with the prior to the king. The prior said, 'I willingly accept your advice, but take care brother Gerard to be courteous as well as frank. I have discovered that the king is crafty and his mind is almost unfathomable. It is possible that by postponing his assistance he is testing us.' . . .

Taking with him therefore Gerard and another monk named Einhard, a very old but exemplary monk, the prior went to the king, who received them as reverently as if they had been angels from Heaven. He was very gracious when they explained their business, and made lavish promises, apologising for the delay and undertaking that everything should soon be completed. He did not, however, offer them the money or give any guarantee that it would be forthcoming. Then the fiery brother Gerard, remembering his first intention and not the warning he had received, turned furiously upon the king. 'Whatever you may finally decide, lord king, about completing or not completing the work you have begun, is no concern of mine, for I shall trouble you no further, but take my leave and return to my hermitage at Chartreuse. You think you are being generous if you provide us with bread, for that at least we have. I prefer to return to my barren Alpine crags, rather than to struggle with a man who regards anything spent on his salvation as so much waste. Keep the treasure you love so much. . . .' Such rebukes and even worse Gerard is said to have used to this mighty monarch. . . . The holy and courteous prior . . . cautioned the monk to speak less bluntly, and either to moderate his language or be silent altogether. He, however, with the assurance of a good conscience, old age, and noble birth, took no notice of what was said to him as long as he could still find fresh words with which to rebuke the king and tell him what he thought of him. . . .

In the meantime the king seemed lost in thought. His face did not change and he said nothing but listened silently and calmly until the speaker had exhausted himself. . . . For some time there was a deep silence. The prior lowered his head in confusion, and the king looked covertly at him, guessing his discomfort from his manner. At last he began to speak. 'You are lost in thought, reverend father. What do you have in mind? Will you go away too and leave me to possess my kingdom in peace?' He replied gently in a low voice: 'I have not lost confidence in you lord king. Rather I pity the distractions and occupations which prevent you from concerning yourself with the salvation of your soul. You are busy, but with God's assistance you will yet complete the good work you have begun.' The king then embraced him, and said with an oath, 'By my soul, as long as I am alive you shall not leave my kingdom. I will take counsel with you on what concerns the salvation of my soul.' He immediately sent the money and ordered that the buildings should be finished as speedily as possible.[1]

In 1186 Henry pressed upon Hugh of Avalon the bishopric of Lincoln, (and paid the cost of the consecration ceremony).[2] Indeed he conceived such an affection for the saintly Hugh and accepted rebukes from him with such good grace that there were many who were convinced that Hugh must be the king's natural son.[3]

Adam of Eynsham, though he knew the king only at secondhand from his hero Hugh, always spoke of Henry II with warmth. Few others did. Henry II was not in fact an easy man to know well. Walter Map, who was close to him and held him in affection, nevertheless criticised him for cutting himself off from everyone but his intimate friends. It

---

[1] Adam of Eynsham, I, 46–9, 54–5, 64–8.

[2] *Ibid.*, 103.

[3] *Ibid.*, 69. Henry allowed Hugh to escape the consequences of a crime hardly less serious than murder – the excommunication of a senior royal official, *ibid.*, 116–18.

did not help his reputation – which suffered anyway from the shadow cast on it by the murder of Becket. The chroniclers of the time were not sure how to place him. Gerald of Wales said that he had many great qualities, but hinted that his performance did not match up to his promise, and after Henry's death he wrote about him more viciously, producing a lengthy tract, *On the Instruction of Princes*, designed to show how he had abused the advantages God gave to him.[1] Ralph Niger, who suffered as a partisan of Becket, conceived so violent a hatred of Henry that he could write nothing of him save with poisoned prejudice. Even the habitual reticence of Gervase of Canterbury can barely conceal his dislike of the man.[2] Roger of Howden passes no comment. Ralph of Diceto, dean of St Paul's, did his best as a friend of the king to underline his generosity of mind; but he seems to be writing on the defensive, as if he knew men would find it hard to believe him.[3] Only time rescued Henry II from the calumny of contemporaries. William of Newburgh, writing in the next generation, and one of the most judicious of medieval chroniclers, says that Henry was almost universally disliked in his own day, but that when men had experience of his sons' reigns they began to appreciate how well off they had been: 'Indeed the experience of present evils has revived the memory of his good deeds, and the man who in his time was hated by all men, is now declared to have been an excellent and beneficent prince.' In Newburgh's view his virtues were tainted by his debauchery, and he never sufficiently repented of his treatment of Archbishop Becket; but at least he was humane, and 'in wielding the sword for the punishment of evildoers and the preservation of the peace and quiet for honest men, showed himself a true servant of God'.[4]

It is perhaps not surprising that contemporary chroniclers had such difficulty in reaching a balanced judgement about Henry II: he was a man of such contradictory qualities, so volatile, and, as Hugh of Avalon said, so crafty and unfathomable that no one could be sure of assessing him correctly. Unlike Becket he was careless of his reputation, and seems to have revealed himself fully only to his intimate friends. He never, to judge from the chronicles, explained his motives in public; and his recorded utterances are either caustic remarks which only the gullible would take seriously, or words spoken in anger which are no true guide to his considered course of action. Something of the difficulty

---

[1] Cf. Warner, introduction to *Giraldi Cambrensis Opera*, VIII, xxiiff.

[2] Cf. Stubbs, introduction to *The Historical Works of Gervase of Canterbury*, I, xlvii-xlix.

[3] e.g. Ralph of Diceto, I, 395.   [4] William of Newburgh, I, 280, 283.

of understanding this complex man is revealed – probably unintention-
ally – in a story told by William FitzStephen of an encounter between
the king and the bishop of Worcester shortly after the coronation of
Henry the Younger in 1170. Bishop Roger, who was a younger son of
the empress's half-brother, Earl Robert of Gloucester, and therefore the
king's cousin, had been summoned to attend the coronation, despite the
fact that he was well known as a fearless defender of the exiled archbishop of Canterbury. He was in Normandy at the time and made his
way to Dieppe to cross the Channel; but Queen Eleanor and the
seneschal of Normandy, fearing that he might be going only to protest
at the archbishop of York performing the ceremony, refused to allow
any transport to be provided for him. He was still in Normandy when
the king returned from England, and they met on the road three miles
out of Falaise. Henry did not know that Bishop Roger had been prevented from crossing and denounced him angrily:

> 'What a traitor you have proved to be,' he said, 'I sent you a personal
> invitation to my son's coronation, and told you when it would be; but you
> did not come. You can have no regard for me or my son's honour. I'll see
> that you lose the revenues of your see for this. You are not your father's
> son. To think that we were both taught by him the essentials of good
> behaviour.'
> 'That is fine, coming from you,' replied Bishop Roger. 'What do you care
> that my father, Earl Robert, fought for you sixteen years against King
> Stephen, and even suffered imprisonment on your behalf. Little good has
> it done my elder brother. The earldom of Gloucester was worth a thousand
> knights until you cut it down to two hundred and forty. And as for my
> younger brother – you have reduced him to such penury that he has had
> to take service with the Knights Hospitaller. That's how you treat your
> kinsmen and friends. That's what people receive for serving you. Take my
> revenues if you will; although I should have thought you might have been
> satisfied with those of the archbishop and the vacant bishoprics and abbeys
> – surely that's enough on your conscience.'
> A member of the party who thought to please the king, bitterly reviled the
> bishop; but the king turned on him angrily and abused him soundly, say-
> ing, 'You miserable lout; do you think that just because I say what I like
> to my kinsman and bishop, it gives you any right to dishonour him with
> your tongue. I don't want to hear a word against him.' So they came to
> their lodgings, and after dinner the king and the bishop had a friendly
> talk about what might be done about the archbishop.[1]

[1] William FitzStephen, III, 103–6. The rendering above is a very free translation
of the story told by William FitzStephen, who was himself giving a Latin rendering
of an exchange which was no doubt delivered in colloquial French.

There was, however, one fault in Henry FitzEmpress which even his well-wishers chose to pass over in silence than try to excuse: he was an oath-breaker. 'He was always ready to break his word,' says Gerald of Wales; in slipperiness he outdid Proteus, wrote Becket.[1] Becket's friends could never bring themselves to trust what Henry said. It was a major factor in the failure to find a basis for reconciliation. It was possible to argue that there was clear proof for all to see. Henry had promised Northumbria to the king of Scots, but refused to let King Malcolm have it.[2] He deprived King Stephen's son, William, of the castles and manors he had promised him in the Treaty of Winchester.[3] He never fulfilled the promise he made to the bishop of Salisbury, before he became king, to restore to him the castle of Devizes.[4] He cheated King Louis over Margaret's dowry in the Vexin.[5] He broke his word at the truce of Montmirail to take no further action against the rebels of Poitou and Brittany.[6] It was not surprising, then, that some men could believe that he had defrauded his brother, Geoffrey, of Anjou and Maine.[7] Yet there are two points which may be made in mitigation of Henry's duplicity. The first is that King Louis, that 'most pious and most Christian king', was far worse: he callously proclaimed truces which he broke – at least no one died from Henry's breaches of faith.[8] The second is that Henry could justify (if not excuse) his oath-breaking on the ground of a superior duty – the duty to recover and defend the 'rights' that fell to him as king, duke or count. Henry the Pretender might make promises which Henry the King could not be expected to observe. Perhaps he stole a march over King Louis in the matter of the Vexin, but the Vexin really belonged to him anyway; it was Louis who was the usurper craftily extracting it from him in the days of his adversity.

Henry's repudiation of the promises he made before becoming king was the counterpart to the repudiation of the grants which Stephen made to the prejudice of the economic and jurisdictional rights of the

[1] Gerald of Wales, V, 304; Archbishop Becket in a letter to the bishop of Ostia, *Materials for the History of Becket*, VII, 124, cf. *ibid.*, 249, 251; John of Salisbury in *Johannis Saresberiensis Opera Omnia*, II, 202.

[2] *See* above, ch. 4, pp. 182–3.

[3] Robert de Torigny, 192–3; cf. Round, *Studies in Peerage and Family History*, 170.

[4] *Materials for the History of Becket*, VII, 241; cf. Saltman, *Archbishop Theobald*, 40.

[5] *See* above, ch. 3, pp. 88–90.

[6] *See* above, ch. 3, p. 110, and Herbert of Bosham, III, 438.

[7] *See* above, ch. 2, pp. 45–6.

[8] Cf. e.g. Roger of Howden, *Gesta*, I, 54; William of Newburgh, I, 192–4.

Crown. As William of Newburgh reports: King Henry 'commanded that all crown lands alienated through the weakness of King Stephen should be surrendered entirely by those who held them. Those who possessed royal towns and manors offered in justification charters which they had either extorted from King Stephen or been given for services rendered; but these availed them nothing. The grants of a usurper,' he commented, 'cannot be allowed to prejudice the rights of a lawful king.'[1] It is easy to see, in fact, that Henry held that alienations of crown property, whether by a usurper or a pretender, were alike unreasonable and therefore invalid. Henry even deprived his chamberlain, William Maudit, of the royal manors of Harborough and Bowden and the constableship of Rockingham castle, with which his services had been bought in 1153.[2] No exception could be allowed to this primary principle – just as no exceptions were allowed to the demand for the surrender of royal castles in 1155: the policy was the same for the king's friends as for his opponents.[3]

This doctrine that unreasonable alienations were void no doubt earned Henry II many enemies; but it had a parallel in canon law. Bishops were held to have no right to alienate the property of their see – they held it in trust for their successors. The diocese of Ely had suffered from baronial encroachments in Stephen's reign, and Bishop Nigel was commanded by the papacy to recover what had been lost: as Pope Eugenius III wrote to him in 1150, the grants which his predecessors had been obliged to make were *irrationabiliter* and therefore void.[4] Later kings of England were to swear at their coronation not to alienate the *iura regni* – the rights which devolved with the Crown. What Henry II swore at his coronation is not known for certain, but clearly this was the principle he embraced. That it was taking root in contemporary thinking is revealed in a lawbook of the period that goes by the name of the *Leges Edwardi Confessoris*:

> The king ought to preserve and defend all lands and honours, all dignities and rights and liberties of the Crown unimpaired, and ought to restore to

---

[1] William of Newburgh, I, 103. Cf. *Gesta Abbatum Monasterii Sancti Albani*, I, 123: 'Edictum igitur ab ipso promulgatur, quatenus omnes terrae quae per totam Brittaniam in dominium praedecessorum suorum, Regum Angliae, secundum juramentum hominum suorum, quolibet tempore habitae sunt, sine alicujus contradictione redderentur, futurisque temporibus in dominio suo, successorumque suorum, servarentur.'

[2] Richardson, 'The coronation oath in medieval England', 155.

[3] *See* above, ch. 3, p. 60.

[4] Richardson, *op. cit.*, 151–2, quoting British Museum, Cotton MS. Tiberius A, vi, f. 117v.

their previous condition those rights of the realm that are lost, damaged, or strayed, and recover what is owed by all men.[1]

In effacing the effects of Stephen's usurpation and his own need in adversity to buy what was his by right, Henry was ruthless but not vindictive. Malcolm of Scotland received some compensation for the loss of Northumbria in the grant of the earldom of Huntingdon which his father had held under Henry I.[2] The bishop of Salisbury had the loss of Devizes made good by the grant of other revenues.[3] Stephen's son William had his loss softened by many small marks of Henry's favour, and remained immensely powerful, for, as Robert de Torigny reports, 'the king confirmed to him all that Stephen his father had held in the year and on the day upon which King Henry his grandfather was alive and dead'.[4] The last phrase is significant: the situation at Henry I's death was the touchstone of what was right, the yardstick by which claims were measured. It is a phrase which appears frequently in the records of Henry II's reign: 'Let it be as it was on the day of my grand-father's death', 'Let them hold as well and as freely as they did in the time of King Henry my grandfather'. This is the recurring phraseology of charters and even occurs in common law writs:

> The king to *so-and-so* greeting. I prohibit you from unjustly vexing *so-and-so* or permitting him to be vexed, in respect of his free tenement which he holds of you in *such-and-such* a vill, or from demanding or allowing to be demanded, customs and services which he is not bound to do for you, or which his ancestors neither did or were bound to do in the time of King Henry my grandfather. . . .[5]

It is the message of Henry's proclamation at the beginning of his reign:

> Know that for the honour of God and Holy Church, and for the common restoration of my whole realm, I have granted and restored and by this present charter confirmed, to God and to Holy Church, and to all my earls, barons, and vassals, all concessions, gifts, liberties, and free customs *which King Henry my grandfather granted and conceded to them.* Likewise all evil

---

[1] Liebermann, *Die Gesetze der Angelsachsen*, I, 635: 'Debet . . . rex omnes terras et honores, omnes dignitates et iura et libertates corone regni huius in integrum . . . observare et defendere, dispersa et amissa regni iura in pristinum statum et debitum viribus omnibus revocare.'

[2] Barrow, introduction to *Regesta Regum Scottorum*, I, 10, cf. *ibid.*, 190, doc. 128.

[3] Saltman, *Archbishop Theobald*, 466.

[4] Robert de Torigny, 193. Henry knighted Earl William in 1158, *ibid.*, 196; cf. Pipe Rolls 2–4 Henry II *sub* 'Warenń comes'. He died in the king's service on the expedition to Toulouse in 1159, Robert de Torigny, 206.

[5] *Glanvill*, XII. 10, cf. IX. 14, and XII. 16.

customs *which he abolished and relaxed*, I also grant to be relaxed and abolished in my name and that of my heirs.[1]

And for a succinct summary of Henry II's fundamental policy we need look no further than the charter he granted to the citizens of Exeter confirming 'all the rightful customs which they had in the time of King Henry my grandfather, *revoking all evil customs which have arisen there since his day*'.[2] The revocation of 'evil customs' of recent growth involved the recovery, restoration, and defence of all the Crown's rights, territorial, economic, and jurisdictional. It was a single policy which embraced politics, government, and the Church's claim to liberty. It formed the justification for the expedition to Toulouse, the campaigns in Wales, the intrigues in the Auvergne; it provided the impetus for the development of the exchequer and the machinery of the general eyre, and it provoked the Constitutions of Clarendon and the breach with Becket.

To say that this was Henry II's fundamental policy is not, of course, necessary to imply that it was his only policy. It might have been merely the prelude to the implementation of more ambitious schemes. Archbishop Becket and his supporters were to argue that Henry's defence of the 'ancient custom' of the realm in matters ecclesiastical was but the first step towards the extinction of the Church's liberties. They were wrong. Would it also be wrong to say that Henry II had no political ambitions beyond the defence of the rights he acquired by birth and marriage? It would seem so.

Henry II has been accused of aiming at world domination, or at the very least of trying to supplant the Holy Roman Emperor.[3] This is nonsense. Gerald of Wales does, it is true, hint darkly at it in a tortured and tendentious passage.

> Not only did he, in his boldness, enlarge his ambit to the French, by abusing the obligingness of that simple and saintly man King Louis, but also to the Roman Empire, at the time when Emperor Frederick and his subjects were in daily warfare and inexorable discord, being often invited as much by the whole of Italy as by the city of Rome, preparing indeed a way for himself for it through the valleys of Maurienne and the Alps.[4]

It is a wise rule, however, always to discount Gerald's laboured hints unless there is evidence to support them. The evidence is slight. Arch-

[1] Stubbs, *Select Charters*, 158.
[2] Ballard, *British Borough Charters*, I, 6: 'Sciatis me concessisse civibus meis Exoniae omnes rectas consuetudines quas habuerunt in tempore Regis Henrici avi mei remotis omnibus pravis consuetudinibus post avum meum ibi elevatis.'
[3] Principally by Hardegen, *Imperialpolitik König Heinrichs II von England*.
[4] Gerald of Wales, VIII, 157.

bishop Becket's letter-writing circle picked up a story that Henry had offered money to the cities of Milan, Cremona, Parma, and Bologna.[1] But even if the report is true it is more important to note that, as Gerald of Wales admits and Peter of Blois confirms, the initiative came from Italy.[2] The Lombard League was looking for an alternative to Barbarossa. Many people came to Henry II for help in their own troubles. They were received politely and refused with courtesy. Gerald of Wales made so bold on one occasion to upbraid Henry for his lukewarm response to the offer of the throne of Jerusalem brought to him by Patriarch Heraclius in 1185. Gerald told him that he ought to feel honoured that so important a man had travelled so far to bring him the offer 'by-passing the emperors and all the other kings of the world'. But Henry had no such illusions: 'If the patriarch or others come to us,' he replied, 'it is because they seek their own advantage rather than ours.'[3] That he dallied at all with the offer from the Lombard League was because he found it momentarily useful: Becket's circle thought he was trying to intimidate the pope, and they were probably right.

If any proof is needed that Henry II's foreign policy was extremely limited in purpose it will be found in the history of the proposed marriage alliance with Maurienne. In 1173 Henry concluded an agreement with the count of Maurienne for the marriage of his youngest son, John, to the count's daughter, Alice. The count, who had no son, traded his extensive territories in Savoy for a son-in-law and five thousand marks in cash.[4] The marriage never took place: the great war of 1173-4 intervened, and before it was over the intended bride had died. This need not have been the end of the project: the agreement provided that if the count's eldest daughter should die, his second daughter would be substituted on the same terms.[5] Henry, though he had already paid two thousand marks, declined to take up the option. It was not worthwhile any more: the proposed marriage settlement had been intended to bring pressure upon the count of Toulouse; but the threat of it had been sufficient to induce the count of Toulouse to offer his homage.[6] John could be saved for more useful purposes: he was in 1176 betrothed to the heiress of the honor of Gloucester, and a future planned for him in Ireland.

Nor can any grand design be traced in the marriages of Henry's daughters. Matilda (born in 1156) was married in 1168 to Henry the

[1] *Materials for the History of Becket*, VIII, 26, 30.
[2] Peter of Blois, letter 13, *Patrologia Latina*, CCVII, 340.
[3] Gerald of Wales, VIII, 207.   [4] *See* above, ch. 3, p. 117.
[5] Roger of Howden, *Gesta*, I, 38.   [6] *See* above, ch. 3, p. 117.

Lion, duke of Saxony; Eleanor (born in 1161) was married in 1176 to Alphonso VIII, king of Castille; and Joan (born in 1165) was married in 1177 to William II, king of Sicily. Matilda's marriage was part of a design in Henry's troubled days for counterbalancing Louis's marriage alliance with the house of Blois.[1] There is no sign that it had any more positive function in recruiting help against Louis; and indeed, the other half of the plan – a marriage to Emperor Frederick's youngest son – fell through because Henry could not bring himself to recognise the emperor's anti-pope.[2] Eleanor's Spanish marriage served no very useful purpose except perhaps to preserve Castille's neutrality, and that, while it may have been important earlier in the reign hardly mattered to Henry in the rosy days of triumph. Joan's marriage can have done no more than cement the good relations England had always enjoyed with the Normans of Sicily. It could bring no real advantage to Henry, and at the time of the marriage Henry knew very well that it could not. When the dreadful storm clouds had gathered in 1173 he had written to King William of Sicily, as he also wrote to the pope, asking for support. King William replied with sympathy, with indignation at the conduct of Henry's sons, and with prayers for his victory, but adding, frankly, that 'the inconvenience of distance does not permit our power to afford any assistance'.[3] It can, in fact, be no more argued from this evidence that Henry was intending to build up an empire of influence by marriage than that Louis VII was when he married his youngest daughter, Agnes, to Emperor Alexius of Constantinople. Henry was really doing no more than marrying off his daughters as suited their station in life. In this respect he did rather better for his daughters than Louis did for his. Agnes was the exception to the rule that Louis betrothed his many daughters to barons of France: to the count of Blois, the count of Champagne, to Henry the Younger, prospective duke of Normandy and count of Anjou, and to Richard, the prospective duke of Aquitaine.[4] Henry might, in fact, have done better to follow Louis's example; but then Henry had to try harder than Louis for he was, as R. L. Graeme Ritchie has observed, a king without a pedigree. That he was the son of a count no one chose to remind him: it was as 'Henry son of Matilda the empress' that the chroniclers knew him, he was 'Mac na-L'imperasi' even to the Irish, and it seems to have been

[1] See above, ch. 3, p. 104.   [2] See above, ch. 3, p. 104 n. 3

[3] Roger of Howden, *Chronica*, II, 48, For Henry's appeal to Pope Alexander III *see Recueil des Actes de Henri II*, II, 8–10.

[4] Alice, though betrothed to Richard, never married him; she eventually married the count of Ponthieu.

as Henry FitzEmpress that he thought of himself.[1] But apart from her imperial title, who was Matilda but the granddaughter of a Norman bastard? Henry had to do something to establish the prestige of his kingship. Having Edward the Confessor canonised was a matter to which he gave close personal attention; marrying his daughters well was another.[2] Henry was no doubt gratified by his success, and so too, to judge by the enthusiasm of the chroniclers, were his subjects.

Henry II's diplomacy was active but not very purposeful. Much of it was simply the exchange of courtesies and gifts between rulers who, in the international climate created by a busy papacy, the crusades, and burgeoning trade, realised that no ruler was any longer a law unto himself.[3] So far as Henry's diplomacy was directed towards the cementing of alliances, it had no very striking results. The negotiations with Germany came to little beyond the marriage of Matilda to Henry the Lion, duke of Saxony; and after the breach between Frederick Barbarossa and Henry the Lion this itself merely meant that Henry II had to find a home for an exile.[4] The alliance with the count of Barcelona, contrived as part of Henry's menace to Toulouse, seems to have been allowed to lapse after its purpose was served. The traditional alliance with Flanders followed a wayward course. To some extent this was inevitable, for the counts of Flanders were pulled three ways: by their trading connections with England, by their long-standing rivalry with the dukes of Normandy, and by their status as vassals of the king of France.[5] They were tempted to dabble in the political affairs of their neighbours, sometimes with unhappy consequences, and frequently found themselves with conflicting obligations. Henry I had made a treaty with Count Robert in 1103, whereby in return for an annual subsidy the count promised a thousand knights in military service –

[1] Ritchie, *The Normans in Scotland*, 354–5. Henry is described as 'filius Matildis' in the Treaty of Falaise of 1174, and in the memorandum of an agreement made before Henry himself in his court at Caen in 1183, *Recueil des Actes de Henri II*, II, 250.

[2] *Gesta Abbatum Monasterii Sancti Albani*, I, 159: 'Abbae Westmonasterii Laurentius ... historiam de Sancto Rege et Confessore, Edwardo, scribi eleganter procuravit, ab ipso collectam de diversis antiquis tractatibus; et in unum corpus redegit, ad petitionem Regis Henrici.' The pope canonised Edward in February 1161, and the ceremony of translation was held at Westminster on 13 October 1163. Cf. Bloch, 'Introduction à la vie de Saint Edouard le Confesseur', and Scholz, 'The canonization of Edward the Confessor'.

[3] For the details see the introductions by Round to the printed pipe rolls from 22 Henry II onwards.

[4] Henry duke of Saxony suffered forfeiture in 1182, and thereafter spent much time at the court of his father-in-law, e.g., Roger of Howden, *Gesta*, I, 249, 287, 288, 291, 316, 318, 319, 323; II, 56, 62.

[5] Dept, *Les Influences Anglaise et Française dans le Comté de Flandre*.

it was one of the early examples of a money-fief.[1] Henry II renewed it in 1163 with Count Thierry (1128–68) and his son; but this treaty seems more designed to secure the neutrality of Flanders in the event of war with the king of France than a league of alliance.[2] It did not always work, and Henry II did not do so much as he might have done to make it work. Count Philip (1168–91) felt that he was being deprived of his due rights in England, and Henry did nothing to assuage his grievance beyond sending him some deer from the New Forest.[3] Count Philip thought that he could obtain what he desired from Henry the Younger and became one of his principal allies in the great war. It was not until he realised that the ambitions of King Philip Augustus were a serious danger to him that, at the very end of Henry's reign, the count of Flanders sought an alliance with England.[4] Even more significant are the alliances Henry II did not make. There is no sign of any league against Louis. Count Theobald of Blois seems to have been ready to throw in his lot with Henry about 1159, but Henry allowed Louis to woo him away.[5] He made no move to inhibit Louis's ambitions in the Auvergne or Berry by forming alliances or even offering bribes to the counts of Sancerre or Forez, or to the seigneur of Bourbon.[6] There was certainly nothing to compare with the ring of alliances Richard I was to weave around the Capetian royal demesne. In short, there can be only one conclusion about Henry II's foreign policy: that he did not have any worth the name. It follows that his primary, and indeed almost exclusive concern was with the integrity of the political rights he acquired by birth or marriage.

Of course, even this purpose could carry menace for the Capetians, and it is perhaps understandable that King Louis VII should fear that Henry's intentions would do irreparable harm to the kingdom of France. But just what he feared, and why, is not easy to say. It could be supposed that Henry wished to separate his continental dominions from their traditional allegiance, create a new political entity, and leave

---

[1] *Foedera*, I, Pt I, 7; Kienast, *Die Deutchen Fursten*, 24 n.2.; Lyon, *From Fief to Indenture*, 34–5.

[2] *Foedera*, I, Pt I, 22–3; *Recueil des Actes de Henri II*, I, 375–81.

[3] Pipe Roll 17 Henry II, 35, 147.

[4] Their relations are surveyed by Dept, *op. cit.*, 21–3. Omitted from the references given there is the story that in 1177 the count, looking for assistance for his projected crusade, promised not to allow his nieces to marry without Henry's consent. Nevertheless he arranged marriages for them against Henry's wishes, Roger of Howden, *Gesta*, I, 133, 136, 269.   [5] *See* above, ch. 3, p. 90.

[6] There was, however, a border dispute with the lord of Bourbon-l'Archambault which led Henry II in 1170 to take possession of the castle of Montlucon, cf. Chénon, 'Les origines et les premiers seigneurs de Montlucon'.

the king in Paris merely with the rump of a kingdom. But such a supposition gains no support from the history of the oaths of allegiance Henry swore to Louis. Medieval oaths of allegiance came in a variety of shapes and sizes. There was a major distinction between fealty (*fidelitas*) and homage (*homagium*). An oath of fealty was little more than a solemn promise to be faithful – to act with fidelity. Homage on the other hand proclaimed the one who swore to be the vassal, the 'man' (*homo*) of the one to whom he swore. But oaths of homage took many forms. Homage could be sworn 'against all other men' or with reservations. It could bind the vassal to many obligations or to few. There was invariably in all oaths of homage the implication that the landed endowment the vassal enjoyed belonged in some sense to the lord to whom the oath was sworn; but in what sense the land belonged to the lord was often hard to determine – until lawyers of the later twelfth century had been at work analysing, codifying, clarifying, and systematising. Before then, oaths of homage could confirm to the lord either the most particular rights of supervision and control, or only the vaguest overlordship – an overlordship of honour which left the vassal in virtual independence. How the oath was to be interpreted depended upon the form of words in which it was sworn, on past history, and on the realities of power that inevitably, at bottom, determined the relationship of lord and vassal.

Where homage was concerned the art of politics lay in the construing of oaths and the imposition of meanings. It was in the construing of oaths that the king of England had difficulty with the king of Scots, and it was just such a problem that the king of France had with the duke of Normandy. History gave to the dukes of Normandy a jealously guarded inheritance of independence. Kings of France would have been rash to set foot in Normandy without invitation. Normandy was accountable as part of the kingdom because the dukes did homage to the king, but it was a homage which barely reduced the duke below the status of an equal. It was sworn only at the border between their respective domains (in the language of later documents it was an *homagium in marchia*), and was held to confer on the king only an overlordship of honour, and to bind the dukes to no more than a personal allegiance. It was rarely sworn, and most often only at the conclusion of hostilities. This tradition, going back, it seems likely, to the formation of the Norman duchy at the end of the tenth century, was clearly formulated by Robert de Torigny, about 1149, in these words:

> In the agreement which was made between the Franks and the Normans in the time of Richard I . . . it was ordained that the count [*sic*] of the

Normans should not perform service to the king of the Franks for the land of the Normans, nor do him any other service, unless the king of the Franks should give him a fief [sc. elsewhere] in France from which service was owed. Wherefore the count of the Normans should, concerning Normandy, do homage and fealty to the king of the Franks only to the extent of [sc. preserving] his life and earthly honour [*de vita sua et de suo terreno honore*]. Similarly the king of the Franks should promise [sc. to preserve] the life and honour in all his possessions [*facit fidelitatem de sua vita and de suarum rerum honore*] of the count of the Normans; and there should be no difference between them save for this, that homage is not done by the king of the Franks to the count of the Normans, as the count of the Normans does it to the king of the Franks.[1]

In short, the leader of the Normans owed no more than a personal allegiance to the king of France, and while the difference in the oaths sworn indicated that the king was acknowledged as overlord, there was no admission that Normandy itself was a fief of the French Crown.

It was a natural ambition of the kings of France to try to invest the oath with greater significance. They sought, as any astute lord would, to take advantage of any difficulty the vassal might encounter. If the language of the chroniclers may be trusted, Henry I, in seeking to guarantee the safe succession to Normandy of his son William Audelin, allowed him to do homage to King Louis in a form of words which at least suggested that he was to hold Normandy as a fief of the French Crown.[2] Stephen, it seems likely, did the same in 1137 when he sought to guarantee the succession for his son Eustace.[3] It is possible that Geoffrey of Anjou did so too when he sought to have Henry recognised by the king as duke of Normandy in 1151, and this oath had the added significance that it was sworn at Paris and not *in marchia*.[4]

It would not be surprising if Henry II had sought to repudiate such oaths sworn in adversity; and, indeed, the language of the Treaty of Ivry of 1177 closely reflects the form of words in which Robert de Torigny had expressed the traditional relationship of king and duke. Louis and Henry declare themselves to be friends (*amici*). They each swear to preserve 'the life, limbs, and earthly honour' of the other. Henry refers to Louis as his *dominus*, and Louis refers to Henry as his *homo et fidelis*, but they seek to resolve their differences not in the court of the lord, but by arbitration in the manner of rulers of sovereign states.[5] All

---

[1] Lot, *Fideles ou Vassaux?*, 261; Lemarignier, *Recherches sur l'Hommage en Marche*, 97 n.89.

[2] Lemarignier, *op. cit.*, 91–2 and n.65.　　　[3] *Ibid.*, 92–3 and n.70.

[4] *Ibid.*, 94.　　　　　　　　　　　　[5] *Ibid.*, 98–100, *see above*, ch. 3, pp. 145–6.

this suggests that Henry was preserving the virtual independence of Normandy, and moreover that he was extending the status of the dukes of Normandy, at least by implication, to the other titles that he held. On the other hand, there is evidence which tends to show that Henry did not insist on sticking rigidly to the provisions of an antiquated formula, and that he was willing to purchase peace for his dominions by indulging to some extent the desire of the kings of France to strengthen the tie of homage. There is, for example, the frequency with which oaths were sworn, not merely by himself, but also by his sons, not always on the border, and not always merely in ratification of peace.[1] The homages which Henry the Younger did in 1169 for Anjou and Brittany (separately from the homage for Normandy) confirmed that these at least were held as fiefs of the Crown.[2] Similarly with the homage which Richard swore for Aquitaine. Indeed it may be said that the fact that Henry II held other lands as fiefs of the French Crown compromised his peculiar status as duke of Normandy. He was not always careful to keep them separate when swearing homage: in 1183, according to Roger of Howden, 'he performed homage and fealty for all his holdings across the water to Philip king of the French, for which he never previously wished to do homage'.[3] Ralph of Diceto sensed the danger in Henry's status as, say, count of Anjou, being confounded with his status as duke of Normandy and king of England. He was alarmed when Henry the Younger attended the coronation of King Philip in 1179, insisted in his chronicle that he was there by special invitation as a brother-in-law, and interpolated a passage designed to remind his readers that the kings of England and France were equals.[4] It cannot be said that Henry II seriously prejudiced the traditional status of the dukes of Normandy: King John was later to claim that he could not, as duke of Normandy, be summoned to attend the court of the king of France, and King Philip admitted it.[5] Nevertheless, if Henry II moved at all on the

[1] The occasions are listed by Lemarignier, *op. cit.*, 100ff.

[2] Indeed, Robert de Torigny, 240, says that on this occasion 'concessit ei rex Francorum ut esset senescallus Franciae, quot pertinet ad *feudum* Andegavenae'.

[3] Roger of Howden, *Gesta*, I, 306: 'In quo colloquio Henricus, rex Angliae, fecit homagium et ligantiam de omnibus tenementis transmarinis Phillippo regis Franciae, cui nunquam antea homagium facere voluit,' cf. *Chronica*, II, 284: 'Henricus . . . devenit homo Philippi regis Franciae de omnibus terris suis transmarinis; cui nunquam ante tempus illud homagium facere voluit.'

[4] Ralph of Diceto, I, 438–9. Robert de Torigny, 287, confined his note of the event to a few words designed to minimise the significance of the attendance of a representative of King Henry; he says nothing of Henry the Younger's active part in the ceremony. Cf. Roger of Howden, *Chronica*, II, 94, who says that he carried the crown in procession 'de jure ducatus Normanniae'. [5] Ralph of Coggeshall, 136.

question of homage it was in the direction of confirming his status as a vassal of the French Crown, perhaps of admitting that his homage was something more than a declaration of personal allegiance, and certainly not in the direction of attempting to detach his continental dominions from the French kingdom.

Of course, it is likely that Louis VII and Philip II placed little confidence in Henry's performance of homage: he had devalued his oaths too often for men to trust in his good faith; but actions spoke more loudly than words in the middle ages, and Henry did much in the matter of homage for which the Capetian kings should have been profoundly grateful. On the other hand they could have argued that the very existence of Henry's 'empire' prejudiced the progress of the Capetian monarchy: that the union in the hands of one vassal of so many provinces created a situation in which the king, however much formally honoured, would always be the lesser power within the kingdom. How far such a fear would be justified depended, of course, on the permanence of the political authority that Henry II wielded. Did he intend it to be permanent?

Historians have often used the phrase 'the Angevin empire', and in doing so have implied that Henry's various dominions were welded together into a unity which bears comparison with the build-up of lesser 'feudal empires' by earlier provincial rulers – with the union of Anjou and Maine, for example, with the absorption of the counties of Mortain, Alençon, and Eu into the duchy of Normandy, or with the federation of the counties in Aquitaine and Gascony under the authority of the counts of Poitou. But such an implication cannot be sustained. It is true that there is some evidence which suggests that Henry II regarded his continental dominions as constituting some kind of unity. In September 1177 he held court at Verneuil in Normandy and promulgated an edict designed to limit the responsibility of vassals for debts contracted by their lords. 'This statute and custom the king enacted,' relates Roger of Howden, 'and ordered to be observed throughout his dominions, namely in Normandy, Aquitaine, Anjou, and Brittany, as being universal and established.'[1] It is unlikely, however, that this was anything more than a matter of convenience. Such evidence as this is too slight to tip the balance against the evidence to the contrary. There were five quite separate provincial administrations for England, Nor-

---

[1] Roger of Howden, *Gesta*, I, 194; *Recueil des Actes de Henri II*, II, 63–4; Yver, *Les Contrats dans le Très Ancien Droit Normand*, 220; cf. Powicke, *The Loss of Normandy*, 25–6. Similarly, the Assize of Arms, made at Le Mans at Christmas 1180, was ordained 'for the whole of his lands across the sea', Roger of Howden, *Gesta*, I, 269.

mandy, greater Anjou, Brittany, and Aquitaine. Though reforms begun in one might be passed to another there is no sign of any attempt to unify them. Each was normally governed by men native to the province.[1] In fact, so far as the 'empire' can be said to have had any unity

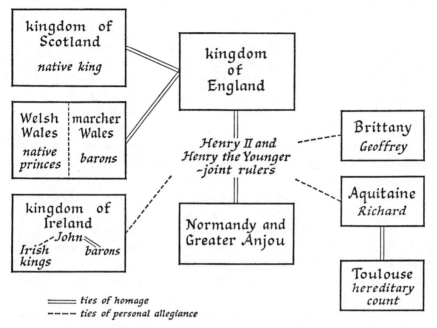

11. The structure of the Angevin commonwealth

at all, it was a unity which rested solely in Henry's peripatetic court and household. So far as the political future was concerned, Henry's intentions were made perfectly plain in the arrangements announced at Montmirail in 1169, and in his will drawn up in fear of death in 1170. The continental dominions were to be divided into three parts. Geoffrey was to be duke of Brittany, Richard was to be duke of Aquitaine, and the eldest, Henry, was to be duke of Normandy and to unite

---

[1] There are a few important exceptions to this principle. Richard of Ilchester, a baron of the English exchequer, was for a few years after 1176 seconded to the seneschalship of Normandy, apparently to reorganise its administration; but when his work was done he made way for a Norman and returned to England, Haskins, *Norman Institutions*, 174–6; Boussard, *Le Gouvernement d' Henri II*, 513. Henry imported some Englishmen and Normans into the administration of Aquitaine; but this seems to have been an exceptional measure for an exceptional situation, and the strangers were never numerous, cf. Boissonade, 'Administrateurs ... anglo-normands en Poitou'.

with it in his person the county of Anjou and its dependencies (that is to say, he was to have Henry II's own inheritance from his father).[1] This political division is reflected in Henry's monetary policy: Angevin money became the standard for greater Anjou and Normandy, in Aquitaine the policy was to make the coinage of Poitou the standard, Brittany was left to its own devices.[2]

Subsequent history disguised Henry's intention. Henry the Younger predeceased his father by six years; Richard was eventually to succeed to the whole, and John after him. But Henry himself steadfastly refused to allow that his dominions should be united in Richard's hands, and Richard had to fight him for them.[3] In short, if the territories to which Henry acquired a title by birth or marriage can be called an 'empire' at all, it was emphatically 'Henry's empire' and not 'the Angevin empire'. In reality, however, 'Henry's empire' was no more than a loose confederation of client states. In his mature conception (c. 1184) it was to be a 'commonwealth' of seven internally self-governing dominions linked merely by dynastic ties and oath-takings: the inherited unit of England, Normandy, and Anjou under his eldest son, Aquitaine under his second son, Brittany under the third, Ireland under the fourth, Welsh Wales (*pura Wallia*) under its native princes, Scotland under its native king, and Toulouse under its hereditary count. In his wars with the king of France it was not the acquisition of Louis's lordship that he was seeking but the security of his own. In his victories he demanded no more than an honourable peace for himself and security for his children. Yet King Louis had reason to be fearful. The very consolidation of Henry's rights inhibited Capetian expansion, particularly in Berry, the Auvergne, and Toulouse. Moreover, there was the success with which Henry brought a remarkable degree of firm government to lands which most men would have thought ungovernable. The real danger was that the Capetians would be obliged to remain for ever a second-class power within the kingdom. Herein lies an explanation for Louis's persistence in a struggle which brought him defeat and humiliation: if he could not fight to win there were still advantages for him in spoiling operations. And who is to say that his efforts were without effect – that the strains and stresses of defensive warfare and fomented rebellions did not undermine the Angevin commonwealth from its inception, and contribute decisively to its collapse twenty-five years after

[1] The Young King did homage separately to Louis for Normandy and Anjou, Gervase of Canterbury, I, 207–8; Robert de Torigny, 240–1.

[2] Boussard, *op. cit.*, 302–8.

[3] *See* below, ch. 14, pp. 496ff.

Henry's death? To say this is not to belittle Henry II's achievement, but to give Louis VII credit for pursuing the policy of his predecessors in putting persistence before pride and gnawing away at obstacles in the dogged hope that one day the obstacle would come tumbling down.

It was just as well that Henry II's political ambitions were limited to the recovery of his rights, for major military campaigns were not his strong point. His reign provided three examples: the Toulouse expedition of 1159, the Welsh expedition of 1165, and the Irish expedition of 1171. For these Henry called upon all available military resources, and made vast and expensive preparations. The preludes were lengthy, the armies ponderous, the campaigns slow, and the results either negligible or not worth the money expended on them. By contrast his defensive campaigns and police operations were bold, swift, almost entirely successful, and achieved with a remarkable economy of effort. He was famous in his own day as a taker of castles, and only the more showy glory of his son Richard has effaced the memory of it. Henry's achievement was to make the impregnable pregnable, and to do it in a matter of days. The conventional wisdom of contemporary warfare – 'First waste the land, deal after with the foe' – was ignored by Henry II.[1] The lightning raid, the rapid investment, the headlong and shattering assault – these were the characteristics of Henry II at war. They were first revealed at Malmesbury in 1153: 'he threw himself straight into the siege, for delay was not his way, and soon took it'.[2] After the protracted sieges and stalemate of the civil war this must have been surprising; but the speed with which Henry could reduce his opponents' castles continued to cause astonishment however many times it was repeated. His brother Geoffrey's partisans were quickly tumbled out of Chinon in 1155 though 'its strength was such that nature seemed to vie with human art in fortifying and defending it'.[3] Thouars was reputed to be 'an impregnable castle on the border between Poitou and Anjou'; but in three days in 1158 Henry had reduced it to submission.[4] In 1160 Count Theobald of Blois turned his castle of Chaumont-sur-Loire into a veritable arsenal of men and supplies; but it could not stand in Henry's way, and he made thirty-five knights and eighty sergeants prisoner.[5] In the following year he went into Aquitaine 'and among other energetic exploits he laid siege to Castillon-sur-Agen, a castle fortified by both

[1] This was the advice of Count Philip of Flanders to William king of Scots in 1174, Jordan Fantosme, line 451.
[2] Henry of Huntingdon, 286.   [3] William of Newburgh, I, 114.
[4] Continuatio Beccensis, 319–20; Robert de Torigny, 198.
[5] Robert de Torigny, 200.

nature and artifice, and took it in less than a week – to the wonder and terror of the Gascons'.[1] In the war of 1166–8 the strongly fortified castle of Lusignan was unable to withstand him, and the castles of the Bretons fell like skittles.[2] In the great war of 1173–4 Henry was more cautious than usual, for the main danger was the threat of invasion; but once he was freed from this he took the rebels' castles as a man might pluck fruit.

Henry II's military success was founded on his use of mercenaries. There was nothing in itself new about employing mercenaries – those who could afford to had been buying their services for a generation or more. The early twelfth century was fertile in military tactics, as men with ideas and money tried to break the dominance of the orthodox cavalry charge. Knights were a devastating but clumsy weapon. The charging Frank, said the Turk, could smash a hole through the walls of Babylon. The way to stop him was by military art: the ambush, harassing archers, the force held in reserve for the unexpected counterstroke, the close-packed phalanx of spearmen upon which the horsemen would impale themselves. Mercenary foot soldiers (*routiers* as they were known, and recruited principally in the Low Countries) were in demand by leaders who could pay for them. King Stephen had fought and nearly won the civil war with them. What Henry II did was to refashion the army – to make mercenary footmen the mainstay of his military power, not merely tactical auxiliaries. He fed them, clothed them, armed them, and above all had them specially trained and equipped for siege operations.

Henry's mercenary force was not an all-purpose army. It was more in the nature of a special force for internal police duties. On his few offensive expeditions he felt it necessary to call out considerable feudal cavalry forces, for mercenary infantry had weaknesses as well as advantages. They were effective (when disciplined) for defensive actions in the field; they were more useful (when well paid) than conscripts or short-service feudal troops for garrison duties; they were excellent (when properly equipped and trained) for siege operations, or for use as short-range mobile shock troops. But their offensive capacity was limited by their heavy demand on provisions and supplies, for they could not forage or live off the country as easily as cavalry forces. They were vulnerable to surprise attack while on the march, and could safely advance only while in battle formation if a force of enemy cavalry were in the vicinity: Henry moved very warily to the relief of Verneuil in

[1] Robert de Torigny 211.
[2] *Ibid.*, 228, 232, 235–7.

1173, for the French were there in strength and knew he was coming.[1] On the expeditions to Toulouse, to Wales, and to Ireland there was plenty of cavalry to reconnoitre and provide a protective screen; but the sluggishness of those expeditions is no doubt attributable to the heavy supply trains that infantry demanded when operating far from their bases. Despite the preparations and the forward dumps at Shrewsbury the army ran out of victuals in the mountains of Powys in 1165. It seems indeed that Henry II never really mastered the problem of combining foot soldiers and cavalry for offensive operations.[2] And if Henry II failed to solve a problem it was probably because he did not really give his mind to it. His main arsenals in France were at Rouen, Chinon, Poitiers, Nantes, and Bordeaux, which indicates that (apart from the necessary defence of the Vexin) his mind was chiefly on internal policework.[3]

The frailty of the traditional castle in the face of Henry II's siege-engines and storm troops involved a transformation of society. For two centuries in western Europe, authority had been largely divorced from power. This was a consequence of castle-building, for the invention of the castle and its refinement gave a decisive advantage to defenders over attackers. A few men in a well-found castle could defy many times their own number, and petty feudatories could set at naught the authority of great rulers.[4] A castle did not have to be impregnable, it merely had to be strong enough and sufficiently provisioned to withstand a few months' siege. Even if the defenders could not count upon allies to come to their relief, they could count on the attackers going away when their food supplies gave out, their short-term military service expired, the harvest approached, or the weather turned foul. Castles could be taken by main-force, starvation, or treachery, but usually only with difficulty and after many fruitless attempts. The Capetian kings took a hundred and fifty years to reduce the petty barons of their demesne lands to a semblance of order. By the late eleventh and early twelfth centuries power and authority were being painfully remarried by rulers such as William the Conqueror of Normandy, Fulk Nerra and Geoffrey Martel

[1] Roger of Howden, *Gesta*, I, 51–5.

[2] Cf. the comments of Gerald of Wales, V, 394–7.

[3] The military assessment given above is based upon Boussard, 'Les mercenaires au xiime siècle: Henry II Plantagenet et les origines de l'armée de metier'; Prestwich, 'War and finance in the Anglo-Norman state'; Verbruggen, *De Krijgskunst in West-Europa in den Middeleeuwen*; Hollister, *The Military Organization of Norman England*; Smail, *Crusading Warfare*; Powicke, *Military Obligation in Medieval England*.

[4] For example, in 1138 nine men held at bay the army of David king of Scots, Richard of Hexham, 156–7.

of Anjou, and the Capetian king Louis the Fat; but their efforts were on a comparatively small scale and there was no guarantee of their permanence. It was Henry II's military revolution which swung the balance decisively against disorder by harnessing wealth to the defeat of defiance. The only defence against his mercenary troops was to match his force with like force, or to build stronger, more elaborate, and vastly more expensive castles of stone. In short, Henry put up the cost of defiance. Indeed, he put it beyond the reach of most men. Only the mightiest of vassals, such as the counts of Angoulême, enriched by tolls on trade, could hope to keep pace with the advance in military techniques.[1]

Henry's successful sieges were a deterrent to defiance; but he did not rely on this alone to swing the balance of power firmly in favour of the ruler. He embarked, from early in his reign, on a systematic programme for strengthening and rebuilding his own castles, and for neutralising the dangerous strongholds of his barons if he could not acquire them by war or other means than war. In England the enforced recovery from baronial hands in 1155 of Scarborough, Bridgenorth, and Gloucester, and a heavy expenditure on the reconstruction of Scarborough, were only the beginnings of a policy that was to be pursued with increasing vigour throughout the reign. Well over £20,000 was spent on castle works in thirty-three years. Some ninety or so castles were kept in a state of repair, some thirty or so were refashioned, six of them drastically. Over £1,000 was spent on each of the castles at Newcastle-upon-Tyne, Nottingham, Orford, Windsor, Winchester, and Dover. The reconstruction of Dover indeed absorbed £6,400 during the reign and cost nearly £7,000 before it was finished in 1191. In the two years preceding the great war thirty castles received attention and nearly £3,000 was spent on them.[2]

Henry II's castle strategy is well illustrated in his dealings with Hugh Bigod, earl of Norfolk. Earl Hugh was one of the most powerful barons in England, with numerous estates, mainly in the eastern counties, which owed the service of more than a hundred and sixty knights to the Crown. Although he took his title from Norfolk his major power was in Suffolk, and it is not without significance that his earldom was sometimes known as the earldom of East Anglia. He had three castles in Suffolk, at Framlingham, Bungay, and Walton; and it was his persistent ambition to entrench his authority further north by gaining control of the royal castle at Norwich. The hostility of King Stephen to his

[1] Cf. Boussard, 'Les mercenaires au xiime siècle', 189, 195, 223.
[2] Brown, 'Royal castle-building in England, 1154–1216'.

ambition prompted Hugh Bigod to identify himself with the Angevin cause, but he was really engaged in a personal struggle with the house of Blois for dominance in East Anglia. It was a struggle which survived the accession of Henry of Anjou, and the rivalry of Hugh Bigod and William of Blois forced King Henry in 1157 to the drastic action of dispossessing both of them of their castles. He was probably driven to it by the frailty of royal power in East Anglia to hold the balance between rival factions; but as an example of high-handed royal intervention it could not be regarded as a satisfactory solution to the problem of holding influential barons in check. The death of William of Blois in 1159 eased the problem slightly, for the escheat of the honor of Boulogne gave the king legitimate control of the minor castles of Eye and Haughley in Suffolk. About 1165 Henry restored Framlingham and Bungay to Earl Hugh on payment of a large fine, but retained Walton and began the construction of a mighty new royal castle – with a novel polygonal keep – at Orford. It was finished just in time for the onset of the great war. Earl Hugh was one of the leaders of the rebels. During the war he captured Haughley and Norwich, but did not dare to attack Orford, and it prevented him bringing effective resistance to the rebel cause elsewhere. In 1174 he was obliged to submit and give up all his castles. Henry had Framlingham razed to the ground. He sent one of his best engineers to see to it personally.[1]

On the continent, of course, Henry had to devote much of his attention and expenditure to strengthening the defences of his frontiers with the rest of France, including the construction of a great earthwork on the open plain of the upper Avre in Normandy, the reconstruction of castles in the Vexin, and the purchase from Hervé de Gien of two fortresses on the border with Blois.[2] But on the continent too, Henry had a deliberate castle strategy for the preservation of internal order. The evidence is too fragmentary for it to be reconstructed in detail; but Robert de Torigny tells enough to reveal the strategy at work. The pacification of Brittany was signalled by the construction of a new castle at Pontorson on the border of Normandy. Henry marked out the foundations himself shortly before leading his army to take possession of Nantes in 1158, thus securing the two chief points of entry to Brittany.[3] He kept a watchful eye on the baronial strongholds in the marchlands between Normandy, Maine, and Brittany, and between Anjou and

[1] *See* above, ch. 3, pp. 66ff. and Brown, 'Framlingham castle and Bigod'.
[2] Robert de Torigny, 242, 243. On the defences of Normandy, *see* Powicke, *The Loss of Normandy*, 184ff.
[3] Robert de Torigny, 197.

Poitou – strongholds which had been essential to defence when they stood on the frontier between rival lordships, but which had become a dangerous anachronism in the days of Angevin hegemony. Thouars was retained in his own hand after its capture in 1158. The tower of Dol and the castle of Combourg in the marchland of Brittany were seized by Henry's men after their owner died in 1162. Fougères was levelled to the ground after its capture in 1166.[1] In 1162 Geoffrey of Mayenne was obliged to surrender Gorron, Ambrieres, and Neuf-château-sur-Colmont.[2] In 1166 William Talvas, lord of Bellême, was deprived of Alençon and Roche-Mabile, on the grounds of misrule.[3] And in 1169 Henry built himself a new castle at Beauvoir near Mamers in the notoriously disorderly upland district where Maine met Normandy and Perche.[4]

It is not surprising that men such as Hugh Bigod, Juhel of Mayenne, William Talvas, and Ralph de Fougères joined the rebel cause in the great war – they were making a desperate attempt to redress the balance of power before it was too late. They failed: it was too late. Henry II's castle strategy and use of mercenary foot soldiers survived triumphantly the test of the great war. But if Henry's policy put up the cost of defiance, it also put a heavy price on the preservation of order. Stone-built castles were vastly more expensive than the traditional motte-and-bailey stronghold of timber and earthworks. Mercenary foot soldiers might be cheaper per head to hire than mounted knights, but mounted knights could be got for nothing by the terms of feudal tenure (at least for short periods of service), and infantry, to be effective, had to be recruited by the thousand, whereas cavalry armies were numbered merely in hundreds. The power of rulers, wrote Henry II's treasurer, 'rises and falls as their available wealth flows or ebbs; those who lack it are a prey to their enemies, and those who have it prey upon them'.[5] It seems an obvious truism, but it was Henry II who first made the truth of it obvious. Louis VII's spoiling operations failed because he could not match Henry II in the conversion of authority into military power. He tried hard to match him: the opening of the great war and the siege of Verneuil were accompanied by quite extraordinary attempts to raise supplies throughout the whole of France that heeded him rather than Henry.[6] But Louis had to abandon the

[1] Robert de Torigny, 198,, 214, 223 228.
[2] *Ibid.*, 212.
[3] *Ibid.*, 227.   [4] *Ibid.*, 243.
[5] *Dialogus de Scaccario*, 1.
[6] Ralph of Diceto, I, 372.

use of mercenaries – the resources of the French Crown were not yet sufficient to sustain the effort.[1]

The conversion of authority into power was the secret of Henry II's success. Hitherto the increase of a ruler's power had seemed tied to the expansion of his authority. All the builders of feudal 'empires' were expansionists.[2] Perhaps this was why it seemed inevitable that Henry would be an expansionist also. But expansion was dangerous if it outstripped the means of control by contemporary techniques of government. There was a law of diminishing returns in medieval 'empire' building.[3] The territories which came to Henry as the result of two marriages – the marriage of his father to the heiress of England and Normandy, and his own marriage to the heiress of Aquitaine – were almost beyond the possibility of effective control. In other hands than his they almost certainly would have been. Henry II's consolidation and defence of his authority in these vast dominions rested upon his mastery of the art of warfare, and this in turn rested upon his ability to turn his capital resources into available wealth. Henry's technique for enhancing his wealth was not conquest and plunder but efficient management. This meant, above all, the efficient management of England, for England was his principal source of wealth. Of course, if this had been all, Henry II might have been remembered simply as an efficient exploiter; but it was not all, for it was Henry's genius to make efficient management synonymous with sound government.

[1] Cf. Boussard, 'Les mercenaires au xiieme siècle', 195.
[2] Cf. Le Patourel, 'The Plantagenet dominions', 294.
[3] Cf. Galbraith, 'Nationality and language', 116.

Part II

THE GOVERNMENT OF ENGLAND

Chapter 6

THE PATTERN
OF ENGLISH GOVERNMENT

The monarchy is at once the most important and the most elusive feature of the medieval polity. Its origins and attributes are too diverse for it to be easily comprehended within the bounds of a definition or reduced to a simple generalisation. The English kingship of the twelfth century was compounded of various elements. Pre-eminently the king was the protector and military leader of his people. The old conception of the king as the personification of a tribal folk had faded, but victory in war was still commonly regarded as the first criterion of successful kingship.

> No one can doubt how splendidly, how vigorously, how skilfully our most excellent king has practised armed warfare against the malice of his enemies in time of war, for now his praise has gone out to all the earth and his mighty works to all corners of the world.
>
> He not only brought strong peace with the aid of God's grace to his hereditary dominions, but also triumphed victoriously in remote and foreign lands.[1]

Such are the typical comments of contemporaries on the reign of Henry II. Closely associated with this conception was the notion of the king as the mystical repository and very principle of peace and order in the realm: 'When King Henry I, the peace of his country and the father of his people, came to his last days and paid his debts to death, the grievous misfortune changed the entire face of the realm to upheaval and utter confusion.'[2] There was too in the English monarchy an element of theocratic kingship – the king as the chief instrument in the divine scheme for the ordering of the world, the king as God's representative and judgement-deliverer. The Anglo-Saxons' confident assumption that the king was the Vicar of God had lately encountered clerical opposition. Gratian reminded his readers that popes had deposed kings, and the Church demoted the oil used for the unction at the coronation

---

[1] *Glanvill*, 1; Gerald of Wales, VIII, 156.   [2] *Gesta Stephani*, 1.

ceremony from the chrism (which was used for the unction at the ordination of a priest) to the more ordinary 'holy-oil'. But many people still thought of their king as touched with a priestly character, and, more than that, as endowed with a divine gift for the healing of the scrofula.[1] Kings, too, purposefully kept alive the notion of divine sanction. The litany *Christus vincit Christus regnat Christus imperat* was chanted before English kings on ceremonial occasions. 'And twenty-five shillings for the clerks who chanted *Christus vincit* before the king at Pentecost,' records the exchequer account for 1188.[2] 'King by the grace of God' becomes a common element of royal titles in the twelfth century, and was used by Henry II from 1173: 'Henry by the grace of God king of the English, and duke of the Normans and Aquitanians, and count of the Angevins'. And in addition, the king in post-Conquest England was a feudal suzerain, supreme disposer of the principal source of medieval wealth and power – land, and recipient of homage from his tenants-in-chief as well as fealty from all his subjects. The king's right overrides all other feudal right: 'It should be noted,' records a twelfth-century law-book, 'that if an heir holds in chief of the lord king, then the lordship belongs wholly to the lord king, whether or not the heir has other lords; the lord king can have no equal, much less a superior.'[3] The obligations of feudal vassalage were sometimes used politically to inhibit dissent. It was as a disobedient vassal that Henry II dispossessed Archbishop Becket and pursued him with his vengeance:

> Know that Thomas who was archbishop of Canterbury has been judged publicly in my court by full counsel of the barons of my realm to be a wicked and perjured traitor to me. . . . Help me avenge my dishonour on my great enemy.[4]

Writers of the twelfth century who reflected upon the nature of monarchy found themselves in the difficulty of having to reconcile ingrained notions that kings were accountable only to God, with the conviction that kings should be subject to the dictates of law and custom. They did not succeed very well. Among English writers of Henry II's day, John of Salisbury distinguished between the true king and the tyrant. The true king was to be known by his respect for law and the liberties of his people; a ruler who trampled upon his subjects' rights and reduced law to his will was only a usurper of royal authority. Yet he

---

[1] Letter of John of Salisbury, *Patrologia Latina*, CXC, 274; Bloch, *Les Rois Thaumaturges*; Kantorowicz, *The King's Two Bodies*.
[2] Pipe Roll 34 Henry II, 19, cf. Kantorowicz, *op. cit.*, 174.
[3] *Glanvill*, VII. 10, 84.   [4] *Materials for the History of Becket*, V, 134.

would not deny that even a tyrant might be an instrument of God's will, and he could not accept that anyone was justified in slaying a tyrant to whom he was bound by an oath of fealty.[1] The less reflective author of the *Dialogus de Scaccario* takes it as axiomatic that subjects have no right to question or condemn the actions of kings: 'For those whose hearts are in the hand of the Lord, and to whom God himself has committed the sole care of their subjects, stand or fall by God's judgement and not man's.' Yet his treatise betrays his conviction that government should proceed by due process of law: exchequer law was to him admirable because it was settled and known, and he speaks scathingly in contrast of the arbitrary character of forest law.[2] Similarly the author of the *Tractatus de Legibus et Consuetudinibus Angliae* does not question the king's supreme power, but he regards it as a special merit in Henry II that 'he does not scorn to be guided by the laws and customs of the realm' and that his court was impartial.[3] Absolutism, indeed, had little place in the twelfth-century conception of kingship, despite the beguiling influence of the revived study of Roman civil law; but this was probably not so much because of a generally acknowledged conception of limited monarchy, but because kings lacked the means, the instruments of government, to make absolutism a practical reality. Respect for established privileges and liberties, a degree of deference to the counsel of the influential, were unavoidable even for a king bent on reform.

Medieval writers about the nature of monarchy are deceptive guides to what medieval kingship was really like. They will say what they think monarchy ought to be, but they do not analyse monarchy as it was. In reality there was no such thing as medieval monarchy; there were a number of monarchies and each was *sui generis*, the product of history, peculiar circumstances, and personalities. Of course a monarchy might be influenced by theoretical expositions to some extent (though much less than idealogues might wish); there might be importation of foreign notions and practices, and there was certainly some borrowing and imitation; but in the twelfth century the differences were more striking than the similarities between, say, the monarchies of England, France, Ireland, Scandinavia, Germany, Scotland, Sicily, Spain, or the Holy Land, not to mention Byzantium.

[1] John of Salisbury, *Policraticus*, Bk III, ch. 15, Bk VIII, chs 17–21.
[2] *Dialogus de Scaccario*, e.g., 1, 59–60.
[3] *Glanvill*, Prologue, 2. There are limits to royal authority: 'The king is accustomed to pardon forfeiture and outlawry, but he should not seek to infringe upon the rights of others', *ibid.*, VII. 17, 91.

Some historians have devoted much attention to ceremonies of coronation in an attempt to extract a meaning from the symbolism, and principles of kingship from the coronation oaths that kings swore.[1] These ceremonies certainly have an intrinsic interest, and often reveal the attitudes of the clergy who organised them. Churchmen were commonly equivocal towards an institution which they knew they could not do without, which they needed to buttress with divine sanction, but of which they were jealous, and sometimes feared. It is doubtful, however, if we can learn from such studies much about the practical realities of contemporary kingship. Kings were never more vulnerable than before they were crowned, and were more complaisant to the Church the day before the coronation than they were ever likely to be afterwards. Moreover, coronation ceremonies rapidly settled into a pattern that concealed realities. There were indeed in western Europe of the twelfth century only two basic patterns of coronation *ordo*, and these were copied with scant regard for their appropriateness. The element of election in an English coronation ceremony was a sham, though appropriate enough in the German ceremony from which it was derived. It is true the French kings laid great emphasis on the divine grace conferred by the ceremony of unction, but they did so, we may suspect, to solace their pride for lack of more effective authority. There was no unction, and indeed no ecclesiastical coronation at the installing of the king of Scots until 1331, although Scottish kings do not seem to have felt themselves to be lacking any essential element of regality in consequence.[2] English kings dated the beginning of their reign from the day of their coronation, which could be taken as an acknowledgement that their royal authority began with their public acceptance by Church, lords, and people; but in practice there was no interruption of royal business in the interregnum. The coronation oath which they swore was traditionally three-fold: to protect the Church, to do justice to their subjects, and to suppress evil laws and customs. The imprecision of these promises is patent. They may be read as obligations, but no more than a twist of interpretation was needed to turn them into prerogatives. Indeed, when Henry II added a fourth promise – to protect the rights of the Crown – he was converting the oath into the proclamation of a programme.[3]

Henry II was not indifferent to the ideology of kingship. He was

---

[1] The most detailed studies of English coronation ceremonies from this point of view are Schramm, *A History of the English Coronation Ceremony*, and Richardson, 'The coronation in medieval England'.   [2] Ritchie, *The Normans in Scotland*, 186 n. 1.
[3] Cf. Richardson, 'The coronation in medieval England', 151ff.

certainly ready to defend its dignity as he saw it. Bishop Hilary of Chichester was rash enough on one occasion to argue that a king could not lawfully confer privileges upon churches or take them away without papal approval. Henry, we are told, waxed wrath: 'You think by sophistry and guile to overturn the authority of the royal prerogatives which God has given me. I charge you now by the fidelity and oath which bind you to me, to submit yourself to correction for these presumptuous words against my royal Crown and dignity.'[1] Here was Henry wielding the stick of his feudal suzerainty to secure acceptance of his divine authority. Then again, when his sons came to make peace after the great war, King Henry the Elder would not allow King Henry the Younger to do homage, 'because he is a king'.[2] His eldest son had been crowned and so was a member of the charmed circle. Yet on the other hand the chronicler Roger of Howden informs us that Henry II abandoned the ceremonial crown-wearings which his predecessors had made traditional. There is evidence to show that this cannot altogether be true; but it is a remarkable assertion for Howden to have made if completely without warrant.[3] It may be that Henry II was impatient of the pomp and ceremony of regality and could only occasionally be brought to enact the traditional rituals. It would be quite in character for him to have preferred the substance of power to the symbols of authority – enough to exercise authority rather than to parade it. At bottom kingship was still what a king was capable of making it, and what his subjects were prepared to accept. The abrasion of the two would in time strike the sparks of constitutional theories and promote a coherent conception of sovereignty. Until then kingship was a living, changing thing, carrying a part of the past with it, but moulding the future too. Henry II was notably a moulder of the future, yet he had to work within the framework of necessary consent, and with the instruments of government that lay readily to hand.

There were three ways, basically, in which government could be carried on in the middle ages. It could be done by delegating royal authority to prominent landholders. Landholders disposed of economic power and had jurisdiction over their vassals. Inevitably they had great influence in the regions where they held estates, and it was convenient to allow

---

[1] *Chronicon Monasterii de Bello*, 91–2.   [2] Roger of Howden, *Gesta*, I, 79.

[3] Roger of Howden, *Chronica*, I, 216, supported by Ralph of Diceto, I, 302; but compare the reference to the services of the earls of Leicester, Arundel, and Norfolk performed 'in coronationibus et sollemnibus festis regum Angliae' (1186), Roger of Howden, *Gesta*, II, 3, and the reference to the singing of the *Laudes* at Pentecost in 1188, Pipe Roll 34 Henry II, 19.

them to exercise some portion of – or perhaps most of – the authority and jurisdiction of the Crown even over men who were not their vassals. This was the situation in France by usurpation of royal authority, and in the kingdom of Jerusalem by design. Government by this means was cheap and convenient, but it involved a severe political disadvantage: the more effective the authority of the great feudal landholders the more likely the kingdom was to disintegrate into feudal power blocs.

Alternatively, government could be exercised through removable officials. Byzantium and the kingdom of Sicily showed the effectiveness of the method. Authority there was exercised through royal agents – men whose standing and authority were derived principally from their master, and not from their share in the economic power of the realm. The disadvantage of the method was that it required a well-ordered fisc, for officials had to be paid for their services; and there was always the danger that officials could become independent local despots unless there were effective central machinery for their control. In short, the most sophisticated method of local government required a highly sophisticated structure for government as a whole.

The third method was to entrust local government to the popular institutions of local communities – those which had arisen, often spontaneously, as a social response to the disadvantages of anarchy. The method could be surprisingly effective, as Anglo-Saxon England and tenth-century Germany, in their different ways, showed. It was particularly satisfactory if local popular institutions were guided in their operations by royal agents (such as the Anglo-Saxon sheriff), and were subject to some coordinating authority which could introduce modifications into traditional practices (as the Anglo-Saxon king and *witan* did). The major disadvantage was that the amount of effective government that could be exercised this way was slight. The method would keep the peace, but would not readily secure real justice. Custom and social pressures ruled, and royal authority was only an occasional intervention, not a constant force. Flagrant misrule or the perversity of local communities could be met only be crude methods, such as the harrying of Dover by King Edward the Confessor. Moreover the success of the method required a strong community sense, and this could be undermined by social and economic pressures tending towards feudalism. These three methods were not of course exclusive of each other. Indeed a combination of two of them was both desirable and common. The remarkable feature of Norman England was that all three were operated simultaneously.

*   *   *

There can, of course, be no government without control over men. In twelfth-century England, as in any society without a police force or a standing army, necessary control was derived primarily from social bonds. The kindred group and the local community exercised social pressures which helped to create and uphold standards of public order. But a particularly important social bond – for it held together the most politically prominent men of the realm – was the bond created by the conditions of feudal land tenure. Twelfth-century England was, in some of its most notable aspects, a land of lords and vassals. Vassalage, the personal dependence of one free man upon another, was cemented by the oath of homage. Homage established a mutual obligation: an obligation upon the lord to protect his vassal and to provide for him a sufficient endowment (usually in land) to maintain his status in society, and an obligation upon the vassal to render his lord counsel, service, and customary aids. Vassals of lords might themselves grant out some of their endowment as fiefs and become the lords of other vassals, and hence were created chains of obligations between the free landholders of a feudal society. The performance of homage was as solemn as the ordination of a priest; the bond created was indissoluble save by death or a formal ceremony of renunciation as solemn as that of homage itself. But the real sanction behind it was the landed endowment that went with it: the faith-breaking vassal was liable to forfeiture of his fief and the disinheritance of his heirs. The relationship of lord and vassal was, it is true, often weakened by the ever-increasing complexity of the pattern of landholding. Marriage, inheritance, and, further, grant could blur the lines of vassalage. A man might become the vassal of several lords. A great lord might find himself holding a fief of a lesser lord. But the importance which society attached to the relationship is shown by the insistence that every vassal must have one lord to whom he owed a special allegiance: 'A man may do several homages to different lords for the different fiefs held of those lords; but there must be a chief homage, accompanied by an oath of allegiance, and this homage is to be done to that lord of whom he holds his chief tenement.'[1]

The network of lordship and vassalage was an important element in the government of the realm. For one thing it provided through the courts which lords held for their vassals a machinery for the administration of the land law: inheritances, dowries, marriage portions, family

---

[1] *Glanvill*, 104; cf. *Dialogus de Scaccario*, 83: '. . . his liege lord, as he is commonly called (that is to say the one to whom he is so closely bound by reason of his lordship, that he cannot owe service to another lord, except the king, to that lord's prejudice)'.

settlements, partition among heiresses, the guardianship of heirs who were minors, such matters as these were governed by the custom of the honor (as regulated by the custom of the realm) and fell within the proper jurisdiction of the honorial court. Secondly, the obligation on vassals to render and on lords to heed counsel was held to be the basis upon which wise policy was framed. This applied as much to the court which the king held for his tenants-in-chief as to any lesser lord. In so far as the medieval state had any constitutional principle this was it.

In addition to honorial jurisdiction any lord who retained land in demesne – exploited directly and not subinfeudated to a vassal – had jurisdiction over his peasants in his manorial courts, and was also responsible for seeing that they were brought to justice, when required, in the public courts. For the most part the jurisdiction exercised by landlords through their honorial and manorial courts was concerned with the internal polity of their estates – with the social and economic relations between their men, and between their men and themselves. But most men, most laymen at least, were also subject to the jurisdiction of the public, communal, courts of the shire and of the administrative sub-division of the shire known as the 'hundred' (or as the 'wapentake' in those parts of England which had once formed part of the Danelaw). Here a royal official, the sheriff or his deputy, presided, for the main-tenance of the communal courts was a royal concern. 'I desire and require,' insisted King Henry I, 'that all men of the shire should attend the meetings of the shire and hundred as was customary in King Edward's day.'[1] Yet these courts were not, strictly speaking, royal courts, save when specially convened at the king's command. In their normal meetings they were an expression of the tradition of communal self-government upon which the strength of the Anglo-Saxon state had rested. Contemporaries rarely speak of the 'shire court' or 'hundred court', but simply of 'the county' or 'hundred'. Kings speak this way. 'I order that my shires and hundreds shall meet as they were wont to do in the time of King Edward.' 'Let it be as the men of the hundreds shall judge.' 'Let him be not dispossessed save by the just judgement of the county.' 'The king to the sheriff greeting. Put before me or my justices that plea which is being pleaded in your county.'[2] The sheriff did not sit in judgement in the county court or in the hundred court: he, or his deputy, presided, organised the business, and executed the

---

[1] Stubbs, *Select Charters*, 122; cf. the 'laws' attributed to William I, *ibid.*, 99.

[2] Stubbs, *Select Charters*, 99 (William I); Van Caenegem, *Royal Writs*, 452, no. 78 (Henry I), 470, no. 109 (Henry I); *Glanvill*, 61 (Henry II).

judgement. The judges of the court were those who were bound to attend as custom decreed. The whole *comitatus*, the men of the shire in their regular sessions every four or six weeks, arbitrated in disputes, tested rival claims by the memory of their older members, put criminals to trial by the customary procedure of ordeal, shared out the county's assessment to taxation, heard the king's proclamations or orders read out by the sheriff and no doubt discussed their implications. The hundred court, meeting sometimes as often as once a fortnight, seems to have enjoyed the same sort of general competence as the shire court, although it probably in practice confined itself to lesser business of a local nature. Its special concern, however, was with police work. It was at this level that the 'hue and cry' was administered, that those suspected of serious crime were named for later trial, and that those who had no lord to go surety for them were put under pledge to keep the peace. Such men were grouped in tens under a tithing man: they had to go surety for each other, and pay a fine if they did not produce an erring member to stand to judgement when he should. Twice a year the sheriff would hold a specially full session of the hundred court and 'view the frankpledge' to see that the tithings were properly organised.

It is possible that when the Normans were new to England the shire courts had wilted in the face of strangers who felt more at home in the feudal courts of the great lords who now ruled the land. But the shire courts did not wilt for long. They survived and grew to flourish partly because masterful Norman kings were not prepared to see them die, but even more perhaps because of the peculiar feudal geography of England. The great estates which supported the dignity of a tenant-in-chief of the Crown were collectively known as his 'honor', but the most striking fact about most English honors was that the many manors of which they were composed were widely dispersed. Consider, for instance, the medium-sized barony held by William de Curci in Henry II's reign. The *caput* of the honor was at Stoke Curcy (now Stogursey) in Somerset, but the rest of the manors that made up the honor were mainly in Northamptonshire and Oxfordshire, with some in Devon, Wiltshire and Essex.[1] The larger honor of Peverel of Nottingham had manors spread over ten counties.[2]

[1] Cf. Farrer, *Honors and Knights' Fees*, I, 103–45. Tenants owing the service of twenty-five-and-a-quarter knights had been enfeoffed by the death of Henry I, and tenants owing another four-and-one-fifth knights since then, *Red Book of the Exchequer*, I, 224–5.

[2] Farrer, *op. cit.*, I, 146–259.

This situation was largely an accident of history, but it had far-reaching consequences. The interests and resources of a great lord were dispersed with his estates – no doubt often to his advantage, but also to the advantage of the Crown and the realm. Provincial separatism was inhibited, and the ability of a rebellious baron to concentrate his power was restricted. Crown and barons had a common interest in the preservation of law and order throughout the realm, but it was a common interest which focused on the communal courts more than on the feudal courts. Feudal custom insisted on the legal integrity of the honor whatever the geographical realities, but the dispersal of vassals and the difficulty of bringing them frequently together inevitably weakened the influence of the honorial courts. Moreover, by the middle of the twelfth century many tenants-in-chief had acquired through marriage, inheritance, or grant, additional honors or parts of honors, but these could not be amalgamated into a single scheme of lordship: as a contemporary law-book insists, a lord who held several fiefs could not compel a vassal of one honor to attend at the court of another honor.[1] An identity of interests between a great lord and all his vassals, then, could not easily be sustained. The honorial court had a long life and retained a hold upon the minds of men, but almost from the moment of its creation in England it bears the marks of artificiality which time would make ever more prominent. The natural association of land-holders of the middling and lower ranks was with their neighbours, who very often were men of other lords. Their common interests allied them in the shire court, their quarrels were fought out there, their rivalries took shape there. They worked together there on the county's business and the king's business, and gradually forged there that community of feeling which would, by the close of the thirteenth century, make the 'knights of the shire' a factor in the political life of the country.

Too sharp a distinction should not, however, be drawn between shire and honor, or between public and private jurisdiction. For one thing landlords commonly exercised franchisal as well as feudal jurisdiction. That is to say, they enjoyed, with royal permission, the privilege (the 'franchise' or 'liberty') of sharing some part of the jurisdiction which would otherwise belong to the public courts. Franchisal powers could be narrow or wide. The franchise of *infangentheof*, for example, gave its holder no more than the right to hang a thief caught on his demesne with stolen goods on him. A wider franchise

---

[1] Leges Henrici Primi, LV, 1, Stubbs, *Select Charters*, 126. On the dispersal of honors and its consequences *see* particularly Lennard, *Rural England*, 28–39, Stenton, *Anglo-Saxon England*, 619ff.

was the 'view of frankpledge' which put into private hands the sheriff's power to supervise the tithings, and, of course, to take the profits from the pleas that were normally held before the sheriff at his twice-yearly inspection. In the widest kind of franchise, control over a whole hundred or group of hundreds might be put in private hands. Franchises could give a lord prestige and standing with his peers; in giving him police powers over the peasants on his lands they could help to consolidate estate discipline; in giving him, as they sometimes did, jurisdiction over the men of a particular neighbourhood, whether they were his tenants or not, they could enhance his local influence. Besides which they could be financially profitable. It seemed natural then for lords to seek them and the Crown to grant them – at a price.[1] But if a sheriff's authority could be limited by franchisal rights, he in turn had jurisdiction over some matters which might seem more properly a matter for feudal courts. He had, for example, jurisdiction over pleas of land when lords' courts could be shown to have defaulted, over complaints that lords were demanding more services from their vassals than was due, and over claims by peasants to be freemen whom lords wished to treat as serfs.[2] In addition, by decree it seems of Henry I, pleas between men of different lords had to go for settlement to the shire court.[3] The intertwining and penetration of feudal, franchisal, and royal or public jurisdictions was thus an inescapable fact of English government. Its complexity was in practice such that it defies analysis and description, and could at the time often be mastered only by those with local knowledge.

In exercising franchisal jurisdiction (usually through a steward or bailiff) a lord could expect a financial return from the profits of justice. Similarly a sheriff could expect to profit himself from the many pleas which were classified as *placita vicecomitis*, besides gathering revenue for the Crown from the pleas that by custom or royal decree were labelled *placita coronae*. The pleas of the Crown were miscellaneous. They included, as might be expected, insults to the royal dignity, treason, breaches of safe-conducts, injury to the king's servants, encroachments on royal property, and damage to the king's highway; but they also included the more serious crimes such as homicide, arson, rape, house-breaking, robbery, false-moneying, or harbouring outlaws, and also the royal perquisites of treasure-trove, shipwreck, and the beasts of the sea that were stranded on the coast.[4]

---

[1] Cf. Painter, *Studies in the History of the English Feudal Barony*, ch. 4.
[2] *Glanvill*, 140–1.   [3] Stubbs, *Select Charters*, 122.
[4] Cf. the list given in the Leges Henrici Primi, X, 1, Stubbs, *Select Charters*, 125. The 'pleas of the sheriff' are less certain, being for the most part what were neither

The supervision of the judicial work of shire and hundred, the enforcement of court decisions (by distraint if necessary) and the collection of court fines, were a major part but only a part of a sheriff's duties. He was the authority for the preservation of the peace, he arrested criminals and pursued outlaws. He supported the authority of the ecclesiastical courts by imprisoning delinquents, if called upon to do so. He was responsible for local defence, he led the shire levies against invasion or rebellion, and was often, though not always, in charge of royal castles in the county. He published royal enactments and pronouncements, levied taxes, exacted services owed to the Crown, and acted as the royal debt-collector. He took possession of lands which escheated to the Crown by forfeiture or default of heirs; and he executed the judgements of the king's own court. In short he was at once the focus of local government in the shire, and the agency for the exercise of royal authority there. He was also guardian of the royal estates within the shire. Sometimes royal manors would be in the hands of bailiffs or custodians who accounted for their charge directly into the king's chamber; but more commonly the royal manors were administered by the sheriff who contracted to manage them and pay an annual rent. In the language of the day he was the *farmer* of the royal manors, and the annual sum he was required to pay was known as his *farm*. He would be allowed to spend from the *farm* as necessary for the execution of the king's business, and pay in the balance to the king's treasury. What profit he could make from the royal manors in excess of his *farm* went to pay his servants and into his own purse.[1]

For most men at the beginning of Henry II's reign government must have seemed almost entirely a matter of local government. Shire courts, hundred courts and manor courts – it was these which filled their horizons and constituted the authority that controlled their lives. For the comparatively small numbers who held land by military tenure there were the honorial courts too, and through these it might have been possible to feel the pull of forces which shaped the political life of the realm, but for the most part only remotely. For most men an awareness of the king's government at work would chiefly come when the king required all men to be taxed. England was remarkable among the kingdoms of western Europe in having a system of national taxation. The Anglo-Saxons had developed it to fight the Danes or pay them off, and it was still known as danegeld and levied on the old Anglo-Saxon

pleas of the Crown nor appropriated to some franchise. They included petty larcenies and assaults.   [1] Cf. Morris, *The Medieval English Sheriff*.

basis of assessment. Beyond this, royal government was likely to be a living force in the shires only when the king intervened to right a wrong. It was the king's duty before God to uphold good laws and customs and to see that justice was done. Usually this meant making sure that someone else did it; but sometimes when justice could not be had by normal means the king would intervene with instructions to the sheriff or local justiciar, or someone trusted by the king would come specially to hold inquiries in the shire and decide what should be done. Anyone could carry a plaint before the king and complain of lack of justice either from the feudal or public courts. But the king's court was distant and frequently on the move, and obtaining the king's ear could be expensive. Usually it was only the rich or influential, or people with time to be persistent (such as monks) who would invoke royal intervention. A strong king such as Henry I was a check upon injustice, for there was always the possibility that he would intervene personally, and even sheriffs and powerful lords feared the king's wrath; but there were many grievances which were not remedied because of the difficulty of doing anything about them. It is a measure of Henry II's achievement that by the end of his reign royal government had changed from being an occasional to being a pervasive force in the shires.

The great questions of state – war, treaties, changes in the customary law, problems raised by the changing attitudes of the Church, together with problems arising from the honors – were matters for the king to decide with the advice of his tenants-in-chief. The Norman kings commonly held great feasts at Easter, Pentecost, and Christmas, attended by all the great men of the realm, at which, among other things, discussions would be held on outstanding issues: then would the king seek counsel as to what he ought to do, or muster consent to what he had decided to do. Of course special meetings might be summoned for urgent business; but whether or not the barons had been specially summoned there was always work for the king's court to do: castles needing custodians, dioceses needing bishops, heiresses to be married off, suitors seeking favours, diplomacy to be conducted, charters to be drawn up or confirmed, decisions on a host of minor matters to be made. On these the king would take counsel with those who happened to be present: trusted advisers whom he liked to have near him, officials and servants, barons who were at court on business or pleasure. In the giving of counsel and the process of decision-making there was no distinction in principle between a great gathering and a small, or between a formal one and an informal one. The *curia regis* was an elastic body and admits of no precise definition.

If in the process of decision-making the king turned for assistance to his *curia*, in the process of translating the royal will into action he turned for assistance to the royal household. In the early twelfth century there was very little machinery of central government that is not identifiable with or closely associated with the royal household. Royal government indeed was largely built upon what had once been purely domestic offices. Once upon a time, when government was still primitive and casual, kings had called upon their chaplains to pen letters for them. By Henry I's day the chancery was a highly efficient writing office through which the king's will was expressed in a flow of writs, and the chancellor an important and highly rewarded official, but he was still responsible for organising the services in the chapel royal. Similarly the chamberlains were still responsible for personal attendance upon the king in his privy chamber, and took care of the valuable furs, jewels, and documents, as well as his bedlinen in the chests of the *garde-robe;* but they also ran the household's financial departments, servicing its needs for money whether it might be for the daily domestic economy, the king's almsgiving, or the mounting of a military campaign. The chamberlains would arrange to have money brought in from a convenient castle-treasury (the chief treasury was at Winchester), or collect it directly from sheriffs or the king's debtors, or arrange loans with the usurers. And having brought the money in, the chamber would supervise the spending of it.

There were four other departments of the household. The steward presided over the hall and kitchens and was responsible for supplying the entourage and guests with food. The butler, similarly, had duties in hall and cellars and saw to the supply of wine and ale. The marshal was a *major-domo*, arranging the pay and allowances of all household servants, supervising the work of ushers, watchmen, fire-tenders, and the outside servants such as messengers and huntsmen. The constable organised the bodyguard and escorts, arranged for the supply of castles, and in time of war saw to the muster of royal forces. Steward, butler, and marshal had only a peripheral connection with administration and government, but their constant presence, their inevitable intimacy with the king, made them a part of the inner circle of counsel, a repository of confidence, and not infrequently involved them in wider affairs of state.

One of the marshal's duties was to arrange lodgings for the king's court as it moved about from palace to hunting lodge, from castle to manor house. It was made more arduous by Henry II's notorious lack of settled plan. Henry I was methodical, Henry II unpredictable. The peripatetic court was a habit from the days when it was simpler for the king to go to live on his estates than to have their produce carted to him. By Henry II's time the food rents had for many years been converted into money payments; but the peripatetic habit survived the necessity, partly because it had become an established pattern of life, but also because it was politically and administratively useful. This was how the king made himself known, how he showed himself to his people, how he kept in touch with feeling in the provinces, and communed with his barons and sheriffs. But as an administrative device, royal visitation – the king's eyre – though useful, was too haphazard, too irregular. The great lack in early Norman government was effective links between the king's court and the government of the shire.

There can be little doubt that the early Norman sheriff was too powerful. This was both because of the wide range and magnitude of his functions, and also because of the wide discretion which had of necessity to be left to him in the discharge of his duties. The Anglo-Saxon sheriff had been inhibited by the presence in the shire court of two men of greater standing and influence: the earl and the bishop. But this triumvirate had been undermined by the creation of separate ecclesiastical courts, and by William the Conqueror's policy – for sound political reasons – of divorcing the earl from the shire from which he took his title. In the twelfth century one of the few links an earl retained with the shire was his right to the third penny of the profits of justice there. Moreover, the Anglo-Saxon sheriff had usually been a man of comparatively humble social standing; his Norman successor, on the other hand, was often a baron with extensive local interests. Again, the Conqueror's policy was sound enough in its political context: England was for a generation a country only partly conquered and precariously held. The sheriff was for a while pre-eminently an agent of military government, and it was inevitable that the Conqueror should entrust the shires to members of his military aristocracy. They stood or fell together, and this, if nothing else, served to keep them loyal. But as the Norman conquest came to be an accomplished fact, the self-interest of baronial sheriffs became less of an asset and more of a danger to the Crown. In one pair of hands the delegated powers of the sheriff could become assimilated to the powers of the landlord, the office become hereditary in the same way that the fief had virtually become hereditary.

Under William Rufus, and more especially under Henry I, sensible moves were made to counter such developments, and at the same time to improve the Crown's financial return from the shires. As opportunity offered or could be created, the shires were taken out of baronial hands and entrusted to humbler men whose ambition made them eager for royal favour and whose future was therefore mortgaged to the Crown.

'Justices' were appointed in the counties to be coadjutors of the sheriffs in the administration of the law, and in particular of the pleas of the Crown.[1] We read too in the chronicles and records of Henry I's time of 'justices of all England', or 'chief justices', who made visitations of the shires and temporarily suspended the authority of the sheriffs and local justices, or who, in the absence of the king abroad, conducted judicial proceedings which would normally have been brought before the king himself.[2] Most important of all, a new institution was devised and grafted on to the ancient institution of the king's treasury. Twice a year the principal officers of the *curia regis* and household met together with men who were specially appointed to be 'barons of the exchequer'. The name 'exchequer' was derived from the chequered cloth which was spread on the table before them. On it were set counters representing sums of money, and moved after the manner of an abacus, so that even the unlettered could see at a glance the state of the account which was being audited. One by one the sheriffs were brought before this tribunal, and taken item by item through their accounts. They had to justify the allowances they claimed from their *farm*, explaining discrepancies and shortcomings, submit their actions to judgement, and receive instructions. It was an ordeal before which sheriffs quailed; so much so, indeed, that one sheriff of Henry I's day made a name for himself simply because he managed to appear with a smile on his face.[3]

In the creation of the exchequer and the itinerant justices is to be seen the first sign of an emerging centralised bureaucracy and the development of links between king and countryside. A session of the exchequer was a special session of a specialised part of the *curia regis*, linked with the household by the presence of the chancellor, chamberlains, constable, and marshal. The itinerant justices carried the *curia regis* into the shires, and fed the exchequer with information which sharpened the efficacy of its audit.

The trend towards the creation of a centralised bureaucracy was

---

[1] The office of shire justice is somewhat obscure; the evidence is ably analysed by Cronne, 'The office of local justiciar in England'.

[2] Richardson and Sayles, *The Governance of Medieval England*, 174ff.; West, *The Justiciarship*, 22–3; Reedy, 'The origins of the general eyre in the reign of Henry I'.

[3] Round, *The Commune of London*, 123. On the early history of the exchequer *see* Poole, *The Exchequer in the Twelfth Century*; the work of the developed exchequer is discussed further below, pp. 267ff.

fostered by the absences of the king abroad. Henry I's frequent and sometimes prolonged preoccupation with the affairs of Normandy made inevitable the erection of a viceregal authority to watch over England while the king was away. His pressing need for English money for the prosecution of his continental ambitions required that the viceregal government be efficient. In the earlier part of Henry I's reign the queen was invested with the authority of regent, but she was advised, and the royal administration controlled, by a group of ministers trusted by the king for their loyalty and competence. After the death of the queen and of Henry I's only legitimate son, the outstanding member of this group of ministers, Roger, bishop of Salisbury, was himself empowered as viceroy. No special regency council was appointed to advise him, for a *curia regis* of sorts remained behind in the king's absence in the persons of the 'barons' of the exchequer. Roger presided at the sessions and made the exchequer the central instrument of his administration. He was 'second to the king', we are told; he was 'strong and controlled England'.[1] His work as viceroy bears some resemblances to that of the chief justiciars of Henry II's reign; but the comparison cannot be too closely pressed. No office with clearly defined powers crystallised about Roger; he had no formal title, his position depended on the personal trust which Henry I placed in him, and his dominance over the administration rested to some extent on his family connections – a nephew (some said son) was chancellor, another nephew was treasurer and bishop of Ely, and yet another kinsman was bishop of Lincoln and confidant of the king. Roger's pomp and arrogance were resented; his dependence upon the confidence of the king made him vulnerable, and when King Stephen gave heed to the envious and resentful and withdrew his confidence Bishop Roger's authority collapsed and no one replaced him.[2]

The development of central government under Henry I was precocious and justly admired, but it had its weaknesses. It was predatory. The abilities of the resourceful men whom Henry I recruited were directed less to creating a sound structure of government than to devising means for channelling the wealth of the country into the king's coffers and their own purses.[3] The links forged between *curia regis* and local community served principally to improve the exploitation of the Crown's rights. There remained a contrast between the sophistication of

---

[1] Anglo-Saxon Chronicle, 251; Henry of Huntingdon, 245; cf. William of Newburgh, I, 36.   [2] Cf. West, *The Justiciarship*, 13–27.

[3] Cf. Southern, 'The place of Henry I in English history'; Stenton, *The First Century of English Feudalism*, 218ff.

exchequer procedure and the somewhat primitive administration of justice. No developments are detectable in the procedure for dealing with the plaints of subjects. If the king's favour were turned to someone who complained of injustice it found expression in a bald executive order:

> Henry king of the English to Geoffrey steward of Count Stephen and his ministers, greeting. I command you and order that you restore possession of the church of Hough to Robert Bishop of Lincoln, as it was given to him by Count Stephen, and he shall hold it in peace until the count returns. And if anything has been taken thence let it be restored promptly. And unless you do it, Osbert the sheriff of Lincoln shall do it speedily. Witness Nigel d'Oilli At Windsor.[1]

There is little in the nature of just judgement here beyond the king's assessment of whether the plaintiff was worthy of his writ (and that as like as not rested on partiality or the proffer of money). It was little more indeed than government by threat. Fear of the king was the mainspring of government in Henry I's reign. In King Stephen's day the mainspring broke.

It is not easy to estimate the extent of the dislocation of government in Stephen's reign, but its enfeeblement is not in doubt. There is a superficial appearance of continuity in the machinery and methods of administration, but the dismissal of Roger of Salisbury and his clan of administrators in 1139 robbed the government of much of the expertise on which its efficiency depended. Sessions of the exchequer were probably held, but civil war deprived it of the chance to be thorough. The control of local government was attenuated: sheriffdoms passed back into baronial hands, and the local justiciarships became an adjunct of provincial power. Stephen issued writs in the same imperious phraseology as those of his predecessor, but the threats were empty, the sanction slight. Contemporaries speak harshly. 'Stephen became king, but his justice was little regarded and he who was strongest got most.'[2] 'He was soft and easy-going and did no justice.'[3] 'In King Stephen's time justice was banished from the kingdom and everything open to plunder; for those who had been despoiled it seemed wisest to cling fast to whatever they had left lest that too should be taken, for it was quite impossible to recover what had already been seized.'[4]

[1] *Registrum Antiquissimum of Lincoln*, I, 46, no. 71.
[2] *Chronicon Monasterii de Bello*, 106.
[3] Anglo-Saxon Chronicle, 263 (AD 1137).
[4] *Chronicon Monasterii de Bello*, 121, cf. 135.

Some of the consequences can be seen in the chronicles of religious houses: the recovery of usurped property and rights preoccupied them in the early years of the next reign.[1] The restoration of law and order seemed indeed the most notable feature of the accession to power of Henry FitzEmpress. The abbot of Battle had trouble in King Stephen's day with a powerful neighbour who appropriated the patronage of a church belonging to the abbey. 'Now royal justice was sought, then ecclesiastical, but iniquity abounded so much that justice could not be had in those days. But when King Stephen died and King Henry the pacifier succeeded, strife was put to flight and long-banished peace recalled; and the abbot, perceiving that justice was beginning to flourish in its old vigour, judged the moment opportune to prosecute his suit.'[2] William of Newburgh tells how peace-loving men pinned their hopes on Henry: 'after the miseries they had endured people hoped for better things from their new monarch, especially as he gave signs of prudence, resolution, and a strict regard for justice, and from the very outset bore himself like a great prince. . . . In the early days he gave serious attention to public order and exerted himself to revive the vigour of the laws of England, which seemed under King Stephen to be dead and buried.'[3] The hope was not misplaced. Some seventy years later the memory was still green in Warwickshire of how a local trouble-maker had been dealt with: the story was told to royal justices who were investigating a disputed claim which had its origin in the troubled times of King Stephen. Warin of Walcote, 'a simple itinerant knight who fought in the war', had lived by plunder. He became captivated by the charms of the daughter of Robert of Shuckburgh, and after her brother was killed in the war he came with a gang of men and abducted her.

> In time, after the death of King Stephen, when the peace of King Henry was proclaimed, Warin fell into poverty because he could not rob as he used to; but he could not refrain from robbery, and went everywhere and robbed as before. And King Henry, having heard complaints about him, ordered him to be taken. At length, when he was sought out and ambushed, he came and hid himself at Grandborough in a certain reedy place, and there he was taken and brought before the king at Northampton; and King Henry, wishing to set an example to others to keep the peace, ordered

---

[1] The chronicles of Abingdon and Battle are particularly instructive. Even powerful tenants-in-chief could find it difficult in the absence of royal authority to exact their feudal services. For some of the effects on clerical tenants-in-chief see Helena Chew, *The Ecclesiastical Tenants-in-Chief*, 149. Cf. *Red Book of the Exchequer*, I, 237.

[2] *Chronicon Monasterii de Bello*, 113.   [3] William of Newburgh, 101-2.

him, by the counsel of his barons, to be put in the pillory. And there he was put, and there he died.[1]

Yet if Henry could be said to have 'restored ancestral times' (the phrase is from the chronicle of Battle Abbey), the value of it should not be exaggerated. Disorder abated and gave justice a chance to flower; men could again put their trust in the efficacy of royal writs; but the machinery of justice remained ponderous and slow, and its operation was not helped by the king's prolonged absences abroad. In the first eight years of his reign Henry II was in England for two periods of about a year each. In the period from the coronation to the beginning of the great war, he spent only a third of his time in England, and twice was abroad for more than four years at a stretch. During this time there was no vicegerent in England with the status and authority of Roger of Salisbury. Whatever Roger's ability and loyalty to Henry I, experience had seemed to show that his example was unwelcome to the baronage as a whole, and Henry reverted rather to the practice of the earlier years of his grandfather's reign. Members of the royal family were appointed as regents: Queen Eleanor, the king's mother Matilda, and the heir to the throne were all called upon. They had power to act in their own name or the king's, and on occasion did so; but their authority seems in practice to have been largely formal. The king's government in England was in fact managed by a group of ministers, the chief of whom were Robert earl of Leicester, Richard de Lucy, and Thomas Becket (when he was not, as often, in personal attendance upon the king).

Whether by accident or design, these three were representative of the principal classes in the community. The earl was the son of Robert de Beaumont, who had fought at the battle of Hastings and been made earl of Leicester by William the Conqueror. His wife was the daughter of an earl of East Anglia. His twin brother, Waleran, was count of Meulan in Normandy. His cousins were earls of Warwick. With the death of Ranulf earl of Chester, in December 1153, he was left as the most powerful of the English earls. His qualifications for high office were not, however, confined to his feudal eminence: his experience of government was profound, and had been acquired at the best source, for he spent his youth at the court of Henry I. He was a man of some education, obtained, initially, it seems, at the abbey of Abingdon.[2] When he accompanied Henry I to meet the pope at Gisors in 1119 he is

---

[1] *Rolls of the Justices in Eyre for Gloucestershire, Warwickshire, and Staffordshire, 1221–2*, 167.

[2] *Chronicon Monasterii de Abingdon*, II, 229.

said to have astonished the cardinals with his learning; and John of Salisbury wrote with respect of his views on kingship.[1] Richard de Lucy, in contrast, had none of Robert de Beaumont's advantages of birth and upbringing. By the middle of Henry II's reign he had become an important baron in his own right; but this was largely the result of grants which rewarded his administrative services. His family background was that of the fairly well-to-do knightly class – the class which supplied the men to run the honors of the tenants-in-chief, and which was the mainstay of the shire courts. But Richard de Lucy followed in the footsteps of men of middling or lowly rank whom King Henry I had recruited, and hitched his fortune to the royal service. He served Stephen faithfully, and Henry II after him, earned for himself the nickname of 'the loyal', and by 1166 held lands which returned the service of thirty knights. Thomas Becket, in yet sharper contrast, came from the merchant class of London, found his way into that other training school of administrators – the household of Archbishop Theobald – and seemed destined for a career of ecclesiastical service until Henry II called him to be his chancellor.[2]

The earl of Leicester and Richard de Lucy were both called 'justiciar', although until his death in 1168 it was the earl who cut the more commanding figure. It is tempting to suppose that they divided the king's government between them, and indeed the evidence does suggest that the earl was the king's representative in the administration of royal justice, while Richard de Lucy concerned himself chiefly with exchequer business. But it is unlikely that there was a formal division of labour, for the earl presided at the exchequer when he happened to be present at its sessions, and it was Richard de Lucy who went on the first of the revived judicial eyres in 1166. Thomas Becket was, as chancellor, often with the king in France; but when in England he could issue writs for the payment of moneys from the king's treasury just as the justiciars did. None of them – the regents, the justiciars, or even Thomas Becket – however, had much power to act entirely on their own initiative. On all major issues, and many minor ones, they acted on the authority of writs sent from the king ('by writ of the king from oversea' is the frequent tag to their own orders). In short they were agents of the king's will and not true vicegerents. The delegation of royal authority was as yet in its infancy.

[1] John of Salisbury, *Policraticus*, II, 74.
[2] On the justiciars and the early government of Henry II *see* West, *The Justiciarship*, 31ff.

Chapter 7

RECOVERY AND RECONSTRUCTION

Know that for the honour of God and holy Church, and for the common restoration of my whole realm, I have granted and restored . . . to God and holy Church, to all my earls, barons, and vassals, all concessions, gifts, privileges, and free customs, which King Henry my grandfather granted and conceded to them. Likewise all evil customs which he abolished and mitigated, I also grant to be mitigated and abolished in my name and in that of my heirs. . . .

[Coronation charter, 1157][1]

Henry king of the English . . . to all northerners who come to the port of Grimsby and to all other ports of Lincolnshire, greeting. I order you to pay to my reeves of Lincoln all the rights and customs which you were wont to pay in the time of King Henry my grandfather. . . .

[Charter to the citizens of Lincoln][2]

. . . Wherefore I will and order that the aforesaid burgesses of Nottingham shall have and hold the aforesaid customs well and in peace, freely and quietly and honourably and fully and entirely, even as they had them in the time of Henry my grandfather. . . .

[Charter to Nottingham, c. 1157][3]

. . . Know that I have granted to my citizens of Winchester all the privileges which they had in the time of Henry my grandfather. And I order that they have and hold all their purchases and pledges and their tenements according to the custom of the city, as freely, quietly, and honourably, as ever they did in the time of King Henry. And if other customs have unjustly arisen in the war let them be suppressed. . . .

[Charter to Winchester, c. 1155–8][4]

. . . I am unwilling to allow any change to stand which anyone has made upon my demesne since the time of Henry my grandfather. . . .

[Charter to St Peter's church, Northampton, c. 1155–8][5]

[1] Stubbs, *Select Charters*, 158.   [2] *Calendar of Charter Rolls*, III, 7.
[3] *Records of the Borough of Nottingham*, 2.
[4] Furley, *City Government of Winchester*, 178.
[5] Stenton, 'Acta Episcoporum', 4: '. . . Nolo enim quod aliqua mutacio stabilis sit que facta sit irrationabiliter de dominiis meis ab alio quam a rege Henrico avo meo. . . .'

Proclamations, writs, and charters all made manifest Henry II's intention to 'restore ancestral times'.[1] There could be no doubt, either, of the king's will to do as he proclaimed. Monks who gave thanks for the recovery of lost rights found that the king's intention was a two-edged weapon that might force them to defend, if they could, the rights they claimed as their own. St Albans, for instance, had its dependent church of Luton seized by royal officers as part of the ancient jurisdiction of the Crown.[2] The abbey of Thame had to surrender part of the royal manor of Faringdon which it had received in King Stephen's day.[3] Battle Abbey found that forest officers laid three of its manors under payment to the sheriff for making clearings (*assarts*) in the king's forest, and the abbot had to send one of his monks to the exchequer to plead the privileges of the abbey's charters. The chief forester, says the abbey's chronicle, was 'vexing the whole country with endless and unusual inquiries'.[4] This is a glimpse, rare in the first decade of the reign, of the king's government at work. Doubtless the king's rights were sometimes pressed aggressively, leaving the holder to prove that his claims were legitimate; but for the most part inquiries into encroachments on royal rights (*purprestures*) were made by due process of law through the oaths of jurors sworn locally for the purpose, much as the Domesday Inquest had been conducted.[5]

But however firm the intention, restoring the country to what it had been in the last days of Henry I after years of civil war and disorder, was a slow process and had to compete for the attention of the king's ministers with other urgent tasks of government. Henry's political problems, the defence of Normandy, the restoration of order in Anjou, the expeditions to Brittany, Wales, and Toulouse, all demanded money at a time when the royal revenues, disordered from the civil war, were still encumbered by debts contracted by Henry on his way to the throne.[6] It is a mark of the government's urgent need for money that it

---

[1] *Chronicon Monasterii de Bello*, 106.

[2] *Gesta Abbatum Monasterii Sancti Albani*, I, 123. As the chronicler explains: 'Edictum igitur promulgatur, quatenus omnes terrae quae per totam Brittaniam in dominium praedecessorum suorum, Regum Angliae, secumdum juramentum hominum suorum, quolibet tempore habitae sunt, sine alicujus contradictione redderentur, futurisque temporibus in dominio suo, successorumque suorum, servarentur.' The abbey, however, recovered the church on application to the king, *ibid.*, 123–4.

[3] *Ancient Charters*, I, 85–6, no. 52.

[4] *Chronicon Monasterii de Bello*, 110–11.

[5] *Gesta Abbatum Monasterii Sancti Albani*, I, 123; *Dialogus de Scaccario*, 93; *Glanvill*, IX. 11, 114.

[6] Cf. Jenkinson, 'William Cade, a financier of the twelfth century', 215ff.; Richardson, 'The chamber under Henry II', 605ff.

had to revive the danegeld, an ancient tax levied on an antiquated assessment riddled with exemptions. But the desirability of a fundamental reorganisation of the royal finances was not neglected even from the beginning. The hunting down of encroachments on royal property in the form of *assarts* and *purprestures* was one part of it – and made to yield an immediate return in fines and rents for retention. The re-stocking of royal manors in the second year of the reign was another.[1] Moreover, senior ministers of the Crown, such as the justiciar Richard de Lucy and even the chancellor, Thomas Becket, are found holding sheriffdoms and bailiffries at the beginning of the reign, perhaps with the purpose of learning at first hand about the sources of revenue.[2] In the fourth year a major reform of the coinage was attempted.

Debasement of the coinage was, of course, a perennial problem of the middle ages. The Crown had for long been accustomed to counter it in two ways: by fairly frequent recoinage, and by requiring the payment of certain fixed revenues in *blanched* money. In blanching, a random sample of the coins offered in payment was tested for silver content, and a supplementary payment exacted to cover any deficiency revealed at the test. Blanching, however, was a cumbersome process appropriate only for large payments, and convenience, if nothing else, obliged the Crown, in practice, to accept many payments by the face value of the coin, by weight, or at a fixed rate of discount of a shilling in the pound (which was known as payment by 'tale'). The loss involved in such payments was especially serious when, as in the early years of the reign, the regular revenues were disorganised and deficient and the Crown was largely dependent upon special taxes and aids for survival. Firm control over the coinage had lapsed in Stephen's day. The coins minted under his authority had, it is true, been of good quality; but there had also been much irregular minting, and the coins of the empress and her son were deplorable.[3] The collection of geld in 1156 must have emphasised the problem with a shoal of bad pennies, and before the next great quest for money, on the eve of the Toulouse campaign, a major reform

[1] e.g., Pipe Roll 2 Henry II, 8, 17, 19, 21, 24, 26, 29, 30, 34, 35, 36, 38, 40, 43, 44, 47, 48, 49, 51, 54, 62.

[2] e.g., Henry of Essex appears in the pipe rolls as sheriff of Bedfordshire in 1155, Richard de Lucy as sheriff of Essex and Hertfordshire in 1155-6, Simon FitzPeter as sheriff of Bedfordshire and Buckinghamshire in 1156-8, and of Northamptonshire in 1155-9, Richard du Hommet as sheriff of Rutland in 1155-6 and of Sussex in 1156. Thomas 'the Chancellor' rendered account for the *farm* of Berkhamsted until he was made archbishop, and Richard de Lucy accounted for Colchester, Windsor, and Wargrave in the early years of the reign.

[3] Cf. Elmore Jones, 'Stephen Type VII'.

of the English coinage was put in hand. The purpose was to drive poor coins out of circulation and to establish a uniform currency throughout the realm. At the same time the practice of changing the design of the coins every few years was abandoned, and a standard pattern introduced, known to numismatists as the 'cross-and-crosslets' type from the design of the reverse.

There can be little doubt that the reform improved the revenue from taxes and rents, and probably helped trade too; but it cannot be reckoned among the more notable achievements of the reign. The design of the coins was uninspired, and the workmanship of the surviving examples rarely rises above the mediocre. Moreover, the moneyers who struck the new coins in more than thirty mints and who changed the old coins at a discount, were left without adequate royal supervision, and only a small fraction of the profit from coining and exchanging was drawn off for the benefit of the royal revenue.[1] It was not indeed until the latter part of the reign that a satisfactory royal control was applied to the coinage. By then a great deal of experience in administering coinages had been gained in Henry's continental provinces, and it was with the direct help of experts from across the Channel that a proper reform was put in hand in England in 1180.[2] The new coins, known as 'short-cross', were of superior design – and round too, as Ralph of Diceto ironically remarks.[3] In the years since 1158 the number of mints had declined from about thirty to ten, probably as a result of deliberate policy. At eight of these, and at another place which had not previously had a mint, large sums of money were spent on the erection of royal exchanges (*cambii regis*).[4] The striking of coins was divorced from the business of exchanging them: the moneyer remained an independent craftsman who contracted for the privilege of producing new coins, but the exchanger was a royal official and much the more important of the two. It was in exchanging rather than in coining that the greatest profits were to be made, and these were now largely diverted to the royal treasury.[5]

[1] Royal revenue from mints and moneyers is discussed by Allen, *A Catalogue of Coins in the British Museum: The Cross and Crosslets Type of Henry II*, lxxviiff.

[2] Recoinage was, it seems, decided at Oxford in January 1180, to begin at Martinmas, Allen, *op. cit.*, lxxii-lxxiii. Richard of Ilchester brought the *cambitores regis* of Tours, Le Mans, and Normandy to England in the spring, *Magni Rotuli Scaccarii Normanniae*, I, 38, 623.

[3] Ralph of Diceto, I, 283. The new coins were designed by Philip Aymer of Tours; they were copied in Germany, Oman, *The Coinage of England*, 136.

[4] e.g., Pipe Roll 26 Henry II, 15: 'and to Philip Aymer £50 for the construction of a *cambium regis*, by royal writ', cf. *ibid.*, 30.   [5] Allen, *op. cit.*, lxxxviii-xcv.

In the light of the coinage reform of 1180, that of 1158 appears as a makeshift, a useful but clumsy measure which speaks of a government not as yet able to undertake central control. The records of the annual audit of sheriffs' accounts at the exchequer – the one major source of information about government in the early years of the reign – tell a similar story. Between 1158 and 1180 the number of items on the sheriffs' accounts increased three- or four-fold, and the amount of money for which they accounted more than doubled.[1] The rolls from the early years of the reign are slim and confused. Entries are blundered, and the rolls reveal some uncertainty even as to how much the sheriffs owed on their regular items of revenue.[2] The exchequer had, it seems, been functioning in the latter years of Stephen's reign, but it must have been only a shadow of Henry I's exchequer. According to Richard FitzNigel 'its expertise (*scientia*) had almost perished during the long years of civil war'.[3] Henry II had to persuade his grandfather's treasurer, Bishop Nigel of Ely, to come out of retirement and advise on proper procedures.[4] It cannot have been easy for Bishop Nigel to work with men such as Robert earl of Leicester, who had been responsible for the downfall of himself and his administrative colleagues in 1138 – Henry indeed had to appeal to him several times before he consented – but under his guidance the exchequer recovered a punctilious routine, the sheriffs were brought more firmly to account, and the pipe rolls became more orderly. By the time of his death in 1169 the exchequer had recovered to the full the efficiency of Henry I's day, and was once again sending out emissaries into the shires to supervise the work of the sheriffs, and to feed the king's ministers with the information upon which effective government rests. Its workings in the 1170s are set out for us in a guidebook to exchequer practice, written by Bishop Nigel's son, Richard. Henry appointed him treasurer sometime before 1160, and he held the office for nearly forty years.[5] 'I was sitting one day at my

---

[1] Figures have been calculated by Ramsay, *A History of the Revenues of the Kings of England*, I, 191. They should, however, be treated with extreme caution, cf. Fawtier, 'L'histoire financière de l'Angleterre au moyen âge'. The pipe rolls do not reveal the full extent of the revenue. They listed outstanding debts due for collection by the sheriffs, but payments made in full before the summonses were issued do not appear. Some items of revenue by-passed the sheriffs and the exchequer.

[2] The pipe rolls survive in an unbroken sequence from the second year of the reign, but extracts from a roll from the first year may be read in the *Red Book of the Exchequer*, II, 648ff. On the early rolls and the evidence for the operation of the exchequer in Stephen's reign see Turner, 'The sheriff's farm'.

[3] *Dialogus de Scaccario*, 50.   [4] *Loc. cit.*

[5] On Richard 'of Ely', Richard 'FitzNigel', or Richard 'FitzNeal', as he is variously called, see Richardson, 'Richard FitzNeal and the *Dialogus de Scaccario*', 161–6.

turret window overlooking the Thames,' he relates 'when someone approached me and said very earnestly, "Master, have you not heard that knowledge and treasure buried away are both useless?" "Yes," I said. And he went on "Why then do you not teach others that knowledge of the exchequer for which you are famous, and put it into writing lest it should die with you?"'[1] And so, with protestations of the author's inadequacy and trepidation, the *Dialogus de Scaccario* came to be written, in the form of a conversation between *Magister* and *Discipulus*.

As the first attempt anywhere in medieval Europe to explain administrative practices, the *Dialogus* is a unique and precious document, indicative of the way Henry's men took a pride in the task they were trying to perform. But its importance should not be overrated, for it was essentially a manual of instruction for apprentices in the mysteries of office practice. It could be wished that it says much more than it does about those whom the king appointed to be 'barons of the exchequer', for it was upon these men that the governance of England chiefly rested. The *Dialogus* does, however, say enough to show that there was, twice a year, a joint meeting at the exchequer of treasury officials with senior officers from the chancery, the chamber, and the constable's department, together with some of the king's privy counsellors, under the chairmanship of the justiciar, to ensure that the royal will was being discharged fully and expeditiously, and to resolve any points of difficulty that might have arisen in the attempt to carry out the king's commands. The twice-yearly review of the sheriffs' accounts was an appropriate occasion on which to do this, since much of the king's business was executed by the sheriffs on the instructions transmitted by writs prepared in the chancery, and the sheriffs 'returned' these writs to the exchequer to warrant the expenditure they had incurred. The chamberlains and the constable were closely involved since it was they who made the arrangements for discharging the king's business – turning his wishes into explicit instructions to appropriate agents. The chamberlains dealt with civil business for the most part, and the constable supervised military matters and the payment of the king's servants and mercenaries. The constable's assistant, the marshal, arranged for the conveyance of writs and summonses. The officers of these household departments had, of course, many other things to do, and it was possible for instructions to become garbled or to miscarry. A joint session of representatives of the several departments, each armed with the departmental records and memoranda was, therefore, a useful check upon what had happened.

[1] *Dialogus de Scaccario*, 5.

Moreover, it was necessary to make sure that the sheriffs had not mis-interpreted their instructions or failed to carry out their duties. The sheriffs, for their part, needed an opportunity to consult those who enjoyed the king's confidence and could act on his behalf, for they often encountered difficulties in trying to carry out their instructions. An exchequer session was then, in essence, a meeting of a specialised part of the king's *curia* to determine whether, in the words of the *Dialogus*, 'the sheriffs have acted wrongly', and to make decisions (*judicia*) on the 'doubtful or troublesome questions which continually arise'. This was the higher learning of the exchequer 'which lies not in calculations but in judgements of all kinds'.[1] Richard FitzNigel, however, does not go into this in detail: it would, he remarks, require a separate treatise. His chief purpose in the *Dialogus* was to explain the more routine aspects of the exchequer's work, and those with which he, as treasurer, was more closely concerned – the method of drawing up the elaborate summonses which specified the items on which the sheriff was expected to account, and the procedure for examining the sheriffs when they came to the exchequer in answer to the summons.

The audit of a sheriff's accounts – which Richard FitzNigel terms a *conflictus* – was conducted by the treasurer and the chancellor's clerk. It was by no means a simple business. Indeed it was part of the ex-chequer's task to reduce to some semblance of order and common form a diversity of payments 'which reach the treasury in different ways, are due on different accounts, and are demanded of the sheriffs in different fashions'.[2] The uniformity of entries on the pipe roll conceals, in fact, a rich diversity of local custom. The practice of allowing the sheriffs to contract for the management of royal manors at a fixed annual rate – known as the *farm* of the shire – relieved the exchequer of any need to inquire too closely into the issues of the king's demesne lands, but did not absolve it from concern with the way the manors were managed. The exchequer had to ensure – if necessary by independent inquiry – that the capital assets were not wasted, and that the estates were properly stocked, for the king expected to be able to call upon his sheriffs for supplies for his household, for his garrisons, and for his campaigns. The sheriff would, of course, be credited with the cost of supplies and transport, and exchequer would allow a deduction from the *farm*, after checking the counterfoils and copies of writs brought to the session from the departments of royal household. The sheriff might also have been instructed to pay tradesmen and creditors, to send money directly to the chamber for the king's personal needs, or to carry out

[1] *Dialogus de Scaccario*, 15.   [2] *Loc. cit.*

repairs and building work on the king's estates, and would have to warrant his expenditure when claiming a deduction from his *farm*. In the case of repairs and building constructions independent assessors had to view the work and report on its cost since it was not possible for the king's writ authorising it to specify in advance exactly how much should be spent.

> For 100 bacons supplied to the castle of Caerleon, 100 shillings authorised by the king's writ. And for 100 axes sent to Ireland, 22s 11d. And for two horses sent to Ireland, 60s. And for finding ships to carry the king's treasure to Ireland, with the wine and cloth which Stephen de Turon sent to the king, and paying the seamen of the aforesaid vessels, £29 10s 1d, authorised by the king's writ.

> Payment of £20 to Ralph of Haverhill for attending to the king's hawks, authorised by the king's writ. And for thirty cartloads of lead for the construction of the castle at Dover, £21 17s 6d, authorised by the king's writ. And cartage of the same from King's Lynn to Dover, 27s 8d, on the authority of the said writ. And for the building work at Norwich jail, 45s 6d, by the king's writ and by view of Walter Scur and Gilbert Poche.[1]

Besides answering for his *farm* the sheriff had to answer for the collective taxes which were imposed from time to time on the shires, on towns, or on royal manors. It might take him several years to collect payment in full, but the balance due was regularly set down to him. He was also required to collect, but was not held personally responsible for, the debts contracted by individuals. These private debts were incurred either because a man had suffered a pecuniary penalty for some fault or misdemeanour, or because he had made a financial bargain with the king for having some favour or privilege. The king was open to offers on anything that was saleable – an office, the wardship of a minor, the marriage of an heiress, the services of his court, even his good will. The purchaser would come to the king or his deputy and strike a bargain and the chancery would set it down in the fine roll and send a note of it to the exchequer which would enter it on the summons to the sheriff.

> Ralph of Lund and Alice his wife owe seven marks for the favour of having their plea against Jordan Haircun about land at Timble heard in the king's court.

> Ralph Pinc owes one mark amercement for his defective custody of the forest at Egglestone.

[1] From the accounts of the sheriff of Gloucestershire, Pipe Roll 18 Henry II, 119, and the accounts of the sheriff of Norfolk, Pipe Roll 30 Henry II, 2.

Walter Coterall owes 30s, being the balance of the 100s which he offered for having the land which belonged to his brother-in-law.

The bishop of Durham owes 500 marks as a penalty for having heard a lay plea in the ecclesiastical court.

Geldwin of Nerford pays five marks instalment on the sum of £15 which was agreed as his payment for the privilege of entering upon his inheritance.

Matthew son of William has a debt of half a mark for selling wine contrary to the regulations.

Adam de Port owes £407 7s 9d of the 1,000 marks which he offered for his inheritance and for the inheritance of his wife in Normandy, and that the king put aside his anger towards him and receive his homage.

Socha of Dunham owes £22 10s for having confirmation of the privileges which he had in the time of King Henry I.

Geoffrey the Fleming owes 20s amercement for bringing a false claim in the king's court. [i.e., he lost his case.]

Adam Decannarius has offered 100s that he may be allowed to marry his daughter, who is in the king's gift, to Norman de Redmain.[1]

Debtors were usually allowed to pay in instalments, or to defer payment for several years; but when the day of reckoning came the sheriff would either collect what was owed, or distrain for it upon the debtor's chattels. If the sheriff was unable, after diligent search, to find sufficient chattels to discharge the debt, he was allowed to swear an affidavit at the exchequer that the debtor was insolvent, and would then be excused his failure to satisfy that item on his summons. But whatever happened, the exchequer never forgot a debt while there was even a faint hope of recovering it. Its persistence and patience were extraordinary. For example, the pipe roll for the sixth year of Henry II's reign notes that the sheriff of Yorkshire, Bertram of Bulmer, owed £14 6s 8d arising out of pleas held in the county by a royal justice.[2] Bertram reduced the debt to £9 6s 8d, but before he had paid off any more he died. Nevertheless the exchequer went on setting down the debt year after year:

Bertram of Bulmer owes £9 6s 8d concerning the old pleas of William FitzJohn; but he is dead.[3]

[1] These examples are drawn from Pipe Roll 30 Henry II, 36–7, 82, 97, 105, 101. The entries have been paraphrased in the light of cognate entries on earlier rolls.
[2] Pipe Roll 6 Henry II, 16, cf. 7 Henry II, 36.
[3] This entry first appears on Pipe Roll 10 Henry II, 37.

Presumably the sheriff of Yorkshire tried fruitlessly year after year to levy it upon his predecessor's estate. In the twenty-second year of the reign this regular item on the pipe roll is followed by a note:

> The debt should be demanded from Geoffrey de Neville who has the daughter of Bertam and the inheritance.[1]

At last the exchequer began to collect: in the twenty-third year Geoffrey de Neville paid off half the debt, and the following year he cleared it.[2] It had been on the rolls for nineteen years.

Sheriffs encountered all kinds of problems in their attempts to collect what was owed to the king, and reported them when they attended at the exchequer. If the problem required deliberation the senior members of the board – the 'barons' – would either retire from the accounting table to an inner room to frame a ruling, or would defer it for discussion later, perhaps when more of the barons could be present or when the advice of the king himself could be taken. There were, in fact, two sessions of the exchequer each year, and only at the second was the sheriff's account brought to a close and the pipe roll drawn up. At the first session, known as the 'view of accounts', the sheriff would pay in half his *farm* and explain any problems he had encountered in trying to discharge the other requirements set out in his summons. If an immediate answer could not be given, the treasurer's clerk would take a note of the problem on the *memoranda roll* for later discussion by the barons, and their ruling would be incorporated in the summons to the second session beginning at Michaelmas.[3] Some of these memoranda survive from the later years of the twelfth century:

> £19 are required from Hugh Bardulf as arrears on the *farm* of Dorset and Somerset. The sheriff says that Hugh paid the money to William of St Ledger constable of Carmarthen and Robert FitzPagan, and was authorised to do so by a writ of the justiciar who has since died, and the writ cannot be found. *Let it stand over until Hugh comes.*

> Speak with the lord king about the £145 10s 8d arrears of rent on the silver mines at Carlisle, outstanding for many years, which have not been rendered because of defects in the mines – so the sheriff says.

> The steward of the abbot of Westminster comes to the exchequer and complains that the sheriff of Worcester has not rendered the £8 which the

[1] Pipe Roll 22 Henry II, 100.
[2] Pipe Rolls 23 Henry II, 69 and 24 Henry II, 64. For a similar case, also from Yorkshire, see Pipe Roll 32 Henry II, Introduction, xxv.
[3] *Dialogus de Scaccario*, 72.

abbot is accustomed to receive, and which are allowed to the sheriff on his account. *A writ is made summoning the sheriff to answer for the breach of faith.*

Consult about the three marks which were demanded from Roger FitzElias and Christiana his girl-friend for having licence to reach an agreement with John FitzNigel. The sheriff says he does not know who they are. *The sheriff should find out who they are.*[1]

These, of course, are the *minutiae* of accounting; but it was from consideration of such problems that the barons elicited points of principle and gradually formed a corpus of exchequer law. It is not a subject upon which we are well informed; but some of the questions to which the barons had addressed themselves may be deduced from the examples of exchequer practice given in the *Dialogus*. For what debts of his predecessor in office is a sheriff liable? The barons ruled that the man in office must account for the public debts, since he alone had power to distrain upon individuals. May a sheriff distrain indiscriminately upon a debtor's chattels? No: he must instruct the brokers to observe an order of sale, beginning with his surplus crops and his luxury goods, and reserving to the end his equipment and beasts of burden. The debtor must be left sufficient necessaries of life for himself, his family, and his household, and the brokers must not touch food prepared for use. If the debtor were a knight he must be left a horse to maintain his dignity, and if he served personally in the wars his armour was exempt from distraint. Is a husband liable for the debts contracted by his wife during a previous marriage? Yes, unless she had died and has an heir to her property. Since usury was forbidden to Christians, could the Crown confiscate the property of a Christian usurer? Not while he lives for he might repent, but on his death all that he had falls to the king. Does an acquittance couched in general terms cover a particular debt? No: even if the king wrote to say 'acquit him in full', the exchequer would not acknowledge it, for the acquittance must specify how much was to be allowed. 'That is a most unfair quibble,' protests the *Discipulus*. 'I entirely agree,' says the *Magister*, 'but I am telling you what the practice is, not perhaps what it ought to be.'[2] The exchequer was nothing if not punctilious.

'We are, of course, aware,' wrote Richard FitzNigel in the introduction to the *Dialogus*, 'that kingdoms are governed and laws upheld primarily

[1] These examples are taken from *Memoranda Rolls 1 John*, 65, and *10 John*, 42, 53, 63. The passages printed in italics are the notes of the barons' decisions.

[2] These examples, a few of many, are culled from the *Dialogus de Scaccario*, 105, 110-12, 114-15, 99, 106.

by prudence, fortitude, moderation, and justice, and the other virtues which rulers must strive to cultivate. But there are times when money can speed on sound and wise policies, and smooth out difficulties, just as skilful negotiation may.'[1] It was Henry II who revealed to western Europe that a ruler's power was to be reckoned more by the amount of revenues he could command than by the number of vassals he could muster. The wonder was that the money flowed in such abundance.

In the view of a contemporary and independent observer, Gerald of Wales, it was the income from proffers, penalties, and taxes which kept Henry II solvent: 'By the time of Henry II so much land had been granted from the royal demesne . . . that the returns to the English treasury amounted to barely £8,000 a year. One may marvel that King Henry and his sons nevertheless abounded in wealth, despite their many wars. The reason is that they took care to augment their revenue from rents by casual income, and relied more on subsidiary than basic sources of profit.'[2] There is much truth in this, although it cannot suffice as an explanation. The figure of £8,000 is probably a fair estimate from the sheriffs' *farms* at the beginning of the reign, but much was done between 1154 and 1165 to enhance the return from this basic source of income. The *farms* of the shires were first fixed on the basis of old and sometime outdated information, and it seems that some manors were undervalued; but errors, when they became known, were rectified by charging 'increment'.[3] Moreover, lands which had been lost to the royal demesne not by grant but by inadvertence, were recovered by diligent inquiries. These losses fall into two categories. There were, first, lands, which had been filched from royal control by encroachment (*purprestures*): 'It often happens,' as the *Dialogus* explains, 'that through the carelessness of the sheriff and his officers, or perhaps because of the disorders of a long war, that those who live beside Crown lands occupy some portion of them and treat them as their own.'[4] And secondly, there were lands that had at one time been granted out, but which should have reverted to the king because of the death of the holder without heirs of his blood (*escheats*). Those who held land with no superior lord except the king might come from all ranks of society, and whereas the default of heirs to a great barony might be well known to everyone, only unceasing vigilance could keep trace of the holdings of

---

[1] *Ibid.*, 2.   [2] Gerald of Wales, VIII, 316.

[3] The pipe rolls reveal, e.g., that increment of £100 was charged upon Norfolk and Suffolk, £22 5s 6d upon Nottinghamshire and Derbyshire, £40 on Warwickshire, and £10 plus four hawks upon Buckinghamshire and Bedfordshire.

[4] *Dialogus de Scaccario*, 93.

humble knights and sergeants.[1] There are signs of a systematic and thorough search for *purprestures* and *escheats* in the first decade of the reign. It seems likely that as they were identified by local juries of inquest they were taken over and held for the king by special commissioners, who accounted for the rents directly to the chamber. But in 1165, when, it may be supposed, the search had been completed, the rolls of the commissioners were handed over to the exchequer, and the rents thereafter demanded from the sheriffs on their summonses.[2] Under the heading *De Propresturis et Escaetis* on the Pipe Roll of 11 Henry II there are over seventy new items of account. Since the lands designated *purprestures* had once formed part of the demesne lands which the sheriff farmed, the rents now separately demanded constituted, in effect, an increase in the *farm* of the shire. The task of tracking down fresh losses from the royal demesne was taken over from the special commissioners by 'justices itinerant' – agents of the exchequer, who, reviving a practice of Henry I's day, began to make regular visitations of the shires with wide commissions of inquiry.[3]

Nevertheless, despite these recoveries, it remains true, as Gerald of Wales says, that Henry II's financial needs could not be satisfied by the revenues of royal manors. At the time of the Domesday Survey over a quarter of England was *terra regis*, the king's own. The history of the royal demesne in the following century is obscure, but what evidence there is suggests that grants had diminished it by half. That is not to say, however, that the royal revenue had been halved. For one thing, the vast demesne lands of the Conqueror were inefficiently exploited, and better estate management could improve the return from reduced holdings. The disadvantage of fixed *farms* for the shires could be offset partly by withdrawing some manors from the *farm* and having them managed directly by bailiffs. Secondly, grants from the royal demesne were not necessarily permanent losses, since the lands granted might revert to the king through forfeiture or escheat for lack of heirs. The

---

[1] Sergeants, like knights, held by service not rent. Originally, no doubt, the term was confined to those who held by a military service less exalted than that of a fully equipped knight, but in the course of time a large variety of tenures by non-military service came to be classed as sergeanty tenures. *See* Poole, *Obligations of Society*, 57ff. Barons too sometimes had difficulty in keeping hold of all land which belonged to them, cf. Helena Chew, *The Ecclesiastical Tenants-in-Chief*, 148–9.

[2] *See* above, p. 263. Two of the commissioners who supervised purprestures and escheats may perhaps be identified in Simon FitzPeter and Dean Guy whose rolls are cited on Pipe Roll 12 Henry II, 32.

[3] Cf. *Dialogus de Scaccario*, 65: 'the *farm* cannot be reduced, but is frequently augmented by the devoted labour of the justices'.

honors which reverted were kept separate from the rest of the king's estates and farmed by bailiffs who accounted for them at the exchequer in much the same way that the sheriffs accounted for the shires. These reversions might subsequently be granted, but they often augmented the royal revenues for several years. Some, the honors of Eye, Peak, Stogursey, Witham, and Long Crendon, for example, remained in Henry II's hands for the greater part of his reign.[1] Thirdly, the grant of land from the royal demesne to be held by feudal tenure did not deprive the king of all future receipts from it, for in transforming him from landlord into overlord it left him residual rights in feudal dues and perquisites – the right to demand the military service of a fixed number of knights or money in lieu, the right to ask for aids, the wardship of minors, and the marriage of daughters and widows.

In order to make the most of such rights the exchequer needed all the information it could obtain about fiefs held of the king in chief, about the holders and their families, about their lands and their tenants. Domesday Book, though still an invaluable work of reference, was dated, and so too was the information collected by Henry I's exchequer. In the later years of Henry II's reign the itinerant justices were given the task of supplying the exchequer with facts; but the first major attempt to revise the exchequer's records was made in 1166 by direct application to the tenants-in-chief. They were commanded by the king to send in sealed returns listing the sub-tenancies which they had created on their lands, the amount of knight service owed by them, and the names of the tenants. No chronicler speaks of it, but something of the nature of the inquiry is revealed in the return of the archbishop of York:

> . . . Your majesty has commanded that all your vassals, both churchmen and laymen, who hold of you as tenants-in-chief in Yorkshire, shall inform you by sealed letters patent, how many knights each has who has been given a fief under the old enfeoffment, that is to say had been enfeoffed by the death of King Henry your grandfather, and how many have been enfeoffed under the new enfeoffment, that is to say, since the death of your grandfather, and how many are owed from the demesne of each; and the names of all these men are to be written in the return . . . .[2]

The returns, known as the *Cartae Baronum*, survive in two transcripts made at the exchequer. They give an almost complete picture of the

---

[1] The examples cited appear in the pipe rolls as the honors of Eye, of William Peverel, of William de Curci, of the Count of Boulogne, and of Earl Gifford. The pipe roll of the last year of the reign lists over thirty honors in the king's hand, several of them being vacant bishoprics and abbeys.   [2] *Red Book of the Exchequer*, I, 412.

tenurial arrangements of the great honors at one moment of time at the beginning of Lent 1166 – and not only the great honors, but of small fiefs too which were technically held in chief of the Crown, since no other lord stood between the holder and the king. There was no set form for reply: the king had posed four questions and each tenant-in-chief answered them as he thought best. There is a variety in the returns which bring an unwonted touch of humanity to the records of government. The bishops tended to send in elaborate replies: their writing offices knew how such documents should be drawn, they carefully rehearse the terms of the king's command as it came to them, they greet him with the full solemnity of his titles, and they are anxious not to prejudice posterity. The archbishop of York concludes:

> And since, my lord, I claim from some of these men more service than they render at present, and others are withholding services . . . I humbly beg that this my return be not allowed to harm me or my successors by preventing the church from recovering or preserving its legitimate rights. Farewell, my lord.[1]

The lay lords were usually more terse and direct.

> To his dear lord Henry, king of the English, Hugh de Bayeux sends greeting. The old enfeoffments on my fief, namely on the day when King Henry your grandfather was alive and dead, are as follows . . . .[2]

Some have the flavour of personal replies; others read like the handiwork of stewards.

> This is the result of the inquiry which the abbot of Ramsay made into the holdings of his knights at the king's command. . . .[3]

And there are the untutored replies of humble up-country lords who said their piece in simple words, and, as like as not, had the parish priest set it down for them in writing.

> To his lord Henry, king of the English, Robert Caro sends greeting. I Robert Caro hold five carucates of land for the service of one knight. And from this fief my brother William holds a third part and does me service for it, as from the time of King Henry I. Farewell.[4]

> To Henry king of the English, his most revered lord, William son of Siward sends greeting. Your order, promulgated throughout England, has come to me, as to others, through the sheriff of Northumberland, that we should inform you about our fiefs and the holding of them, which we

---

[1] *Red Book of the Exchequer*, I, 415.
[2] *Ibid.*, 387.   [3] *Ibid.*, 370.   [4] *Ibid.*, 443-4.

hold from you. And so I am letting you know by this letter that I hold from you a certain village, Gosford by name, and the half of another which is called Milton, for the fee and service of one knight, which I faithfully perform to you, as my ancestors have done to your ancestors: and I have enfeoffed no one on it but hold it as my demesne.[1]

To his dearest lord Henry, king of the English, William son of Robert sends greeting. You should know that I hold of you the fief of one poor knight; and I have not enfeoffed anyone on it since it is barely enough for me, and thus my father held it. Farewell.[2]

The *cartae* of such men as these take us to the grass roots of life in twelfth-century England, to simple squires with family holdings, sometimes barely able to support the dignity and duties of knighthood. The *cartae* of the barons, on the other hand, speak of great estates, much of which had been parcelled out in sub-tenancies owing the service of perhaps two, three, five, or more knights. In some cases a baron had to hire additional knights if the king demanded service (and these would then be said to be a charge 'upon his demesne'); but in many cases the sub-tenancies owed more knights to the baron than the baron owed in service to the Crown. Earl Ferrers, who claimed to hold his honor by the service of sixty knights, had created sub-fiefs owing the service of sixty-nine and one-third.[3] The tenants of the abbey of Bury St Edmunds were assessed at the service of fifty-two knights and three-quarters, but, as the return reminded the king, 'the church owes the service of no more than forty knights'.[4] The surplus may have been a simple precaution to ensure a sufficiency to meet the Crown's demands; but it is more likely, as the fractions of 'knight's fees' bear witness, that to reckon the value of a fief in terms of knight service was simply an accepted form of making tenurial arrangements. In practice the service was often commuted to money payments, as indeed might be the service owed by the barony to the Crown.

The purpose of the inquiry was not immediately obvious – perhaps, indeed, it was kept deliberately obscure.[5] It is curious that although the king had spoken with his barons in council only a few weeks previously, several of the returns testify that the king's command was made

---

[1] *Ibid.*, 440.
[2] *Ibid.*, 362–3. The 'knight's fee' (or fief) of which the *cartae* speak was not a territorial unit of a standard or commonly agreed size or value, but simply a tenancy which was deemed to owe the service of one knight.
[3] *Ibid.*, 340.
[4] *Ibid.*, 394.
[5] Tait thought that Henry II 'tricked' the barons, 'Knight-service in Cheshire', 458.

known through the sheriffs.[1] The most informative *carta*, that of the archbishop of York, notes that the king asked for the names of the tenants 'because you wish to know if there are any who have not yet done you allegiance'. This was an important consideration: the English monarchy was distinguished from the French, for example, by the insistence of English kings on reaching behind their tenants-in-chief to demand the allegiance of all men. William the Conqueror began it when, on Salisbury Plain in 1086, he took oaths from 'all men of any standing in England, whosoever vassals they were'.[2] Rolls were kept of those who had sworn allegiance. Doubtless, in the troubles of Stephen's reign, many heirs to mesne fiefs and those newly enfeoffed had been missed. But this is an adequate explanation only of the last of the king's commands: give the names of your vassals.

If the purpose of the other questions was uncertain in 1166, it became obvious in 1168. In that year Henry II levied an aid for the marriage of his eldest daughter. This was one of the customary feudal aids, which a lord might levy without having to ask the consent of his vassals. The amount of money which Henry sought to collect in 1168, however, seems related not so much to the cost of marrying Matilda to Duke Henry of Saxony, as to the political and military problems confronting him on the continent: Poitevin and Breton rebels were in league with King Louis, and open war had broken out in the summer of 1167. It was a war largely fought, on Henry's side, with mercenaries, and the aid *ad maritandum filiam regis* was a help towards paying for them. It was in fact levied as if it had been a *scutage* – the payment in lieu of military service – for the rate was fixed at one mark per knight's fee. But instead of asking each baron to pay at the standard rate in the number of knights he owed in service to the Crown (his *servitium debitum*), a new assessment was attempted, using the information supplied in the *Cartae Baronum*. If the baron had created on his estates sub-fiefs which owed more in knight service than he himself owed to the Crown, his contribution to the aid was calculated on the total number of knights' fees he had in fact created.

This was reasonable. The military obligation of the tenants-in-chief had been fixed at the time the honors were created; but in fixing these *servitia debita* the size of the fiefs granted had been only one consideration among several: caprice, friendship, gratitude, or necessity might all have played a part. In consequence, the *servitia debita* were not an

---

[1] Cf. the return of William son of Siward cited above, p. 276.

[2] Anglo-Saxon Chronicle, 217; Stenton, *The First Century of English Feudalism*, 111–3; Cronne, 'The Salisbury Oath'.

accurate guide to the real resources of the honors. Using them as a basis for assessing taxes and aids was convenient but far from equitable, and far less productive than the Crown could wish. To take an example: the archbishopric of Canterbury owed a service of sixty knights, the archbishopric of York a service of seven – figures which were grossly out of proportion to the disparity of their endowments. On both more knights' fees had been created than were required to discharge the obligation to the Crown. By 1166 Canterbury had sub-fiefs which returned a military service of eighty-four knights and three-quarters, and York forty-three and a half. When the king demanded scutage at so much per knight of the *servitium debitum*, they could legitimately pass on the demand to their tenants. The archbishop of Canterbury would then make about forty per cent profit, and the archbishop of York well over five hundred per cent. It was this profit which the Crown was attempting to acquire in 1168.

The attempt was, however, tempered by the recognition that there might be resistance. In setting down the debts on the pipe roll the exchequer adopted one of two formulae. For example:

Gilbertus de Munfichet debet xxx. *l. et x.s.* pro militibus suis de veteri feoffamento, et ix.*s.* et IIII.*d.* de novo.

Gilbert Mountfichet owes £31 10s for his knights of the old enfeoffment, and 9s 4d for those of the new enfeoffment.

Episcopatus Lincolniensis debet xl. *l.* de militibus quos recognoscit de debere Regi. Idem debet xxviii.*l.* de milites quos non recognoscit se debere Regi.[1]

The bishopric of Lincoln owes £40 in respect of the knights which it acknowledges are owed to the king. It owes £28 in respect of the knights which it does not acknowledge are owed to the king.

The difference in the form of entry for a lay baron and a churchman represented a real difference in the way they were treated. In each case the assessment is set down in two parts, but the assessment is differently divided. The lay barons were assessed first on the number of knights' fees created by the death of Henry I (*de veteri feoffamento*), and secondly on the number created since then (*de novo*). The *servitium debitum* was ignored unless the baron had created less knights' fees than were necessary to discharge his obligation to the Crown. The ecclesiastical baron, on the other hand, was assessed first on his *servitium debitum* (which is said to be 'in respect of the knights which he acknow-

[1] Pipe Roll 14 Henry II, 38, 64.

ledges he owes'), and secondly on the number of fees actually created over and above his obligation.

The king was being cautious – and clever. His grandfather, Henry I, had, as a matter of fact, also tried to increase his barons' liability to aids. The Pipe Roll of 1130 (the only one to survive from the reign) reveals that he too had demanded payment on the actual number of knights' fees created.[1] Henry II was simply attempting to revive his grandfather's practice and bring it up to date; but it seems that he expected opposition and was prepared to make concessions. The churchmen, in particular, could be expected to resist any attempt to increase demands upon church property. In the circumstances of 1168, and the dangerously poised feud with Becket, an argument with the Church over taxation was something he would wish to avoid. He was prepared in practice, then, to accept payment on the *servitium debitum* (about which there could be no argument) and set the rest down as an unrequited debt. But in the case of the lay barons the least he was prepared to settle for was payment on all the fees created by the death of his grandfather – for on this his grandfather's own precedent could be cited in justification. So the exchequer set this down separately from the demand for payment on the fees created since then (which he was far less likely to get). There was indeed resistance to the full demand: the debts remained on the rolls year after year – not only for the aid of 1168, but for the subsequent scutages similarly assessed. In the end the king had to be content with partial success along the lines he seems to have anticipated in 1168: the lay barons, on the whole, were persuaded to pay on the old enfeoffments but not on the new, while the ecclesiastical barons were left paying, by and large, on the old *servitium debitum*.[2]

Even so, the *Cartae* remained very useful to the exchequer – useful enough to deserve being copied out twice in the thirteenth century. It is not hard to guess why. If the king had to forgo collecting scutage and aids on new enfeoffments from his tenants-in-chief, he was still able to collect in full when, for any reason, the honor was in his hands

---

[1] Hollister, *The Military Organization of Norman England*, 203.

[2] There were exceptions to this generalisation: for example, the archbishop of York came to acknowledge that the *servitium debitum* of seven knights was absurdly low, and accepted an assessment of twenty knights, though this was still far short of the number of knights' fees created. The *Cartae* and the attempt to reassess liability to taxation are discussed by Round, *Feudal England*, 189ff., and his introduction to Pipe Roll 33 Henry II, xxvff.; Helena Chew, *Ecclesiastical Tenants-in-Chief*, 17–23; Hollister, *op. cit.*, esp. 203, 266–7. For a late tradition on Henry's concession see *Register of Bishop Swinfield of Hereford (1283–1317)*, 414ff.; Helena Chew, *op. cit.*, 22–3.

– and the *Cartae* told the exchequer from whom to collect. Moreover, the information about the sub-fiefs gave the Crown a fair indication of the feudal resources of an honor, and so enabled the king to put a realistic price on it when charging relief to an heir, putting it out to wardship, or marketing an heiress. In short, the lasting importance of the *Cartae* was that they equipped the government to exploit more fully the residual rights of the Crown over lands granted out as fiefs to tenants-in-chief.

The debts arising from the aid *ad maritandum filiam regis* were dropped from the pipe rolls only in 1187. The exchequer did not give up easily. But how hard the debts had been pressed we cannot say. From the chroniclers there is nothing at all to be learned of the whole affair. Were it not for incidental information to be gleaned from one or two of the *Cartae*, and the curious form of the entries relating to the aid on the pipe rolls, this important episode in the administrative history of the reign would pass without notice. There were at least three other crucial developments in this period, 1165–6, but they too are ill-attested, and known almost exclusively by deduction from entries on the pipe rolls. The first of these is indicated on the roll for 1166 by penalties 'for disseisin contrary to the assize'. Disseisin was the forcible dispossession of a man from his land or from other rights. Nothing further is known for certain about the circumstances or nature of this assize, but it may be assumed that the king had issued some form of edict which had the effect of making disseisins punishable in the shire court. At the time this probably seemed no more than an attempt to repress a particular kind of disorder; but having taken an interest in the matter the Crown was to develop from it, within a very few years, a wholly new category of civil jurisdiction.[1] The second major development was the attempt, in the Assize of Clarendon, to improve the administration of criminal jurisdiction, and to increase the financial return to the Crown from it. The third was the revival of the general eyre.

The chronicler, Roger of Howden, gives in his *Historia Anglorum* the text of what has commonly been taken to be an 'assize' – a modification of the customary law – made at a council of king and barons held at Clarendon early in 1166. There was, undoubtedly, an assize made at Clarendon in 1166, and the text which Roger of Howden gives is almost certainly a reasonably faithful transcript of a document prepared in the royal chancery; but the provisions of this text cannot be reconciled with the evidence of the exchequer records, and, moreover, they

[1] This topic is discussed in more detail below, ch. 9, pp. 336ff.

presuppose a judicial organisation which was not in existence in 1166.[1] The explanation for this perplexing problem is probably that the document copied by Howden derives not from the early months of 1166 but from a slightly later period, and describes a developed form of the administrative procedures devised to give effect to the changes in the law decided upon at Clarendon.

Nevertheless, despite the lack of a text of the earliest form of the Assize of Clarendon, it is possible to speak with a fair degree of confidence about the nature of the changes involved from the evidence of the pipe rolls and from references to it in other sources.[2] The sheriff and county justices (who were responsible for pleas of the Crown) were ordered to make searching inquiries into those who were suspected of having committed murder, robbery, or theft, and those who were suspected of harbouring such criminals. They were to make the inquiries through juries of *presentment*. These juries were not created by the Assize of Clarendon – they were an ancient institution in many parts of the country. They consisted of representatives of the basic units of local government – the hundreds and village communities – who testified under oath to all crimes committed in their neighbourhood, and indicted those they suspected as responsible. What the Assize did was to insist upon this procedure being adopted everywhere systematically, and to require the juries to testify not only about crimes committed since the last presentation, but about all those suspects who had escaped justice 'since the lord king became king'. Those who were thus indicted of serious crime were to be dealt with in a special way. In the first place, the accused were to be put on trial not as the shire court saw fit according to its customs, but by a specified form of trial: the

---

[1] Roger of Howden, *Chronica*, II, 248. The difficulties in the way of accepting Howden's text as deriving from early in 1166 are set out by Richardson and Sayles, *The Governance of Medieval England*, 438ff. Their suggestion that it is a concoction by Howden is, however, contradicted by the survival of an independent text in almost identical terms in Bodleian MS. Rawlinson C. 641, printed by Stubbs in an appendix to his edition of Howden's *Chronica*, II, cii–cv (trans. in *English Historical Documents*, II, 408–10). The arguments of Holt on this point, 'The Assizes of Henry II: the texts', seem to me convincing, although I am not persuaded by his further attempt to salvage the traditional date by explaining away the conflicting evidence of the pipe rolls. That the decisions taken at Clarendon were subject to modification is suggested by the appearance of yet another version in summary form in the preamble to the Assize of Northampton of 1176. It has to be remembered that the texts are not 'legislation' in the modern sense, but 'administrative acts' by the king and his ministers giving practical expression to decisions taken in principle by the great council.

[2] e.g., some of it was re-enacted in the Assize of Northampton of 1176.

ordeal of water.[1] Secondly (and this must have seemed at the time the most radical aspect of the Assize), the sheriffs were to conduct their inquiries, hunt down suspects, arrest them, and bring them to trial, without any regard for the rights and privileges claimed by the holders of franchises. In other words, lords who enjoyed franchisal rights, and privileged communities such as boroughs, were forbidden to exclude the sheriff, as they normally did, when he was about this business, and were not allowed to claim jurisdiction over the criminals arrested. Thirdly, those who were accused by the juries of presentment and convicted of felony by the ordeal were to forfeit their chattels to the king. The lands of the felon reverted to his lord, but his chattels were sold off by the sheriff and the proceeds paid over to the king's treasury.

It seems likely that the Assize was not at first envisaged as a permanent change in the law of the realm. It seems to have been regarded as a special measure to deal with special categories of crime in a special way, which would continue only so long as the king thought necessary to clear up the backlog of unpunished crime, and to reduce the country to better public order. But ten years later, after the procedures had been modified and improved in the light of experience, they were re-enacted at a great council held at Northampton, and the law further changed to make punishments more severe and so enhance the value of the measure as a deterrent. The new provisions were retrospective – reaching back to gather in criminals who might have escaped justice during the upheavals of the great war of 1172–3, and indeed right back to the enactment of the Assize of Clarendon. Like its predecessor, the Assize of Northampton was to remain in force 'so long as it shall please the lord king'; but no more is heard of re-enactment, and the procedures already devised came gradually to be accepted as a normal part of the administration of justice.

Although fundamental changes in the law required the assent of the barons if they were to be effective, the king and his ministers freely made changes in the administration of the law; and it was these rather

---

[1] The various forms of ordeal as methods of trial are described by Sayre, *Cases in Criminal Law*, 28–32, and Plucknett, *Concise History of the Common Law*, 111. A medieval description of the ordeal of water, as translated by Sayre, reads: 'Let the hands of the accused be bound together under the bent knees after the manner of a man who is playing the game of *Champ-estroit*. Then he shall be bound around the loins with a rope strong enough to hold him; and in the rope will be made a knot at the distance of the length of his hair; and so he shall be let down gently into the water so as not to make a splash. If he sinks down to the knot he shall be drawn up and saved; otherwise let him be adjudged a guilty man by the spectators.'

than changes in the substantive law which were to transform the face of English justice, and, indeed, of English government.

Within a few months of the promulgation of the Assize of Clarendon, Richard de Lucy, one of the justiciars, and Geoffrey de Mandeville, earl of Essex, set out on a tour of inspection – a 'general eyre'. Their visitation of the shires leaves a trail in the pipe rolls. For example, on the first account on the Pipe Roll of 12 Henry II, that for Lincolnshire, there is a subheading: *De Placitis Comitis Gaufridi et Ricardi de Luci.* Beneath it debt follows debt. There is a man who went surety for another's appearance in court, but the other has fled, and the man who pledged him is fined one mark. There is a man who made a false claim and he owes forty shillings. There is another who absented himself for a judicial duel and is fined one mark. There is a man who disseised another against the king's assize, forty shillings. There are dozens whose offence is unspecified, but the amounts they owe are set down against their names for the sheriff to collect. Wapentake by wapentake (for the king's justices are in the old Danelaw where hundreds were called wapentakes) cases come before the court and are noted, some at one mark for a lesser offence, twenty shillings for a middling one, forty shillings or even five pounds for the more serious. There are one hundred and five of them altogether, and over £250 is due to the king. If it were all collected it would be enough to hire roughly twenty knights or one hundred and sixty-five foot soldiers for a whole year.[1] Lincolnshire, of course, was a large county, but there are comparable entries for the other counties visited. Half of England, mainly the east and north, had been brought to account for defaults and misdeeds before Earl Geoffrey fell sick and died at Carlisle in October 1166.

This was not the first time in the reign that royal justices had been at work in the shires. As early as the second year the sheriff of Devon accounted for debts incurred 'in respect of *murdrum* fines and pleas conducted by Henry of Essex'.[2] The *murdrum* was a fine imposed upon a district in which a furtive killing had occurred and no one brought to trial. Imposing it was normally the duty of the sheriff and county justice. Henry of Essex, however, was the king's constable, and he seems to have taken over a meeting of the shire court and to have heard the normal business that came before it. The pipe rolls indicate that he heard pleas throughout southern England, joined in Kent by the chan-

---

[1] Pipe Roll 12 Henry II, 7–10. The pay of a knight was commonly, at this period, eight pence a day, that of a foot soldier one penny a day, Poole, *Obligations of Society,* 52, 78.

[2] Pipe Roll 2 Henry II, 47.

cellor, Thomas Becket.[1] They were both, of course, barons of the exchequer, and they may have gone to gain experience at first hand of the business of the shire courts. During the next ten years there is some evidence of royal commissioners in the shires hearing pleas, but it is slight. The chancellor seems to have been at work in Huntingdonshire in 1158.[2] William FitzJohn, an administrator of high standing with King Henry, was hearing pleas – largely civil pleas it seems – in the west country and in Yorkshire in 1159 and 1160.[3] In 1163 there are signs that Richard de Lucy was hearing pleas in that outpost of Angevin rule, Carlisle, and possibly in Northumberland too.[4] There was doubtless much work to be done establishing the king's government in these territories, only recently released to Henry II by Malcolm of Scotland. In the same year the chief forester, Alan de Neville, was making a most thorough investigation into offences against the forest law throughout the Midlands.[5] There may have been more such visitations: the entering up of the pipe rolls in these years is too capricious for it to be assumed with confidence that these occasional references represent the entire activity of royal commissioners.[6] But it is certain, for the pipe rolls could hardly have failed to indicate it, that there was no systematic visitation of the shires to inquire thoroughly into all the king's rights, and to bring offenders to book for defaults in the administration of local government. The visitation of Earl Geoffrey and Richard de Lucy was the first such 'general eyre' to be attempted since the reign began, and probably the first since the death of Henry I.

[1] *Ibid.*, 31–2, 47, 54–5, 57–8, 60–1, 65. In addition, the earl of Leicester is mentioned as hearing pleas in Buckinghamshire and Bedfordshire, and he and the chancellor in Lincolnshire, *ibid.*, 22–3, 26. It seems likely that these were special commissions to hear pleas of land. [2] Pipe Roll 4 Henry II, 164.

[3] Some long-standing debts on the pipe rolls, which are said to be *de placitis Willelmi filii Johannis*, can be equated with entries not so described on the roll of the fifth year: cf. Pipe Roll 6 Henry II, 28, 51, 59, Pipe Roll 9 Henry II, 58, with Pipe Roll 5 Henry II, 27, 42, 21, 31. Other references are Pipe Roll 6 Henry II, 59; Pipe Roll 7 Henry II, 36, 49. [4] Pipe Roll 9 Henry II, 10–11, 44.

[5] He certainly heard pleas of the forest in Oxfordshire, Pipe Roll 9 Henry II, 48–51, and the similarity of entries on the accounts for Buckinghamshire and Bedfordshire, Leicestershire and Warwickshire, Cambridgeshire and Huntingdonshire, and Northamptonshire, suggests that he was hearing such pleas there too, cf. *ibid.*, 15–20, 31–3, 36–7 (with explicit reference to forest offences), 63–5. The debts recorded are very numerous.

[6] The unusual concentration of *murdrum* fines for Wiltshire, Norfolk and Suffolk, and Hampshire in 1158, for Wiltshire again and possibly Dorset in 1160, and for Essex and Hertfordshire in 1161, point to a visit by a representative of the royal majesty, although none is mentioned by name, Pipe Roll 4 Henry II, 117–19, 126–30, 133–4; Pipe Roll 6 Henry II, 18–20; Pipe Roll 7 Henry II, 66–9.

Doubtless one of the motives for their eyre was to see that the Assize of Clarendon was being properly administered, that the new procedures were being applied, that criminals were not only indicted but brought to trial, that ordeal pits had been dug, that gaols were being constructed to hold arrested criminals pending trial.[1] Many of the fines they imposed were for defaults in criminal justice. But the real work of administering the Assize fell upon the sheriffs and county justices. At Michaelmas 1166, after less than a full year of the new procedures, the sheriffs accounted at the exchequer 'for the chattels of those who fled or who perished at the judgement of water'. The total proceeds from the sale of felons' chattels amounted to more than £323. But it should have been more, for some of the sheriffs had been remiss. One of the most striking features of the Pipe Roll of 12 Henry II is that the sheriffs of those counties which had been visited by the two royal justices invariably reported greater numbers of felons who had fled or failed at the ordeal than the sheriffs of counties which had not yet been visited. The disparities are startling. The sheriff of Essex and Hertfordshire reported the names of thirty-one felons, the sheriff of Lincolnshire thirty-nine, the sheriff of Norfolk and Suffolk one hundred and one, the sheriff of Yorkshire one hundred and twenty-seven. All these were on the route of the justices. By contrast the sheriff of Gloucestershire reported eight, the sheriff of Hampshire four, the sheriff of Wiltshire three, the sheriff of Worcestershire one (he handed in sixteen shillings). The sheriff of Shropshire paid in nothing at all, for as the pipe roll notes, 'the Assize was not enforced in that county'.[2] The efficacy of visitation could not have been more clearly demonstrated.

The death of Earl Geoffrey brought the eyre to an end before its work was complete, but a year or so later, at the beginning of 1168, a fresh visitation was begun on a more elaborate plan: several teams of justices divided the country between them, and in the course of the next three years visited every shire, some twice.[3] They can only have confirmed what must already have been suspected: that the sheriffs were less diligent and less honest than the Crown had a right to expect. One consequence was that the administration of the Assize of Clarendon was taken out of the hands of the sheriffs and county justices and entrusted to the itinerant justices.

[1] The pipe rolls show numerous allowances to the sheriffs for the construction of gaols.

[2] Pipe Roll 12 Henry II, 60. The reports of the other sheriffs are indexed in the printed volume under *Aque, nomina eorum que perierunt in judicio.*

[3] Cf. Richardson, 'Richard FitzNeal and the *Dialogus de Scaccario*', 168; Doris Stenton, 'The development of the judiciary, 1100–1215', *Pleas before the King or his Justices*, III, liv–lvi.

And when a robber or murderer or thief or receiver of them has been arrested . . . if the justices are not about to come soon enough to the county where they have been taken, let the sheriffs send word to the nearest justice by some well-informed person that they have arrested such men, and the justices shall send back word to the sheriffs informing them where they desire the men to be brought before them: and let the sheriffs bring them before the justices. And with them the sheriff shall bring from the hundred or village where they have been arrested, two lawful men to bear the record of the county and of the hundred as to why they have been taken, and there before the justices let them stand trial.[1]

This is the procedure described in Howden's supposed text of the Assize of Clarendon, and it agrees well enough with what is known of later practice. When it was introduced is obscure, but it could have been during the eyre of 1168–70.[2] For the itinerant justices to take on the administration of the Assize was a crucial step: it made them an indispensable part of the government of the country, and set them apart even from the busy justices of Henry I's day. Once this step had been taken their functions rapidly expanded. The county justices gradually disappear from the records: presumably no new appointments were made. The sheriffs soon lost much of their discretionary power, and became closely tied to preparing business for the itinerant justices to attend to.

The king returned briefly to England in the spring of 1170 (one of his rare short visits between 1166 and 1175) and set on foot a new eyre with a special commission to inquire into malpractices in local government. It quickly gained for itself the title of the 'Inquest of Sheriffs'.[3]

The articles of commission are known from two contemporary copies.[4] Maladministration of the Assize of Clarendon figures prominently:

Concerning the chattels of those who fled or who were undone through the Assize of Clarendon, inquiry should be made as to what action was taken,

---

[1] Roger of Howden, *Chronica*, II, ciii and 249; Stubbs, *Select Charters*, 170.

[2] The pipe rolls for these years offer no certain guidance on the point. On many shire accounts the sheriff's returns for the proceeds of the sale of forfeited chattels appear immediately after the entries relating to the eyre, which suggest that the sheriff was simply carrying out the instructions of the justices; but for shires which the eyre had not recently visited, the sheriff can also be found accounting for the chattels of felons, which suggests that the sheriff himself had been administering the Assize. It may be that the new procedures were introduced piecemeal, and that it was only gradually that the sheriff was eliminated from the process of trial of the accused.

[3] Gervase of Canterbury, I, 216; Pipe Roll 19 Henry II, 182: *de Inqusitione vicecomitum*.

[4] Gervase of Canterbury, I, 217–19; Bodleian MS. Rawlinson C. 641, printed in Stubbs, *Select Charters*, 175–8, trans. in *English Historical Documents*, II, 438–9. The

and what arose from it in each hundred and vill, and let it be accurately and carefully written down. And similarly, inquiry should be made as to whether anyone was unjustly accused under that Assize for reward or promise or out of hatred or in any other unjust way, and whether any of the accused were released or a charge withdrawn for reward or promise or favour, and who accepted a bribe, and this likewise should be written down.

But this was only one item in a catalogue which brought all the sheriffs' activities under scrutiny. The inquiry covered their financial dealings since 1166:

Inquiry should be made as to what and how much the sheriffs or their bailiffs have received from each hundred and each village and each man, since the lord king crossed to Normandy . . . and let inquiry be made about allegations, their cause, and the evidence for them.

It extended to the way they had managed the royal manors:

Let inquiry be made about the king's demesne, whether the buildings are enclosed with ditches and hedges, whether there are granaries, cowsheds, sheepfolds, and other outhouses, and whether they are stocked as the lord king commanded before he crossed the sea.

It reached back to the aid *ad maritandum filiam regis*:

And let inquiry be made about the aid for marrying the king's daughter, as to how much was contributed from the several hundreds and villages and from each man . . . and to whom it was delivered.

The sheriffs and their subordinates were not the only officials to come under scrutiny: inquiries were also to be made into payments to royal messengers and into the activities of the forest officers. But most remarkable of all the articles is this:

Similar inquiry should be made concerning archbishops, bishops, abbots, earls, barons, sub-tenants, knights, citizens, and burgesses, their stewards and servants, as to what and how much they have received, since the king's last departure, from their lands, from each hundred and village and from each of their men, by a judgement [of their court] or without judgement; and let the justices write down all these exactions and their causes and occasions.[1]

---

justices were also instructed, it seems, to promulgate new regulations about essoins and essoiners, *see* Doris Stenton, *Pleas before the King or his Justices*, I, 151–3.

[1] Gervase of Canterbury, I, 217–9; Stubbs, *Select Charters*, 175–8.

For a king of France or a king of Germany to have contemplated such an inquiry would have been unthinkable. Even to an Englishman it was an 'inquisitio mirabilis'.[1] The whole financial exploitation of the country and the manner of it, in whosoever's interest, whether just or unjust, for the four years of the king's absence, was to be set down in writing and in detail. It might almost be thought that the king was asking the impossible, were it not that fragments of the returns survive.[2] It so happens that all but one of the fragments concern baronial estates, but these are quite sufficient to show the astonishing pertinacity of the inquiry and the labour of the clerks in writing it all down.

> . . . The men of Kenninghall on the demesne of the earl of Arundel, gave the earl on two occasions, of their own free will, ten marks for the defence of the Welsh marches: and they voluntarily gave five marks to discharge the earl's debts to the Jews. . . .

> Fifteen days before the Purification of the Virgin next following, it will be four years since the servants of the earl of Arundel seized four hundred and five sheep belonging to Matthew of Candes and drove them as far as Snettisham and kept them fourteen weeks. On the journey two died. They had in their charge eighteen ewes and eighty lambs: and a sum of two shillings was paid over to these servants. In fact nothing was due to the earl. The earl's bailiffs say in justification that they seized the aforesaid chattels for default of service by Anelald of Bidon. The earl himself admits what was done and complains of Anelald. . . .

> For a certain scutage the earl of Clare had thirty shillings, and again a second time a further thirty shillings; and for the said moneys the earl's servants seized a certain horse. But although they have received the moneys they still retain the horse. . . .

> In the hundred of Milford and the half-hundred of Dereham and in the soke pertaining to the fief of the bishop of Ely, the bishop had eighteen marks and then a further six marks, which Achard his reeve received, and this was a grievance. . . . During the bishop's illness, Achard the reeve and Payn the priest increased the *farm* to eight pounds, and as a result the men were so heavily burdened that unless it is rectified they will all be paupers. . . .

> The verdict of the men of Mileham. When the village came into the custody of John L'Estrange and Ralph his brother, there were in the village

---

[1] Gervase of Canterbury, I, 219.

[2] *Red Book of the Exchequer*, II, cclxvii–cclxxxiv (identified by Round, 'The Inquest of Sheriffs'); *see* also Tait, 'A new fragment of the Inquest of Sheriffs', and Helena Richardson, 'An Anglo-Norman return to the Inquest of Sheriffs'.

only sixteen ploughs, and now, as they testify there are twenty-eight. Moreover the men of the village say, in respect of men newly enfeoffed, and of woodland, and of the other things that are in the custody of John L'Estrange and Ralph his brother, the village has been improved to a value of more than forty marks of silver. And all the men of the vill testify to this on oath.

. . . In the period between the king's crossing to Normandy and the making of this assize, Walter of Sapiston was reeve of Robert de Valognes at Fakenham, and through his mismanagement the lord's hay crop perished; and so, by the verdict of a jury, he paid forty shillings in compensation to his lord. . . . Afterwards he was two marks short in his accounts, and these he paid back to his lord, after judgement. . . .[1]

One can only marvel at the authority of the English Crown which made this possible, and at the insatiable appetite of Angevin government for information. On the other hand it is perhaps no small wonder that England was soon to be engulfed in a baronial revolt.

But as to what the king or his exchequer intended to do with all the information, there is neither explanation nor clue. Even the consequence for the sheriffs is not altogether certain. Roger of Howden says that King Henry dismissed almost all the sheriffs from office before he made everyone, earls, barons, knights, freemen, and even peasants, swear on the gospels that they would tell the truth about the exactions of the sheriffs and their officers. 'But the people of England suffered grievously in consequence, since after the inquiry the king restored certain of the sheriffs to their places, and they were thereafter much harsher than they had been before.'[2] He has almost certainly misrepresented the facts. The sheriffs must have remained in office as the inquiry proceeded, for one of the articles reads:

And after they have been examined, my sheriffs and officers shall be employed about my other business, and they shall swear to apply themselves lawfully to the inquiry to be made throughout the lands of the barons.

On the other hand, when the results of the inquiry became known, almost all the sheriffs were dismissed. By the time the next pipe roll was drawn up at Michaelmas 1170, twenty of the sheriffs had been

---

[1] Red Book of the Exchequer, II, Appendix A, nos 4, 8, 21, 47, 50, 55, 46.

[2] Roger of Howden, Gesta, I, 4–5. In the shorter text, Chronica, II, 4, Howden suggests that they were fined – the king, he says, 'redemit eos'. The only visible trace on the pipe rolls is a fine upon the former sheriff of Warwickshire and Leicestershire: 'Willelmus Basset debet 100 marcas pro fine quem facit cum Rege de Iurata facta super eum de Inquisitione vicecomitum Angliae', Pipe Roll 19 Henry II, 182.

changed. Only six continued in office, and four of these were members of the king's household who had presumably discharged the duties of the office by deputy.[1] It was a turning point in the history of the office. The practice, common in the early years of the Conquest and briefly revived under Stephen, of allowing great barons to acquire hereditary control of the shires, had been abandoned from the beginning of Henry II's reign; but the sheriffs were still for fifteen years drawn largely from the ranks of local magnates. They contracted to do the king's work, and were held on a leash by the exchequer; but they did the work in their own way, almost entirely as they themselves saw fit. After 1170, however, the sheriffs were usually recruited from among the *ministeriales*, men who had made a profession of the royal service and knew its ways. The sheriff of the later twelfth century was, in fact, less the discretionary agent of a distant authority, and more the trained local officer of a centralised bureaucracy, less the military governor of a province and more the resident magistrate. The change would have come about even without the clean sweep of 1170, for the office was bound to lose its appeal to the class that had hitherto monopolised it, as its powers were trimmed and its prestige dimmed.[2] It was one thing for the sheriff to have to go to be examined before the king's court at the exchequer, it was another to have the king's court coming to the shire in the persons of the itinerant justices and eclipsing his glory with a greater majesty.

It is arguable that in restoring the exchequer and its *scientia*, in the despatch of justices on eyre, and in the recruitment of men who owed nothing to feudal eminence and everything to royal service, Henry II was doing no more than building his house after the fashion of his grandfather's mansion. There can be no denying that the basic design was Henry I's; but imitation led to no mere revival, no hasty reconstruction of a tumbled structure, but to an unhurried act of fresh creation. The revival of the general eyre was the culmination of a long period of preparation, during which the government had sharpened its techniques, tightened its procedure, recovered lost rights by systematic

---

[1] For the details see Stubbs, introduction to *Gesta Regis Henrici Secundi*, II, lxviii–lxix, reprinted in *Historical Introductions to the Rolls Series*, 132–3. It is not always easy to tell whether a shire was being administered by deputy, for as the *Dialogus de Scaccario*, 82, explains, even if a deputy attended in place of the sheriff at the exchequer, 'the wording [of the pipe roll] will be exactly the same as if he were sitting at his account in person'.

[2] That is not to say, with Painter, that the sheriff became the 'errand boy of the administration', for this is to belittle the extensive functions which the sheriff performed on his own account; cf. Doris Stenton, *English Justice*, 80.

inquiry, assembled vital information, and gained first-hand knowledge of the work of local government in the course of forays into the shires by some of the king's chief ministers. It was ready to revive the general eyre in 1166, and having revived it surged forward to take on a larger share of the work of actually administering the country than any previous government had thought possible. Tasks which sheriffs and county justices had performed imperfectly were taken over by the royal justices; new functions were rapidly developed, for the king and his advisers perceived that regular visitations of the shires opened up possibilities for solving problems which had long gone without adequate remedy.

The method of dealing with disseisin, for example, passed quickly through three stages. When the king first resolved to take firm action against disseisors in 1165 or 1166, prosecution had of necessity to be left to the officers and institutions of local government; but then, within a few years, the itinerant justices took it over from the sheriffs inquiring into disseisins through the machinery of presentment; and finally (and this was to prove a momentous step), those who had been disseised were offered an opportunity of bringing a private action to be heard before the king's justices. The instrument of trial was a jury which testified as to those facts of the matter which would enable the justices to reach a speedy verdict. This was the action of *novel disseisin*. The form of the action and the writ which set it in motion were capable of adaptation to other kinds of plea, and a family of actions soon developed on the basis of *novel disseisin*.[1] These actions, the *petty assizes* as they were called, were designed to give possession to the party who had reasonable grounds for being in possession; they did not, however, decide finally whether he had an indefeasible right to be in possession. Actions of right were a more solemn affair, determined by traditional procedures, and the royal justices were at first empowered to hear only those pleas of right which concerned small holdings and raised no dubious points of law.[2] A machinery was soon devised, however, which enabled the

[1] Changes in the methods of dealing with disseisin have been much obscured by the unwarranted assumption of many historians that there was no development – that the culminating stage of the process, the action of *novel disseisin*, was devised right from the beginning of the king's concern with disseisin. In consequence all references to 'disseisin' or to 'disseisin against the king's assize' on the pipe rolls have been interpreted as references to the assize of *novel disseisin*. In fact they could not be so, because these references occur on the pipe rolls before the justices were making regular visitations of the shires. Once this confusion has been cleared up it becomes much easier to interpret the evidence both for the emergence of the petty assizes and for the activities of the justices. *See* below, ch. 9.

[2] Assize of Northampton, clause 7: 'Let the justices determine all suits and rights

justices to be commissioned to hear any case 'which ought to be, or which the king is willing should be, tried in the royal court'.[1] The originating writ in these cases was the writ *praecipe*, but unlike the writs for the petty assizes, which were issued without question, the writs concerning right were writs of grace, and granted only if the king or his deputies deemed it proper to grant it. The convenience of an action held locally before the justices was thus combined with firm control by the central government. In 1179 Henry II went a step further and offered the use of a jury in actions for right, as an alternative to the traditional procedures which culminated in a judicial duel. This was the *grand assize*, and was open to the defendant in any action for right.[2] If the defendant opted 'to put himself upon the king's grand assize' the case was transferred for a hearing before the royal justices. Between 1166 and 1179, it may be said, the era of the English Common Law had begun.

The essence of the new procedures was a division of functions between the sheriff, the jury of local men, and the royal justices. They were effective only in concert, and no one element was given decisive authority. The sheriffs took the preliminary steps in setting up the case for trial, the jury 'found' a verdict by answering questions of fact, the royal justices supervised the trial, interpreted, if necessary, the answers of the jury, ruled upon questions of law or referred them to higher authority, and pronounced the decision of the court. The sheriffs executed the decision. These procedures combined the maximum of necessary authority in determining pleas and enforcing the law, with the minimum of necessary discretion in reaching a judgement, and hence solved the problem which had long troubled Henry II: how to delegate royal authority to subordinates without endowing them with too much power.

Henry showed considerable caution in the early years of his reign even in allowing the justiciars, Robert earl of Leicester and Richard de Lucy, to act on his behalf on their own initiative. In everything that was not a matter of routine, and in much that was, they were controlled in his absence by regents, and directed by instructions sent from the king himself. As regents Henry appointed either his wife or

---

pertaining to the lord king and his crown through the writ of the lord king [i.e., the *writ of right*, see below, p. 334] or of those who shall be acting for him, of half a knight's fee or under, unless the dispute is so great that it cannot be determined without the lord king, or is such that his justices shall refer to him, or to those acting for him, by reason of their uncertainty in the case.'

[1] *Glanvill*, I.5, 5.   [2] *See* below, pp. 352ff.

his eldest son.[1] A change came with the great war of 1173–4 in which Henry was betrayed by his family and saved by his administrators. Robert earl of Leicester was by then dead, and it was Richard de Lucy who contained the rebels in England, kept the government going, supplied the king with money, and fought off invaders, while Henry himself was prosecuting the war on the continent. The justiciarship was not, thereafter, to lose the authority and prominence which it then achieved. The justiciar was allowed to authorise expenditure from the treasury, and to issue writs which had equal force with the king's. In a very real sense the justiciar became, from the middle of the '70s, the king's *alter ego*. It was the same throughout the Angevin dominions: the chief administrators in the several provinces, the *seneschals* as they were known on the continent, became viceroys who could govern without waiting upon the king's commands. This was partly because Henry had learned to trust them, it was partly because of the perfection of methods of accounting and control, and it was partly because the king was learning, by devising standard procedures, to reduce to routine much of what had previously required his personal attention.

In 1178 Richard de Lucy retired from the justiciarship of England to the house of canons he had founded at Lessness in Kent, there to take thought for the good of his soul in the few months which remained to him of life.[2] His place was taken by Ranulf de Glanvill, a man who, like Richard de Lucy, came from the lower ranks of the landed classes, and had made a career for himself in the royal service.[3] He had a reputation for self-interest, but his loyalty to Henry had been demonstrated in 1174 when he helped to organise resistance in the north to the Scots invasion, and had captured King William.[4] He brought to the justiciarship long experience as a sheriff, as custodian of escheats, and as a royal justice; and he applied his first-hand knowledge to developing the machinery of the eyre. Unlike his predecessor, he went out on every eyre himself, on one or other of the circuits, and there can be little doubt that he deserves much of the credit for perfecting the procedures on the judicial side. To Roger of Howden, who himself served as a royal

[1] Cf. West, *The Justiciarship*, 31–4.

[2] Ralph of Diceto, I, 425–6; Gervase of Canterbury, I, 277, 293; Roger of Howden, *Gesta*, I, 238, *Chronica*, II, 190 (under 1179).

[3] On his background and career *see* West, *op. cit.*, 54ff.

[4] *See* above, p. 135, and Roger of Howden, *Gesta*, I, 65. He had been dismissed as sheriff of Yorkshire after the Inquest of Sheriffs in 1170. Howden tells a story of his persecution of Gilbert of Plumpton for carrying off an heiress whom Glanvill wished to dispose of himself, *ibid.*, 314–16.

justice at the end of the reign, Ranulf de Glanvill was the man 'whose wisdom established the laws which we call English'.[1]

At the time Richard de Lucy retired there are signs that the rapid expansion of the duties of the justices was producing serious difficulties. When King Henry returned to England in the summer of 1178 after a year in France, the eyre which had begun in 1176 was in its last stages. Henry, so Roger of Howden relates, 'inquired about the justices whether they had dealt well and properly with the men of his kingdom, and learned that the land and its people had been overmuch burdened by the multitude of justices, for they were eighteen in number'.[2] Howden is almost certainly misleading about this, as he is misleading about the Assize of Clarendon and the consequences of the Inquest of Sheriffs. That there were complaints is probable; but that they were complaints about too many justices is unlikely. Indeed, on the next eyre, beginning in the following year, even more were appointed.[3] The true cause for complaint is probably revealed on the pipe rolls which show that time after time in the course of the eyre, the justices had been unable to complete their business in one shire before having to move to another, and had deferred the unfinished business until they returned to Westminster for a session of the exchequer, and had concluded it there.[4] People in eight counties had had their business deferred to the exchequer. This did not happen again. In the following years a variety of remedies was tried. Circuits were reorganised and more justices appointed.[5] The general eyre was in 1186 supplemented by a special commission to hear judicial business alone.[6]

Doubtless part of the difficulties experienced in 1176–8 stemmed from the eagerness of people to bring pleas before royal justices. The perfection of the procedures under the petty assizes must have speeded up the

---

[1] Roger of Howden, *Chronica*, II, 215. For his work as a justice see Pipe Roll 31 Henry II, 73, Pipe Roll 33 Henry II, 17, 88, 95, and Barlow, 'Roger of Howden'.

[2] Roger of Howden, *Gesta*, I, 207.   [3] Cf. *ibid.*, 238–9.

[4] This is the clear implication of the headings *De placitis eorundem ad scaccarium* following the entries under the headings of the justices in eyre, Pipe Roll 23 Henry II, 31, 32, 45, 112; Pipe Roll 24 Henry II, 4; Pipe Roll 25 Henry II, 8, 45, 124. There is one such heading on the Pipe Roll of 26 Henry II, 50, but this is a repeat of an entry on a previous roll. There are no similar entries on any of the later rolls.

[5] See Doris Stenton, 'The development of the judiciary', *Pleas before the King or his Justices*, III, Introduction, Appendix 1. The chronicle evidence is defective and garbled.

[6] This is to be inferred from the entries under the heading *Nova placita et nova conventiones per Hugonem de Morewich et Radulfum Murdac et Willelmum le Vavassur et Tomam de Husseburn* on Pipe Roll 32 Henry II. They are much more restricted in scope than the normal entries for an eyre.

hearing of pleas, but is likely at the same time to have stimulated litigation. What did most in the end, however, to relieve pressure on the
eyres and to prevent their other work being too much impeded by
judicial business, was the creation of a central tribunal to which litigants
might bring their pleas without waiting for the justices to come to the
county. In a sense there had always been such a tribunal in the king's
court which met at Westminster for a session of the exchequer. Litigants
had in the past offered the king large sums for the favour of bringing a
plea *ad scaccarium*.[1] The trouble was that by 1178 a session of the exchequer was itself becoming heavily burdened with the financial
business generated by the eyres, and when the exchequer was not in
session the 'barons' had dispersed either to attend upon the king or to
serve as justices itinerant. It seems likely that the king found a solution
to this in 1178 by commissioning a few members of his *curia* to remain
at Westminster to hear litigation brought by one of his subjects against
another. This, at least, is a plausible interpretation of a difficult passage
in Howden's chronicle.[2] After relating that Henry heard complaints
about the eyre on his return from France, he adds that 'on the advice
of the wise men of the realm', the king 'chose five only, namely two
clerks and three laymen, who were all members of his private household [*de privata familia sua*]. And he commanded that these five should
hear all the complaints of the kingdom [*omnes clamores regni*] and should
do right; and that they should not depart from the royal court [*a curia
regis*] but should remain there for the purpose of hearing the complaints
of the people [*ad audiendum clamores hominum*], with the proviso that if
any case should come before them which they could not bring to a
decision, it should be brought to the king and determined as might
seem good to him and the wiser men of the realm.'[3] It is possible that
as a purely temporary expedient Henry attached a few justices to

---

[1] e.g., Pipe Roll 14 Henry II, 197: 'Robertus de Hasting' reddat compotum de
106s 8d ut placitum quod fuit inter eum et Radulfum Moin differatur ad Scaccarium';
cf. *ibid.*, 102; Pipe Roll 15 Henry II, 66; Pipe Roll 17 Henry II, 73.

[2] Cf. Adams, *Origins of the English Constitution*, 168–70, and *Council and Courts in
Anglo-Norman England*, 214–47. Van Caenegem, *Royal Writs*, 30, accepts Adams' view
that a separate court was established for common pleas. On the other hand Chrimes,
Administrative History of Medieval England, 49 n.1, is reluctant to admit this interpretation, and the existence of any central court other than the exchequer is flatly
denied by Richardson and Sayles, *The Governance of Medieval England*, 173–215. Doris
Stenton, *English Justice*, 75–6, reads Howden's words as a reference to a temporary
expedient to deal with urgent pleas, and sees 'nothing revolutionary in this measure'.
There is no warrant for the suggestion of Stubbs, *Constitutional History*, I, 644–5, that
the court of King's Bench was then established.

[3] Roger of Howden, *Gesta*, I, 207–8.

himself to hear pleas: he had done this before when he was touring England immediately after the great war.[1] But it seems on the whole more likely that we have here the germ of what was a little later to be known as 'the Bench' and later still as 'the Court of Common Pleas'.[2] It was an appropriate occasion for it, and 'common pleas' (that is to say, cases in which the Crown was not a party) is an apt translation of 'clamores hominum'. But even if Henry II was in 1178 making special provision for judicial business, there can be no suggestion that he was creating a new court: even when men came to speak of taking their cases before 'the Bench', they were referring to nothing more than a session of the king's court to hear a particular category of business, just as the exchequer was a session of the king's court to deal with another category of business. Until long after Henry was dead it was often the same men who dealt with both kinds of business. Richard FitzNigel, for instance, who rarely went out on eyre, sat as one of the justices to hear civil pleas when he was not, as treasurer, conducting the audit at that other manifestation of the king's court, the exchequer.[3] In official parlance such men were simply justices of the king's court. But if it were necessary to distinguish a case brought before justices at Westminster from one brought before justices in eyre, the former would be referred to as justices of the 'chief court' (*capitalis curia*), or of 'the court of the lord king at Westminster', or 'the court that meets at Westminster at the place where the exchequer meets' (*in curia regis apud Westmonasterium ad scaccarium*).[4] And if there were justices who remained at Westminster to hear *clamores hominum* they were simply the nucleus of

---

[1] This seems to be the implication of references to *Placita et conventiones per Willelmum fitz Radulfi, Bertram de Verdun, et Thomam Basset in curia regis* on Pipe Roll 21 Henry II. A few months later they were on eyre as justices itinerant.

[2] *Glanvill*, XI. 1: attorneys were customarily nominated 'coram iusticiis domini regis in banco residentibus', cf. *ibid.*, VIII. 1. The phrase is significant, although it is doubtful if there was yet any real distinction between the king's court *in banco* and *ad scaccarium*: the distinction is between the places where the *curia regis* might meet within the palace of Westminster. It seems likely that the term 'bench' (*bancus*) was first used to distinguish the secretariat which dealt with judicial matters from the secretariat which dealt with financial business, and was first transferred to the place where the justices met, and later applied to the justices themselves. Cf. Flower, *Introduction to the Curia Regis Rolls*, 31 ff.

[3] He appears as one of the justices *in curia regis apud Westmonasterium* in numerous final concords, e.g., *Feet of Fines of the reign of Henry II*, nos 1–4; *Early Yorkshire Charters*, II, 239, 494; V, 74.

[4] These phrases are culled from *Glanvill*, and from final concords, e.g., *Cartularium Monasterii de Rameseia*, II, 383; *Feudal Documents from Bury St Edmunds*, nos 224, 229, 232; *Early Yorkshire Charters*, II, 239, 494; Dugdale, *Originales Juridicales*, 92; Madox, *History of the Exchequer*, I, 213, n.p; *Final Concords of the County of Lincoln*, II, 329.

a wider body of men appointed to be justices in the king's court, which expanded or contracted as the eyres went out and returned, or as an exchequer session opened or closed. Doubtless there were members of the king's court who developed an expertise in the common law, as there were others who were expert in exchequer procedure. It was some such member who at the close of Henry II's reign wrote a *Treatise on the Laws and Customs of England* describing in detail the sophisticated procedures of the *curia regis*, whether it was *ad scaccarium* or with the justices in eyre.[1] But specialists were on the whole less useful to Henry II than men of general competence and wide experience.[2]

Those who went out on a general eyre performed a remarkable variety of tasks which were listed for them in the *Articles of the Eyre*. These *Capitula Itineris* show a continual process of development, and did not become stereotyped before the middle of the thirteenth century. Unfortunately no copies of the Articles, *eo nomine*, survive for the eyres of Henry II's reign, but there is sufficient evidence to show that their later development was, by and large, an elaboration and refinement of a basic pattern already evolved by the 1180s.[3] The justices on eyre promulgated and enforced new legislation. They assessed taxes (in the form of tallages and aids) on towns and royal manors. They adjudged both civil and criminal pleas. They sought out encroachments on royal rights of all kinds. They passed in review the ways in which the local communities of shire and hundred, township and vill, had performed or failed to perform their public duties, and they imposed penalties for laxness, or concealment, or corruption. They endeavoured to bring to light and punish the errors, inefficiencies, and malpractices of local officials and their servants. They gathered information about outlaws, about 'escheats, churches, lands and women in the gift of the lord king', about those who owed homage but had not performed it, or about anything else in which the king or exchequer were interested.[4] They might be instructed to perform special tasks which were not normally part of the eyre: in 1176, for example, they helped to deal with the

---

[1] In the thirteenth century this treatise was attributed to Ranulf de Glanvill, but there is no contemporary warrant for his authorship. Several possibilities have been suggested; *see* Hall, introduction to *Glanvill*, xxxi–xxxiii. The treatise is discussed below, ch. 9.

[2] It was not easy to find men of the right calibre to man the eyres, says Ralph of Diceto, I, 434–5.

[3] On the eyres and the *Capitula Itineris*, *see* Helen Cam, *Studies in the Hundred Rolls*. Although not specifically described as *Capitula Itineris*, the surviving text of the Assize of Northampton takes the form of instructions to the justices about to go on eyre.

[4] The quotation is from the Assize of Northampton, clause 9.

aftermath of the great war, taking oaths of fealty from everyone, 'from the earls, barons, knights, and freeholders, and even villeins, who wished to remain in the kingdom', and making sure that 'the castles which have been destroyed are well and truly demolished and that those which are due for destruction are razed to the ground'.[1]

The information collected on the eyres for Henry II's reign has almost all perished; almost but not entirely, for there survives in the Public Record Office some *Rotuli de Dominabus et Pueris et Puellis* from 1185. These are undoubtedly some of the returns of the justices in eyre to an inquiry they were instructed to make about 'women and maidens in the king's gift, and minors who are in his wardship'.[2] There are twelve rotulets for twelve counties, and for each shire the information is arranged hundred by hundred, taken down, no doubt, as the representatives of each hundred came forward to testify on oath. For example:

Buckinghamshire. Roll of matrons and maidens in the king's gift, and of boys who are in his wardship in Buckinghamshire.

Hundred of Stoke

William of Windsor, son of William of Windsor the elder, is a ward of the lord king; and as arranged by him, he is in the custody of Hawise of Windsor, his mother, and has been for nine years with his land, namely Horton and Eton. The aforesaid William is eighteen years old. Horton is valued at £14 a year with this stock, to wit, two ploughs of seventeen oxen, and four plough-horses, five sows, one boar, five cows and a bull. Eton is valued at £10 a year with this stock, to wit, one plough of eight oxen, and one plough-horse, and two cows.

Hawise of Windsor is in the gift of the lord king, and, apart from the aforenamed heir, has seven daughters, of whom two are abroad, two are nuns, three are in the gift of the lord king. The jurors do not know the age of the said lady since she was born abroad.

The daughters of Stephen the forester are in the gift of the lord king in the village of Iver. Geoffrey Wood (as arranged by Thomas Basset) has the sisters and their mother in wardship with half-a-virgate of land which is their inheritance in the village of Iver; and he holds the half-virgate by the military service which pertains to half-a-virgate of land; and the value of the said land is half a mark.[3]

[1] Assize of Northampton, clauses 6 and 8.
[2] Cf. 'Form of Proceeding on the Judicial Visitation, 1194', clauses 4 and 5, in Stubbs, *Select Charters*, 253.
[3] *Rotuli de Dominabus et Pueris et Puellis*, 35.

Here juxtaposed are the heir of a noble honor which stretched over several counties and owed in all the service of twenty knights to the Crown, his widowed mother from overseas, and the unnamed widow and daughters of a humble forest officer who held a morsel of land by sergeanty tenure. The justices made no social distinctions and knowingly overlooked nothing in their pursuit of the king's rights.

The work of the justices was at once judicial and financial, political and administrative, supervisory and executive. The twelfth century did not distinguish such functions: the king's government was as yet indivisible. The general eyre was a powerful engine of government. It was to run, much developed and enlarged, for over a hundred years. At the end of the thirteenth century, weighed down by the multifarious tasks laid upon it, it was brought to a halt. Alternatives were sought in a variety of commissions of more limited scope; but none were to prove so effective a means of carrying royal authority to the country or holding local communities so firmly in the grip of royal government as the *iter ad omnia placita* – the general eyre which Henry II had fashioned.

Chapter 8

THE KING'S GOVERNMENT

Walter Map, gossip writer, courtier, ambassador, and itinerant justice, professed to find the *curia regis* an elusive concept: 'I speak of the court, but what the court is God alone knows, I do not.'[1] He had reason to feel uncertain: the *curia regis* manifested itself in many guises and in many places at once. The court of the justiciar or the court of an itinerant justice was not an agency of the *curia regis*, it *was* the *curia regis*.

> This is the final concord that was made in the court of the lord king at Westminster during the Easter session of the exchequer in the 23rd year of King Henry II . . . before Ranulf Glanvill justiciar of the lord king, and Richard the treasurer, and Hubert Walter, and Master Robert of Inglesham, and Thomas of Hurstbourne, and Hugh of Morwick, and William Rufus the steward of the lord king, and Michael Belet and other loyal men of the lord king. . . .[2]

> This is the final concord made in the court of the lord king at Norwich . . . before Roger FitzReinfred, and William Rufus and Michael Belet, justices of the lord king. . . .[3]

Such use of the term could lead to confusion; but it advertised the unity of the king's government.[4] It was the same on the continent, where too, perhaps surprisingly, we hear of the *curia regis*, despite the fact that Henry had no monarchical authority there. 'The court of the lord king Henry FitzEmpress meeting at Caen' in January 1183 was presided over by William FitzRalph, seneschal of Normandy.[5] The rights of the abbey of Marmoutier in Touraine were proved 'in the court of the lord Henry king of the English' before the seneschal of Anjou.[6] The monks of Savigny appealed 'to the court of the lord king at Rennes'

---

[1] Walter Map, I, 248. He was an itinerant justice in England in 1172–3 and 1184–5, and an ambassador to the pope in 1178, Pipe Roll 19 Henry II, 154; Pipe Roll 24 Henry II, 106; Pipe Roll 31 Henry II, 128, 146, 166.

[2] *Early Yorkshire Charters*, V, 74.

[3] *Feudal Documents from Bury St Edmunds*, no. 227.

[4] For examples of difficulties created *see Dialogus de Scaccario*, 32, 34.

[5] *Recueil des Actes de Henri II*, II, 250; cf. Introduction, 349.   [6] *Ibid.*, I, 335.

in Brittany, and came to an agreement 'in curia domini regis' before the seneschal of Rennes.[1] Clearly the *curia regis* existed wherever a delegate of King Henry acted in his name. It also, of course, existed wherever King Henry himself happened to be. This could be anywhere, for the king and his household were continually on the move. In the thirty-four years of his reign Henry II spent Christmas at twenty-four different places.[2] He crossed the English Channel at least twenty-eight times and the Irish Sea twice.

Sea travel was far from easy. In 1154 Henry was delayed by contrary winds for a month when wishing to cross the Channel for his coronation.[3] In December 1162 he was delayed for two months at Barfleur.[4] He spent several weeks at Pembroke in 1171 waiting to cross to Ireland, and nearly a month at Wexford on the return journey.[5] In April 1170 a convoy of ships bearing the king, his household, and many noble families to England for the coronation of the Young Henry, was struck by a fierce storm: five vessels went down, with a loss, it is said, of nearly four hundred lives.[6] Many were drowned in the Channel in the bad winter of 1177–8, including the chancellor of the Young Henry.[7] The king spent Christmas in 1181 at Winchester and hoped to cross to France for a meeting with King Philip as soon as the festivities were over, but it was mid-Lent before he was able to do so.[8] Land travel presented less dramatic difficulties, but that too cannot always have been easy, especially when heavy rains made the river fords impassable, for bridges were few, and the royal household had a heavy baggage train. But despite all the difficulties the king kept on the move. His progress was in effect a royal eyre. 'He does not,' wrote Peter of Blois to a friend in Sicily, 'remain in his palace as other kings do, but going about the provinces, he investigates the deeds of all, judging those most strictly whom he had appointed judges of others.'[9]

As the king journeyed, the *curia regis coram rege* absorbed the local

---

[1] *Recueil des Actes de Henri II*, Introduction, 350.

[2] Bermondsey (1154), Westminster, (?) Bordeaux, Lincoln, Cherbourg, Falaise, Le Mans, Baieux, Cherbourg, Berkhamsted, Marlborough, (?) Oxford, Poitiers, Argentan, Argentan, Nantes, Bures, Dublin, Chinon, Caen, Argentan, Windsor, Angers, Angers, Winchester, Nottingham, Le Mans, (?) Winchester, Caen, Le Mans, Windsor, Domfront, Guildford, Caen, Saumur (1188).

[3] Gervase of Canterbury, I, 159.   [4] Robert de Torigny, 216.

[5] Roger of Howden, *Gesta*, I, 25, 29.

[6] Gervase of Canterbury, I, 216; Roger of Howden, *Gesta*, I, 4, *Chronica*, II, 3; Ralph of Diceto, I, 337; Robert de Torigny, 244.

[7] Robert de Torigny, 275; Ralph of Diceto, I, 422, cf. 424.

[8] Roger of Howden, *Gesta*, I, 284–5.

[9] Peter of Blois, *Opera*, I, 195.

curia regis for the period of its sojourn and released it again when it moved on.

> This is the final concord made in the court of the lord king at Clarendon ... before the lord king and John his son, and Ranulf de Glanvill, and Hubert dean of York, and Ralph archdeacon of Hereford, and Robert of Inglesham archdeacon of Gloucester, and Jocelin archdeacon of Chichester and Master Thomas of Hurstbourne and Michael Belet. . . .[1]

The justiciar, a number of prominent royal clerks, and barons of the exchequer have joined the king at his favourite hunting lodge in Wiltshire: but they are just such a group of men who might have witnessed an agreement to terminate a suit by compromise in the *curia regis apud Westmonasterium* or the *curia regis* on eyre.

If there were numerous barons present, court merged into council, and if the barons had been specially summoned the chroniclers might talk of a meeting of the 'great council' (*magnum concilium*). Great councils were summoned for momentous business: to discuss the possibility of a crusade, for instance, to advise the king on his arbitration between the rulers of Castille and Navarre, or to assent to changes in the law.[2] The Assize of Northampton was made 'in the presence of the bishops, the earls, and the barons of the land'; the *grand assize* was introduced 'concilio procerum'.[3] The council was still the *curia regis*, but it was a session of the *curia* with a public face, whether specially summoned or convened with only those barons who happened to be present.[4] Whether business was brought before a council because the assent of the barons was necessary or simply for the sake of publicity is not always clear. Some kinds of business which did not necessarily concern the whole realm were nevertheless thought to be better done in public. The abbot of Battle Abbey, founded by William the Conqueror at the site of his victory near Hastings, came one day to Henry II and showed him a foundation charter which had decayed with age. The king said it ought to be renewed. The abbot asked that it be done

---

[1] *Cartularium Monasterii de Rameseia*, I, 121 (February 1187).

[2] e.g., Roger of Howden, *Gesta*, I, 336, 139, 107.

[3] *Ibid.*, 107, cf. Assize of Northampton, clause 7: 'Let the justices hold the assize for wicked robbers and evildoers throughout the counties they are about to traverse, for this assize is enacted in accordance with the advice of the king, his son, and his vassals'; *Glanvill*, 28.

[4] For a great council as *curia regis*, *see*, e.g., Roger of Howden, *Gesta*, I, 139. The rebels of 1173–4 were banned from coming to the *curia* unless they had been specially summoned, *ibid.*, 93. It was 'in curia mea a plenario baronum regni mei concilio' that Becket was condemned as a traitor, letter of Henry II to Louis VII, *Recueil des Actes de Henri II*, I, 385.

by means of a charter of confirmation, but the king said 'I may not do so without a judgement of my court' (*nisi ex judicio curiae mea*). The abbot consulted the justiciar, Richard de Lucy, who advised him of a proper time to make his request, and promised him that 'if our judgement is asked you will get the unanimous support of the whole court'. So the abbot raised the matter again 'when the king was sitting in the midst of his magnates'. The king asked for the views of the magnates whether he might do as requested or not, and Richard de Lucy spoke up and said, 'It would be proper to renew this charter of Battle, my lord, if it please you, for even if all its charters had perished, we ourselves ought to be its charters, for we owe our fiefs to that victory at Battle. And since you ask for our judgement as to whether you should do it or not, we adjudge that the charter should be renewed by a confirmation on your authority. . . .' So the king called his chancellor and dictated the form that the confirmation was to take.[1]

As the body of the king's vassals the council gave assent (*assensus*); it was duty bound to give him advice (*consilio*) when he asked for it; as a court, his 'full court' as it was sometimes called, it rendered judgements (*judicia*).[2] The giving of assent (*consent* is perhaps too strong a word) is the one distinctive feature of the council of magnates. The rendering of judgements it shared with all manifestations of the ubiquitous *curia regis*. The tendering of counsel it shared with those whose advice the king chose to seek. For besides the formal counsel of the *magnum concilium* there was the informal counsel of those whom the king consulted in the daily business of government and administration. There was in the twelfth century no inner or privy council as an institution, no body of sworn counsellors as there was in the thirteenth century, but there was a group, loosely formed and constantly shifting, of those who enjoyed the king's confidence, whose experience he valued, whose opinions he respected. They might be barons by inheritance, such as Robert earl of Leicester, or men from the lower ranks, such as Ranulf de Glanvill, or men with no background at all such as Ralph Brito, an obscure Breton, or Richard of Ilchester of whose parentage no one seems to have been sure; and they might be rewarded for loyal service with heiresses, escheats, archdeaconries, or bishoprics. Some of them

---

[1] *Chronicon Monasterii de Bello*, 164–5. The king, it is said, dictated a new form of wording: charters of confirmation normally incorporated the phrase 'as the earlier charter testifies', but Henry II ordered this to be omitted, and devised a formula which made the new charter fully authoritative even if all earlier charters should perish. The abbot prudently had several copies made in the chancery.

[2] A charter of the bishop of St Malo refers to an agreement reached 'in plenaria curia domini regi Angliae' at Chinon in 1182, *Recueil des Actes de Henri II*, II, 227.

were office holders, *ministeriales*, in chamber or chancery perhaps, and some were simply *amici*, the king's friends. It is probable that many of their names elude us, for intimate counsel was not a matter of record; but some come before us in letters of recommendation, or the comment of a chronicler, characterised as *familiares regis*. Ralf archdeacon of Llandaff, for instance, is described by Gerald of Wales, as 'clericus familiaris' of the king.[1] When news came of the murder of Becket, writes Roger of Howden, the king despatched to Rome the archbishop of Rouen, the bishops of Evereux and Worcester, Richard Barre 'and certain others of his clerks and *familiares*' who were to speak there 'on behalf of the king and his kingdom'.[2] The king himself described two messengers sent to the pope as 'our clerks and *familiares* in whom you may repose full confidence'.[3] The king's decision in 1177 to summon his English barons for services in Normandy was said to have been taken 'per consilia familiarum suorum'.[4] *Familiares* is a word which defies adequate translation: a *familiares* was an intimate, a familiar resident or visitor in the household, a member of the *familia*, that wider family which embraces servants, confidants, and close associates.[5] There were, so far as can be seen, few who were simply courtiers, for the king employed his *familiares* on a variety of administrative tasks. The more important of them could expect to serve a term as barons of the exchequer or itinerant justices, and so help the king to keep in touch with his provincial governments, supplementing with their first-hand knowledge the information that reached him by way of the copy of the pipe roll which the chancellor brought back from the Michaelmas session of the exchequer, the endorsed writs returned by the sheriffs and put in the marshal's charge, or the rolls of information that he specially asked for (even the names of outlaws were sent to the king).[6] The functions of the *familiares*, indeed, make nonsense of any attempt to describe the king's government simply in terms of offices or institutions.

* * *

[1] Gerald of Wales, IV, 219.

[2] Roger of Howden, *Gesta*, I, 19.

[3] *Recueil des Actes de Henri II*, I, 435. In 1166 the clergy of the province of Canterbury, in a letter to the pope, speak of 'fideles et familiares regis specialiter assistentes secretis is quorum manu consilia regis et regni negotia diriguntur', *Materials for the History of Becket*, V, 507, cf. *ibid.*, I, 35, IV, 114.

[4] Roger of Howden, *Gesta*, I, 138.

[5] On the topic of familiar counsel it is impossible to improve upon Jolliffe, *Angevin Kingship*, 166–88.

[6] On the chancellor's roll *see Dialogus de Scaccario*, 17–19; on the writs preserved by the marshal, *ibid.*, 20–1, 33, 90; on the names of outlaws sent to the king, Assize of Northampton, clause 12.

Regarded superficially, Henry II's administration consisted of two overlapping but distinct elements: a household element, and what, for want of a better term, may be called a provincial element. The household administrative element, consisting of the chancery and chamber, supplemented to some extent by the office of the constable and marshal, was constantly with the king and conducted his business with any part of his dominions. The second element, on the other hand, was separately reproduced in each of the component parts of the Angevin 'commonwealth'. In England, where it is best known, it consisted of a central court, the *capitalis curia* or *curia regis apud Westmonasterium*, presided over by the justiciar and discharging its financial and judicial tasks through the exchequer, its subordinate treasury, the emerging 'bench', and the itinerant justices. How far it also controlled the administration of the forest – areas where the rights of the individual landholders were restricted by the superior claims of the beasts of the chase – is doubtful: the *Dialogus* says that 'the whole organisation of the forests, and the punishments of forest offences, is outside the jurisdiction of other courts, and solely dependent upon the decision of the king, or of some officer specially appointed by him.'[1] It is unlikely that the forest officers were entirely beyond the justiciar's control; but with this possible exception, the justiciar (or his counterpart on the continent – the seneschal) was in supreme control of the provincial administration during the king's absence. The structure of the offices, as it appears in the records of government, might, then, be represented on a diagram (see opposite page).

Such a diagram has a limited usefulness. It reveals something of reality: this, no doubt, is how the structure of offices appeared from the outside, to merchants, sheriffs, petitioners, who had dealings with it. It probably, too, would be an intelligible picture to lesser clerks and servants who worked in one office or another, and drew their pay on its livery roll. But it does not adequately represent the way the administration, particularly in its upper reaches, worked in practice. No diagram can show, without confusion, how the royal household penetrated into the justiciar's domain at a session of the exchequer. It cannot reveal the real relationship of the chief officers, nor delimit their actual functions, nor show how, under Henry II, offices were successively magnified, diminished, or dispensed with. There were two justiciars in England until 1168, and none at all for more than a year after Richard de Lucy's retirement.[2] Thomas Becket as chancellor was, it is said, 'second only to the king'; he ran a great household to which

[1] *Dialogus de Scaccario*, 59.
[2] Cf. West, *The Justiciarship*, 55-6.

many magnates sent their sons for training, crossing the sea 'with six or more vessels in his train'.[1] He directly took a hand in administration of England when the king was out of the country, authorising payments by writs in his own name.[2] But none of Becket's successors had such

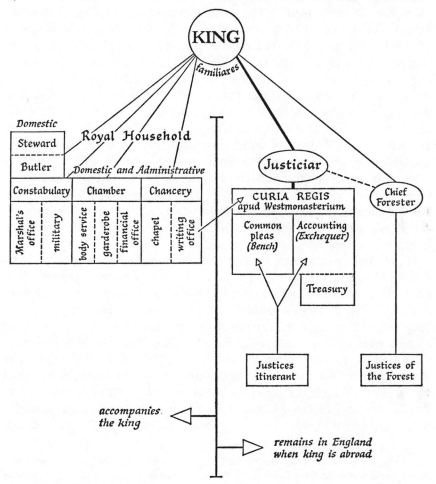

12. The relationships of the chief agencies in Angevin government

eminence or disposed of such authority. It is doubtful even if there was a chancellor, *eo nomine*, for many years after Becket resigned: Geoffrey Ridel can be seen performing some of the functions of the office but no record gives him the title. The simple principle that the chancellor

[1] William FitzStephen, III, 41, 22.
[2] Pipe Rolls 2–4 Henry II, 83, 89, 112, 140; Pipe Roll 8 Henry II, 1, 53, 64, 67.

and the chancery followed the king, even if a detachment of clerks was
left behind to assist the justiciar, is not borne out in consistent practice:
in 1173, according to Ralph of Diceto, Ralph de Warnerville was
appointed 'chancellor of ¦England' and Walter of Coutances 'vice
chancellor in *curia regis*'.[1] The administrative assumption (made for
instance in the *Dialogus*) that there was only one constable who journeyed with the king and had specific duties in the household and exchequer, takes no account of the fact that there were at times at least
two.[2] To speak of 'the' chancellor, or 'the' constable, or 'the' justiciar
in Henry II's reign, is, indeed, simply to use a convenient abstraction.
To take abstraction a stage further, and to attempt to delimit the
functions of office-holders, is to ignore the men who filled the offices
and the unlimited range of duties they performed in practice. Henry II
appointed officers as he needed them, or perhaps quite often simply to
assure his servants the fixed emolument of office, but he used them
freely without much regard for their 'official' functions. The Angevin
administration, in its upper reaches at least, was not really a bureaucracy, nor even a hierarchy of offices, but a network of men – a rather
intricate network.

If one looks to the men instead of the offices, it becomes difficult to
classify them, such is the variety of work they perform and titles they
bear. How is one to classify Ralph FitzStephen? He appears as a witness
to many royal charters, dignified with the title of 'chamberlain': he was
only one of the chamberlains, for there are several who bear the title
of *camerarius* simultaneously. He is to be found ferrying money across
the Channel, taking charge of the baggage of the duke and duchess of
Saxony when they visited England, attending to the needs of the captive Queen Eleanor, or supervising the building of the house of Car-
thusian monks which the king founded at Witham – all of which duties
might, conceivably, fall to him as a *camerarius*. But he is also to be found

---

[1] Ralph of Diceto, I, 367.

[2] Richard du Hommet (or de Humez) appears in witness lists to charters as *con-
stabularius* at the same time as Henry of Essex appears in the pipe rolls with the same
title. Cf. *Recueil des Actes de Henri II*, I, 82, 111, 541, and Pipe Roll 2 Henry II, 14–16.
They appear together as witnesses to a charter of Henry II to William de Vesci made
at Rhuddlan, *The Percy Cartulary*, 294 n. 8, in which Richard du Hommet is qualified
as 'constable of Normandy'. Richard du Hommet appears as 'constable' until he
retired to a monastery in 1180, and was succeeded by his son William. Henry of
Essex was accused in 1163 of having betrayed the king by casting away the royal
standard in an ambush on the Welsh campaign, cf. e.g., Jocelin of Brakelond, 69–71,
Ralph of Diceto, I, 310. He seems to have had no successor as constable 'of England'
(if indeed this is what he was). Information about the constables is gathered by
Boussard, *Le Gouvernement d'Henri II*, 344 and n. 6.

as sheriff of Gloucestershire for several years, very frequently as an itinerant justice, as custodian of part of the honor of Richmond, and as the assessor of taxes on the forests of Sherwood and Chippenham.[1] If one speaks of Manasser Bisset, is it as steward of the household or baron of the exchequer and itinerant justice?[2] Or of Richard du Hommet: sheriff of Rutland for most of the reign, but constable 'of Normandy' too, from 1154 to 1180.[3]

There were many men who held no household office yet were clearly great with the king and were active in administration ('majores de regni,' in a phrase of the Dialogus, 'qui familiarius regiis secretis assistunt').[4] Take Hugh de Cressy: in 1176 he was pressed into service as an itinerant justice, as any man around the king might be; in 1180 he is to be found on the Norman rolls in charge of Rouen; but he appears little on the rolls and might be thought of small account, were it not that he appears time and time again in the witness lists of royal charters.[5] He was one of the *familiares*, undignified by any great office yet close to the king, and ready for any kind of business: in 1184, for example, he was sent out to recruit mercenaries for a campaign in Poitou.[6] There were many such men who in terms of the confidence reposed in them by the king ranked among the highest in his government, yet whose importance would go unrecognised but for the frequency with which they attest royal charters. It is only from such evidence that we may detect the true prominence in the king's service of men such as Hugh de Gundeville, Robert Marmion, Richard de Canville, Gerard de Canville, Saher de Quincy, Fulk Painell, William FitzHamo, Thomas Bardulf, Robert de Stuteville, Gilbert FitzReinfred

[1] Cf. charters in *Recueil des Actes de Henri II*, and the Introduction to that work, 417; Roger of Howden, *Gesta*, I, 108; Pipe Roll 18 Henry II, 118; Pipe Roll 22 Henry II, 43, 141, 188; Pipe Roll 25 Henry II, 7; Pipe Roll 26 Henry II, 131; Pipe Roll 27 Henry II, 129; Pipe Roll 30 Henry II, 20–1, 26, 70, 92; Pipe Roll 30 Henry II, 206, 215; Pipe Roll 33 Henry II, 194; Madox, *Formulare Anglicarum*, 217, no. 357. Cf. Darlington, introduction to *Cartulary of Darley Abbey*, I, xxii–xxiv.

[2] He appears as 'dapifer' to Henry both as duke of Normandy and king of England, until his death in 1177. But Humphrey de Bohun also appears with this title, having served both Stephen and Matilda in that capacity. For Manasser Bisset's appearance in other capacities, see, e.g., *Feudal Documents from Bury St Edmunds*, nos 227, 230.

[3] Cf. *Recueil des Actes de Henri II*, Introduction, 429–31.

[4] *Dialogus de Scaccario*, 15.

[5] Cf. charters in *Recueil des Actes de Henri II*; *Calendar of Documents Preserved in France*, Eyton, *Itinerary of Henry II*; *Magni Rotuli Scaccarii Normanniae*, I, 70; Roger of Howden, *Gesta*, I, 170; *Rotuli Dominorum*, 2, 54; Pipe Roll 21 Henry II, e.g., 13; Pipe Roll 22 Henry II, e.g., 200; Pipe Roll 32 Henry II, 168; Haskins, *Norman Institutions*, 327, 334.

[6] *Magni Rotuli Scaccarii Normanniae*, I, 15.

or Robert of Harcourt, to name but a few. There were barons among them, and knights and men of humble origins, for social status mattered less to Henry II than loyalty, diligence and ability. Some of them might for a time be entrusted with an administrative task, put in charge of a strategic castle, given a bailiffry, made responsible for a shire, appointed as baron of the exchequer in England or in Normandy, sent to help the king's sons in Brittany, Poitou, or Ireland, or commissioned as an itinerant justice; but such is the variety of their work that it is impossible to label them as belonging to this or that branch of the king's government. Bertram de Verdun, for example, was a knight of the Avranchin, sometime custodian of Pontorson, sheriff of Warwickshire and Leicestershire from 1169 to 1184, itinerant justice, sent on a mission to Spain in 1177, despatched to clear up the dangerous muddle in Ireland in 1185, guardian of the heir to the earldom of Chester. Clearly he was a man of many parts (he was put in charge of Acre on the Third Crusade and died at Joppa); but again he was a man who when not entrusted with a special task was to be found constantly with the king and numbered among his most intimate counsellors.[1]

There were, of course, men in the royal service whose activities were more restricted. Richard FitzNigel appears to have performed no other duties than those required by the office of treasurer, or by his status as a member of the *curia regis* at Westminster. Or, to take a less prominent example, William Basset sometimes attests charters of the king, but only when the king is in England. For the rest he confined himself to his function as baron of the English exchequer, although that admittedly called from him a variety of duties: assessing tallages, visiting shires on the eyre, or hearing pleas which men brought to the king's court at Westminster. But in the higher reaches of Henry II's government such specialists were more the exception than the rule. The administrative offices of chancery, chamber and exchequer were the few fixed points in an ever-shifting kaleidoscope of men about the king and in his service – a few fixed points where business could be reduced to routine. And even here, among the chancery clerks and chamberlains and 'barons' of the exchequer, were men who were readily called to other tasks, and merged imperceptibly with those who had no fixed duties at all, but served the king in whatever way he desired, giving counsel, negotiating a treaty, taking charge of his chil-

---

[1] Roger of Howden, *Gesta*, I, 107, 157: 'misit in Hyspaniam quosdam de familiaribus suis, scilicet magistrum Johannem Cumin, et Bertranum de Verdun, et Robertum de Salobesbiria'; Gerald of Wales, I, 65; *Recueil des Actes de Henri II*, Introduction, 359–60.

dren, communicating his private views to the pope, raising an army of mercenaries.[1]

Henry used *familiares* to fill gaps in the administrative structure of his 'commonwealth', and to provide links between its several parts and himself. Through them the king was able to keep in his hand all the strings of government. Of particular significance is the way he used Richard of Ilchester. Richard's origins are wrapped in obscurity. That he was a kinsman of Gilbert Foliot, bishop of London, and was born in the diocese of Bath is about all that is known for certain. Even his surname is elusive: 'Toclyve', 'Tokelin', 'Poore', are some of the patronymics bestowed on him; the name 'd'Ilchester' seems to have been derived from a piece of the royal demesne granted to him in Somerset.[2] It would seem that for him as for many another clever young man, clerical orders offered a way of escape from the disadvantage of humble origins, and the path of a royal clerk the surest of all. Already in the second year of Henry's reign he is mentioned several times in the pipe roll as '*scriptor curie*' – a puzzling designation, but one which places him close to the king.[3] To the abbot of St Albans, at about the same time, he was 'one who has the king's ear' and could be asked to help in recovering a benefice seized by the Crown as part of the royal demesne.[4] High on the list for preferment at the king's hand, he appears from 1163 as archdeacon of Poitiers, or to those who recognised his uniqueness, simply as 'the Archdeacon'.[5] In the crisis with the bishops over the Constitutions of Clarendon he was one of the king's chief advisers and carried his views to Rome and to the court of the German emperor. Yet he was not a time-server, and seems to have kept clear of many of the passions and animosities that the conflict provoked. Archbishop Becket spoke of him venomously, as was his wont, but John of Salisbury respected him and worked through him to try to mitigate the king's anger, and to the monks of the cathedral church at Canterbury he was 'a friend and protector of the convent in its troubles'.[6] When Becket's death cleared the way to fill the vacancies in English bishoprics, King Henry nominated him to the electors of Winchester in the notorious

---

[1] e.g., Roger of Howden, *Gesta*, I, 138; Pipe Roll 12 Henry II, 100–1; *Recueil des Actes de Henri II*, I, 435; *Magni Rotuli Scaccarii Normanniae*, I, 15.

[2] Information about him is gathered by Kate Norgate, article in *Dictionary of National Biography*, and Duggan, 'Richard of Ilchester, royal servant and bishop'.

[3] Pipe Roll 2 Henry II, 30, 122; cf. 31, 47, 121.

[4] *Gesta Abbatum Monasterii Sancti Albani*, I, 123–4.

[5] Cf. Pipe Roll 11 Henry II, 4; Pipe Roll 13 Henry II, 34.

[6] *Materials for the History of Becket*, V, 331–4, 347–52; *Patrologia Latina*, CC, 1396, cf. CXC, 1003–5.

writ, 'I order you to hold a free election, but forbid you to elect anyone but Richard my clerk'.[1] Even so he had the support of sticklers
for canonical propriety, and even Bishop Bartholomew of Exeter, who
had stood by Archbishop Becket with fair zeal, spoke up for him at
Rome. Besides his labours for the king in the conflict with the
Church, and such incidental tasks as arranging for the Young Henry's
coronation, he had become a power in the administration in the late
'60s, baron of the exchequer from at least 1165, and an itinerant justice
on every eyre until he became a bishop. As a bishop he retired from the
eyres but not from the exchequer, unless it was to attend upon the
king in England or Normandy or to venture forth on an embassy.
And sometimes, instead of his going to the king, the king came to him,
as when, in 1182, Henry stayed at Richard's manor house at Waltham
in Hampshire.[2] He witnessed the king's will, and the king witnessed his
benefactions. For two years, 1176–8, he was seconded to the administration of Normandy, and seems, in the temporary capacity of seneschal, to have had the task of reorganising its financial and judicial
procedures along the lines that had by then become standard practice
in England. When William FitzRalph took over as permanent seneschal,
Richard returned to his seat at the English exchequer. Although, as
familiaris, he was on call for whatever royal business required his special
talents, it was at the English exchequer that he performed his most
regular royal service, and the manner of it is peculiarly indicative of
Henry II's way with his administration. Richard bore no special title
at the exchequer, but he had a special seat, and spoke with an authority that could modify exchequer practice.[3] Richard FitzNigel explains
in the *Dialogus*:

> On the right hand side of the justiciar sits the present bishop of Winchester:
> he sits ex officio, but his place has only recently been created. . . . Before
> his promotion, when he held a slightly lower position in the king's court,
> he proved himself trustworthy and industrious in attending to the king's
> business, and adept and efficient at preparing rolls and writs. Wherefore a
> place was given him near the treasurer, so that he should, jointly with him,
> attend to the writing of the roll and all such matters. He is without doubt
> a great man and concerned with many important tasks.[4]

It is a pity that the *Dialogus* is not more explicit about the functions of
Richard of Ilchester at the exchequer, but something may be gleaned

---

[1] It was made notorious by the Young King who reported it to the pope when at
odds with his father, *Recueil des Historiens des Gaules et de la France*, XIV, 645.

[2] *Memorials of St Edmunds Abbey*, I, 227. In 1186 the king visited him at Marwell,
Ralph of Diceto, II, 41.   [3] *Dialogus de Scaccario*, 17, 74.   [4] *Ibid.*, 17, 27.

from the pipe rolls. They speak now and then of *rotuli archidiaconi* – of special notes kept by Richard of Ilchester. They are cited in support of a claim upon a sheriff for a rent from a piece of royal demesne which the sheriff was reluctant to acknowledge; they record what has been happening about large arrears of rent from the *farm* of Norfolk and Suffolk which had been caught up in the king's repayment of loans; they are drawn upon for information about the royal tin mines in Cornwall.[1] Such slender evidence gives no certainty, but it seems that Ilchester's special concern was with the unusual, the non-routine items of account, the points which might be missed in the press of business at the exchequer. Richard FitzNigel says all too little, but he does, when talking of Richard of Ilchester, make the pregnant remark that the treasurer could not be alert to everything.[2]

Richard of Ilchester was not the only man to hold an extraordinary position at the exchequer. Directly opposite him sat Master Thomas Brown; he too was there by special ordinance of Henry II – 'contrary to the ancient custom of the exchequer', as Richard FitzNigel, with his love of traditional routine, was careful to point out.[3] Thomas Brown had lived for many years in the Norman wonderland of Sicily, had been great in the counsels of King Roger II and privy to his confidential business. But finding himself spurned by King Roger's successor, he had accepted a long-standing invitation from Henry II to return to his native land, and had been given a seat at the exchequer. He was not one of the barons, but was 'associated with them in all important business'.[4] The *Dialogus* is reticent about his functions, but does reveal that he had a clerk, who perched on a high stool behind the treasurer's scribe so that he could look over his shoulder and copy down whatever he required ('quod oportet excipiat').[5] Thomas Brown was specially privileged: the king had ordered that the roll which he kept should be accorded equal authority with the two official versions of the pipe roll known as the treasurer's roll and the chancellor's roll, and that he could carry it about with him wherever he wished. In it, so it is said, were written 'the laws of the realm and the king's private business'.[6] He also had a clerk in the treasury of receipt in the lower exchequer 'who sits next to the treasurer's clerk and has full freedom to take notes of all receipts and expenses of the treasury'.[7] This is little enough; but

[1] Pipe Roll 13 Henry II, 34; Pipe Roll 11 Henry II, 4; Pipe Roll 22 Henry II, 151.
[2] *Dialogus de Scaccario*, 27.
[3] *Ibid.*, 18, 35.
[4] *Ibid.*, 35–6.   [5] *Ibid.*, 18.
[6] *Ibid.*, 35.   [7] *Loc. cit.*

it can hardly be doubted that Thomas Brown formed a special and personal link between the king, the exchequer, and the treasury.

Some historians have seen in Ilchester and Brown the forerunners of officials of the exchequer known as *King's Remembrancer* and *Lord Treasurer's Remembrancer*. It may be so; but the differences are important. Ilchester and Brown owed their status at the exchequer to the king's confidence in them as persons. The later remembrancers performed well-defined functions within the established procedures of the exchequer; Ilchester and Brown, on the other hand, stood quite outside the established procedures, *preter antequam consuetudinem*. They were the freelances of a king who always seems to have preferred to recruit freelances than to rely exclusively on customary services. Later kings found themselves hampered by the strict office routine of a formalised exchequer, but not Henry II – he may have brought Bishop Nigel of Ely to restore traditional practices, but he did not allow them to fetter himself. Thomas Brown's roll was to be as authoritative as the two official rolls, for the king would have it so.[1]

Flexibility was the keynote of Henry II's administrative system. It had to be flexible because he did so little to encourage the growth of a bureaucratic hierarchy. Expansion there was, of course, but it was an expansion within the framework of the administrative institutions that he inherited. It is perhaps surprising that no thought seems to have been given to developing or creating new offices or new posts with defined functions and demarcated spheres of authority. That there was not seems less a matter of policy than of attitude. Just as in the political control of his vast territories Henry II preferred rather informal family arrangements, so too in administrative control he seems to have preferred a loose structure and informal methods that sat lightly upon his desire to retain much of the substance as well as the theory of personal rule.

In the course of the next century the amorphous body of *familiares* and *ministeriales* resolved itself into private secretaries and remembrancers, keepers of the privy seal, wardrobe officers, and sworn privy counsellors, all labelled and docketed and drawing their fixed liveries. The wonder is that Henry II's flexible system did not collapse into chaos. Messengers hurried back and forth across the Channel; petitioners appeared before the *curia regis* at Westminster and were not sure whether to call it the *scaccarium*, or they appeared before the *curia*

[1] *Dialogus de Scaccario*, 19: 'Par enim est auctoritas illius duobus rotulis ratione scripture quia sic placuit eius auctori'.

regis with the king and were given writs to take to someone else; writs were sued from chancery, or the chancery detachment with the justiciar or from the clerks of the justices itinerant; the chamber picked up money from whatever resources were to hand in Sussex or Yorkshire, the Avranchin, or Poitou; *familiares* came hither and thither, transmitting instructions by word of mouth, commandeering this or requisitioning that, and levying their expenses wherever was convenient.

> *Memorandum:*
> In the Fine Roll it was found that Robert de Walterville agreed to a fine of twenty marks for having custody of the land and heir of Geoffrey of Martin, and in another roll it was found that he agreed to a fine of forty marks concerning the same fine, and it was not known if both fines should stand or not.

One hand, it seems, did not know what the other hand was doing; but the exchequer is there to identify the problem and seek an answer.

> *Note:*
> The justiciar has ruled that the fine of forty marks should be adhered to.[1]

It was the exchequer which saved flexibility from chaos. The punctilious routine, the meticulous procedures, the reluctance to change anything, that are revealed so clearly in the pages of the *Dialogus de Scaccario* were not typical of Henry II's government. The exchequer itself was not typical. It was possible to write a book about it simply because much of its business was highly formalised. It is doubtful if a book could have been written about the workings of the chancery or chamber. Even the *Dialogus* did not venture into the inner room where those privy to the mind of an undisciplined king tried to resolve the problems of his government. The treasurer confined his treatise to the auditing chamber where life was orderly, tried not to notice the intrusion of Richard of Ilchester or Thomas Brown into the routine of the past, and ventured barely a word about that amorphous, indescribable, and immensely powerful body, the *curia regis ad scaccarium*. But the auditing machine which he describes with loving care was the gyroscope that kept the whole structure of government and administration on an even keel.

'The exchequer shares with the king's court in which he administers justice in person the privilege that its records and judgements may not be impugned.' Mistakes made by the clerk when writing the pipe roll might be struck out but not erased, 'and the pipes should be made of

[1] *Memoranda Roll 1 John*, 47.

sheepskin, on which it is difficult to make an erasure without its showing plainly'. Mistakes could be corrected only 'by the assent of all the barons and in their presence'; and once the exchequer has risen only the king himself could change anything. The itinerant justices should make sure that their own rolls 'are correct and in order' when they handed them over to the treasurer, for once this had been done 'not even the justices themselves may alter one jot, although they should all agree to it'. Not even the justiciar could alter a royal writ presented at the exchequer. The pipe roll must be above reproach, both the treasurer's copy and the chancellor's.[1] These were rules of the exchequer, part of the necessary disciplines which brought order out of confusion. It was at the exchequer that business conducted by the royal household or by the provincial administration was brought into view and reconciled; it was at the exchequer that the king's administrative writs came to rest; it was at the exchequer that all men were brought to account; it was at the exchequer that explanations were called for from all the king's agents, and questions asked until answers were found; it was at the exchequer that muddles were straightened. The chancellor, frequently having to absent himself from sessions of the exchequer, tried, it seems, to escape responsibility for what was written in his copy of the pipe roll, but the barons, so the *Dialogus* reveals, would not allow it.[2] They could not allow it: the rolls incorporating their decisions had to be sacrosanct, because so little else was. The chancellor had to shoulder responsibility for what was done in his name, or the vital links which the exchequer forged between itinerant household and provincial administration would be chafed to breaking point. The exchequer consisted of an inner core of expertise and an outer ring of those knowledgeable about the king's business, under the control of those privy to royal policy and capable of interpreting its intentions. It was not the focus of government; it was the eye of the storm.

[1] *Dialogus de Scaccario*, 14, 31, 28–9, 77–8, 91, 92.
[2] *Ibid.*, 19.

Chapter 9

ROYAL JUSTICE

The practice of English law was transformed in Henry II's reign. There was no revolution, there was not even, so far as we can detect, a conscious plan of reform. In a manner that is typical of Henry II, nothing was abolished: the transformation was effected by setting up alongside the old an alternative, in which old practices were rationalised and selected precedents fused together with the transmuting touch of intelligence. There was, so far as can be seen, no long gestation, such as preceded the contemporary transformation of ecclesiastical legal practice, no slow digestion of the lessons of history, no absorption of Justinian's summation of Roman law, no deep reflection upon the principles of jurisprudence. English legal practice was transformed by the practical decisions of busy men responding intelligently to practical problems that were nothing new in themselves, but which had never before encountered an authority that made a habit of asking not simply what needed to be done, but how it could be done better. Better meant more simply, more rationally, more efficiently, and more effectively. This attitude alone was yeast to the dough of an English legal system which, for all its hoary virtues, was immensely complicated, and frequently irrational, clumsy and slow.

Twelfth-century England was well supplied with courts of law. There were the courts of the vill and the manor, hundred courts and shire courts, borough courts, honorial courts and the ecclesiastical courts of archbishops and bishops, and the newer courts of archdeacons, and, of course, there was the court of the lord king. In general terms it is fairly easy to distinguish the competence of each. The humble court of the vill enforced the village by-laws. The manor court was the landlord's private estate court, hearing cases which arose out of the unfree tenures of his peasantry. The hundred court dealt with the petty crimes of lowly men in the neighbourhood of a few vills. The shire court, in its judicial aspects, was largely concerned with more serious crimes: felonies, accusations against freemen, tort and pleas of debts. The borough court performed similar functions to the shire court within the bounds of the township and according to the terms of its charter of incorporation. Pleas of land, however, and all that arose out of land holding, such as inheritance, dower, and a vassal's obligations to his lord, were the peculiar province of the honorial court, the court which a lord summoned for the free tenants of his fief. The ecclesiastical courts, in the words of an edict of William I, were the proper tribunals for 'causes which concern the cure of souls' – a sweeping phrase, for by the notions of the time it covered matrimonial and testamentary causes, promises made on oath, besides the discipline of the clergy and correction of sinners. The king's court – a court which met whenever and wherever the king chose to convene it – was the greatest honorial court in the land, for it was there that the tenants-in-chief brought their pleas; but it was also the supreme court for the enforcement of all the king's rights, and the final court of appeal from all lesser jurisdictions.[1]

In reality, however, the situation was much more confused than such simple distinctions might suggest. To which court a man took his plea depended only partly on the nature of the plea: it depended partly on his status, and partly on the nature of his tenure. A case which a villein might bring in the hundred court, a freeman might bring in the shire court, and a clergyman might bring in the ecclesiastical court. The Church's claim, indeed, to try all manner of causes in which a clergyman was involved threatened to turn the ecclesiastical courts into a parallel instead of a 'peculiar' jurisdiction. Among secular courts too, however, the lines of demarcation were often blurred, and there could be competition for competence within the same area of the law. The courts of vill and manor merged into one another when village and manor were coterminous and controlled by one lord. Manorial courts handled certain categories of criminal business if the lord had a franchise for it from the king. On the other hand, even so basic a topic of manorial economy as the status of a peasant, whether he be free or serf, was a matter for the sheriff in the shire court. Pleas of land, too, might be heard in the shire court if the litigants were vassals of different lords, or if it could be shown that a lord had defaulted in giving justice in his own court. Pleas of land might even be heard in the ecclesiastical courts if the land in question was held 'in free alms', instead of by some secular service.[2]

[1] Cf. Leges Henrici Primi, XXX. 14: 'no man may dispute the judgement of the king's court, but men who are acquainted with the plea may appeal against the judgement of other courts'.
[2] Even here the distinction was not always clear, cf. Poole, *Obligations of Society*, 6–7.

Competing and overlapping jurisdictions were a source of serious trouble in the twelfth century. The strife between Henry II and the Church over the competence of the ecclesiastical courts is merely the most notorious example of a struggle that went on daily between almost all courts. Jurisdictional disputes, indeed, frequently impeded the operation of the courts, and astute litigants could indefinitely protract the prosecution of suits by pleading now here, now there, or by contesting the competence of the tribunal before which their opponents had brought them. This situation was to a great extent the consequence of William the Conqueror's equivocal attitude to the kingdom he acquired. He came not to destroy but to preserve, for he came in the guise of a true heir challenging a usurper for the throne of Edward the Confessor; but he was obliged in the end to conquer England, and in order to hold it had to Normanise it. Intention and necessity were never formally reconciled. The Normans who took over from English lords inevitably brought Norman practices with them; but these did not supplant the practices of the old English state – they were casually combined with them. It might have happened in England, as it had long ago happened on the continent, that the public courts would become absorbed into the private jurisdictions of great lords. This, indeed, was a fate which frequently overtook hundred courts, but it did not happen to the shire courts, for strong-handed Norman kings jealously preserved the shire courts as vehicles for royal authority. Nevertheless, the all-embracing competence of the Old English shire court was broken apart and diminished by the piecemeal erection of other courts with narrower but in some ways more compelling jurisdiction. Continental ideas of ecclesiastical propriety led first to a ban on 'any sheriff or reeve or official . . . interfering with the laws that pertain to the bishop', and then to the erection of separate church courts.[1] The eviction of English landowners and their replacement by Normans on new conditions of tenure led inevitably to the erection of courts in which lords administered to their vassals the law of the new tenures by procedures with which they were familiar.

The substantive and procedural law administered in the Old English courts, already complicated by a still undigested admixture of Scandinavian elements, was further confused by the introduction of Norman influences and principles. A Norman at litigation with another Norman would normally plead before his lord's court on the basis of Norman land law; but when claiming the rights of his Anglo-Saxon predecessors might find himself obliged to plead in the shire court by the formulae

[1] Stubbs, *Select Charters*, 99–100.

and principles of King Edward's day. King William insisted on it: 'It is my will and command,' he said, 'that all shall have and hold the law of King Edward in respect of all their lands and all their possessions.' So spoke the true heir; but the conqueror was obliged to add, 'together with all those decrees which I have ordained for the welfare of the English people'.[1] It was one thing, however, for William to insist on the *legem Eadwardi*, it was another thing to know what that law was. The Norman settlers found it puzzling. Some tried manfully to reduce it to writing in the early years of the twelfth century but got little further than transcribing the laws attributed to Anglo-Saxon kings. This was not enough, for such legislation was simply the modification of a deep substratum of customary, unwritten law. The bravest of them, the anonymous author of the *Quadripartitus* and the *Leges Henrici Primi*, who at least tried to write a textbook of contemporary legal practice, succeeded only in confusing himself and posterity.[2] It is understandable that he failed in his attempt: almost every positive statement which could be made about English law in the early twelfth century was subject to qualifications and exceptions; there was no definable framework into which a discussion of law might be cast, no single point of entry into the diversity and peculiarity of local custom. A sensible man could do only as the author of the *Tractatus de Legibus et Consuetudinibus Angliae* did seventy years later when discussing litigation about land-holding: 'such pleas,' he said, 'are tried in the courts of lords, in accordance with the reasonable customs of those courts, which are so diverse and numerous that they cannot readily be reduced to writing'.[3] The author of the *Tractatus* was able to push the problem aside because he was writing primarily about the law administered in royal courts. That he could produce a book which is a model of clarity, and which describes a law that was clear, rational, precisely formulated, and common to the whole country is a measure of the achievement of King Henry II.

The diversity of the old customary law was not its only drawback: there was the almost insuperable problem of proof. Procedure is the darkest of all aspects of the old customary law, but something may be gleaned from chronicles, cartularies, and memorials of law-suits. Proceedings began either with public accusation of a crime by a jury of twelve men sworn for the purpose, or by a formal complaint delivered orally by the plaintiff and formally denied by the defendant. In the

---

[1] Stubbs, *Select Charters*, 99.
[2] Cf. Plucknett, *Early English Legal Literature*, 19ff.
[3] *Glanvill*, XII.6.

presence of two parties litigation might proceed by 'alternate pleadings' with the parties introducing arguments to support their own case or demolish that of their opponents, buttressed perhaps by the testimony of those who claimed to know the truth.[1] There was, however, no examination of witnesses and little testing of evidence. Documents, it is true, might be entered in support of a claim, and if accepted as genuine would be held to constitute incontrovertible proof; but documents could too easily be lost, destroyed, or forged, and in a society not yet wholly committed to the written word the absence of documentary proof could not be bar to a man's claim or to his defence. The two methods of proof commonly employed were by oath or ordeal. The court might require one or other or both of the parties to 'wage their law' by bringing in a specified number of oath-helpers. He who swore falsely might expect the vengeance of God, but this could be of little satisfaction to a man who lost his case because of it. The ordeal was another but more immediate request for the intervention of God. In the ordeal of water the innocent had to hope to be preserved from drowning even though it was necessary for him to sink to prove his innocence. In the ordeal of iron innocence was demonstrated by the rapid and clean healing of the hand blistered by carrying hot metal. The Normans favoured a duel between the parties as a form of ordeal and brought it with them to England. In criminal cases it had to be fought between accuser and accused, but in civil cases the court might permit the substitution of champions. The ordeal at least had the advantage of decisiveness, but men of the twelfth century were less convinced than their predecessors of its efficacy in proving guilt or innocence. It was not until 1215 that the Church finally withdrew the sanction of its authority from all forms of ordeal, but scepticism had long since weakened confidence in its use.[2] Anglo-Saxon justice had not favoured the use of the ordeal in civil litigation, but preferred instead, when possible, to try to reach a judgement on the testimony, under oath, of men who might be presumed to know the facts of the matter at issue. References to the verdict of jurors – men put on oath to tell the truth as they knew it – are quite numerous among the legal memorials of Anglo-Norman England. This device of the judicial fact-declaring jury was, suitably adapted, to become a key element in the procedures devised for the royal courts in Henry II's reign. Little is known of how the jury actually functioned in the earlier period, but

[1] Leges Henrici Primi, XXIX.
[2] Cf. Baldwin, 'The intellectual preparation for the canon of 1215 against ordeals'. See, e.g., the criticism of the judicial duel in Glanvill, II.7.

what evidence there is suggests that it was usually employed with the consent of the parties, and that the parties themselves selected the jurors.[1] It was, it seems, basically a form of arbitration. Alternatively the court might appoint arbitrators, or it might suggest to the parties that they reach a compromise, itself ratifying the agreement they proposed. Compromise and arbitration had a long history; even before ordeals fell into disrepute they seem to have been the methods of concluding litigation which courts preferred: partly it was a recognition that truth was elusive, but partly it was a reluctance to create a legacy of bitterness by the harshness of a decisive judgement. An honourable peace seemed preferable to the sort of rough and ready justice that might drive the disappointed party to the violence of self-help.

It would probably be a mistake to criticise the weaknesses of Anglo-Norman justice. It was something that the courts functioned at all. Anglo-Saxon England, indeed, developed to a remarkable degree a respect for law and judicial process, and a readiness to seek rational means of disposing of disputes.[2] Norman discipline coupled with Anglo-Saxon sophistication probably helped to make the processes of law and order a little less unsatisfactory in early twelfth-century England than in other parts of western Europe. Moreover, many of the stories of lack of justice come from monastic chronicles, and the monasteries were a special case. Wealthy monasteries were prone to be pillaged, and had no other means of defending themselves than litigation. Their archives preserved the memory of rights, and, conscious that they held their property in trust for posterity, they were disinclined to accept compromise or arbitration if there were any prospect of securing, sometime, somewhere, a favourable verdict on their claim. Nevertheless the deficiencies were serious. Compromise may show good sense, but frequently cloaks injustice with the mantle of peace. The proliferation of courts and the overlapping of jurisdictions robbed men of that certainty which a satisfactory judicial system demands. The lack of adequate methods of proof, the possibility of evasion and delay put a premium on persistence which lesser men could rarely afford. Furthermore, the arrival in England of a military aristocracy noted throughout Europe for its aggressiveness and acquisitive instincts, undoubtedly corrupted the sophistication of Anglo-Saxon justice, substituting for the subtle social pressures which regulated the Old English state, a crude and overbearing wilfulness sustained by retinues of knights.

The situation would undoubtedly have been much worse but for the

[1] For a review of the evidence *see* Van Caenegem, *Royal Writs*, 69–77.
[2] On the Anglo-Saxon achievement *see* Doris Stenton, *English Justice*, 6–21.

intervention of strong-minded kings. William the Conqueror and Henry I had a passion for order, or at least a dislike for disorder as an insult to their kingship, which amounted, in practice, to the same thing. They were highly conscious of the prerogatives of kingship, and discharged its duties more vigorously than many Anglo-Saxon kings, who did not have to try so hard to prove that they were truly kings. It was the duty of a Christian king, as the Church frequently reminded everyone, to remedy the deficiencies of the law and protect the defenceless. The Norman kings were not great legislators, but they readily atoned for their own violence by suppressing it in others. Adopting the device of the Anglo-Saxon writ they issued peremptory orders for the righting of wrongs, often with as little regard of the formalities of the law as those who had committed the wrong. The king might intervene to help a petitioner obtain a hearing by commanding the holder of an appropriate court to entertain the plea, under threat of someone else doing it instead, 'so that I hear no further complaint thereof for lack of right'.[1] Or he might intervene to ensure that the hearing a plaintiff received was a fair hearing, by ordering, for example, that he be put in possession of the disputed property before pleadings began, for customary procedures quite properly gave advantages to the man in possession.[2] Or he might intervene to insist that a petitioner achieved possession of his proven rights, for it was one thing to gain a favourable judgement, and quite another to have it executed.[3] Or he might arbitrarily command that a wrong be righted without any reference to the hearing of a plea before a competent court.[4]

In none of these ways was the king actually doing justice, he was discharging his duty by ensuring that someone else did it. It is not the intervention of the king's court but the intervention of the king by means of an executive order. The king's court, although prepared on occasion to convene as a judicial tribunal to hear appeals from any quarter, was primarily concerned, in Maitland's phrase, with 'the great men and the great causes'.[5] It is possible that Henry I tried to intervene more positively in the administration of justice through the agency of the itinerant justices who visited the shires in pursuit of the king's rights. The one surviving pipe roll from the reign, that for 1130, provides evidence stretching back over several years, which shows the justices

---

[1] Van Caenegem, *Royal Writs*, 413ff.   [2] *Ibid.*, 439ff.
[3] *Ibid.*, 508ff.; cf. 493, no. 154, a writ to uphold a compromise.
[4] *Ibid.*, 444ff. Some of the writs cited in this section, however, while not referring to a judgement, do perhaps presuppose it.
[5] Pollock and Maitland, *History of English Law*, I, 108.

not merely dealing with pleas of the Crown and other of the king's lucrative rights but hearing pleas of land too.[1] It is possible that these civil pleas were the consequence of petitions to the king which had been referred to the royal justices for a hearing locally. But it is more likely that most of them were pleas which happened to be at litigation in the shire court when the royal justices arrived, for the effect of the justices' arrival was to suspend the jurisdiction of the sheriff and convert the shire court for the time being into a royal court. It was an advantage, no doubt, to litigants to have the hearing of their plea presided over by a royal justice, but there is no sign that it led to any modification of the traditional procedures. Royal justice in the first decade of Henry II's reign is indistinguishable from that of the earliest years of the century. To the numerous complaints of lack of justice in Stephen's reign, Henry responded with equally numerous writs ordering someone else to see that the plaintiff got a hearing, or that his plea was dealt with justly, or that judgement was executed.

Henry, king . . . to the sheriff of Derby greeting. I order you to cause the abbot and monks of Burton without delay and justly to have the customs which they claim in Derby, as they are able to prove through lawful men of the district. And unless you do it the earl of Leicester shall have it done, that I hear no complaint thereof for want of right. Witness Jocelin de Balliol. At Burton.[2]

Henry, king . . . to Hugh de Neville greeting. I command and order that you shall without delay and justly reseise the monks of St Andrew's Northampton, of their land of Newton and of their men, and justly give back to them their chattels which you have taken thence. And unless you do it my justice of Lincolnshire shall do it. And let me hear no further complaint thereof for want of right. Witness the chancellor. At Northampton.[3]

Henry king of the English and duke of the Normans and of the Aquitanians and count of the Angevins . . . to the bishop of Norwich, greeting. I order you to cause William, abbot of Holme, to have fully and entirely and justly the advowson of the church of Ranworth, as he justly ought to have it and as it was recognised by the oath of lawful men. And unless you do it, the archbishop of Canterbury shall have it done, so that he does not lose his right for lack of right or full justice. Witness Warin FitzGerald the chamberlain. At St Jean d'Argély.[4]

[1] Richardson and Sayles, *The Governance of Medieval England*, 176–80.
[2] Burton Cartulary, 11; Van Caenegem, *Royal Writs*, 421, no. 18.
[3] Van Caenegem, *op. cit.*, 461, no. 95, from an unedited Northampton cartulary.
[4] *Register of St Benet of Holme*, I, 17; Van Caenegem, *op. cit.*, 514–15, no. 196.

These examples are typical of many. It is difficult to classify or differentiate them for although they display, as might be expected, a certain amount of common phraseology, they are not reduced to standardised formulae for the various purposes required. Each writ is *ad hoc*, each is unique, for we are still in the era of unsystematic royal intervention. The amount of royal justice that was done, in the sense of the actual hearing of pleas by the king or his agents, was minimal. The king has his chief justiciar, who, particularly in the absence of the king abroad, sees to the transmission and execution of writs. There are royal justices at the king's court of the exchequer who, besides hearing pleas which arise out of their financial business, might sometimes be commissioned to hear cases brought on appeal.[1] Royal commissioners are sometimes down in the shires to hear pleas brought to the attention of the king which are better dealt with locally, or they might, as William FitzJohn seems to have done in 1159–60, hear pleas pending in the shire courts in the course of a visitation to investigate the work of local officials. But such direct interventions in the dispensing of justice were only occasional and extraordinary. They served to remind men that the king would not knowingly allow injustice or lack of justice to prevail. The trouble was that only a small fraction of the defaults of justice reached the ears of the king; and furthermore that even when the plaintiff had armed himself with a royal writ, he had not necessarily surmounted all the obstacles that his opponents could erect.

The chronicler of Battle Abbey tells a story which illustrates some of the defects in the administration of justice. The story starts in the latter years of Henry I's reign. The abbey then purchased three virgates of land at Barnhorne in Sussex from a tenant of Withelard de Balliol. Withelard approved the transaction and made a gift of an adjoining plot of land, which was confirmed by his own lord, the count of Eu, and by King Henry I himself. But when the land had been much improved by the efforts of the monks, the lord of the manor of Barnhorne began to demand a return for the favour conferred. When the abbot firmly refused, the lord of the manor deprived the monks of the property and mortgaged it to a money-lender in Hastings. 'The abbot and his agents took this very hard, and started a variety of weighty appeals for justice, but since King Henry died abroad they were unable to secure restitution of their rights. King Stephen succeeded, but in his time justice was little regarded: he who was strongest got most, and thus, as everyone

---

[1] The barons of the exchequer were sometimes commissioned to do justice to a plaintiff when the addressee of a royal writ failed to do so, Van Caenegem, *op. cit.*, 418, no. 13.

for a time held on to what he had seized as if by right, the abbey was unable to recover Barnhorne despite many attempts.' But after Stephen's death Henry II 'restored ancestral times', and Abbot Walter, who was a brother of the justiciar, Richard de Lucy, obtained a friendly hearing at the royal court. King Henry sent a writ to the overlord of the fief, the count of Eu, telling him to do full right to the abbot, and that if he failed to do so the sheriff of Sussex would, so that the king should hear no further complaint for want of right. 'But Gilbert de Balliol, who was then lord of the manor, put up many excuses to avoid having to answer, although he was repeatedly summoned and required to do so by the count, the sheriff, the abbot and his men. Much time was thus spent in fruitless effort, but the abbot had no wish to abandon his purpose, and after frequent applications to the king, sometimes in person, and sometimes through friends, secured the transfer of the case to the royal court. But the lord king was crossing back and forth between England and Normandy busy about his own business, and it still proved impossible to bring the matter to a satisfactory conclusion, although the case was for long ventilated before the justices who deputised for the king in his court, and despite the fact that the king by his mandates and writs very often required that full justice be shown the abbot.' Finally, however, the king came to stay for a while at Clarendon, and importuned yet further by the abbot, had the parties brought before him. On behalf of the abbey it was explained how the land at Barnhorne had been acquired partly by gift and partly by purchase, and how it had been taken away, and how much fruitless effort had been expended in trying to recover it. With the king's permission the deeds of purchase and gift and the charters of confirmation were read aloud. Gilbert de Balliol, in reply, began by challenging the authenticity of the deeds on the grounds that he could see no seals attached. But this argument availed him nothing, for as Richard de Lucy, the justiciar, pointed out, it had not in the past been the custom for every petty knight to have a seal. So Gilbert tried next to challenge the confirmation of Henry I. Then the king took the charter with his grandfather's seal on it into his own hands and said 'By the eyes of God, if you can prove this charter false you will make me a rich man in England. If the monks by a charter and confirmation such as this would lay claim to this very palace of Clarendon, which I delight in above other, I would be obliged to give it up to them entirely.' The abbot and his friends were then told to confer together as to whether they wished to rest their case on any other grounds than the charter: but they, heartened by the king's comments, returned to say that they desired no other proof, and would claim neither more nor less than the charter contained. Gilbert de Balliol had nothing to say, so, 'by unanimous consent of the whole royal court', judgement was given for the abbot. By the king's order writs were then sent to the four knights who at that time jointly held the sheriffdom of Sussex requiring them to restore to the abbey what it had recovered in court, 'the land itself being first ascertained, and its bounds walked by twelve loyal men of those parts, who knew its boundaries, and who should speak the truth about it upon oath'.[1]

This story is interesting as one of the few surviving descriptions of a hearing before the king himself, but it is even more interesting as a revelation of the ineffectiveness of a series of royal writs in the face of an opponent who was prepared to exploit to the full the opportunities for delay and evasion. It would not have been surprising if a weaker plaintiff, without the resources and influence of Battle Abbey, had given up in despair. There was no follow-through from the issue of a royal writ to the conclusion of a case; too much was left to the persistence of the plaintiff. And this was not all, for further defects in the operation of royal justice before Henry II got to work to reform it are revealed in a story told by the chronicler of St Albans abbey.

St Albans had for neighbours in Hertfordshire the influential family of Valognes, lords of Bennington. In the Conqueror's day Abbot Paulus had allowed Peter of Valognes to enjoy the use of the abbey's wood at Northam, and successive abbots had renewed the privilege to successive heirs. This was rash: long-continued possession could begin to look like hereditary right. So when in 1158 Abbot Robert heard that Peter of Valognes the younger was nigh unto death he sent two monks to ask for restitution of the wood. Peter readily acknowledged that his family held the wood not by hereditary right but simply by the generosity of St Albans, and in the presence of his knights who were standing about his bed he made it over to the monks. That very night he went the way of all flesh and the abbot took possession of the wood. Peter's successor, his brother Robert, was reluctant to see the wood go, and frequently begged the abbot to let him have it, but in vain. So Robert went to King Henry in France and besought him to order that the wood be conceded. The king was then planning his expedition to Toulouse, and being anxious to recruit his barons' support went so far as to give Robert a writ saying that he was not to be unjustly deprived of possessions that his ancestors held by hereditary right. Returning to England, Robert confronted the abbot with the king's writ. The abbot had it

[1] *Chronicon Monasterii de Bello*, 105-9.

read aloud in his court and then pointed out that it was of no avail to Robert since no question of hereditary right was involved. Robert, annoyed at still being frustrated, then went to the earl of Leicester, 'who presided over the hearing of pleas in England', and drew his attention to the conclusion of the king's writ to the abbot which read 'And un-less you do it, Robert earl of Leicester shall do it, lest he is further vexed for want of right'. So the earl instructed the sheriff of Hertfordshire to summon the abbot to answer the complaint at Northampton. But the abbot, 'being unwilling to be adjudged by the earl' (*nolens comitis sisti judicio*), sent one of his monks instead. The earl took the abbot's absence amiss and summoned him again. When he still did not appear the earl condemned him, adjudged the wood to Robert of Valognes 'by judgement of the royal court' (*in judicio curiae regiae*), and instructed the sheriff of Hertfordshire to put Robert in possession 'by royal auth-ority'. Then Robert, calculating that he would enjoy it for only a short time 'since he possessed it unjustly', started cutting down the timber. When the abbot discovered that irreparable damage was being done he hastened to the earl of Leicester and besought him to restrain Robert, but the earl simply reiterated his judgement. So the abbot went to Queen Eleanor 'who was then in England' and begged her to send a writ to Robert of Valognes condemning the damage he was causing. She did so, and Robert desisted for a time, though not for long. Meanwhile the abbot had sent messengers to acquaint the lord pope with the mischief and a letter came back addressed to Theobald archbishop of Canterbury and Hilary bishop of Chichester, instructing them to require Robert of Valognes to restore the wood or do full justice to the monks within thirty days. If he failed to do so they were to excommunicate him. But 'the bishops feared to bind Robert with the chains of anathema since King Henry II had forbidden his bishops to pronounce sentence of excommunication on any of his barons'. So the abbot took counsel again and despatched one of the monks to the king, who was then with his army before Toulouse. He was to ply the king with entreaties, gifts, and promises, beseeching him to write to the earl of Leicester instructing him to bring Robert of Valognes to judgement in his court over the wood at Northam, according to the tenor of the charters which the abbey possessed. The king could not be persuaded to agree, but he did write to the earl of Leicester requir-ing him not to allow Robert of Valognes to cut down, sell, or give away any of the timber from the wood pending his own return to England. Robert reluctantly yielded to an order from the earl; but the abbot was still worried that St Albans might lose its wood, and after taking counsel with the brethren decided to go himself to the king. He found him in Normandy after his return from Toulouse, and offered him £100 for a writ to the earl of Leicester that, summoning both parties into his presence, he should hear pleadings about the proprietary right on the basis of the charters of Archbishop Lanfranc and others, and pronounce a definitive sentence in the case. The abbot's cause prospered, the earl of Leicester received a writ from the king, and Robert of Valognes was cited to appear within forty days. On the appointed day, at London, Simon the prior of St Albans appeared on behalf of the abbot, but Robert of Valognes neither appeared nor sent anybody. The earl was somewhat vexed that the abbot had not appeared in person, and told the prior to make sure he attended to answer the second summons at Leicester. But the abbot was then at Tynemouth on his way to Scotland and from there took ship to reach the abbey of Dunfermline. There a messenger found him, arriving breathless with letters from Simon the prior. As soon as he read them the abbot mounted his horse, without even waiting for a meal, and hurried south; but hurry as he would the length of the journey and the diversions caused by rivers made him a day late in arriving at Leicester, and he had to make his apologies to the earl. Simon the prior was there, but Robert of Valognes did not appear, so judgement was again put off. A third time Robert was cited by the earl. On the appointed day the abbot came but again his adversary absented himself, so the earl confiscated the wood and issued a fourth and final citation. Yet again Robert of Valognes did not appear, or send anyone to represent him, or make an excuse, so the wood of Northam was finally adjudged to the abbot by Robert's default.[1]

The caution in bringing the case to judgement and the numerous citations are understandable: no one would wish a plea concerning land to be settled hurriedly, or without making every effort to get both parties into court. But the absence of the king abroad added grievously to the delays and expense involved. Most remarkable of all, however, is the limitation imposed upon the authority of the earl of Leicester as justiciar: he had power to hear pleas of a sort, he could issue orders which had the force of royal authority, but he could act only on specific instructions from the king himself. The king will allow him an inter-locutory jurisdiction but is extremely reluctant to allow him to decide

<hr />

[1] *Gesta Abbatum Monasterii Sancti Albani*, I, 159–64. A further example is the case of Anstey v. Francheville, which began in 1158 and did not reach a conclusion until 1163, *see* Patricia Barnes, 'The Anstey case'; Hall, *Court Life under the Plantagenets*, ch. 7; Doris Stenton, *English Society in the Early Middle Ages*, 36–8, 191–2.

the principal cause at issue. Even the abbot, although in the end he purchased permission for the earl to determine the case, was reluctant at first to submit himself to the earl's authority. This too is understandable: the case was between tenants-in-chief of the Crown and it was reasonable to argue that no one but the king should have discretionary power over their landholding. Yet the case was not difficult; the plea could have been determined not only by the examination of charters but by the testimony of those who had heard the dying testament of Peter of Valognes the younger – had satisfactory procedures existed for bringing such evidence to bear.

The basic problem, indeed, was how to delegate royal authority without at the same time putting too much discretionary power into the hands of agents. Until this could be solved, royal justice would have to remain very much under the control of the king himself; and appellants would be put to the expense and time-consuming trouble of seeking an audience. That the problem was solved by Henry II is clearly revealed in a lawbook produced towards the close of the reign. Its full title is *The Treatise on the Laws and Customs of England* (*Tractatus de Legibus et Consuetudinibus Angliae*). The author of it is not known for certain, but it has for long been attributed to Ranulf de Glanvill, who was justiciar of England from 1180 to 1189; and the treatise is commonly known by the short title of *Glanvill*.[1] The situation it reveals is dramatically different from that which appears in the stories told by the chroniclers of Battle Abbey and St Albans. The king's court has multiplied itself like an amœba, so that there is now not only a court which travels with the king himself, but also a 'chief court' (the *capitalis curia* as *Glanvill* calls it) which resides at Westminster, and a royal court which is carried periodically to the country as a group of royal justices traverses a circuit of the shires.

The court with the king (*coram rege*) remained, as in earlier days, a loosely organised royal tribunal for the great causes, and for pleas in which the king was specially interested, meeting as the king chose and flexible in its procedures. But the other royal courts, as described in *Glanvill*, operate much more systematically. They hear pleas which are brought before them by fixed procedures, set in motion by a plaintiff who has applied to the king's chancery for a standardised writ appropriate to the kind of action he wishes to bring. The progress of the action was controlled at crucial points by precisely formulated writs to the sheriff, instructing him to put the disputed property under royal protection pending a decision, to empanel a jury and have it view the

[1] On the question of authorship see the introduction to Hall's edition, xxxff.

property in advance of the justices' arrival, to ascertain a point of fact material to the plea, to summon a 'warrantor' to support if he can a claim by the defendant, and so on. There are more than thirty such writs in *Glanvill*, all in common form and requiring only the insertion of the names and details appropriate to a particular plea. They are followed by the writs, fewer in number but equally precise, terse, and peremptory, ordering the execution of judgement. In most cases it was unnecessary for the royal justices to hear much, if any, pleading to the action: they put a few basic questions to the jury, gave judgement according to their replies, apportioned penalties, and passed on to the next plea.

> The assize comes to recognise if William Fiskerton unjustly and without judgement disseised the prior of Ormsby of his free tenement in Lincoln, within the time limit of the assize. The jurors say that he did so disseise him. Judgement: the prior shall have his seisin, and William is in mercy for the disseisin. Damages 10s. Amercement 1 mark.

> The assize comes to recognise if Knot the father of Alan was seised in his demesne of the fief of one bovate of land with its appurtenances in Sansthorpe on the day on which he died, etc. Which land Gilbert of Sansthorpe holds. The jurors say that Knot did die seised of it, but in villeinage, for he was a villein. Judgement: Gilbert shall hold, and Alan son of Knot is in mercy for a false claim. Alan's amercement: half a mark. His sureties are Warin of Langton and Daniel Thornlord.[1]

These are typical laconic entries upon some of the earliest surviving assize rolls. Several hundred cases could be disposed of in the two or three weeks which the royal justices spent at the shire court. Not all cases, of course, were straightforward. The justices might have to use their discretion as to whether an action should proceed: it might be dismissed because it had been improperly brought, it might be postponed if the necessary preliminaries had not been carried out. And if it involved issues which the justices could not resolve on the spot, it might be referred to the court at Westminster which had more time to unravel complications.

Although *Glanvill* describes the court at Westminster as the 'chief court', it should not be thought of as a superior court, or as a court of appeal. It was simply the headquarters court, from which the circuit justices set out and to which they returned on completing their commission; but it was a court in regular session with always a nucleus

---

[1] *The Earliest Lincolnshire Assize Rolls*, nos 250 and 50. Although these rolls are from the reign of King John, the actions recorded follow the pattern described in *Glanvill*.

of justices who did not go on tour. It was a court at which the justices could confer and take more weighty advice before reaching a judgement, or to which the circuit justices could refer a case for the consideration of some point of principle. It was a court which might tie up the loose ends of cases left unfinished in the shires. It was also a court to which a man might take a plea – if he could afford the expense – without waiting for the justices to visit his shire court. It was, indeed, the centre of a web of judicial administration which in the space of a few years transformed the face of English justice.

It is not easy to say when the transition took place. The *Tractatus* is not concerned with history: it is a practical handbook for the guidance of those apprenticed to the law, and for all those who had dealings in the royal courts. It alludes in passing to royal decrees of which no other record survives; but this only serves to demonstrate how scanty is the evidence upon which to base a reconstruction of the development of royal justice.[1] The chroniclers' evidence is scrappy and confused; and they seem, indeed, not to have realised what was happening until it had happened. It is improbable, in consequence, that the line of development will ever be fully traced; but there are signs and hints which permit a possible reconstruction.

The starting point was almost certainly the imposition of a rule to bring a measure of royal control over litigation about land-holding. *Glanvill* explains that,

> According to the custom of the realm, no one is obliged to answer concerning his freehold in the court of his lord unless there is a writ from the king or his justiciar.[2]

Since *Glanvill* describes it as a 'custom', some historians have supposed that the rule was immemorial; but ten or twenty years' usage was quite sufficient in the middle ages for a decree to become assimilated to 'custom', and the circumstances of Henry II's accession made it imperative that some such rule, if it did not already exist, should have been introduced in the early years of the reign.[3]

The way the civil war ended created difficulties for Henry when he

[1] Examples are given below, p. 359 and n. 2.

[2] *Glanvill*, XII.25, 148 (cf. XII.2, 137): 'Nemo tenetur respondere in curia domini sui de aliquo libero tenemento suo sine precepto domini regis vel eius iusticie capitalis.'

[3] For discussions of the problem of dating the rule *see* Plucknett, *The Legislation of Edward I*, 6–7; Van Caenegem, *Royal Writs*, 223–5; Doris Stenton, *English Justice*, 26–9.

became king. It had been brought to a close not by a crushing victory, but by the compromise of the Treaty of Westminster of 1153. There could be no expropriation of the defeated to reward his supporters, for there were, in fact, no victors and no vanquished. Disputes between rival claimants to lands and titles, which had often done much to determine allegiances during the war, were not resolved by the triumph of one side over the other. Yet there were nevertheless gainers and losers. As the chronicler of Battle Abbey said of the years of disorder, 'he who was strongest got most, and everyone held on to what he had seized as if by right'.[1] Henry II's inclination was to proclaim a return to the *status quo ante bellum*; and certainly, so far as the recovery of royal rights was concerned, the situation at the death of Henry I was the only test. But it was impossible in practice to make this the principle for everyone. Quite apart from the claims of his supporters, the new king's monarchy rested on the help of men, such as the earl of Leicester and Richard de Lucy, who had profited in the service of Stephen. Expediency dictated selective discrimination and a dual standard; some men were allowed to claim their rights by proving tenure at the death of Henry I, but for others a veil was drawn over what had happened in the interval, and the coronation of Henry II made the limit of legal memory.[2] An example is provided by the history of the FitzAlan family, which, at the death of Henry I, held of the honor of Richmond a fief valued at thirteen knights' fees. During the civil war Ruald Fitz-Alan, then constable of Richmond, remained loyal to Stephen, and Empress Matilda expropriated him and granted the fief to her own supporter, Richard de Rollo. But later, King Stephen recovered control of half of the fief and restored it to Ruald. At the accession of Henry II there were, then, two men, each claiming the whole fief but each holding half of it. Was the new king to confirm or repudiate the charter of his mother? He resolved the dilemma by a reasonable compromise and decided to leave matters as they were: each was confirmed in the half he held.[3]

---

[1] *Chronicon Monasterii de Bello*, 106.

[2] Cf. above, ch. 3, pp. 62ff. *Glanvill* illustrates, without explaining, this dual standard, II.3, IV.6, 23, 46. In later years the royal courts commonly refused to countenance claims based upon tenure in Stephen's reign but sometimes accepted claims based on the situation in Henry II's day, cf. *Curia Regis Rolls*, IV, 217, with e.g., III, 182, IV, 125, VII, 261.

[3] *Curia Regis Rolls*, VI, 147–8; Flower, *Introduction to the Curia Regis Rolls*, 157–8; *Early Yorkshire Charters*, V, 89, 91–2, 95–6. Henry II, *c.* 1170, confirmed to Ruald FitzAlan the lands of the honor of Richmond which had once belonged to Henry FitzMorini, *Recueil des Actes de Henri II*, I, 441.

What, however, of men who were not tenants-in-chief of the Crown?
It was only natural that they would resort to the courts of the barons
in the hope of recovering by litigation what they had lost in the fortunes
of war or the misfortunes of disorder. Henry II could hardly allow lords
in their courts to determine the outcome of the civil war; yet he could
not simply prohibit all litigation about what had happened in Stephen's
reign, for to have done so would have been to deny justice to helpless
victims. Here, too, the king had to discriminate, and to do so the
Crown had to have some mechanism of control over litigation in
baronial courts. For this purpose the perfect instrument was the rule
that a claimant had to obtain a writ from the king or his justiciar
instructing the lord to do justice, before a defendant could be obliged
to stand trial. This approached the problem indirectly but decisively,
and with a neat economy of effort. It put the onus on the plaintiff to
notify the Crown of intended litigation, and saved the Crown having
to intervene in litigation which had begun by giving it a power of veto
over whether the action should start. For a plaintiff with a reasonable
claim the inconvenience was counterbalanced by the advantage of
a royal writ commanding the lord to do justice; and even for the lord
there was an advantage in having the Crown impose some discipline
over the prosecution of suits in his court.

The imposition of the rule, however, had several consequences which
may not have been foreseen at the time. First, the natural inclination
of defendants to refuse to answer unless their opponent had secured a
royal writ, increased the number of writs which had to be issued and
stimulated the royal chancery to devise a standard formula. Secondly,
the issue of writs commanding lords to do justice obliged the Crown
to reconsider the procedures to be adopted if the lord defaulted.
Thirdly, the imposition of the rule had the unwelcome consequence of
prompting some men to seek redress of their grievances by extra-legal
means.

The issue of a writ commanding a lord 'to do full right' in his court
to a plaintiff was nothing new. It was known as the 'writ of right' (*de
recto*), and was an expression of the king's duty to see that all men
secured justice. For some years after the accession of Henry II, the
chancery continued, as it had done in previous reigns, to draw up a
writ for each particular case. Here is an example of such a writ issued
about 1162 by the justiciar on instructions from the king:

> Robert earl of Leicester to Reginald de Warenne, greeting. I order you to
> do full right without delay to Robert de Mandeville concerning the land
> of Digswell and its appurtenances, which has belonged to William de

Mandeville, his brother, which he claims to hold from you. And unless you do it, Robert de Valognes shall do it, and unless he does it, I shall have it done myself. Witness, Geoffrey Labbe. By the king's writ from overseas.[1]

This should be compared closely with the following example of the developed form of the writ:

Henry, by the grace of God king of the English . . . to the abbot of Thornley, greeting. I order you to do full right without delay to Richard FitzAdam concerning one virgate of land in Twyell, which he claims to hold from you by the free service of five shillings a year, and of which Roger de Bachelor deprives him. And unless you do it, the sheriff of Northampton shall do it, that I hear no further complaint thereof for lack of justice. Witness, Ranulf de Glanvill. At Geddington.[2]

At first glance these writs are very similar; but the differences are significant. First, there is a development in precision: the specification of the service rendered and the naming of the defendant fix the claim exactly. Secondly, the earlier writ nominates a major baron, or failing him the justiciar himself, who had to be approached for help by the plaintiff if the lord defaulted; whereas the later writ follows what became the invariable practice and names the sheriff. *Glanvill* explains the standard procedure of the later years of the reign if the lord's court defaulted. The plaintiff lodged a complaint before the shire court and produced his writ authorising the sheriff to act. The sheriff then appointed one of his servants and four or more knights of the shire to accompany the plaintiff to the lord's court, there to hear him declare on oath that he had not received justice. The shire court then took cognizance of the plea, and the lord's court was debarred from recovering jurisdiction or contesting the judgement.[3] The standardised writ and the procedure are simple enough, but in devising them the king and his ministers were learning, for the first time, how to make the processes of law both efficient and effective.

A more troublesome problem was the man who took the law into his own hands, and avoided the necessity of applying for a writ *de recto* by simply driving out the occupant of the land in dispute. There was a special terminology for this: the occupant of a freehold was said to be

[1] Quoted by Madox, *History of the Exchequer*, I, 34, from Westminster Abbey Muniments, no. 1886. For examples of earlier writs commanding lords to 'do right' *see* Van Caenegem, *op. cit.*, 418ff.

[2] Van Caenegem, *op. cit.*, 424, no. 24, from the unedited Red Book of Thornley. Cf. *Glanvill*, XII.2–5, 137–8.

[3] *Glanvill*, XII.6–7, 139.

in seisin, and the man who deprived him of it was said to *disseise* him, or to commit an act of *disseisin.* It would, of course, be open to the man deprived to seek restitution in the lord's court; but he would now be in the position of having to seek a writ *de recto.* Moreover, since custom gave procedural advantages to the man in possession, the man who had been deprived would find himself involved in protracted as well as solemn and ponderous judicial processes for the recovery of right.

It might seem that disseisin was obviously wrong, and that it should itself have been actionable at law. Contemporaries, however, had an equivocal attitude towards disseisin. It was not thought to be necessarily wrong. Custom, for instance, allowed it as a proper form of coercion if a tenant failed to render the services due to his lord. Moreover, men were not yet fully persuaded that wrongs should be righted only by recourse to the courts. A man, it was felt, should be prepared to fight for his rights, and have recourse to the courts only if self-help failed. Customary law, therefore, did not frown upon a man who forcibly deprived another – provided he had right, as well as might, on his side. It was only 'unjust disseisin' which was held to be wrong.

Earlier kings, when appealed to for help by a man forcibly deprived of seisin of a freehold, commonly acted by simply 'disseising the disseisor' – restoring the man who had been deprived so that he would not suffer the procedural disadvantages of being the plaintiff in an action for right. Henry II, however, from quite early in his reign, began to tackle the ambiguity about disseisin which lay at the heart of the problem. His first step, taken sometime between 1156 and 1160, was to decree that disseisin was unlawful unless the justice of the disseisor's case had first been demonstrated to the satisfaction of a court – in other words, that a proper disseisin should only follow upon judgement.[1]

The next step, taken in 1166 or possibly a little earlier, was the proclamation of an 'assize' on the subject, which changed the customary

---

[1] The edict is lost and the date uncertain, but clear evidence for it is to be found in a letter of Archbishop Theobald which may be dated between 1156 and 1161. It tells of an action brought in the archbishop's court by Earl William and his clerk Osbert to recover the church of Hinton, which was being held by Ernald of Devizes. The archbishop himself was responsible for putting Ernald in possession: he had done so, apparently, as a procedural step before the question of right was brought to trial. To counter this the plaintiffs had complained to the king that Osbert had been disseised without judgement, and were given a writ ordering the archbishop 'to restore to Osbert the church of which he had been deprived contrary to the king's edict', *Letters of John of Salisbury,* I, 162–3, no. 102. See also *ibid.,* 189, no. 115 – which must have been written before 22 August 1160 – for a reference to an *edictum regis* which had been trangressed by the abbess of Amesbury in ejecting a priest from possession of a church.

law. Henceforward a disseisin made 'unjustly and without judgement' was to be treated as a breach of the king's peace, punishable in the same way as 'pleas of the Crown'. No text of this 'assize' has survived, and the chroniclers do not refer to it; but its nature may be inferred from references on the pipe rolls to monetary penalties imposed 'for disseisin against the king's assize' (*pro disseisina contra assisam regis*).[1] Offenders seem to have been dealt with at first by the sheriff and local justice; but after the regular eyres had been properly organised, the pursuit of disseisors almost certainly passed to the itinerant justices. The instructions to the justices who were about to set out on eyre in 1176 included the item:

> Let the justices make inquiry about disseisins contrary to the assize, committed since the lord king returned to England after making peace with his son.[2]

The third step was to be of crucial importance in the history of the English common law. A legal process was devised to give the man who had been disseised a swift action for the recovery of seisin. When this was introduced is uncertain. It cannot have been before the development of regular eyres, for the royal justices who visited the shire courts were an essential element in the judicial process. Nor does it seem to have been in existence when the first eyre after the great war was commissioned in January 1176, for only the older process of punishing disseisors is referred to in the surviving text of the commission. But it must

---

[1] e.g., Pipe Roll 12 Henry II, 65; Pipe Roll 13 Henry II, 48, 134; Pipe Roll 14 Henry II, *passim*. In addition to the fines specifically *contra* (or *super*) *assisam regis*, there are references to fines *pro disseisina* or *pro disseisina super breve regis*. There are no references to fines for disseisin on earlier rolls. The earlier the roll, however, the less specific it tends to be, so that 1166 cannot be taken as beyond doubt the date for the assize, though it seems likely. The king was out of England from January 1163 to *c.* May 1165, and departed again in March 1166. Some historians, approaching the history of Henry II's dealings with seisin by a different route, have supposed that the phrase *contra assisam regis* refers in some way to the 'assize' of *novel disseisin* (discussed below); but this is one of the less plausible guesses that may be made about this ill-documented subject. Another is Van Caenegem's suggestion that Henry II was conducting in 1166 a 'drive' against disseisin which was not repeated until 1176; on this *see* Doris Stenton, *English Justice*, 38ff.

[2] Assize of Northampton, clause 5; Stubbs, *Select Charters*, 180. This too has been taken to imply the existence of the assize of *novel disseisin* (*see* previous note, and below, p. 338 n. 1), but to do so is to distort the meaning of words. How the justices discharged their commission is not revealed, but it seems probable that they elicited the information from the juries of presentment which came before them to testify upon oath about crimes committed in the neighbourhood; this is to be inferred from references to penalties imposed upon hundreds and vills 'pro disseisina concelata', e.g., Pipe Roll 14 Henry II, 133, 164.

have followed shortly afterwards.[1] Indeed, the reports of the justices who went on circuit in 1176 about the condition of the country after the years of disorder during the great war may have been the spur which urged on the king and his advisers to find a means of swift redress for those who were forcibly deprived of their freehold.[2]

The new process was known as the *assize of novel disseisin*. Both the action and the writ which set it in motion were elegantly simple. The heart of the action was the use of a jury (known as a 'jury of recognition') to answer questions of fact put by a royal justice. There were two questions. First, had the plaintiff, as he alleged, been disseised of the freehold in question, unjustly and without judgement, within the time limit laid down? Secondly, did the person who was alleged by the plaintiff to have committed the disseisin in fact do so? Judgement was given according to the jurors' replies. The losing party, whether plaintiff or defendant, was adjudged to be 'at the king's mercy', and the justices decided what monetary penalty (known as an *amercement*) was appropriate. A successful plaintiff might be awarded damages to compensate him for the loss of revenues he had suffered.

Since the jurors said all that was required for judgement, pleadings to the action by the parties were unnecessary, and were not normally allowed. And since pleading was unnecessary, the action could proceed and judgement be given even if the defendant absented himself. This in itself was a major revolution in litigation: under the traditional procedures, in which the declarations and counter-declarations of the

[1] The first explicit reference on the pipe rolls is in 1181, although less precise terminology on earlier rolls may conceal payments for the issue of the writ, cf. Van Caenegem, *Royal Writs*, 294. Many historians have assumed that *novel disseisin* appeared much earlier than 1176. It may have done so: the new action did not make the pursuit of disseisin by the justices unnecessary, so that clause 5 of the Assize of Northampton ordering the justices to make such inquiries (quoted above, p. 337) does not in itself disprove the existence of the writ. On the other hand the Assize of Northampton is remarkably comprehensive, and if the justices were in 1176 to hear actions brought on writs of *novel disseisin*, the lack of any mention of it is, to say the least, surprising.

[2] The itinerant justices commissioned in January 1176 were instructed to confine their inquiries into disseisin to the period since the king's return to England after the great war – a period of about eighteen months. This was understandable: they had enough to occupy their attention in the pursuit of more serious crime and the king's rights, without concerning themselves with every breach of the king's peace in time of war. Indeed, they were also instructed to ignore 'cases of petty thefts and robberies which have been committed in time of war, as of horses, and oxen, and lesser things' (Assize of Northampton, clause 1). But understandable though this may have been, it doubtless raised a clamour from those who had suffered disseisin and found no other means of redress.

parties to the action were an essential element, plaintiff and defendant were each allowed three reasonable excuses for non-attendance, and the case would be postponed until both parties were present in court, or until it became clear that one of them was defaulting deliberately.

The swiftness of the action of *novel disseisin* was further enhanced by having some of the necessary procedural steps completed before the justices arrived. In these preliminary processes the sheriff was the royal officer in charge. He first made sure that the plaintiff meant business (and was not, for example, merely trying to harass his opponent) by taking security from him that he would prosecute his suit. The sheriff then put whatever was in dispute under royal protection, and arranged for the shire court to elect a jury of twelve law-worthy men of the neighbourhood. The defendant had to be summoned to the election, and could, if he wished, offer reasonable objections to the choice of jurors; but if he failed to attend, the jury was appointed without him. The jurors were then sent to inspect the freehold to which the plaintiff laid claim, and the defendant could attend the 'view' if he wished, but again received only one summons. Finally the defendant was summoned to appear before the justices of the king on the date appointed for them to hear the jury declare the facts of the matter (to 'recognise' the facts, or to make a 'recognition', in contemporary language). This last summons gave the defendant no option: he was required to pledge his land and the word of his friends to the sheriff's satisfaction that he would attend, and he would be punished if he did not.[1]

These procedural steps were authorised in the writ of *novel disseisin* which the plaintiff purchased from the royal chancery. The writ was a model of precision and economy. The standard form, as given in *Glanvill*, was as follows:

> The king to the sheriff, greeting.
>
> N. has complained to me that R. unjustly and without judgement has disseised him of his free tenement in *such-and-such* a vill since *my last journey to Normandy*. I command you, therefore, that if N. gives you security for prosecuting his claim, you are to see that the chattels which were taken from the tenement are restored to it, and that the tenement and the chattels remain in peace until *the Sunday after Easter*. And meanwhile you are

---

[1] In legal language, the defendant was required to offer 'gage and reasonable sureties'. In other actions for the recovery of seisin which developed on the model of *novel disseisin* the defendant was simply summoned; and in civil actions generally sureties alone were accepted as sufficient security. That the defendant in an action of *novel disseisin* had to offer gage (*vadium*) probably reflects the king's previous concern to treat disseisins without judgement as punishable offences against his peace, *see* Van Caenegem, *Royal Writs*, 322.

to see that the tenement is viewed by twelve free and lawful men of the neighbourhood, and that their names are endorsed on this writ. And summon them by good summoners to be before me or my justices on *the Sunday after Easter*, ready to make the recognition.

And summon R., or his bailiff if he himself cannot be found, on the security of gage and reliable sureties, to be there to hear the recognition. And have there the summoners, and this writ, and the names of the sureties. Witness, etc.[1]

It is remarkable how little was left to chance or put at the mercy of avoidable error. Every item in this procedure had been carefully thought out. The jury, for instance, had to be selected from men who were both 'free' and 'lawful' (*liberos et legales*). It was normal to insist that a man selected for jury-service should be *legalis* – that is to say, untainted by infamy or a reputation for untruthfulness, and hence law-worthy, a man whose oath could be accepted without question. Law-worthiness, however, knew no distinction of status, and a serf might in principle be as *legalis* as a freeman; but it was a sensible precaution to exclude serfs from juries 'of recognition', for they might be swayed by their lords, and could not be punished for perjury so readily as free-men.[2] As an extra safeguard against malpractice, the sheriff had to ensure that those who delivered the summons to the defendant were in court, so that the justices could check, if necessary, that the proper procedural steps had been carried out. Moreover, the writ, endorsed with the names of the jurors, had to be surrendered by the sheriff to the justices (it was said to be 'returnable'). With it in their hands, the justices had all the information necessary for proceeding with the case.

The device of the returnable writ was an innovation, and a clear illustration of the quest for perfection in procedure which is character-istic of Henry II's legal reforms. There was a tradition current in the middle of the thirteenth century that the wording of the writ of *novel disseisin* had occupied the king and his advisers for many sleepless nights.[3] It could well be true.

Besides procedural precision, there was another element in the action of *novel disseisin* which was crucial to its success as a major reform of the law. This was the isolation of a simple, clear issue to lay before

---

[1] *Glanvill*, XIII.33, 167–8 (the passages printed in italics were variable). Variants of the writ were available to men deprived in other ways of the full enjoyment of their rights, *ibid.*, XIII.34–7.

[2] Odegaard, 'Legalis homo', cf. Morris, *Constitutional History*, 169.

[3] Henry de Bracton, *De Legibus et Consuetudinibus Angliae*, IV.6 (ed. Twiss, III, 38): 'multis vigiliis excogitata et inventa'.

the jury. The jurors were not asked the difficult and probably obscure question of whether the plaintiff had a better right than the defendant to the property in question; they were simply asked whether the plaintiff were disseised of it unjustly and without judgement. Seisin was much more readily ascertainable than right. The man 'in seisin' was the 'sitting tenant', and the fact of his seisin could be established in several ways. The formal act by which a lord put him into possession might be within the memory of the neighbours who served on the jury. But failing that, there were other simple tests of whether he had been enjoying seisin, such as his receipt of rents from sub-tenants, or his sale of crops grown on the land. It was the purpose of the action of *novel disseisin* to establish such facts and to determine whether the plaintiff had lost the seisin which he formerly enjoyed by the intrusion of the defendant. On the basis of these facts, as 'recognised' by the jury, judgement could be given, restoring the plaintiff or rejecting his claim.

The action of *novel disseisin* was, however, strictly limited to determining whether an unlawful act of disseisin had recently taken place. It did not dig more deeply to ask whether the man who had been enjoying seisin was really entitled to it. It could be that he or his ancestors had acquired seisin by some deceit or intrusion in the past, and it could be that the man who tried to gain possession by ejecting his rival had a better claim to it. Since such questions were left unresolved, a decision about recent disseisin could not be, and was not, regarded as a bar to further litigation about the matter. The losing party was at liberty to try to recover the property by applying for a writ *de recto* and taking it to the appropriate court. But although the purpose of *novel disseisin* was limited, it was nevertheless of major importance, for it forced disputes about land-holding into the courts, curbed the disorder of self-help, and provided a quick remedy for a tenant improperly ejected.

Novel disseisin soon became a model for other actions in the royal courts using a 'jury of recognition', and known as 'recognitions', or, later, as 'petty assizes'. The assize of *darrein presentment* determined who should exercise the right of patronage to an ecclesiastical benefice by inquiring into who presented an incumbent at the last vacancy.[1] In an assize *utrum* the jury had to decide whether the tenancy of a clergyman

---

[1] *Glanvill*, XIII.19–22, 161–3, discusses not merely the action but some important procedural points which might arise from it. The incentive for devising *darrein presentment* was probably the new canon law of the Lateran Council of 1179 that a bishop should intervene to provide a parson to any church left vacant for three months, *Sacrorum Conciliorum*, XXII, col. 227, clause 17.

was held by an ecclesiastical or secular form of tenure, as a preliminary to deciding whether a dispute about it should be tried in an ecclesiastical or secular court.[1]

The most important of the other 'recognitions' was, however, that of *mort d'ancestor*. It was important both to litigants, who sought the writ in large numbers, and because it led to major developments in judicial practice. It was concerned with transmitting the seisin of a dead man to his true heir, and the writ was sought by anyone who believed he had been deprived of his inheritance.

The protection of inheritance was an awkward problem in a feudal society. Indeed, feudal tenure conveyed, in principle, no right of inheritance: on the death of a vassal the fief reverted to the lord, who could, at least in theory, regrant it to anyone he wished. In practice, however, the desire of all men to be succeeded by their heirs prevailed against theory; and in England in the twelfth century a lord granting a fief was expected to confirm it not merely to the grantee but also to his heirs.[2] Nevertheless, the notion persisted that the succession of an heir was a favour conceded by the lord; and by customary feudal law, the succession of the heir was not recognised until he had performed homage to the lord and agreed to pay a fee for the privilege – a payment known as 'relief' (*relevium*). The rights of heirs were not, therefore, in practice secure, unless lords could be obliged by some effective means to receive the homage of the true heir and accept a reasonable rather than an extortionate relief.

The plight of deprived heirs was, we may well suppose, a matter which touched Henry II deeply. He himself, until the age of twenty-one, had been, as he always claimed, the 'rightful heir' seeking his inheritance against a usurper. Indeed, his noticeable reluctance to decree forfeiture, even for a vassal who made war upon him, may be interpreted as a distaste for disinheriting the rebel's heirs.

---

[1] It is probable that juries had been used to determine this question ever since, in Stephen's day, ecclesiastical courts had acquired jurisdiction over tenures in *frankalmoign*, and that Henry II's reforms consisted in making it an issue to be resolved before royal justices by a standardised procedure modelled on *novel disseisin*. On the earlier history of the action *see* Warren, 'Royal justice in England in the twelfth century', 172–3. *Glanvill*, XIII.23–5, 163–4, says little about the assize *utrum* apart from giving text of the writ and remarking that the recognition proceeded in the same manner as other recognitions. In practice the assize was not always merely a preliminary action to determine jurisdiction: if the point at issue was whether the holding should render secular services, the verdict of a jury that it was held in 'free alms' would resolve the point. For further discussion *see* Thorne, 'The assize *utrum* and canon law in England'; Van Caenegem, *Royal Writs*, 325–50.

[2] On the evolution of the heritable fief *see* Bloch, *Feudal Society*, ch. 15.

If a deprived heir sought the king's assistance, he might be given a writ commanding the lord to receive 'justly and without delay the homage and reasonable relief' of the plaintiff, or to answer for his refusal before the king or his justices.[1] Clearly, however, the heir was better placed to defend his rights if he were actually in possession of the inheritance – if, for example, he were living in the house of the deceased and sustained by the produce of the home farm. He might not be able to receive the rents and services of sub-tenants, and would suffer other legal disabilities until his right had been established by the lord; but he could at least afford to wait patiently for the lord to accept his homage, and in the meantime attend to the testamentary bequests of the deceased. Moreover, as the man in possession he was better able to fend off rival claimants.

It was to help in this way that Henry II, in 1176, took steps to ensure that the presumptive heir could secure seisin of the inheritance even against the wishes of a hostile lord. The instructions to the justices who early that year set out on eyre, included a statement of what the law ought to be and how the justices should apply it:

If any freeholder has died, his heirs should remain possessed of such seisin as their father had of his fief on the day of his death; and they should have his chattels from which they may execute the dead man's bequests; and afterwards they should seek out the lord and pay him the relief and anything else that is due from the fief. . . . And if the lord of the fief should deny the heirs the seisin of the said deceased which they claim, the justices of the lord king shall cause an inquiry to be made by twelve lawful men as to what seisin the deceased had on the day of his death; and as that inquiry establishes it, so shall restitution be made to his heirs. And if anyone shall do anything contrary to this and is convicted of it, he shall be at the king's mercy.[2]

---

[1] *Glanvill*, IX.5, 109, gives the standard form of the writ; and for the punishment of a defaulting lord *see* Pipe Roll 31 Henry II, 72: 'Radulfus de Multhalt debet lx marcas quia non cepit homagium Johannis de Lisewis'.

[2] Assize of Northampton, clause 4; Stubbs, *Select Charters*, 179–80. Many historians have assumed that this clause marks the inception of the action of *mort d'ancestor* as described in *Glanvill*, but such an assumption will not survive a scrutiny of the texts. There is no indication in this clause that the justices shall act on the authority of a royal writ previously addressed to the sheriff: the implication of the wording is that the justices shall proceed upon an oral complaint. Moreover the action envisaged in these instructions lies against the lord who is detaining the inheritance, whereas the action described in *Glanvill* was directed against the man 'who holds the land', which could of course be the lord, but might also be a tenant to whom the lord had conveyed it. There is no suggestion in *Glanvill* that in the latter case the lord should be called to account; but clause 4 of the Assize of Northampton decrees punishment for

Clearly the concern here was to prevent the disseisin of the deceased's family (referred to collectively as 'the heirs') before the formal installation of the rightful heir; and the justices were instructed to deal with anyone who deprived the family of seisin in a similar way to their pursuit and punishment of other disseisors.

It is more than probable, however, that these instructions had an unforeseen and unfortunate side-effect. In trying to help the family of the deceased against a hostile lord, the king had created a problem for the lord who wished to act correctly, but who did not know who the rightful heir was. This was a problem which might not often arise in the case of major fiefs and of families well known to the lord and his court; but every great lord had numerous minor fiefs upon his estates, and he could hardly be expected to know the identity and whereabouts of the next of kin of everyone of his lesser tenants. His difficulty would be all the greater if the tenant died without heirs of his body. The Crown recognised this as a problem, and *Glanvill* says that 'whenever a lord entertains a doubt concerning the heir of his tenant, as to whether he be the rightful heir or not, he may retain the land until the facts be lawfully proved to him'.[1] But how much trouble could a lord and his court be expected to take over small inheritances and insignificant tenants?[2] The issue was of far greater consequence to the claimant than to the lord; and the lord had to reckon with the possibility of harassment by the king's justices and the necessity of demonstrating to their satisfaction that delay in granting seisin was justified. It seems likely that the threatening words of the instructions to the itinerant justices in 1176 had the effect of prompting even conscientious lords to deliver

the lord who denied seisin to the heir, and in speaking of him as *attaintus* reveals that he is being thought of as a criminal. It seems clear, indeed, that this clause was concerned with the hostile lord who deliberately denied to an heir the enjoyment of his rights, and did not cover (as did the action of *mort d'ancestor*) the mistaken grant of a fief to a man who was not the true heir. Indeed, the action contemplated in this clause is closer to the pursuit of disseisors (which occupies the following clause) than the action specified in the writ of *mort d'ancestor*. It is, furthermore, worthy of note that *Glanvill* echoes the words of the Assize of Northampton when writing about marriage portions, heirs, and wardships in Bk VII, but not when writing about *mort d'ancestor* in Bk XIII: 'Heirs of full age may, immediately after the death of their ancestor, remain in their inheritance; for although lords may take into their hands both fief and heir, it ought to be done so gently that they do no disseisin to the heirs. Heirs may even resist the violence of their lords if need be, provided they are ready to pay them relief and to do the other lawful services', *op. cit.*, VII.9, 82.

[1] *Glanvill*, VII.7, 90.

[2] One of the most striking features of the assize rolls is the smallness of the tenements at issue in the majority of actions of *mort d'ancestor* – sometimes as little as half a bovate (about five acres), a toft, or a few furlongs.

seisin to the first applicant who could show a reasonable claim. But what was to be done if afterwards another claimant presented himself who insisted that he was the nearer heir? The lord could not simply dispossess the man to whom he had given seisin, for he might then find himself accused of an unjust disseisin. All he could safely do was to offer the new claimant an action for right in his court.[1] Unfortunately, customary procedures made this a lengthy and hazardous course, which a man might be reluctant to embark upon for the sake of a few acres, especially since custom gave procedural advantages to the man in possession.

The answer to this problem was a swift action to test the claimant's assertion that he was closer in kinship to the dead man, using a jury of local men to pronounce upon the claim, and, if they found in his favour, to transfer seisin to the claimant. Only the king could provide such a remedy, and it seems that Henry II did so before 1179, for in the pipe roll for that year there appears a payment by a certain Hugh Stanton 'for having a recognition concerning the death of his father-in-law'.[2]

A typical writ to initiate such an action is given in *Glanvill*:

> If G. the son of O. gives you security for prosecuting his claim, then summon by good summoners twelve free and lawful men from the neighbourhood of *such-and-such* a vill, to be before me or my justices on *a certain day*, ready to declare on oath whether O. the father of the aforesaid G. was seised in his demesne as of fee [i.e., that the tenancy in question was heritable and had not been sub-let] of *one virgate* of land in that vill on the day he died, whether he died after my first coronation and whether the said G. is his nearest heir. And meanwhile let them view the land. And you are to see that their names are endorsed on this writ. And summon by good summoners R., who holds the land, to be there to hear the recognition. And have there the summoners and this writ. Witness, etc.[3]

---

[1] If the lord had received homage for the tenement and was then confronted by another claimant, customary law required him either to warrant it to the man whose homage he had taken or give him equivalent lands in exchange, *Glanvill*, IX.4, 107.

[2] Pipe Roll 25 Henry II, 82. The lapse of time between the Assize of Northampton and the appearance on the pipe rolls of even this oblique reference to *mort d'ancestor* has troubled those historians who supposed that the new action began in 1176. The explanation of the development of the action offered above avoids this problem. The delay in the appearance of a reference on the pipe rolls does not, however, give decisive support to this argument since the pipe rolls are inadequate guides to the appearance of writs. For an alternative interpretation *see* Doris Stenton, *English Justice*, 43ff.

[3] *Glanvill*, XIII.3, 150. The details, of course, were variable; and there were standard variations for an ancestor who died while on pilgrimage, or who entered a monastery, or for an heir under age, *ibid.*, XIII.4–6.

This was the writ of *mort d'ancestor*, and the action upon it was similar to that on *novel disseisin*. After the jury had answered the questions specified in the writ, the justices gave judgement according to the tenor of their replies, and might levy a monetary penalty upon either an unsuccessful claimant for making a false claim, or upon an unsuccessful defendant for unjustly detaining the property. This new action in the royal court would be welcome not only to the deprived heir, but also to the lord, for – except in the case of a lord who himself detained the inheritance – it relieved him of liability and of any necessity for justifying his action in having admitted the tenant. At the same time it was salutary to lay the tenant under threat of a penalty for 'unjust detention', for it would deter men from hurrying to do homage to a lord in prejudice of a nearer heir. *Mort d'ancestor*, then, dealt swiftly with the problem of deciding between rival claimants, one of whom had managed to acquire seisin; but at the same time it also covered the problem which the king had tried to deal with in the instructions to the justices in 1176. The phrase 'he who holds the land' caught the lord who had refused to admit any claimant, while exonerating the lord who in good faith admitted a claimant whose right subsequently appeared open to challenge. Altogether the writ of *mort d'ancestor* was a brilliant piece of drafting.

Although the procedural steps were similar to those already devised, there were important differences in the course of the action which reveal that *mort d'ancestor* was no mere mechanical adaptation of *novel disseisin*. It was realised that there could be factors involved which would not be elicited by the standard form of the questions to the jury. The tenant was therefore allowed to enter objections. Before the questions were put to the jury he was asked if he wished to show cause why the assize should not proceed. He might, for example, admit that the claimant was next of kin, but allege that he was a villein and so incapable of succeeding to a freehold. He might assert that the claimant was a bastard, or that the dead man held seisin wrongfully and that it had been adjudged to himself in another court. There were many such 'exceptions' which the court might entertain, and the case would either be dismissed, or be made to turn on the new question of fact alleged by the defendant, which could then be put to the jury. The practice of allowing the defendant to plead 'exceptions' seems to have been something rather new in English law, and was to prove a fruitful field for lawyers' ingenuity in later years.[1]

Since it was thought reasonable to allow the defendant to enter

[1] Cf. Pollock and Maitland, *History of English Law*, II, 611ff.

objections, he was, contrary to the practice under *novel disseisin*, given three opportunities to appear in court. Provided he gave acceptable excuses for non-appearance, the assize would be held over; but if he failed to answer the third summons it would proceed without him, for the intention to provide a swift action was not to be unduly impeded. It was not unreasonable to restrict the latitude shown to the defendant, for, as with the other petty assizes, the decision in an action of *mort d'ancestor* was not irreversible. It determined merely the question of who should enjoy seisin on the basis of neighbours' knowledge of the recent history of the tenement and its holders. It did not seek to penetrate behind recent facts, and therefore left open the possibility of further litigation. It might be that the man who was not the nearest heir to the dead man had a better title to the tenancy than the deceased. The assize of *mort d'ancestor* would not help him, but did not prevent him from bringing an action for right against the man who had acquired seisin. Indeed, the early assize rolls reveal that the justices sometimes felt sympathy for the losing party in an action of *mort d'ancestor* and offered him a writ *de recto* without charge if he wished to have it.[1]

In the great majority of cases, however, in which the dispute was simply about which of the parties was the nearest heir, the decision in an action of *mort d'ancestor* must in practice have been final. To this extent the royal courts were taking over from lords' courts the function of determining the descent of fiefs. Indeed, the encroachment of the royal courts in determining land-holding proceeded further, for the justices would often allow the parties to arrange a compromise instead of prosecuting the assize to its conclusion. It might be that the jury despaired of deciding who was the nearest heir; or the parties themselves might come to realise that it was fairer to divide the inheritance. Even if one of the parties was sure that the jury would decide in his favour, he might nevertheless offer his rival a compromise to dissuade him from pursuing the matter further by troublesome litigation on a writ of right.

Settling a dispute by a reasonable compromise was, of course, nothing new; but the royal justices brought to it in the royal courts a greater discipline in reaching and formulating a reasonable compromise, and a model way of setting out the terms of the agreement in writing. The formulae for a *final concord*, as it was called, were evolved in the later years of Henry II's reign and subsequently saw little change. At first the concord was drawn up in the form of a two-part chirograph: the agreement was written out twice on one piece of parchment, and

[1] e.g., *The Earliest Lincolnshire Assize Rolls*, cases 190, 289, 377.

the two parts were then separated by an irregular cut through the word CHYROGRAPHUM, so that the authenticity of one part could subsequently be tested by marrying it to its partner. Once drawn up in approved form, the final concord put an end to further litigation about the matter. If necessary, the justices would testify to the agreement in the royal court, and either party could seek an injunction to have the other party abide by it. If the agreement were broken the offender would have to answer to the king. The finishing touches were put to the device a few years after Henry II's death, with the decision to draw up the chirograph in three parts and retain one in the royal archives. The 'feet of fines', as they are called, gave the royal courts certified records which could be called in evidence, and have also provided genealogists and local historians with an invaluable source of information.

It was soon perceived that the final concord could be used as a form of conveyance – a means of transferring property with greater security than that offered by the customary charter, and with the added advantage of enforcement in the royal courts. For this purpose a writ, such as the writ of *mort d'ancestor,* would be sought from chancery to start an action in the royal courts, but with the intention from the first of seeking leave of the court to reach an agreement. A simple sale of land could be effected in this way: the seller agreeing in court to make over the land to the purchaser in consideration of a 'compensation' which the justices approved as reasonable, and the transaction would then be embodied in a final concord. How soon such fictitious suits made their appearance is hard to say, for the form of the agreement assumes that there had been a genuine dispute, but it would not be surprising if it were soon after Henry II's justices had perfected the formulae of final concords.[1]

The distinction drawn above between swift but limited actions for the recovery of seisin, and protracted but decisive actions for establishing 'right', needs to be examined more closely. In the language of Roman law a sharp distinction could be drawn between 'mere possession' (*possessio*) and 'proprietary right' (*proprietas*). This is a terminology which *Glanvill* sometimes uses, and which a modern writer finds almost

---

[1] On final concords and the procedures involved *see Glanvill,* VIII.1–5, 94–9; Pollock and Maitland, *op. cit.,* II, 94–105; Foster, introduction to *Final Concords of the County of Lincoln,* II; Margaret Walker, introduction to *Feet of Fines for the County of Lincoln, 1199–1216*; Jessup, introduction to *Kent Feet of Fines*; and Flower, *Introduction to the Curia Regis Rolls,* 266–75.

indispensable. But such a clear distinction cannot be made to fit the circumstances of feudal land tenure. In twelfth-century England only the king had proprietary right. All other landlords were tenants of one sort or another, holding directly or indirectly of the king. They were not, strictly speaking, property *owners* but property *holders*. The 'right' of medieval law (the *ius*, as they called it) was a conditional and limited right, foreign to both Roman and modern conceptions of proprietorship. One cannot therefore simply equate the medieval term *saisina* with the *possessio* of Roman law, nor equate *ius* with *proprietas*. There was, of course, a distinction which could be drawn in medieval law, but it was a distinction between different qualities of possession. Henry II's petty assizes looked into recent facts to test who had a presumptive right to be in possession, but anyone dissatisfied with this verdict could seek a writ *de recto* for an action to decide whether this presumption was justified, and to establish who had a greater right (*maius ius*) to be in possession.

It was not easy to know for certain who had a good right to be in possession, for comparatively few men in the middle ages had titledeeds to the property they held. Some could produce charters; but a charter was not a necessary or even a usual part of a valid conveyance of rights, and in any case charters could be, and frequently were, forged. If a charter were drawn up it was usually at the request of the grantee, and even then was not a form of conveyance, but simply a record or confirmation of the formal ceremony by which the transfer of rights was made.[1] Charters were sought by those who liked to have a written record, and particularly by those who built up extensive holdings from numerous grantors. Monasteries, for example, would have large collections of charters. But for most people in a generally illiterate society, charters were of limited usefulness, so much so indeed that few men of the knightly class in the earlier middle ages would even have a seal.[2] They had, however, other methods of proving their rights. Whoever made a grant would be expected to 'warrant' it to the grantee; that is to say, he would, on request, appear in court to testify

[1] Charters of this time contain some such phrase as: 'Know all men, that I *have* given and by this charter confirmed. . . .'

[2] Cf. above, p. 326. A partiality for the use of written documents as evidence was, however, undoubtedly spreading in Henry II's day. The Crown itself encouraged it by, for example, the device of the final concord, and by keeping copies of its own grants and confirmations of private charters on the rolls of the chancery. In 1182 Oger FitzOger sought security of the final concord he had obtained by offering half a mark to have it enrolled on the pipe roll, *see* Pipe Roll 28 Henry II, 107–8 (this, of course, was before the development of the three-part chirograph).

to the grant he had made. Even after his death the grant could be attested by those who had witnessed the original ceremony of transfer, or who had heard it warranted.

Eventually, of course, the support of warrantors lapsed, and the remembrance of the original grant passed beyond the memory of the living. If all else failed, a dispute between rival claimants could be put to the test of 'trial by battle' – a judicial duel fought out by the parties themselves or by champions. But there was another possibility of demonstrating right which men thought reasonable, and that was by a history of unbroken seisin of the tenement, passing from one generation to the next, as far back as anyone could remember. It might not prove *ius* conclusively, but it created a strong presumption of a greater right (*maius ius*) than anyone else could allege. It may be said, then, that in practice *saisina* and *ius* merged: unsullied seisin was the outward and visible sign of an abstract *ius*. Hence the need to safeguard continuous seisin, and hence the popularity of the petty assizes as a means of swiftly rectifying an interruption of seisin.

The swiftness of the petty assizes was secured by not seeking to penetrate too deeply into the history of seisin. A time limit within which the action must be brought was specified in the writ, so that the facts inquired into would not be beyond the certain memory of the neighbours who constituted the jury. The justice secured by the petty assizes was therefore equally limited, and the judgement could not be forced upon the losing party as definitive: he had to be allowed, if he wished, to pursue his claim to superior right by other means. Although this would normally be done in the court of the lord of the fief in dispute, Henry II did not neglect it; indeed, his most far-reaching reforms were in the methods of pursuing superior right in the royal courts.

Litigation over land held directly of the Crown was, of course, always and exclusively a matter for the king's court; but he might also open his court to undertenants who complained that they had been unable to obtain their rights in lower courts.[1] The king's own court, however, must have been the most inconvenient of all courts for the pursuit of right: Henry II's long absences abroad and his daily preoccupation with matters of state were frustrating to all but the most persistent of litigants. Yet persistence was often necessary, especially for litigants with hostile lords. In the early years of the reign the king sometimes allowed the justiciar or the senior officers of the exchequer to deputise for him in hearing and determining suits; but the heavy payments which petitioners had to make for the privilege suggest that per-

[1] Cf. *Glanvill*, I.5, 5.

mission was not lightly granted.[1] Alternatively the king might avoid the necessity of judicial process in his own court, and simply order that a wrong be righted. An example of this occurs in a dispute between the monks of Durham and the Muschamp family. The monks claimed that Thomas de Muschamp (who held the barony of Wooler in Northumberland until he entered a monastery) granted them the manor of Heatherslaw. Eventually the barony passed into the hands of Cecily de Muschamp and her son, who denied the manor to the monks, apparently relying on their inability to produce a charter. They complained to the king, who commanded the following writ to be issued:

> Henry, king of the English, duke of the Normans and Aquitainians, and count of the Angevins, to Cecily de Muschamp and Thomas her son, greeting. If the monks of Durham are able to demonstrate that Thomas de Muschamp senior gave in alms to God and St Cuthbert the manor of Heatherslaw and seised the monks thereof with his sword, then I order that you seise them thereof without delay or argument, and that you should allow them to hold it in peace and justly.
> Witness, Reginald earl of Cornwall. At Bridgenorth.

The king had simply decided that the dispute could be put to the test by inquiries among those who had seen the monks invested with the manor by Thomas de Muschamp senior. The holders of the barony could determine this for themselves, and no further argument was necessary. But the monks were not given satisfaction, and the king had to intervene again:

> Henry, king of the English, duke of the Normans and Aquitainians, and count of the Angevins, to Cecily de Muschamp and Thomas her son, greeting.
> I am astonished and greatly displeased that you have not done what I ordered in my other writs concerning the manor of Heatherslaw, which the monks of Durham claim. Now, however, I firmly order you on pain of forfeiture to execute my commands without delay, so that I hear no further complaint about it for want of full right.
> Witness, Reginald earl of Cornwall. At Northampton.[2]

[1] Cf. e.g., Pipe Roll 14 Henry II, 102: 'Monarchi Elyiensis ecclesie debent xl marcas ut Barones de Scaccario mandent Regi in Normanniam quod ipsi disracionaverunt terra de Stoka versus Rogerum de Monte Canesi et uxorem ejus in curia sua.' Robert of Hastings owed £5 10s 8d 'ut placitum quod fuit inter eum et Radulfum Moin differatur usque ad Scaccarium', ibid., 197. Robert FitzErnisus owed five marks 'ut placitum quod est inter illum et Hugonem Malebisse sit coram Justic ad scaccarium', Pipe Roll 17 Henry II, 73. See also above, p. 329.

[2] Raine, History and Antiquities of North Durham, appendix, 141, nos 782–3; Van Caenegem, Royal Writs, 435, nos 47, 47a.

The more sophisticated government of Henry II's later years could not countenance such crude and unsatisfactory methods; and the development of a permanent corps of royal justices, on eyre or at Westminster, made an alternative procedure possible. It was set in motion by a writ known from its opening word as the writ *praecipe*. An example given in *Glanvill* takes the following form:

> The king to the sheriff, greeting.
> Command [*Praecipe*] N. to render justly and without delay to R. *one hide of land in such-and-such a vill*, which the said R. complains that the aforesaid N. withholds from him. If he does not do so, summon him by good summoners to appear before me or my justices on *the day after the octave of Easter*, to show why he has not done so. And have there the summoners and this writ. Witness, etc.[1]

The writ is now addressed to the sheriff (who can ensure that the accused is left in no doubt as to what is expected of him) and was returnable to the royal justices. It is impossible to know how many such writs were returned by the sheriff with a report that the accused had done all that was required of him, for none have survived from Henry II's reign. Probably most people at the time, as later, took the view of *Glanvill* that the writ *praecipe* was simply 'a writ of summons'.[2]

Once brought into court, the case followed a carefully prescribed course. If the plaintiff prosecuted his suit, and if the defendant did not default, enter a convincing 'exception', or offer a compromise, the issue would be tested by the judicial duel. Those at least were the possibilities available until 1179. In that year Henry II offered an alternative to trial by battle – the trial of the issue by a jury of twelve knights of the shire. This was known as the king's *grand assize*. As soon as the plaintiff had stated the terms of his case, the tenant could, if he wished, decline battle and 'put himself upon the king's grand assize'.[3] Trial by

---

[1] *Glanvill*, I.6, 5. Other forms of the writ *praecipe*, e.g., for the recovery of an advowson, or of homage and relief, or for breach of a final concord, are given *ibid.*, IV.2, VI.15, VIII.4, IX.5, X.2, X.4.

[2] *Ibid.*, I.5, 5. If it were simply a 'breve de submonitione', it may be thought surprising that it did not take the form of a straightforward summons to answer a charge in the royal court: Angevin writs did not usually waste words. The explanation may lie in the origin of the writ in earlier royal orders to make restitution; but it may also lie in a wish to avoid directly undermining the authority of baronial courts. The man who was summoned before royal justices on a writ *praecipe*, appeared to answer to a breach of a royal command, and not specifically to answer an accuser whose case could have been brought before an honorial court. On the baronial attitude to the writ *see* below, ch. 10, pp. 370–1.

[3] *Glanvill*, I.6, 26–8. The plaintiff had to accept the grand assize if the defendant chose it, unless both were descended from the same stock, in which case the issue

jury could only take place in the royal courts, for only royal authority could empanel a jury; but the use of the grand assize was not restricted to suits which began in a royal court. In any other court the defendant in an action over freehold could stay the proceedings by 'putting himself upon the king's grand assize', and seek a 'writ of peace' which forced the plaintiff to reopen his suit in the royal court.[1]

The grand assize was a solemn and cautious business, properly so, for freehold rights should not lightly be put in jeopardy. The defendant was allowed three reasonable excuses (*essoins*) for postponing his answer to the original summons, and three more for putting off his consent to the selection of the jury. But he could not essoin himself on the day the jury were to deliver their verdict, since judgement could be given whether he were there or not.

Great care was taken over the selection of the jury: the sheriff nominated four knights who appeared before the royal justices to elect a jury of twelve law-worthy knights of the neighbourhood 'who best know the truth of the matter'. The twelve were then sent to 'view' the disputed property, and returned to court at a later date to 'recognise' on oath before the royal justices which of the parties had the 'greater right'. It was the greater right, the *maius ius*, not an absolute right, upon which they pronounced, for the remote hope of certainty was sensibly set aside, and it was to questions of seisin and the descent of the tenement that they addressed themselves. Doubtless they conferred together at 'the view' and consulted neighbours, for although they were required to base their decision on what they personally had seen or heard, or had been told by their fathers, there was nothing to prevent them refreshing their memories.[2] The verdict of such a jury was, indeed, more like that of a public inquiry than the opinion of a modern jury formed from the answers of witnesses cross-examined in court.

Glanvill speaks of the grand assize as 'a royal benefit conferred on the people by the clemency of the king, acting with the advice of his magnates', and says that justice 'may be more easily and quickly obtained' by the assize than by the traditional procedures. It was possible, indeed, for the process to be speeded, with the consent of the parties or by the

---

would be decided by calling for evidence as to which was the nearer heir. On the date *see* Round, 'The date of the grand assize', 268–9.

[1] *Glanvill*, II.8–11, 29–31. The writ of peace directed the sheriff to prohibit the lord from holding the plea in his court unless battle had been offered and accepted – the tenant was not allowed to change his mind.

[2] *Ibid.*, II.11, 30; II.17, 34–5. If the twelve were not unanimous, further jurors were added until twelve could be found to declare in favour of one party or the other.

direction of the justices, for royal authority could modify established procedures as convenience and equity required. Nevertheless the grand assize was quick only by comparison with the traditional process, and a case would not have been considered unduly protracted if two years elapsed before judgement were given.[1] Hence the popularity of *mort d'ancestor* or *novel disseisin* as preliminary actions: they ensured that the party with a reasonable presumption of right should enjoy seisin until a final verdict could be given.

To read *Glanvill* is to be impressed not only by the lucidity and forensic skill of its author, but also by the clear logic of the new royal law, the ingenuity of the decision to base actions upon seisin, the fool-proof commonsense of its procedures, and the economical precision of the writs which governed the crucial steps of the judicial process.

Criminal law did not show the same progress towards the development of rational processes. There were royal reforms here too, but they were chiefly directed towards making the law a more effective deterrent to serious crime. Before Henry II took the matter in hand, the prosecution of criminals was undertaken before the sheriffs and local justices in shire and hundred courts, or before the officials of baronial franchises or the courts of boroughs. Crime was brought to the attention of the court in two ways: either by a private appeal lodged by the injured party, or by public accusation. The machinery for making public accusations is obscure, and probably varied widely. In the late 1160s, however, Henry II standardised it, and required those who were accused of more serious crimes to be brought for trial before the royal justices itinerant. Juries 'of presentment' were to be elected, consisting of twelve lawful men from each hundred and four from each vill, who were put under oath to declare what crimes had been committed in their localities. They were also required to indict those they suspected of being responsible for serious crimes, and those who harboured suspects.[2]

In the early stages of Henry II's drive against crime, it seems that

---

[1] *Glanvill*, II.7, 28; II.12, 31–2; Flower, *Introduction to the Curia Regis Rolls*, 130–2.

[2] The indictable offences were probably at first murder, robbery, and theft, cf. Assize of Clarendon, clauses 1, 2, 4, 11, 13, and *Historiae Dunelmensis*, Appendix, 1, no. xxxi; but they had been extended to cover forgery and arson by the time of the Assize of Northampton, cf. clause 1. The juries, it seems, were also sometimes required to present cases of treasure trove, *Glanvill*, XIV.2, 173. It is possible that the instructions on what was required from the juries by way of presentment varied from eyre to eyre, cf. Naomi Hurnard, 'The jury of presentment and the Assize of Clarendon', 401–2.

the presentments were made before the sheriffs, who reported to the justices the names of those suspects they had been able to arrest; but the Assize of Northampton of 1176 reveals that by then the juries were required to repeat their presentments of crime and indictments of suspects before the justices themselves. The change was probably a consequence of the revelations of inefficiency and malpractice by sheriffs brought to light by the great Inquest of 1170.[1] It meant that for the first time the central government was able to gain a clear impression of the amount of serious crime in the country, and the figures seem to have been disturbing. The king's treasurer, Richard FitzNigel, wrote in the *Dialogus de Scaccario* that crime was rife, and he thought that greater prosperity, and the drunkenness which went with it, had induced a crime wave.[2]

In the circumstances, it is perhaps not surprising that in the trial and punishment of criminals the emphasis was upon deterrence. The Assize of Clarendon in 1166 changed the customary law, which allowed some of those accused of crime to purge themselves by swearing oaths with the support of oath-helpers, or by the ordeal of hot iron, and insisted that all those arrested upon indictment by juries of presentment should go to the ordeal of water. This form of ordeal seems to have been regarded as particularly undignified, and was previously reserved for serfs.[3] Anyone who failed at the ordeal was condemned either to be hanged, or to be mutilated by the loss of a foot and banished from the realm within forty days. Ten years later, by the Assize of Northampton, punishments were made even more severe. Mutilation of those convicted by the ordeal was extended to the right hand as well as the foot; and those who survived the ordeal but were notoriously suspect of a 'base felony' were obliged to leave the realm within forty days. Even those of better reputation who survived the ordeal, but who had been suspected by a jury of presentment, had to find sureties for good behaviour.[4]

[1] Compare clauses 4 and 6 of the Assize of Clarendon with clauses 1 and 7 of the Assize of Northampton; and on the Inquest of Sheriffs *see* above, ch. 7, pp. 287ff.

[2] *Dialogus de Scaccario*, 87. Evidence does not survive from Henry II's reign to provide reliable estimates, but assize rolls from the early years of the thirteenth century reveal that even after fifty years of stern repression the volume of crime was still enormous. In 1202, for example, the justices visiting Lincolnshire received reports of 114 homicides, 89 robberies, mostly with violence, 65 woundings, and 49 cases of rape, Poole, *Obligations of Society*, 82. Since there had been an eyre in the county the previous year, these must have been recent crimes.

[3] Cf. *Glanvill*, XIV.1, 173. On the form of the ordeal of water *see* above, p. 283 n.1.

[4] Assize of Northampton, clause 1. The *Dialogus de Scaccario*, 97, describes it as 'the more severe assize which the king has appointed to repress crime'.

These draconian measures were not, however, the whole story of the reform of criminal law in Henry II's reign. *Glanvill* unfortunately treats cursorily of criminal pleas, but nevertheless reveals that the royal justices employed more sophisticated methods of reaching a verdict. Speaking of cases brought upon indictment by the juries of presentment, *Glanvill* says: 'The truth of the matter shall be investigated by many and varied inquiries and interrogations, and arrived at by considering probable facts and possible conjectures both for and against the accused, who must in consequence be either completely absolved or made to purge himself by the ordeal.'[1]

No evidence survives from Henry II's reign to show how the justices handled criminal cases in practice; but the earliest eyre of which there is record, that for Wiltshire in 1194, has details of a case which shows the justices at work. The jurors of the hundred of Brenchburg reported that a man named Reginald had been killed at Langford, and that a certain Waleran and Philip had been arrested for the crime and imprisoned at Salisbury, pending the justices' arrival. The body had been identified by Reginald's parents, but they did not know who killed him. The jurors, however, gave as their opinion that Waleran killed him, and that Philip was with him at the time. The justices asked the jurors what grounds they had for this belief, and they said that the bailiff of the hundred, and many other people, had found Richard before he died, and asked him who had attacked him. He said that Waleran had, and that if he lived he would prove it against him. He had not mentioned Philip, and Philip would not have been suspected had it not been that when the bedel went to attach him as a witness, he had fled to sanctuary with Waleran and refused to leave when the bedel required him to do so. Waleran and Philip were then brought before the justices and protested their innocence, which they offered to prove as the court might direct. The justices ruled that Waleran should go to the ordeal of water, but that Philip should be held in custody until it were seen what befell Waleran at the ordeal.[2]

The royal justices had to consider other criminal cases besides those laid before them in the indictments of the juries of presentment. A private individual could prosecute a criminal suit by lodging an 'appeal' against the person or persons he believed had injured him.

---

[1] *Glanvill*, XIV.1, 171.

[2] *Three Rolls of the King's Court in the Reign of Richard I*, 100–1. Many of the entries of indictable offences on the early rolls simply record that those suspected had fled, so that the justices were confined to sequestrating the chattels of the fugitives, and punishing those who ought to have secured the appearance of the accused in court.

Many minor cases of this kind must have been brought before the shire court and pass without record; but if the offence alleged was a serious crime (a felony), it would be reserved for a hearing before the royal justices. Even lesser, non-indictable offences might be held over for a hearing before the royal justices, if the accuser chose to allege in his appeal that the offence he complained of was 'against the king's peace'.[1] In an 'appeal of felony' the accuser had to be prepared to maintain his accusation 'by his body' – that is to say, by engaging, if the court willed, in judicial combat with the accused.

The earliest surviving eyre rolls show that, in practice, the royal justices were very cautious about appeals, and preferred if possible to search out the truth by other means, and very commonly either faulted the appeal in order to quash it, or persuaded the appellor to withdraw his appeal. The judicial duel was rarely fought. Indeed, it seems that the justices regarded with some suspicion allegations that a felony had been committed which the juries of presentment had not seen fit to report, and tried to ferret out the truth of the matter. An eyre roll of 1202 for Lincolnshire reports such a case:

William FitzHawise appeals Richard of Somercotes of having broken into his house, against the king's peace, and robbed him of twenty shillings, a cape, a surcoat, twenty-five fowls, and twenty shillings' worth of corn, and of having wounded him in the head with a wound which he shows. And this he offers to prove as the court should require.

And Richard comes and denies the breach of the king's peace, the housebreaking, the wound, and the robbery. He admits, however, that he did come to a house which William claims to be his, but which in fact belongs to himself since it reverted to him on the death of Roger his villein. And he took from there certain chattels which had belonged to his villein, but which passed to him on his villein's death. And he offers the lord king twenty shillings to have an inquest whether this be so or no.

And William says that Richard speaks unjustly, for Roger never possessed that house nor those chattels, for it was owned by William himself, and the chattels belonged to him.

The jurors, being questioned as to whether Roger had held that house in villeinage from Richard, say that it was so. Also the coroners and the whole shire court testify that William never showed any wound until now; and the wound that he shows is fresh.

---

[1] *Glanvill*, I.2, 4: 'The crime of theft . . . belongs to the sheriffs, and is pleaded and determined in the shire courts. If lords fail to do justice, then sheriffs also have jurisdiction over brawling, beatings, and even wounding, unless the accuser states in his claim that there has been a breach of the peace of the lord king.'

And so it is decided that the appeal is void: Richard should be acquitted, and William is in mercy for a false claim.[1]

Although this case was brought before the royal justices thirteen years after Henry II's death, there is no reason to doubt that before the end of his reign the justices similarly allowed cases brought on appeal to rest on a point of fact which could be put to a jury; certainly they did so in civil cases. It seems likely, too, that they might allow the accused to object to an appeal on the ground that it had been brought maliciously. In King John's reign there was a simple remedy for this: the accused sought a writ *de odio et atia* which required a jury to say whether the accusation had been made 'out of hatred and spite'. If so, the appeal was automatically quashed, and the jury had in effect returned a verdict of 'not guilty'. That some such way of having an action stopped was possible in Henry II's day is suggested by an entry on the Pipe Roll of 1178: 'Nicholas of Ufton acknowledges that he owes half a mark since he was convicted of having appealed Thomas Fagflur out of hatred.'[2]

In 1215 the Church removed its sanction from all forms of ordeal. In consequence the problem of arriving at a verdict in criminal cases could have been extremely awkward; but after forty years or so of judicial experience of getting at the truth of a matter by rational means, the government of the day in England felt confident in leaving the problem to the discretion of the justices on eyre. The justices were accustomed to asking juries of presentment why they suspected those named in their indictments, or empanelling a jury from those of the locality who were present in court to speak to some point of fact material to the case. It was a short step to take to put to the jurors the question of whether they thought the accused guilty as charged.[3] It was in this way that the trial jury was evolved in the course of the thirteenth century; but it might not have happened if informal methods of handling both cases and jurors had not been common practice long before the method of ordeal had to be abandoned.

Much of the English common law was to be judge-made law, and it owed its origin to that combination of royal authority and a sensible if circumscribed discretionary power which the royal justices carried with them from Henry II's day. Some latitude could be allowed to the justices because they were part of a closely woven web of supervision and control. The problems they encountered were the subject of con-

[1] *Earliest Lincolnshire Assize Rolls*, case no. 561, 98–9 (slightly abridged).
[2] Pipe Roll 24 Henry II, 104. Magna Carta (1215), clause 36, provided that the writ should be issued free of charge.
[3] Cf. Plucknett, *Concise History of the Common Law*, 114ff.

stant debate among themselves, and their rulings were fashioned out
of their common experience as they conferred with colleagues on the
bench at Westminster, as they argued and discussed in the ante-
chambers of the royal palace where exchequer and bench had their
offices, or in the houses which they commonly rented from the Confessor's abbey hard by. *Glanvill* reveals the discussion of just such a
problem which had still then not been resolved:

> What is the law on the matter if the plaintiff in a plea of right fails to
> appear in court or essoin himself when the defendant is there and waiting?
> Different people give different answers to this. Some say that the plaintiff
> shall lose only his costs and expenses, and that though the action should
> cease, he may begin the plea again. Others say that he should forfeit his
> case with no right to reopen it, and should be at the king's mercy for con-
> tempt of court. Others, however, say that he should be amerced for the
> default, but that it should be at the royal pleasure whether or not he may
> proceed with the plea.[1]

The king, of course, might be asked for a definitive ruling. *Glanvill*
several times refers to such decisions, of which no other record survives.
For example:

> Note that a certain constitution has been ordained for good and equitable
> reasons, which rules that when the four knights appear in court on the
> appointed day ready to elect the jury of twelve, the court may expedite
> the proceedings by directing the four knights to make their election even
> if the defendant absents himself.

> It has been ordained that clerks presented to churches by patrons who
> usurped the right of patronage by violence in time of war, shall not be
> deprived of the benefice for their lifetime.[2]

That the development of the English common law owed much to the
royal justices is abundantly in evidence; that it also owed much to
Henry II personally, though less surely warranted, can hardly be put
in doubt. The 'leap forward', as Doris Stenton has called it, derived its
impetus from his will. The assize on disseisin and the decision to take
more than a financial interest in the administration of criminal justice,
emerged from his close attention to English affairs in 1163–6. The
formulation of the actions on seisin, the beginnings of a judiciary,
and the grand assize, are to be ascribed to the period of his long sojourn

---

[1] *Glanvill*, I.32, 20–1. For another example *see* VII.1, 72–4.

[2] *Glanvill*, II.12, 31; IV.10, 50; cf. II.19, VIII.9, XIII.11. In addition rules were
framed on essoining, apparently in 1170; they are printed in Doris Stenton, *Pleas
before the King or his Justices*, I, 153.

in England in the years from 1175 to 1180. The great lawyer of the thirteenth century, Henry de Bracton, recorded a tradition that Henry II and his advisers spent sleepless nights 'excogitating and devising' the writ of *novel disseisin*. The tradition echoes the words of a contemporary, Walter Map, who wrote that Henry II was 'a subtle deviser of novel judicial processes'.[1] The *capitalis curia*, to which *Glanvill* constantly alludes, carried with it the impress of Henry II's methods of administration. It is no mere fancy to see the court at Westminster as a reflection of his personality: busy and decisive, yet always ready to listen to arguments, and adept at finding solutions to awkward problems. With Henry's household, as with the central court, it was 'school every day and the discussion of *questiones*'.[2]

The reign of Henry II was, as F. W. Maitland, the most renowned of legal historians, has said, 'a critical moment in English legal history'. The customary law was no longer adequate for the needs of a changing society, and the revived study of Roman Civil Law had made men aware of the possibilities of rational jurisprudence. In Maitland's view, it was a moment fraught with peril, for Henry II might have turned for guidance to the principles of Roman law before they were thoroughly understood, and have distorted English traditions by trying to graft on to them alien institutions.[3] There was a danger, too, of imitating the inquisitorial methods which the Church was developing in the ecclesiastical courts. This was a very real danger, since some of Henry II's most able advisers were originally trained in the service of the Church. It could have imparted to the administration of royal justice an authoritarian bias from which only revolution could have rescued it. But Henry II chose instead to take English customary law, trim it, knead it, reshape it, and give it the transforming touch of genius.

Henry II and his advisers may appear, superficially, to have been merely supplementing existing legal processes; but in fact they were erecting the basic framework of a structure capable of continuous expansion and adaptation. It was this capacity for adaptation and

---

[1] Henry de Bracton, *De Legibus et Consuetudinibus Angliae*, IV,6 (ed. Twiss, III, 38); Walter Map, 237. A bitterly hostile critic said that Henry II 'abolished the ancient laws, and every year made new laws which he called assizes', Ralph Niger, 168. In fact, Henry II abolished nothing: the new processes were offered as an alternative to, not in substitution for the traditional procedures.

[2] Letter of Peter of Blois, printed in *Materials for the History of Becket*, VII, 573.

[3] Pollock and Maitland, *History of English Law*, II, 673: 'There was a danger of an unintelligent "reception" of misunderstood and alien institutions. There was a danger of a premature and formless equity.'

change which distinguished the new common law from the old customary law. Royal justice drew deeply upon the resources of tradition, but fashioned from them new components for a rational system of law. The principles which informed the old law (largely Anglo-Saxon principles) were fundamentally sound; but they were encapsulated in a formulation which owed its sanction to its immemorial antiquity. Royal authority liberated them, and enabled them to pass into and supply the ground rules for that system of English common law which was eventually to rival systems which borrowed wholesale from the great corpus of Roman Civil Law. It is remarkable that what is so often regarded as a characteristically English achievement should have owed its inception to a Frenchman from Anjou.

Chapter 10

KING AND SUBJECTS

'I seem to gather from what you have said,' remarks the Apprentice half way through the *Dialogus de Scaccario*, 'that any knight or other discreet man may be appointed to a sheriffdom or other bailiffry by the king, even if he hold nothing of him in chief, but is the vassal of another.' And the Master replies, 'It is within the king's power to require the services of anyone, if he have need of him'.[1]

The relationship of lord and vassal could not stand in the way of the relationship between king and subject. It is one of the crucial features of Henry II's reign that this was more than a principle; he made it a fact, reaching across the feudal structure to forge links between the central government and the men of the shires which were never thereafter to be shattered. Long before the knights of the shire were summoned to attend the king's parliaments, they came to attend the king's court, and the king's court came to them. As jurors in judicial cases and administrative inquiries, as summoners and essoiners, as sheriffs, undersheriffs, and bailiffs, the ordinary freemen of the shires were woven into the fabric of English government. This had at least two important consequences. In the first place it produced what A. B. White has aptly called 'self-government at the king's command', and avoided that bureaucracy of officials by which the Church then, and other rulers later, sought to solve the problems of local government.[2] In the second place the alliance of Crown and freemen inhibited the development of forces which might have broken the realm up into fragments: in England, in contrast to elsewhere, the great fief and the municipality were never to overshadow the shire and the Crown as focuses of loyalty. In short, Henry II helped to forge a nation.

All this is the more remarkable in that at the beginning of the reign the opposite might have been expected. It was more likely that the realm of England would, as Germany did after a civil war, disintegrate into principalities. Early Norman England had never been entirely free from the danger of empire-building by great barons, to the detriment

[1] *Dialogus de Scaccario*, 84.

[2] White, *Self-Government at the King's Command*; cf. Naomi Hurnard, 'The Jury of Presentment and the Assize of Clarendon', 409.

of the monarchy. Several satrapies had been founded by royal favour or political necessity and grew to threaten the integrity of the kingdom. The danger had been averted only because the early Norman kings were more ruthless even than their barons, and had broken ambitions and confounded conspiracies by forfeitures and enforced escheats. In the shifting kaleidoscope of family fortunes there had in fact been little opportunity for the consolidation of feudal power blocs. But opportunities waited. William the Conqueror and his sons had, too, striven to inhibit in England the processes by which the great continental seigneuries had been formed: they prohibited warfare between their vassals, allowed castles to be built only with their permission, and resisted the identification of the English earldom with the continental countship. These were salutary policies, but they seemed at the time the self-interested prejudices of authoritarian rulers. On the whole these early Norman kings had managed to limit the earldom to a title of dignity rather than an office of power, despite its Old English antecedents. They had elevated some of their barons above others in status by naming them earls, but had withheld from them real control of the shires from which they derived their titles. Yet to do so seemed to fly in the face of nature. In the Latin of the day, the earl was a *comes*, the sheriff a *vicecomes*, and the shire itself a *comitatus*. This seemingly natural equation came close to fulfilment in the years of anarchy. As Stephen and Matilda vied for support they created earldoms. There were eight earls in 1135, more than twenty by 1154, and their identification with shire government had come to seem normal rather than exceptional.[1]

Moreover, civil war disrupted the control which earlier kings had exercised over castle-building and the armed rivalries of their vassals. In consequence, feudal empires were forming. The power of the earl of Chester stretched deep into the Midlands, penetrated Lancastria, absorbed Staffordshire, and was firmly planted in Lincolnshire. The bounds that the earl saw for himself were those of the old kingdom of Mercia.[2] The Beaumont family spread wide its tentacles: Robert Beaumont controlled Leicestershire and had a claim on Hereford, his twin brother Waleran thought of Worcestershire as his own, their younger brother Hugh pursued a claim to Bedfordshire, their brother-in-law Simon de Senlis established himself in Northampton.[3] Gloucester,

[1] Cf. Davis, *King Stephen*, 129–44. More shires were under baronial control than appears from a mere count of earls: for example, Durham was completely controlled by its bishop, and William of Ypres was earl of Kent in all but name.

[2] Cf. Cronne, 'Ranulf de Gernons, earl of Chester', and *The Reign of Stephen*, 174ff.

[3] Cf. Davis, *op. cit.*; Fox, 'The honor and earldom of Leicester'; White, 'The career of Waleran, count of Meulan and earl of Worcester'.

Hereford and Shropshire seemed to be drawing together into a great affinity on the Welsh march. Hugh Bigod was to the chronicler Henry of Huntingdon the *consul* of East Anglia.[1] Northumberland had virtually dropped away from the kingdom of England after Stephen granted it to a son of the king of Scots. Men such as William d'Aumale in Yorkshire, Alan the Black count of Brittany and earl of the castlery or 'shire' of Richmond, Hugh du Puiset bishop and virtually 'earl' of Durham, seemed the arbiters of provincial destinies. Henry of Blois, the prince-bishop of Winchester, practically controlled Hampshire, was lord of strategically important castles, and thought of himself as a kingmaker.

Henry I's reign had given shape and force to the English monarchy, but had not bound the realm inseparably together. The ruthlessness with which he crushed families whose loyalty he distrusted left a legacy of bitterness, and unexpired hopes of recovery; his building up of one of his satraps to balance another – his bastard son Robert of Gloucester as a counterpoise to his nephew Stephen of Blois, the Beaumont family as a counterpoise to the earls of Chester – drew the battle lines of the civil war which followed his death. If King Stephen had been succeeded by a man with a less clear sense of monarchical authority and of how it was to be achieved, and with less determination to achieve it than Henry of Anjou, it seems likely that England would have become a gathering of earldoms, instead of an organisation of shires. Yet Henry too on the eve of his accession seemed to confirm the trend by his remarkable confirmation of all that Earl Ranulf of Chester had won for himself, and the grant of much to which he aspired.[2] The Treaty of Winchester which ensured Henry's succession to Stephen seemed at the same time to build peace on the preservation of the existing situation, and to guarantee a great appanage for Stephen's son William, already count of Boulogne and earl of Surrey. But it was soon to appear that Henry regarded the treaty simply as a formula for peace and not as a blueprint for his reign. The demolition of unlicensed castles was an agreed part of the treaty, but nothing prepared the earls for the new king's demand for the surrender of the castles which they held as custodians for the Crown, nor for his swift campaigns against those who refused his demand, whether former foes such as William d'Aumale, or former friends such as Roger of Hereford and Hugh Mortimer.[3] The earldom of Essex was revived as a reward for Geoffrey son of Geoffrey de Mandeville, who had died in revolt against Stephen, but Henry at the same time demolished its

[1] Henry of Huntingdon, 273.

[2] *Regesta Regum Anglo-Normannorum*, III, 65–6; cf. the comments of Stenton, *First Century of English Feudalism*, 241–2.   [3] *See* above, ch. 3, pp. 59–60.

castles.[1] Northumberland was recovered from Malcolm king of Scots, despite the promises which Henry had made to his father, and was kept without an earl.[2] The appanage created for Stephen's son was curtailed, and after his death on the expedition to Toulouse, Henry gave his widow, together with the earldom of Surrey, to his own illegitimate brother Hamelin, and retained for himself the rest.[3] Ten of the earldoms created by Stephen or Matilda were either not recognised by Henry or were allowed to lapse when their holder died. He made no new creations, so the number of earls steadily declined. In 1154 there were twenty-four earls; by the beginning of the great war there were sixteen: by the end of the reign there were twelve.

Even the earldoms which survived were trimmed of power and influence. Earl Ranulf of Chester died in December 1153, and his honors and his heir passed into the wardship of the king until Hugh came of age in 1162. Nothing more was heard then of the concessions which Duke Henry had made to his father. He was not given the additional earldom of Stafford which had been promised in 1153, nor the earldom of Lincoln which he coveted, despite the fact, or perhaps because of the fact, that his greatest feudal power lay in Lincolnshire.[4] Hugh Bigod, whose support had done much to secure the throne for Henry, was confirmed in the earldom of Norfolk and Suffolk, which Stephen had sought to deny to him, but he had to relinquish control of the government of the shires and was deprived of his castles. He bought back his castles, but was denied possession of Norwich and his grander hopes of a province of East Anglia, and had to see a powerful royal castle of an ingenious new design rise at Orford to challenge his stronghold of Framlingham.[5] The Beaumont influence declined. Waleran retreated from Worcestershire and Hugh from Bedfordshire. Earl Robert of Leicester was not allowed that control of 'the city, castle, and the whole county of Herefordshire' which Stephen had granted him in 1140, despite the fact that his rival for the earldom of Hereford, Roger FitzMiles, surrendered it to Henry in 1155 when he retired to a monastery.[6] For

---

[1] Pipe Roll 4 Henry II, 132.

[2] *See* above, ch. 4, p. 182.   [3] *See* above, ch. 3, pp. 66ff.

[4] The earldom of Lincoln lapsed with the death of Gilbert de Gant in 1156. It was conferred on the son of Earl Hugh of Chester in 1217.

[5] Cf. Brown, 'Framlingham castle and Bigod'. Hugh Bigod accounted for Norfolk and Suffolk at the exchequer at the beginning of the reign, but only until the third year, cf. Pipe Roll 3 Henry II, 75–6.

[6] For Stephen's grant *see* Regesta Regum Anglo-Normannorum, III, 437. The earldom of Hereford lapsed. For Waleran *see* White, 'The career of Waleran, count of Meulan and earl of Worcester'. For Hugh *see* Davis, King Stephen, 135.

Earl Robert of Leicester, of course, the curb to the territorial ambitions of the Beaumont family was amply compensated by the enormous influence and power which he exercised as justiciar, but which he could not transmit to his heirs. His successor as earl of Leicester, Robert Blanchemains, was one of the chief rebels of 1173. His co-conspirators were the earls of Chester and Norfolk. In a real sense the rebellion in England was the attempted *revanche* of the earls. It failed; and after the great war not a single earl was to be found in the inner counsels of Henry II.[1] The earls were diminished; the great luminaries of the reigns of Henry I and Stephen eclipsed.

Henry II's ascendancy over the earls was given an almost symbolic demonstration at the meeting of the great council in January 1177. The lands of the greater rebels were then in the king's hands and one of the vassals of Earl Robert sought the break-up of the honor of Leicester by claiming that he himself should hold his fief directly of the king:

> At the council William de Cahagnes made known to the king that he ought to hold of the Crown in chief the barony which he held of Robert earl of Leicester. His argument, however, was based on crooked reasoning, for his real purpose was to win the favour of the king, who was ill-disposed towards his lord. And when the aforesaid earl of Leicester came on the day appointed him to answer, and had listened to all which his adversaries had to say, he replied that although his great-grandfather, and his grandfather, and his father, and even he himself had charters and privileges of kings of England – of William and of Henry I – referring to his lands and specifying the sub-fiefs which had been formed upon them, and although the predecessors of William de Cahagnes had consistently held that fief of his predecessors, nevertheless he was loath to plead about any tenement, either that or any other, against the king's will [*contra regis voluntatem*], but instead declared that it and all his other holdings should be at the king's mercy. And when the king heard him speaking so dutifully, he was moved to tenderness, and restored to him all his tenements in their integrity, as they were fifteen days before the outbreak of war – save that the king retained in his own hand the castle of Mountsorrel, and the castle of Pacy, which were the only two of all his castles that remained standing.[2]

---

[1] Of the earls who were influential in Henry II's service in the early years of the reign, Geoffrey earl of Essex died in 1166, Robert earl of Leicester in 1168, and Reginald earl of Cornwall (an illegitimate son of Henry I) in 1175.

[2] Roger of Howden, *Gesta*, I, 133–4. It seems that William de Cahagnes's attempt to win the king's favour redounded to his discredit: in this same year he was debited at the exchequer with a fine of a thousand marks 'that the king might set aside his anger towards him and confirm his charters', Pipe Roll 23 Henry II, 95.

Earl Robert had doubtless been well-schooled by his friends in how to turn the king's hostility; but nonetheless his deference was a public acknowledgement that Henry II had mastered the earls. They too were his subjects; and their honors were at his mercy. At the same time it should be recognised that to be at the king's mercy was not for the barons the disaster it had been under Henry I or Stephen. Henry II offered little threat to the integrity of their ancestral lands and their family fortunes. Disputed claims arising from the civil war between Stephen and Matilda were settled with remarkable impartiality, and where necessary by reasonable compromises.[1] The principle of hereditary succession, eagerly sought in the twelfth century but implicitly denied in the wilful acts of Henry I and Stephen, was firmly established during Henry II's reign. The protection of *seisin* in his judicial reforms gave a security which helped the transition from feudal tenure to the hereditary ownership of land.[2] It is true that Henry II was dilatory in hearing and deciding pleas of land brought in his court by barons: it is a charge which his enemies brought against him, and which his friends could defend only by the excuse that it was a legacy of his mother's malign influence.[3] But, on the other hand, there were none of the arbitrary political forfeitures which had marked and marred the reign of his grandfather. There were not even justified forfeitures. No one could have objected if Henry II had deprived the earl of Chester, the earl of Leicester, the earl of Norfolk, and the earl of Derby for rebellion during the great war: it would indeed have been the perfect opportunity to destroy the major earldoms if this had been his intention. But it was clearly not his intention: all the rebel earls received their lands back, sooner or later.

Henry could afford to be lenient with rebel barons, partly because the great war had shown the futility of rebellion, and partly because his governmental measures had weakened the baronial grip on the political and social life of the country. Henry I had dispensed favours, privileges, and powers to barons because he needed their support; he had destroyed them when he feared them. Henry II did not fear them, and as royal authority grew, he ceased to need them. Their custodianship of castles was being treated as an anachronism; their local influence was being eroded by the activities of royal officials; their ambitions could

[1] Cf. Davis, 'What happened in Stephen's reign', 10–11.
[2] Cf. *ibid.*, esp. 11–12; Thorne, 'English feudalism and estates in land'. Thorne, however, unduly postpones the acceptance of the hereditary principle: he is arguing from legal sources, and the lawyers lagged behind political realities.
[3] Cf. e.g., Gerald of Wales, V, 304; Walter Map, 238, 241.

no longer be achieved by bargaining with the Crown for their services. They could buy favours, but nothing that amounted to real power. Ralph of Diceto, dean of St Pauls, perceived therein the deeper causes of the rebellion of 1173. Unfortunately he cast his explanation in elliptical terms, but his general meaning is tolerably clear: the rebels joined themselves to Henry the Younger, he says,

> not because his was the juster cause, but because the king, his father, with a view to enhancing the royal dignity, was trampling upon the necks of the proud and haughty, because he was overthrowing the mistrusted castles of the country, or bringing them under his control; because he was firmly insisting that those who were occupying properties which were known from old to pertain to his table as to his treasury [*quae suam ad mensam quasi ad fiscum pertinere noscuntur*] should be content with their own patrimony, and was even compelling them to do so; because he was condemning those guilty of treason to exile, was punishing robbers with a capital sentence, was deterring thieves in the pillory, and inflicting a loss of money on oppressors of the poor.[1]

These are dark phrases; but there can be little doubt that behind them lurks the implication that the restoration of order after the civil war, the recovery of *purprestures*, the Assize of Clarendon of 1166, and the searching inquiry into local government in 1170, had aroused deep resentments, at least among the more reactionary of the barons.

Henry II put a hedge around the barons, a hedge of royal controls and royal officials. The political influence which barons had attempted to erect as a supplement to their economic power was circumscribed. Their engrossment of public functions was arrested. The balance of power within the body politic was tilted steeply and irreversibly in favour of the monarchy and monarchical institutions. Some historians have supposed that Henry did more than this: that he was not content merely to fashion and strengthen royal government, but that he set out deliberately to cripple the authority which the barons exercised as of right within their fiefs and franchises. Professor Joüon des Longrais, for instance, has argued persuasively that the new legal procedures were cunningly devised to undermine the judicial function of the seigneurial courts, and to draw away by a sleight of hand much of their jurisdiction to the royal courts.[2] Maitland held that Henry II mounted an attack upon the franchises, invading and devitalising them so that the terms

---

[1] Ralph of Diceto, I, 371.

[2] Joüon des Longrais, *La Conception Anglaise de la Saisine*, and 'La portée politique des réformes d'Henri II en matière de saisine'.

in which their charters defined their franchisal powers became 'nothing better than an unintelligible list of obsolete words'.[1] Stubbs believed that the whole tenor of his policy was anti-feudal.[2] None of these views should be accepted without qualification, although each enfolds a kernel of truth.

Professor Joüon des Longrais is right to insist that the petty assizes did more in practice than provide a swift preliminary action to protect possession pending the more lengthy and laborious action on who had the juster claim to the property in question. It is fallacious, as he points out, to equate *seisin* with the simple *possessio* of Roman law, for *seisin* was a wholly medieval concept which embraces a strong presumption of right.[3] The attempt at the time to draw this fallacious equation was, he argues, a veil drawn across the attempt of the Crown to tempt litigation away from seigneurial courts. Few, he holds, who lost at the petty assizes would avail themselves of the proffered opportunity to pursue the matter further on a writ of right to the lord's court since they had already lost more than half the battle.[4] The earliest surviving evidence does indeed seem to show that actions upon seisin were commonly regarded as decisive, and there can be no question that the royal courts were, in fact, deciding many cases which might have been brought in seigneurial courts. But the suggestion that Henry II dressed up the petty assizes to delude the barons into thinking that they were no more than preliminary actions about possession is unwarranted.

The equation of *seisin* with *possessio* and of *ius* with *proprietas* came naturally, if mistakenly, to those who had a passing acquaintance with Roman law, and was employed by lawyers in an attempt to explain the disquieting fact that English law seemed to recognise two different types of action for what was basically the same thing; but there is no evidence that the Crown deliberately tried to confuse its critics or dull baronial understanding of what was happening by a spurious analogy with an alien system of law.[5] If the king were waging covert warfare on baronial

---

[1] Maitland, *Domesday Book and Beyond*, 283.

[2] e.g., Stubbs, *Constitutional History of England*, I, 508.

[3] Joüon des Longrais, *La Conception Anglaise de la Saisine*, 45: 'Il ne nous semble pas possible de concevoir la saisine comme une pure possession romaine. La saisine est une conception absolument propre au moyen âge. C'est une jouissance toute pénétrée d'éléments du droit, elle se fond avec le droit sous toutes ses formes, et ne s'en distingue pas dans sa nature.'

[4] Joüon des Longrais, 'La portée politique des réformes d'Henri II en matière de saisine', 563.

[5] It is true that *Glanvill* sometimes, although not always, drops into the terminology of Roman law when talking about the petty assizes – it was difficult for anyone

courts it is strange that the royal justices not infrequently reminded litigants that the *recognitio* of a petty assize was not necessarily final if they wished for a writ of right: and it is stranger still, if the king hoped that his actions on seisin would prove a substitute for actions on right, that he provided a much more rational procedure for pursuing right in the grand assize. It is true, of course, that if the defendant put himself upon the grand assize the case was transferred from the seigneurial to the royal court, but this procedure was introduced with the concurrence of the barons.[1] Furthermore, there is no evidence that the barons as a whole resented or regretted what Professor Joüon des Longrais believes to be the political implications of Henry II's legal reforms; on the contrary, in Magna Carta they were to seek the more frequent visitation of the shires by royal justices for the holding of the petty assizes.[2] The surviving evidence is quite inadequate to show the effects of the new royal justice on seigneurial courts: it is more than possible that it stimulated litigation in all courts; and if, on the other hand, it did in fact draw litigation away from the seigneurial courts, it is unlikely that the barons resented it, for opening their courts to civil actions was a burdensome duty which brought little if any financial profit, and, save in the few cases of serious disputes between important vassals, the outcome of the cases mattered to them little if at all. To have the right to hold a court was a valued mark of status, but the right and the status symbol were not greatly affected by the amount of business transacted. It is clear from the assize rolls that the overwhelming majority of actions of *mort d'ancestor* – the most popular of the petty assizes – were brought by humble claimants with humble claims, commonly a few bovates of land or a share in a mill, for whom the traditional procedures culminating in trial by battle were too laborious, too expensive in time and effort, and too perilous. It seems likely indeed that the king's legal reforms generated a mass of litigation that might not otherwise have been brought at all. The one aspect of the royal judicial procedures to which the barons did object in Magna Carta was the issue of the writ *praecipe* 'in such a way that a freeman may lose his court'.[3] Since the writ *praecipe* had the effect of summoning a defendant to answer in

---

attempting to write a treatise upon law to avoid it. It was a terminology which sometimes occurred to monastic chroniclers (cf. Doris Stenton, *English Justice*, 172); but it is clear that their understanding of *saisina* was better than their understanding of Roman law.

[1] *See* above, p. 353.
[2] Magna Carta (1215), clause 18, cf. Articles of the Barons, clause 8.
[3] Magna Carta (1215), clause 34.

the royal court without any reference to his lord or his lord's court, it is remarkable that the barons did not ask simply for its abolition. It was, probably, because the issue of the writ had become *de cursu* – that it was readily being issued at the request of a plaintiff without any reflection upon its appropriateness – that it provoked the temperate baronial reaction; in King Henry's day it is more likely that the writ was granted to the plaintiff only as a matter of grace.[1] All in all, it would be hard to sustain a case that Henry II set out to undermine the authority of seigneurial courts and that the barons resented it. Nevertheless, there can be no doubt that in practice baronial justice was devalued by the obvious superiority of royal justice, and that the barons had to recognise that the Crown had pre-empted progress.

Maitland's belief that Henry II's legal reforms involved a radical diminution in the franchisal powers of the barons is mistaken on two counts. In the first place he overestimated the scope of the franchises which existed in Henry II's day, since he started his argument from the false premise that the privileges which the greater Anglo-Saxon lords enjoyed, and which their Norman successors took over from them, conferred powers and exemptions equivalent to the continental 'immunity'. On the continent, a great lord, a duke of Normandy or a count of Anjou, for example, enjoyed complete powers of jurisdiction over all men subject to his authority without any interference from royal officials. But in England such exalted privilege was almost unknown – there was no real need for it while the public institutions of shire and hundred retained their vitality. As a result of his false premise Maitland could only explain the decline of what in fact had never existed by supposing that Henry II's transformation of royal justice had robbed the old privileges of meaning.[2] Secondly, Maitland did not observe that Henry II and his sons were quite ready to grant fresh franchisal powers. Nonetheless, Maitland rightly sensed that something had changed in the course of Henry II's reign, and that the franchises occupied a somewhat different status in the ordering of the realm after his reign than they had before.

The franchises of the twelfth century are not, as it happens, a subject on which it is possible to speak with much certain knowledge, but research in the seventy years since Maitland wrote has made the general

[1] On the writ *praecipe* see above, p. 352. On the purpose of the clause in Magna Carta *see* Naomi Hurnard, 'Magna Carta, clause 34', modified by Clanchy, 'Magna Carta, clause 34'.

[2] Cf. Naomi Hurnard, 'The Anglo-Norman franchises', and Helen Cam, 'The evolution of the medieval English franchise'.

lines of the situation a little clearer. 'Franchise' was a word of wide scope and multifarious application.[1] It could give the lord and his men and his lands exemption from some or all of the local taxes, from tolls, from payments for pasturage, from the *murdrum* fines and communal amercements. It might free them from 'suit of court' at hundred or shire or the forest courts, from jury service, or from contributing to the up-keep of castles, bridges, roads, and parks. In some cases the taxes, fines, levies, and services were rendered to the lord instead of to the sheriff or king. The sheriff might hold 'view of frankpledge' in the normal way, but the profits of the petty police jurisdiction be payable to the lord instead of going into the *farm* of the shire; or in some cases the sheriff himself might be excluded from the 'view' and the jurisdiction be exercised by the lord's bailiff. The lord might be allowed jurisdiction over certain types of crime, or over criminals caught in certain places. He might, if he were specially privileged, be allowed all the jurisdiction of a hundred court or group of hundreds. The 'three hundreds of Oswaldslaw' belonged to St Oswald and the bishops of Worcester. The two hundreds of the Isle of Ely, the hundred-and-a-half of Mitford in Norfolk, and the five hundreds of Wicklaw in Suffolk, all belonged to St Etheldreda and the church of Ely. St Cuthbert held sway over all the men of Durham, ruling from the grave in the persons of his successors in the land of the living, the bishops of Durham. The greater jurisdictional peculiars, or 'liberties', excluded the sheriff from most or all of his functions and sometimes even, although rarely, excluded royal justices too. The lordships in Wales created by the Marcher barons were completely private: the king's writ did not run there. These were exceptional; but in England there were some regions – Ridesdale, parts of Richmond, the honor of Wallingford, for example, and one or two counties – where seigneurial government virtually replaced that of the king, although not so completely as in Wales. There are no returns in the pipe rolls for Durham, for Cheshire, or for Cornwall until 1176, for in these counties there was no royal sheriff, and all normal profits, the farms, the taxes, the amercements, the chattels of felons, went to the bishop of Durham, the earl of Chester, or the earl of Cornwall. The origin of such exalted privileges is obscure, but probably relates to a time when these were the wilder, underpopulated, and, it may be suspected, virtually ungovernable fringes of the realm. The justification for treating them differently from the rest of the country had greatly diminished by

[1] There is a useful analysis of franchisal rights in Painter, *Studies in the History of the English Feudal Barony*, 91–123, and a detailed study of an extensive franchise in Miller, *The Abbey and Bishopric of Ely*, 199–246.

the middle of the twelfth century; yet Henry II respected their traditional privileges. Cornwall, it is true, was brought into the normal shire
organisation after the death of Earl Reginald without legitimate heirs,
but Henry made no move to demolish the great liberties of Chester or
Durham, even though there was no lack of opportunity: Earl Hugh was
guilty of manifest treason in the great war, and Bishop Hugh du Puiset
was suspected of it. Both had their castles seized for a while but their
jurisdictional privileges survived.[1] Indeed, so far from seeing legitimate
franchises abolished or whittled down, the later twelfth century is a
period of franchisal growth. It is true that old privileges were devalued:
exemptions from the sheriff's jurisdiction, for instance, were of no avail
as the Crown directly assumed responsibility for a wider range of criminal cases; but the new procedures, the new regulations, and new royal
officials provided Henry II and his sons with more exemptions to sell.
They did so partly from motives of immediate profit, but partly also, it
may be suspected, to soften the impact of thrusting royal government.
The right, for example, of the bishop of Ely to the proceeds of a danegeld levied on his tenants lapsed with the end of that antiquated tax, the
value of his privilege to 'plead all the pleas which the sheriff pleads'
diminished as the sheriff's jurisdiction diminished; but the regular eyres
of the Crown's itinerant justices brought him increased returns from his
share of the amercements laid on vills and hundreds and juries for
defaults, and he retrieved something of the prestige and protection of
his liberty by acquiring the right to have his own officers discharge
everything which preceded and succeeded trial.[2]

There was a danger that an unrestricted growth of franchisal rights
would weave a web of exclusions so fine in mesh that royal government
would be hampered to the point of ineffectiveness. It was a danger that
could arise either from an improvidence in the sale of privileges by the
Crown, or from surreptitious usurpation, by forgery, assumption, or a
partial definition of ancient ambiguities. There was a tendency among the
barons to make the fief the unit of local government.[3] There was a ten-
dancy among them to assume that their status conferred rights without
the necessity of a special grant: Roger Bigod, the third earl of Norfolk,
for instance, asserted certain privileges on the ground that the count of

---

[1] There are excellent studies of the bishopric of Durham by G. V. Scammell, *Hugh
du Puiset*, and of the liberty of Durham by Lapsley, *The County Palatine of Durham*, and
Jean Scammell, 'The origin and limitations of the Liberty of Durham'. There is no
comparably detailed study of Chester, but many pertinent observations by Barraclough, 'The earldom and county palatine of Chester'.

[2] Cf. Miller, *op. cit.*, 201–5.

[3] I owe this observation to Painter, *op. cit.*, 100.

Guisnes had them, and that his status as an earl in England was comparable to that of the count in France.[1] Such dangers could only be averted by a vigilant Crown, and it was Henry II who set the pattern of royal policy. The *Quo Warranto* proceedings of the thirteenth century, which systematically investigated the legitimacy of claims to franchises, have their antecedents in the activities of Henry II's justices: 'Gilbert Brunus owes five marks since he claimed a liberty which he cannot prove', 'The men of the Isle of Wight owe £100 for twice failing to appear before the justices' – apparently they claimed unsuccessfully that the Isle had formed part of the onetime honor of Roger de Montgomery earl of Shrewsbury, and did not owe this duty.[2] The thirteenth-century lawbook which insists that franchise holders exercised merely a delegated jurisdiction from the Crown was in fact propounding a new theory, but it derives from the practice of Henry II in overriding franchisal rights *pro necessitate*.[3] 'Let there be no one,' says the Assize of Clarendon, 'within his castle or outside it, not even in the honor of Wallingford, who shall deny entry by the sheriff to his court or his land to take the view of frankpledge and to see that all are under pledge. . . . And let there be no one in a city, or a borough, or a castle or without, not even in the honor of Wallingford, who shall forbid the sheriff entry to their land or their jurisdiction to arrest those who have been accused or are notoriously suspect of being robbers or murderers or thieves or receivers of them, or outlaws, or those accused of forest offences, for the king commands that all shall aid the sheriffs to capture them.'[4] This was probably a special provision for a special occasion, but it was a forceful expression of a new dogma, that the king will not allow franchisal privileges to stand in the way of effective government. The bishop of Durham seems to have tried to claim that the provisions of the assize could not apply to his exalted liberty, but even he was brought to allow the entry of a royal justice to see that the assize was being enforced.[5] Moreover the new judicial writs gained entry to Durham, although they were there executed by the bishop's officers.[6] 'It is my wish,' said Henry in a charter to

---

[1] Painter, *op. cit.*, 93–4; Matthew Paris, *Chronica Majora*, V, 85–6.

[2] Pipe Roll 32 Henry II, 16 (there are ten similar entries following); Pipe Roll 16 Henry II, 126; cf. Painter, *op. cit.*, 110.

[3] Henry de Bracton, *De Legibus et Consuetudinibus Angliae*, ff.14, 55d (edited Woodbine and Thorne, II, 58, 167); cf. Helen Cam, 'The evolution of the medieval English franchise', 438–40.

[4] Assize of Clarendon, clauses 9 and 11.

[5] *Historiae Dunelmensis*, l, no. xxxi.

[6] King John's charter to the men of Durham in 1208 confirmed their right to plead in the court of the bishop according to 'the common and right assize of the realm of

the bishop, 'that the land of the Blessed Cuthbert should have its liberties and ancient customs as best it ever had them', but all the same the bishop was being reminded that his liberties did not stand outside the realm.[1] Furthermore the investigation into the activities of baronial bailiffs, as part of the Inquest of Sheriffs in 1170, was at the very least a warning that the king would not allow the exercise of private rights to pass without scrutiny. It was a portent of his grandson's threats to barons that he expected them to preserve the king's peace and do justice effectively within their liberties, 'that we may not be obliged to lay our hands upon your liberty because you have failed'.[2] This was the inner implication of Henry II's policy. Although, in short, he eschewed abolition, professed respect for ancient rights, and granted new ones, it is clear that the holders of liberties moved with less freedom in his day and after, and that franchisal authority was distinguished from feudal authority. The franchises survived, they multiplied, but only as complications in the administrative process, not as private enclaves, withdrawn from the common law and the common government of the realm.

William Stubbs's description of Henry II's policy as 'anti-feudal' bears the stigma of anachronism.[3] Henry could not be anti-feudal without destroying the society in which he lived. Fief-holding and the mutual obligations of lord and man appear to have seemed to him, as to other men, the natural framework of the social order. After all, the rights conferred by fief-holding still constituted the basic mechanism for exploiting land – the fundamental sources of medieval wealth. The pursuit, definition, and exploitation of the rights of lordship were essential elements in Henry II's own ascendancy, and if he sought to discipline feudal barons and trim the excesses of their *de facto* power, he did so by insisting on his *de iure* authority as their feudal overlord. On the continent, after all, the only resources of his authority were the obligations inherent in the homage and jurisdiction which derived from feudal *dominium*, for monarchical authority, such as it was in France,

---

England'; they were not to answer for their freeholdings except by writ of the king or his justiciar, as they had done in the time of Henry II; the sheriff of Northumberland could intervene to see that they were treated justly, *Rotuli Chartarum*, 182; cf. Jean Scammell, 'The origin and limitations of the Liberty of Durham', 459–60.

[1] *Historiae Dunelmensis*, Appendix 1, no. xxxi.

[2] *Close Roll 1234–37*, 556; cf. Helen Cam, *op. cit.*, 438; Miller, *The Abbey and Bishopric of Ely*, 243–4. As Helen Cam remarks, from Henry II's day 'privilege was insensibly being turned into an obligation, the exemption into a burden'.

[3] Stubbs, *Constitutional History of England*, I, 508.

resided in the Capetian rulers at Paris, and not in Henry of Anjou.[1] Even if Henry II could have conceived an attack on feudalism he would have been a fool as well as an anarchist to have tried it. Nor does he seem to have perceived the possibility of creating a counterpoise to the economic power of the baronage by fostering the interests of the trading communities of the towns. Richard FitzNigel speaks scathingly in the *Dialogus de Scaccario* of 'those who condescend to trade' and there is little sign that his master thought differently.[2] Henry II, it is true, seems to have appreciated the increasing economic importance of the towns, most of which were deemed to form part of the royal demesne, and provided the Crown with an effective means of profiting from their prosperity by developing a new form of tax, known as tallage, out of the older, haphazard 'aids' and 'gifts'. He was ready to confirm, at a price, the trading privileges, guild organisations, and tenurial customs which had already been established; but he seems to have set his face against granting towns the autonomy from shire government which they craved, and would allow only limited concessions even of the right to account separately at the exchequer for their share of the shire *farm*. The massive sale of privileges to chartered boroughs by which his sons augmented their revenues is indicative both of the eagerness of towns to buy and the reluctance of their father to take advantage of it.[3] In the long run Henry II's hesitancy to humour the assertiveness of the new mercantile classes was probably beneficial to the community of the realm as a whole, for it postponed the administrative autonomy of the borough until royal government had so developed that it could entertain the creation of 'local authorities' without the dire political consequences which so often attended municipal autonomy on the continent. Henry II's attitude to the towns, then, is hardly indicative of any coherent 'anti-feudal' policy. If anything, he was as concerned to protect royal government against the encroachment of municipal franchises as he was against the encroachment of baronial franchises, and saw the burgesses' desire to make the town a unit of local government with as much displeasure as the barons' desire to make the fief the unit of local government. But one can speak of his policy as anti-municipal with no more justification

---

[1] For the jurisdiction inherent in feudal lordship *see* Jolliffe, *Angevin Kingship*, 23ff.

[2] *Dialogus de Scaccario*, 108, cf. 109: '. . . But if a knight or other freeman should so far demean himself (which God forbid) as to acquire money by engaging in trade. . . .'

[3] Cf. Young, *The English Borough and Royal Administration*; Jolliffe, *Constitutional History of Medieval England*, 314ff.; Hoyt, *The Royal Demesne*, 107ff. Richard of Devizes, 49, writing after Henry II's death, describes a commune as 'a tumult of the people, the terror of the realm, and the horror of the priesthood', and says that Henry II would not have allowed one for a million silver marks.

than one can speak of it as anti-feudal, for to do so is to place the wrong emphasis upon Henry's intentions: it was not that he was anti-anything so much as that he was seeking to promote the efficacy of royal institutions.

Moreover, it is perhaps significant, and it is certainly curious, that, apart from the tallage, Henry II apparently devoted little attention to the development of non-feudal forms of taxation. The Norman kings inherited from their Anglo-Saxon predecessors what had been in its day a remarkably precocious system of direct taxation under the name of the *danegeld*, levied on a territorial assessment known as the *hidage*, in which every local community (and homestead) was reckoned at so many *hides*. Henry II levied the geld in the early years of his reign but allowed it to lapse after 1162. It had probably outlived its usefulness in its old form: the *hidage* assessment no longer accurately reflected economic conditions, and so many exemptions had become customary that administering the tax was cumbersome, and the returns amounted to no more than three-fifths of what was possible.[1] Levying it may well have seemed hardly worth the trouble; yet it is hard to believe that it was beyond the competence of Henry II's government to revise the assessment, or beyond its ingenuity to devise alternatives to the *hidage* as a basis for taxation. Indeed, the possibility of levying taxes on income or on wealth was not unknown in the middle of the twelfth century. The ecclesiastical tithe, after all, was a form of tax on revenues. In 1166 King Louis VII of France persuaded Henry to join him in raising an aid for the succour of the Holy Land throughout their respective dominions in the form of a small percentage of the value of each man's moveable property—a crude but effectively simple means of assessing wealth. But this useful precedent was not pursued for nearly twenty years. In 1185 and in 1188, the kings of England and France agreed to levies upon their subjects' incomes and chattels in aid of the Holy Land. That of 1188 was particularly heavy, and was known to contemporaries as the 'Saladin Tithe'. Each man was required to contribute ten per cent of the value of his revenues and movable goods (with the exception of certain categories of property such as the horses and armour of knights and the books and vestments of the clergy). Collectors were appointed in each parish and given the power to investigate suspected cases of dishonesty: 'And if anyone to their knowledge has given less than he ought, four or six lawful men shall be chosen from the parish who shall declare upon oath what amount he ought to have declared; and this sum shall then be added to the smaller amount he had given'. The method of assessment, specified in the king's ordinance, was well thought out, and the

[1] Cf. Ramsay, *Revenues of the Kings of England*, I, 194.

use of a local jury as a check upon fraud was a typically neat device of Angevin government. The proceeds amounted to twice the sum collected as danegeld in 1162.[1] It is not surprising therefore that the Saladin Tithe should have formed a precedent for all later forms of royal taxation of property; what is surprising is that Henry II should for so long have neglected the example of 1166 and been content with tallages upon the royal demesne, with attempts, not altogether successful, to improve the returns from scutages and aids levied on the knight service of the barons, with casual income from incidental features of feudal tenure, such as the sale of wardships and marriages, and with the profits of justice. It may of course have been a deliberate act of policy to avoid the unpopularity of direct taxation. The Saladin Tithe did indeed provoke bitter resentment even though it had a pious purpose; and William of Newburgh found it a mark of merit in Henry that 'he never imposed any heavy tax on England or his continental possessions, until the recent tithe for the Holy Land'.[2] All the same the heavy dependence upon feudal revenues which the neglect of direct taxation entailed cannot easily be reconciled with the assumption that Henry II's general policy was basically 'anti-feudal'.

On the other hand, it cannot be denied that the importance of the feudatories and of the feudal organisation of society was considerably diminished in the course of Henry II's reign, nor that certain of his policies, if not specifically anti-feudal, were markedly non-feudal. The commandeering of castles diminished the status of the barons at the same time as it curtailed their opportunities for rebellion. The changes in military techniques and the wholesale recruitment of mercenaries undermined, though they did not yet wholly eliminate, the *raison d'être* of a military aristocracy. It was being deflected, in fact, into becoming an aristocracy of special service and distinctive tenure. And much as Henry respected honorial courts and franchisal jurisdiction, the greater efficacy of royal justice and the growing insistence upon the standards of royal government in the exercise of private right sapped the baronial

---

[1] That a tax was levied in 1185 has sometimes been doubted by historians, but is demonstrated by Cazel, 'The tax of 1185 in aid of the Holy Land'. The text of the Saladin Tithe is given by William of Newburgh, I, 273–4, Roger of Howden, *Gesta*, II, 30–1, *Chronica*, II, 335–6, printed in Stubbs, *Select Charters*, 189, and trans. in *English Historical Documents*, II, 420–1. On the amount raised in England, Gervase of Canterbury, I, 422, gives the improbable figures of £70,000 from Christians and £60,000 from Jews; cf. Round, 'The Saladin Tithe', Mitchell, *Taxation in Medieval England*, 119–22.

[2] William of Newburgh, I, 282. For protests about the tithe *see* Ralph of Diceto, II, 73; Ralph of Coggeshall, 25; *Historiae Dunelmensis*, 13; Gervase of Canterbury, I, 422–3; Gerald of Wales, VIII, 253.

share in local government of much of its vitality. Feudalism was to become a fossil embedded in the landlaw; many developments contributed to this, including changes in economic circumstances, a freer land market, and the increasing reluctance of rear-vassals to perform their traditional obligations; but the process begins with Henry II's governmental reforms. Above all Henry's insistence on calling upon the resources of the community as a whole in the work of government contributed decisively to the creation of a community of the realm, transcending feudal relationships in its identification of royal interests with the interests of all subjects. His Norman predecessors had appreciated the value of the English monarchy's claim upon the allegiance of all men, and had cherished it as an alternative to the hierarchy of feudal homage as a source of authority; but Henry II was the first to turn it into an instrument of policy. 'Summon by good summoners twelve free and lawful men of the vicinity to be before me or my justices ready to make this recognition': such was the conclusion of the original writs, so was achieved what Jolliffe has felicitously called 'the coordination of king and country'.[1]

Moreover, Henry II could detach himself sufficiently from feudal forms of thinking to turn from the knight service supplied by barons as a condition of tenure, not merely to the recruitment of mercenaries, but to the arming of all freemen for the defence of the realm at the king's command. The Assize of Arms of 1181 specified the arms and armour to be borne by each freeman according to his status, but even more significantly it also required 'each and every one of them to swear that he will bear these arms in the king's service as he may command'.[2] The very notion, the form of the ordinance, and the distinctions of status instead of tenure, all hark back to pre-Conquest England. The author of the *Dialogus de Scaccario* remarks that by his day it was scarcely possible any longer to distinguish Englishmen from Normans, at least among freemen; he might have added, had he been able to recognise it, that the military régime of the Norman rulers was itself becoming merged, indeed submerged, in the living traditions of the English monarchy.[3] It

[1] Jolliffe, *Angevin Kingship*, 139.
[2] Roger of Howden, *Gesta*, I, 278–80, *Chronica*, II, 261–3; Stubbs, *Select Charters*, 183–4, trans. in *English Historical Documents*, II, 416–7. Richardson and Sayles, *Governance of Medieval England*, 439 n. 3, and *Law and Legislation*, 99–100, have argued for dating the Assize of Arms to 1176. Howden's date is, however, independently supported by Gervase of Canterbury, I, 297. There was a similar assize for the continental dominions which Roger of Howden dates to Christmas 1180, *Gesta*, I, 269. On the significance of the Assize *see* Powicke, *Military Obligation in Medieval England*, 54–6. [3] *Dialogus de Scaccario*, 53.

is impossible to say for certain whether Henry's policy promoted such a transformation or reflected, intelligently, a natural process of merger; but in any case it did represent a major shift in emphasis from feudal to non-feudal elements in the community. Henry II did not strike at the roots of feudalism, but he did encourage other plants which would in time grow to choke it. To this extent Stubbs, in the penetrating way that characterised his historical insight, laid bare a vein of truth; but to describe Henry's policy as 'anti-feudal' was to be guilty of a terminological solecism. It obscures too much, distorts too much, and omits too much. Stubbs's mistake was to try to comprehend in a simple phrase a policy which in its complexity and subtlety defies generalisation – a policy which in its commonsense pragmatism set little store by consistency and barely noticed contradictions and paradox. Paradox was implicit in Henry II himself, for he was a conservative who made a revolution.

The revolution did not pass unnoticed. Ralph Niger is the spokesman of those to whom Henry II and all his works were anathema: the brief passages which he devoted to the reign in his short chronicles are diatribes of unparalleled ferocity against a man who, it is implied, had corrupted and perverted the traditional way of life. Henry appears as a seducer and a tyrant, sacrilegious and unprincipled, who hated men of dignity and noble birth as if they were vipers, who cheated them of their inheritances, devalued their charters, strangled them with unprecedented exactions, cast them into servitude, and elevated the meanest servants to take over their positions of authority. By him the very foundations of the state were undermined, for 'he abolished the ancient laws, and every year made new laws which he called assizes'.[1] Such a travesty of the facts, of course, destroys Ralph Niger's credibility as a critic. In the savagery of his onslaught he was taking revenge on Henry for the exile he had suffered as a partisan of Archbishop Becket; but there were doubtless others who found in his words an expression of their own resentment of the changes which Henry II wrought upon society. William of Newburgh relates that it was only with the passage of time that Henry II's excellence as a ruler came to be acknowledged, and that 'in his own day he was hateful to nearly everyone': the treacherous and ungrateful, he adds, carped unceasingly at his failings and could not bear to hear of his good qualities.[2]

[1] Ralph Niger, 92–3, 167–9.
[2] William of Newburgh, I, 283. One man, Ralph d'Aubeney, could not contain his hostility, and threw a stone at the king when he was at Bedford castle, *Curia Regis Rolls*, IV, 270.

Yet it would be wrong to interpret such hostility and resentment as evidence of a general baronial opposition to the whole tenor of Henry II's rule. There is in fact no traceable consistency in baronial attitudes to Henry II, or to his policy of pursuing royal rights and enhancing the efficiency of royal government. The rebellion of a man such as Hugh Bigod, earl of Norfolk, may be seen as an attempt to preserve an older order in which baronial ambition had scope to deploy itself; but his contemporary and equal, Robert earl of Leicester, was, as justiciar, one of the chief agents in the restoration of monarchical authority after the disorder of Stephen's reign. Their sons steered opposite courses in the great war of 1173–4: the younger Robert of Leicester was Bigod's confederate in rebellion, but Bigod's son stood to arms with the king. Moreover, however much resentment there may have been by individuals, it is significant that Henry II could muster an effective weight of baronial opinion behind him in his major reforms: they were effected, after all, at great councils, with, as the chroniclers record, 'the advice and assent of the archbishops, bishops, abbots, earls, and barons'.[1] It is true that the impact of his measures was softened by Henry's tactical caution, by his professed respect for ancient liberties and legitimate privileges; it is true that the deeper consequences of his reforms in the paramount ascendancy of royal government were in practice obscured by his apparent conservatism, by the ambivalence of his policy in retaining the old beside the new, and the impenetrable subtlety of his paradoxical pragmatism. Yet it is of the greatest moment for English history that even when the consequences had become apparent, the barons did not seize the opportunities presented by the absence of King Richard or the revulsion against King John to enforce reaction. They accepted what King Henry had schooled them to accept; the demands presented to King John are as important for what they do not say as for what they do say; and in its silence the Great Charter approves the efficient machine of royal government which Henry II had fashioned.

Nevertheless, the acceptance of an efficient, watchful, resourceful, and ever expanding central government was not the same thing as acceptance of the will of individual kings acting above and beyond the bounds of accepted or acceptable law. The hatred and distrust of Henry II which Ralph Niger distortingly mirrors and William of Newburgh disapprovingly records, may have been provoked by an incoherent resentment at an ill-perceived but consciously felt shift in the balance of

---

[1] Cf. the heading to the Assize of Clarendon, Stubbs, *Select Charters*, 170; the heading to the Assize of the Forest, *ibid.*, 186; the text of the Assize of Northampton, clause 7, *ibid.*, 180; and the comments of *Glanvill*, 28, on the grand assize.

power between Crown and barons; but as the confusing steam of resentment evaporated and the working out of Henry's reforms revealed their beneficence, disapproval fastened quite properly, not upon royal government itself, but upon the arbitrary power which kings arrogated to themselves in administering it.

Henry II, by his improvement in military techniques, his administrative procedures and judicial devices, had tamed baronial tyranny and brought the great feudatories within the bounds of discipline and law; but he left unresolved the cognate problem of monarchical arrogance. Indeed, his decisive victory over baronial rebellion in a sense created the problem, for hitherto kings, if not inhibited by the fear of God or respect for law, had in practice been restrained by the imminence of rebellion. The balance of power between king and barons had in fact been a sort of primitive safeguard against royal tyranny, a crude substitute for a constitution. Henry II had upset this balance of power, and in doing so opened the way to the exclusive pursuit of royal interests. The old-style struggle for baronial independence was virtually over; but a new kind of struggle to impose restraints upon monarchy was just beginning.

It cannot be said that the real objections to Angevin government achieved articulate expression in Henry II's own day. The nearest approach to any comprehensive statement of grievances which has survived, is the protest which Gerald of Wales records, and which he attributes to Roger Asterby, a Lincolnshire knight. Sir Roger, according to the story, was bidden in a dream by St Peter and the Archangel Gabriel to warn King Henry to obey seven commandments. If he did so and went on crusade he would reign happily for another seven years, but if he failed to do so he would die miserably within four. Gerald records the headings of the seven commandments:

> First, the three promises which he made at his coronation to maintain the Church of God.
>
> Secondly, concerning the observance of the just laws of the realm.
>
> Thirdly, that he would condemn no one to death without judgement, even though he were guilty.
>
> Fourthly, in the matter of inheritances, that they should be restored and justice done.
>
> Fifthly, concerning the rendering of justice freely and without cost.
>
> Sixthly, concerning services rendered to his officials.
>
> Seventhly, concerning the Jews; that they should be expelled from his dominions with only enough money to pay their fare and support their

families, after their securities and title deeds had been taken from them and restored to their owners.[1]

It is not easy to deduce the real causes of complaint from these summaries and the only one of them to be specific, the last, does not encourage belief that the rest are free from prejudice. One might, indeed, be inclined to dismiss them out of hand were it not that they dimly foreshadow clauses of Magna Carta. Moreover, grievances which they hint at, and which the Charter formulates with greater clarity, may be illustrated from unimpeachable sources of Henry's reign.

The clearest example is the fifth commandment, 'concerning the rendering of justice freely and without cost'. 'To no one,' King John was made to say in 1215, 'To no one will we sell, refuse, or delay, right or justice.'[2] Gerald of Wales more than once denounced Henry II as 'a seller and delayer of justice'.[3] Raph Niger naturally echoes the charge.[4] But it cannot have been an accusation born entirely of senseless prejudice, for the author of the *Dialogus de Scaccario* hastens to enter an earnest defence:

> Some offerings are made for future advantage, as when a man offers money to the king to obtain justice; not, of course, to ensure that justice is done – so you must not lose your temper with us and say that the king sells justice – but to have it done without delay. The king does not always accept such offers, even though he may seem to depart from propriety. To some he does full justice for nothing in consideration for their past services, or merely from kindness of heart; but so far as others are concerned (and it is only human nature) neither prayer nor payment will bring him to assent. . . . In cases in which such offerings are concerned, the king has ordained that applicants shall not be required to tender their offerings until justice had been done, whether judgement is for them or against them.[5]

The defence is reassuring: the king does not sell judgements, and he has ruled that judgement should precede payment; but the defence admits half the charge – that the king might accept payment to hasten trial, or might condemn a man to infinite delay. Henry's justice was discriminatory.

William de la Mare accounts for £2 for having right in a fief of two knights fees against Robert of Cirencester.

---

[1] Gerald of Wales, VIII, 183–6.
[2] Magna Carta (1215), clause 40. For an echo of the third 'commandment' *see* clause 39, on the sixth 'commandment', clauses 28, 30, 31, and on the seventh 'commandment', clauses 10–11.
[3] Gerald of Wales, VIII, 160, cf. V, 304.
[4] Ralph Niger, 169.   [5] *Dialogus de Scaccario*, 120.

Peter of Marton owes five marks for having right against the earl of Warwick concerning land in Linton and Whitewell.

Robert de Prendergast accounts for three marks for the hastening of his right [*pro recto festinando*] against William of Binbrook concerning land at Binbrook.[1]

The payments are small – a little oil to the slowly grinding wheels of government; but acceptable offers could be punitive. It cost Guy of Buckland thirty marks 'for having right' about a portion of his wife's inheritance, and Reginald Basset owed a hundred marks 'for having right in land according to the charters of his predecessors'.[2]

The pipe rolls abound in such entries. How many applicants were refused we do not know; but it is clear that justice was not easily obtained even by those who deserved well of Henry. Sir Robert's plea that inheritances should be restored and justice done receives justification not only from Walter Map's admission that his hero was dilatory in determining great causes, but also from the accumulation of escheats in the king's hand towards the end of the reign, and in particular from the history of the Bigod inheritance.[3] Earl Hugh of Norfolk died in 1177 and the entire inheritance was claimed, with the earldom, by his eldest son, Roger Bigod, who had sided with Henry II in the great war. But the claim was disputed by his widow and second wife, who asserted that Earl Hugh had intended to divide the property, assigning his ancestral lands to his eldest son by his first marriage, but all his 'purchases and perquisites' to his younger son by his second marriage. Henry heard the pleas in court at Windsor, promised to give judgement, 'with the counsel of his earls and barons according to right and the custom of the country', and meanwhile seized 'all the treasure of the earl' into his hand, and kept the earldom in suspense.[4] But judgement remained undelivered on Henry's death twelve years later. It was from King Richard, within the first few weeks of his accession, that Roger Bigod obtained the earldom. The motive for procrastination was not, then, always hostility, nor even the caution of a cautious king; it was also, it may be suspected, a disagreeable avarice.

The financial motive is unmistakable in the treatment of vacant bishoprics and abbeys. The king's right to appropriate, in the case of a

---

[1] Pipe Roll 26 Henry II, 115; Pipe Roll 27 Henry II, 45; Pipe Roll 30 Henry II, 18.
[2] Pipe Roll 22 Henry II, 145, 183.
[3] Walter Map, 238, 241. Cf. Pipe Roll 34 Henry II, 1–17, for a *rotulus honorum* listing estates in the king's hand.
[4] Roger of Howden, *Gesta*, I, 143–4; cf. *Curia Regis Rolls*, I, 93.

vacancy, the revenues which normally went to the bishop or abbot was well established in English practice, for the theory was that the bishops and principal abbots held their lands as baronies of the Crown; but nothing could justify the deliberate withholding of the royal licence to elect a successor simply so that the king could continue to enjoy the revenues.[1] Even so well-disposed and generous a critic as William of Newburgh, who defended Henry against the charge that he was greedy for money on the ground that 'the excessive wickedness of the times' demanded a strong monarchy, felt bound to exclude from his defence the king's augmentation of his revenues by prolonging ecclesiastical vacancies.[2] He had good cause for disquiet: the see of London was kept vacant for two-and-a-half years, Salisbury for nearly five years, Lincoln for over six years, and York for nearly eight years.[3]

Henry II was evidently less solicitous of others' rights than of his own; and worse than this was capable of abusing rights which belonged undoubtedly to the Crown. The most obnoxious example of this is the treatment sometimes meted out to the widows of tenants-in-chief. The king, like any other feudal lord, had control over the marriages of heiresses and widows. It was a necessary safeguard against the conveyance of property into the hands of enemies; but at the same time the rule offered possibilities of abuse by the lord. Henry I had promised in his coronation charter that:

> If the wife of one of my tenants shall survive her husband, she shall have her dower and marriage portion, and I will not give her in marriage unless she herself consents. . . . And I require that my barons shall act likewise towards . . . the widows of their men.[4]

He had not in fact kept his promise; but it is hardly a defence of Henry II that he followed his grandfather's practices instead of his principles. The widow of a Yorkshire baron was in 1182 sold for two hundred marks.[5] The widow of William de Heriz paid £50 to avoid a similar fate.[6] Countess Matilda, widow of Earl William of Warwick, had to pay

---

[1] Cf. Margaret Howell, *Regalian Right in Medieval England*; Constitutions of Clarendon, clause 12.

[2] William of Newburgh, I, 280–1.

[3] Margaret Howell, *op. cit.*, Appendix A listing the revenues appropriated by the Crown. I have excluded from the examples quoted vacancies which were unavoidably prolonged by the exile of Archbishop Becket.

[4] Henry I's coronation charter, clauses 3–4, Stubbs, *Select Charters*, 118.

[5] Pipe Roll 28 Henry II, 46: 'Radulfus de Alben' reddit compotus de 200 marcas pro ducenda matre Edwardi Ros'.

[6] Pipe Roll 28 Henry II, 17: 'Aelina que fuit uxor Willelmi de Heriz reddit compotus de £50 ut non cogantur nubere nisi cum voluerit'.

seven hundred marks 'to have the land of her father, and her dower, and that she should not be married except to someone of her choice'.[1]

There are, it is true, not many such examples on the pipe rolls of Henry II's reign; but that there were any at all seems all the more blatant an iniquity in that the king's court administered to other men the strictest rules for the protection of widows, their dower, and their marriage.[2] It is a valid charge against Henry II that he ignored, in the royal interest, the developing notions of propriety and justice, and indeed the rules of custom and law, which he obliged his subjects to respect. Proof that there was, in effect, one rule for the king and another for the subject is afforded by the practice in the payment of relief by heirs when entering upon their inheritance. Hardening custom fixed a reasonable relief at the rate of £5 for each knight's fee which the inheritance owed in service to the lord. The king's court recognised and enforced the custom – but only so far as under-tenants were concerned. As *Glanvill* explains:

> According to the custom of the realm a reasonable relief for a knight's fee is one hundred shillings, but for baronies there is no certain figure laid down, for the tenants-in-chief in making satisfaction to the lord king for their reliefs are at his mercy and pleasure.[3]

There was no consistency in the sums demanded: for example, although William Brito paid forty marks on an inheritance of fifteen knights' fees, and William de Montacute paid a hundred marks on one of ten knights' fees, William Bertram paid £200 for a mere three knights' fees.[4] Some of the reliefs demanded were exorbitant: Robert de Lacy, for example, paid a thousand marks for the honor of Pontefract and so did Richard de Gant for his inheritance.[5] It is one of the paradoxes of Henry's reign that he who did so much to define and protect the rights of heirs, and to erect the developing principles of succession into rules of law, should have kept the heirs of tenants-in-chief at the mercy of his uncertain pleasure. Magna Carta was to fix the rate for baronies at £100.[6]

---

[1] Pipe Roll 31 Henry II, 76; cf. Magna Carta (1215), clauses 7 and 8.

[2] Cf. *Glanvill*, Bk VII.

[3] *Glanvill*, IX. 4, 108; cf. *Dialogus de Scaccario*, 96: if the inheritance is held in chief of the Crown, 'there is no fixed amount which the heir must pay to the king: he must make what terms he can'.

[4] Pipe Roll 24 Henry II, 39; Pipe Roll 23 Henry II, 83.

[5] Pipe Roll 24 Henry II, 72; Pipe Roll 31 Henry II, 91. Fulk Painel paid 1,000 marks for the honor of Bampton, Pipe Roll 26 Henry II, 94, and William de Briouze paid 1,000 marks for part of the honor of Barnstaple, Pipe Roll 23 Henry II, 188.

[6] Magna Carta (1215), clause 2.

An element of financial extortion entered into Henry II's dealings with his barons – and it extended beyond his exploitation of the Crown's undoubted rights. The most sinister of all the payments entered upon the pipe rolls are those 'for having the king's good will'.

Hamo de Masci accounts for £100 *pro habenda benevolentia regis.*
Gervase Paniel owes 500 hundred marks *pro habenda benevolentia regis.*
Gilbert FitzFergus accounts for 1,000 marks *pro habenda benevolentia regis.*

Robert Trenchant owes 300 marks for having the king's goodwill, and that he might have peace from the complaints which Robert of Briddlesford has brought against him, and since he gave in marriage a certain woman without the king's permission.[1]

The instances are numerous, the explanations rare. Sometimes, as in the case of Robert Trenchant, the cost of purchasing the king's goodwill was a form of punishment for a misdemeanour, but a punishment without judgement of a court, for an offence of which the king was sole judge. More often, we may suspect it was the punishment for a crime which no court would recognise: the crime of being uncooperative, of failing the king in his need or desire.[2] The converse of the king's *benevolentia* was his *malevolentia,* the expression of his anger and ill-will.

Geoffrey Ridel owes 300 marks for offences against the forest law, and since the lord king is putting aside his anger towards him [*quia dominus rex remittit ei iram suam*].

Ralf of Badwell [de Betteville] accounts for 100 hundred marks for having peace from the king's ill-will [*pro habenda de malevolentia regis*].

Adam de Port accounts for one thousand marks for relief of his land and the inheritance of his wife in Normandy, and that the king should set aside his indignation towards him [*ut rex indignationem suam ei remittat*] and receive his homage.[3]

Anger and ill-will were the attributes of personal monarchy. John of Salisbury might argue in his contemporary treatise on the nature of government that princes should act against the delinquent 'unmoved by any passion but by the disciplined arbitrament of law', but he was arguing against the contemporary facts of life.[4] When a friend sought to dissuade Henry from revenge on his enemies, the king, it is said, replied,

[1] Pipe Roll 23 Henry II, 59; Pipe Roll 22 Henry II, 106; Pipe Roll 25 Henry II, 31; Pipe Roll 24 Henry II, 111.   [2] Cf. Jolliffe, *Angevin Kingship,* ch. 4.
[3] Pipe Roll 23 Henry II, 94; Pipe Roll 14 Henry II, 28; Pipe Roll 20 Henry II, 135.
[4] John of Salisbury, *Policraticus,* IV, 2 (edited Webb, I, 239): 'Princeps delinquentes rectissime punit non aliquo iracundiae motu sed manusuetae legis arbitrio'.

'Am I not to be allowed to be angry when passion is part of man's character and a natural attribute? I am by nature a child of anger: how therefore should I not be moved to anger? God himself was moved to anger.'[1] The speech may have been put into Henry's mouth, but it chimes with the words of one of his charters: 'If anyone should attempt to infringe or quash this grant, or in any way presume to threaten it, he will incur the disfavour, anger, and indignation of Almighty God and me.'[2] Withdrawal of the king's favour brought harassment and despair to an erstwhile courtier in Arnulf bishop of Lisieux.[3] It was the king's anger which inadvertently condemned Archbishop Becket to death. At the very least the king's ill-will brought inconvenience and expense, for it postponed justice, put up the price of inheritance and cut a man off from profitable marriage, wardships, and the purchase of privileges. Its seriousness was compounded by the expansion of royal government and the ever-increasing intervention of the Crown in the lives of its subjects. Royal favour was the passport to prosperity, a key which unlocked doors, an insurance against adversity, the *sine qua non* of baronial peace of mind.

The wrath of kings might carry them beyond law to distraint, disseisin, and imprisonment without judgement. It might be the impious wrath of hatred or pious wrath at the frustration of legal process, but both seemed indefensible to the better minds of the age, such as John of Salisbury. Arbitrary distraint and disseisin were instruments of tyranny. There was a time, not long distant, when arbitrary action by well-meaning lords was a harsh necessity which wrought order out of disorder and rescued justice from injustice; but with the peace which Henry brought and the sophistication of judicial process, no one, save wilful kings, could any longer believe that there was justification for its use by the Crown any more than by other lords. 'No freeman,' King John was brought to say in Magna Carta, 'shall be arrested or imprisoned or disseised or outlawed or exiled or in any way destroyed, neither will we set forth against him or send against him except by the lawful judgement of his peers or by the law of the land.' The fault lay not in King John alone. The evidence for Henry II's reign is fragmentary but revealing.

[1] 'Dialogus inter Regem Henricum Secundum et Abbatem Bonevallis', ed. Huygens, 99–100, lines 79–82; in *Patrologia Latina*, CCVII, 978. The conversation may be apochryphal, but the words were chosen by one who knew Henry II well – Peter of Blois.

[2] *Recueil des Actes de Henri II*, II, 244: 'Si quis vero hanc prescriptam donationem meam infringere vel cassare attemptaverit, vel aliquo modo imminuere presumpserit, omnipotentis Dei malivolentiam, iram, et indignationem incurrat et meam'.

[3] Barlow, introduction to *The Letters of Arnulf of Lisieux*, l–lx, cf. above, ch. 5, p. 211.

Within a few months of King Henry's death, his son Richard accepted a proffer of a hundred marks by the canons of Chichester for the restoration of a prebend 'Whence the king's father disseised them', a proffer of £100 by Henry de Monfort, 'for having seisin of Wellesbourne from which he was disseised by will of the king's father', and a proffer of eighty marks by Robert Belet 'for having his inheritance of Coombe with the park valued as £9 7s whence the king's father had wilfully disseised him'.[1] Several years later the jurors in a grand assize testified that Robert Belet had been disseised of all his lands because 'the lord king Henry was angry with him over a sparrowhawk'.[2] Adam of Hale and his brothers petitioned King John 'to have seisin of the lands of their father in Shoreham from which their father was disseised, and was imprisoned by the will of King Henry, for no other reason than that he was with the Blessed Thomas in his persecution'.[3] In Henry III's reign, Warin Montchesney, being summoned to show by what warrant he held a manor which had once formed part of the royal demesne, explained that it had never been Crown land although it had for some time been under royal control, since King Henry II had disseised his ancestor, William Montchesney, of all his lands 'for taking a wife without the king's permission', and the manor had not been recovered until his father obtained it from King Richard.[4] On Henry II's death his son and heir, Richard, proclaimed an amnesty for prisoners and outlaws, declaring, *inter alia*, that 'all who had been taken for forest offences should be liberated and quit, and that all outlawed for forest offences should return to the peace quit of former forfeitures for the forest; and that all others who had been taken and detained by will of the king or his justiciar, who had not been detained by the common law of shire and hundred or on an appeal, should be quit'.[5]

* * *

[1] Pipe Roll 2 Richard I, 129, 43–4, 155.

[2] *Curia Regis Rolls*, IX (AD 1220), 332: '. . . contigit quod dominus rex Henricus iratus fuit cum ipso Roberto Belet occasione unius espervarii, ita quod dominus rex disseisivit ipsum Robertum de omnibus terris suis. . . .'

[3] Pipe Roll 5 John, 103.

[4] *Curia Regis Rolls*, XIII (1227–30), case no. 56, 248. For further examples *see Bracton's Note Book*, cases 39, 769, and cf. Magna Carta (1215), clause 52. The allegations of Ruald FitzAlan and Peter FitzHerbert that their ancestors had been disseised by Henry II (*Curia Regis Rolls*, V, 148; V, 177, 287, 296) related to Henry's attempts to resolve competing claims arising from the civil war of Stephen's day.

[5] Roger of Howden, *Gesta*, II, 74, *Chronica*, III, 4. At Easter 1183, according to Roger of Howden, Henry, apprehensive of another conspiracy, took and imprisoned those whose loyalty he doubted, including the earl of Gloucester and the earl of Leicester and his wife. In 1189, Richard restored to the earl of Leicester the land which his father had taken from him, *Gesta*, I, 294; II, 75.

Of all aspects of royal government it was the administration of the special areas known as 'Forest' which provoked the most vocal criticism in Henry's day. According to the biographer of St Hugh of Lincoln,

> the worst abuse in the kingdom of England, under which the country groaned, was the tyranny of the foresters. For them violence took the place of law, extortion was praiseworthy, justice was an abomination and innocence a crime. No rank or profession, indeed, in short, no one but the king himself, was secure from their barbarity, or free from the interference of their tyrannical authority.[1]

The chronicler of Battle Abbey was especially incensed by Alan de Neville, the king's chief forester,

> who by the power with which he was endowed most evilly vexed the various provinces throughout England with countless and unaccustomed persecutions. And since he feared neither God nor man, he spared no men of rank whether ecclesiastics or laymen. . . . This Alan so long as he lived enriched the royal treasury, and to please an earthly king did not fear to offend the king of Heaven. But how much gratitude he earned from the king whom he strove to please, the sequel showed. For when he was brought to his last, the brethren of a certain monastery, hoping, it seems, to secure something of his substance for their house, besought the king to allow them to carry away his body to their burial place. Whereupon, the king revealed his sentiments towards him in these terms. 'I,' he said, 'will have his wealth, you shall have his corpse, and the demons of hell his soul.'[2]

Even Walter Map, a royal servant himself, thought the forest officers the most disreputable:

> they eat the flesh of men in the presence of Leviathan, and drink their blood. . . . They fear and propriate the lord who is visibly present: the Lord whom they do not see, they offend without fear. I do not mean to deny that there are in this vale of misery some merciful judges. It is of the wilder majority that I speak.[3]

The Forest was not, as has sometimes been supposed, a strictly private preserve of the Crown, from which other men and their rights were rigorously excluded. It is true that much of it was wilderness, scrub and tangled woodland, but the bounds of the Forest also embraced culti-

[1] Adam of Eynsham, I, 114.
[2] *Chronicon Monasterii de Bello*, 110, 111–12.
[3] Walter Map, 5–6. Cf. the reference to 'Alan and his gang' in the *Dialogus de Scaccario*, 58–9.

vated land, homesteads, village communities in woodland clearings, and even townships. Some of it was royal demesne, but the lands of many other lords fell within the bounds of the Forest. Their rights were not extinguished there, but they were circumscribed, overlaid by royal rights, and they and their men subjected to forest law. It is uncertain how much of England was Forest in the twelfth century, but it may have amounted to nearly a third. Practically the whole of Essex was Forest, and so was much of Berkshire, Hampshire, and Wiltshire. Most other counties had Forest areas, although Norfolk, Suffolk, Kent and the northern parts of Lincolnshire were free of it. Nor was the Forest an area under the direct rule of royal officers administering forest law to the exclusion of common law and the normal organisations of shire and hundred: on the contrary, to be subject to forest law was to be subject of an additional, not a different, form of law and government. The nature of the Forest is indeed best understood on the analogy of modern Nature Conservancy Acts and regions designated as Areas of Outstanding Natural Beauty in which agrarian life goes on, but under special restrictions. The special restrictions of the Forest, however, were designed for the king's advantage alone. 'In the forests,' explains the *Dialogus de Scaccario*,

> are the privy places of kings and their great delight. Thither they go for hunting, and having laid aside their cares, to enjoy a little quiet. There, away from the continuous business and incessant turmoil of the court, they may for a little time breathe in the gracious freedom of nature. And that is why those who despoil it are subject to the royal censure alone. . . . The king's Forest is a safe abode for wild animals, not of every sort, but of the sort that dwell in woodland, and not everywhere but in places suitable for the purpose . . . in the wooded counties, where wild beasts have their lairs and plentiful feeding grounds. It makes no difference to whom the woods belong, whether to the king or the barons of the realm; the beasts have freedom and protection wandering almost where they will.[1]

In the areas designated Forests the beasts of the chase – red deer, the fallow deer, the roe, and the wild boar – could be taken only by the king or by those who had his warrant; anyone else, even if the woods, the heath or the marshes were his, was restricted to hares and coneys, foxes and wolves, badgers and wildcats, but could hunt even those only if he had the royal licence. Protection of the beasts inevitably involved protection of their environment, and it was this (the *vert* of forest law) which caused the most irksome restrictions for those who had lands and habita-

[1] *Dialogus de Scaccario*, 60.

XII Royal Forests (*not all forest names are given*)

Note: there is insufficient information to establish the bounds of the Forest in Henry II's day. The above map is sketched from information gathered by Margaret Bazeley for the thirteenth century, after the areas subject to forest law had been somewhat reduced.

tions within the Forest. The cutting of timber, even the gathering of firewood, was subject to strict regulation; clearings to extend cultivation even in a man's own woods were severely limited. Pigs could be sent to forage in the woods only under supervision and on payment for the privilege, and were barred altogether when the deer were fawning. To take a cart off the highway, to carry bows and arrows, to lead dogs without a couple, even to own a dog which had not been 'lawed' by the trimming of its claws on the forefeet, were serious offences.[1] Henry II, it is said, was more lenient than his grandfather in punishing transgressors, but even he prescribed imprisonment for a third offence.[2]

The king's love of hunting was, of course, a principal reason for the existence of the Forest. 'He was most knowledgeable about dogs and birds,' says Walter Map, 'and a very keen follower of hounds.'[3] 'He was addicted to the chase beyond measure,' says Gerald of Wales. 'At crack of dawn he was off on horseback, traversing the wilderness, plunging into woods and climbing the mountain tops.'[4] 'He delighted in the pleasure of hunting as much as his grandfather,' says William of Newburgh, 'and more than was right.'[5] His favoured residences, at Clarendon and Woodstock, were hunting lodges. Yet the imposition of forest law in areas which the king rarely if ever visited, Amounderness in Lancashire, for example, Delamere and the Wirral in Cheshire, or Pickering in Yorkshire, are indications that the king's pleasure was not the only reason. The other reason was economic advantage. The Forest, of course, provided a useful revenue from fines for offences, rents for pannage and pasturage, and the sale of privileges and exemptions. But it was also important for its produce. Venison, fresh or salted, was sent to the king's household, to his favoured friends, and garrisons. Timber was supplied for building his houses and castles – and the high cost and difficulty of transporting timber made local supplies desirable. Charcoal burners, licensed of course, converted wood into fuel for the smelting of iron, and iron-smelters and smiths with portable forges followed the charcoal burners. Woodland manufacture produced large quantities of roofing shingles, arrows, iron arrow-heads and quarrels.[6] It is doubtful if the Crown exploited the Forest as thoroughly in the twelfth century as it

[1] On forest law and customs see Manwood, *Treatise of the Lawes of the Forest*; Margaret Bazeley, 'The Forest of Dean and its relations with the Crown during the twelfth and thirteenth centuries'.

[2] William of Newburgh, I, 280, cf. Roger of Howden, *Chronica*, II, 247; IV, 65–6.

[3] Walter Map, 237–8.   [4] Gerald of Wales, V, 302.

[5] William of Newburgh, I, 280.

[6] Cf. Margaret Bazeley, *op. cit.*, 219ff.

might have done; but forest law, and the Crown's power to designate areas as Forest at will, enabled it to pre-empt the development of hitherto untapped resources, and hindered the efficient exploitation of their own woods by other lords.

'The whole organisation of the forests,' the *Dialogus de Scaccario* explains, 'the punishment, pecuniary or corporal, of forest offences is outside the jurisdiction of the other courts, and solely dependent upon the decision of the king, or of some officer specially appointed by him.'[1] It called for an army of royal servants: foresters, woodwards, verderers, agisters, regarders and the justices who conducted forest eyres. Forest law was administered through forest courts parallel to, but distinct from, the courts of hundred and shire and of justices in eyre. Much of the vocal complaint about the forest in the twelfth century is about the activity of forest officers and forest courts. This is probably misleading. It is true that forest officers had unique opportunities for petty tyranny and extortion, and Magna Carta was to condemn their 'evil customs'.[2] It is true, too, that forest eyres produced a huge revenue from fines, but the fines on individuals, although numerous, were not usually very heavy. The main complaints, it has to be noted, come from monastic chroniclers, and the monks had two special sources of grievance: in the first place, they were among the chief sufferers from the activity of the royal foresters in reimposing forest law in areas which had slipped from under it during the disorder of Stephen's reign; and in the second place, they were incensed that forest officers treated the clergy just like laymen. It was no consolation that a papal legate agreed to Henry II's request that the privileges of clergy should not apply to those apprehended for forest offences.[3] For most men subject to forest law, however, the objection was probably not so much the tyranny of godless forest officers, for poaching was itself good sport and local officials could often be bribed, as the inconveniences and disabilities which the law entailed – the burden of attendance at forest court, the denial of access to good forage and timber, the hindrance to bringing virgin land into cultivation, and above all the serious restriction on the development and exploitation of a man's own lands. Yet even these objections did not go to the heart of the matter. Remarkably, it was the king's treasurer, Richard FitzNigel, who put his finger on it: forest law was not true law at all but the expression of arbitrary will. 'The Forest has its own laws,' he writes in the *Dialogus de Scaccario*, 'based, it is said, not on the common law of the realm, but on the arbitrary decision of the ruler; so that

---

[1] *Dialogus de Scaccario*, 59.   [2] Magna Carta (1215), clause 48.
[3] Cf. Gervase of Canterbury, I, 257; Roger of Howden, *Gesta*, I, 105.

what is done in accordance with that law is not called "just" without qualification but "just according to forest law".'[1]

It is possible that the disapproving tone which Richard FitzNigel always adopted when referring to the Forest was provoked by the exclusion of forest officers from control by the exchequer: the sheriffs accounted for forest fines, but any question arising about the administration of the Forest had to be referred to the chief forester or the king himself.[2] Nonetheless, the revelation that in court circles forest law was criticised, is a reminder that it was Henry's government itself which taught men to recognise the defects within it. The precision, sophistication, and impartiality of exchequer law and common law sharpened the contrast with the arbitrariness of forest law, and showed up in stark nakedness the occasions when the king acted at will to disseise, distrain upon, or imprison a man. It was, after all, the king's government which provided a remedy against unjust disseisin by anyone else; it was the king's own courts which provided actions for the recovery of property unlawfully distrained.[3]

Royal power under Henry II could be discriminatory, violent, arbitrary, wilful, and selfish – for monarchy was still personal, and it was Janus-faced. Nonetheless, its weaknesses should not be allowed to obscure its virtues; and in the long run its customary impartiality, its respect for legal principle, its equation of right and law, and its sense of justice, were more important in moulding the traditions of English government than its lapses into tyranny. As the prologue to the *Tractatus de Legibus et Consuetudinibus Regni Angliae* justly remarks: 'The royal court is so impartial that no judge there is so shameless or audacious as to presume to turn aside in the slightest from the path of justice or to digress in any respect from the way of truth. For there, indeed, a poor man is not oppressed by the power of his adversary, nor does favour or partiality drive any man away from the threshold of judgement.'[4] Of Henry II himself it was said that 'he was so just in his judgements that whoever had a good case was anxious to have it tried before him, whereas whoever had a bad one would not come before him unless he were dragged'.[5] 'Let no one,' warns Richard FitzNigel, commenting on the Assize of Clarendon, 'venture to oppose the king's ordinance made, as it is, in the interests of peace.'[6] In 1177 London was disturbed by rob-

---

[1] *Dialogus de Scaccario*, 60; cf. the description of forest taxes as *illiciti*, 104.

[2] Cf. *Memoranda Roll 1 John*, lxxviii, n. 2.

[3] Cf. *Glanvill*, XII.12, 142, and Painter, *Studies in the History of the English Feudal Barony*, 107.   [4] *Glanvill*, 2.

[5] Walter Map, 253.   [6] *Dialogus de Scaccario*, 101.

beries perpetrated by the well-born. The justiciar, Richard de Lucy, intervened and captured one of them, who betrayed his accomplices. Among them, relates Roger of Howden, 'was a certain prominent and most wealthy citizen of London, John Senex by name, who, failing to purge himself at the ordeal of water, offered the king five hundred marks of silver to save his life. But since he had been condemned by the judgement of water, the king refused to accept the money, and ordered that sentence should be passed, and he was hanged.'[1] But at the same time, royal justice was vigilant against abuse and the pipe rolls record amercements upon communities or local officials who overreached themselves:

> Silvester FitzSimon accounts for 20 marks since he sent Warin FitzBaldwin unjustly to the judgement of water.

> The village of Malden accounts for 3 marks for hanging a thief without the view of a royal officer [*pro latrone suspenso sine visu servientis regis*]. Gerard the reeve accounts for 5 marks for the same.[2]

Even criminals were entitled to be executed properly: there was to be no lynch law in England.

Magna Carta was to condemn the defects of royal government by the high standards which that government had itself inculcated; and it was Henry II who taught his subjects the remedy against the abuse of power – the rule of law. This was his greatest paradox.

[1] Roger of Howden, *Gesta*, I, 156.
[2] Pipe Roll 29 Henry II, 23; Pipe Roll 31 Henry II, 17.

Part III

HENRY II AND THE CHURCH

Preface

THE PROBLEM OF
INTERPRETATION

It is not easy to avoid allowing the topic of Henry II's dealings with the Church to be dominated by his quarrel with Archbishop Becket. The sheer volume of information about Thomas Becket's life, the course of the quarrel, and the justifications the archbishop offered for his stand, is compelling in its copiousness. Moreover, it is plausible to assume that Thomas Becket, as a result of his five years' intimacy with the king while he was his chancellor, knew better than anyone what Henry's intentions were towards the Church. It seems reasonable, in consequence, to assume that although Thomas Becket was archbishop for only eight of the thirty-four years of Henry II's reign, the period of his tenure of the see of Canterbury brings the whole of Henry's ecclesiastical policy into focus.

This may be a plausible assumption, but it is nevertheless unacceptable. For one thing it would be like assuming that Henry II's Welsh policy can be read from the wholesale revolt of the Welsh upon his demand for homage in 1163. Henry's policies matured – and in any case, policy cannot always be read from tactics. Henry II's tactics from 1159 to 1164 plunged him deeply into trouble with many people: with the king of France, the Welsh, the Scots, the Bretons, the Poitevins, and with the bishop of Poitiers as well as with some of the English clergy. They were tactics spawned of an overweening, youthful self-confidence. Henry, it is as well to remember, was just twenty-six when he embarked on the ill-starred expedition to Toulouse, and was barely twenty-nine when, against advice, he made Becket archbishop of Canterbury. Henry was a brash young man, but the brashness slipped away with youth.

Thomas Becket was the companion of Henry's youth and of most of his youthful indiscretions. He never really knew the mature king: his self-imposed exile in 1164 came too soon for that. The resistance which Henry encountered in the early 1160s (and would have encountered even without Becket) was the turning point in the development of his policies. The solid achievements of his reign begin with the *annus mirabilis* of 1166. His true greatness as a ruler begins only to emerge in his response to the problems which his youthful impatience had itself done much to evoke. Hitherto he had pursued, by somewhat crude means, the restoration of what he took to be his grandfather's position and prerogatives; but from the later 1160s he was appreciating the inner subtleties of his grandfather's policies, refining out the principles that lay beneath them, and applying the principles in new fashions to the realities and needs of his own day. The archbishop's quarrel with the king proved irreconcilable because his conception of the king's intentions remained crude and narrow. Most people who were closely involved came to realise this, but not Becket himself. He was left out on a limb; and while he became acutely conscious of his isolation he remained unable to understand why. He blamed treachery, envy, intrigue, the guile of the king, the machinations of royal agents, papal cowardice, anything; but when even friends deplored his intransigence, his denunciations of the king's supposed intentions became increasingly detached from reality, and his self-justification ever more hysterical. He brought a violent death upon himself because he could not bring himself to admit that his reading of the situation had been mistaken, his sufferings largely self-inflicted, and his obstinacy misguided.

Thomas Becket belongs to an early phase of Henry II's career, and one which, in the context of the whole, seems untypical. Perhaps what helped to make it untypical was Chancellor Becket's own enormous influence as the intimate adviser of the young king. 'Being,' as William FitzStephen writes in his *Life of St Thomas*, 'a man of diligence and experience in many and great affairs, he so discharged the onerous duties and obligations of office to the praise of God and the well-being of the whole realm, that it seems doubtful whether he served the king with greater distinction and efficiency or to greater advantage in peace or in war. . . . When business was over, the king and he would sport together like boys of the same age; in hall or in church they sat together, together they rode out. . . . Never in Christian times were there two men more of one mind or better friends.'[1]

Yet it may be doubted whether Thomas Becket was altogether a good influence on the young Henry. The obstinate insistence upon the unequivocal acknowledgment of rights, and the preference for grand gestures, which mark the whole of Becket's career, are peculiarly characteristic of Henry's activities in the early years while Becket directed his hand. The young Henry behaved as a man seemingly convinced that the world would fall at his feet if he challenged it with determina-

[1] William FitzStephen, III, 18, 24, 25.

tion, confident of the righteousness of his cause. Becket went his way even unto death with just such a conviction; but Henry learned that the world had to be wooed, not browbeaten. It may be that Henry's early love of Becket sprang from a shared temperament, but it was the archbishop who pursued intransigence to the meretricious glory of a martyr's crown, the king who learned to bend and manipulate, to concede with grace and recover by stealth, to persuade where he could not force, to defer before he was obliged to fight, to achieve his ends by clever compromise, circuitous routes, or, as many contemporaries seem to have believed, by sleight of hand. The temperament of Henry, the very mode of his kingship, changed almost out of recognition; Becket, the older man by some fifteen years, was left behind, uncomprehending. There would have been a breach between them even if they had not found a quarrel over the liberties of the Church and the prerogatives of Canterbury: the memory of close friendship lingered on to embitter their enmity, but the mature king and the mature churchman had become incompatible. Becket was too rigid, too narrow, too *simpliste* in his methods, and probably too upright a man, to be boon companion to the complete statesman and exponent of *realpolitik* that Henry became. Becket belongs rather to the period of Henry's apprenticeship, fortifying by his counsel, and furthering with his zeal, a young man's fancy for simple solutions dressed up as grand adventures, and his faith that Jericho will fall to the sound of the trumpet. Toulouse was Henry's Jericho; but its walls did not fall as his trumpets blew and his armies marched and marched about. The expedition to Toulouse was the culmination of Becket's career as chancellor. It was he who was prominent in organising it, pledging the king's faith freely to raise money for it; it was he who was prominent in the conduct of it, leading a large force of mercenaries in the king's service and himself unhorsing a famous French knight; it was he who remained behind to besiege the castles of the Cahorsin, when the king returned, thwarted, to Normandy. The expedition, however, seems to have been a turning point for Henry, and the beginning of a quest for other methods of securing his ends. There were to be no more chivalrous *chevauchées*. New methods required new men. In moving his chancellor from the court to Canterbury Henry was, consciously or unconsciously, shaking off a tutelage he had outgrown.

The famous quarrel, then, marks the end of an era, and for that reason alone cannot be assumed to illustrate the essential nature of Henry's developed policy. In espousing the cause of clerical liberty Becket may indeed have known what he was about, for in denouncing what he took to be Henry's ecclesiastical policy he was denouncing that narrow conception of royal rights which, it is likely, he himself had helped to foster in the young king's mind: he thought he knew what Henry would do because that is what he would have done in Henry's place. Henry, it is true, responded to Becket's challenge with brusque demands – it was his wont at the time – but there is every reason to believe that, could he have escaped the personal animosities which the quarrel provoked, he would have retreated from the attempt to browbeat the clergy as quickly as he retreated from his contemporaneous attempt to browbeat the Welsh princes. The humble submission of the clergy would have suited his purpose, but his basic purpose was not the humble submission of the clergy: it was the defence of royal interests, and these, as he subsequently discovered, could be secured by means which the Church could accept, or at least tolerate. Becket mistook the means for the end.

Henry soon realised his mistake; Becket never realised his, and his posthumous reputation disguised it from the world. It must never be forgotten that his biographers were writing after the murder in the cathedral, and the nature of his death determined their interpretation of his life. They were writing not of Becket the archbishop but of Becket the martyr. Martyrdom excused a multitude of defects, and the miracles at the tomb were taken to prove not merely that Thomas Becket was a saint, but that Archbishop Becket had been right. Hence, for them, Henry's intentions must have been as nefarious as the archbishop's stand proclaimed them to be. But can we accept the premises of their argument?

The beam of light cast by Becket's biographers on Henry II's ecclesiastical policy is bright but narrow; it is cast obliquely and distorts, throwing monstrous shadows from innocent objects. More uniformly illuminating is the correspondence of participants in the quarrel, massively preserved; but this too leaves pools of darkness in the very places where one might hope to descry Henry's intentions. For the king resolutely refused to be drawn into argument about principles, and in his passionate desire to be rid of an archbishop who, he believed, had betrayed his trust, dealt his cards to win tricks but carefully concealed his hand. The correspondence tells of manœuvres and debating points, persuasions and threats, excuses and justifications; but he who would read Henry's mind must learn to read between the lines.

Z. N. Brooke, in a memorable series of lectures in 1929–31, offered an interpretation which is graphic, all-embracing, and internally consistent. Henry II's attitude to the Church, he suggests, was in line with that of his predecessors since the Norman Conquest, and his purpose was to preserve the prerogatives he had inherited. William the Conqueror had acknowledged papal leadership of the Church, but was determined to be master in his own house. He had erected a barrier of rules and regulations to exclude papal intervention, which also had the effect of keeping out the teaching of the high clericalists who had gathered around Pope Gregory VII. Henry I had maintained the barrier, but with difficulty: two great disputes within the English Church in his day had made communication with Rome necessary, and some reformist doctrine had come in over the wall, but it was cleverly rendered harmless, and England effectively 'isolated' from 'papal interference'. During Stephen's reign, however, the barrier had been breached all along the line, and in an atmosphere of free intercourse with Rome the English Church had become infected with an aspiration to ecclesiastical liberty. Henry II saw a duty to restore royal control:

> His object was to rebuild the barriers again, and by excluding the papal authority to revive the royal in its old form. But he had to act with caution. He was indebted for the ease of his coronation to the Pope and Archbishop Theobald, and had to be careful not to antagonise them by too sudden a reaction. . . . When Theobald died in 1161 the opportunity for which he had been waiting seemed to have arrived.[1]

But Henry's chosen instrument – Thomas Becket – betrayed him, precipitating a quarrel which was to transform the relations of Church and State in England.

Subsequent research, taking up themes which Z. N. Brooke suggested, has diminished the force of many of his arguments and cast serious doubt on the validity of his thesis. Nevertheless, in suggesting a consistent line of policy between Henry II and his grandfather, Brooke had found the thread which leads through the labyrinth of the source material. This is the thread which must first be taken up.

[1] Brooke, *The English Church and the Papacy*, 198–9.

Chapter 11

CHURCH AND STATE IN NORMAN ENGLAND

Many aspects of William the Conqueror's ecclesiastical policy are hung about with doubt, either for lack of evidence or from the difficulty of interpreting such evidence as there is, but of its general lines and basic assumptions it is possible to speak with a fair degree of confidence. It was characteristic of the Conqueror's England that 'all things spiritual and temporal alike waited upon the nod of the king' (as Eadmer put it).[1] William's native imperiousness was reinforced, so far as the Church was concerned, by conceptions of the divinely appointed function of the lay ruler to direct and control ecclesiastical life within his dominions – conceptions that were daily called into question at the court of Pope Gregory VII, but which were deeply implanted by Byzantine tradition, Carolingian practice, and habits of thought of the Scandinavian homeland of the Normans and of the Anglo-Saxon England they conquered. In practice, William's dominance was strengthened by the close ties which bound the leading bishops and abbots to him; their selection rested upon his personal choice or at the very least upon his explicit approval, and on appointment they placed their hands between his and became his feudal vassals. In exercising the functions of their office the bishops were subject to a web of customary restrictions, of which the near-contemporary Eadmer selects two as typical: a council of bishops could not 'lay down any ordinance or prohibition unless these were agreeable to the king's wishes and had first been approved by him', nor could any bishop, except with the king's permission, 'take action against or excommunicate one of his barons or officials for incest or adultery or any other cardinal offence or even when guilt was notorious lay upon him any penalty of ecclesiastical discipline'.[2]

William seems to have conceived of the church within his dominions as forming a *Landeskirche* or regional church, subject to his own authority, with the counsel of his own ecclesiastical advisers, but nevertheless forming an integral part of Christendom as a whole, of which the

---

[1] Eadmer, *Historia Novorum*, 9.　　　　[2] *Ibid.*, 10.

bishop of Rome was the spiritual head. Such an attitude was normal in the eleventh century and had history on its side; but it was already in William's own day archaic by the standards of the reformers who dominated the papal curia. Two aspects, in particular, of the new thinking at Rome were subversive of the traditional conception of the relations of Church and State: the desirability of excluding laymen from any function in the *ecclesia* (as distinct from the wider body of baptised persons, *Christianitas*), and the necessity of papal direction of ecclesiastical affairs throughout Christendom. William's respect for papal headship of the Church undoubtedly involved the recognition that the bishop of Rome (in addition to being the supreme arbiter in matters of faith) could discharge functions which no lesser ecclesiastical authority could perform – the creation of episcopal sees, for example, or the deposition of bishops – but such exceptional powers, required only infrequently, were a very different matter from papal intervention in the everyday life of local churches.

Such novel notions brought no confusion to the English church in William's lifetime, partly because the papacy, out of appreciation for the efforts of the king and Archbishop Lanfranc to enforce decent standards of order and discipline, did not press its views to the point of open dispute, and partly because English churchmen lacked sympathetic understanding and probably even simple knowledge of what those views were and the arguments in support of them. Some of the customary restrictions which William imposed on the clergy helped to ensure that the papacy was kept at arm's length: if prelates were summoned to attend the papal court or general councils they could not obey without his licence; he would not allow anyone to receive a letter from the pope unless it had first been shown to him; he would not allow papal legates to visit his dominions without his permission; even the recognition of a newly-elected bishop of Rome had to await the king's approval.[1]

Z. N. Brooke argued that such restrictions constituted a 'barrier' interposed to prevent 'papal interference' in the ecclesiastical affairs of the Anglo-Norman realm, and that in affirming these rules William's successors were concerned to maintain such a 'barrier'.[2] But the Conqueror's rules were not a set of absolute prohibitions: they were restrictions against contact with Rome without his approval. The

---

[1] Cf. *ibid.*, 10; Hugh the Chantor, 108; Anselm, *Opera*, IV, 106. For recent discussions of William I's ecclesiastical policy, *see* Douglas, *William the Conqueror*, 317–45; Cantor, *Church, Kingship, and Lay Investiture in England*, 29–34.

[2] Brooke, *The English Church and the Papacy*, Pt 2.

qualification is important and renders the metaphor of a 'barrier' inapposite and misleading. It would be more accurate to say that the Conqueror interposed a net or sieve. His rules amounted to an insistence that in certain matters he must be consulted, and a claim to exercise a discretionary power of veto. It is possible that the Conqueror, wishing to insulate his realms from the revolution at Rome, applied his rules in a way that had the effect of creating something akin to a barrier, but even if this is true it cannot be assumed that his successors, in adopting his rules, necessarily adopted an identical intention or sought to create a similar effect. Much, in fact, in the life of the English Church was to depend on the way kings chose to exercise the discretionary power they claimed, and in the event the continued enforcement of the customs of the Conqueror was not incompatible with moving, to some extent, with the theological times.

However William the Conqueror looked upon these restrictive customs it can hardly be argued that Henry I regarded them as designed to hold the Church in his dominions fast in its traditional mould. Though Henry instructed one pope after another in the customs of his realm in matters ecclesiastical, insisted upon his right to enforce them, and did so without hesitation, a profound change nonetheless overtook Anglo-papal relations and the attitudes of Anglo-Norman churchmen during his reign.

The notion of lay theocracy which had informed the attitudes and actions of William I and Archbishop Lanfranc was largely abandoned. Exponents of it were not wanting, and its language continued to colour royal actions and pronouncements for several generations, but there is little sign that either William II or Henry I regarded it as an essential ingredient in monarchial authority.[1] The issue was posed squarely by the papacy in its attempt to erase the habit of centuries by prohibiting bishops from receiving the symbols of their office at the hands of a lay ruler. Henry I's response to papal pressure was negotiation, not the confrontation of ideologies, and in the compromise that negotiation procured, he showed himself ready to abandon any show of conferring episcopal authority.

[1] e.g. King William Rufus deferred to Anselm's argument that if he were to receive the *pallium* from the king's hand it would appear that it was in his gift rather than St Peter's, and allowed the bishop who brought it from Rome to lay it on the altar at Canterbury, from whence the archbishop took it up, Eadmer, *Historia Novorum*, 71–2. The same was done by Archbishop Ralph in 1115, *ibid.*, 230. Henry I seems to have raised no objection to a change in the coronation *ordo* which diminished the implication that at his anointing the king acquired sacerdotal authority, Cantor. *op. cit.*, 139–46.

By the end of Henry I's reign, dealings with the papal curia and papal intervention in the affairs of the regional church had become an accepted part of its everyday life – still, certainly, not so common as both were to become as the century progressed, but nonetheless representing a transformation of the situation in the Conqueror's day. Sometimes a change startled contemporaries: as when a papal legate was allowed to tour the country at will and to hold a council at London.[1] The two notorious and protracted disputes of the period arising from Archbishop Anselm's acceptance of the papal ban on the investiture of bishops by the lay ruler, and the resistance of successive archbishops of York to Canterbury's demand for an oath of obedience, inevitably involved close dealings with the papal court. English ecclesiastics began to go there quite frequently as exiles, litigants, witnesses, or royal envoys.[2] The exiled Archbishop Anselm, when not residing with that assiduous exponent of high-Gregorian ideals, Hugh of Fleury, archbishop of Lyons, spent much time living near the pope 'and having, as it were, a common establishment'.[3] Archbishop Thurston of York, unable to return to England for having accepted consecration at the pope's hands contrary to the king's wishes, spent many months in the pope's company 'like a cardinal or chaplain'. The members of the curia came to seem to him like 'colleagues and messmates' and 'in councils, trials, and judgements, he was, as it were, one of themselves and in almost all their secrets'.[4] It would be hard to imagine a more radical training in the higher flights of papal policy for an erstwhile royal clerk, who had known the favour of William Rufus and the trust of Henry I.

The disputes also evoked a stream of papal letters to England, and the appearance of full transcripts (even of letters addressed to the king) in the writings of Eadmer and Hugh the Chantor shows that little if any attempt can have been made to suppress knowledge even of those that gave clear expression to unwelcome views, or set out in detail the arguments against traditional practices.[5] How far such letters set English churchmen thinking along new lines about the relations of Church,

---

[1] Hugh the Chantor, 121: 'The legate, having gone about and through England almost to the Scottish border, celebrated a council at London . . . a thing which no Roman legate had ever done in the time of either William.'

[2] e.g., Hugh the Chantor, 13, 47, 50, 68, 71, 74, 82, 111, 121f.

[3] Eadmer, *Historia Novorum*, 112.

[4] Hugh the Chantor, 84, 91, 81.

[5] Cf., e.g., Eadmer, *Historia Novorum*, 128–32. According to Eadmer (*op. cit.*, 137) Henry did on one occasion attempt to keep the contents of a papal letter secret, but this led people to assume that it was not to his liking, and 'the more carefully it was then kept secret, the more widely it was published abroad a few days later'.

State, and papacy can only be a matter for conjecture. Their interest for an understanding of the royal ecclesiastical policy lies in their apparently open dissemination. It would seem that the king harboured no narrow fears about the contamination of his subjects by outside influences, for he might, if he had wished, have done more than he did to restrict knowledge of them. Hugh the Chantor tells an instructive anecdote: an informer told the king that Archbishop Thurston had received a latter from Rome, and the king, annoyed that the archbishop had not, as custom required, asked his leave before accepting it, summoned Thurston to come to court and explain himself; but then the king forgot about it, and the archbishop himself had to remind him of the letter and reveal its contents.[1] Clearly the king adhered to his restrictive rules, but the mesh of the sieve was fairly wide.

More indicative, however, of a change in Anglo-papal relations than the numerous letters about the two great disputes which inevitably involved correspondence with Rome, is a papal letter on a trivial matter which Eadmer thought to copy into his *Historia Novorum* because he hoped 'it may in the future be of use to someone in dealing with a like matter'. The letter is addressed to the bishop and clergy of the church of Exeter and bids them respect the tradition which required monks to be buried within the precincts of their monastery and desist from preventing the monks of St Martin of Battle in the city from following so ancient and laudable a practice.[2] In the very triviality of the subject of this letter lies its importance. In appealing to the pope to intervene on their behalf, the monks of Exeter have absorbed the notion, still as yet novel, that the papal court will hear any cause, not simply those that lie beyond the competence of lesser ecclesiastical jurisdictions or which are referred to it on appeal from other courts – that, as the canon lawyers put it, the pope was universal ordinary. Precious as it is as an early example of papal intervention in the minor disputes of distant churches, it does not stand alone as an indication of a new readiness of English churchmen to turn to Rome for assistance. In the late 1120s Bishop Urban of Llandaff carried to Rome a lawsuit over the boundaries of his diocese – an awkward matter to settle at a great distance from the disputed lands and in the absence of competent witnesses, and, as Mrs Cheney has remarked, not the kind of case that would readily be taken to the papal courts if the idea of appealing to Rome had not become fairly well established.[3] And in addition to taking their causes to the

---

[1] Hugh the Chantor, 108, 110.   [2] Eadmer, *Historia Novorum*, 136–7.

[3] Mary Cheney, 'The Compromise of Avranches and the spread of canon law in England', 178–9.

papal court the subjects of King Henry I, in ever increasing numbers, applied to it for bulls of protection and privilege, seeking to put churches and abbeys directly under papal jurisdiction.[1]

Yet this contact with Rome and the acceptance of the papacy as a factor in the ordinary life of the regional church went on within the framework of the restrictive rules that King Henry I not only inherited from his father's reign but frequently applied. Archbishop Thurston asked many times for permission to go to Rome and was regularly refused it.[2] He was reminded of the custom that no one should accept a letter from the papacy without the king's knowledge and permission.[3] The canons of the Council of London of 1125 were issued, as the archbishop is careful to state, with the king's approval.[4] The king prevented one legate from entering England and showed another every courtesy except cooperation in his mission.[5] He told Pope Calixtus II plainly when he met him at Gisors in 1119 that by English custom papal legates were welcome only when they came at the king's request to deal with matters which were beyond the competence of the local hierarchy.[6]

Examples are numerous of the application of the Conqueror's customs in ecclesiastical affairs from the later as well as the early years of Henry I's reign, and leave no doubt as to his persistent intention to maintain them. Yet there can equally be no doubt that they were applied strictly *ad hoc* and for what the king considered good cause without any general intention to isolate his realms from the rest of Christendom or to insulate it from papal 'interference'. Certainly their application frequently obstructed papal dealings with the English Church; but it is significant of Henry's attitude to the papacy that he was most anxious to secure recognition of the legitimacy of the customs from successive popes, and, it would seem, was not denied it. We learn, for example, from Eadmer that in 1104 a royal envoy at Rome sought that 'the pope should with the authority of the apostolic see confirm to King Henry all the customs and usages of his father and brother'. After the envoy had presented arguments in favour of the concession, some members of the curia said that what they had heard 'must be admitted to be reasonable and that the wishes of a man of such eminence

---

[1] Cf., e.g., Cantor, *op. cit.*, 314–16. Cf. also Eadmer's defamatory anecdote about Bishop Herbert of Norwich (*Historia Novorum*, 132–3): in journeying to Rome as a royal envoy the bishop secured the annulment of a papal bull which had conferred on the abbey of Bury St Edmunds immunity from episcopal jurisdiction.

[2] Hugh the Chantor, 39, 47, 52, 61. For other examples of the operation of this rule *see ibid.*, 27, 36, 57, 62, 66, 68.

[3] *Ibid.*, 108.

[4] Eadmer, *Historia Novorum*, 141–2.

[5] *Ibid.*, 239, 295–6.

[6] *Ibid.*, 258.

should on no account be disregarded', and the pope, 'while altogether prohibiting the investiture of churches, granted the king a number of other usages which his father had had'.[1] In 1119 the king personally requested Pope Calixtus II to concede to him 'all the customs that his father had had in England and Normandy'.[2] And when declining to allow legate Peter to pursue his commission in England in 1121 the king told him that he did so in virtue of customs conceded by the apostolic see.[3] When, in 1164, Henry II submitted the Constitutions of Clarendon for confirmation by the pope he did so, unwisely as it turned out, but quite in accord with the policy of his grandfather.

Henry I, it would seem, regarded his status *vis-à-vis* the papacy as analogous to that of a feudal franchise holder. The rights he claimed were exceptional indeed, but they were to be thought of as privileges granted by one who had the authority to make such a grant; and in seeking confirmation of his 'liberty' or 'immunity' the king tacitly disavowed any intention of asserting independence, for the franchise holder enjoys a dependent liberty.[4]

For William the Conqueror, it may be, the customs were valuable for their own sake as an expression of royal authority in the Church; but for Henry I their value seems to have been purely practical. Their justification was that they protected royal interests; and in this they were on a par, precisely, with rules enforced against the tenants-in-chief, such as the prohibition on them marrying off their sons and daughters without royal consent. The necessity of securing the king's consent before receiving papal letters or appealing to the Roman court, ensured that the king had direct knowledge of what was afoot and gave him a chance to consult the interests of the Crown. The discretionary power of veto implicit in these rules enabled him either to parry a threat to those interests or to impose delays while he prepared a countermove or opened negotiations.[5]

The papacy's acceptance of the privileged position of the king of England (though doubtless reluctant and certainly only provisional)

---

[1] Eadmer, *Historia Novorum*, 152–4.

[2] *Ibid.*, 258, cf. Hugh the Chantor, 78–9.

[3] Eadmer, *Historia Novorum*, 295. A papal legate is said to have granted William Rufus that no papal legate should be sent into England without his permission, and that papal letters should not be accepted without his consent, Hugh de Flavigny, *Chronicon*, *Monumenta Germaniae Historica: Scriptores*, VIII, 475.

[4] The suggestion was first made by Davis, 'England and Rome in the middle ages', 115.

[5] Cf., e.g., his intervention in the dispute between Canterbury and York, Hugh the Chantor, 121–6, and his intervention in Archbishop Thurstan's attempt to assert jurisdiction over Glasgow, *ibid.*, 129.

was made easier because Henry I showed himself reasonable in the exercise of discretionary power and was not disposed to see a threat to royal interests in every change that the spirit of reform provoked. Henry I was far from being the ideal ruler the papacy might have prayed for, but he was a blessing beside the awful example of the German emperors. It could always be said of him that he protected his interests by negotiation and compromise, not by withdrawing his allegiance from St Peter's rightful successor in favour of an anti-pope. Henry, for his part, while not an active reformer like his father, lent his support to those who were striving for decency and order in the Church. The canons of the Council of London of 1102, to which he gave his approval, would have gladdened the heart of Pope Gregory VII himself, and the royal clerk who compiled the *Leges Henrici* could quote that prop of the reforming programme, the *Pannormia* of Ivo of Chartres, without any sense of disloyalty or incongruity.[1] What the king was concerned to guard against, however, was change getting out of hand. The 'customs' established by his father provided just the control mechanism that he needed.

At the very beginning of his reign Henry I was faced with a crisis which threatened to undermine the Anglo-Norman state William the Conqueror had created in England. Archbishop Anselm, in exile from the bitter persecution of William Rufus, had attended the Easter Council of 1099 in St Peter's at Rome, and had heard Pope Urban himself pronounce anathemas against laymen who invested clergy with churches, clergy who so received churches, bishops who consecrated them, and all clergy who did homage to laymen for ecclesiastical estates. The prohibition of lay investiture had been a staple ingredient of papal pronouncements for twenty years, although there is no sign that it had as yet penetrated to England. The ban on homage on the other hand had not been heard before the latter years of Urban II's pontificate, but it was a logical culmination of the radical reformers' desire to detach the clergy from all secular obligations. For Urban its desirability was reinforced by a heightened sense of the sacramental functions of the priesthood: the hands of priests, he argued, were more privileged than those of any angel, for in the sacrament of the altar they resurrected their Lord; could it be right that hands so honoured should be made subject to hands contaminated by plunder and the shedding of blood? Such a thing was an abomination.[2] For Anselm, the man of obedience,

<hr/>

[1] Cf. Cantor, *op. cit.*, 277–8.

[2] Eadmer, *Historia Novorum*, 114. For the struggle over lay investiture in England *see* Southern, *St Anselm and his Biographer*, 63–80, and Cantor, *op. cit.*

Urban's anathemas left him no choice but to refuse homage to Henry I, and to decline to consecrate the bishops the new king had created. Pope Paschal II was adamant that it must be so: his letters to the king harped on the intolerable impiety of lay investiture. The king, however, fixed instead upon the prohibition of homage: to concede this point, he said, would be to forfeit half his kingdom.[1] He was exaggerating – the ecclesiastical tenants-in-chief held about a quarter of the land of England – but the exaggeration was pardonable. After years of tortuous negotiations and delays – carefully engineered by the king – a compromise was reached which separated the two things: the king gave up the ceremony of investiture but retained the homage of bishops and abbots who held lands of the Crown. The king's surrender of the right of investiture may be seen as a turning point in the long history of theocratic monarchy; but, if anything, the papal concession of the right of the king to take homage from his clergy was even more momentous. It meant the abandonment of the attempt at a clear separation of clergy and laity: henceforth the line of separation was to be drawn instead between the spiritual and secular aspects of the clerical *persona*. The sharp distinction between the Church and the World harboured by the revolutionaries of the Gregorian era now dimmed, and the clergy found themselves with dual loyalties to Church and State – loyalties that were demanding but yet ill-defined. There were infinite possibilities of dispute about what was secular and what was spiritual, but the history of Church and State for the rest of the middle ages was to be less one of the major clashes than of relatively minor buffetings leading to the gradual definition and adjustment of a complex relationship.

In coping with this situation Henry I and his successors could draw a comforting lesson from the course of the so-called Investiture Contest. It had strikingly revealed that despite the emphatic and even peremptory tone of papal edicts, the papacy was not in fact a monolithic organisation whose commands had either to be accepted submissively or repudiated at peril. Paschal II, like Urban II, had regarded the homage of ecclesiatics to the laity as an abomination: 'It is intolerable,' he wrote to Anselm 'that a clerk who has been received into the order of God and has advanced beyond the dignity of laymen should do homage to a layman for earthly wealth.'[2] Yet he had retreated; and he retreated because he failed to carry the papal curia with him. It is easy, when reviewing the development of papal government in the middle ages, to see in it a single line of policy developed with clarity and pursued with

[1] Eadmer, *Historia Novorum*, 120.
[2] Anselm, *Opera*, IV, 126–9, letter no. 223.

consistency; but the reality was otherwise. Despite superficial appearances and theoretical discussions to the contrary, the Church was in fact managed by the collective leadership of the papal curia, a collective leadership which reflected many shades of opinion and attitude. A pope might publicly speak his mind, but policy was actually shaped by prolonged internal debate which often led to the triumph of compromise over principle, and even the repudiation of a pope's pronouncements.[1] If men of the twelfth century learned to speak of papal authority in unequivocal terms, they also learned to expect that its exercise might produce effects which were neither consistent nor permanent. It produced an ambivalence of mind in some of them. John of Salisbury will in one work hesitate to criticise Rome, 'which by the high authority of God is the parent and nursing mother of faith and life and, fortified by privilege from heaven, can neither be judged nor blamed of men,' while in another he will dismiss with scorn the work of a particular pope. 'I am at a loss to explain,' he writes in his *Memoirs of the Papal Court*, 'why so many of Eugenius's decisions were revoked, unless for these two reasons: first that he had merited it by so readily revoking the judgements of his predecessors, not to mention his fellow-bishops, and secondly that he was too ready to rely on his personal opinion in imposing sentences.'[2] Hence the necessity of negotiation and persistence. We should guard against the assumption that conflict implies a challenge to papal authority. The *conflictus* is the medieval method of discussion: in the schools, in the exchequer, in the papal court.

If the king had to reckon with the papacy as an important and increasingly active, if somewhat erratic, factor in ecclesiastical life, so too did his bishops. And here again, acceptance of papal supremacy was not necessarily accompanied by blind submission to every papal edict. The resistance of the bishops was, it is true, compromised by their greater vulnerability to papal displeasure, and by a growing consciousness of the corporate identity of all clergy. Even the more secular-minded of the bishops could be moved by St Paul's proclamation that 'the Church should be free'; but although the papacy was teaching that this ambiguous slogan meant that the corporate body of the clergy should be free

---

[1] Cf. Southern, *St Anselm and His Biographer*, 167, 172–3; White, 'The Gregorian ideal and St Bernard of Clairvaux', 321ff.

[2] John of Salisbury, *Policraticus*, VIII, ch. 17 (ed. Webb, II, 354), *Historia Pontificalis*, 51. Cf. his sharp strictures on Pope Eugenius III's absolution of the count of Vermandois from an excommunication incurred for bigamy, *Historia Pontificalis*, 12–13.

from lay interference, few bishops could for long remain unaware that the corollary of the papal argument was greater centralisation of the Church, and the substitution for lay interference of papal interference – with, as its consequence, the subversion and diminution of time-honoured episcopal jurisdiction. The twelfth century indeed sees the rise in an acute form of that problem of the relationship of the bishop of Rome to all other bishops of the Roman obedience which has persisted until the twentieth century. One of the results of the emergence of the problem in the twelfth century was a curiously ambivalent attitude of the hierarchy to the papacy; and Europe was to be treated to the spectacle of bishops who would hasten to Rome in furtherance of their own interests, but who would be equally ready to put obstacles in the way of papal mandates they did not like, or seek, as the lay power so often did, to circumvent them by ingenuity.

The invasion of episcopal authority was the most disturbing but not the only disadvantage of unfettered papal supremacy. The papacy had begun to encourage appeals to itself as universal ordinary before it had developed an adequate machinery for coping with them, and abuse of the primitive procedures to frustrate the ends of justice or delay decisions indefinitely provoked criticisms of the papal curia which are almost as commonplace as complaints about its venality.[1] Moreover, papal intervention could work to confuse or complicate situations, since the papacy, always more mindful of the judgement of history than the criticism of contemporaries, would, if uncertain of its ground or of the most expedient policy to pursue, speak with Delphic ambiguity or procrastinating indecisiveness.[2]

No one in England was sooner or more acutely aware of such disadvantages than the archbishops of Canterbury. The successors of St Augustine stood heir to a tradition, jealously guarded and assiduously fostered by the undying corporation of the monks of the cathedral church. This tradition taught that the British Isles had always stood apart as an entity detached from the Mediterranean-centred civilisation of ancient and early medieval times – it was another world, an *alter orbis*. Gregory the Great was held to have acknowledged – and sanctified – this tradition by the authority over the whole British Church

---

[1] For illustrations of the weaknesses in the system for exercising papal jurisdiction, *see* Cheney, *From Becket to Langton*, 63ff.

[2] For an example of this difficulty in a major issue *see* the accounts of the dispute between Canterbury and York given from opposite sides by Eadmer and Hugh the Chantor; for another *see* Southern, *op. cit.*, 126–7: the abbot of Fécamp had the greatest difficulty in obtaining an answer to the question of whether an altar should be reconsecrated if it had been moved.

which he entrusted to St Augustine.[1] It was a tradition fortified by Anglo-Saxon pretensions to an *imperium* of all Britain, and given concrete expression by Archbishop Lanfranc's virtual assertion of patriarchal status for Canterbury. There was no suggestion of independence of Rome in this, indeed Bede's *Ecclesiastical History* fostered the idea that the Church in England was in a special sense the daughter of Rome; but implicit in manifestations of the tradition was the notion that the archbishop of Canterbury inherited a delegated papal authority throughout the British Isles. Eadmer puts the notion clearly when he relates (not without suspicion of fabrication) that when Archbishop Anselm was in exile, Pope Urban II introduced him to the curia as 'one who is almost our equal, being as it were pope and patriarch of the *alter orbis*'.[2]

Unfortunately for the proponents of this tradition the authority claimed was never clearly acknowledged by all of those supposedly subject to it, particularly in Wales, Scotland, and Ireland. The archbishops of York resolutely refused to accept a permanently subordinate position, and there was the problem posed by the arrival of papal legates armed with an authority more direct and more concrete who threatened to supplant, if only temporarily, the authority the archbishops of Canterbury claimed.[3]

Archbishop Anselm, a man by personal inclination and monkish habit disposed to welcome papal commands as an opportunity to demonstrate Christian obedience, was pushed from his inclination by the papacy itself. The papal retreat from the prohibition of clerical homage, for which he had endured years of exile, left him with a sense of betrayal. The ground which he took to be so firm had shifted under his feet.[4] The papacy's shufflings and evasions in the matter of the dispute between Canterbury and York prompted him to the extremity of declaring that if the papacy gave comfort and support to the archbishop of York, 'I could on no account remain in England, for I neither ought nor can suffer the primacy of our Church to be destroyed in my lifetime'.[5] His

[1] Cf. Southern, 'The Canterbury forgeries'.

[2] Eadmer, *Vita Sancti Anselmi*, 105 and n. 2. Cf. Anselm, *Opera*, V, 400, letter of the Pope to Anselm: 'we behold in you the venerable *persona* of St Augustine the apostle of the English'.

[3] Eadmer, writing of the arrival of a papal legate in 1101, relates that 'all were astonished, as everyone knew that it was unheard of in Britain that anyone should exercise authority over them as a representative of the pope save only the archbishop of Canterbury', *Historia Novorum*, 126. Cf. Anselm, *Opera*, IV, 2, letter no. 214.

[4] Cf. Southern, *St Anselm and His Biographer*, 170–9.

[5] Anselm, *Opera*, III, 152, letter no. 451; Southern, *op. cit.*, 135–8.

protests over the despatch of a papal legate to England induced the pope to promise not to send another with an authority over Canterbury while he remained archbishop.[1]

With such an example before them it is small wonder that his lesser successors welcomed the royal 'customs' as a mechanism for the protection of their 'rights' and jurisdiction as well as the Crown's, and turned for help to the king when they failed to get it, or despaired of getting it, or preferred not to seek it from Rome. When in 1116 a papal legate arrived in Normandy and showed King Henry I his letters of commission for England, Archbishop Ralph of Canterbury hurried over to remind the king of 'the ancient custom and liberty of the realm', and the legate got no further; and when three years later Henry met the pope at Gisors and talked with him of the customs of the realm, he defended the proper jurisdiction of the native hierarchy against the intrusion of legates.[2] Moreover, although the king might act in church affairs with an assumption of authority that high papalists would altogether deny him, he could get things done where Rome could only hope and plead.[3] Only the king could manage, when he wished, to still the noise and rancour of Canterbury's dispute with York.[4] Henry himself proposed, and the pope accepted, a neat solution to the problem of Canterbury's authority: legatine powers were conferred on the archbishop by the papacy. Not that Canterbury could be entirely satisfied with this: just as the king's claim to a privileged status *vis-à-vis* the papacy needed frequent renewal, so too did the archbishop's status as legate, but it secured protection for 'customs' and 'rights' while avoiding the big issues of principle and ideology. In this it may be said to typify Henry I's approach to the ecclesiastical problems of his day. This was the attitude, this was the policy, that Henry II was to take as his model.

The last decade or so of Henry I's reign is marked by a peaceability and deference to the king's wishes in matters ecclesiastical, which, though it differed greatly from William the Conqueror's secure dominance, probably appealed to Henry II both as proper and as his birthright. It was Henry I's achievement that the traditional royal

---

[1] Southern, *op. cit.*, 31; Cantor, *op. cit.*, 150-1.

[2] Eadmer, *Historia Novorum*, 239, 258.

[3] On the matter of the enforcement of clerical celibacy, Eadmer remarks, somewhat ruefully it seems, that 'the king, whom many fear more than God, bound them by his law, whether they liked it or not, to become, at least in the sight of men, upholders of the Council of London', *Historia Novorum*, 213.

[4] Cf. Hugh the Chantor, 29-30, 109, 111, 122-3, 130.

habit of intervention in Church affairs had suffered no significant diminution; but the big change from William I's day was that papal intervention was now accepted as its normal concomitant. He seemed to have established a convenient *modus vivendi*, but the absence of contentious issues in the working relations of king, Anglo-Norman hierarchy, and papacy, in the later years of the reign was something of an illusion – an illusion born of special circumstances which the king profited from but had not created and could not control.

One of these circumstances was the state of canonical studies. Some of the Gregorian reformers had seen with acute perception that canon law could supply weapons both for the defence of the *Libertas Ecclesiae* and for its extension. It was in fact to do much more than this: it proved to be a powerful instrument for the spread of papal jurisdiction; it provided a rationale for changing papal primacy into papal monarchy; and in the hands of its practitioners throughout Christendom it presented a corrosive challenge to the methods, content, and applicability of folk and feudal law. At the end of the eleventh century it had been difficult to say what the Church's law was, for it was uncodified and confused – a core of pious or partisan fabrications surrounded by a pulp of local custom. Some of the most brilliant intellects of the early twelfth century applied themselves to systematising, rationalising, and interpreting the evidence for it. But it cannot be said that it was yet possible, by Henry I's death, even to perceive what canonical jurisprudence was one day to become. Indeed the early canonists probably exacerbated confusion and rendered students even less certain than before, by discovering conflicts in the evidence and by revealing the complexities of the problems involved. Despite, then, the intellectual excitement and interest it aroused, canon law in the early twelfth century remained an academic pursuit which touched the ordinary life of the Church little if at all. Canon law could still have been ignored in the 1120s in a way that would have been hazardous in the 1140s and impossible in the 1160s.

Even more crucial than the state of canon law, however, was the state of the papal curia. Behind the serene and grandiloquent phraseology of papal letters lurked muddle and doubt. This was, principally, the result of a strong reaction against Gregorian ideas. The reaction took two forms. There were those who deplored the political aggression of Gregorianism. Such disapproval had always been strong, but it had formerly dissipated and discredited itself in support of imperial antipopes, or had stood aloof until the noise of battle died away. But sweeping back from the provinces to Rome in the 1120s it spoke with a louder voice now that some of the consequences of violent Gregorianism had manifested themselves. Even those who professed undivided loyalty to the ideal of papal ascendancy could boggle at the bland, or blind, assumption of an Urban or a Paschal that the world must be broken apart in order to liberate the Church. Doubts about the assertions of Gregorians who adopted the extreme views of Cardinal Humbert are reflected in the political theories of the mid twelfth century, many of the most prominent of which defend a positive, if circumscribed, contribution from the lay power to the life and direction of the Church.[1]

The other form of the reaction was promoted by those, chiefly monks, who, while persuaded of the vital and central role of the papacy, deplored its concern with temporal authority, and desired to make it a power-house of moral and spiritual influence. With the loud voice and dominating personality of St Bernard of Clairvaux behind it, this point of view elbowed its way into the curia in the 1130s. The monument to Bernard's influence on the Europe of his day is the general recognition accorded to his candidate, Innocent II, after the double election to the apostolic see in 1130. The respectable and properly elected Anacletus was overborne by the Bernadine protégé; but the victory of monastic idealists was soon eroded by the pervasive temptations and pressures of the papal office. Power readily corrupts the most ascetic of intentions. But the clamour of rival attitudes and rival candidates kept the papacy introverted for a decade, and more than usually solicitous of the favour of princes.[2]

Canon law and papal policy had, however, begun to clarify themselves by the time of Henry II's accession. It was the work of the great canonists of the early twelfth century to convert the detritus of a thousand years of Church law-making into a comprehensible legacy. Their efforts reached an apogee and a fulfilment with the appearance, about 1140, of Gratian's *Concordia Discordantium Canonum*. This work almost immediately joined the select band of writings universally accorded a short title or nickname: to the twelfth century Gratian's work was known as the *Decreta*, and to all succeeding generations as the *Decretum*. It provided a systematic exposition of a vast corpus of ancient law, and did it so thoroughly that further attempts at codifying the past were unnecessary. Thereafter the emphasis in canonical studies shifts from

---

[1] These political theories were a consequence of, and did not create, the changed climate of opinion. For a useful summary supported by quotations, including several from unpublished MSS, *see* Pacaut, *La Théocratie*, 114–36, 251ff.

[2] There has been much confusion among historians as to the relationship of St Bernard to Gregorian ideas. I am persuaded by White, 'The Gregorian ideal and St Bernard of Clairvaux'.

compilation and codification to commentary and exegesis. But the *Decretum* was far more than a canonical encyclopaedia, for Gratian used his texts as raw material for refining out legal principles and constructing a rational system of canonical jurisprudence. No longer could Roman Civil law claim to be unique in its comprehensiveness and scientific formulation.

The importance of Gratian in the history and development of canon law is beyond question. The influence of the *Decretum* (or, more likely, potted versions – *Summae* – of it) on young clerks who encountered canon law in the schools or the *familia* of an up-to-date bishop is harder to assess but as likely as not just as important. One of the chief lessons that it taught was the justification and necessity for papal legislative sovereignty. The principal problem facing the early canonists was that of reconciling contradictory or conflicting edicts promulgated in the past. They came to acknowledge that some law-making was better than other law-making and then had to establish a proper principle of discrimination. They were obliged to recognise two kinds of law: necessary law, such as that propounded in scripture, which they regarded as immutable; and convenient law, which the Church formulated in the interests of discipline and the cure of souls, and which might be varied according to circumstances of time and place. They had to draw distinctions between principles of law and particular applications of principles. They had to recognise the inevitability of dispensation from the rigour of the law, relaxations of it *pro temporum necessitate* or *pro personarum qualitate*. But, pursuing in this way the resolution of apparent contradictions in the substantive law of the past, they were brought to feel the necessity for an authoritative source of law, an agency for the definitive resolution of doubts, and a final control upon the exercise of dispensatory powers. The conclusion of scholars such as Ivo of Chartres, Bernold of Constance, and Gratian was that such functions were inherent in the papal office.[1]

The influence of such studies, and especially of the *Decretum*, was probably, then, on the one hand to make the clergy of the mid twelfth century conscious of their membership of a corporate body, a *societas*, whose constitutional rules could be authoritatively defined; and on the other hand to make them aware that the particular local customs that

[1] The early history of the canon law has in recent years called forth numerous studies. For short summaries see the prefatory chapters to Duggan, *Twelfth Century Decretal Collections*, and *The Canon Law of the Church of England: being the report of the Archbishops' Commission on canon law*; for more extensive treatments *see* Fournier and Le Bras, *Histoire des Collections Canonique en Occident*; van Hove, *Prolegomena ad Codicem Iuris Canonici*; and Plöchl, *Geschichte des Kirchenrechts*.

enfolded them might only be inherited concessions to the hardness of times past. If custom conflicted with a canonical principle, newly appreciated or authoritatively defined, no amount of royal appeal to past acceptance by the Church would suffice to stifle criticism. It might be that continued departure from strict principle could be justified, but the judgement of such necessity would henceforth be held to lie with St Peter's vicar.

The moot point in the middle of the twelfth century was whether the papacy was capable, in practice, of discharging the functions with which the canonists endowed it. By the end of the century there were to be no doubts on the score: lawyer popes like Alexander III (1159–81) and Innocent III (1198–1216) both asserted and demonstrated its capability. With Alexander III, indeed, canon law and papal policy achieved a unity of purpose: legal sovereignty became both the ground of papal monarchy and the method of achieving it. Alexander III, however, succeeded to a papacy already reinvigorated by the short but influential pontificate of an Englishman who became pope as Adrian IV in 1154, a week or so before Henry of Anjou became king of England. Adrian IV brought to an end a generation of hesitancy at Rome – not all at once or by the declaration of a radical papal programme, but by the confidence and sense of purpose he imparted to papal activity. There is, it is true, not much in the conflict between him and Emperor Frederick Barbarossa that arouses sympathy for either side: it lacks the tragic proportions of the conflict between Gregory VII and Emperor Henry IV, and seems too contrived on foundations of prestige and politics; but Adrian's readiness to challenge and meet challenges is itself an indication of a new hardness in the papal line and of a boldness in making clear-cut decisions that would have startled the latter days of King Henry I.[1]

If a new assertiveness from Rome was one factor Henry II had to reckon with in his dealings with the Church, another was the effect of Stephen's reign. That the relations of Church and State established in Henry I's reign were compromised in Stephen's is beyond question, but in what ways precisely is not easy to assess. Stephen was not so ready to make concessions to the Church as is sometimes supposed. Even at the beginning of his reign, when the circumstances of his accession obliged

---

[1] Adrian IV awaits a modern biographer. For an important, although one-sided contribution see Ullmann, 'The pontificate of Adrian IV', and for a survey of his pontificate, Raymonde Foreville in *Histoire de l'Église*, ed. Fliche and Martin, IV, Pt II.

him to bid for clerical support, he was circumspect in making grants. His charter of 1136 promised 'freedom to holy Church', but like Henry I when making a similar grant in 1100, he interpreted freedom to mean particular liberties and the extent of the freedom he envisaged was defined in the clauses which followed. Though much more extensive than Henry's promises, and reflecting an awareness of canonical rectitude, they were formulated with cautious imprecision and ambiguity. In any case Stephen soon showed that he intended to have his way with the Church whenever it suited him to do so, and churchmen had to recognise that his promises were worthless.[1] Stephen's intention of perpetuating the old-established 'customs' is exemplified on more than one occasion: John of Salisbury, for example, tells us that he would not even allow a papal legate to pass through England on his way to Ireland, and that he avoided papal excommunication for forbidding the archbishop of Canterbury to attend the Lateran Council of 1148 only by the earnest pleas of the archbishop himself.[2] But Stephen's control of affairs, in Church as well as State, was undermined and impeded by political events; and in practice his interventions were fitful, sometimes interrupted, and not infrequently ineffective. It is possible that, in consequence, his interventions came to seem like arbitrary harassments in the proper conduct of ecclesiastical affairs by the clergy themselves, instead of a normal part of the working relations of Crown and Church – as under Henry I. If this surmise is correct, then Henry II had the difficult task of reducing to normality a situation that abnormality rendered intolerable, and to do it in the face of the clear opposition of a canon law much more clearly formulated and better appreciated than formerly.

Even more seriously hurtful to the Crown's position, however, was the clumsiness of Stephen's interventions and his failure to appreciate the real nature of his predecessor's policy and the foundations upon which it rested. In Henry I's hands the peculiar Anglo-Norman customs were a mechanism of control intended to protect vital royal interests, but applied with discrimination for clear reasons, and with little inclination to make a fuss about side-issues. The smooth operation of the mechanism was acknowledged to require papal acquiescence, and the resolution of

[1] Cf. William of Malmesbury, *Historia Novella*, 20: 'pene omnia . . . perperam mutavit'; Henry of Huntingdon, 258: 'Haec principaliter Deo vovit, et alia, sed nihil horum tenuit'. *See* also Saltman, *Archbishop Theobald*; Isabel Megaw, 'The ecclesiastical policy of Stephen . . . a reinterpretation'; Cronne, *The Reign of Stephen*, 125ff.; and for a discussion of Stephen's apparent renunciation of the issues of vacant sees, Margaret Howell, *Regalian Right in Medieval England*, 29–32. The text of Stephen's charter of 1136 is printed in Stubbs, *Select Charters*, 143–4.

[2] John of Salisbury, *Historia Pontificalis*, 6–7.

difficulties seen to depend upon close accord between the king and the native hierarchy. The functioning of Henry I's system demanded subtlety and fine judgement as well as firmness. Subtlety and fine judgement were qualities that Stephen lacked, and for firmness he substituted arbitrary acts of violence.[1] He appears to have had a crude conception of the Crown's established prerogatives as rights to be defended like pieces of property, with little consciousness of the wider ends they were designed to serve. He accepted the papacy much as Henry I had done, but gave no hint of recognising that the special relationship which Henry claimed needed frequent renewal and careful cultivation. His dealings with Rome were ham-handed and his enforcement of the ancient restrictions unnecessarily provocative. He antagonised the native clergy by his violent persecution of the bishops of Salisbury and Lincoln for reasons that are obscure but savour of personal animosity, and neglected either to cultivate supporters among the existing bishops, or to manipulate elections so as to secure the appointment of effective adherents. Though he defended the Crown's right to exercise a measure of control over elections to episcopal sees and the most important abbeys, he did so with little ulterior interest save that of trying, usually fruitlessly, to promote the interests of his numerous, and worthless, nephews.[2]

Stephen's greater concern with his *right* to participate in elections than with the *need* to participate is illustrated in the promotion of Theobald of Bec to the archbishopric of Canterbury in 1138: the proceedings were conducted in such a way that contemporary chroniclers could believe that King Stephen made Theobald archbishop, but the choice was in fact made by the monks of the cathedral priory, and accepted by the king, it would seem, for no better reason than that he had nothing to say against him.[3] Such indifference to so crucial an appointment is further marked in his acquiescence in the appointment of the bishop of Winchester to the legatine office and hence to overlordship of the two provinces of Canterbury and York. The bishop of Winchester, Henry of Blois, was Stephen's brother, and a man whose extraordinary ambitions were almost, but not quite, matched by his ability; but whatever justifications might be offered for Stephen's acceptance of his appointment as resident legate, the promotion of cordial relations between Church and State cannot have been one of

[1] Cf. Davis, 'What happened in Stephen's reign'.
[2] For episcopal elections during the reign *see* Saltman, *op. cit.*, 12–13, 90–126; Raymonde Foreville, *L'Église et la Royauté en Angleterre*, 9–13.
[3] Cf. Saltman, *op. cit.*, 7–13.

them, for the king and his brother differed in almost everything save a common desire for the preferment of scions of the House of Blois.[1]

In obtaining the legateship for Theobald's predecessor, King Henry had simultaneously ensured that Canterbury exercised the authority it craved and the Crown found convenient, short-circuited much of the bothersome discord with York, and interposed a tame papal representative for the unpredictable ones Rome had hitherto sent direct. In discarding these advantages, and at the same time humiliating Canterbury by the erection of one of its suffragans as a rival, Stephen revealed a shocking imperceptiveness and a deplorable lack of considered policy. Stephen's political weakness disfigured the superstructure of Henry I's Church–State edifice; his maladroit interventions called into question the validity of its design; the shallowness of his policy threatened to undermine its foundations.

Yet the reign was not without features that redounded, in the long run, to the benefit of the Crown, for it revealed some of the disadvantages of lax or spasmodic royal control of church affairs, and the lessons were to linger in the minds of men who were to live on through the crucial first two decades of Henry II's reign. The first and most obvious of these lessons was that the normal processes of ecclesiastical life could falter and fail when strong kingship was lacking even temporarily. The most striking illustration of this was in the diocese of Ely. The see of Ely had been created by Henry I's reign out of part of the sprawling and unwieldy see of Lincoln because, as Archbishop Anselm told the pope, 'one bishop is not enough for performing fully those duties which can only be performed by one of episcopal rank'. The intricate negotiations inseparable from such a project were facilitated by cooperation between archbishop, king and pope, and although Henry I exploited the resources of the new see, as he exploited others, to save the royal purse by securing the appointment as bishop of his treasurer, Nigel of Ely, the creation of the diocese could be seen as an example of the operation of Henry's *modus vivendi* with the Church at its best.[2] During Stephen's reign, however, the arrangements were wrecked and the see left crippled for many years as powerful laymen, unchecked by the Crown, intruded themselves into the bishop's estates. Papal denunciations were powerless to cure a situation which King Henry would not have tolerated for a month.[3]

---

[1] For Henry of Blois *see* especially Voss, *Heinrich von Blois*; Knowles, *Episcopal Colleagues of Archbishop Becket*, 34–7; Cronne, *The Reign of Stephen*, ch. 4.

[2] Eadmer, *Historia Novorum*, 195–6; Anselm, *Opera*, V, 388, letter no. 441.

[3] Cf. Miller, *The Abbey and Bishopric of Ely*, 167ff.

The second lesson, and one perhaps less expected, was that papal intervention in English ecclesiastical affairs, uncontrolled by a local authority, could be as disruptive as the interference of rapacious barons. The scene of the lesson was the archiepiscopal see of York.[1] In 1140 the chapter of York had to find a successor to Archbishop Thurston and encountered difficulties. One of its candidates was vetoed by King Stephen because of his kinship with the king of Scots – a perfectly proper use of the royal power of veto. Another of its choices, acceptable to the king, was vetoed by the pope, because the candidate wished to hold the archbishopric in conjunction with the abbacy of Fécamp. Again the veto was reasonable, though the papacy often winked at such a situation – indeed its legate in England, the bishop of Winchester, was also abbot of Glastonbury. That it stood upon the point this time was probably due to the influence of St Bernard, who acted on behalf of the strong Cistercian interests in the northern province. It was the interference of Cistercian abbots, far exceeding what was legitimate, that did most to prevent an easy solution to the problem of providing a pastor for York, for the Cistercians, with all the pious arrogance for which they were already becoming notorious, seem to have been convinced that no one short of a Cistercian monk could be adequate for the task.

At this point a king who appreciated ecclesiastical realities would have intervened to bring the parties to the election together in his chapel and by pressures subtle or open, and probably both, persuade them to fix their choice on some respectable if undistinguished candidate, as like as not some deserving royal clerk; but King Stephen contented himself with sending an oral message proposing the name of William FitzHerbert, one of his many nephews, already treasurer of the Church of York, and by general repute an amiable but idle young man. Accepted by a majority of the electors (though fiercely opposed by the rest), William hurried to the king and was invested with the temporalities of the see, a few days before the political situation was thrown into confusion by the defeat and capture of Stephen at Lincoln. The dissidents naturally appealed to Rome, accusing William of an unchaste life, simony, and intrusion; and in the absence of other voices from England which in normal circumstances might have been heard in such a matter, the issue was joined before the pope by William himself and a powerful party of Cistercians. The way was open for the untrammelled exercise of papal authority; but the opportunity only served to reveal with startling clarity how difficult it was for the papacy to get at facts

[1] For the story which follows *see* Knowles, 'The case of William of York'; Poole, 'The appointment and deprivation of St William, archbishop of York'.

and reach a firm decision in just the kind of critical and contentious issue for which its exercise of authority was most to be desired. The case dragged on for six years before William was declared deposed, and in that time he had secured consecration but been denied the bestowal of the *pallium* – the symbol of the right to exercise his archiepiscopal jurisdiction. The laity of the diocese were largely on William's side, and a party of enthusiasts had sought vengeance on his enemies by wrecking Fountains Abbey. A new election at York again threw up rival candidates, and the papacy intervened in favour of Henry Murdac, the Cistercian abbot of Fountains; but so great was the resentment of the local clergy that for over half of the six years he occupied the see he was unable to take up residence in his cathedral city. In the meantime, William FitzHerbert, matured by the controversy, retired, with a dignity and fortitude that were to be remembered to his honour, to the cathedral monastery at Winchester. In 1153 Murdac died and a new pope, Anastasius IV, putting magnanimity before respect for his predecessor's decisions, restored William to the archbishopric. A few weeks later William was dead and quick rumour accused an enemy in the chapter of having poisoned him. The trial of the accused, claimed by the church courts, dragged on well into the reign of Henry II and never reached a formal judgement, bringing yet more discredit upon the processes of ecclesiastical justice. Even this is not the end of a remarkable tale, for miracles were reported from William's tomb, and in 1227 he was canonised.

The fame of the persecuted archbishop of York, though clearly persistent in the north, was soon to be eclipsed by that of an even more dramatic story from Canterbury, yet it would not be surprising if it encouraged men to reflect that even royal management of episcopal elections might be preferable to the disorder which the papacy had been unable to prevent York suffering for ten years, and for which, indeed, it was partly to blame. Archbishop Theobald of Canterbury had wisely kept aloof from the unseemly wrangle in the north, but on Archbishop William's death he intervened to manage the next election firmly but discreetly – with the king's support and in his presence. In Roger de Pont l'Évêque, York acquired an archbishop of distinction and ability. The pope had no hand in the appointment, for considerable care was taken to make his intervention unnecessary.[1]

Clergy of moderate views asked, in the mid twelfth century, for their

---

[1] Saltman, *op. cit.*, 122–3; Raymonde Foreville, *op. cit.*, 13. In the see of Durham also there were severe disorders which only the intervention of Archbishop Theobald served to quieten, Scammel, *Hugh du Puiset*, 8–19.

opinion on the relations of Church and State, would commonly reply in some such phrases as 'Both are so bound together by the very necessity of their nature that each derives great strength from the other', or 'Kings cannot attain salvation without the church, nor can the church without royal protection obtain peace'.[1] Such anodyne remarks make little appeal to students of ecclesiastical ideologies; but to ordinary men of Henry II's reign, the nineteen winters of Stephen's had seemed to put their justification beyond dispute.

Several incidents of Stephen's later years reveal the trend of episcopal thinking. In 1148 the king incurred the justified displeasure of the papacy by his clumsy attempts to reassert, as part of his general recovery of authority, the ancient customs of the realm in the matter of contact with Rome. An interdict was pronounced on England. Almost to a man the English bishops ignored it.[2] They, like the lay barons, were weary of the *tempus werre*. A king recovering his power was rather to be encouraged than repulsed, even if some of his particular acts might be deplored. In John of Salisbury's phrase, 'the clergy preferred peace to duty'.[3] As King Stephen, anxious for the coronation of his son Eustace, showed himself more and more disposed to be cooperative, the bishops gladly sought his help in restoring order and discipline to a Church shaken in its life and morals as well as its property by years of political insecurity. The canons of the Council of 1151 speak frequently of royal authority; of papal authority never.[4] But the bishops were not prepared to extend their new-found cooperation with Stephen to the coronation of his son Eustace, for a surer prop of royal authority than he stood at hand in Henry of Anjou. When the succession question had first been raised, Cardinal Gregory of St Angelus advised Pope Eugenius to opt for Eustace rather than Henry, saying that it would be easier for a ram to be held by his horn than a lion by his tail. But the pope was not persuaded, and the English bishops were almost unanimous in preferring the lion.[5] The critical question which remained to be determined was how much of their coveted canonical freedom they were prepared to barter for the necessity of peace and the benefits of cooperation.

[1] Arnulf of Lisieux, *Letters*, 76, cf. 101; Ralph of Diceto, I, 335, and Rotrou, archbishop of Rouen to Pope Alexander III, *Materials for the History of Becket*, Epistolae, VII, 86.

[2] Cf. Saltman, *op. cit.*, 28–9.

[3] John of Salisbury, *Historia Pontificalis*, 46.

[4] Cf. Saltman, *op. cit.*, 33–6, 547–9.

[5] *Materials for the History of Becket*, Epistolae, VII, 242; cf. Saltman, *op. cit.*, 36ff.

Chapter 12

ARCHBISHOP THEOBALD

The first difficulty which any attempt to understand Henry II's ecclesiastical policy encounters is the contrast between the apparently amicable relations while Archbishop Theobald lived, and the sudden plunge into conflict after the elevation of Thomas Becket to Canterbury in 1162. It is not easy to decide if the inconsistency was real or only apparent, or, if there was an inconsistency, to account for it.

Z. N. Brooke plausibly suggested that although Henry II's basic objective was to re-establish full royal control over ecclesiastical affairs, he was in the early years of his reign inhibited by the debt of gratitude he owed to Archbishop Theobald and to the pope for the ease of his succession, that he could 'not act otherwise than with caution at first', and bided his time until he could acquire an archbishop more amenable to his purpose.[1] Many historians have accepted Brooke's interpretation without question; and certainly it seems that a politic respect for Theobald's influence was a factor in the situation, at least so far as England was concerned. Nevertheless there are grounds for suspecting that Brooke's explanation is at best inadequate. In the first place the province of Canterbury was only one among several ecclesiastical provinces covered or trenched upon by Henry II's wide dominions: there were seven in all, until the acquisition of Ireland added another four. Theobald's influence may be held to extend to the province of York in virtue of his office as papal legate for England, and because Archbishop Roger de Pont l'Évêque was his protégé, but the fingers of his influence did not stretch across the Channel. It could be argued that the possibility of Henry II controlling ecclesiastical affairs in the provinces of Bourges and Auch was too remote to be of any account, and not worth the trouble of trying; but that still leaves the important provinces of Rouen, Tours, and Bordeaux, which between them covered the heartland of Henry's continental dominions. Moreover there were, in parts at least of these provinces, traditions of control by the lay ruler upon which Henry could draw, which were barely less strong than the tradition

[1] Brooke, 'The effect of Becket's murder on papal authority in England', 215, *The English Church and the Papacy*, 199.

of the early Norman kings in England. To none of the continental archbishops did he owe any debt of gratitude, and upon none of them was he seriously dependent for political support. Nevertheless, Henry II's behaviour towards the Church in his continental dominions does not appear to have differed materially from his behaviour towards the Church in England.[1] Secondly, there is evidence which will not allow us to suppose that Henry avoided raising contentious issues of the relations of Church and State in his dealings with Archbishop Theobald, nor that, having raised them, he allowed Theobald to dictate his policy. That the contentious issues did not lead to open conflict must owe something at least to the flexibility of Theobald's responses to Henry's challenges.

Thomas Becket certainly would not have subscribed to the view that in the early years of the reign Henry was biding his time in his dealings with the Church. In a letter to the pope in 1170 he vigorously rebutted the charge of those who blamed his obstinate dogmatism as the cause of Henry's aggressive proclamation of the *avitae consuetudines*. On the contrary, he counterclaimed, Henry had from his first assumption of power assaulted the liberty of the Church as if by the right of inheritance (*quasi de jure hereditario*). Was I archbishop, he asked, when the king penalised the bishop of Exeter for entering an appeal to Rome by taking from him the wealthy chapelry of Bosham and giving it to Arnulf of Lisieux? And how did the bishop of Chichester fare when he cited papal letters in the suit against the abbot of Battle? Was he not bent to the king's will and obliged to make peace with the impenitent abbot in the royal court? And who was responsible for preventing Achard, bishop-elect of Séez, from taking possession of his see, even though his election had been confirmed by the pope? By what authority did the king then make Achard bishop of Avranches instead? And what of Froger, *non electus sed intrusus* into the see of Séez? All these things, claimed Becket, had taken place before his own promotion.[2] He had a case, for his charges, though tendentiously framed, are corroborated by independent testimony.[3] But although Becket was justified in claiming that before he became archbishop Henry's policy had revealed itself, the suggestion that this policy was one of brutal assault upon the Church's liberty should be treated with caution. Becket was always

---

[1] For a useful summary *see* Shaw, 'The ecclesiastical policy of Henry II on the continent'.

[2] Paraphrased from *Materials for the History of Becket*, Epistolae, VII, 241–3.

[3] Corroboration of the charge about the chapelry of Bosham is provided by the pipe rolls, e.g., Pipe Rolls 2–4 Henry II, 61; Pipe Roll 7 Henry II, 14; *see also* Arnulf of Lisieux, *Letters*, 174, note a, and Introduction, liv; for the other charges *see* below.

more concerned to win an argument than to clarify a situation, and a close examination of the evidence suggests that Henry's interferences with ecclesiastical freedom were not so blatant as Becket would have liked the pope to believe, or as at first glance they might appear.

For only one of the examples cited by Becket are the facts adequately known to us, and here, certainly, the impression left by the full story is somewhat different from that Becket sought to create. The attempt by the bishop of Chichester to assert jurisdiction over Battle Abbey, and the efforts of the monks there to defend their exemption from episcopal authority finds many parallels in the England, and indeed the Europe, of the time. Arguments over rights between bishops and monks, like those between bishops and archbishops, between king and bishops, or between king and pope, all reflected the intense interest of the twelfth century in the reappraisal of law and custom, and in the definition of spheres of jurisdiction. Newly appreciated principles clashed with the facts of history, and the needs of the past had all too often given rise to incompatible precedents. The attempt to discipline life with law was one of the noblest endeavours of twelfth-century Europe, but passionate litigation was an inevitable by-product of it.

Battle Abbey had a special claim upon the protection of the Crown, for it was founded by William the Conqueror in thanksgiving for the victory of Hastings: it was at once both a royal *Eigenkloster* and a Norman war-memorial.[1] King Stephen had professed his desire to maintain its rights as fully as those of the Crown itself.[2] And Richard de Lucy could declare before Henry II's court that the abbey was a symbol of that victory from which the king derived his title to the throne:

> Wherefore I maintain that the abbey ought to be held in high regard both by you and by all us Normans, inasmuch as it was on that spot that the most noble King William, by God's grace and with the aid of our ancestors, acquired the right from which you, my lord king, at present hold the crown of England by inheritance, and by which all of us have been richly endowed.[3]

Nevertheless the king hesitated to reject, at the abbot's request, the bishop's demand for canonical obedience until the facts had been thoroughly sifted, and delayed a consideration of the matter for many

---

[1] According to the abbey's chronicler, the king spoke of the abbot of Battle as 'his own chaplain', and Richard de Lucy, addressing the king on behalf of the barons, spoke of the abbey as 'the monument of your triumph and of ours', *Chronicon Monasterii de Bello*, 84, 86–7, cf. p. 100.

[2] *Ibid.*, 71.

[3] *Ibid.*, 86–7, cf. 88–9.

months.[1] When at length he came to give the matter his full attention, a preliminary investigation made it clear that, so far as the Crown was concerned, the question turned on the authenticity of the foundation charter of William the Conqueror and its confirmation by Henry I. These fully supported the abbey's claim to be free of subjection to the diocesan, and if they were to be accepted as authentic the case had to go against the bishop, for no king could lightly overturn rights guaranteed by his ancestors, and certainly not a king such as Henry II who made the defence of ancient rights the cornerstone of his policy. Indeed, Henry II had at his accession expressly promised to uphold all liberties confirmed by his grandfather's charters.[2] An examination of the abbey's charters satisfied the king as to their authenticity, but he nevertheless gave the bishop of Chichester an opportunity to present his side of the argument in full court. The bishop, however, could allege little that was material to the point at issue: he did not seek to assert that the charters were forgeries, or that their true import differed from that alleged by the abbot. He offered a few dubious and unconvincing precedents designed to show that the abbey had admitted episcopal jurisdiction in the past; but he rested his case principally upon a theoretical argument. The abbot's charters were worthless to him on the point of the abbey's freedom, he contended, for in purporting to grant it the founder was acting *ultra vires*: no layman could confer ecclesiastical liberties and dignities, save with the permission and confirmation of the bishop of Rome. The argument was a sound one by the canonical standards of the mid twelfth century, but hardly by the customary practice of the eleventh. The abbey's charters had been ratified by Archbishop Lanfranc and other bishops, including the bishop of Chichester of the day. Many privileges by which the Church set much store would have foundered if attempts were made to apply the standards of a later age to one which knew them not. The bishop's argument, too, might have been more tactfully presented: it seemed to the king that he was dismissing royal charters as frivolous, and an outburst of wrath was only to be expected. It is noteworthy, however, that although the king spoke in anger, he said nothing to impugn papal authority; his one concern was to defend his own:

> You think by subtelty and guile to overthrow the strength of the royal prerogatives which God has given me. I charge you by the fidelity and oath by which you are bound to me, that you submit yourself to correction

[1] Early in the reign the abbot prayed confirmation of his charters, but the king withheld it at the intervention of Archbishop Theobald, *ibid.*, 73.

[2] Coronation charter, 1154, Stubbs, *Select Charters*, 158.

for those presumptuous words against my crown and dignity. And I further beseech the archbishops and bishops here present to do me justice upon you, as appropriate to the rights of the royal crown granted to me by the Most High. It is clear that you oppose my royal dignities, and are striving to deprive me of privileges due to me by ancient right.

The bishop hastened to apologise, and professed his anxiety to uphold the Crown's honour and dignity; and although the king grumbled that such honour as the bishop offered was hardly worth having, he allowed him to proceed with his case. When it became clear, however, that the bishop had no further argument of substance to advance, the king forbore to give judgement against him but instead, after consultation with the assembled bishops and barons, persuaded him to renounce voluntarily all his claims upon the abbey – a way of settling the matter which would hold good in ecclesiastical courts. Nor did the king venture to ratify the agreement by his own charter: ratification was left to Archbishop Theobald, who performed it in his joint capacity as archbishop and papal legate. The conclusion of the dispute was the exchange of kisses of peace between the parties and between the king and the bishop of Chichester.[1]

The papal letters, which as Becket later told the pope had availed the bishop nothing in the matter, had been introduced into the debate not by the bishop but by the king's chancellor – Thomas Becket himself – who, speaking on behalf of the abbot, alleged that the bishop had procured a papal letter to reduce the abbey to subjection. There was no mystery about the letter – the abbot had it there in his hand. It was in fact nothing more than the kind of letter popes frequently issued when a complaint was made which seemed reasonable, but about which nothing was known for certain – a cautiously worded command (much as the king himself might issue in similar circumstances) which left plenty of opportunity for the recipient to say that he was under no obligation to comply since the facts of the matter had been misrepresented.[2] The chancellor's purpose in introducing the letter into the debate was obviously to bring discredit on the bishop by suggesting that he had attempted to circumvent royal authority by means of a papal mandate. The bishop denied, and denied on oath, that he had

---

[1] *Chronicon Monasterii de Bello*, 84–104. Theobald's charter of ratification is printed in Saltman, *Archbishop Theobald*, 243, charter no. 11. For a discussion of the case *see* Knowles, 'The growth of exemption', Pt 1, 218–25, Pt 2, 431–6.

[2] *Chronicon Monasterii de Bello*, 102; the letter itself is reproduced on p. 78. For similar royal intervention *see* the case of Robert of Valognes versus the abbot of St Albans, above, ch. 9, pp. 327–8.

procured such a letter or caused it to be procured. The abbey's chronicler relates that Archbishop Theobald crossed himself in astonishment at the bishop's oath, believing him to have told a lie; but it is quite possible that he had sworn the literal truth. Bishop Hilary of Chichester seems to have pursued the subjection of Battle Abbey out of a sense of duty, but he did so with a noticeable lack of enthusiasm. The abbey's chronicler makes it plain that there was little ill-will generated during the dispute. The bishop himself had offered to negotiate a compromise with the abbot before the hearing began in the royal court, and his friendly action on an earlier occasion in offering the abbot the kiss of peace during mass, after having formally excommunicated him for disobedience, was cited against him as the hearing proceeded.[1] After his compromise had been rejected, he made out a case as best he could, but with what seems to have been little conviction. It is more than likely that the prime instigator of the move to reduce Battle Abbey to subjection was not in fact the bishop but the cathedral chapter of Chichester, and the indications are that it was the chapter which procured the papal letter to the abbot.[2] To suggest, as Becket did to Alexander III in 1170, that Bishop Hilary had rested his case on papal authority and had it brusquely overborne by the king was nothing less than a mischievous falsehood.

The Battle Abbey case, as told in great detail by the abbey's chronicler, reveals Henry II determined to defend both his right to hear a case that involved an ecclesiastical issue as well as the question of the authenticity of royal charters, and as equally determined that the development of papal jurisdiction should not menace the prerogative of the Crown; but it also shows the king acting with considerable moderation in the face of provocation. His outburst of wrath was brought under control, and Bishop Hilary did not suffer for what Archbishop Theobald described in court as his ill-advised remarks which appeared derogatory to royal dignity. And in the end the king allowed the confirmation of the abbey's liberties to be an ecclesiastical fact instead of a royal one. It tells, in short, that Henry was touchy about his royal dignity, but not insensitive to clerical aspirations and ready to go some way to indulging them.

It might be supposed that Henry's readiness on this occasion to curb his wrath and to accept that gaining his way should not be achieved at the cost of unnecessarily inflaming clerical sentiments, are attributable to the presence and influence of Archbishop Theobald; but Henry

---

[1] *Chronicon Monasterii de Bello*, 90, 74, 100.
[2] *Ibid.*, 77ff.

exhibited much the same attitude in his relations with the Church on the continent when Theobald was not at hand to persuade and mollify. Becket, in his letter to the pope in 1170, made great play with Henry's refusal to accept Achard as bishop-elect of Séez and his intrusion of Froger; but here, as in his reference to the case of Battle Abbey, it is likely that he misrepresented the situation by a selection from the facts. Séez was a trouble-spot, and had been for many years. The previous election of a bishop in 1144 had provoked from Henry's father, Count Geoffrey, a violent reaction which in some quarters was remembered as his greatest crime.[1] Count Geoffrey's wrath had been provoked by the failure of the cathedral chapter to seek from him the customary licence to proceed with the election, although the omission seems to have been prompted not by exalted notions of ecclesiastical liberty, but by the eagerness of a faction in the chapter to steal a march on their opponents by hurriedly choosing a bishop before all the electors arrived. Count Geoffrey eventually repented of his persecution of the bishop-elect, was reconciled to him by Pope Eugenius III personally, and allowed those servants who had done the bishop physical violence to be punished in the church courts. But when, as seems probable, the circumstances were repeated in 1157, with those who had been out-manoeuvred on the previous occasion now determined that a man of their own choice should be appointed whether Henry approved or not, further trouble was inevitable. Precedents had a way of hardening rapidly into custom in the middle ages, and Henry had to act decisively if he were not to allow his successors to be denied the right of being consulted.[2]

Of course, Henry's action at Séez in forcing his almoner, Froger, upon the electors and finding another bishopric for Achard at Avranches, was inexcusable by canonical standards; but it should be recognised as exceptional. Against it should be set evidence which creates a very different impression. At Bordeaux, for example, Henry attempted to persuade the electors to choose as the new archbishop John de Side, a scholar of Poitiers, by entering the room where the election was being held; but when the electors refused to proceed in his presence, he withdrew and Raymond de Mareuil was chosen instead.[3] Even more remarkable is the story of the election to the see of Angers in 1156. In Count Geoffrey's day it had been the custom that the count selected a

---

[1] Gerald of Wales, VIII, 160, 301, 309, compared it with the murder of Becket.

[2] For Séez see Barlow, introduction to Letters of Arnulf of Lisieux, esp. xxxiv–xxxv.

[3] Imbart de la Tour, Les Élections Épiscopales dans l'Église de France du IXe au XIIe siècle, 464 n. 1.

new bishop from three candidates nominated by the cathedral chapter; but on this occasion the chapter made a stand on canonical rectitude and insisted on selecting a bishop for itself. Henry's response was not a show of violence but an appeal to the papacy to uphold established custom. Pope Adrian IV, however, when he heard about the custom, was horrified that it should ever have existed, and in the presence of the envoys utterly forbade it in future. Henry acquiesced and gave his assent to the chapter's choice.[1] Learning his way from these collisions in the early years, Henry seems to have evolved a method of promoting his interests in episcopal elections while avoiding trouble. When the see of Angers next fell vacant in 1162 he acted circumspectly: canonical forms of elections were respected, but he persuaded the chapter to fix its choice upon Geoffrey Moschet, one of the clerks of his chancery.[2]

Becket's biographers accepted his assertions that Henry's intention to persecute the Church (by which they invariably meant the clergy) had been revealed before Becket became archbishop; but their stories, like his, must be treated with caution. Take, for instance, the story told by William FitzStephen to illustrate his contention that, 'the king had long before, in the time, that is, of Archbishop Theobald, taken against the clergy of England generally'.[3] When the king visited the north of England in 1158, he relates, a burgess of Scarborough laid before him a complaint that a rural dean had blackmailed his wife by threatening to prosecute for adultery. The dean was summoned, and appeared before the king, in the presence of Richard de Lucy and other barons, Archbishop Theobald, the bishops of Durham and Lincoln, and John aux Bellesmains, a protégé of Archbishop Theobald who was then treasurer of the cathedral chapter of York. On being examined, the dean asserted that there had been witnesses to the woman's guilt, but he was unable to produce or name them. Since he might therefore be presumed to have disregarded a royal edict that rural deans (as well as the officials of lesser secular courts) should not bring charges unsupported by the testimony of worthy men of the neighbourhood, the king demanded judgement upon him.[4] The barons and clergy retired to deliberate, and John aux

---

[1] Boussard, *Le Comté d'Anjou*, 97–8; *Regesta Pontificum Romanorum*, no. 10174.

[2] Robert de Torigny, 215; Boussard, *op. cit.*, 98.

[3] William FitzStephen, III, 43–5.

[4] William FitzStephen does not specify the nature of the king's edict (*constitutio*) to which he refers. It has been supposed that this edict, otherwise unknown, prohibited the extortion of money by judges. The only basis for this assumption is William FitzStephen's report that in calling for judgement on the dean, the king remarked that 'archdeacons and rural deans extorted more money in a year by such means than he himself received'. William's account, however, deserves closer scrutiny. His

Bellesmains offered his view that the dean should be obliged to return the money he had extorted and then be committed to the mercy of his diocesan, the archbishop of York, for punishment. 'What then,' asked Richard de Lucy, 'will you adjudge to the lord king, whose law has been broken?' 'Nothing,' replied John, 'for the accused is a clerk.' 'I cannot associate myself with such a sentence,' said Richard, and withdrew with the rest of the lay barons. When the clergy returned to the king's presence the verdict they pronounced was along the lines suggested by John aux Bellesmains. The king angrily turned on Archbishop Theobald, denouncing the sentence as perverse (*falsa*) and fixing a day for rehearing the case. It was never brought to conclusion, however, adds William FitzStephen, for, learning of the death of his brother, the king went overseas before the appointed day arrived. This story had often been used as an illustration of a hardening of the king's attitude against the Church's claim that the clergy should be amenable only to ecclesiastical discipline. But any attempt to interpret the incident must allow that two years later, when a citizen of London complained to the king that he had been despoiled by a rural dean in the diocese of Exeter, Henry committed the case to Archbishop Theobald, bidding him to see that justice was done.[1]

Such contradictory evidence may appear perplexing, but the perplexity arises only if it is assumed that Henry had conceived, or was developing, a doctrinaire attitude towards his prerogatives as ruler and the conflicting claims of the Church. But the continental evidence suggests that this simply is not true, and that on the contrary Henry's

---

words suggest that it was not the accusation of extortion but the accusation that charges of adultery had been brought *sine alio accusatore*, which was contrary to the king's *constitutio*. This, together with the dean's defence that originally a deacon and a layman had been party to the accusation, suggests that the edict referred to was the counterpart in England of one which Henry issued a few months later in Normandy. According to the Continuatio Beccensis, 327, Henry, at Falaise at Easter 1159, ruled 'ut nullus decanus aliquam personam accusaret sine testimonio vicinorum circumanentium, qui bonae vitae fama laudabiles haberentur'. A similar rule was imposed on secular judges. Cf. Constitutions of Clarendon, clause 6: 'Laici non debent accusari nisi per certos et legales accusatores et testes in praesentia episcopi. . . .'

[1] John of Salisbury to Bartholomew archdeacon of Exeter, *Letters*, I, 193: 'If what he says is true, our friend has been despoiled by one of your deans and endured wrongs such as no citizen of London should suffer. Our lord the king has given instructions that the dean and his accomplices should be summoned and that the lord archbishop should try the case; but because he has special confidence in your wisdom and justice, he entrusts the case to you in order that you may serve the cause of God in the person of a poor man . . . faced by a more powerful adversary. Otherwise the archbishop is bound by the king's command to do justice to our fellow citizen, which will cause your dean no small trouble.'

attitude at this time was singularly undoctrinaire. To maintain the proposition that Henry was bent on destroying the *libertas ecclesiae*, Becket and his biographers had to select and distort the evidence. The truth, indeed, was complex, and lent itself to partisan fabrications. In the Battle Abbey case the king had shown, in quotable phrases, that he was watchful over his interests and could be irked by clerical pretensions; only the pertinacious inquirer would observe that nevertheless the king had shown himself ready to accept a formula for peace which preserved the dignity of both Crown and Church. As an indication that Henry II was prepared to try to accommodate himself to the Church's developed conceptions of canonical propriety, the Battle Abbey case does not stand alone.

Henry ignored Stephen's promise, as he ignored all Stephen's promises, to entrust the property of vacant bishoprics to administrators from the diocese; but instead of absorbing the income from the property into the royal revenue, he placed it at the disposal of the most prominent clergyman in his service, Chancellor Thomas Becket.[1] And as to the elections to vacant bishoprics there are signs that Henry expected to be consulted and might exercise his influence, but that he did not insist on forcing upon the electors unwelcome nominees.[2] The election of a new bishop to Exeter in 1161 offers clear evidence on the point. The see lay vacant for a year, its revenues in the custody of Chancellor Becket. The king was being pressed by the powerful FitzHarding family of Gloucestershire to nominate a scion of the house. He went as far as suggesting the name of Henry FitzHarding to the canons of Exeter, but they rejected it.[3] The king besought Archbishop Theobald to use his influence on behalf of FitzHarding, but the archbishop instead persuaded him of the unworthiness of the candidate.[4] Archbishop Theobald had his own candidate, acceptable to the electors, in Bartholomew archdeacon of Exeter, an eminent theologian and canon lawyer. Chancellor Becket was recruited to petition the king on his behalf.[5]

---

[1] John of Salisbury to Thomas Becket, 1160: 'There is a rumour that the king has placed at your disposal the revenues of the three bishoprics now vacant', *ibid.*, I, 223. The absence from the pipe rolls of accounts for the vacant bishoprics, and the demand from Becket in 1164 that he should account for the issues of vacant bishoprics and abbeys (Herbert of Bosham, III, 299) suggests that the chancellor's custody of ecclesiastical property was more extensive than John of Salisbury supposed. Cf. Margaret Howell, *Regalian Right in Medieval England*, 32–3.

[2] For an analysis of the evidence for episcopal elections in England in the period 1155–61, *see* Saltman, *Archbishop Theobald*, 126–32.

[3] *Letters of John of Salisbury*, no. 128, I, 122.

[4] *Ibid.*, no. 128, I, 223, and no. 133, I, 242.

[5] *Ibid.*, no. 128, I, 222–3, 225.

Henry delayed for several months, but eventually gave his assent, and Bartholomew became bishop of Exeter.

That royal influence and royal intervention were factors with which the clergy had to reckon, there can be no doubt, despite the king's prolonged absences on the continent. John of Salisbury, Archbishop Theobald's secretary, wrote darkly to a friend of the 'satellites of the court' who 'oppose the king's authority to every effort of the Church'.[1] Archbishop Theobald, passing on a plaintiff's appeal to the papal court, remarks that, 'There he will say things which he dared not say in England', because his opponent 'is a servant of the king'.[2] The Archbishop sought the cooperation of the bishop of Coventry over a dispute in which the king was interested, reminding him that, 'In this way you will be able to retain the king's favour, which is most necessary [qui per necessarius est]'.[3] The abbot of St Albans, who had obtained papal letters commanding the archbishop of Canterbury and the bishop of Chichester to excommunicate Robert of Valognes if he did not restore property seized from the abbey, discovered that 'the bishops feared to bind Robert with the chains of anathema since King Henry II had forbidden his bishops to pronounce sentence of excommunication against any of his barons'.[4] Royal writs were the long arm of royal authority. The bishop of Coventry found himself confronted by a royal command to postpone a case in which he was about to pronounce sentence.[5] The archbishop of Canterbury, having rebuked the abbess of Amesbury for ejecting Jordan, treasurer of Salisbury cathedral, from the church of Froyle, found himself obliged to write again, more peremptorily, because 'the authority of the king compels me to punish a wrong done to the Holy Roman Church and an affront to the king's majesty, not to say to ourselves'. In his first letter he had expressed his readiness 'to wait in patience for you to make speedy reparation of your errors'; but in the second there was to be no delay: 'We instruct and command you that, in accordance with the mandate of our lady the queen which you have received, you suffer Jordan to hold the church, as he held it by apostolic authority at the time when the king went overseas.'[6]

There is, however, little justification for regarding such interventions as wanton interference with the processes of ecclesiastical government. In most of the known cases it was the clergy themselves who invoked royal intervention. The abbot of Battle sought recovery of a dependent

---

[1] Ibid., no. 94, I, 144.   [2] Ibid., no. 81, I, 128.
[3] Ibid., no. 104, I, 165–6.
[4] Gesta Abbatum Monasterii Sancti Albani, I, 163.
[5] Letters of John of Salisbury, no. 53, I, 91.   [6] Ibid., nos 114, 115, I, 188, 189.

church 'now in the royal courts, now in the ecclesiastical'.[1] The bishop of Lincoln sought from both the pope and the king that the abbot of St Albans should acknowledge his authority.[2] Moreover, Archbishop Theobald's correspondence, which provides much of the evidence for royal intervention, also demonstrates that the king was disposed to leave the final judgement to the ecclesiastical authorities: he was not interfering, but intervening to see that justice was done. When, for instance, a complaint reached the king that the bishop of Coventry, endeavouring to induce some discipline into a royal foundation of canons at Lilleshall, had acted unfairly, the king asked the archbishop to bring the matter to 'final judgement'.[3] The royal writ which ordered the bishop of Coventry to postpone a case in which he was about to pronounce sentence, had been sought by a clerk who complained that the bishop had improperly heard his adversary during an adjournment of the case. Henry did not attempt a ruling or try to draw the case into his own court: he simply ordered a postponement and allowed the archbishop to reopen proceedings.[4] This case went, in fact, on appeal to Rome. So too did the case of the man who feared to plead in England because his adversary was 'a servant of the king'.[5] Evidently he did not fear reprisals for making an appeal without royal permission.

There is indeed ample evidence in all the relevant sources of the freedom with which appeals were made to Rome, without the necessity of prior approval by the king. There was, it is true, a royal writ of 1159 to Archbishop Theobald and the clergy of the realm forbidding them to leave the country for the purpose of prosecuting appeals until a decision had been taken on who should be recognised as the lawful successor of Pope Adrian IV.[6] But this was an exceptional ban in the exceptional circumstances of a papal schism. Indeed, the fact that the ban was necessary is an indication that free intercourse with Rome was accepted as normal. Archbishop Theobald approved of royal intervention to prevent the English Church being split by the schism, and expressed alarm to the king that despite his ban he had allowed some to go to Rome.[7]

[1] *Chronicon Monasterii de Bello*, 113.
[2] *Gesta Abbatum Monasterii Sancti Albani*, I, 138, 143–4.
[3] *Letters of John of Salisbury*, no. 104, I, 165; on the Lilleshall case *see* Letter no. 105.
[4] *Ibid.*, no. 53, I, 91–2.   [5] *Ibid.*, no. 81; *see* above p. 437.
[6] Printed in Saltman, *Archbishop Theobald*, 543.
[7] *Letters of John of Salisbury*, no. 116, I, 191. The renunciation at the request of the king of an appeal to Rome by Roger priest of Ingatestone (referred to in Letter no. 132), which is sometimes cited as an example of royal interference, should probably be related to this temporary ban.

On the other hand there can be no doubt that Henry II expected that those who had dealings with the papal curia would do no injury to the Crown or the realm, and that he reserved the right to obstruct appeals or frustrate papal mandates if his rights were trenched upon. A prudent litigant would seek the king's approval before making an appeal, or like Bishop Hilary of Chichester repudiate a papal mandate which was likely to offend the king.[1] The evidence is insufficient to allow a reasonable estimate of the extent to which Henry II obstructed appeals or frustrated papal mandates. Some of the evidence that does survive is open to question: the accusation, for instance, which Pope Adrian IV levelled at Archbishop Theobald of 'conspiring with the king to bury appeals', arose out of the long and bitter struggle which the archbishop was having to secure the obedience of the abbot of St Augustines, Canterbury, and was prompted by the malice of the archbishop's enemies.[2] It is probably unnecessary, however, to look further than a story told by the biographer of the abbots of St Albans for an illustration of Henry's general attitude and the basis for his discrimination against some papal mandates.

Abbot Robert of Gorham, in company with the abbots of many prominent monasteries, was assiduous in seeking from the papacy privileges for his house and exemption from episcopal jurisdiction. As a tenant-in-chief of the Crown, the abbot of St Albans, of course, ranked equal with the bishops in the council of the king, and it seemed natural to seek or assert ecclesiastical equality. In 1155 Abbot Robert was a member of an embassy which the newly crowned King Henry II sent to the newly elevated Pope Adrian IV, and while at Rome he had seized the opportunity to secure outstanding privileges, fortified by a letter from the king requesting the pope to treat the abbey's business as favourably as his own.[3] The validity of the abbot's claim to exemption

[1] Concrete evidence of the king's approval having been sought is not easy to come by, but an example is provided in the case of Anstey v. Francheville, Patricia Barnes, 'The Anstey Case', 19. For the bishop of Chichester's repudiation of a papal mandate, see above pp. 431–2.

[2] Thomas of Elmham, *Historia Monasterii Sancti Augustini Cantuariensis*, 412. *Letters of John of Salisbury*, nos 8–11, tell of Archbishop Theobald's difficulties with the monks of St Augustines and of their friends at the papal curia. The archbishop's reply to the pope that 'we would remind you that it is open to anyone to make an appeal' (*ibid.*, no. 12, I, 20) was somewhat disingenuous and should not, perhaps, be taken as evidence of the true situation in England. It was not the obstruction of appeals but the frustration of papal instructions which most concerned the pope.

[3] *Gesta Abbatum Monasterii Sancti Albani*, I, 126. The rest of the story is told on 135–47. See also Knowles, 'The growth of exemption', 213–18, and Richardson and Sayles, *The Governance of Medieval England*, 292–3, 299–300.

from diocesan control was subsequently challenged by the bishop of Lincoln in appeals to both the king and pope. The king sent a writ from France ordering the erection of an ecclesiastical commission, consisting of three bishops and the abbot of Westminster, under the chairmanship of the justiciar, Earl Robert of Leicester, which was to hear the parties and report on the relations between the bishop of Lincoln and the abbot of St Albans in the time of King Henry I. The case was, however, eventually adjourned for hearing before the king himself. In the meantime the bishop's appeal to Rome had resulted in a papal mandate to the abbot, ordering him to testify before judges-delegate who were to report on the case for the pope's judgement. When the king heard of this he was extremely annoyed with the abbot ('concepit magnam indignationem contra abbatem'), supposing that the abbot had sought it to avoid royal jurisdiction. The abbot sent messengers to plead his innocence, pointing out that the judges-delegate were more likely to favour the bishop than himself, since one was the bishop of Norwich who was engaged in a similar dispute with Bury St Edmunds, and the other was the bishop of Chichester who similarly sought the subjection of Battle Abbey. The king was persuaded and placated, but he insisted that the abbot should produce for his inspection all the abbey's privileges, both old and new. The monks were greatly alarmed at this, 'For they feared that the king would tear up any which displeased him'. The abbot tried to appear before the king without his charters and bulls, but was made to fetch them. The king personally examined them and viewed with favour the foundation charter of King Offa and the privileges granted by Pope Calixtus, which had been confirmed by his grandfather. But when he read in a bull of privileges granted by Pope Celestine that the abbey was to render to the supreme pontiff an ounce of gold anually, the king protested angrily: 'This article, my lord abbot, is contrary to our dignity; you had no right to make my church tributary to the see of Rome without my assent, nor ought the pope to have required it.' The abbot replied that it had been done not by himself but in the time of a predecessor. 'Whoever did it,' replied the king, 'it was done without warrant of law [contra juris ordinem factum est]'. He then turned to the other privileges, asking to see those to which the bishop of Lincoln objected, including the abbot's privilege of wearing episcopal vestments. As he handed the king the bull which conferred the privilege of wearing the mitre, the abbot was apologetic, saying that Pope Adrian had granted it for love of St Albans without being asked. The king, however, was unconcerned: 'We would not need much persuasion to feel content,' he said, 'if all the abbots of our kingdom appeared in mitres.' The right, he pointed out, which the abbot of St Albans enjoyed to perform episcopal functions preceded and did not follow from the wearing of a mitre. When the bishop of Lincoln was called upon to present his side of the argument, he admitted that his case rested not upon documents but solely upon prescription. 'The documents, as we believe,' said the king, 'overrule prescription.' He went on to point out that the abbot alleged that the rights he claimed inhered in the abbey from its foundation, and only the negligence and apathy of his predecessors had led to its subjection to the church of Lincoln; but now, by the favour of the bishops of Rome, it had been restored to its birthright. 'It is the function of popes in such cases,' remarked the king, 'to intervene, and as they should see fit to restore, on the authority of St Peter, each one to its pristine state.' He advised the bishop to consult with his cathedral chapter and decide whether to contest the case or come to some settlement. When the bishop had departed, the king suggested to the abbot that he should offer a piece of land to the church of Lincoln in return for the bishop's renunciation of the rights which he claimed over St Albans – ten pounds' worth of land he thought would do. On this basis a settlement was effected. The bishop formally renounced his claim to jurisdiction. Charters setting out the renunciation and the grant of a vill were exchanged, and confirmed by charters of the king and archbishop. Between the beginning and end of this dispute Archbishop Theobald had died; the archbishop who witnessed and ratified the settlement which the king had engineered was Thomas Becket.

The chronicler's detailed account of these proceedings speaks eloquently of the deep respect in which the authority of the twenty-nine-year-old king was held, of his complete command of the situation, and of his mastery of the principles involved. It tells that, like his grandfather, he would brook no slight to the dignity of the Crown, but was disinclined to make a fuss over side-issues. He acted throughout with propriety. He did not question the pope's right to issue bulls which affected the status even of a royal foundation, though he expected those bulls to respect the royal dignity. He handled judiciously the awkward problem created by the pope's appointment of judges-delegate. He did not complain of papal interference, but directed his annoyance at the person he supposed to have created the awkward situation. The abbot, when he appeared before the king, said that he was prepared to plead either before the king's *curia* or the judges-delegate, but thought that he should defend himself before one tribunal and not both. The king, turning to the archbishop of Canterbury, who sat beside him, said, 'What the abbot says is reasonable; for it would hardly be consonant with the honour of our majesty, if an action decided in our court should be adjudged again in the consistory of the lord pope'.[1] Again there was no challenge to papal jurisdiction as such; and by arranging a compromise by the parties which avoided the necessity of pronouncing a formal judgement, the king avoided a confrontation with papal authority in a manner which preserved the dignity of each.

It seems clear that Henry II took the view that ecclesiastical and royal jurisdiction were complementary and should cooperate. He was not prepared to see the traditional rights of the Crown impugned, and did not, for his part, wish to contest the authority of the Church. He seems to have supposed that the troublesome competition which might be caused by the unclear line of demarcation between the two jurisdictions, could be averted by sensible give-and-take, with neither side trying to claim an exclusive jurisdiction. He expected his interests to be respected, as he in turn was prepared to accommodate himself to the clergy's notions of canonical propriety. Problems in the relations of Church and State should be resolved by arrangement between the king and ecclesiastic leaders, and not made the occasion for proclaiming principles.

There is good reason to believe that Archbishop Theobald shared the view that the two jurisdictions should be complementary and not competitive.[2] For all his defence of the Church's liberty, and despite his profound respect for the Holy See, Archbishop Theobald was not persuaded of the propriety either of untrammelled access to the Roman curia, or of the intervention of the papacy in the normal affairs of local churches. His letters to popes expressed, politely but firmly, the conservative view that papal authority should be invoked only for matters which were beyond the competence of local authorities, or to rectify their errors. The phrasing of the letters is doubtless that of his secretary, John of Salisbury, but the archbishop's mind must lie behind such remarks addressed to the pope, as:

[1] *Gesta Abbatum Monasterii Sancti Albani*, I, 150–1.

[2] Cf. *Letters of John of Salisbury*, no. 116, I, 190, Archbishop Theobald to Henry II: 'When the members of the Church are united in loyalty and love, when princes show due reverence to priests and priests render faithful service to princes, then do kingdoms enjoy that true peace and tranquillity which must always be the goal of our desire. But if they clash one against the other, in all their might, then the vigour of the secular power will be impaired no less than the ecclesiastical.' This, however, is a rhetorical preamble, composed by John of Salisbury, to a letter about the schism in the papacy, and should perhaps be treated as no more than rhetoric.

... it is essential for all men to have recourse to you when they are in the grip of some necessity *from which they cannot free themselves by their own efforts.* ...[1]

Swein appealed to your court ... *despite the fact that we were prepared to do justice to both parties.*[2]

... After carefully examining these witnesses and finding they agreed pretty closely in their evidence, we took their oath and were about to give judgement ... when William, *without alleging any hardship and illegally, as it seemed to us,* made an appeal to your most excellent consistory. ...[3]

Even such a remark as, '... But you to whom the final decision has *rightly* [*ut oportuit*] been reserved ...', carries the implication that although the pope had full authority to hear any plea, not every appeal was justified.[4] Undoubtedly part of Theobald's reluctance to accept the development of papal jurisdiction was the inconvenient consequences it often in practice entailed. There is a tartness in the postscript to one letter which reads:

In addition we beg you to give us a ruling on the punishment to be inflicted on those who forge your letters: it is difficult for us to await your advice on individual cases of this kind every time they arise.[5]

There is indignation in another as to the ease with which the papal curia could be deceived into making erroneous decisions:

... Nicholas, the bearer of these letters, has in defiance of all law ... been deprived by our venerable brother David, bishop of St David's, of the archdeaconry which he canonically possessed, on account of letters which a certain Jordan, perhaps unknown to you, secured from your clemency by lying entreaties, to the amazement of the whole English Church. This man, Holy Father, is that open perjurer, covered with public infamy by a previous charge of murder, who was condemned for forging papal letters by your predecessor Eugenius and deprived of his office and benefice. For a long time ... he lay hid in remote places ... until he learned that Pope Eugenius had been taken from the world. We therefore entreat your majesty that, after consideration of the wretched poverty of the bearer and the justice of his cause, you will of your mercy punish the outrageous crime of which he has been the victim and that, after restoring him to his office, you will give orders that the case should run its natural course through the channels of the law – unless, that is, you decree that the sentence

---

[1] *Ibid.*, no. 57, I, 97.   [2] *Ibid.*, no. 68, I, 110.   [3] *Ibid.*, no. 84, I, 132.
[4] *Ibid.*, no. 71, I, 114. Cf. nos 64 and 65, in which the archbishop expresses regret at having to pass on appeals which he regarded as attempts to evade his judgement.
[5] *Ibid.*, no. 57, I, 98.

passed by your predecessor shall be nullified, and that a man already condemned should deserve freedom to plead his cause rather than punishment.[1]

It was, moreover, the disastrous intervention of the papacy in elections to the archbishopric of York which prompted Theobald to arrange for the election of Roger de Pont l'Évêque in 1154 in a way which gave no grounds for further papal intervention.[2] But there seems to be a deeper reason for Theobald's ambivalent attitude to the exercise of papal authority: a conviction that properly constituted ecclesiastical authorities in the provinces and dioceses should be allowed to discharge their duties, arranging matters in the light of their better knowledge of local circumstances, unhampered by unnecessary papal involvement. In expressing reluctance to pass on appeals to Rome made by litigants in his court, Archbishop Theobald was suggesting that he was perfectly competent to settle the matter.[3] He took a similar view of some of the appeals which came to his own court from lower courts. To the bishop of Chichester he wrote:

> The transgressions of malicious persons are best punished by those who have intimate knowledge of the merits of the parties concerned and have received power from the Lord to correct them thoroughly. . . . That disputes within your jurisdiction find their way to us, is a sign of weakness or negligence. . . .[4]

This attitude of Theobald goes far to explain his amicable relations with Henry II. The desire of each to uphold his authority, his 'power received from the Lord', gave them a common interest in minimising differences, and in disposing decisively of problems which concerned them both, in mutual accord. The scandal of open conflict could only result in the honour of one or the other being besmirched. Henry II, unlike Stephen, was astute enough to wish to resolve differences in private before public action was resolved upon, and it is likely that problems were discussed privily through the agency of the friend and servant which Theobald and Henry had in common – Thomas Becket. It is hardly to be expected that such consultations would be a matter of record, but a hint of the process at work may be caught in a postscript to a letter from the archbishop to Chancellor Becket: '. . . Let us know what is the will of our lord the king and your advice concerning the

---

[1] *Letters of John of Salisbury*, no. 86, I, 134–5.
[2] *See* above, ch. 11, p. 425.
[3] *Letters of John of Salisbury*, nos 64, 65, 68.　　　　　　　　[4] *Ibid.*, no. 61, I, 102.

monk who claims to be abbot of Boxley'.[1] An indication of the confidence which the king reposed in the archbishop is his release to him of control of an election of an abbot of a great monastery who would rank as a baron of the realm: to the monks of Evesham, Theobald wrote, '. . . we have obtained from our lord the king permission that we may, in accordance with the precept of the sacred canons, set over you a worthy shepherd'. The monks were notoriously factious and a contested election could readily have resulted in the intervention of Rome. It was in the interests of both archbishop and king that a trustworthy man should be appointed, whose election should be unchallengeable. The appointment of a monk of Canterbury to be the new abbot suggests that the archbishop had his own candidate to impose, although the supervision of the election was entrusted to the bishops of Coventry and Worcester, and the abbots of Pershore and Winchcombe. Theobald's letter to the monks concluded with a stern warning against prevarication: 'Let none of you think that he may fly to our lord the king for refuge; for any delay in your salvation will sorely vex him, and he has appointed us as his vicegerent in the matter that there should be no such delay. Farewell.'[2]

The advantages which Theobald recognised in a king who could impose his authority were demonstrated in the months following the double election of Victor and Alexander to the papacy in 1159. The normal processes of appeal to Rome were of course undermined by the uncertainty as to where authority lay, and there was a real danger of some English clergy adhering to one and some to the other contender for the papal throne.[3] The archbishop sheltered behind the custom of the realm that no pope should be recognised in England without the royal assent: 'While the matter is in suspense,' he wrote to the king, 'we think that it is unlawful in your realm to accept either of them, save with your approval. It is far from desirable that the English Church should be torn asunder after the example of the Church of Rome and by so doing give occasion for a conflict of Church and State.'[4] At the same

---

[1] *Ibid.*, no. 129, I, 225.

[2] *Ibid.*, no. 109, I, 173–4. There had been a disputed election in 1149, and Theobald's intervention had been overridden by an appeal to the pope, Saltman, *Archbishop Theobald*, 84.

[3] *Letters of John of Salisbury*, no. 116, I, 190, Archbishop Theobald to the king: 'Some of us are prepared to approach or visit Alexander, while others are for Victor.' The bishops of Winchester and Durham were said to favour Victor; the archbishop himself, after a short period of impartiality, came out strongly for Alexander, *ibid.*, nos 122, 124; Saltman, *Archbishop Theobald*, 45ff.

[4] *Letters of John of Salisbury*, no. 116, I, 190.

time he was anxious that Henry II should not, as his grandfather had done, make his own decision: 'And if it please you in a time of such peril to the whole Church of God, your majesty should take counsel with your realm and decide nothing to its prejudice without the advice of your clergy.'[1] There were rumours, alarming to Theobald, that Henry might opt for Victor, who had the support of the German emperor; but the king acceded to the archbishop's prompting and requested the English clergy to tender their advice.[2] The archbishop acted with strict propriety: as he reported to the king after holding a council at London, '. . . on the issue before us we gave no definite judgement, since that was not permitted; nor did we make any decision to the prejudice of the royal majesty, for that would have been wrong; but as was both permissible and right and in accordance with your majesty's command, we have, God being our witness and our judge, framed our advice'.[3] Henry delayed announcing his decision to reap from it the maximum political advantage, but it was in accordance with the advice tendered: that Alexander should be recognised.

It is possible that at the very beginning of his reign Henry had sought a formal understanding with the papacy on the relations of Church and State. An embassy consisting of the bishops of Le Mans, Lisieux, Evreux, and the abbot of St Albans waited upon Pope Adrian IV, to discuss 'ardua negotia regalia'.[4] No more, unfortunately, is known of it; and if Henry was seeking some approval for the exercise of prerogatives enjoyed by his predecessors, he was certainly disappointed.[5] But it mattered not: with an archbishop such as Theobald to work with him, Henry did not need a concordat.

[1] *Letters of John of Salisbury*, no. 122, I, 202.
[2] *Ibid.*, nos 122, 124, 125.
[3] *Ibid.*, no. 125, I, 216–17.
[4] *Gesta Abbatum Monasterii Sancti Albani*, I, 126.
[5] Cf. Raymonde Foreville, *L'Église et la Royauté en Angleterre*, 89.

Chapter 13

ARCHBISHOP THOMAS BECKET

There is no good reason to suppose that Henry II was seriously dissatisfied with the working relationship of *regnum* and *sacerdotium* in the first eight years of his reign. Royal interests had been consulted and respected. That is not to say, however, that he expected to continue with the *ad hoc* resolution of difficulties. It is more than likely that by the early 1160s he wished to introduce clearer definitions into the relationship of Church and State: the quest for clarification and definition is a characteristic of these years of the reign. Henry II disliked ambiguity as much as he disliked disorder. The continental Church as well as the Church in England began in these years to be constrained to observe sets of rules derived from Henry's predecessors or fashioned from the practice of the past. In Normandy the policy is signalled by the demand in 1162 for observance of the Lillebonne decrees of William the Conqueror, and in Poitou in 1163 by the issue of instructions to the new bishop of Poitiers for the observance of the ruler's prerogatives in the conduct of ecclesiastical jurisdiction.[1] The king's proposals at the Westminster council of October 1163 for the adequate punishment of members of the clergy who committed crimes, and the constitutions formulated at Clarendon in January 1164, were part of a general process of review of the interaction of ecclesiastical and royal government and of the marking out of boundary lines. It was a process which could easily give rise to disputes – disputes which could readily become acrimonious if the king's conception of the interests of the state became entangled with questions of royal prerogative, or if the clergy feared that his proposals trenched upon ecclesiastical self-government – threatened, as they would have put it, the *libertas ecclesiae*. It needed an archbishop in whom the king had confidence to steer a course through such dangerous waters – one who had a sympathetic understanding of the king's objectives, but who could deflect him from collisions with the Church over what the clergy regarded as essential to her liberty. Archbishop Theobald was such a man, and his death in April 1161, at the moment when King Henry was beginning to give more attention to ecclesiastical problems, was a serious loss.

[1] *See* above, p. 95, and below, p. 516.

It should not be assumed that Henry II was opposed to ecclesiastical self-government, or that Thomas Becket was his chosen instrument for an assault upon it. Even in the most bellicose phases of the struggle to come Henry sought nothing more than safeguards for what he regarded as royal interests, which might be injured by unfettered ecclesiastical jurisdiction. The Church's objection was that the form of the safeguards he demanded offended canonical principles, but not that his concern was itself reprehensible. The charge that Henry was bent on the destruction of the Church's liberty, if not of the Church itself, was simply Becket's attempt at self-justification after the breach between them. Most of the English bishops were never convinced of it, and the pope himself was persuaded only briefly and with hesitation. In the end it proved possible to satisfy almost all Henry's requirements without serious injury to the Church's essential 'liberties'.

What Henry II probably hoped for was that the province of Canterbury would provide a model for the elaboration of a concordat with the papacy; and it may be argued that he wanted Thomas Becket as Archbishop Theobald's successor because he thought Becket was the man most likely to continue and expand Theobald's policy. There are many reasons why he should have thought so. Thomas Becket was Theobald's chosen agent in the royal household, and his joint position as chancellor to King Henry and archdeacon of Canterbury ('my archdeacon' as Theobald continued to call him) was a symbol of that working cooperation between Church and State which both Henry and Theobald desired.[1] It is true that Becket's zealous prosecution of his duties as chancellor and his vigorous defence of royal prerogatives sometimes gave Theobald cause for apprehension, but the archbishop's confidence was retained to the end.[2] Indeed it is possible that Thomas Becket was Theobald's own choice as his successor.[3] On the other hand, even though Henry had reason to be gratified by Becket's zeal as chancellor, he could have had no illusions about his deep-seated piety and his basic sympathy for the Church's highest claims. Becket was a keen and efficient administrator who filled the office of chancellor with dignity and style; he kept a good table and a lively household to match that of any baron in the land, and could hawk and hunt with the best of them; he conducted diplomacy with panache and success.[4] Here was

---

[1] *Letters of John of Salisbury*, I, 198, 200   [2] *Ibid.*, I, 221–3, 224–5.

[3] This suggestion is strongly advanced by Raymonde Foreville, *L'Église et la Royauté en Angleterre*, 101, 104, although there is no unequivocal evidence to support it.

[4] William FitzStephen, III, 22–32. For Becket's eye for a fine hawk, *see* Roger of Pontigny, IV, 56–7.

a leader of men whom others would follow as the weak follow the strong. Yet here would be no worldly prelate: for all his parade of pomp and munificence Becket was personally frugal and, above all, chaste. It was a matter of sport in the young and lusty Henry to tempt him to the pleasures of the flesh, but no one could contradict the biographers' insistence on his purity. And if he connived at Henry's indulgences, he nonetheless banished from his own household an adulterous servant whom he had once called friend.[1] He paid for the lavishness of his household by acquiring, as it was easy for the royal chancellor to do, several wealthy benefices which were in the king's gift; but he sought out those benefices to which no cure of souls was attached and so avoided the sin of pluralism; moreover, much of the wealth he acquired is said to have been dispersed in gifts and almsgiving.[2] He publicly objected to the proposed marriage of King Stephen's surviving daughter Mary to Matthew of Boulogne, because she was a professed nun.[3] He opposed and reputedly thwarted the proposed marriage of Henry II's youngest brother William to the widowed countess of Warenne, heiress to the earldom of Surrey, on the grounds of their consanguinity.[4] There could be little doubt, indeed, that Chancellor Becket never shook off the training he had received in Theobald's household in the defence of God's law.

Voices, it is said, were raised against Henry's choice of Thomas as Theobald's successor.[5] Herbert of Bosham reports that when the king disclosed his intention Thomas himself warned that it could give rise to strife between them: 'I knew that you would demand many things – for already you presume much in ecclesiastical matters which I never bear unmoved.'[6] Henry himself seems to have hesitated, for several months passed with only rumours to say that Becket was to be the next archbishop. England was not lacking in churchmen whose reputation would have fitted them for the primatial see; there was even an outstanding candidate in Gilbert Foliot, renowned as a man of letters and an ascetic, who seemed destined for ecclesiastical eminence;[7] but there was no one

[1] William FitzStephen, III, 21; *Thómas Saga Erkibyskups*, I, 50; William of Canterbury, I, 5–6.   [2] e.g., William FitzStephen, III, 23.

[3] Herbert of Bosham, III, 328; IV, 332. Sometime before 1158 Henry II granted a charter to 'Marie filie regis Stephani et monialibus suis', *Recueil des Actes de Henri II*, I, 144.

[4] William FitzStephen, III, 142; Stephen of Rouen, 676.

[5] e.g., *Materials for the History of Becket*, Epistolae, V, 410.

[6] Herbert of Bosham, III, 181.

[7] Cf., Knowles, *The Episcopal Colleagues of Thomas Becket*, 37ff.

who seemed so clearly as Thomas Becket to possess the qualities which King Henry required in an archbishop of Canterbury. What Henry wanted in an archbishop was understanding, loyalty, and cooperation; but what he needed was the kind of loyalty which offers wise advice and persists in it, not the loyalty of concurrence and submission. A puppet in the seat of St Augustine would have been the surest way to provoke opposition from a bench of bishops who were remarkable, almost all of them, for owing their promotion to ecclesiastical rather than royal influence.[1] This would not have been the way to win respect for royal interests and promote cooperation between *regnum* and *sacerdotium*. But Becket was no puppet; he was the nearest approach Henry could find or hope to find to a man cast in the mould of Archbishop Theobald, and this, together with their mutual friendship, is sufficient reason for the king's nomination of Thomas Becket to the electors of Canterbury. Only thus, Henry may well have thought, could the contentious problems in the relations of Church and State, which were already beginning to engage his attention, be resolved without an open breach with the highest ecclesiastical authorities.

Henry, of course, had mistaken his man, and felt himself cruelly deceived; but his misjudgement was not perhaps so wildly wrong as the common account would have us believe. Indeed, one of the chief difficulties in the traditional account is that it requires us to suppose either that Henry utterly, and uncharacteristically, misread Becket, or alternatively that Becket performed a startling about-face from champion of the royal prerogative to champion of ecclesiastical liberty. That Becket changed was assumed by his biographers who either tried to explain it as a miracle of conversion, or were driven to argue that he had dissimulated as chancellor in order to save himself for the defence of the Church in her direst need. Others less sympathetic denounced him as a hypocrite. John of Salisbury in his *Life of St Thomas* rather feebly suggests that as chancellor he had been acting under orders. Z. N. Brooke has ingeniously suggested that Becket was the consummate actor who not merely plays but actually lives a part.[2] And Dom David Knowles has argued with sensitive subtlety that Becket released as archbishop the true self which, as chancellor, he had submerged under

---

[1] Cf. Knowles, *The Episcopal Colleagues of Thomas Becket*, 7–9.

[2] Brooke, *The English Church and the Papacy*, 193: 'The only explanation of him that seems to me to fit the facts at all is that he was one of those men who, exalting to the full the rôle they have to play, picture themselves as the perfect representatives of their office, visualising a type and making themselves the living impersonations of it; actors playing a part, but unconscious actors.'

his tendencies to worldliness.[1] The diversity of explanations emphasises the problem; but it is a problem engendered by the assumption that Henry conceived of Thomas as the pliant agent of his supposed machinations against the Church.

The supposition that Becket was thought by Henry to be another Theobald rescues us from half the difficulty. Henry was mistaken – blinded perhaps by his impetuous affection for Becket – but his mistake consisted simply in his failure to recognise that Becket lacked Archbishop Theobald's mature flexibility and his judicious assessment of the realities of power. It would be asking too much of the thrusting young Henry to have expected him to realise that Theobald's policy was born in large part of the wisdom of the aged, who have witnessed peril and change, and who, knowing that the world will go on long after they are dead, will presently bear with patience much of what they hope will in better times abate. It would also be asking too much of Henry to have expected him to perceive the deeper nature of Becket's personality. Thomas Becket was a man who strove to please, but striving to please was simply a reflection of his will to succeed; and success for him lay not in worldly prosperity or even in glory, for his austere inner self saw these merely as the trappings of success, but in proving to himself that nothing was beyond his competence. He was fundamentally a proud, self-centred man. His biographers and correspondents will speak of him with admiration and respect, but affection is noticeably a quality that he did not draw from them.[2] Only two people are known to have given him affection: Archbishop Theobald and King Henry, and from each of them in turn he drew away.

If proof be needed that even after he had secured an archbishop of his choice at Canterbury, Henry II's policy, like that of his grandfather, was of mutual accommodation with the Church, it will be found in his response to the pope's summons of bishops to a council in 1163. Pope Alexander III had been driven from Italy by Emperor Frederick Barbarossa, and had taken refuge in France where his authority, and not that of the emperor's puppet pope, had been acknowledged since 1160.[3] As a manifestation of this authority Alexander convened a general council to meet at Tours in March 1163. The city of Tours lay within Henry's dominions, although ecclesiastically its position was

[1] Knowles, 'Archbishop Thomas Becket: a character study', *The Historian and Character*, 110.

[2] A point observed by Knowles, *op. cit.*, 105.

[3] Barlow, 'The English, Norman, and French councils called to deal with the papal schism of 1159'.

somewhat anomalous: the archiepiscopal province of Tours took in Greater Anjou and Brittany, but the right of receiving the homage of the archbishop – and hence the patronage of the see – lay with the king of France.[1] It was, however, with, as the pope wrote, 'the advice and desire of the kings of the French and of the English' that the council was summoned to Tours.[2] The archbishops and bishops of the provinces of Canterbury and York attended the council in full force, 'with the permission of the king', as Ralph of Diceto noted in his chronicle.[3] The 'ancient custom of the realm' required, of course, that bishops should not attend general councils without the king's assent. It had not always been given, or had been given grudgingly to a small delegation. Indeed, Henry II's assent to the full attendance of the bishops at the council of Tours in 1163 is in striking contrast to King Stephen's action when the last general council had been convened by Pope Eugenius III at Rheims in 1148. He had expelled the papal messengers who brought the summons, and had nominated three bishops to attend on behalf of the Church in England. The ports were watched to prevent others going, but Archbishop Theobald slipped across the Channel in an unseaworthy boat (accompanied, incidentally, by his clerk Thomas Becket) and attended the council in defiance of the royal ban.[4] There is no explanation for Henry II's liberal attitude in 1162 other than a general desire to establish amicable relations with the highest ecclesiastical authorities. His generosity reaped an immediate reward: Pope Alexander wrote to him after the council, returning thanks for the full attendance of the English archbishops and bishops and declaring

> that on account of this no detriment or disadvantage ought to come upon him or his successors, nor by reason of this should a new custom be introduced into his realm, or the privilege [dignitas] of the realm be diminished in any degree.[5]

This, it may be believed, was precisely the way Henry hoped the relations of Church and State could be conducted: a liberal interpretation

---

[1] On the relationship of the archbishopric of Tours to the French Crown, see Pacaut, Louis VII et les Élections Épiscopales dans le Royaume de France, 64–5.

[2] Letter of Alexander III to the king of Aragon, 7 December 1162, Raymonde Foreville, L'Église et la Royauté en Angleterre, 115 n. 2.

[3] Ralph of Diceto, I, 310. The only absentees were the bishops of Winchester, Lincoln, and Bath, who were excused because of infirmity.

[4] Saltman, Archbishop Theobald, 25–7, 141. At the Lateran Council of 1139 Archbishop Theobald had been an official representative, accompanied by four bishops and four abbots, Richard of Hexham, 177.

[5] Foedera, I, Pt I, 44; Regesta Pontificum Romanorum, II, no. 10834.

of the ancient customs on his part, with a clear acceptance of those customs on the Church's part, and an acknowledgement of the royal interests they protected.

That relations rapidly deteriorated was initially not Henry's fault but Becket's. Becket's behaviour in the first month of his archiepiscopate is puzzling, for it seems at first sight gratuitously offensive to the king. None of the issues involved was the least unusual, and if the problems were real enough, there were none that could not have been settled, probably to his advantage, by the process of negotiation which his predecessor had pursued with Henry. That sparks might fly was only to be expected from the volatile nature of the Angevin temper, but Henry was always more reasonable in decision that in debate. Becket, however, made no attempt at negotiation. It almost seems that he was deliberately picking a quarrel with the king. But perhaps, in the early months after his consecration, he was thinking not so much of the impression his actions might make on the king as the impression he intended to make on the monks of his cathedral chapter and the bishops of his province, proving to them that he could cast off the royal servant and put on the good churchman. The key to understanding Becket's behaviour is probably to be found in the process of his election as archbishop. In all the detail that is given of Thomas's life by his biographers, from his conception in his mother's womb to his bloody death in Canterbury cathedral, there is no important period so dark as the long months during which the chair of St Augustine stood vacant. Perhaps this should not be surprising, for the process by which Thomas Becket became archbishop was the weakest spot in his armour as a champion of ecclesiastical liberty.[1] At bottom his election was improper. It is true that canonical procedures were carefully observed: the election was made in due form by the monks and ratified by the bishops of the province. But everyone knew that he was made archbishop by the will of King Henry, and even the observances of the canonical decencies could provide no escape from the edict of Pope Adrian IV in 1156 prohibiting the consecration of a bishop 'who had not been freely elected and without previous nomination by the secular power'.[2] It was no secret that the monks of Canterbury had taken the advice of the

[1] That his partisans were aware of this is revealed by the anxiety of some of them to believe that at the council of Tours he had surrendered the archbishopric into the pope's hands and received it back from him. Cf. William of Newburgh, I, 140.

[2] *Regesta Pontificum Romanorum*, II, no. 10139. According to Alan of Tewkesbury, II, 343, Becket himself later admitted to the pope that his appointment to Canterbury had been less than canonical.

justiciar Richard de Lucy before reaching their decision.[1] It was this that Becket had to live down.

The bishops were later to claim that they had strenuously opposed the king's nomination of his chancellor.[2] Becket replied to their accusation that his election had been unanimous: 'Look at the form of the election, the consent of all who were concerned in it, the consent of the king expressed through his son and through his emissaries, the consent of his son himself and of all the nobility of the kingdom. If anyone of them spoke against it, or opposed it in the least, let him speak who knows, let him proclaim it who is conscious of it.'[3] But his reply is disingenuous: he is referring to the public ceremony of formal election held before the Young Henry at Westminster on 23 May 1162. There indeed the solemn election before the clergy and people was made without opposition.[4] But of course it was, for the royal government had been at pains to ensure that all opposition was overborne before the final ceremony was performed in public. The delay of over a year after the death of Archbishop Theobald is at least partly to be explained by the extent of the opposition. Bishop Foliot was later to remind Becket that Richard de Lucy had been instructed by the king to warn the monks and bishops that unless they elected his chancellor they would provoke his anger and find themselves treated as his enemies:

> We know what we are saying and you know it too, for we anticipated that the Church was about to be smothered, and we in a manner raised our voice against it, for which we heard a sentence of proscription passed against us. . . . But what the king commanded with so much earnestness, what he argued on with such powerful representations, and you, as was known to all, were so bent upon, whilst all your friends and creatures were using threats, promises, and blandishments to promote it, who was there that dared to oppose it?[5]

[1] Roger of Pontigny, IV, 14–16: 'But after they had been in session together . . . they came to the conclusion that nothing could be decided without the advice of Richard de Lucy and the bishops, who were fully acquainted with the king's wishes, on which the whole question of the election must depend.'

[2] *Materials*, Epistolae, V, 410, cf. V, 524.

[3] *Ibid.*, V, 498.

[4] Ralph of Diceto, I, 306–7, is quite explicit: 'In the presence of Henry, son of the king, and the justiciars of the realm, Thomas, archdeacon of Canterbury and chancellor of the king, was solemnly elected archbishop without anyone speaking against it. The election was made *sine aliqua contradictione*.'

[5] *Materials*, Epistolae, V, 524–5. On the authenticity of this letter, sometimes doubted, *see* Knowles, *The Episcopal Colleagues of Thomas Becket*, 171 ff.; Morey and Brooke, *Gilbert Foliot and his Letters*, 166ff.

Moreover, the cathedral chapter of Canterbury was far from united in accepting the king's nomination of his chancellor. On receiving the royal licence to proceed with an election at the hands of the justiciar and three bishops, the prior of Canterbury had summoned several of the more senior monks to confer with him apart. Roger of Pontigny relates that 'after they had been in session together to consider the message they had received, they came to the conclusion that nothing could be decided without the advice of Richard de Lucy and the bishops who were fully acquainted with the king's wishes'. The matter had first been considered by the prior and the senior monks who deliberated apart for some time before deciding that they must follow the advice of the king's commissioners. They then, says Roger of Pontigny, 'with one mind and one voice chose the chancellor to be shepherd and bishop of their souls'.[1] The monks, he says, 'did indeed for some time hesitate over the election, not because they failed to recognise that Thomas was a virtuous man, but because he did not wear the monastic habit, for up to that time the church of Canterbury had almost always had for pastors men who wore the religious habit and observed monastic rule'. Herbert of Bosham, however, reveals that when the recommendation of the senior monks was made known to the whole chapter there was an acrimonious debate about it.[2] According to Edward Grim the hostility of the monks was still evident when Thomas came to them as their archbishop, 'murmuring that contrary to custom he came to the choir in the garb of a secular priest'. Thomas heard of the criticism from a member of his household who reported a dream in which 'a person of terrible countenance had ordered him in menacing tones "Go tell the chancellor" – withholding the name of archbishop in his indignation – "that unless he change his garb forthwith, I shall oppose him all the days of his life" '.[3] So Thomas visited the house of Augustinian canons at Merton where as a boy he had been sent to school and there 'laid aside his costly clothes and silk garments and took on the black cap and white surplice of a canon regular'.[4]

This story is told by the hagiographers as an example of Becket's humility and change of life; but as a grand gesture to win over those who were recently his opponents but upon whose support his dignity now rested, it is typical of the actions of the new archbishop. He filled the early months of his archiepiscopate with grand gestures; that some of these gestures proved offensive to the king seems almost incidental – Becket was proving himself, justifying his election as archbishop to the

[1] Roger of Pontigny, IV, 15–16.
[2] Herbert of Bosham, III, 183.
[3] Edward Grim, II, 368.
[4] *Thómas Saga Erkibyskups*, I, 84.

electorate, striving to please those on whose respect his reputation would depend. To prove himself a success as a member of Archbishop Theobald's household it had been necessary only to please Theobald. To prove himself a success as chancellor it had been necessary only to please King Henry – and Theobald was left to bewail that his arch-deacon gave thought to him no more. But to prove himself a success as archbishop it was necessary to please the monks of his cathedral chapter, the bishops of his province, the people, and the pope. The king would have to make the best of it. Several of his gestures offended nobody, and are commonly ignored by those who are looking for the origin of the conflict with the Crown, but they were all part of the same attitude and policy. He declared that the day of his consecration, the octave of Pentecost, should be a new feast day, the festival of the Holy Trinity – and the Church in England still counts the Sundays of summer and autumn as 'Sundays after Trinity' instead of 'Sundays after Pentecost'.[1] At the Council of Tours he promoted the cause of Archbishop Anselm for canonisation (which was not in fact approved until 1494).[2] In October 1163 he conducted a magnificent ceremony at Westminster Abbey for the translation of the bones of Edward the Confessor to a new shrine.[3] He hastened to defend the jurisdiction traditionally claimed by Canterbury, entering an immediate appeal to Rome against the pretensions of York, and demanding a profession of obedience from Gilbert Foliot when he was translated from the see of Hereford to that of London early in 1163. In the latter Becket overreached himself, for Foliot had already as bishop of Hereford made a profession of obedience to Canterbury.[4]

Becket's provocative actions towards King Henry and the lay barons were simply the counterpart to these more strictly ecclesiastical gestures. As soon as he received from Pope Alexander the *pallium* (a confirmation of his authority as archbishop), although significantly not before, he resigned the royal chancellorship, saying that he was 'insufficient for one office let alone two'.[5] Henry had apparently no inkling of Becket's intention to resign and was mortified: the emperor of Germany had an archbishop for chancellor, why not the king of England? It was a useful symbol of the close alliance of Church and State. In a sense they were swapping gestures; for the archbishop to have remained chancellor would only have been a piece of make-believe. The chancery

---

[1] Gervase of Canterbury, I, 171   [2] Cf. *Materials*, Epistolae, V, 35–6.
[3] Herbert of Bosham, III, 261; for the date *see* Hutton, *Thomas Becket*, 78 n. 1.
[4] *Materials*, Epistolae, V, 44–5, 56–7.
[5] Ralph of Diceto, I, 307; William of Canterbury, I, 12.

was a busy department always of necessity travelling with the king, and it needed an active head even if his title was merely that of a deputy. Henry retaliated to Becket's gesture of resignation by doing without a chancellor *eo nomine* until after the archbishop's death. The work of the office was performed by Geoffrey Ridel, who was in fact chancellor in all but name; and to drive the point home Henry insisted on installing Ridel in the benefice which Becket had held while chancellor – the archdeaconry of Canterbury.[1] This was the first sign of a dangerous posturing which was to inveigle the two of them deeper and deeper into irreconcilable conflict. But Becket's gesture was grander: by resigning even the nominal office of chancellor he proclaimed his independence.

More specific was the archbishop's demand that Roger de Clare, earl of Hertford, do him homage for the castle and bailiwick of Tonbridge in Kent. A reasonable case could certainly have been made in favour of the subjection of Tonbridge to the barony of Canterbury, and Becket had every right, indeed a clear duty, to try to recover property which had once belonged to the archbishopric; but it would have been more proper and it might have been more effective, if he had brought an action for recovery in the royal court. The barony of Clare was one of the greatest in the land, and to antagonise Earl Roger was rash; but Becket chose the dramatic gesture of demanding that the earl perform homage.[2] It did him no good with the baronage, and was not even successful, but it no doubt sounded well to the monks of Canterbury, ever solicitous for the property of Augustine, and to those bishops who had lost property from their sees in the civil war, and to the papal curia which had recently been reminding English bishops that they should not countenance alienation of church property.[3]

It was in pursuit of a similar right that the archbishop presented a clerk named Laurence to the parish church of Eynsford, in Kent, although the lord of the place, William of Eynsford, claimed the right of presentation. William expelled Laurence's men, and the archbishop

---

[1] Ralph of Diceto, I, 308.

[2] *Ibid.*, I, 311; William FitzStephen, III, 43; Gervase of Canterbury, I, 174.

[3] The homage of the earl of Clare for Tonbridge was finally obtained by Archbishop Hubert Walter in King John's reign, Gervase of Canterbury, II, 409. The most notorious example of the depredation of church property in the civil war was the see of Ely, and the earl of Clare was involved in it. In 1156 Pope Adrian IV ordered Bishop Nigel of Ely to recover the lost property under threat of suspension. The matter had been raised at the council of Tours, *Papsturkunden in England*, II, no. 92; cf. *Letters of John of Salisbury*, nos 39–43, I, 71–8; Raymonde Foreville, *L'Église et la Royauté en Angleterre*, 87–8.

excommunicated him. According to William FitzStephen, 'The king straightway wrote to the archbishop that he should absolve him. The archbishop replied that it was not the king's place to give orders either to absolve or excommunicate any man. The king contended that it pertained to his royal prerogative that no one who held of him in chief should be excommunicated without his being consulted.'[1] The king of course was quite right, for this was one of the well-known customs of the realm. Archbishop Theobald had declined to excommunicate Robert of Valognes even when a papal mandate commanded it since the king 'had forbidden his bishops to pronounce sentence of excommunication on any of his barons'.[2] Moreover, if Becket wished to claim the right of presentation to Eynsford church there were proper legal procedures for doing so; in intruding Laurence, even if he believed himself justified, and then resorting to excommunication without trial of William's claim, he was guilty of an unjust disseisin. Archbishop Theobald had found himself in similar difficulties when, as a purely procedural step before a court hearing, he had ejected an alleged intruder from the parsonage of Hinton; this was held to be 'contrary to the king's edict' forbidding disseisin before judgement, and a royal court had ordered the man's restoration.[3] Becket may well have had this in mind when he took the action he did over Eynsford: he was making a public gesture of disapproval of any interference with ecclesiastical jurisdiction, even such well-meaning interference as King Henry's attempts to prevent disseisin without trial.

Even more surprising, and somewhat obscure, is the archbishop's objection to the king's proposal at a council at Woodstock in July 1163 that a customary payment to sheriffs, known as the 'sheriffs' aid', should in future be rendered at the exchequer. This was, presumably, part of the king's efforts to improve the revenue from the shires beyond the fixed and antiquated *farms*. Becket spoke out against it saying he would pay the aid to the sheriff if he deserved it, but not as a contribution to the royal revenue. 'The king,' so Edward Grim relates, 'taking ill this answer of the archbishop, said "By the eyes of God, it shall be given as revenue and entered in the royal rolls: and it is not fit that you should gainsay it, for no one would oppose your men against your will". The archbishop, foreseeing and being aware that by his sufferance a custom

---

[1] William FitzStephen, III, 43. There is no evidence other than this testimony that William of Eynsford was a tenant-in-chief of the Crown, although he was an important sub-tenant of several major baronies.

[2] *Gesta Abbatum Monasterii Sancti Albani*, I, 163; *see* above, ch. 9, p. 328.

[3] *Letters of John of Salisbury*, no. 102, I, 162–3; *see* above, p. 336 n. 1.

should be brought in whereby posterity might be harmed answered, "By the reverence of the eyes by which you have sworn, my lord king, there shall be given from all my land or from the property of the church not a penny".'[1] The justification offered by Edward Grim is not easy to understand, for no one would have suffered directly by the change except the sheriffs, and the king was probably right in assuming that the sheriffs could well afford the loss. If the story is correctly told, Becket was being obtuse and cantankerous; and his final assertion that not a penny would be paid from his lands was quite improper, for the debate was not about the obligation to pay but to whom it should be paid. It may be that the account of the biographers is garbled, but it sounds like another unilateral declaration of independence.[2]

Of course, if Henry were looking to Thomas Becket as to another Theobald to rally the Church behind him in cooperating with the Crown on the really important issues of the relations between Church and State, it was to his advantage that the archbishop should proclaim his independence and demonstrate that he was no mere puppet. It may be for this reason that Henry reacted mildly, for him, to Becket's offensive actions. The biographers of Becket dwell on the king's harsh words of anger, but the important point is that they were words not deeds. Becket, for instance, was persuaded to absolve William of Eynsford, 'For which,' the king is reputed to have said, 'I owe him no thanks'; but at least he resorted to persuasion and did not arraign the archbishop for contravening the law of the land.[3] And although Henry rounded on Becket for opposing him at the council of Woodstock, he did in fact drop the matter of the sheriff's aid. Nevertheless the king could not but be disturbed by the tenor of some of Becket's actions and words which seemed to undermine the whole basis of cooperation between Church and State. These early encounters were, however, over peripheral issues; the crucial question was whether Archbishop Becket would persist in this posture and refuse cooperation on matters which lay closer to the heart of Henry II's reforming programme.

The test came over the attempt to deal adequately with those members of the clergy who were suspected of having committed crimes.

---

[1] Edward Grim, II, 373-4; cf. William of Canterbury, I, 12; Roger of Pontigny, IV, 23-4; Garnier of Pont-Sainte-Maxence, lines 751-70.

[2] The uncertainty as to what was at issue in this dispute was compounded by a previous generation of historians who, following William Stubbs (Constitutional History, I, 462, and his preface to the Gesta Henrici, II, xcii), supposed that the payment referred to was the danegeld. This confusion was cleared up and the auxilium vicecomitis identified by Round, 'The alleged debate on Danegeld (1163)'.

[3] William FitzStephen, III, 43.

Criminous clerks were not a rare phenomenon. The clergy, it should be remembered, constituted a substantial proportion of the population in the twelfth century, perhaps as much as one in six. Many of these were not and never would be ordained to the priesthood. The Church had need of large numbers of men in minor orders; and, moreover, many of those who entered the ranks of the clergy to gain education subsequently used that education not in the service of the Church but in the service of lay masters who needed men who could read and write. The king employed many clerks in his administration. The rewards of such service might be a benefice in the gift of a patron, but the majority of clerks remained unbeneficed. It may be suspected that the lives of many clerks in secular service approximated closely to those of laymen, and that indeed many of those in minor orders were married. The way of life of parish priests was often hardly to be distinguished from that of the peasants among whom they worked, and even though Church law refused them leave to marry, this usually in practice simply meant that their wives were unrecognised and their children illegitimate: Gerald of Wales speaks of 'the houses and hovels of parish priests filled with bossy mistresses, creaking cradles, newborn babes and squawking brats' as far from uncommon.[1] The general run of parish clergy were ill-trained and often barely literate: there was no seminary system, training was commonly picked up by apprenticeship, and examination before ordination was perfunctory. Nor was there as yet any regular system of inspection – of visitation by archdeacon or bishop – to enforce the standards which canon law professed. It was not even easy for a bishop to keep track of his clergy, and vagabond clerks were a constant source of anxiety. The efforts of the ecclesiastical authorities, reiterated in almost every church council of the period, to require clerks to be distinguished from laymen by dress, manner of life, and celibacy, were a basic element in an urgent attempt at reform, but reform worked only slowly. With so many clerks assimilated so closely to the manner, habits, and lives of laymen, it is not surprising that in an age of violence, clerks too should often be guilty of violent crime. To many church reformers it seemed right in principle as well as desirable in practice that clerks should be subject only to ecclesiastical discipline whatever their fault, and indeed that such a principle was fundamental to the attempt to separate the clergy from the world. But to many laymen this must have seemed like putting the cart before the horse: until the Church had achieved proper control of clergy, clerks who behaved like laymen should be subject to lay penalties for offences against secular law.

[1] Gerald of Wales, IV, 313.

For Henry II the problem of criminous clerks was part of the wider problem of how to master prevalent crime, and his intention was stern repression and condign punishment. His concern with it was shortly to issue in the Assize of Clarendon, and the wholesale reorganisation of the methods of dealing with serious crime. It had long been in his mind: and the reason why the subsidiary problem of criminous clerks had not been thrashed out with Archbishop Theobald is probably to be found in Henry's prolonged absence on the continent from August 1158 until January 1163.[1] He had indeed been in England for only twenty-nine months since his coronation in December 1154. The primary problem of government in this first decade of the reign had been the restoration of royal authority and the recovery of rights and of property alienated from the Crown; but the king's duty to ensure to every man the peaceful enjoyment of property and his protection from crimes of violence was next upon the agenda for reform.[2] For Becket, however, the king's concern over criminous clerks was part of a different problem – the more fundamental question of clerical immunity from secular jurisdiction. To him the problem of criminous clerks was one for the Church itself to solve, if necessary with secular help, but without secular interference.

The king could have argued, and doubtless did argue, that the Church had been given more than sufficient opportunity to put its own house in order and had failed to do so. At the beginning of his reign he had allowed himself to be persuaded, somewhat reluctantly, to concede a clerk accused of murder to the jurisdiction of the ecclesiastical authorities. The clerk in question was Archdeacon Osbert of the diocese of York, accused of poisoning his archbishop, William FitzHerbert.[3] The accusation had first been made before King Stephen by a member of the household of the late archbishop. Osbert denied the charge and claimed that as a clerk he was 'not subject to lay jurisdiction, but only to that of the Church'. King Stephen, however, insisted, despite the opposition of the bishops, that the case lay within his jurisdiction because of the atrocity of the crime, and because he was himself in York when the alleged offence was committed; Theobald reported to the pope, 'we just and only just succeeded in recalling the case to the judgement of the Church'.[4]

How far Henry's concession of the case to ecclesiastical jurisdiction was in accord with or contrary to the previous custom of the realm is

---

[1] Cf. Saltman, *Archbishop Theobald*, 160–1.
[2] *See* above, ch. 7.
[3] *See* above, ch. 11, p. 425.
[4] *Letters of John of Salisbury*, no. 16, I, 26–7.

not readily apparent. Before the Conquest there had been no separate ecclesiastical courts in England: the bishops administered church law, and, it seems likely, took special cognisance of accusations against clerks, but they did so in the shire and hundred courts. The Normans, who had rather more up-to-date notions of canonical propriety, introduced a crucial change. William the Conqueror ordained that:

> ... no bishop or archdeacon shall henceforth hold pleas relating to the episcopal laws [*episcopales leges*] in the hundred court; nor shall they bring to the judgement of secular men any matter which pertains to the government of souls, but anyone cited according to the episcopal laws, for whatever cause or fault, shall answer at the place which the bishop shall appoint and name. ...[1]

But in separating lay and ecclesiastical jurisdictions, William I did not divide into two categories the persons subject to those jurisdictions: laymen were subject to ecclesiastical law for offences which imperilled their souls, and the clergy, it may be presumed (for there is no mention of clerical immunity) remained subject to secular law for secular offences. The claim that the clergy were to be subject to ecclesiastical jurisdiction alone, for whatever fault, derived not from the Conqueror's ordinance, but from hardened views of clerical privilege. Such views drew sustenance from the supposed decrees of church councils, forged in the ninth century to protect the Frankish clergy from heavy-handed lay lords; and were strongly promoted by the high-clericalist reformers during the so-called Investiture Contest.[2]

In England early in the twelfth century the anonymous compiler of the *Leges Henrici Primi* states unequivocally that:

> ... The bishops should have jurisdiction of all accusations, whether major or minor, made against those in holy orders. ...[3]

It is not clear, however, whether the author of the *Leges* is saying what the law is or what it ought to be. Cases are known from the early Norman period of members of the clergy pleading immunity from secular jurisdiction, which at least shows that the notion had taken hold, but in the cases which are known the plea was firmly rejected.[4] It may

---

[1] Stubbs, *Select Charters*, 99–100, trans. in *English Historical Documents*, II, 604–5.

[2] Cf. above, ch. 11. On the influence of the False Decretals, *see* Brooke, *The English Church and the Papacy*.

[3] Leges Henrici Primi, LVII, 9; 'De illis, qui ad sacros ordines pertinent, et eis, qui sacris ordinibus promoti sunt, coram prelatis suis est agendum de omnibus inculpationibus, maximis et minoribus'; Stubbs, *Select Charters*, 126.

[4] e.g., the trial of Bishop Odo of Bayeux before the court of King William I, Orderic Vitalis, III, 188–92; and the trial of William of St Calais, bishop of Durham,

be that they are known because they were exceptional cases; but it is clear that the high-clericalist claims were frequently disregarded from the fact that King Stephen could make a concession of clerical immunity in his charter of 1136:

> . . . Jurisdiction and authority over ecclesiastical persons and over all clerks and their property, together with the disposal of ecclesiastical estates, shall lie in the hands of the bishops. . . .[1]

Stephen's charter is not free from ambiguity, and Stephen's promises not free from duplicity; but it was presumably upon this clause that Archbishop Becket was relying when in 1163 he informed the Pope that 'the clergy were hitherto *by special privilege* entirely exempt from lay jurisdiction'.[2] The case of Archdeacon Osbert shows that this cannot be altogether true, although since King Stephen advanced special reasons for taking cognisance of the case, it may be that he admitted the general principle. Nevertheless, whatever Stephen's intentions, it is likely that church courts had in practice dealt with criminous clerks in his reign, if only because of the difficulty secular courts must have had, at a time of dislocation of royal authority, to compel the attendance of clerks. Of course, an argument from Stephen's promise or from what had happened during his reign would not weigh with Henry II, for the time of the usurper was a time of 'unlaw'.[3]

Whatever the practice in the immediate past, Henry II was able to look back to a time when the clergy in England had, despite their claims to immunity, been amenable to secular jurisdiction at least for serious crimes.[4] It is possible that a distinction had been drawn between trial and punishment: clerks being tried in the church courts but handed over to the secular authorities for punishment – even the high claim of

---

before the court of King William II, Symeon of Durham, I, 170–95, trans. in *English Historical Documents*, II, 609–24.

[1] Second charter of Stephen, 1136, Stubbs, *Select Charters*, 143, trans. in *English Historical Documents*, II, 403–4.

[2] *Materials*, Epistolae, V, 49. For a comment on this clause of Stephen's charter, *see* Richardson and Sayles, *The Governance of Medieval England*, 289. It should be noted that although the clergy claimed exemption from secular jurisdiction in criminal matters, they nevertheless sought the protection of secular law for their civil rights, and pleaded about property in civil courts. Their argument in practice seems to have been that the persons of the clergy were privileged, but not necessarily their property, unless it could be described as specifically ecclesiastical property.

[3] Cf. Pollock and Maitland, *History of English Law*, I, 449.

[4] It is noticeable that neither Becket nor his partisans ever claimed that the clause on criminous clerks in the Constitutions of Clarendon, or indeed any of the other clauses, were contrary to the ancient custom of the realm.

the *Leges Henrici Primi* does not preclude that. Nevertheless, Henry II had conceded both trial and punishment to Archbishop Theobald in the case of Archdeacon Osbert, and this presumably set the pattern during the king's prolonged absence. It was, it seems, a concession which he came to regret. The trial of Osbert served only to demonstrate the deficiencies of the ecclesiastical courts in reaching prompt and decisive judgements. After more than a year of delays and forensic debate, the accusation was neither proved nor disproved, and the attempt to test Osbert's innocence finally by requiring him to support his oath with the oaths of three archdeacons and four deacons was frustrated by the appeal of the accused to Rome. Eventually he was deprived of his archdeaconry and reduced to the status of layman, but twenty years later he was still claiming that this was improper and that Pope Adrian IV had acquitted him of the charges.[1]

The ecclesiastical courts were in fact claiming a jurisdiction which they were not as yet competent to discharge. A generation more of expert endeavour was needed to clarify the law and tighten the procedures of trial. As Archbishop Theobald himself admitted, the case against Archdeacon Osbert faltered 'owing to the subtlety of the laws and the canons'.[2] The ecclesiastical courts had even more trouble than the secular courts in finding a satisfactory method of proof, for in eschewing the crude and drastic secular methods of ordeal, they were driven back on compurgation – the swearing of oaths with the assistance of oath-helpers. Moreover the ecclesiastical courts had inadequate powers for sentencing criminals, for the Church's law was more attuned to finding penance for sin than punishment for crime, and, since it would not condone 'judgements of blood', had no equivalent to the secular sentences of mutilation or execution. One way out of the dilemma when dealing with those guilty of heinous crime – as with incorrigible heretics – was to hand them over after trial for punishment by the secular authorities; but whether this could properly be done with those who as clerks still had a claim upon the protection of the Church, was a question which had no certain answer.

The inadequacy of ecclesiastical discipline was the burden of many complaints reaching the king when he returned to England in 1163. He was told that since his coronation more than a hundred murders had

---

[1] Letter of Archbishop Theobald to Pope Adrian IV (1156), *Letters of John of Salisbury*, no. 16, I, 26–7, and Appendix III, 258–62; Knowles, 'The case of St William of York', 92–4; Morey, 'Canonist evidence in the case of St William of York', 352–3; Clay, 'Notes on the early archdeacons in the Church of York', 277–9, 286.

[2] *Letters of John of Salisbury*, no. 16, I, 27.

ILLUSTRATIONS

Section II

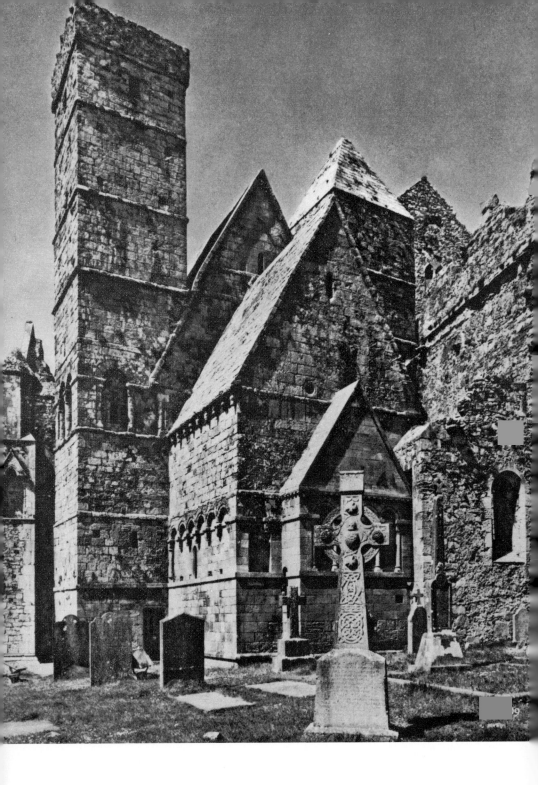

14   Cormac's Chapel at the Rock of Cashel, in what is now Co. Tipperary. Henry II was at Cashel on 6 November 1171 to preside over a council of Irish bishops which approved reforms in Irish churh law (*see* above, pp. 115, 198). Cormac's Chapel was then of recent construction, begun in 1127 and consecrated in 1134.

Cashel was anciently the seat of the kings of Munster, but was vacated by King Murchetach O'Brien in 1011 to make way for the newly created archbishopic of Cashel in the first major attempt at establishing an episcopal hierarchy for Ireland. A cathedral was built on the site in the early years of the twelfth century, and the adjoining chapel added later. The latter was one of three churches built by King Cathel MacCarthy of Desmond as an act of penitence. His mentor was Bishop Malchus of Waterford-Lismore. Malchus had in his early days been a Benedictine monk at Winchester Cathedral; his return to Ireland as a bishop was sought by King Murchetach O'Brien as part of the king's attempts at reforming the Irish Church, and he was consecrated by Archbishop Anselm of Canterbury in 1096 (*see* above, p. 191 and n. 2.) Malchus became the first archbishop of Cashel, but retired again after a few years to Waterford. He died in 1135.

Cormac's Chapel is a fine piece of Romanesque architecture of a kind very unusual in Ireland at the time. Influences from Germany, Normandy, and England can be traced in its design (*see* Francoise Henry, *Irish Art in the Romanesque Period*, pp. 169ff.). It could be said to symbolise the attempts to remodel the Irish Church along continental lines.

15 (*overleaf*).   Examples of English coins from Henry II's reign. In the twelfth century there was no equivalent of the modern Royal Mint. Coins were struck at local mints in many parts of the country by moneyers who contracted to do the work; and much of the profit of coining went to those who held the privilege of having a 'mint'. In Henry II's day the Crown exercised control to the extent of licensing mints, and by requiring the moneyers to use authorised dies; the coinage was thus standardised, and the moneyer had to take responsibility for the quality of the coins he struck. The name of the moneyer and of the mint from which he worked had to be stamped on the reverse of the coin. The dies issued to moneyers were individually engraved, and had to be replaced when they were wore out, so that minor variations occur even within a nominally standard 'type' of coin. The controls were, however, inadequate to prevent poor workmanship, and the coins issued between 1158 and 1180 were generally badly struck, although in terms of weight and fineness of silver reasonably good standards were maintained. In 1180 there are administrative reforms which reduced the number of mints, ousted most of the moneyers, and gave the Crown a better return from the profits of exchanging old money for new. At the same time a new type of coin was introduced. Examples of the two types are illustrated.

15i. 'Cross and Crosslets' type (sometimes known as the 'Tealby' type from the large hoard found at Tealby, Lincolnshire, in 1807), issued between 1158 and 1180 (approx. 19 mm. diameter).

(a) Obverse. The king's head is turned slightly to the right; he is shown crowned, and with a moustache, bearing a sceptre in his right hand. The legend (somewhat obscured in this example) reads + HENRI (cus) REXANGL(orum). [This is also reproduced on the half-title page of section I of the Illustrations.]

(b) Reverse. A cross with smaller crosses between the arms of the main cross. The legend indicates that this coin was struck at Canterbury by a moneyer named Goldhavoc.

15ii. 'Short Cross' type, issued after 1180 (approx. 18 mm. diameter). It was continued with only minor variations by Henry II's successors for nearly a century.

(a) Obverse. The king is shown full face, with a short beard and curly hair, and with a diadem on his head and a sceptre in his right hand. The legend reads HENRICUS REX. [This is also reproduced on the half-title page of Section II of the Illustrations.]

(b) Reverse. A cross with quatrefoils between the arms. The legend indicates that this coin was struck at York by a moneyer named Isaac – that Isaac the Jew made famous by Sir Walter Scott in *Ivanhoe*.

15iii. Examples of halfpenny and farthing of the 'Short Cross' type. The only denomination of coin to be struck in England was the silver penny of approximately $22\frac{1}{2}$ grains Troy weight. Since such coins were of considerable value at the time, currency of lower demoninations was privately made by cutting pennies into halves or quarters. Examples shown are

(a) A halfpenny from the mint of London.

(b) A quarter-penny from an unidentifiable mint.

16 The beginning of the Pipe Roll for the 30th year of the reign of Henry II. It shows the beginning of the account for the counties of Norfolk and Suffolk, which were administered as one unit. The amount the sheriff has paid in respect of his *farm* is recorded in the first line. Then follow the allowances to be set against his *farm*. First are the payments of alms to hospitals and religious orders; secondly, deductions in respect of grants which the king has made from demesne lands; and thirdly, the payments which the sheriff has been authorised to make by royal writs. This last section (marked with an arrow) is the source of the second of the paraphrased quotations from pipe rolls on page 269.

17 A Carta of 1166: a return to the royal inquiry into tenancies by military service. The *Cartae Baronum* are for the most part known only from transcripts made at the exchequer in the thirteenth century. This is one of the rare surviving original returns, that of Hilary, bishop of Chichester. The return lists the names of the tenants of the bishopric who hold land by military service. Most of the tenancies are very small: the names of several men are grouped together as holding lands jointly valued at one 'knight's fee'. In other returns such men were usually listed separately as holding a fraction of a knight's fee. (Actual size: 280 × 150 mm.)

18 A section of the *Rotuli de Dominabus et Pueris et Puellis* of 1185). Part of the duties of the itinerant justices was to make inquiries about those who should be in the wardship of the Crown, i.e., the widows and children under age of deceased tenants-in-chief. The information collected by the justices was deposited at the exchequer, and these returns are the only ones to survive from Henry II's reign. Under the sub-heading 'hund' de Stokes' are the entries which are quoted, in translation, above, p. 299.

19 The original writ of right cited in translation on pages 334–5. It is a writ of the justiciar, Robert earl of Leicester, acting on instructions from the king overseas. Like all writs of the period it is undated; but internal evidence suggests it was issued about 1162.

20 A writ ordering reseisin, dated to the first decade of the reign. It shows the king intervening to secure the restoration to the canons of Lincoln of land of which they claimed to have been deprived. Though it orders the sheriff to ascertain the facts of the matter by the testimony of a jury, there is no sign of the procedural precision and judicial process which characterised the later writs. The wider strip cut at the bottom is the 'tongue' to which the royal seal was attached (traces of which remain). The narrower strip is the 'tie': the writ was folded for delivery into a small bundle and tied with this narrow strip of parchment, the seal hanging out of the bundle on the tongue. Actual size: 15 cm × 8½ cm. Later judicial writs were not retained by the plaintiff; they were handed to the sheriff and subsequently 'returned' to the royal justices. These later writs are known from transcripts, but no originals have survived from Henry II's reign.

21 Incidents from the life of Archbishop Becket, as illustrated in an anonymous *Life of St Thomas* written in French verse early in the thirteenth century, perhaps at St Albans.

i. At Vézelay at Whitsun, 1166, the archbishop denounces the 'depravities' contained in the Constitutions of Clarendon and excommunicates the king's agents.

ii. The archbishop at Montmirail in January 1189 addresses the kings of England and France, and receives insults.

iii. The archbishop's return to England on 1 December 1170. Some of those on the shore kneel for his blessing, others are hostile.

22   The Cistercian abbey of Pontigny, on the river Serein, between Troyes and Auxerre, not far from Sens. It was founded in 1114 and the surviving buildings erected in the mid twelfth century. Archbishop Becket was offered refuge here after his flight from England and his meeting with the pope at Sens. He took up residence in November 1164 and lived here for two years, occupying himself in the study of canon law, much to the alarm of John of Salisbury, who counselled instead the study of the Psalms and works of devotion. A Life of St Thomas was subsequently written here, commonly attributed to the monk Roger who acted as the archbishop's personal servant during his stay at the abbey.

23 *opposite*   The murder of Archbishop Becket: the earliest known representation of the events of 29 December 1170. It is quite likely also to be the most authentic, for it occurs in a late-twelfth-century manuscript which was probably written at Canterbury. The manuscript contains correspondence relating to the archbishop compiled by Alan of Tewkesbury, who was a monk of the cathedral and prior there from 1179–1189. The illustration immediately precedes a copy of a letter which John of Salisbury wrote, giving an account of the murder.

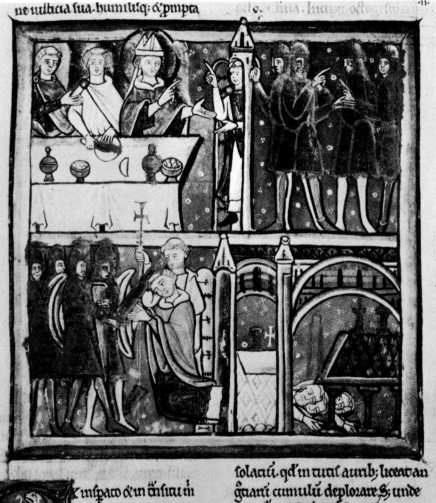

·11·

K inſpaco & in tñſitu in
ch gña ppitiante nup
innotuit: qd ad nos e
rat latoz pſentiu tñ
tur. Cautus g duum
e miniſtratã occaſione ſebendi ad
amicu eā gtiam arripui: arbittꝰ
in longe calamitatis magnu da

ſolaciu qd in tutis auribꝰ; liceat an
gtiant cumulu deploꝛare S; unde
ſumet exoꝛdiu: Ha dicendi parit
mopia: matia copioſa & exuberant.
& q uiſi tepe nro malitia excreuit
ſet ad ſumu: fide excedit. Publica
anguſtias an domeſticas deploꝛa
boꝛ S; gualeſ mundꝰ agnotuit ſua
quêq; miſeria punit acriꝰ: ñ foꝛte

24 The murder scene, with the four knights, Thomas wounded in the head, and the
cross-bearer at the same time wounded in the arm, occurs frequently in the iconography of St Thomas. The same scene appears carved in stone on one of the roof
bosses in the nave of Exeter Cathedral. It was executed in the fourteenth century.
The carving is slightly disfigured by two holes bored subsequently to take hanging
lamps.

25 Henry II's burial place: the abbey church of Fontevrault, between Chinon and
Poitiers in the borderlands of Anjou and Poitou. Henry II's tomb is on the far right.
The other tombs are of Queen Eleanor, King Richard I, and Isabella of Angoulême
(King John's second wife).

Though commonly referred to as an abbey, Fontevrault was in fact a mixed
community of nuns and monk-priests, ruled over by an abbess. The contemplative
nuns were the major element in the community, ministered to by lay sisters and monk-
priests.

Fontevrault was founded about A.D. 1010 by Robert of Arbrissel, an itinerant
preacher of renown, who gathered disciples around him. It soon became the most
celebrated nunnery in north-west France, attracting particularly the daughters of
royal and noble families. It was generously patronised by King Henry II and Queen
Eleanor. In 1177 Henry II arranged for twenty-four nuns to be transferred from
Fontevrault to the ancient nunnery of Amesbury in Wiltshire, which had become
scandalously disordered. Amesbury then became the English equivalent of Fontevrault as a house in which well-born women took the veil. Fontevrault was also the
inspiration for the English Order of Sempringham.

Fontevrault is now secularised. The surviving buildings are of several periods, but
the nave, shown here, was erected in the early twelfth century.

26 Effigy on the tomb of Henry II at Fontevrault.

been committed by clerks, as well as innumerable cases of theft and of robbery with violence which had escaped the rigours of secular justice.[1] Notorious cases were brought to the king's attention. Philip de Brois, a canon of Bedford, was acquitted in the court of the bishop of Lincoln on a charge of murdering a knight. The sheriff of Bedford, dissatisfied with the verdict, attempted to reopen the case in the royal court and was furiously abused by Philip. Informed of the matter, King Henry angrily demanded justice both on the charge of homicide and on a fresh charge of disrespect to one of his officers.[2] He tried to insist, it is said, on a trial in the secular court of a clerk of Worcestershire who was accused of seducing a girl and killing her father, and of a clerk of London who stole a silver chalice from the church of St Mary-le-Bow.[3] The archbishop seems to have realised that such demands posed a challenge to his standing with the bishops on the defence of the Church's liberties, and he acted with resolution in deflecting the king from his intention and rescuing all three cases for adjudication in the ecclesiastical court. At the same time he seems to have appreciated that there was valid ground for criticism of the ecclesiastical courts in that their customary sentences were no deterrent to crime, and he attempted to appease the king by securing harsher punishments for clerical criminals. A priest of the diocese of Salisbury who was unable to purge himself of a charge of homicide was, on the archbishop's instructions, not merely deprived of his benefice but committed for life to strict confinement in a monastery.[4] But Becket overreached himself in having Philip de Brois banished, and the clerk who stole the chalice branded, for not only were such sentences unknown to canon law, they were a flagrant usurpation of the authority committed only to royal justices.[5]

The problem of criminous clerks could not be solved by the archbishop's discretionary intervention, and his arbitrary actions made it inevitable that the king would seek a more satisfactory solution in the imposition of a standard procedure. He raised the matter at the royal council which had been summoned to meet at Westminster on

[1] William of Newburgh, I, 140.
[2] The affair of Philip de Brois is recorded by most of Becket's biographers but with such varying detail and interpretations as to make it impossible to give a satisfactorily coherent account of it. See, e.g., William FitzStephen, III, 45; Herbert of Bosham, III, 265–6; Edward Grim. II, 374–5; William of Canterbury, I, 12–13; Roger of Pontigny, IV, 24–5. Cf. also Ralph of Diceto, I, 313.
[3] William FitzStephen, III, 45–6.
[4] Herbert of Bosham, III, 264–5.
[5] William FitzStephen, III, 45–6; cf. Herbert of Bosham, III, 267.

1 October 1163.[1] After the bishops had had their say, he intervened, according to one account, to remark:

> We have been silent awhile and have meekly observed the attitudes you bishops adopt towards our royal authority and the government of this country. And as we have listened to your views, we have been wondering and humbly searching our mind, as to what fault you should find in us that you should deem us less worthy than other kings, our predecessors, to wear a secure crown; for they, each in turn, enjoyed legal powers and royal prerogatives which no learned man hitherto sought to subtract from the honour of the Crown.[2]

According to Herbert of Bosham: 'the king demanded that clerks seized or convicted of great crimes should be deprived of the protection of the Church and handed over to his officers, adding that they would be more prone to do evil unless after incurring a spiritual penalty they were subjected to physical punishment'.[3] If this report be accurate, it would seem that the king was picking his ground carefully, avoiding a demand for trial in the secular court, and insisting only on an additional secular punishment after trial in the ecclesiastical court. He advanced arguments first from common sense: a man who could commit an outrageous crime while in holy orders would make light of being degraded, if this were to be his only punishment; and furthermore as a man dedicated to higher things the guilt of a criminous clerk was all the more serious than that of a layman who committed a similar offence, and hence it was appropriate that the punishment should be more severe. He then challenged the view that canon law was opposed to such a procedure:

> Now you bishops maintain that it is written in your canons that such unworthy men should be protected and withheld from proper punishment, and you think that you alone are able to understand Roman law and Church law; but we know better that there are men sufficiently learned in both laws who are capable of demonstrating your misunderstanding and utterly refuting your arguments.[4]

The king's advisers then cited canonical texts concerning clerks guilty of serious crimes which contained the judgement: 'Traditur curiae' –

---

[1] Whether the council was summoned for this purpose alone, as some of the biographers seem to imply, is doubtful, Knowles, *The Episcopal Colleagues of Thomas Becket*, 56–7.

[2] *Thómas Saga Erkibyskups*, I, 146.

[3] Quoted from Quadrilogus, IV, 299; *see* also Herbert of Bosham, III, 266.

[4] *Thómas Saga Erkibyskups*, I, 148; Herbert of Bosham, III, 266; Quadrilogus, IV, 299.

'Let him be handed over to the court'. This phrase, they argued, could only mean that a degraded clerk should be handed over to the secular authority for punishment. And this was only reasonable since the secular authority alone had power to impose condign punishments for serious crimes, the ecclesiastical authority being confined to anathema, suspension from office, and banishment from the altar.[1]

Becket, after conferring with the rest of the bishops, spoke at length against such views. According to Herbert of Bosham, he began with an unequivocal defence of the clergy as a separate estate and claimed that they should not be drawn into subjection to any temporal authority: 'The clergy, by reason of their orders and distinctive office, have Christ alone as king. . . . And since they are not under secular kings, but under their own king, under the King of Heaven, they should be ruled by their own law, and if they are transgressors, they should be punished by their own law, which has its own means of coercion.' It was not appropriate that an ordained clergyman should suffer the normal punishments of mutilation, 'lest in man the image of God should be deformed'. To be degraded, deprived of orders and privileged status was punishment enough. When the canonical texts spoke of the 'traditio curiae' they were referring to the symbol of degradation – the transfer of the former clergyman back to secular jurisdiction. Only if he committed a subsequent crime would he, however, be subject to secular jurisdiction. It would be iniquitous to impose on him an additional penalty for the crime for which he had been degraded, for as St Jerome had said in his commentary on the prophet Nahun, 'God does not judge twice in the same case'.[2]

Which side had the better argument in canon law is a nice question. The fact of the matter was that the canonical tests were imprecise and ambiguous, and the commentators uncertain or contradictory. The king's case was best supported by the law of the Christian Roman Empire. The *Corpus Juris Civilis* allowed that a clerk might be examined before a secular magistrate, who, if he approved the charge, should set the record before the local bishop; and the bishop, if he accepted the justice of the case, should deprive the clerk of honour or rank, leaving him to the secular magistrate for sentence.[3] But the ecclesiastical texts, gathered by the canon lawyers, were more concerned to protect the

---

[1] Herbert of Bosham, III, 266–7.

[2] *Ibid.*, 268–72, cf. 281; Anonymous of Lambeth, IV, 96–7; Summae Causae inter Regem et Thomam, *Materials*, Epistolae, IV, 202–4; cf. William of Canterbury, I, 28–9; Edward Grim, II, 385–8.

[3] Corpus Juris Civilis, Novellae, cxxiii, c.21.

clergy from secular authority (some, indeed, of the texts had been forged for that purpose), and when they referred to the 'traditio curiae' they limited the occasions and retained the initiative in the Church's hands. To this extent Becket was more in line with the canonical tradition than Henry's advisers; but in suggesting that it was improper for clerks ever to be handed over for punishment by the secular authority he was on very unsafe ground. In his firm rebuttal of the king's proposal Becket was assuming that canon law was much clearer on the subject than was warranted. Even Gratian had hesitated to speak with certainty on the implications of the texts before him. The only honest course for Becket would have been to admit doubt and to suggest submitting the question to the pope. Whether his stand would have been approved is doubtful: the papacy was naturally anxious to protect clerical privilege, but was also mindful of the harm done to the Church's interests by criminous clerks, and was eventually to lean towards Henry's views on how they should be dealt with.[1] Becket simply assumed he was right; and from the course of his argument he assumed he had to be right because the dignity of the clerical order apparently demanded that he should be. Yet whatever the principles involved, it was axiomatic that the Church's law could and should be adapted to the hardness of the times. Criminous clerks were a real and serious problem, yet Becket offered no satisfactory way of dealing with them.

The remarkable, and decisive, fact, however, was that the rest of the bishops were apparently unanimous in support of Becket on this issue. They, it seems, were at least hoping he was right. Secular jurisdiction over clerks was, of course, a topic on which they were peculiarly sensitive. The strength of their resistance to Henry's proposal is perhaps a measure of their awareness that criminous clerks were the weakest point in their defences: if they gave way over this their whole position might be breached.

That is not to say, necessarily, that the bishops approved the line of argument propounded by Archbishop Becket before the council. Tactically it was a mistake. Set to counter a dubious if not erroneous interpretation of canon law, Becket, in his characteristically drastic way, advanced a case based upon an unnecessarily provocative proclamation of the untouchability of the clergy – 'they are, as it were,

---

[1] For an analysis of canon law and the conflicting views of commentators *see* Duggan, 'The Becket dispute and criminous clerks'. It seems to me, however, that Duggan overstates the case for Becket's interpretation, and that his meticulous analysis emphasises, rather, the uncertainty of contemporary canonists.

set apart from the nations of men'.[1] It was not even a wholly relevant argument: the king was not proposing that the secular courts should try an accused clerk, or even punish a guilty one – merely that they should punish a former clerk, tried by the ecclesiastical courts and degraded from his orders. Becket's supporting contention, that secular punishment following degradation was an improper double punishment, was not an entirely novel argument, but it found little support in contemporary canon law, and was ultimately to be rejected by the highest ecclesiastical authorities.[2] It would have been wiser to have confined the counter-argument to a rebuttal of the interpretations advanced by the king's advisers, to have pointed out the perilous uncertainties of the existing canon law on the treatment of criminous clerks, and to have proposed a working arrangement for dealing with offenders pending the resolution of the difficulty by the highest authority.

It may be that the bishops thought that unanimity was more important than the actual arguments used, and that by a united stand they could dissuade the king from his novel and disturbing resort to canon law. They certainly did succeed in deflecting the king from citing canon law against them, but in so doing they forced him back on tradition. If they would not admit that canon law allowed the delivery of criminous clerks for punishment by royal authority, were they prepared to deny that their predecessors had allowed it to his predecessors? He demanded to know how they stood on the 'customs' of England – were they ready to abide by them? The bishops went into private conference, and again resolved on a united stand. With Becket as their spokesman they said they would observe them, *saving their order*. In response to the king's angry demand that they should promise without qualification, Becket justifiably pointed out that bishops on assuming office swore fealty to the king in life and limb and earthly honour *saving their order*, and that in the term *earthly honour* were comprehended the royal customs.[3] But the damage had been done: Henry, after testing each bishop's resolve individually, declared that they had formed

---

[1] Herbert of Bosham, III, 268: '. . . quasi a gentium nationibus segregati'.

[2] For the most sympathetic interpretation of canonists' support for Becket's contention, *see* Duggan, *op. cit.*, 15–18. Becket's stand helped to persuade Pope Alexander III to condemn a double penalty in his decretal *Licet praeter* of about 1178; but this was drastically modified by Pope Innocent III in his decretal *Novimus expedire* of 1209, which allows, with safeguards, a degraded clerk to be handed over for punishment by the secular authority, Decretales Gregorii IX,II.1.4 and V.40.27; cf. Duggan, *op. cit.*, 23–5.

[3] The justification for Becket's argument is admitted in the Constitutions of Clarendon, clause 12.

a conspiracy, that poison lurked in the phrase 'saving their order', and that it was a mere sophistry. He stormed out of the meeting and next day departed for London without a further word to the prelates.[1]

The course of the council of Westminster does not suggest that Henry had resolved on a campaign to subject the Church in England to his undivided authority. The demand for adherence to the 'customs' only followed the failure to persuade the bishops that the proposed procedure for dealing with criminous clerks had the support of canon law. A king bent, as has been alleged, on erecting 'a ring-fence round his kingdom', would have insisted from the first on the observance of all the customs and dismissed continental canon law as an irrelevancy.[2] It was Becket's dogmatic stand and the bishops' united front, leaving no loophole for possible compromise, which made a resort to the customs inevitable. And once having been forced to resort to the customs, it was obviously essential for the king to insist on unqualified observance.

When his anger had cooled, Henry made one more attempt to avoid an open breach. He summoned Becket to join him at Northampton and as the archbishop approached the town, rode out to meet him and turned aside into a field where they could converse alone. In the story told by Roger of Pontigny, who probably heard it from the archbishop himself, the king appealed to gratitude and affection;

'Have I not raised you from the poor and humble to the pinnacle of honour and rank? It hardly seemed enough for me unless I not only made you father of the kingdom but also put you even before myself. How can it be that so many favours, so many proofs of my affection for you, which everyone knows about, have so soon passed from your mind, that you are now not only ungrateful but oppose me at every turn.'

'Far be it from me, my lord,' said the archbishop. 'I am not unmindful of the favours which, not simply you, but God the bestower of all things has deigned to confer on me through you, so far be it from me to show myself ungrateful or to act against your wishes in anything, so long as it is agreeable to the will of God. . . . You are indeed my liege lord, but He is lord of both of us, and to ignore His will in order to obey yours would benefit neither you nor me. . . . Submission should be made to temporal lords, but not against God, for as St Peter says, "We ought to obey God rather than men".'

To this the king replied 'I don't want a sermon from you: are you not the son of one of my villeins?'

[1] Herbert of Bosham, III, 273–5.
[2] The quotation is from Duggan, *op. cit.*, 1, cf. Knowles, *The Episcopal Colleagues of Thomas Becket*, 133.

'It is true,' said the archbishop, 'that I am not of royal lineage; but then, neither was St Peter. . . .'

The archbishop protested his loyalty saying, 'I am ready for your honour and good pleasure, *saving my order*'. The king insisted that he omit the qualifying phrase, but he would not; and so they parted.[1]

Having failed in his personal appeal, the king began to wage diplomatic war. He went to work on both the bishops and the papal curia.

At the time of the controversy with Archbishop Becket, and indeed for the whole first half of his reign, Henry II had no ready-made core of supporters among the bishops. The only members of the episcopate who had served as royal clerks, and owed their promotion to royal favour, were the aged Nigel bishop of Ely, appointed as long ago as 1133, and Thomas Becket himself. This lack, which Henry curiously had not striven very hard to remedy in appointments to the four bishoprics which fell vacant during the first decade of the reign, accounts at least in part for his anxiety to have his chancellor as archbishop of Canterbury, and when Thomas proved false, helps to explain the king's determination to tether the bishops to the rock of the ancient 'customs'. It is perhaps remarkable that Henry ever found any of them willing to cooperate with him and ready to speak up for him at the Roman *curia* against the denunciations of Thomas and the suspicions of the pope. Yet he did, even among those who might have been supposed to cherish more than Becket himself the clerical ideal of freedom from secular interference. In the autumn of 1163 the king, it seems, was able to detach at least three from unstinted support of the archbishop: Roger de Pont L'Évêque, archbishop of York, Gilbert Foliot, bishop of London, and Hilary bishop of Chichester.[2] Roger de Pont L'Évêque was one of the bright lights of Archbishop Theobald's household, who, by his master's favour and adroit manœuvring, was made archbishop of York in October 1154, two months before Henry became king. Gilbert Foliot was an austere monk, trained at the great abbey of Cluny where reform of the Church was taught as a way of life, and early singled out for positions of distinction. It was as abbot of Gloucester that he attended, in 1148, the papal council at Rheims against the will of King Stephen, and was there appointed to the bishopric of Hereford by the pope himself. In 1163 he became bishop of London by the rare exercise of the papal prerogative to translate a

[1] Roger of Pontigny, IV, 27–9.
[2] Edward Grim, II, 377; Roger of Pontigny, IV, 30, is undoubtedly in error in giving as one of the three the bishop of *Lincoln* instead of the bishop of London.

bishop from one see to another. Hilary of Chichester was pre-eminently a canon lawyer who had made his name as an advocate at the papal curia, was appointed to Chichester by the favour of Pope Eugenius III in 1147, and frequently employed as a papal judge-delegate in cases referred on appeal to Rome.[1] These were men whose allegiance to the Church-universal was unhampered by any prior commitment to the king, and unblemished by any taint of the provincial loyalties which had characterised the bishops of Henry I. The calumnies of Becket's biographers obscure their motives in parting company with their archbishop. Roger, it seems probable, was moved by a dislike of Becket conceived while they served together in Archbishop Theobald's household, and driven by a desire to enhance the importance of the archbishopric of York. Gilbert was accused of envy, but denied it with a solemnity which must command respect, although his dislike of Becket is beyond question and seems to spring from an unbending assessment of his archbishop as probably a hypocrite and certainly a fool. Hilary, it may be, was a man who favoured his own talents as a diplomatist, negotiator, and appeaser. Yet when all the qualifications induced by the criticisms of Becket's friends have been entered, the underlying impression which remains is that these three were the first to take the view, increasingly shared by most of the other bishops, that Becket's provocative and intransigent stand was neither opportune nor wholly necessary, and more likely to hinder than promote the Church's interests. They had no reason to favour the king's policies and were as yet unwilling to commit themselves to his cause, but their experience of ecclesiastical politics as well as their inclination were making them despair of Thomas.[2]

Bishop Hilary visited the archbishop and pleaded with him not to be obstinate, arguing that in any case the king had the power to do as he wished without the bishops' consent, but that he had no intention of requiring them to act against the honour of their order.[3] Thomas rebuffed him; but he found it harder to stand out against the pope. Alexander III was still in exile at Sens, readily accessible to English envoys, and susceptible to arguments that the archbishop's intransigence was disrupting the life of the English Church. He sent the highly

---

[1] Knowles, op. cit., 12–14, 24–7, 37–49; Morey and Brooke, Gilbert Foliot and his Letters; Mayr-Harting, 'Hilary, bishop of Chichester'.

[2] For the king's attempts to win over the bishops see, e.g., Edward Grim, II, 377–8; Roger of Pontigny, IV, 29–30; William of Canterbury, I, 14; Garnier of Pont-Sainte-Maxence, lines 850ff.

[3] Roger of Pontigny, IV, 30–1; Edward Grim, II, 378; William of Canterbury, I, 14–15; Herbert of Bosham, III, 276–7.

respected abbot of L'Aumône to Becket with letters from himself and the cardinals counselling restraint and pliancy, reminding him that the schism promoted by the emperor had confused and clouded the face of the Church, and warning him lest the storm which beset the head of the Church should spread down through its members. With the abbot came the Englishman, Robert of Meulun, shortly to be made bishop of Hereford in succession to Foliot, one of the most celebrated theologians and teachers of the day, who had numbered the young Thomas Becket among his many distinguished pupils. Together they assured Thomas that the king had told them personally that never would he require the archbishop to do anything contrary to his order. All that was needed was to remove the apparent slight to the royal dignity; let the archbishop withdraw the qualification from his promise and peace and good will would be restored to the relations between the king and the English Church. Becket allowed himself to be persuaded and went with them to the king at Woodstock. 'You should know,' he said to Henry, 'that I will observe the customs of the kingdom in good faith, and in other respects I will be loyally obedient to you in all things as is decent and just.' From the proud Thomas this was a handsome submission. The king, however, was not satisfied: the offence, he said, had been committed in public and the retraction should be in public also: let the archbishop summon the ecclesiastical dignitaries, and he himself would summon the barons 'so that in the presence and hearing of all this speech should be repeated for my honour'.[1]

The great council of the realm, duly summoned, met at the royal palace of Clarendon in the New Forest in the middle of January 1164.

It is a singular misfortune that those of Becket's biographers who were probably present at Clarendon – William FitzStephen and Herbert of Bosham – treat of events there with a studied brevity, induced perhaps by their inability to explain the archbishop's conduct. The other accounts, although apparently circumstantial, were written many years later from hearsay – the confused memories of what seems to have been a confusing occasion – and they differ too much to give assurance to any attempt to reconstruct what happened. What is clear, however, is that the bishops found themselves confronted by a demand from the king which they had not anticipated. Instead of being asked simply to concur in the archbishop's expected declaration that he would observe the customs in good faith, they found themselves required

[1] So Roger of Pontigny, IV, 31–3; cf. Edward Grim, II, 378–9; Herbert of Bosham, III, 277. On Robert of Meulun and the abbot of L'Aumône *see* Knowles, *Episcopal Colleagues of Thomas Becket*, 29–30, 59–60.

to acknowledge (*recognoscere*) an explicit statement of what those customs were, and to promise 'on the word of truth to the lord king and his
heirs that these customs should be kept and observed in good faith
without evil intent'. And furthermore, before the council ended they
were required to set their seals to a document in which sixteen of the
customs were carefully formulated – henceforth to be known as the
Constitutions of Clarendon.[1] Thomas, it seems, justifiably felt himself
deceived by the previous assurances that all that was required of him
was a formal promise to abide by the customary but unformulated
practices of the past, and hesitated to make his promise, provoking the
king to a furious and fearsome anger. The bishops, however, stood
against the king's anger in support of the archbishop: as in the debate
over criminous clerks they had been confronted with an issue which
united them in resolution if not in policy and attitude. Then suddenly,
on the third day, Becket gave way, made the promise which the king
required, and instructed his suffragans to do likewise. It may be possible
to explain his capitulation as the consequence of a barrage of pleas and
threats, the memory of papal warnings, and an uncertainty engendered
by accusations of perjury; but Becket offered no explanation to his
bishops. He neither took their counsel nor advised them; his capitulation was as impetuous and wilful as his resistance. This much is
asserted in Bishop Foliot's reply to Becket's later accusation that he had
been deserted by his bishops:

> . . . Let us pass in review what took place at Clarendon, where, for three
> whole days, the point was to obtain from us a promise to observe un-
> conditionally the king's privileges and customs. We stood by you then,
> because we thought you were standing boldly in the spirit of the Lord. We
> stood immovable and were not terrified. We stood firm, to the ruin of our

[1] It is not clear from the narrative sources at which point the Constitutions were
produced. The preamble to the surviving text, however, leaves little doubt that a
recognitio (presumably a verbal declaration) of the 'customs and privileges' was first
made before the king, that the bishops were then required to give an oral promise
to obey them, and that a selection of the customs (presumably those most liable to
cause dissension) were then reduced to writing: '. . . By reason of the dissensions and
discords which had arisen between the clergy and the justices of the lord king and
the barons of the realm, concerning the customs and privileges of the realm, this
declaration [*ista recognitio*] was made before the archbishops, and bishops, and clergy,
and earls, and barons, and magnates of the realm. And these same customs were
acknowledged. . . . [The archbishops and bishops] agreed to and *by word of mouth*
steadfastly promised on the word of truth to the lord king and his heirs that these
customs should be kept and observed in good faith and without evil intent. . . . Now
of the acknowledged customs and privileges of the realm a certain part [*quaedem pars*]
is contained in the present document. . . .', Stubbs, *Select Charters*, 163–4.

fortunes, to encounter bodily torment or exile, or, if God should so please, the sword. What father was ever better supported by his sons in adversity? Who could be more unanimous than we? We were all shut up in one chamber, and on the third day the princes and nobles of the kingdom, waxing hot in their wrath, burst into the chamber where we sat, muttering and clamouring threw back their cloaks and shook their fists at us, exclaiming 'Listen, you who set at nought the statutes of the realm and heed not the king's commands, these hands, these arms, these bodies of ours are not our own, but belong to our lord the king, and they are ready at his nod to avenge every wrong done to him and to work his will, whatever it may be. Whatever his commands deriving from his will alone, will be just to us; think again, and incline your thoughts to his command, so as to avert the danger while there is still time.' What was the result of this? Did anyone flee? Did anyone turn tail? Was anyone's spirit broken? . . . Let the truth be told, let the light of day be shed on what then happened in the presence of us all. It was the general of our army who deserted, the captain of our camp who fled: our lord of Canterbury who parted with the company and counsel of his brethren, and deliberating apart for a while, returned to tell us, 'It is the Lord's will that I forswear myself, submit for the present and take a false oath, to do penance for it, hereafter as I may'. We were thunderstruck when we heard it, clinging to each other in astonishment. . . . When the head is faint, the other limbs faint also, drooping from the same weakness. Our lord of Canterbury himself acquiesed in the royal prerogatives and the ancient customs of the realm, and in their being reduced to writing, and when he had unconditionally sworn to our lord the king faithfully to observe them in the word of truth, he obliged us by force to bind ourselves by a similar pledge of obedience. . . .[1]

The failure to stand firm and to persuade the king of the unwisdom of his demands was the root cause of all that followed. Admittedly an angry Angevin was little open to persuasion; but even Angevin anger cooled. The initial unanimity of the bishops in opposition to the Constitutions was a danger signal, which if persistently sounded might eventually have penetrated Henry's wrath. Becket's capitulation allowed the king to suppose that only the archbishop's stiff-necked pride had hitherto hindered their acceptance. But there in the argument over the Constitutions was the whole basis of the disagreement between Crown and Church. It was a serious disagreement; yet however intractable it may have seemed in January 1164, the dispute was susceptible to reconciliation. If someone had told the king that his prerogatives could be safeguarded, but that their practical application needed to be

---

[1] *Materials*, Epistolae, V, 527–9; Gilbert Foliot, *Letters and Charters*, no. 170, 233–4.

reformulated in the light of developing canon law, the bitter confrontation could have been avoided – for this indeed is how the problem was eventually to be solved. Some of the bitterness is undoubtedly attributable to Henry's imperiousness; but at bottom the confrontation was made inevitable by Becket's casting aside of the king's good will, and by his intransigence over criminous clerks.

One way of escape from the dilemma over observance of the customs, canvassed by continental mediators and approved by Empress Matilda, was 'that the ancient customs of the realm should be observed without promise or writing, applying such moderation that neither shall the secular justices detract from ecclesiastical liberty nor the bishops abuse it'.[1] But such a working arrangement demanded a mutual confidence which was impossible after Becket, in his efforts to ingratiate himself with the clergy, had driven the king to distrust him. In his political maturity Henry II might even have accepted a promise to observe the customs *salvo ordine* as a formula for an honourable peace; but in 1163–4 the trouble was not merely that he was as yet politically immature, and still looking for definitive solutions to his problems, but that Becket's behaviour made him suspect the duplicity of sophistry; 'Poison,' he said, according to Herbert of Bosham, 'lay in that phrase, and it was full of guile.'[2] It was ironical that battle lines should have been drawn over criminous clerks, for of all the points in dispute this was the one most susceptible to a compromise which the highest authorities in the Church could have accepted: but Becket's insistence on an absolute form of clerical exclusiveness called into question the whole of Archbishop Theobald's *modus vivendi* with the State, and drove the king to an equally dogmatic stand on the royal prerogatives, which could be defined only as history defined them in the practices of his predecessors.

On the other hand the blame for converting a difficulty into a dispute does not attach to Becket alone. If Becket was responsible for promoting a conflict, Henry was responsible for closing all avenues of compromise. In having the customs written down he departed from the policy of his grandfather. By this action malleable custom acquired the rigidity of law. Henry I had never been so rash: rigidity precluded negotiation. It might be argued in defence of Henry II that the only alternative to an archbishop who could be trusted to respect the customs was to define the king's rights beyond question. But this defence will not bear scrutiny, for the young Henry II had a weakness for defining his rights.

[1] Letter of Nicholas prior of Mont-aux-Malades to Becket (1164), *Materials*, Epistolae, V, 149.
[2] Herbert of Bosham, III, 274.

At this very time, in 1163, he made the same mistake in his relations with the Welsh and the Scots, driving the Welsh to rebellion and the Scots to an unaccustomed coolness by insisting on putting definitions upon relationships which rested on convenient ambiguities. Malcolm IV had previously taken an oath of homage to Henry 'in such fashion as his grandfather had been the man of the old King Henry, *saving all his dignities*'. This is precisely comparable to the bishops' willingness to observe all the rights which his grandfather had exercised over the Church, *saving their order*. Henry II would accept neither. It was only experience of opposition which taught him the saving grace of flexible formulae.[1]

The analogy, however, may be pressed further: Henry II may have been, in both cases, pressing for a definition of his rights, but there is no more reason to believe that he intended aggression against the Church than that he intended aggression against Scotland. It begins to become clear indeed that the suggestion that Henry II had aggressive designs on the Church derives from Becket's attempts at self-justification, as he strove to counter the accusation that he had provoked unnecessary war between Church and State.

Henry may be excused for supposing that the formulation of the customs in the Constitutions of Clarendon was eminently fair and reasonable. Certainly they do not read as a belligerent assertion of the Crown's prerogatives, or necessarily imply a fundamental attack on the liberty and privileges of the Church. For example, in setting out the procedure for the election of prelates who were also barons of the realm (that is to say who held their estates as tenants-in-chief of the Crown) – a procedure agreed by Pope Pashcal, Archbishop Anselm, and King Henry I – the Constitutions do not shy away from allowing that the prelate should swear to preserve the king's earthly honour, *saving his order* – the point which Becket had made at the council of Westminster:

... The lord king ought to summon the more important of the beneficed clergy of the [vacant] church, and the election ought to take place in the king's chapel with the assent of the lord king and the advice of the clergy of the realm whom he shall summon for the purpose. And the clerk elected shall there do homage and fealty to the lord king as his liege lord for his life and limbs and his earthly honour, saving his order, before he is consecrated.[2]

---

[1] Cf. above, ch. 4, pp. 163, 183.
[2] Constitutions of Clarendon, clause 12. There are texts of the Constitutions in *Materials*, Epistolae, V, 71–9; Gervase of Canterbury, I, 178–80; William of Canter-

The rest of the clauses of the Constitutions fall principally into three groups: those which define the machinery of royal control over communication between the English Church and the apostolic see, those which define limitations upon the exercise of ecclesiastical censures, and those which governed the exercise of ecclesiastical jurisdiction, drawing a boundary line in certain areas of litigation in which competence was disputed between the Church courts and lay courts.

Restrictions on the clergy leaving the country without the king's assent were drawn in familiar terms:

> It is not lawful for archbishops, bishops, and beneficed clergy of the realm to depart from the kingdom without the lord king's permission. And if they do so depart, they shall, at the king's discretion, give security that neither in going nor tarrying nor returning will they contrive mischief or injury against the king or the kingdom.[1]

In summarising the Constitutions, one of Becket's biographers, Edward Grim, interprets this as: 'It shall not be lawful for an archbishop or bishop to leave the realm in answer to the summons of the lord pope without the king's leave.'[2] There can be no doubt, of course, that the intention was to control (though not necessarily prohibit) the attendance of English ecclesiastics at the papal court or Church councils abroad; but it is noticeable that the clause itself avoids an offensive reference to the papacy, and is phrased to emphasise the justificatory purpose of protecting the Crown's interest from injury.

Similarly, in defining the procedure of appeals in ecclesiastical causes the Constitutions are careful to avoid an explicit mention of appeals to the papal court:

> With regard to appeals, if they should arise, they should proceed from the archdeacon to the bishop, and from the bishop to the archbishop. And if the archbishop should fail to do justice, the case must finally be brought to the lord king, in order that by his command the dispute may be determined in the archbishop's court, in such wise that it may proceed no further without the assent of the lord king.[3]

This clause does not prohibit appeals to the papal court, but draws them under the control of the royal assent. Significantly, there is no claim that the king may adjudicate ecclesiastical pleas: a litigant who believes that justice has been denied him may apply to the king, but

---

bury, I, 18–23; Stubbs, *Select Charters*, 163–7; for a translation *see English Historical Documents*, II, 718–22.

[1] Constitutions of Clarendon, clause 4.   [2] Edward Grim, II, 380.
[3] Constitutions of Clarendon, clause 8.

the king will command the archbishop to see that justice is done – much as he would command a lay lord to see that a plaintiff received justice by a writ *de recto*. The most interesting aspect of the clause, however, is the insistence that a case should pass through every stage in the hierarchy of ecclesiastical courts within the realm, before any possibility is entertained of an appeal to Rome. The papacy itself did not insist on such a procedure: on the contrary it had developed the practice of giving audience to any petitioner whatever the state of his case in a lower court, or even, indeed, if he had not brought his case in a lower court at all. This change from the older habit of opening the papal court only to the great causes or to appeals of lack of justice elsewhere, was still something of a novelty in Henry II's day. It played havoc with the Crown's desire to keep track of ecclesiastical causes which might affect its interests. By insisting on a discipline derived from the practice of the past, Henry hoped to retain a machinery of control. He may also have hoped to win episcopal sympathy by protecting the jurisdiction of the local hierarchy against papal encroachment.

The Constitutions, indeed, even when applying limitations to the exercise of ecclesiastical authority, were concerned to safeguard and reinforce that same authority. It was made clear, for example, that the measure of protection normally accorded barons and officers of the Crown against excommunication extended also to interdict on their lands:

> No one who holds of the king in chief nor any of the officers of his demesne shall be excommunicated, nor the lands of any one of them placed under interdict, *unless application shall first be made to the lord king*.[1]

This was regarded by the Crown as a necessary safeguard against the obstruction of government; but such protection was not to be applied indiscriminately to anyone who could claim to stand in a special relationship to the Crown, and royal officers were instructed to assist the ecclesiastical authorities:

> If anyone of a city, castle, borough, or demesne manor of the lord king be cited by an archdeacon or bishop for an offence for which he is obliged to make answer to them, and he refuse to give satisfaction at their citations, it is highly proper to place him under interdict; but he ought not to be excommunicated until application has been made to the chief officer of the lord king in that township, that he should discipline him to make satisfaction. And if the king's officer fail to do this, he himself shall be at the mercy of the lord king, and thereafter the bishop may coerce the accused by ecclesiastical justice.[2]

[1] *Ibid.*, part of clause 7.   [2] *Ibid.*, clause 10.

Assistance was offered to the Church against the abuse of lay power:

> If any of the magnates of the realm shall prevent an archbishop or bishop
> or archdeacon from doing justice upon himself or his men, the lord king
> ought to bring him to justice.[1]

Moreover, the resources of local government could be drawn on to
identify offenders:

> Lay men ought not to be accused save by accredited and lawful accusers
> and witnesses in the presence of the bishop, although the archdeacon
> ought not thereby to lose his right nor anything that is due to him. And
> if the offenders be such that no one will or dare accuse them, the sheriff, at
> the bishop's request, shall cause twelve law-worthy men of the neighbour-
> hood on oath in the presence of the bishop, to reveal the truth according to
> their conscience.[2]

In commenting upon the Constitutions, Archbishop Becket accorded
such provisions an oblique approval by ignoring them. His harshest
censures were reserved for what he regarded as lay encroachment on
ecclesiastical jurisdiction. Yet the Constitutions are remarkable for the
narrowness of the royal claims. Nothing was said, for instance, about the
jurisdiction of the Church in marriage, bastardy, or testamentary
questions despite the repercussions they might have on property-
holding. The Constitutions were confined to a few items of jurisdiction
on which the Church, while asserting claims, could not deny some
uncertainty. The Crown claimed pleas of debt, which the Church
courts sought to adjudicate by reason of the breach of faith involved.[3]
The Crown also claimed jurisdiction in disputes about the right of
patronage to benefices in the Church, since such a right was a piece of
property, although the Church was disposed to treat such disputes as
'pertaining to the cure of souls'.[4] If disputes arose as to the nature of
tenancies held by the clergy – whether they were held by the peculiarly
ecclesiastical tenure of 'free alms' or by some form of secular tenure –
it was deemed proper to settle the question by a jury of recognition
in the presence of the king's chief justice; but if the verdict was that the
tenancy was held in 'free alms', any further dispute between the parties
was to be transferred for hearing in the ecclesiastical court.[5] On the

[1] Constitutions of Clarendon, part of clause 13.
[2] *Ibid.*, clause 6.
[3] *Ibid.*, clause 15.
[4] *Ibid.*, clause 1.
[5] *Ibid.*, clause 9.

question of criminous clerks, the Constitutions are cautious to the point of somewhat perplexing circumlocution:

> Clerks cited and accused of any matter shall, when summoned by the king's justice, come before the king's court to answer there concerning matters which shall seem to the king's court to be answerable there, and before the ecclesiastical court for what shall seem to be answerable there, but in such a way that the justice of the king shall send to the court of holy Church to see how the case is there tried. And if the clerk shall be convicted or shall confess, the Church ought no longer to protect him.[1]

The imprecision of the phraseology, so unusual in Angevin enactments, can only be explained as an attempt by the king to adjust his previous demand for the practice of the past to the sentiments of the bishops expressed at the council of Westminster, and to the uncertainties of contemporary canon law. The clause allows that trial shall take place in the ecclesiastical court, it carefully omits any reference to the *traditio curiae*, and tactfully avoids involving the Church in approving or condoning the debatable 'double punishment'. The intention, wrapped in decent obscurity, seems to be this: anyone accused of a criminal offence shall appear before the appropriate secular tribunal, but if he is there able to establish that he is a member of the clergy, the case shall be referred for trial to the ecclesiastical court; a royal officer will, however, accompany the accused to his trial and take charge of him when the Church has found him guilty and 'withdrawn her protection'. The unexpressed implication, of course, is that the former clerk would be held for punishment as a layman.[2]

The solicitude for clerical opinion exhibited by the Constitutions of Clarendon could not, of course, disguise those aspects which may be summed up as royal interference with the free exercise of ecclesiastical authority. Nevertheless it is an earnest of the king's desire – even in the throes of an increasingly bitter conflict with his archbishop – to establish an amicable working relationship between Church and State in England. The Constitutions are not aggressive but defensive – a conservative defence in the face of changing attitudes which it was beyond the king's power to control. To the Church of the later twelfth century – a Church gaining from its reformulated law a new confidence in the exercise of its authority – such conservatism seemed like reactionary oppression. The bishops of Henry II's day had grown up with Gratian's *Decretum*, they had tasted the fruit of clerical freedom in Stephen's day and had

[1] *Ibid.*, clause 3.
[2] *See* Maitland, 'Henry II and criminous clerks'.

found it refreshing, yet at the same time they had learned that the fruit could be bitter and the harvest threatened by disorder.

Many of the bishops were later to reveal that they had some sympathy with Henry II over the 'customs'. Nevertheless the highly significant fact is that they, as much as Thomas Becket, indeed even more than he, were resolute in opposing the king's demands at Clarendon. It is not hard to see why. It was one thing to agree to cooperate with the Crown in the spirit of the 'customs', it was quite another to take an oath to observe them in an explicit formulation, 'in good faith and without guile'. In the first place such an oath was itself without precedent. Secondly, the taking of such an oath without qualification not only cut across their obligations under canon law, but also confounded the principles and practices which were modernising the Church, strengthening it, and making it more efficient: the king was forcing them into an invidious position in which they had no option but to refuse his demand. Thirdly, the precise formulation of the customs precluded the possibility of adjustment to changing conditions or more favourable interpretation, which was still possible while the customs remained a matter of memory, not of record. Fourthly, while the bishops might agree to some working arrangement with the Crown on those matters which were yet subject to canonical uncertainty, they could not be expected to commit themselves unequivocally to any practice in advance of the Church's resolution of its uncertainty: they might privately feel, for example, that the king's proposal on criminous clerks was reasonable, but what would their position be if they took an unqualified oath to the Constitutions and the pope then declared that under no circumstances should a clerk be brought before a secular tribunal? Fifthly, the reasonable operation of the Constitutions depended too much on the caprice of the royal will: the limitations on the clergy's exercise of their authority was precisely defined, but the principles on which the king would grant permission or apply his veto were not. Sixthly, although none of the bishops, it appears, wished to deny the authenticity of the customs, they were the customs of a distant past: by insisting that they should agree to observe ancient practices, the king was insisting that they set aside the practices, the precedents, indeed the 'customs', of thirty years. It might be reasonable to ignore what had happened in the lawless days of King Stephen, but they were also being required to set aside these precedents of the early years of Henry II's own reign, which had seemed to promise some latitude in the application of ancient rules. Consider, for example, the first clause of the

Constitutions on disputes about advowsons – the right of patronage of ecclesiastical benefices:

> If a dispute shall arise between laymen, or between clerks and laymen, or between clerks, concerning advowson and presentation to churches, let it be dealt with and settled in the court of the lord king.

Undoubtedly some such disputes had in recent years been settled in lay courts by the verdict of a jury (which shows that Henry was not over-anxious, as has often been alleged, to appease Archbishop Theobald); but it is equally beyond doubt that the king had sometimes not merely condoned but had actively approved the hearing of such disputes in ecclesiastical courts. Witness this writ to the bishop of Norwich some-time before 1162:

> Henry, king of the English . . . to William, bishop of Norwich, greeting. I order you to cause the abbot of Hulme, without delay and justly, to have that advowson in the church of Repps which he has proved in your court. And unless you do so, the archbishop of Canterbury shall do it. Witness, Thomas the chancellor at Caen.[1]

Archbishop Theobald, while on one occasion accusing the bishop of Norwich of having despoiled someone of the advowson of Ringstead under pretext of a royal command, on other occasions seems to have been glad of the help of the Crown's authority in settling questions of advowson which had long gone without remedy.[2] The convenient co-operation of Church and State achieved by Archbishop Theobald in

---

[1] *The Register of the Abbey of St Benet of Holme,* no. 26, 18; cf. the previous writ, no. 25, in which the king commands the bishop to do full right to the abbot in the matter of the church of Repps. For an example of a verdict of a jury of recognition in a case of advowson, cf. *ibid.,* no. 24, 17 – in this case again recourse was to be had to the archbishop of Canterbury in the event of lack of justice.

[2] *Letters of John of Salisbury,* I, 123–4, no. 78; Saltman, *Archbishop Theobald,* docs 129–31, 350–3; *The Register of St Benet of Holme,* nos 21–4, 16–17. That disputes over advowsons were sometimes settled by compromises arranged by the church is demonstrated by a letter of the bishop of Exeter notifying the king of an agreement reached at Exeter (*c.* 1161), Morey, *Bartholomew of Exeter,* no. 23, 144–6. In the early years of the reign the abbot of Battle pursued the advowson of Middlehall in the royal court, then in the ecclesiastical court, and finally before the pope, who referred it for settlement on apostolic authority in two English bishops acting as judges-delegate, *Chronicon Monasterii de Bello,* 113–15, cf. 116. In a later dispute over the advowson of Mendlesham the abbot sought a royal writ ordering that full justice should be done him, and the abbey's chronicler notes: 'This was done by royal authority, yet without any injury to ecclesiastical rights or dignities, since the royal court had merely to inquire upon whose presentation Alan had been instituted to the church of Mendlesham.' The affair was settled by a compromise arranged before the royal justices, *ibid.,* 122–7.

patient, firm, but undogmatic negotiation, was being cast aside by King Henry in favour of a new dogmatism reviving ancient and apparently long-discarded rules.

This is a formidable list of objections; yet it is doubtful if Henry was made aware of the full force of any of them. He seems to have persisted in thinking that resistance was simply the product of the archbishop's stiff-necked pride, and that the problem had disappeared when Becket capitulated. It is symptomatic of his assumption that his demand for recognition of the *avitae consuetudines* was reasonable, and as acceptable to the papacy of his own day as it had been to the papacy of his grandfather's day, that he immediately sought papal approval. This was part of the plan he conceived for rendering Becket innocuous. The archbishop's instability was inconvenient. As he left Clarendon he had repented of his oath by the wayside, donned the garb of a penitent, imposed a fast upon himself, and abstained from the celebration of Mass.[1] There could be no trust in the value of his oath. So Henry sought to discredit him by gaining papal support, and to circumvent him by obtaining legatine authority for the archbishop of York. It is improbable that a copy of the Constitutions of Clarendon was sent to the pope: it seems more likely that he was simply asked to ratify his predecessors' acceptance of the custom of England.[2] But the pope withheld his approval, and offered an authority as papal legate to York which was so hedged about with qualifications that the king returned the documents in disgust.[3]

Henry attributed his discomfiture to the machinations of Becket, and gave way to that malevolent fury which always consumed him when he believed himself confronted by treachery.[4] He would not rest until he had driven Thomas to resign the archbishopric or had procured his dismissal. The realm of England, Henry is reported to have said, was not big enough for both of them.[5] Becket, no doubt fearing the worst, made two abortive attempts to leave the country, but the king ignored these infractions of the Constitutions of Clarendon, preferring to wait

---

[1] Alan of Tewkesbury, II, 324-5.

[2] This appears from the sequel, *see* below, pp. 490ff.

[3] *Materials*, Epistolae, V, 85-6, 91. The pope gave no reasons for refusing to ratify the customs; he simply said in writing to Becket, 'In the matter of the dignities, though you and others have given your consent to them, yet we could not grant his request', *ibid.*, V, 86.

[4] It is evidence of the king's passion that he would not write to the archbishop directly, but sent summonses to him through the sheriff of Kent, thereby avoiding the necessity of addressing him with the usual salutation, William FitzStephen, III, 51.   [5] *Ibid.*, III, 55.

until he could arraign him on charges which would not allow him to pose as the defender of the liberty of the Church. The intention was to attack Becket on the spot which hurt most – his *idée fixe* that an ecclesiastic should not be subject to secular jurisdiction; and the purpose was to humiliate and wholly discredit him.

Becket provided Henry with his opportunity in September 1164. John FitzGilbert, marshal of the royal household, had laid claim in the archbishop's honorial court to land on the archiepiscopal manor of Pagenham. The case was dismissed, and John had appealed to the king for lack of justice. On being summoned to answer to the appeal before the king's court, the archbishop had sent four knights with letters from himself and the sheriff of Kent explaining the circumstances of the case. The marshal's claim was ill-grounded and his complaint of lack of justice less than honest.[1] It is possible that the archbishop had been summoned not directly, as was customary, but by writ sent via the sheriff of Kent – a petty insult on the king's part – and, as a piece of bravado, Becket had replied in kind, indirectly. But it was foolish as well as improper for the archbishop to treat the matter so lightly. The king's response was to arraign him before the royal council, meeting at Northampton in October 1164, on a charge of contempt of court in having failed to appear in person or to send an excuse for non-appearance which the law recognised as valid. The archbishop could show that the verdict of his court had been justifiable, but he had no adequate defence to the charge of contempt of the king's court. As William FitzStephen put it,

> It seemed to all that, considering the respect due to the king and the oath of liege homage which the archbishop had taken, and the maintenance of his lord's earthly honour to which he had sworn, he had little defence or excuse; because, when summoned by the king, he had neither come nor pleaded sickness or urgent business in respect of his ecclesiastical office. They therefore declared that he should be condemned to forfeit all his goods and movables at the king's mercy.[2]

It was a harsh sentence for what, as Becket himself not unreasonably pointed out, was a failure to attend a first summons – if he had failed to attend after several summonses his offence might have been judged more contumacious. It is indeed a sign that the court felt uneasy that there was hesitation and shuffling over who should pronounce sentence:

[1] Cf. Knowles, *Episcopal Colleagues of Thomas Becket*, 69 n.1.

[2] William FitzStephen, III, 52. It is interesting that some of the biographers tried to claim that the archbishop was sick and had made a valid excuse for non-appearance; but the evidence against seems decisive, cf. Knowles, *loc. cit.*

the barons said that the bishops should do it, 'For he is one of you'; and the bishops retorted that the barons should do it, 'For this is a secular judgement not ecclesiastical; we sit here not as bishops but as barons; you and we are equally barons here'. Eventually an angry king cut short the debate by ordering the very reluctant bishop of Winchester to do it.[1]

According to Herbert of Bosham, Becket's chaplain, the archbishop was not appeased by the bishops' reluctance to pronounce, as bishops, a judgement upon their ecclesiastical superior. His concept of ecclesiastical dignity would not admit such nice distinctions:

> When the archbishop heard that judgement had been passed upon him he said, 'Even if I were to remain silent at such a sentence, future ages will not. . . . It is improper that an archbishop of Canterbury should be tried in the court of the king of the English on such a charge, on account of the dignity of the Church and of the authority of his person, and also because the archbishop is the spiritual father of the king and of everyone in his kingdom. For this reason he ought to be reverenced by all men.' But he complained more of the judgement of his brother-bishops than of the judgement of the lay magnates, declaring that it was truly a judicial innovation that an archbishop should be judged by his suffragans and a father by his sons.[2]

The king's desire to humiliate Becket was working its poison. But Henry had not finished with him yet: he began to make a series of accusations of embezzlement arising from Becket's handling of royal moneys while he was chancellor. To the first charge, of misappropriation of £300 received while he was keeper of the castles of Eye and Berkhamsted, Becket made answer that the money had been properly spent on the king's business, but in hope of settling the matter, offered security for repaying it. But as charges of further misappropriations piled up, he saw there was no escape, for all his movable property had been declared forfeit for contempt of court. He was interrogated about £500 he had borrowed for the campaign against Toulouse, and about a loan of £500 from the Jews raised in the king's name. Then the king required him to account for all the revenues of vacant bishoprics and abbeys which he had administered as chancellor. Becket protested, with justification, that he had been summoned only to answer to the appeal of the marshal, that he needed time to present such accounts, and that

---

[1] William FitzStephen, III, 52–3.

[2] Herbert of Bosham, III, 297, quoted from the shorter version of the Quadrilogus, IV, 312. Cf. the archbishop's letter to the pope, November 1164, *Materials*, Epistolae, V, 139.

in any case he had been given quittance of all outstanding debts as chancellor when he was made archbishop. But the king became insistent, pressing him either to answer or to offer security that he would stand to judgement on his stewardship in the royal court. Days were spent in anxious discussion amid mounting threats of violence as the archbishop vainly sought an avenue of escape or a way of appeasing Henry. He fell sick, wracked with an ague induced by severe mental strain, but recovered quickly and said he would answer the king on the morrow.[1]

It was St Stephen's day, 12 October, and the archbishop first celebrated mass, with its significant *Introit*, 'Princes also did sit and speak against me; but thy servant is occupied in thy statutes'. So would Becket behave, and being Becket he could not omit the melodramatic gesture. It was only with difficulty that his clerks dissuaded him from going to Northampton castle where the council met, wearing the full mass vestments. As he dismounted from his horse in the courtyard of the castle he took the archiepiscopal cross from his cross-bearer and bore it before him. Some of the bishops tried to take it from him, but in vain. 'If the king were to brandish his sword,' said Foliot, 'as you now brandish yours, what hope can there be at making peace between you?' 'I know what I am doing,' replied Thomas, 'I bear it for the protection of the peace of God upon my person and the English Church.'[2]

King and archbishop did not meet: Henry remained in an upper room while Becket sat below with his chaplains holding his cross in silence while bishops and barons passed to and fro between them. The bishops revealed to the king that the archbishop had that morning reprimanded them for giving judgement against him in the civil case of contempt of court, had appealed to Rome against them for doing so, and had forbidden them to judge him on the criminal charge of embezzlement under pain of suspension from office.[3] Not only was this a breach of the Constitutions of Clarendon, it was a breach of the archbishop's oath of allegiance and tantamount to treason. Becket was asked by a formal deputation from the king if he stood by his appeal, and he said that he did, and that he placed himself and the church of Canterbury under the protection of God and the lord pope.

The king pressed the bishops to join with the lay barons in judgement. Amid scenes of mounting clamour and confusion they begged to be excused. They remonstrated with Becket that he had thrust them be-

---

[1] On the archbishop's illness, which seems to have been psychogenetic, *see* Knowles, *op. cit.*, Appendix V, 167–8.

[2] Herbert of Bosham, III, 305; William FitzStephen, III, 57.

[3] Herbert of Bosham, III, 302–3; William FitzStephen, III, 62.

tween the hammer and the anvil: if they ignored his prohibition they were guilty of disobedience to their superior, if they respected it they infringed their oath to the Constitution and transgressed against the king. Some urged him to resign. When he rebuffed all entreaties they returned to the king and offered him a bargain: if he would excuse them from sitting in judgement upon the archbishop they would immediately appeal to Rome against him and seek his deposition, accusing him of perjury and of forcing them to infringe their oath. Henry, doubtless thinking that such an appeal would utterly discredit Becket at Rome, and that a request for his deposition would come more conveniently from the bishops than from himself, agreed.[1]

After the bishops had withdrawn, the rest of the council responded to the king's demand for judgement and then descended to the lower room to acquaint the archbishop with its verdict. But Becket refused to hear: 'Think you to judge me?' he said. 'You have no right to do so. Judgement is a sentence pronounced after trial, and this day I have said nothing in formal pleading. . . . Such as I am, I am your father, while you are magnates of the household, lay powers, secular persons. I will not hear your judgement. . . .' He pushed his way out of the chamber and out of the castle, bearing his cross before him.[2]

That night the archbishop sent to the king for permission to depart and for a safe-conduct. The king replied that he would give answer the next morning. What the king's intentions were remain unknown, for next morning they had become irrelevant: Thomas Becket had already gone.

The council of Northampton reflects no credit on Henry II. It is true that Becket invited condemnation by his contempt of court and his prohibition of the bishops performing their duty to the king by taking part in the deliberations of the council; but Henry had acted throughout with scant regard for decency, legality, or justice. It is a sign of the uneasiness of the best of the barons that even though Becket had put himself unquestionably in the wrong, the justiciar, the earl of Leicester, was reluctant to pronounce judgement: he tried first to shift the task on to someone else, and when obliged to do it himself, deferred announcing the verdict to the archbishop while he span out a recital of all that had happened since Clarendon – until interrupted by Becket's refusal to listen.[3] Henry, not for the first time, or the last, had overplayed his hand. Yet Becket does not emerge with much credit either. His lonely persistence in the midst of harassment and hints of violence,

[1] Cf. Knowles, op. cit., 81–4.
[2] William FitzStephen, III, 67–8.   [3] Ibid., 67.

argues a remarkable strength of will; but it was a strength devoted to preserving his dignity – however much he tried to rationalise it as a defence of the Church. The humiliation, not of being found guilty or of being punished but simply of being put on trial, proved in the end too much for him. To have borne with composure the king's manifest persecution, to have exposed patiently the hollowness of the accusations, and to have suffered perhaps imprisonment on such flimsy charges would have been true martyrdom. But Becket was not yet ready for martyrdom – and never for this kind of martyrdom.

Henry took the advice of the bishops and did not lay hands on Becket's property or ecclesiastical estates while the appeal to the papal curia was pending. He nonetheless pursued Becket with his venom in his flight abroad:

> To his lord and friend Louis, the illustrious king of the French, Henry king of the English and duke of the Normans and Aquitanians and count of the Angevins, greeting and affection.
>
> Know that Thomas, who was archbishop of Canterbury, has been publicly adjudged in my court, by full council of the barons of my realm to be a wicked and perjured traitor to me, and under the manifest name of traitor has wickedly departed, as my messengers will more fully tell you.
>
> Wherefore I earnestly beg you not to permit a man guilty of such infamous crimes and treasons, or his men, to remain in your kingdom; and let not this great enemy of mine, so it please you, have any counsel or aid from you or yours, even as I would not give any such help to your enemies in my realm or allow it to be given. Rather, if it please you, help me to take vengeance on my great enemy for this affront, and to seek my honour, even as you would wish me to do for you if there were need of it.
>
> Witness Robert earl of Leicester. At Northampton.[1]

Henry's expressions of friendship for Louis were wasted. The French king guaranteed to Becket a safe refuge, actuated partly, perhaps, by the piety which the Capetians always affected and sometimes felt, but even more by a keen appreciation of the value of the persecuted archbishop as a pawn in his struggle to bring down the great Angevin.[2] At the very least the protection of the archbishop of Canterbury would advertise a Christian virtue and a defiance of Henry II which could

---

[1] *Materials*, Epistolae, V, 134; *Recueil des Actes de Henri II*, I, 385, no. ccxxxvii.

[2] John of Salisbury, preceding Thomas Becket abroad, had written to him earlier in 1164: 'The French fear our king and hate him equally', *Materials*, Epistolae, V, 99. For the French king's reception of the king's envoys and of Becket's, *see* Herbert of Bosham, III, 332–4.

only reflect glory upon the French Crown. He already had a notable exile, Pope Alexander III himself, ensconced at Sens. If Louis could not hope to match the emperor and the king of England in power it was nonetheless a singular achievement for a French king to cock snooks at both of them simultaneously.

Becket's flight abroad prompted Henry to send a diplomatic mission speedily to the papal curia. The archbishop of York and four bishops went, together with a few lay magnates led by the earl of Arundel, and a group of the king's *familiares*. It was virtually a deputation of the royal council. The purpose was not, it seems, to prosecute the bishops' appeal. The envoys were instructed not to enter into controversy or to remain longer than three days at the curia; if there was to be a confrontation between the king's views and the archbishop's they were to seek that it should take place before a papal legate in England – where the king himself might hope to sway the verdict. In speeches before the pope and cardinals in public consistory members of the deputation spoke of the king's devotion to the apostolic see and advertised his anxiety that the pope should put an end to the dissensions in England caused by the impetuous behaviour of the archbishop of Canterbury; but it is likely that the main business of the delegation was conducted in private – lobbying the cardinals, and when a sympathetic ear was found, suggesting that the archbishop was an impossible man, and that peace could be secured only by his deposition.[1] The pope, however, was circumspect: he would not commit himself to any irrevocable decision before he had heard the archbishop, and although he was agreeable to the appointment of legates, he would not consent to endow them with powers which precluded further recourse to the papal curia.[2]

A few days later Becket himself arrived. His purpose was simple: to salvage his reputation. He could not abstain from melodrama, and for once it stood him in good stead. Throwing himself at the pope's feet he proferred not the usual gift of gold, silver, or jewels, but the chirograph of the Constitutions of Clarendon, spreading it out with his two hands. 'Behold, holy father,' he said, 'the customs of the king of the

---

[1] This is suggested by William FitzStephen, III, 74. The purpose of the deputation is not clearly revealed by the sources, and the reports of the speeches made are not consistent. FitzStephen says that in public nothing was said against the archbishop personally; but this is contradicted by Herbert of Bosham, who was there, III, 335–6, and by Alan of Tewkesbury, II, 337ff. I follow Knowles's interpretation, with its plausible suggestion that the intention was 'to carry the archbishop's position at the rush', *Episcopal Colleagues of Thomas Becket*, 92–4, 111.

[2] Herbert of Bosham, III, 336; Alan of Tewkesbury, II, 340.

English, opposed to the canons and decretals and even to the laws of secular princes, for which we are driven to endure exile.' Rising to his feet he read them out, commenting on them clause by clause.[1] Then, with a finesse worthy of Henry II himself, he produced his master stroke: 'My fathers and lords,' he said to the assembled cardinals:

> Every man ought to speak the truth at all times and especially in the presence of God and yourselves. I freely confess with sighs and groans that these afflictions have befallen the English Church through my wretched fault. I clambered into the sheepfold of Christ, not through Him who is the door, as one summoned by canonical election, but was forcibly intruded by the secular power. And though I accepted this burden unwillingly nevertheless it was human will not divine will which induced me to do so. What wonder then, if it has brought me into such straits. Yet had I, at the threat of the king, renounced the jurisdiction of episcopal authority, as my brother bishops urged me to do, it would have constituted a pernicious precedent, ruinous to the interests of princes and the will of the Catholic Church. I therefore deferred doing so until I should appear before you. But now, recognising that my appointment was far from canonical, dreading lest the consequences should prove the worse for me, realising that my strength is unequal to the burden, and fearing lest I should involve in my own ruin the flock to which, such as I am, I was given as shepherd, I resign into your hands, father, the archbishopric of Canterbury.[2]

So saying he wept and sobbed, removed the archiepiscopal ring from his finger and handed it to the pope.[3]

In private some of the cardinals were for seizing the opportunity of his proferred resignation, seduced, as Becket's biographers believed, by the king's gold; but the recital of the Constitutions of Clarendon, torn from their context in the traditions of English Church life, and with no one to gainsay the archbishop's interpretation, had excited a disapproval which rendered such a course of action indecent. The pope restored to Becket his archiepiscopal ring, saying 'receive anew at our hands the cure of the episcopal office', and thus wiped out the stigma of Becket's irregular promotion.[4] Thereafter Becket was secure in the

---

[1] Roger of Pontigny, IV, 62; Garnier of Pont-Sainte-Maxence, lines 2341ff.; cf. Alan of Tewkesbury, II, 342, Herbert of Bosham, III, 340ff., Edward Grim, II, 403. The quotation is from Roger of Pontigny; other accounts differ in wording but the sentiment is the same.

[2] Alan of Tewkesbury, II, 342–3.

[3] William of Canterbury, I, 46.

[4] Alan of Tewkesbury, II, 344.

knowledge that there was little possibility of his being deprived of Canterbury against his will.

In his rage at being outwitted, Henry wreaked his vengeance on Becket's hapless friends and servants and their kinsfolk in writs to the bishops and sheriffs:

> You know how wickedly Thomas, archbishop of Canterbury, has acted towards me and my kingdom and how basely he has fled. And therefore I command you that his clerks who were with him after his flight and the other clerks who disparage my honour and the honour of the realm shall not receive any of the revenues which they have within your bishopric, except by my order. Nor shall they receive from you any aid or counsel.
>
> I command you . . . to seize into my hand all the revenues and possessions of the archbishop's clerks, as Ranulf de Broc and others of my officers shall direct you. And the fathers and mothers, brothers and sisters, nephews and nieces of all the clerks who are with the archbishop shall be laid under safe pledges with their chattels, until you shall learn my will about them.[1]

It was a mean and tyrannous act which impeded Henry's efforts to reach an understanding with the papacy.

The sequel to the abortive attempt to have Becket relieved of the archbishopric of Canterbury was a stalemate which lasted for six years. The pope strove for a reconciliation which would allow the archbishop to return to England; but Becket would agree to no form of reconciliation which did not thoroughly vindicate him by the public abasement of Henry; and the king, protesting that the archbishop had never been sentenced to exile and was free to return whenever he wished, would agree to the imposition of no conditions.

The pope patiently negotiated year after year by letters and envoys, restraining and even interdicting the archbishop from such extreme measures as the excommunication of the king, and on the other hand cajoling Henry and hinting that he might himself apply an interdict, but all the time looking for an opening created by shifting circumstances, or, less hopefully, for a change of heart. His efforts were punctuated by attempts by Henry or Becket to break the deadlock by more drastic means.

Henry made the first move early in 1165 by entering into negotiations with Alexander's enemies in the German empire. A powerful delegation of German magnates, led by the *eminence grise* of imperial policy, Rainald of Dassel, archbishop of Cologne, visited Henry in Normandy,

[1] *Materials*, Epistolae, V, 151–2.

and went over to England to speak with the queen and council. Two of Henry's most trusted *familiares*, John of Oxford and Richard of Ilchester, accompanied the archbishop of Cologne on his return to Germany and waited upon the emperor's court at Würzburg in May. Their primary and ostensible purpose was to pursue a suggestion made by the German delegation of marriages of one of Henry's daughters to a son of Emperor Frederick, and of another daughter to the duke of Saxony; but they allowed themselves to become involved, presumably not without Henry's connivance, in delicate discussions about the relations of empire and papacy. Alexander III's rival for the papal throne, recognised in Germany as Victor IV, had died the previous year, and there was a distinct possibility that the schism might be ended by the acceptance of Alexander. The imperial council was divided and the emperor wavered; but the archbishop of Cologne, who favoured the continuance of the schism, proclaimed the sympathy and support of the king of England and swung the assembly decisively in favour of the recognition of a new rival to Alexander in Paschal III.[1] It is likely that Henry favoured a marriage alliance with Germany as a threat to King Louis of France, and had hoped incidentally to exploit the negotiations with the German delegation as a means of frightening Alexander into action against Becket, but had instead found himself exploited by the devious Rainald of Dassel. Reports that the English envoys at Würzburg had taken an oath to Paschal were strenuously denied, and Henry himself protested his innocence.[2] Pope Alexander kept his head and refused to be stampeded into concessions to Henry. On the contrary, he chose this moment to declare that the English bishops ought not, at Northampton, to have presumed to sit in judgement on their ecclesiastical superior, and that the sentence of forfeiture of movable property was invalid since the archbishop had no goods save those which belonged to the Church.[3] At the same time, however, he took good care to restrain Becket from exuberance, recognising the danger of his intemperance:

> Since the days are evil and much has to be endured for the circumstances of the times, we beseech your discretion, we advise, we counsel, we urge, that in your whole conduct respecting your cause and that of the Church, you display caution, prudence, and circumspection, doing nothing in

[1] Robert de Torigny, 224; Ralph of Diceto, I, 318; cf. Munz, *Frederick Barbarossa*, 236ff.

[2] For the reports *see Materials*, Epistolae, V, 185–94; for the denial, *ibid.*, V, 194–5; and for Henry's protestations of innocence, *ibid.*, V, 206, and VI, 79–80.

[3] *Ibid.*, V, 178–9.

haste or precipitately, but at the right time and gravely; so that in all possible ways, consistent with the liberty of the Church and the dignity of your office, you will labour to recover the favour and good will of his majesty the king of England. And until next Easter you should uphold the said king in that you should forbear to take action against his person or territories. For then God will give us better days, and both you and we may take proceedings with safety.[1]

When Easter 1166 arrived, the pope confirmed to Thomas the office of papal legate for England, and the archbishop at once adopted his own policy for breaking the deadlock. He wrote three consecutive letters to the king. One is addressed to 'His most revered lord King Henry', another is addressed, 'His lord and friend King Henry', and the third begins 'These are the words of the lord of Canterbury to the king of the English'.[2] In them Thomas progressed from memorials of affection to threats of divine vengeance. In June 1166 vengeance began to strike. On the day of Pentecost, speaking from the pulpit at Vézelay, the archbishop solemnly condemned and annulled the 'depravities' contained in the Constitutions of Clarendon, and excommunicated John of Oxford and Richard of Ilchester for consorting with schismatics, the justiciar Richard de Lucy and Jocelin de Balliol for their drafting of the Constitutions, and others of the king's servants for presuming to lay hands on the property of the see of Canterbury. The king himself, it is said, was excluded from the censures only because it was reported that he was sick, but the archbishop issued dire warnings that he too would suffer anathema unless he speedily gave satisfaction for his injuries to the Church.[3]

Henry's response was a renewed threat to withdraw from his allegiance to Alexander III, made explicit in a letter to the archbishop of Cologne, which, from its presence among the materials collected by Becket's biographers, seems to have been deliberately published.

> I have long desired a legitimate opportunity for withdrawing from Pope Alexander and his perfidious cardinals, who presume to support that traitor Thomas, formerly archbishop of Canterbury, against me. Wherefore by the council of all my barons and with the assent of the clergy, I mean to send to Rome certain great men of my realm, namely the archbishop of York, the bishop of London, the archdeacon of Poitiers, John of

---

[1] *Ibid.*, V, 179–80.

[2] *Ibid.*, V, 266–82.

[3] For John of Salisbury's account of the Vézelay censures *see ibid.*, V, 383–4, for Becket's report of his action to the pope, *ibid.*, V, 386–8, to the bishops of England, *ibid.*, V, 392–7, and the archbishop of Rouen, *ibid.*, V, 400–1.

Oxford, and Richard de Lucy, who publicly and plainly on behalf of me and my whole kingdom and all the other territories which I hold, shall demand from Pope Alexander and his cardinals, and warn them, that they should no longer sustain that traitor to me, but shall so free me from him that I may, with the advice of the clergy, set up someone else in the church of Canterbury. They shall warn them also to declare null and void everything Thomas has done. They shall also demand this, that the pope shall publicly swear to them, on behalf of himself and his successors, to preserve in perpetuity to me and all my successors, the royal customs of Henry my grandfather, secure and inviolate. And if they will not grant me what I ask, neither I, nor my barons, nor my clergy shall show the pope any further obedience, nay rather will openly oppose him and his; and anyone who shall be found on my land adhering to him will be expelled.

And so we ask you, as a dear friend, to send to us without delay Arnold, or Brother Ralph of the Hospitallers, that they may afford safe-conduct on behalf of the emperor to these envoys, both in going and returning through imperial territory.[1]

This time Alexander III was seriously alarmed. The resistance of the north Italian towns to Emperor Frederick and the financial support of the Norman monarchy of Sicily had allowed him to return to Rome; but his political position was by the autumn of 1166 extremely precarious as his money ran low and a German army marched into Italy.[2] The death of King William I of Sicily early in 1166, and the succession of a minor under regency, robbed him of his most generous source of assistance and made him look in desperation to the support of kings such as Louis VI and Henry II. To Becket's intense chagrin, the pope completely undermined the effects of his censures on Henry's servants, forbade the archbishop to take any further action and made his own attempt to break the deadlock, announcing the appointment of two cardinals as legates to try to effect a reconciliation, and earnestly beseeching the king of France to assist as peacemaker.[3] The king's envoys returned from Rome in such exultation that Henry was led to believe that all would be settled according to his own wishes, and Foliot is reported to have exclaimed, 'No longer will Thomas be my archbishop'.[4] Becket rounded on the pope in a letter which not only displays the bitterness of despair, but also betrays his own stubbornness in pride and wounded vanity:

Let us not be put to shame among men, let not our adversaries insult Christ and the Church; let us not be brought to derision among the high-

---

[1] *Materials*, Epistolae, V, 428–9.   [2] Munz, *Frederick Barbarossa*.
[3] *Materials*, Epistolae, VI, 84–6, 123–8.   [4] *Ibid.*, 150–2.

born and the low, when we have invoked you by name, holy father, to watch over us. Not for us, father, not for us, but in the name of our Lord Jesus Christ earn for yourself a great name, restore your glory, and recover your reputation.[1]

Becket, however, as well as Henry, had mistaken the pope's intentions. As chancellor to a previous pope and ambassador extraordinary, Alexander III had developed a finesse in diplomacy which was more than a match for either of them. While placating the king's anger and circumventing the embarrassing consequences of the archbishop's intemperance, he had in fact given away nothing. The prospect of a legation to depose the archbishop kept Henry in hope for several months and Becket in restraint. Henry only realised he had been outmanœuvred when he discovered that the cardinals' purpose was to contrive a compromise, not to pronounce judgement on his enemy, and he stormed out of a meeting with them saying loudly enough for all to hear, 'I hope to God never again to set eyes on a cardinal'.[2] Becket, who all along regarded the legation as a scandal, dismissed all suggestions of compromise with contempt.[3]

For several years time seemed to be on the side of Henry II. The archbishop might die, or be driven by penury to accept another see; Alexander III might be succeeded by one of the cardinals favourably disposed towards the king of England. Becket's friends indeed displayed a lively apprehension about the pope's health. But by the close of 1168 time was rapidly running out for Henry. He was becoming anxious to have his son crowned as joint-king, and history left no doubt that the coronation of English kings was the prerogative of Canterbury. This anxiety was more than a desire to settle the succession: it was an integral part of a comprehensive scheme for the establishment of peace with the king of France. The uneasy truce after the Treaty of Fréteval in 1161 had in 1167 given way to a sharp if intermittent war in which King Louis had sought to exploit all sources of grievance against Henry including Archbishop Becket. Henry crushed the rebellions which Louis fomented or encouraged, but wearying of the waste of effort involved, sought to allay the fears of the French by proposing a dynastic settlement which would dismember the Angevin 'empire' among his sons.[4] The homages of his sons to Louis was one element in the ratification of peace, but the seal was to be set upon it by the coronation of Henry the

[1] *Materials*, Epistolae, VI, 155.
[2] *Ibid.*, 270, cf. 248. For the pope's instructions to his legates *see ibid.*, 232-3.
[3] For Becket's attitude *see ibid.*, 162-5, 245-53, 296-7.
[4] *See* above, pp. 103-9.

Younger and his wife – Louis's daughter Margaret. In these circumstances Archbishop Becket became something of an embarrassment to
King Louis, and his exile an obstacle to the coronation. The peace
negotiations at the border town of Montmirail in January 1169 were
therefore extended to embrace the conflict between Henry and Becket.
Indeed, they were extended further to include relations between France
and the empire, and between the empire and the papacy. Emperor
Frederick had been deprived of the fruits of his victory in central Italy
in the summer of 1167 by an attack of malaria which carried away not
only the bulk of his army but many of his closest advisers, including
Rainald of Dassel, archbishop of Cologne. The venom of the schism had
ebbed with the emperor's fortunes; his whole policy towards Italy was
in 1168 being reappraised, and looking to a rapprochment with the
papacy he was considering asking Alexander III to perform the coronation of his own son, another Henry. The kings of France and England
were looked to as mediators, and German envoys, including Henry II's
son-in-law, the duke of Saxony, came to the conference at Montmirail.[1]

Had circumstances really been ripe for it, Montmirail might have
achieved fame as a conference which settled the peace of Europe: instead it must count merely as one of those abortive attempts at peace
brought about by the naïve hope that problems can be wished away.
Neither Henry II nor Thomas Becket was really ready for reconciliation. Henry was prepared to take back the man he had sought to depose
as archbishop of Canterbury, provided it did not publicly appear that
Becket had won, and Becket was prepared to return provided it did not
appear that he had lost. The mediators worked hard to persuade
Becket that he should make the first move towards securing a real peace
by offering to accept the king's pleasure on the matters of the 'customs',
without any qualification, such as the phrase 'saving his order' which
had so offended the king at the council of Westminster. It appeared
that they had succeeded. Thomas approached the two kings as they
sat amid a great crowd of clergy and laity, and knelt at Henry's feet.
The king took him by the hand and made him rise, and the archbishop
began humbly to entreat the royal mercy on the English Church which
was committed to so unworthy a sinner as himself. 'On the whole matter
which is between us, my lord king,' said Becket, 'I throw myself on
your mercy, and on your pleasure, here in the presence of our lord the
king of France and of the archbishops, princes, and others who stand
round us.' Then he added, to the astonishment of everyone, including
his friends, 'saving the honour of my God'. Henry raged at Becket,

[1] Munz, *Frederick Barbarossa*, 295.

H—R

denouncing him as proud, vain, and ungrateful, and turning to King Louis said, 'Observe, if you please, my lord, whatever his lordship of Canterbury disapproves, he will say is contrary to God's honour, and so will he always have the advantage of me'. King Louis remonstrated with Becket, the mediators pleaded with him, the barons, both English and French, abused him; but Becket calmly but firmly refused to withdraw his qualification, and the assembly broke up in disorder.[1]

King Louis's desire to promote a reconciliation cooled as he lost confidence in the political settlement made at Montmirail, and Becket was soon restored to his favour as a useful irritant to Angevin equanimity. But the pope lost no time in making further strenuous efforts to patch up the quarrel. Indeed he intervened with a swiftness which suggests that he feared that the repercussions of the failure at Montmirail might be damaging to all prospects of a settlement. A series of legates laboured unremittingly but fruitlessly throughout 1169. They found Henry outwardly reasonable, but slippery and evasive when pressed. They found Becket obdurate and demanding punitive action by the Holy See. Henry, when the legates had exhausted pleas and turned to warnings, said that the archbishop could return as soon as he agreed to abide by the Constitutions, but when pressed for guarantees changed his answer. He said he would summon the English bishops and comply with their advice, but when pressed to name the day for a meeting he procrastinated. The legates, complaining that they could not report his answers to the pope because he changed them so often, asked him to set down his intentions in writing, but he refused.[2] Becket said that he was ready to comply with all the king's wishes – except to undertake any obligation, however couched, to observe the customs that did not include the reservation, 'saving God's honour and our order'. He astutely justified his refusal to compromise by reminding the pope of the scene at Sens in December 1164,

> When your holiness absolved me in a special manner from the observances of those usages hateful to God and the Church, and from the pledge which fear and force had extorted from me, and, after a grave rebuke, which, by God's grace shall never pass from my mind, prohibited me from ever again obliging myself to anyone in a like cause, except saving God's honour and my order. You added too, if you are pleased to recollect, that not even to save his life should a bishop bind himself, saving God's honour and his order.[3]

[1] Herbert of Bosham, III, 418–28.
[2] *Materials*, Epistolae, VI, 516–17.
[3] *Ibid.*, 520–1.

As negotiations dragged on Becket became abusive about what he deemed to be the supineness of the papal curia. He tried to force the issue himself by fulminating in the spring of 1169 a new set of excommunications against the bishops of London and Salisbury and several of the king's *familiares*; and in the autumn Henry himself was threatened with excommunication and his realms with interdict.[1] The king retaliated with a set of decrees sealing off the ports, forbidding any communication with the archbishop or pope, prescribing imprisonment for anyone found with a mandate on him, threatening expulsion for anyone who observed a sentence of interdict, ordering all clergy who had gone abroad to return home under threat of expropriation of their revenues, and the seizure of property belonging to anyone who favoured the archbishop's cause. Sheriffs were to take oaths from everyone over fifteen years of age to observe these decrees.[2] But at this point Henry encountered a serious check: the bishops were summoned to London to accept the decrees, but they all either refused, ignored the summons and took refuge in monasteries, or, in the case of the bishop of Chester, disappeared into the Welsh mountains. The archbishop of York, Becket's unflagging opponent, was equally staunch and forthright in his opposition to taking an oath.[3] Becket encountered a reverse too, for the pope showed no disposition to confirm his excommunications, and seemed likely to raise some of them.[4]

It was in these circumstances that the legates brought king and

[1] On the excommunications *see*, e.g., *ibid.*, 541–3, 558–9, 571–3, 576–7, 601–3; VII, 49, 111; and for the king's indignation, *ibid.*, VI, 598–600. For Becket's complaints about papal policy, *see*, e.g., his letters to Alexander III, *ibid.*, VI, 579–82; VII, 122, to Cardinals Albert and Theodwin, *ibid.*, VI, 586–9, and to Cardinal Humbold, *ibid.*, VII, 23ff., 123. For the threatened interdict *see*, e.g., *ibid.*, VI, 100, 102, 104, 109, and for the renewal of excommunications, *ibid.*, 111–16.

[2] Surviving texts of the decrees vary considerably and none is without difficulty. The fullest is Gervase of Canterbury, I, 214–15, with a date for their inception, 9 October. Other versions are given by William of Canterbury, I, 53–5, Roger of Howden, *Chronica*, I, 231–2, and *Materials*, Epistolae, VII, 147–9. Cf. William Fitz-Stephen, III, 102. The suggestion of Knowles, *Episcopal Colleagues of Thomas Becket*, 132–3, that these decrees were a supplement to the Constitutions of Clarendon, and an attempt to realise a long-term aim of insulating England from the Church of Rome, is unwarranted, cf. review by Southern in *English Historical Review*, lxvii (1952), 89–90. There has been some dispute among historians as to the date of the decrees. It is very likely that similar attempts to seal off the ports had been made in the long course of the quarrel whenever the king feared excommunication or interdict; but the date of the decrees cited above is unquestionably 1169.

[3] William FitzStephen, III, 102; cf. Gervase of Canterbury, I, 206; William of Canterbury, I, 55–6; *Materials*, Epistolae, VII, 176–7.

[4] Cf., e.g., *Materials*, Epistolae, VII, 65–6.

archbishop face to face at Montmartre in November 1169. Rapid progress was made, for both sides seemed ready to abandon their stand on the question of the 'customs'; but it is probable that the progress was based more on the growing feeling of the contestants that each of them was likely to lose as much face by trying to continue the struggle as by ending it, rather than on any real desire for reconciliation. It seems, indeed, that both were looking for an excuse to frustrate agreement; and Becket found it when he insisted that Henry should give him a kiss of peace – not, he is reported to have said, that he suspected any treachery on the king's part, but that his vassals might see that enmity was at an end. The king refused; and the only reason he would give was that once in his wrath he had sworn never to grant the archbishop the kiss of peace, and he could not go back on his oath.[1] Becket's response was decisive: no kiss, no peace. It is unlikely that either of them was displeased at the outcome. Since Becket said, in reporting the incident to the archbishop of Sens, that trust could not be placed in Henry's kiss of peace anyway, it seems that his insistence on it was motivated by a desire that Henry should make a public gesture of surrender.[2] That Henry persisted in his refusal on a lame excuse argues that his pride too could not, when put to the test, stomach a semblance of defeat.

Unwilling as he was to make peace for the sake of having his son crowned by the archbishop of Canterbury, Henry was equally unwilling to delay much longer in having it done by someone. He determined that the archbishop of York should do it. The historic rights of Canterbury were evaded by subterfuge. Henry took a stand on the fact that in exceptional circumstances the coronation of an English king had been performed by a prelate other than the archbishop of Canterbury: William I had been crowned by Ealred, archbishop of York, since Stigand of Canterbury was suspected of having gained his see improperly, and Henry I had, after his seizure of the throne, been hurriedly crowned by the bishop of London, since Archbishop Anselm of Canterbury was still in exile, and the archbishop of York failed to arrive in time for the ceremony.[3] Secondly, Henry had in his possession a letter from Pope Alexander III permitting him to have his son crowned by any bishop of his choice. This letter does not survive and is known only from report: but the fact of its existence was admitted by

[1] Herbert of Bosham, III, 449.
[2] *Materials*, Epistolae, VII, 164–5.
[3] There is some doubt in the sources as to who crowned Henry I; the difficulty is resolved by Cantor, *Kingship and Lay Investiture in England*, 135–6.

Becket and is confirmed by a letter of Alexander III to Archbishop Roger of York:

> Since through our dearest son Henry, the illustrious king of England, great help and favours are known to have come to the Church in this extremity of need, and as we love him with the more affection for the constancy of his devotion, and hold him foremost in our heart, so do we the more freely and eagerly desire that which we know will promote the honour, profit and exaltation of him and his. Hence it is that at his request we, on the authority both of the Blessed Peter and ourselves, and by the assembled counsel of our brethren, grant that our dearly beloved son in Christ, his eldest son Henry, may be crowned in England. We command you by apostolic letter that whenever the king our son shall request it you shall place the crown upon the head of his son aforesaid on the authority of the apostolic see; and what therein shall be done by you we decree to remain valid and firm.[1]

This remarkable concession was probably made in June 1161, when Alexander was deeply grateful for his recognition as true pope by Henry a few months earlier, and during the vacancy in the see of Canterbury caused by the death of Archbishop Theobald in April 1161.[2] It is noticeable, however, that the letter applies no limitation to the commission, and Alexander III seems at the time either to have been ignorant of or to have disregarded the historic claims of Canterbury.[3] Becket had campaigned against the commission and eventually persuaded the pope to revoke it by a letter of 1166 to the archbishop of York and the bishops of England forbidding them to injure the rights of the church of Canterbury which, as he had been informed, included the privilege of crowning kings.[4] There is no indication, however, that he also revoked the letter to Henry II, permitting him to have his son crowned by any bishop of his choice. Henry, it seems, toyed with the idea of having it done by a continental bishop; but finally settled upon

---

[1] *Materials*, Epistolae, VI, 206–7; a critical text is provided by Anne Heslin, 'The coronation of the Young King in 1170', 177–8. The letter to Henry II is revealed in Becket's report to the pope of the circumstances of the coronation, *Materials*, Epistolae, VII, 328ff.

[2] There has been considerable disagreement over the dating of this letter; for its attribution to 1161 *see* Raymonde Foreville, *L'Église et la Royauté en Angleterre*, 280–3, and Anne Heslin, *op. cit.*, 168–73.

[3] That the pope was at the time ignorant of such claims is suggested by his later letters to the archbishop of York and the bishops of England in which he says, 'we have heard' of the privileges of the church of Canterbury in the matter of the coronation, *Materials*, Epistolae, V, 323, cf. VII, 217.

[4] *Ibid.*, V, 323.

the archbishop of York, doubtless for the greater insult offered to Canterbury. The prohibition of 1166 was circumvented by the spread of a convincing rumour that the royal embassy which visited the papal curia in January 1170 had secured a renewal of the commission.[1] Becket protested vigorously, and was given strong support by the Pope, who repeated his prohibition with stern threats of the suspension or even deposition of any bishop who ignored it, 'for we have decided that no appeal shall be entertained, and no excuse admitted'.[2] It is extremely unlikely, however, that their letters penetrated the strict security measures which Henry had enforced since the end of 1169.[3] The coronation was therefore performed at Westminster Abbey on 14 June without anyone to gainsay it.[4]

Henry's subterfuges could not of course for long withstand papal displeasure; but they were sufficiently plausible to have the coronation performed without a hitch, and thereby, as he probably intended, to force Becket's hand. The coronation, indeed, changed the situation dramatically. Becket went into full retreat, for Henry had found the chink in his armour. Quite apart from the affront to his *amour propre* was the injury to the rights of Canterbury. A precedent had been created which no amount of papal displeasure or the punishment of those involved could altogether efface. The monks of Canterbury, and probably St Augustine too, would never forgive him for bringing upon their church such dishonour. It was a dishonour all the more bitter in that it was undeserved, for throughout his career as archbishop Thomas Becket had fought for and defended the historic rights of Canterbury with a tenacity equal to that displayed by Henry II in defence of the historic rights of the Crown. This, indeed, is the sub-plot to the main drama of his archiepiscopate, and one which offers a curious and ironical parallel to the campaign waged by the king: curious because it was waged with very similar arguments, ironical because it was pressed with the same disregard for changes in the climate of opinion within the Roman Church. For Thomas, as for Henry, his claims had the sanction of history, and the touchstone of what was proper and decent was what had happened under his predecessors. Lanfranc and Anselm hold the place in Becket's thinking which William I and Henry I hold in the king's. Neither was willing to forgo a tittle of the

---

[1] *Materials*, Epistolae, VII, 227, 229ff.

[2] Becket's letters, *ibid.*, VII, 256–7, 258–61, 262, 263–4; the pope's letters, *ibid.*, VII, 216–17.

[3] *See* above, p. 499, and Anne Heslin, *op. cit.*, 175–6.

[4] There is some confusion over the date: *see* Anne Heslin, *op. cit.*, 165 n. 1.

rights their predecessors had exercised. Yet the claims of the archbishop of Canterbury to a patriarchal jurisdiction over the whole British Church – to regard York as a sub-province and the Celtic churches as dependent – ran counter to the whole movement for the centralisation of the Church. There was no room in this new conception for regional self-government, and even the metropolitan jurisdiction of an archbishop over suffragan bishops was coming to seem an unwelcome obstacle to papal government. It was a trend of thinking which was eventually to give an archbishop in the Roman Church little more than a distinction of dignity, conveyed by calling his see an 'archdiocese'. Of this Thomas Becket apparently perceived nothing. He persisted in regarding all hesitations by the papal curia on the status of Canterbury as the product of the rivalry of York and the malevolence of Archbishop Roger, and strove to overcome it with complaints, protests, and incessant appeals.[1] It is one of the ironies of the situation that the pope, declining to confirm the ancient rights of the Crown, found himself, in his sympathy for the exiled Becket, obliged to confirm the ancient rights of Canterbury – but probably with only little less reluctance. During the vacancy in the see of Canterbury Archbishop Roger had secured privileges – such as the right to have his cross carried before him anywhere in England – which supported York's claim to equal and independent metropolitan status.[2] In 1164, however, at Becket's promptings, the pope first asked Archbishop Roger to refrain from acting on the permission to carry his cross throughout England because of the controversy which had arisen over it, then retracted the permission, explaining to Becket that the phrase 'throughout England' had been an error.[3] Becket claimed that at the meeting of Sens in November 1164 the pope confirmed the primacy of Canterbury, but the papal bull of confirmation was not issued until 1166 or 1167, and even then was a cautious document, repeating almost word for word the bull of Pope Eugenius III to Archbishop Theobald, which itself cautiously refrained from defining the primacy, merely confirming to the archbishops of Canterbury such primacy 'as Lanfranc and Anselm, and their other predecessors possessed'.[4] The only element of the primacy which Alexander III ever clarified was the right of crowning kings of England – which was, of course, a matter of indifference to the papacy.

[1] Cf. Raymonde Foreville, *L'Église et la Royauté en Angleterre*, 276ff.

[2] *Ibid.*, 276–7; cf. *Materials*, Epistolae, VI, 590.

[3] *Materials*, Epistolae, V, 67–9.

[4] The bull is printed *ibid.*, V, 324–5; on the date *see* Raymonde Foreville, *op. cit.*, 283 n.2. For Becket's claim that the pope had confirmed the primacy in 1164, *see* *Materials*, Epistolae, V, 215.

A way round the difficulties caused by disputes over the nature of the primacy and the rivalry of Canterbury and York had been found by Henry I who asked the pope to confer the office of resident papal legate on the archbishop of Canterbury, who might then do by apostolic authority what might be resisted if done on archiepiscopal authority.[1] Such commissions lapsed with the death of the holder and had to be renewed. It is curious that Henry II made no move to secure legatine authority for Becket at the beginning of his archiepiscopate when he still enjoyed the king's favour – an appropriate occasion would have been the council of Tours in March 1163. The fact that Henry did not, casts yet further doubt on the theory that he intended to use Becket as an instrument for the royal control of the Church in England. Instead, after Becket had proclaimed his independence, Henry sought legatine authority for Archbishop Roger of York, but since the papal commission had offered insufficient control over Becket himself, had returned it in disgust.[2] In April 1166 the pope sought to comfort Becket by conferring on him the office of legate for England, but even then excluded the see of York.[3]

Thomas Becket could not be satisfied with such hesitations and equivocations. To him the rights of Canterbury were exalted, ancient, and indefeasible. Legatine authority might be a useful adjunct but it could not be a substitute for the authority which Canterbury possessed as of right. To him Canterbury was the mother church of the British Isles, and stood to the realm of England 'as the head does to the body'.[4] The arguments he used for Canterbury's primacy were familiar from the writings of Eadmer in the previous generation, but Becket brought to their expression a quality all his own.[5] His elevation to the seat of St Augustine made him, he believed, the supreme arbiter of ecclesiastical affairs in the kingdom and hence more exalted than the king, whose jurisdiction was over mere worldly matters: 'For it is to my priesthood,' he wrote to Henry in 1166, 'that God has enjoined the care of the church of Canterbury, and to your rule that he has, for the present, deputed the human affairs of this kingdom [res humanas regni]'.[6] It was the duty, by office and tradition, of the archbishops of Canterbury to be the advisers of princes, and to be the upholders of God's law against their

---

[1] Above, ch. 11, p. 416.   [2] Above, p. 484.   [3] *Materials*, Epistolae, V, 328–9.

[4] *Ibid.*, VII, 394: '. . . . sancta Cantuariensis ecclesia, Britanniarum mater in Christo . . .'; *ibid.*, V, 29: 'Cantuariensis ecclesia quae in regno Anglorum est sicut caput in corpore. . . .'

[5] For an enlightening analysis of Becket's thoughts on the primacy of Canterbury, see Raymonde Foreville, *L'Église et la Royauté en Angleterre*, 231–40.

[6] *Materials*, Epistolae, V, 270.

follies. 'Have you ever heard tell,' he wrote to Cardinal Boso, 'of any other prelate in England than the archbishop of Canterbury having offered resistance to the princes in the defence of the liberties of the Church? . . . Some archbishops of Canterbury have suffered exile and persecution, others have even shed their blood on behalf of the divine law.'[1] Canterbury's right of coronation gave it, he thought, control over succession to the throne. Archbishop Theobald had refused to crown Stephen's son Eustace, and had secured the succession for Henry.[2] In Becket's view, in short, Canterbury stood to the English monarchy as, in the mind of the high-clericalists, Rome stood to the imperial authority. There was no suggestion in this of an independence of Rome: on the contrary Canterbury's rôle was justified by its unwavering fidelity to the Holy See; but the themes running through Becket's correspondence are that Canterbury's cause is God's cause, that the interests of the pope and of himself as archbishop of Canterbury are identical, and that the archbishop of Canterbury is more than a delegate – he is the surrogate of the apostolic see. It is small wonder then that Becket saw in the coronation by York something more than a personal insult: it struck at the roots of Canterbury's divine authority.

The coronation changed the pope's policy too. It is clear from Alexander III's letters that he had hoped to use Henry's anxiety to have his son crowned as a lever by means of which the king could be tipped into making concessions to the Church: this was part of his purpose in forbidding the bishops to take part in the coronation.[3] When Henry broke the lever he forced the pope's hand as well as Becket's. The pope now had no other resort but the use of ecclesiastical censures: he authorised Becket to suspend bishops who had taken the oath to the Constitutions, to excommunicate those who had taken part in the coronation, and to lay an interdict on England.[4] These powers were to be used as the archbishop saw fit in forcing the king into acceptable terms. But Henry had anticipated such action and moved ahead of papal displeasure. The coronation was no sooner completed than he gave notice that he was ready to make peace with the archbishop.[5]

The terms Henry offered were basically those arranged at Montmartre: the peaceful return of the archbishop and the restoration of the property of the see of Canterbury. Becket accepted them at Fréteval

---

[1] *Ibid.*, VI, 57–8. [2] *Ibid.*, V, 57; VII, 330.
[3] Cf. e.g., *ibid.*, VII, 216. [4] *Ibid.*, 358, 382–3.
[5] Letter from Henry II to the archbishop of Rouen, dated at Westminster, *ibid.*, 300. The king returned to Normandy very shortly after the coronation, Eyton, *Itinerary*, 138.

on 22 July 1170 – after a few days of parley between mediators, and less than six weeks after the coronation. He did not even insist on the kiss of peace: it was neither sought nor offered. The clue to his ready response to the king's overtures is to be found in Henry's promise that he might recrown Henry the Younger together with his wife Margaret.[1] In this way his honour could be saved. As for the Constitutions of Clarendon, no one's honour was put in jeopardy on that score for nothing at all was said about them.[2]

At the meeting of the king and the archbishop on the border of Touraine, in a meadow between the castles of Fréteval and Viefui, Henry is said to have behaved as if there had never been any discord between them.[3] But the consequences of the archbishop's six years of exile were not so easily effaced: property of the see of Canterbury long in the hands of custodians had to be identified and recovered, nominees of the king intruded into benefices in the patronage of the archbishop of Canterbury had to be ejected. Becket, reluctant to return to England until all had been settled, left the work to agents. Henry too had to rely on subordinates for he was busy on the continent; and although he seems, from the writs he issued, to have been genuinely intent on carrying out the promises made at Fréteval, he did little to prepare those who had taken his part against the archbishop for the consequences of reconciliation. Becket was demanding full reparation, including the repayment of all revenues derived from archiepiscopal property during his absence. It is not surprising that there were delays, evasions, and disputes, nor that considerable hostility built up against the peace of Fréteval among those who would suffer from the return of a revengeful archbishop.[4] Becket, his entourage, and the pope, seem to have expected Henry to take a more personal and more direct part in securing restitution, and blamed him for the delays, questioning even his good faith.[5] But Henry was preoccupied with affairs in Normandy and Anjou, and moreover fell so seriously sick in August that he was in-

[1] Margaret had not been present at the coronation of her husband, much to the chagrin of her father, King Louis VII, see above, ch. 3, p. 111. A formal coronation of the two was performed after Becket's death by the archbishop of Rouen, in August 1172, a month before Henry's absolution at Avranches, Roger of Howden, *Gesta*, II, 31.

[2] Becket's letter to the pope, *Materials*, Epistolae, VII, 326–38, describes the reconciliation in detail. It is a lengthy attempt to justify his all too prompt agreement. It dwells at length on the rights of Canterbury, and claims that Henry declared: 'I do not doubt that Canterbury is the noblest among all the churches of the west.' For other accounts *see* Herbert of Bosham, III, 465–7; William FitzStephen, III, 107–11.

[3] Becket to the pope, *Materials*, Epistolae, VII, 327.

[4] Cf. Raymonde Foreville, *op. cit.*, 308ff.

[5] e.g., *Materials*, Epistolae, VII, 384–95.

duced to make his will. By November the archbishop was anxious to return to England and Henry intended to accompany him, but he became so distracted by the serious threat posed by King Louis to his interests in Berry, that he sent John of Oxford, dean of Salisbury, instead to accompany Becket across the Channel.[1] John of Oxford was one of the most trusted of the king's *familiares* and had been his principal agent in the war of propaganda and diplomacy against the archbishop. Henry has been accused of a calculated insult or at least of extreme tactlessness in sending a man whom Becket had reviled; but on the contrary it was the best advertisement he could make of his reconciliation with the archbishop. The need for it was revealed when the ship put in to Sandwich on 1 December 1170, for a hostile reception party was barely deterred by the presence of John of Oxford from laying violent hands on Becket. It was led by Gervase of Cornhill, the sheriff of Kent, and by Ranulf de Broc who had administered the property of the archbishopric in the king's name.[2] The biographers speak of a rapturous welcome for the returning archbishop by ordinary people; but the real hostility to the reconciliation at Fréteval in official and baronial circles was demonstrated by the refusal of the Young King to receive him at Windsor.[3]

To this combustible material, Becket himself touched a fuse. On the eve of crossing the Channel he excommunicated, on apostolic authority, the archbishop of York and the bishops of London and Salisbury, who had assisted at the coronation of Henry the Younger. The action itself is not so remarkable as the timing. He had asked for and received from Henry at Fréteval permission to discipline the erring bishops. He had in his possession for several months past a papal bull authorising him to take such action in the name of the apostolic see. He had refrained from using it; instead he had written to the pope pointing out that there were distinctions to be drawn in the nature and degree of guilt of the offenders, and asking for separate bulls to be sent to him to be used at his discretion.[4] The pope had them drawn up for him, but before they arrived Becket had changed his mind, had pronounced the excommunications on the authority of the earlier bull, and had sent word of them across the Channel just before embarking himself.[5]

[1] *See* above, ch. 3, pp. 111–12, and *Materials*, Epistolae, VII, 400.

[2] William FitzStephen, III, 116, 118–9; William of Canterbury, I, 86–8; *Materials*, Epistolae, VII, 403, 410.

[3] William FitzStephen, III, 119–24; Herbert of Bosham, III, 478–83.

[4] *Materials*, Epistolae, VII, 357–8, 382–3, 384–9, 397–9.

[5] *Ibid.*, VII, 403, 410; cf. William FitzStephen, III, 116–17; William of Canterbury, I, 89–95; Herbert of Bosham, III, 471–2.

The only plausible explanation for doing so then, after he had delayed for so long and could with propriety have delayed a few weeks longer, is that, eager as he was to return to England, his pride would not allow him to do so until his chief opponents had been publicly humbled.

The bishops, complaining that it was hardly decent to mar a peaceful return with recriminations, sought the archbishop's absolution. He offered a conditional absolution to his suffragans of London and Salisbury, but insisted that only the pope himself could absolve the archbishop of York.[1] Archbishop Roger persuaded the others that they should stick together, and they crossed to Normandy to seek the king's intervention, or at least his permission for an appeal to Rome. They found Henry at Bures for the Christmas festivities.

It is commonly said that the protests of the bishops at their excommunication and suspension touched off the king's anger, which led to the archbishop's murder. But this cannot be entirely true. Henry probably knew of the excommunications before the bishops arrived; and he had, so Becket himself said, acknowledged the archbishop's right to punish the bishops who had taken part in the coronation of his son.[2] Rather, it seems, it was the nature of the archbishop's act on the eve of his return, and the stories the bishops brought with them of his behaviour in England which did the damage. It was said that he was careering about the country at the head of a strong force of armed knights.[3] It was not so much what the archbishop had done as his manner of doing it which inflamed the king. Nothing had changed, nothing had been learned: here was Becket behaving in the same old self-centred, ham-fisted way. Someone, it is said, remarked to Henry, 'While Thomas lives you will have neither peace nor quiet nor see good days.'[4] It was an undeniably true if provocative remark. Whether Henry actually spoke the famous words 'Will no one rid me of this turbulent priest', there is no means of knowing. The chroniclers and the biographers of Becket tell differing tales. That he uttered some such words is, however, beyond doubt, for Henry himself later admitted responsibility, although disclaiming any intention of wishing to procure the archbishop's death. He had made a similar exclamation when in 1166 he received letters from Becket threatening excommunication and

---

[1] *Materials*, Epistolae, VII, 405–6.

[2] William FitzStephen, III, 127, 133, Herbert of Bosham, III, 466, and Becket's letter to the pope, *Materials*, Epistolae, VII, 332.

[3] William FitzStephen, III, 127; Garnier of Pont-Sainte-Maxence, lines 5066ff.

[4] William FitzStephen, III, 128.

interdict, to judge by the story John of Salisbury picked up of a council meeting at Chinon:

> The king complained exceedingly of the archbishop of Canterbury with sighs and groans: as those who were present afterwards reported, he declared with tears that the archbishop would take from him both body and soul. Finally he said they were all traitors who could not summon up the zeal and loyalty to rid him of the harassment of one man.[1]

This was doubtless a typical expression of the familiar, extravagant, Angevin passion. Nothing then happened beyond a gentle rebuke for his intemperate language from the archbishop of Rouen; and the council passed on to a suggestion from the bishop of Lisieux that Becket's threatened censures might be warded off by an appeal to Rome. But at Bures in December 1170 there were some who took the king's angry words seriously. Four knights of the household slipped away, 'eager to win his favour', as FitzStephen says.[2] Riding ahead of all attempts to recall them, they took different routes to England and met together again at the castle of Saltwood, the headquarters of Ranulf de Broc and the centre of hostility to Becket and the peace of Fréteval.

They were not intelligent knights and probably understood little of what was involved in the dispute.[3] They knew only that the archbishop had to be made to submit to the king's will. There are no signs that they had a plan or even any very clear purpose. Whether they were there to arrest him, deport him into exile again, or kill him, remained in doubt until the end.[4] They first approached him while he was conducting

[1] John of Salisbury to Bartholomew, bishop of Exeter, *Materials*, Epistolae, V, 381. The council meeting was held at the beginning of June; Becket's threatened censures were promulgated at Vézelay on 12 June.

[2] William FitzStephen, III, 130; cf. William of Canterbury, I, 121ff.; Edward Grim, II, 428-9; Herbert of Bosham, III, 487.

[3] As a sample of their intelligence *see* FitzStephen's account, III, 134, of an exchange with the archbishop: 'Reginald FitzUrse: "Do you not recognise that you hold everything from the king?" The archbishop: "By no means; we must render unto the king the things that are the king's, but unto God the things that are God's." At this, as if he had said something extraordinary, Reginald and his companions growled at him and ground their teeth in rage.'

[4] The biographers assume that their purpose was always the same as their deed, but nevertheless report incidents which indicate otherwise. Edward Grim, II, 422, for example, says that they demanded in the king's name that 'you should depart with all your men from the kingdom and the land which lies under his sway'. William FitzStephen, III, 141, describing the struggle in the cathedral only moments before the archbishop's death, says that Becket was first struck with the flat of a sword, and that some cried, 'You are our prisoner, come with us.'

business in an inner room, shortly after he had dined, and sat themselves down sullenly among the monks and clerks gathered there. They were known to some of the archbishop's entourage, indeed two of them had commended themselves to Beckct when he was chancellor. Edward Grim says that they were even offered dinner. They said nothing until the archbishop noticed and greeted them. Then their spokesman, Reginald FitzUrse, broke into demands and threats. He was neither coherent nor consistent, accusing the archbishop of breaking the peace and wishing to deprive the king's son of his crown; insisting one moment that the archbishop should return with them to answer the king, the next that he should depart forthwith into exile.[1] Thomas tried patiently to answer their accusations, replied reasonably to their demands, but with scorn to their threats. The knights were tempted to brain the archbishop there and then with his processional cross, but they thought better of it and retired, calling first to the people who had crowded into the chamber at the sound of raised voices to abandon the archbishop in the king's name, and then, when no one moved, saying 'We command you to take this fellow into custody to prevent his escape'. It was a farcical situation which some found menacing but others attributed to drunkenness. The archbishop went into the cathedral to hear vespers. The knights, however, reacted as men of action, but of low intelligence, will to a situation they could not handle: they determined to do something. They armed themselves and went into the cathedral after him. When they found him, rather more easily than they expected, they drew back 'as though confused and bewildered', says William FitzStephen, who was close by the archbishop – one of only three who remained with him, for the rest fled to sanctuary. In the uncertainty as to what to do, one of the knights struck the archbishop on the shoulder with the flat of his sword, saying, 'Fly, you are a dead man'. But the archbishop faced them with a calm dignity, challenging them to do their worst. What they thought of doing was to drag him out of the church, but this Becket fiercely resisted, and it was in the ensuing melée that he received a blow on the head. As the blood flowed the four knights fell upon him with their swords. Despite their military training they made a butcher's job of it. It was late afternoon when he died, on a dark winter's day, 29 December 1170.[2]

[1] Edward Grim, II, 430ff.

[2] The contemporary accounts, although agreeing in the main, differ considerably as to details. The account above is drawn from the two best sources, those of William FitzStephen, III, 132–42, a clerk of the archbishop who remained with him until the end, and Edward Grim, II, 430–8, a casual visitor to the cathedral who intervened to help the archbishop and was wounded at the first blow.

The biographers of Becket are unanimous in representing the archbishop as expecting violent death, prepared for death, even at the last moment inviting death: 'I am ready,' he said, according to Edward Grim who stood by him at the time, 'to die for my Lord, that in my blood the Church may obtain liberty and peace.'[1] Whether he regarded such a death as inevitable sooner or later and faced it with courage and faith, or whether he actually sought martyrdom, no one can tell for certain.[2] The indications are that the prospect of martyrdom was not unwelcome to him: he resisted attempts to protect him from the knights and would take none of the possible opportunities for escape. When he entered the cathedral the monks attempted to bolt the doors, but he ordered them to be thrown open, saying, according to Edward Grim: 'It is not proper to make a fortress of the house of prayer, the church of Christ, . . . we shall triumph over the enemy rather in suffering than in fighting, for we came to suffer, not to resist.' William FitzStephen had no doubt that escape would not have been difficult: 'Had he so wished the archbishop might easily have turned aside and saved himself by flight, for both time and place offered an opportunity of escape without being discovered. It was evening, the long winter night was approaching, and the crypt was near at hand, where there were many dark and winding passages. There was also another door near by, through which he could have climbed by a spiral staircase to the arched chambers in the roof. . . . But none of these ways of escape would he take.'[3] Thomas Becket did not have to die on 29 December 1170. That he did is partly, to say the very least, because he chose to do so.

That is not to say necessarily that he craved the martyr's crown or thought it would bring him the victory that had eluded him in life. He may have done so, but it is just as possible that he realised that only his own death could resolve the dilemmas which his return posed, and rather than put off the evil hour, he embraced death at the hands of

[1] Edward Grim, II, 436. According to William FitzStephen, III, 140–1, he said, 'I submit to death in the name of the Lord, and I commend my soul and the cause of the Church to God and St Mary and the patron saints of this church.' Both agree that he offered his neck, although he was in fact struck by all four of the knights on the crown of the head.

[2] Edward Grim, II, 434, has no doubts on this score: 'He who had long yearned for martyrdom, now saw that the occasion to embrace it seemed to have arrived.' Knowles, 'Archbishop Becket: a character study', 122, discounts such views, remarking that Becket had rejoiced at his homecoming and was full of the vitality which characterised him all his life; but this is not incompatible with welcoming martyrdom when an opportunity presented itself.

[3] Edward Grim, II, 435; William FitzStephen, III, 140.

the four knights, with resignation but with courage.[1] Quite apart from the hostility aroused by his demands for reparations, it is impossible to believe that he could ever have worked with suffragans such as Gilbert Foliot. Too many bitter words had been exchanged. Indeed in the later years Becket was almost unbalanced in the violence of his sentiments towards the bishop of London: 'Your aim,' he began a letter to him in 1167, 'has all along been to effect the downfall of the Church and ourself'; and he protested to Cardinal Hubert of Foliot's absolution by the Pope in 1170 from the excommunication the archbishop had laid upon him, that 'Satan is unloosed for the destruction of the Church'.[2] Even allowing for the customary extravagance of medieval invective, these were words which could not easily be taken back, or breaches which could easily be repaired. Nor was there any possibility that the superficial reconciliation with King Henry could survive more misunderstandings, let alone disputes. Becket would never surrender, but he was equally determined not to go on his travels again: 'From this day,' he said to the knights when they bid him depart from the kingdom, 'no one shall see the sea between me and my church.'[3] Yet the peace of Fréteval was itself an invitation to further discord for it was a peace built upon ambiguities which, while according victory to neither side, allowed both sides to claim one. The king wrote to his eldest son: 'The archbishop of Canterbury has made peace with me according to my will.'[4] The archbishop wrote to the pope that in his discussions with the king on the matters in dispute: 'on every topic he appeared vanquished'.[5] Here was a prelude to disaster. Moreover, Becket's views on the relations of Church and State had not changed: exile had merely hardened his resolve.

It has been said of Becket's pamphleteering and correspondence that 'in all these utterances and letters, the archbishop studiously lifted the controversy on to the high level of doctrinal and canonical theory, where it might meet and mingle with the great Gregorian controversy of the previous century'.[6] It is true that he had occupied himself in his refuge at Pontigny in the study of law and the writings of the schoolmen

---

[1] The biographers' accounts are susceptible of either interpretation. Knowles remarks, op. cit., 122, that, 'There are abundant indications that even had the four knights not acted, men and forces were in motion that would have borne the archbishop away'. Cf. William FitzStephen, III, 113-14, 123ff.

[2] Materials, Epistolae, VI, 181; VII, 279.

[3] Edward Grim, II, 432.

[4] Ralph of Diceto, I, 339; Materials, Epistolae, VII, 346-7.

[5] Materials, Epistolae, VII, 327.

[6] Knowles, Episcopal Colleagues of Thomas Becket, 150.

– much to the dismay of John of Salisbury, who implored him instead to give his time to devotional works and spiritual exercises.[1] It is true that his studies enabled him to find words for what he wanted to say, enriched his store of allusions, and gave increasing cogency to his arguments; but it is difficult to see in his numerous letters any evidence that he progressed beyond a narrow clericalism, dogmatic and basically unspiritual, despite its trappings of pious sentiment. Becket was not looking to doctrinal and canonical theory for enlightenment, but for justification for the stand he had taken on clerical immunity, which itself was based at least as much on his personal need to prove himself a worthy archbishop as on deep conviction. The necessary justification he found in extremist views of sacerdotal supremacy. These, if they fell just short of the basic error of identifying the Church with the clergy, nevertheless fell easily into the less heinous but no less perilous mistake of identifying the Church's interests with the clergy's interests. Becket, indeed, went further and identified himself personally with the cause of God: he moved easily from complaining that at Northampton, 'I was called before the king's tribunal like a layman', to referring to it as the occasion 'when Christ was judged in my person before the tribunal of the prince'.[2]

There was an old argument in western Christendom about the origin of spiritual and temporal authority. That all authority derived ultimately from God was not in doubt; but did spiritual and temporal authority each descend directly from God, or was one mediated by the other? To Becket this was not a matter of debate, and the answer was beyond question: 'It is certain that kings receive their power from the Church, and the Church not from them but from Christ'. Hence, so he argued to the king in a letter of 1166, 'You have no power to give rules to bishops, nor to absolve or to excommunicate anyone, to draw clerks before secular tribunals, to judge concerning breach of faith or oath, and many other things of this sort which are written among your customs which you call ancient'.[3] The justification for such a theory he set out in a further letter to Henry, in which he paraded the dogmatisms of the high clericalists: the administration of the Church belongs exclusively to the clergy, the clergy themselves are exempt

---

[1] *Materials*, Epistolae, V, 163–4: 'Of much profit indeed are laws and canons; but believe me that now is not the time for them . . . the exercises of the schools increase the pride of knowledge but rarely or never kindle devotion. I would rather that you should meditate on the psalms and peruse the blessed Gregory's *Moralia* than that you should philosophize in scholastic fashion.'

[2] *Ibid.*, 139, 494.

[3] *Ibid.*, 281.

from secular authority, but the government of secular princes is not exempt from clerical supervision:

> God wishes that the administration of ecclesiastical affairs should belong to his priests, not to secular rulers, who, if they are of the faith, he wishes to be subject to the priests of his Church. . . .

> . . . God Almighty has willed that the clergy of the Christian religion should be governed and judged, not according to public laws and by secular authorities, but by bishops and priests.

> Christian kings ought to submit their administration to ecclesiastical prelates not impose it on them. . . . Christian princes should be obedient to the dictates of the Church rather than prefer their own authority; princes should bow their head to bishops rather than judge them. . . .[1]

Such views did indeed put Becket in touch with 'the great Gregorian controversy of the previous century': it was from thence that they were derived – or rather from one segment of it – with little or no modification. Indeed, it is not going too far to suggest that Becket saw himself as another Gregory VII, and that what he wanted was Henry II on his knees begging forgiveness as Emperor Henry IV had been on his knees before Pope Gregory at Canossa.

It is this 'Gregorianism' which most clearly demonstrates Becket's limitations as a theologian and his failings as an archbishop. He was a theological dinosaur. Such theories of clerical exclusiveness and of clerical direction, not only of the Church but of the world, exercise a fascination which the clergy have perennially found hard to shake off; but they were never, even in the days of Gregory VII, Urban II, or Paschal II, entirely dominant, and they had in the early twelfth century suffered a serious reverse – as much from reaction within the Church as from lay resistance.[2] Thomas Becket, however, behaved as if the 'Investiture Contest' had never been settled. His outmoded stand on clerical exclusiveness threatened to reopen the whole delicate question of the status of the clergy within the state. It was a question which popes and other sensible men of affairs prudently preferred to leave on one side, admitting that for practical purposes the clergy had dual loyalties, to their clerical order and to the society in which they lived, to the apostolic see on the one hand and to lay rulers on the other. Where the demands of each conflicted, the problems were to be resolved not solely by reference to ideological principle but by mutual

---

[1] *Materials*, Epistolae, V, 274–5.
[2] *See* above, pp. 417–18.

accommodation in the light of practical necessity. Open warfare was to be avoided not least because it disrupted the life of the Church. Ideology had if necessary to give way to the principle that the Church's government must be carried on, and government often involves compromise. The precept that while the divine law must be preserved intact, the application of that law has to be adjusted to persons and circumstances was dismissed by Becket with a contempt which speaks clearly of his lack of understanding that not only papal government, which he professed to revere, but also the new canon law, which he embraced as a divine ordinance, would have foundered without it.[1] 'They say,' he complained of the bishops, 'that this is not the moment for provoking the king – a subtlety which leads them into servitude.'[2] His recipe for the resolution of clerical difficulties was to strike and to strike hard: as he wrote to Alexander III after the failure of papal mediators in 1169,

> May it please you to deal manfully, for assuredly, if it is your pleasure to put the wicked in fear, you will restore peace to the Church and a perishing soul to God. You have now seen what gentleness can do; now try the other method. In the severity of justice you will most assuredly triumph.[3]

Even some who sympathised with Becket's stand against Henry II as a necessary defence of ecclesiastical liberty could not approve his methods. One such was the man whom Becket addressed even in reproach as his 'dearest friend': John aux Bellesmains. Their careers ran remarkably parallel. They had both been clerks in the household of Archbishop Theobald, and friends, which they both remained, of John of Salisbury. Like Thomas Becket, John aux Bellesmains was set on the rungs of preferment by the influence of his old master, becoming treasurer of York while Thomas was archdeacon of Canterbury. Like Thomas he was marked out by Henry II for appointment to a key ecclesiastical office in the Angevin dominions, being nominated to the bishopric of Poitiers (politically speaking the most important see in Aquitaine) at about the very time that Becket was nominated to Canterbury, and, as in Becket's case, against some resistance from the cathedral chapter. Like Thomas, he gained the king's nomination despite the fact, or

---

[1] *See* above, p. 419.

[2] *Materials*, Epistolae, V, 141.

[3] *Ibid.*, VI, 522. This is one of the milder of Becket's demands for condign action: contemporary usage affronts the modern ear. Cf., e.g., *ibid.*, 254: 'Who shall resist Anti-Christ when he comes if we show such patience towards the vices and crimes of his precursors? By such leniency we encourage kings to become tyrants. . . . But blessed is he who dashed such little ones against the stones.'

perhaps if we read the situation aright, because of the fact that he had shown he would be no royal puppet by publicly defending clerical liberty.[1] Like Thomas he at once encountered difficulties with the king's desire to enforce his prerogatives. He was commanded to observe certain 'customs', principally that he would not excommunicate any baron without seeking first the king's consent. He replied that he must consult his clergy, 'for I could not myself resign a right which the Church claimed upon prescriptive usage'. Having conferred with his clergy, he refused.[2] Unlike Thomas, however, he retained both a reputation as a defender of the Church's authority, and the confidence of Henry II. He also retained the confidence of Archbishop Becket, kept in touch with him when he went into exile, and tried to act as a mediator. But in the end he lost patience with Becket's intransigence. At Montmirail, when Becket had cruelly disappointed hopes of peace, many attacked him, says Herbert of Bosham, 'as ever proud, puffed up, wise in his own eyes, always a follower of his own will and opinion, adding that it was a great misfortune, and an immense hurt and danger to the Church that he had ever been made a ruler in it'. The archbishop guarded his tongue, and muttered psalms to himself, behaving as if he did not hear the insults; but one reproach went home, and that was the reproach of John bishop of Poitiers that he was destroying the Church. To him the archbishop made reply: 'Have a care brother lest the Church of God be destroyed by you.'[3] It was not a danger that John aux Belles-mains ever ran, either by a cowardly surrender to the demands of secular princes or by plunging the Church into useless discord. He opposed the promulgation of the Constitutions of Clarendon, but pro-moted Angevin interests in Aquitaine. He brought out troops to defend Poitiers against the king's enemies, yet insisted on protecting a clerk accused of treason from trial in a lay court.[4] He gained the affection of his flock, the respect of the Poitevin barons, the confidence of the king, and the favour of the papal court. In 1182 he was called by Pope Lucius III to the archbishopric of Narbonne, and translated in 1183 to the even more important archbishopric of Lyons. He retired, eventually, to the Cistercians at Clairvaux, and lived well into his eighties, long enough to be visited by Pope Innocent III and to place in his hands prayers composed in honour of St Bernard.[5]

[1] He maintained that the king had no right to punish a delinquent rural dean 'quia clericus est', William FitzStephen, III, 44–5. See above, pp. 434–5.

[2] Materials, Epistolae, V, 37–41.

[3] Herbert of Bosham, III, 428. Cf. John of Salisbury, Materials, Epistolae, VI, 510.

[4] Ralph of Diceto, I, 407; Roger of Howden, Gesta, I, 122–3.

[5] See Boissonnade, 'Administrateurs laïques et ecclésiastiques anglo-normands en

Given Becket's developed theological views, a real reconciliation with so masterful a ruler as Henry II was quite impossible. Yet it was the manner of Becket's opposition rather than its ideological content which caused the implacable hostility of the king. Henry resolutely refused to be drawn into ideological debate. He did not answer Becket's letters. For him the conflict remained, as it had begun, a conflict of personalities set on a collision course from which neither could retreat without an unthinkable loss of prestige. The story of Henry II and Thomas Becket is indeed a classic tragedy – the story of heroic men with remarkable qualities, undone by equally great flaws of character, flaws of passion and of pride.

Poitou', in which will be found all references not otherwise cited above. For the career of John aux Bellesmains *see* also Pouzet, *L'Anglais Jean dit Bellesmains,* and Clay, 'The early treasurers of York', 11–19.

Chapter 14

THE RESTORATION OF HARMONY

Thomas Becket was victorious in death; but the victory was a triumph for his reputation, not the triumph of his cause.

His fame was instantaneous and widespread. As a man prepared to die for his principles he excited a sympathy which transcended both the man and the principles, and was perhaps more poignantly felt the less the man and his principles were understood. The dramatic transition from magnificent courtier to clerical martyr, heightened and fixed in the mind by the discovery on the corpse of a lice-laden hairshirt, established him as a copybook exemplar of the drama of conversion. His courage and steadfastness unto death marked him out as a martyr in an age uncommonly short of martyrs, and swept him on a wave of popular acclaim to an unusually swift canonisation in March 1173.[1] The stand he took – or was supposed to have taken – identified him with the heroic age of the past in the struggle for the freedom of the Church, and appealed to two groups among the clergy who were at odds with the apparent tendency of the papacy to appease kings – those who from idealism disliked it and those who from innocence or ignorance could not understand it. Moreover, as a man who – for whatever reason – would not give way to the mighty King Henry II, Thomas Becket became a cherished symbol of defiance to all who felt an inarticulate resentment at the heavy hand of the king's authority. So Thomas Becket came to be regarded as a martyr, and as a saint, and as a folk hero. The reality became irrelevant.[2]

To many, in consequence, it became necessary to believe that Becket had been victorious in death, and the myth of the martyr's achievement, erected to comfort them and eagerly cherished, has almost obliterated reality. But not everyone was deceived, especially among contemporaries. Even the partisan Herbert of Bosham confessed that not all had been gained for which his hero fought and died.[3] And Gerald of Wales,

[1] The bull of canonisation is printed in *Materials*, Epistolae, VII, 545–6; *see* Kemp, *Canonization and Authority in the Western Church*, 86–9.

[2] Cf. Brown, *The Development of the Legend of Thomas Becket*.

[3] Herbert of Bosham, III, 546.

who would have been delighted to see King Henry worsted, could not conceal his frank appraisal that there was little to show for the martyrdom, although with his customary eagerness to find someone to blame, he attributed it to the cowardly carelessness of Becket's successors at Canterbury.[1] The appraisal is accurate, the blame unfairly laid, for Becket's cause was foredoomed to failure. In the great attempt of the twelfth-century papacy to orchestrate the clergy into an harmonious instrument for ecclesiastical government upon which the themes of the new canon law could be adequately performed, Becket was a misfit. He was not merely out of tune, but was obstinately insisting on playing the wrong music. He relished the discordant clash of *regnum* and *sacerdotium*, while the papacy sought anxiously for harmonies. Becket's demands for a holy war against the State fell on ears which, while not deaf, were unheeding and impatient. The interests of the age were in law, its elaboration and refinement and enforcement. Through it the lives of clergy and people might be made, gradually, to conform to the principles which earlier and more drastic reformers had proclaimed in vain. There was no time for war: pope and bishops were much too busy. John of Oxford sensed the mood and turned it to the king's advantage when he told the Empress Matilda that Becket was more interested in power than reform.[2]

Nevertheless the murder of the archbishop might easily have precipitated the war he so ardently desired. It did not need the clamour of France for vengeance to make the pope recoil in horror from negotiation with the king of England.[3] As soon as the news reached the papal court at Tusculum he broke off talks with English envoys, declined for a week to broach the subject with his advisers, and refused even to speak with an Englishman. A powerful embassy sent by Henry to defend him against the charge that he had either ordered or desired the archbishop's death waited in vain for an audience. As Easter approached it was rumoured in the *curia* that the pope would on Maundy Thursday pronounce sentence of excommunication against the king and his realm. Panic-stricken, the king's envoys pleaded with cardinals to mediate, and at last were admitted to the pope's presence. There, in full consistory, on Thursday 25 March 1171, they swore that their master 'would abide by the pope's mandate and would himself take an oath upon it'.[4] Pope Alexander pronounced a general sentence of excommunication against the murderers of the archbishop, all who had given them counsel,

---

[1] Gerald of Wales, VII, 70, 72.
[2] *Materials*, Epistolae, V, 146, 149–50. [3] *See* above, ch. 3, pp. 112–13.
[4] An envoy of the king to Richard of Ilchester, *Materials*, Epistolae, VII, 476–7.

countenance, or aid, and all who should receive them or give them shelter; he confirmed the sentence of interdict which the archbishop of Sens had laid upon Henry's continental dominions, and the sentences which Becket had pronounced upon his enemies among the bishops; but instead of laying an interdict upon England or excommunicating the king personally he simply prohibited him from entering a church and announced his intention of sending legates 'to see whether the king were truly humbled'.[1]

More remarkable than the pope's horror is the moderation of his action. Doubtless he was influenced by stories of Henry's deep and apparently sincere remorse. Arnulf bishop of Lisieux wrote that at the first intimation of the murder of the archbishop

> the king burst into loud lamentations and exchanged his royal robes for sackcloth and ashes, behaving more like the friend than the sovereign of the dead man. At times he fell into a stupor, after which he would again utter groans and cries louder and more bitter than before. For three whole days he remained shut up in his chamber, and would neither take food nor admit anyone to comfort him, until it seemed from the excess of his grief that he had determined to contrive his own death. The state of affairs was lamentable and the reason for our grief and anxiety was now changed. First we had to bewail the death of the archbishop, now, in consequence, we began to despair of the life of the king, and so by the death of the one we feared in our misery that we might lose both.[2]

Doubtless, too, Alexander was influenced by the appearance at the papal court of one of Becket's staunchest supporters among the bishops, Roger of Worcester, pleading the king's innocence of the charge of complicity in the crime.[3] Even so, the long delay before the pronouncement of any kind of sentence suggests that the pope was seeking assurances of the king's innocence and humility to justify his own moderation; and the mild sentence on Henry *ab ingressu ecclesiae*, pending the visit of legates, argues strongly that he was anxious not to prejudice the long-term interests of the papacy by precipitate action over the church of Canterbury.

Clearly Alexander III had more hope than ever Becket had wished to allow him, that a negotiated settlement with Henry II was possible, a settlement which would allow scope for the development and consolidation of ecclesiastical government. The pope, it seems, appreciated that

[1] *Materials*, Epistolae, VII, 478. For the sentence of the archbishop of Sens, *see* above, ch. 3, p. 113.

[2] Letter to the pope, *Materials*, Epistolae, VII, 438; Arnulf of Lisieux, *Letters*, 122-3.

[3] *Materials*, Epistolae, VII, 476, 477.

Henry had acted throughout the conflict with what for him was considerable restraint — save only when his personal animosity against Becket was engaged. The king had tried a variety of tactics: flattery, dissimulation, the suborning of cardinals, offers to refer any errors he might have committed to a council of English bishops or to French universities, hints that he might recognise the emperor's anti-pope, throw England into schism and appoint his own hierarchy, or, short of that, fence off his kingdom against the assaults of the archbishop and the apostolic see and retreat into isolation. Yet there were unmistakable signs that even the most serious threats were little more than tactical gestures shrouding a great deal of bluff. It was significant that there were lengths to which Henry would not go. Although he had flirted with the imperialists, he had dallied with them only long enough to remind the pope of the value of his loyalty, and he had withdrawn hastily from the brink of schism when it yawned inconveniently before him. He had sedulously avoided allowing the dispute to take an ideological turn, either by entering a defence of his position in terms which had been familiar in the days of the Investiture Contest — and were still common coin among the imperialists — or by replying to Becket's challenging arguments on the necessity of submission to 'spiritual' authority. As Bishop Foliot pointed out, there was no question of faith or morals involved in the dispute, it was simply a matter of church administration.[1] And Henry was anxious that it should remain a matter of the administration of the Church in England: he did not argue about the customs with the papal curia, or try to defend them on any other principle than that they were part of his rightful inheritance, which might, in the context of the Church as a whole, be peculiar, but which nevertheless had been allowed by previous archbishops and previous popes. He seems indeed to have been anxious from the first to avoid alienating the papacy over the Constitutions if at all possible: references to the papacy were avoided, by careful drafting, in the clauses on appeals and the attendance of English bishops at general councils, and most significant of all, there was no mention whatever of that 'custom of the realm' which had figured so prominently in his grandfather's reign — the ban on the reception of papal legates entering the country without the king's permission. It is true that the Constitutions of Clarendon concluded with the words:

> There are, moreover, many other great customs and privileges pertaining to holy mother Church and to the lord king and his barons of the realm

[1] *Ibid.*, V, 538; Gilbert Foliot, *Letters and Charters*, no. 170, 240.

which are not contained in this document. Let them be safe for holy Church and for our lord the king and his heirs and the barons of the realm. And let them be inviolably observed for ever and ever.[1]

The custom on papal legates was thus discreetly covered; but the omission of so important a practice from the text itself indicates that the Constitutions were restricted to those items on which the archbishop had power to be obstructive or troublesome.

Admittedly, Henry's professed determination to stand by the Constitutions seemed an obstacle to a negotiated settlement. He had, indeed, declared in a letter to the college of cardinals in 1166:

> . . . we will, with the consent of our clergy and barons, willingly redress whatever we have done amiss; but if anyone attempts to impede or abate the rights, customs, and dignities of our realm, we will hold him as a public enemy, for we will not stomach any diminution of the dignities and customs which we have inherited from our predecessors . . . as they were in the days of former Roman pontiffs. . . .[2]

Yet even this was little more than a tactical obstinacy – ruling out any suggestion of a compromise which would involve the recall of Archbishop Becket. Henry was not then ready for reconciliation, and by insisting on the full measure of his sovereignty was exploiting Becket's intemperance in order to prevent a reconciliation, for the archbishop had burned his boats over the 'customs' in the censures of Vézelay.[3] Indeed, even here, in the opening words of the passage quoted, the hint is broadly given that the king might retreat from the letter of the Constitutions – provided his rights and ancient dignities could be safeguarded by other means. Furthermore, in less public correspondence and talks, the king had shuffled his feet over the crucial clause on appeals. Bishop Foliot reported to the pope in 1165 that the king

> . . . had no wish to interfere with appeals to your holiness's court, but merely claimed to himself the right, in civil causes, of first taking cognisance of the case according to the ancient usage of the realm; but that if this should be unacceptable to you he would place no further obstacle in the way of an appeal. Moreover, should it be prejudicial to your authority or honour in any respect, he would submit the matter to correction at the next general council of the Church in his realm. . . .[4]

[1] Stubbs, *Select Charters*, 167.
[2] *Materials*, Epistolae, VI, 81.
[3] That the real purpose was to persuade the cardinals, and through them the pope, to set Becket aside, is strongly suggested by the preceding paragraph of this letter.
[4] Gilbert Foliot, *Letters and Charters*, no. 155, 204–5, *Materials*, Epistolae, V, 205.

Papal legates who attended the king's council at Argentan in November 1167 were told that the king was prepared 'to relax his ban on appeals, having enacted it only to save poor clerks from expense, and being now annoyed to find them ungrateful for it'.[1] These excuses and explanations are patently disingenuous, but they indicate that Henry was not unwilling to shift his position, and lend support to Foliot's contention, ridiculed by some critics, that although the king would not yield to force over the Constitutions, he might be persuaded to modify them in practice.[2]

The question of how the Constitutions were to be applied was, indeed, the major imponderable in the dispute about them. Becket and his supporters, believing Henry to be of Protean guile, would set no store by his expressions of good will towards the Church, and the pope doubtless had much sympathy with their attitude. Yet it seems that Becket, in his quest for self-justification, consistently misrepresented Henry II's basic attitude to the inherited rights and dignities of the Crown. There is no good reason for doubting that Henry regarded the encroachments of the 'free' Church of King Stephen's day upon the royal privileges of the past as on a par with encroachments upon the lands and perquisites which of old belonged to the royal demesne. The latter were hunted down, identified with precision, and the royal right asserted; but discovery was not made the ground for abolition – many of the encroachments were allowed to stand, defined as *purprestures*, and rendering the Crown its due in rents.[3] Similarly, the customs of the realm in matters ecclesiastical were part of the king's true inheritance: 'customs' and 'dignities' are closely linked in the text of the Constitutions, and in Henry's mind when speaking about them. They were, as he said when writing to the college of cardinals in 1166, part of his 'honor', but were conceived more as pieces of property than abstract rights.[4] There is no reason to doubt that, as with *purprestures*, the assertion of the royal right was compatible with the continued enjoyment, under control, of the advantage which usurpation had brought. The crux of the problem was whether the Church could be content with royal indulgence. To Becket and his supporters the answer was definitely not: the Church could not be beholden to anyone for the liberty which Christ, as he said, had won for her; and, furthermore, it was not for the secular power to

---

[1] As reported to Archbishop Becket, *Materials*, Epistolae, VI, 272.

[2] Gilbert Foliot, *Letters and Charters*, no. 170, 242; *Materials*, Epistolae, V, 542. The bishop of Lisieux expressed a similar opinion, Arnulf of Lisieux, *Letters*, no. 42, 72–3.

[3] *See* above, ch. 7, pp. 273–4.

[4] *Materials*, Epistolae, VI, 81; William of Canterbury, I, 13.

lay down the rules.[1] The answer of the pope, however, was a more qualified No: he could not allow the king to dictate the terms of a concordat – as he had tried to do in the Constitutions of Clarendon – but he would not rule out the possibility of a concordat altogether, or obstruct the possibility of negotiations by defining conditions in advance. It is this caution which presumably accounts for Alexander III's ambivalent attitude towards the Constitutions.

That the pope strongly disapproved of the Constitutions is, of course, beyond question; and that he expressed his disapproval publicly after Becket's dramatic recital of the text at Sens in November 1164 is equally certain.[2] But it is improbable that he condemned them with the authoritative finality which Becket would have wished. The archbishop's biographers, it is true, assumed that he did. Roger of Pontigny, for example, says that 'the pope then condemned those constitutions in perpetuity, and consigned those who observed them or insisted upon them to eternal anathema'.[3] Edward Grim asserts that at Sens the pope, 'condemned to perpetual anathema the text which had been read, the instigators of it, and anyone who should give assent to it'.[4] Yet if the pope had indeed pronounced such a comprehensive anathema, Becket's own condemnation of selected clauses at Vézelay in June 1166, and his general excommunication of those who observed or required the observance of these 'perversities', would have been both superfluous and impertinent.[5] John of Salisbury later claimed that the archbishop had been acting on apostolic authority; but it is noticeable that the pope's bull confirming the excommunications which Becket pronounced upon his enemies at Vézelay had nothing whatever to say about the Constitutions.[6] Moreover, the comprehensive anathema recorded by Becket's biographers cannot be squared with the English bishops' con-

---

[1] Cf. *Materials*, Epistolae, V, 280.

[2] *Ibid.*, VI, 390.   [3] Roger of Pontigny, IV, 64.

[4] Edward Grim, II, 404. Herbert of Bosham, who was present but who wrote of it many years later, uses more elliptical language, III, 342: 'Vir apostolicus easdem praenominata consuetudines . . . in audientia cardinalum, nobis praesentibus, reprobavit, et ab ecclesia in posterum damnandas censuit'.

[5] Cf. *Materials*, Epistolae, V, 387–8.

[6] *Ibid.*, 257, 392. John of Salisbury's account of the meeting with papal legates in November 1167 and of the archbishop's reply to their suggestion that he might consider pledging himself to observe the ancient usages of England, should be compared with Becket's own account to the pope, *ibid.*, VI, 249–50. Becket, although saying that Holy Church condemned the Constitutions, does not specifically claim papal authority for his own condemnation at Vézelay; he gives as his reasons for refusing the legates' suggestion that none of his predecessors had given such an undertaking, and that the pope had absolved him from his oath to the Constitutions.

tinued observance of the Constitutions. It cannot have been that they were ignorant of the true situation, for they were in frequent contact with the papal court, and Bishop Foliot indeed corresponded with the pope himself on the implications of the clause on appeals.[1] Moreover, the papal legates sent to effect a reconciliation between Becket and Henry persisted in trying to find a formula which would bind the archbishop to observe the Constitutions under cover of some circumlocution. Becket protested to the legates Simon and Bernard in 1169 that he could not be expected to observe the Constitutions unconditionally, 'since some of them have been condemned by the apostolic see'.[2] This, it is true, points to some form of papal condemnation, but not one which the negotiators regarded as an insuperable obstacle. In any case Becket's own words do not suggest the root and branch anathema which some, at least, of his biographers believed in. Shortly afterwards Becket was to be found beseeching the pope not to require him to enter into any obligation to the customs, and trying to deter him by warning that 'if the required customs prevail the authority of the apostolic see in England will utterly vanish away, or be minimal'.[3] It can hardly be doubted, then, that Becket's partisans have exaggerated the extent to which Alexander III committed himself against the Constitutions, and have blurred the distinction between his criticism (trenchant though it may well have been) and formal anathema. 'Condemnation' is, after all, an imprecise word.

On the other hand, the pope undoubtedly took the strongest exception to the oath which the English bishops had been required to swear: he not only absolved Becket from his oath, but tried to insist that the oaths of the bishops should be set aside before permission could be given for the coronation of Henry the Younger.[4] Furthermore, he obliged Archbishop Roger of York to repudiate the oath before allowing him to purge himself of complicity in the murder of Becket.[5] According to one of the sources for the terms of Henry's reconciliation with the Church in 1172, the king was required to 'relax the oath which the bishops took to the Constitutions and promise not to exact it in the future'.[6] The pope's objection was one which the English bishops would gratefully echo for, as they asserted, they had resolutely resisted the oath until

[1] *Ibid.*, V, 176, 205. Cf. the pope's letter to the bishop of Worcester in 1168, *ibid.*, VI, 390.

[2] *Ibid.*, 491: 'quia aliquae earum a sede apostolica condemnatae sunt'.

[3] *Ibid.*, 515.

[4] *Ibid.*, VII, 216.

[5] *Ibid.*, 500, 502.

[6] Cardinals Albert and Theodwin to the archbishop of Sens, *ibid.*, 522.

obliged to take it at the archbishop's command.[1] It seems likely that the pope's objections to the Constitutions were, indeed, basically similar to those of the bishops themselves: that the oath was unprecedented and bound the English clergy to a one-sided version of ancient customs which were in some respects offensive to developed notions of canonical propriety, and in many more respects an impediment to church government. On the other hand, there is no reason to doubt either that he shared their general view that open and prolonged conflict was even more obstructive to church government, and to be avoided, if necessary, by some concessions to the king's anxiety to protect his own interests.[2] This is far from Becket's cataclysmic view of the Constitutions as 'heretical depravities', utterly destructive of the Church's liberty, and to be resisted at all costs.[3] Becket's attempt to represent the dispute as a fundamental conflict of ideologies has appealed to those historians who are tempted, as some contemporaries were, to identify the English situation with that in the Empire; but such a conception was at variance with the Anglo-Norman tradition, with the temperament of the king, and with the attitudes of a majority of the English and Norman clergy. It was an interpretation which even the pope was reluctant to accept, press him as the archbishop might.

The one clause upon which the pope seems to have felt more strongly than the English bishops – and it is hardly surprising – was the clause imposing royal control on the pursuit of appeals beyond the jurisdiction of the local hierarchy. This was the one clause on which from the beginning he sought to change the king's mind, and it was to be the one clause on which he demanded a positive concession before peace could be made.[4] The king's defence, that he intended merely to restrict abuses, could not be acceptable. More reassuring was the fact that even in the difficult years of the dispute with Becket, the king had allowed appeals to the Roman court – and not only on matters arising from the dispute itself, but also upon points of canon law which had arisen in the course of ordinary litigation in the church courts in England.[5] These at least showed that the king did not intend to veto all resort to the Roman

---

[1] *Materials*, Epistolae, V, 529. It was presumably for this reason that the Pope made a special point of the archbishop of York's repudiation of any participation in the oath to the Constitutions: he could not advance the same excuse as the suffragans of Canterbury.

[2] For comments upon the attitudes of the English bishops to the relations of *regnum* and *sacerdotium see* Morey and Brooke, *Gilbert Foliot and his Letters*, 175–87; Cheney, *From Becket to Langton*, chs 2 and 4; Mayr-Harting, 'Hilary, bishop of Chichester'.

[3] e.g., *Materials*, Epistolae, V, 401.   [4] Cf. *ibid.*, V, 175; VII, 517.

[5] Cf. Mary Cheney, 'The Compromise of Avranches and the spread of canon law

curia. But even this reassurance could not be satisfactory, for the heart of the pope's concern with this clause of the Constitutions lay in its obstruction to the development of the papal court as a court of 'first instance' – hearing cases brought directly to Rome without resort to the courts of the local hierarchy.[1] Papal authority was developing, as royal authority was shortly to develop, through the agency of its comprehensive claims to jurisdiction; and the hearing of any kind of case was as vital to the elaboration of a common law for the Church as it was to be for the common law of the English realm.[2] With Alexander III the Roman Church had become evolutionary instead of revolutionary, and although this meant that it was less overtly aggressive in the pursuit of its claims, it nevertheless meant that it could brook no such obstacle to the evolutionary process as was implicit in Henry's resort to antiquated procedures as a means of protecting his interests. That is not to say that the interests themselves were necessarily illegitimate or the protection of them always improper. It was the particular means Henry insisted upon which were unacceptable, and his demand for unqualified acceptance of a royal *diktat* which was intolerable. In protecting his own interests the king was trespassing upon ecclesiastical interests, and misusing his royal authority to defend the trespass. This was the burden of a letter addressed by Alexander III to Henry II in 1166:

> . . . as the clergy are distinguished from the laity in manner of life and dress, so also is clerical jurisdiction wholly distinct from lay jurisdiction. Wherefore if you improperly subvert this ordering of society, and if, usurping to yourself the powers which belong to Jesus Christ, you establish new rules oppressive to the churches and the poor in Christ at your pleasure, introducing, even, those customs which you call ancestral, you yourself will, at the unescapable last judgement, be undoubtedly judged in like manner, and the same standards which you have applied will be meted out to you. . . . It is not only decent for you but also expedient not to confound Church and State. . . .[3]

---

in England', 186ff., and the papal decretals *Meminimus* (c. 1167–9), *Inter cetera* (1163–1164), and *Ex parte tua* (1170–1), *Regesta Pontificum Romanorum*, nos 13162, 12254, 11872.

[1] *See* above, pp. 408, 478–9.

[2] Pope Alexander III (1159–81) was a great canonist, and his pontificate saw the consolidation and refinement of existing procedures and rules of law. The problem of the remoteness of the papal court when considering appeals was overcome by the employment of judges-delegate who established questions of fact about a case; but questions of law were reserved for papal decision. For a useful summary of the development of papal jurisdiction in this period *see* Brooke, introduction to *The Letters of John of Salisbury*, I, xxxi-xxxv; and for the operations of the judge-delegate system, Morey, *Bartholomew of Exeter*, 44–78. [3] *Materials*, Epistolae, VI, 553–4.

This is one of the few letters addressed by the pope to the king in the years of crisis, and the only one to allude directly to the Constitutions. Alexander III, like Henry himself, seems to have been reluctant to allow the quarrel between king and archbishop to develop into a quarrel between Crown and papacy.

Historians have commonly assumed that the pope's caution in dealing with Henry II stemmed from an anxiety to retain his allegiance, and that the strength of his support for Becket fluctuated with the fortunes of the imperial party in Italy. Alexander did indeed offer his political difficulties as an excuse against accusations of spinelessness; and the close watch kept on events in the empire by Becket's correspondents suggests that they expected that the archbishop's cause would prosper when the pope's did. But although the ups and downs of the schism undoubtedly influenced the mood of the papal curia and the tone of papal letters, there is no exact correlation between the fluctuations of Alexander III's position in Italy and the vigour of his support for Becket. The schism, indeed, seems to have been only one factor among several in shaping the pope's attitude to King Henry. For one thing, the papal curia itself was far from united on the policy to be pursued.[1] For another, Henry's vacillating attitude towards a settlement of the dispute demanded a variety of diplomatic responses. And, thirdly, Alexander III's interpretation of Henry's intentions seems to have undergone a cautious change, and hence too his assessment of the problem and his response to it. After Becket's dramatic intervention at Sens in November 1164 he had been persuaded that the Constitutions of Clarendon were indeed the cause of the archbishop's exile; and in the light of this adopted many of the delusions which ever since have clustered round the Constitutions – that the king intended, for instance, not merely to control but prevent appeals, or that clerks were to be brought to trial in lay courts.[2] But the conduct of English church government during the years of the archbishop's exile had not lent very much credibility to such views. The king's insistence on nothing less than the Constitutions began to look like nothing more than a tactical move to force the archbishop to climb down. Henry might be obstinate, devious, and evasive, but he had persisted in negotiation and in looking to the papacy for a solution. As a result, his basic fidelity both to Alexander III and the apostolic see began to appear less and less in question, and the pope probably came to regard his blustering threats to change sides in the schism as no more

---

[1] See, for example, the letter of Cardinal William of Pavia to the bishop of London, *Materials*, Epistolae, VI, 46–7.

[2] Cf., e.g., the pope's letter to the bishop of London, *ibid.*, V, 176–7.

serious than his alleged threat to embrace Islam.[1] After all, even the consolation he had given to the pope's enemies in the letter to the imperial chancellor in 1166 had been merely the preamble to a request for safe-conduct for royal envoys on their way to the papal court.[2]

As the pope became doubtful about Becket's self-justificatory interpretation of events, so he began to try to separate the two issues which Becket had run confusingly together. At least from 1167 the papal negotiators tried hard to push the question of the 'customs' to one side, and to concentrate on securing the archbishop's peaceful return to England. The pope had no hesitation in regarding Henry's treatment of Becket as an intolerable persecution. He never entertained the king's disingenuous argument that the archbishop had not been sent into exile but had taken to flight, and that he was generously prepared to overlook this treachery and receive back the archbishop whenever he chose to come: the repudiation of the sentences at Northampton was implicit in all the papal proposals for reconciliation. But at the same time it is clear that the pope came to regard the problem of the 'customs' as one which it would be better to try to resolve piecemeal by negotiation once normality had been restored to English church government. His policy, indeed, was the typical papal policy of being cautious about offending deep-seated susceptibilities, but to be even more cautious about appearing to confirm them. The difficulty in trying to effect a reconciliation was to prevent Becket making an issue of the Constitutions, and to prevent Henry establishing his point that he was entitled to the 'dignities' which his predecessors had enjoyed.

It is indicative of Alexander III's mature policy that he did not insist on a specific repudiation of the Constitutions of Clarendon before allowing Henry II to purge himself of complicity in the murder of Becket. People doubtless expected that he would insist on it and some convinced themselves that he did – to the confusion of contemporaries and posterity; but in fact the Pope rested content with a repudiation by Henry of any 'novelties' he had introduced during his reign (which took care of the unprecedented oaths), and a compromise over appeals.[3] It was on this basis that the future relations of Church and State were to be built.

It is commonly held that Henry deliberately postponed his reconcilia-

---

[1] *Ibid.*, VI, 406.

[2] *See*, e.g., the pope's instructions to his legates, *ibid.*, VI, 201, and Herbert of Bosham, III, 410–11.

[3] Cf. the anonymous report of the terms of the reconciliation, *Materials*, Epistolae, VII, 515, with the legates' own memorandum of the terms, *ibid.*, 517. The terms are discussed below, p. 531.

tion with the Church – that he went to Ireland in 1171 to evade the legates sent to negotiate his absolution, and with the intention of recovering his credit with the papacy by reducing the Irish Church to order. The assumption is unwarranted. Henry had no alternative but to go to Ireland in 1171: the marriage of Earl Richard de Clare to the daughter of King Dermot of Leinster in the autumn of 1170, the death of Dermot the following May and the victory of the earl's men over the forces of the high-king at the battle of the Liffey made Henry II's intervention imperative and urgent.[1] He spent the summer of 1171 preparing an expedition, and sailed from Milford Haven on 16 October. Legates had been commissioned at Rome to examine Henry and, if they found him contrite, to arrange his absolution, within a month of the imposition of the papal sentences at Easter 1171; but they did not leave the papal court until the autumn, and did not reach Henry's dominions until the beginning of December.[2] It is unlikely that Henry heard of their arrival until much later, for bad weather in the Irish Sea had interrupted communications. When he did hear of it he hastened to complete his business in Ireland, and travelled back through Wales, England, and Normandy to meet them with a speed which prompted King Louis to exclaim 'The king of England seems rather to fly than to travel by horse or ship'.[3]

Talks began at the abbey of Savigny on 17 May 1172. Nothing is known of the pope's instructions to his legates or of the course of the negotiations, except that Henry is said to have marched angrily out of the first session saying that he would return to Ireland where there was much requiring his attention.[4] Doubtless the legates had pitched their initial demands as high as they dared, and Henry was giving notice that he was not prepared to buy his absolution at any price. His expedition to Ireland may have had other motives than restoring his credit at Rome, but it had certainly strengthened his hand, for the chequered course of the reform movement in Ireland had shown how necessary to the Church was a strong monarchy. Without it there was little hope of the enforcement of ecclesiastical government. Henry had no serious

[1] *See* above, ch. 4, pp. 193ff.

[2] Raymonde Foreville, *L'Église et la Royauté en Angleterre*, 333–5; the contention of Roger of Howden that there was an earlier deputation of legates may be dismissed as an error.

[3] Ralph of Diceto, I, 351, cf. the report of the legates themselves, *Materials*, Epistolae, VII, 520.

[4] An anonymous report, *Materials*, Epistolae, VII, 514: 'rex ab eis cum indignatione discessit in haec verba: "Redeo," inquit, "in Hiberniam, ubi multa mihi incumbunt" '. Cf. the legates' report of the incident in a letter to the archbishop of Ravenna, Roger of Howden, *Chronica*, II, 38.

intention, however, of breaking off the talks: they were continued by his deputies, and within three days agreement had been reached. On Sunday 21 May 1172 a public ceremony of reconciliation was performed at the cathedral at Avranches. With his hand on a copy of the Gospels, Henry swore that he had neither commanded nor willed the death of the archbishop, but admitted that his anger had prompted his servants to commit the deed, and offered himself ready to do all that the legates should require of him. The terms announced by the legates were:

> That he should at his own expense provide two hundred knights to serve for a year with the Templars in the Holy Land.

> That he himself should take the cross for a period of three years and depart for the Holy Land before the following Easter, unless the pope postponed it, or unless his services were urgently required against the Moslems of Spain.

> That the church of Canterbury should be put in full possession of all the property it enjoyed a year before Archbishop Thomas incurred his anger, and that all who had suffered in the archbishop's cause should be restored to property and favour.

> That he should not impede appeals to Rome or obstruct the papal decision; but that he might take security from anyone he distrusted that they would not damage himself or his realm.

> That he should utterly abolish customs prejudicial to the Church which had been introduced in his reign, and should require no more from the bishops.[1]

A personal penance was also imposed, but its nature was not divulged. After the king had sworn to abide by these terms he was taken to the door of the cathedral and publicly absolved, and was then formally led into it again as a symbolic gesture of his restoration to the bosom of the Church. A week later at Caen, Henry publicly repeated his promises and released the bishops from their oath to observe the Constitutions.[2] The pope ratified the agreement by a bull dated 2 September 1172.[3]

*   *   *

[1] These are, condensed, the terms as set out by the legates in a memorandum to the king, *Materials*, Epistolae, VII, 517–18. In a letter to the archbishop of Sens the legates indicate that a further promise was required: that the king should not withdraw his allegiance from Pope Alexander and his catholic successors, *ibid.*, 521; cf. Roger of Howden, *Gesta*, I, 32; Gervase of Canterbury, I, 238. Henry was subsequently released from his vow to go on crusade, *see* below, p. 538, no. 1.

[2] Reported by the legates to the archbishop of Sens, *Materials*, Epistolae, VII, 522, and to the archbishop of Ravenna, *ibid.*, 523.

[3] Johnson, 'The reconciliation of King Henry II with the papacy: a missing

The clauses of the agreement at Avranches which bear upon the Constitutions of Clarendon are worthy of careful scrutiny. It is unfortunate that there is no authoritative text of them: the legates' report to the pope has not survived, and the papal confirmation survives only as a fragment of a late copy. Nevertheless, there are versions given by the legates in a memorandum to Henry II, by the legates in letters to the archbishops of Sens and Ravenna, and by Henry II himself in a letter to the bishop of Exeter, which exhibit verbal differences, but are in sufficient agreement on points of substance to be acceptable as indicating the true nature of the king's promises.[1] The need for precision is underlined by an anonymous report of the negotiations which asserts that the king swore that he would utterly renounce the perverse statutes of Clarendon and all evil customs which had been brought into the church in his days, and further that he would 'moderate those evils which existed before his time, according to the instructions of the lord pope and the counsel of religious men'.[2] This may possibly have been what the legates initially sought, but it was not what Henry was required to promise. He was not required to abrogate the Constitutions of Clarendon, but simply to release the bishops from their unprecedented oath 'to keep and observe them in good faith and without evil intent'.[3] The Constitutions – or such of them as survived the rest of the agreement – were thus reduced to the status of those laws of the realm, comprehended in the king's 'earthly honour', which bishops, before their consecration, swore to uphold, 'saving their order'.[4] The king was not required to submit the ancient customs of the realm to the judgement of the pope 'and the counsel of religious men', but simply swore to set aside, in the words of the legates' memorandum, 'those customs prejudicial to the

---

document'. It is possible that after the papal confirmation Henry formally repeated his promises, which could account for the date of 27 September instead of 21 May being given for the absolution at Avranches by Roger of Howden, *Gesta*, I, 31–2, *Chronica*, II, 35, and by Gervase of Canterbury, I, 238. It is equally possible, however, that they are simply mistaken and have run together Henry's absolution at Avranches in May with a church council held by the legates at Avranches in September.

[1] *Materials*, Epistolae, VII, 516–23. There are versions in Roger of Howden, *Gesta*, I, 32–3, *Chronica*, II, 35–6, and Gervase of Canterbury, I, 238–9, which are parallel to the legates' letter to the archbishop of Sens.

[2] *Materials*, Epistolae, VII, 515: 'Quod prava statuta de Clarenduna, et omnes malas consuetudines quae in diebus suis in ecclesias Dei inductae sunt penitus dimitteret. Si quae autem malae fuerunt ante tempora sua, illas, juxta mandatum domini papae et consilio religiosorum virorum, temperabit.'

[3] Constitutions of Clarendon, preamble.

[4] Cf. Constitutions of Clarendon, clause 12, and Becket's argument, above, ch. 13, p. 469.

churches of your territories which have been introduced in your time'.[1] These, Henry himself commented (in his letter reporting the agreement to the bishop of Exeter), 'I reckon to be few or none'.[2] This carefully worded agreement clearly left open to further discussion and negotiation the question of what, if anything, was prejudicial, not so much to the Church as a whole, as to the churches of his realms (*contra ecclesias terrae suae*).[3] In short, the agreement at Avranches simply laid down the minimum of general principles within which the relations of Church and State could further be adjusted and their conflicting interests reconciled.

An illustration of the kind of compromise which could be achieved was provided by the clause on appeals. The memorandum of the agreement sent to King Henry said:

> You shall not impede appeals, nor allow them to be impeded; but they shall freely be made in ecclesiastical causes to the Roman Church, in good faith and without fraud or evil intent, so that causes may be dealt with by the Roman pontiff and brought to judgement by him; yet so, that if anyone should be suspect to you they shall give you security that they will not seek the injury of you or your kingdom.[4]

In his report to the bishop of Exeter the king glossed the security clause:

> that those whom I mistrust shall, before leaving the kingdom, swear that in journeying thither they shall not seek injury to me, nor the dishonour of my kingdom.[5]

If Henry's desire was control over, and not the prevention of, appeals to Rome – and the weight of the evidence supports such an interpretation – then he lost little by this ingenious compromise. Royal officials would have to be rather more diligent in watching over the Crown's interests, for by the agreement at Avranches the king had to forgo that automatic control over all cases which anyone wished to take outside

---

[1] *Materials*, Epistolae, VII, 517: 'Consuetudines quae inductae sunt contra ecclesias terrae vestrae tempore vestro penitus dimittetis, nec ab episcopis amplius exigetis'. The last phrase apparently refers to the bishops' oath, cf. *ibid.*, 522, 523.

[2] *Ibid.*, 519: 'quas quidem aut paucas aut nullas aestimo'.

[3] The legates' letter to the archbishop of Sens refers only to 'the churches of his kingdom' (*contra ecclesias regni sui*), *ibid.*, 521.

[4] *Ibid.*, 517: 'Appellationes nec impedietis nec permitetis impediri, quin libere fiant in ecclesiasticis causis ad Romanam ecclesiam, bona fide, et absque fraude et malo ingenio, ut per Romanum pontificem causae tractentur, et suum consequantur effectum; sic tamen, ut si vobis suspecti fuerint aliqui, securitatem faciant, quod malum vestrum vel regni vestri non quaerent.' There are verbal differences in the legates' report to the archbishop of Sens, *ibid.*, 522.

[5] *Ibid.*, 519.

the kingdom which the procedure laid down in the Constitutions had ensured; but in return for this concession the king gained papal sanction not merely for the taking of security but for having cognizance of the plea of anyone he chose to declare suspect, and was thus given an opportunity to prepare a counter argument and enter an interlocutory appeal at Rome.

'How he fears God and is obedient to the Church,' wrote the legates of Henry II, 'his actions sufficiently reveal, and will reveal still more in the future, as we have been given hope to believe.'[1] Henry, in his mature years, knew how to give way graciously, and it won him the confidence of the papacy, indulgence towards his foibles, and its active assistance in some of the political problems which confronted him.

The first manifestation of papal approval came just over a fortnight after the ratification of the agreement at Avranches. From Tusculum on 20 September 1172 Pope Alexander III despatched two bulls to Ireland. To lay rulers of Ireland he wrote commending them for having submitted of their own free will 'to that powerful and majestic king who is a devoted son of the Church', and admonishing them to keep firm and unbroken the fealty they had sworn.[2] To the bishops of Ireland he wrote expressing his 'great joy' at Henry's intervention in Ireland and urging them to give him their cooperation and support:

> If any king, prince, or other man in that land, violating the oath of fealty which he has properly sworn to the aforesaid king, shall rashly go against him, and thereafter basely refuse to accept your admonitions as he ought, you are, without excuse or delay, to strike him with the censure of the Church, relying in so doing upon the apostolic authority. This catholic and most Christian king has heard us in respect of tithes and other rights of the Church, and in restoring to you and to all men those things which pertain to the liberty of the Church.[3]

These were sentiments which must have sounded strangely to Becket's partisans.

The second sign of papal complaisance was the pope's attitude to the appointment of bishops to the sees which had fallen vacant since 1164 and had been left unfilled because of the archbishop's exile. The long vacancies had been a scandal to the Church and a rebuke to the king whose obstinacy had prolonged the archbishop's absence; but the pope

---

[1] *Materials*, Epistolae, VII, 521; Roger of Howden, *Chronica*, II, 38.
[2] *Liber Niger de Scaccario*, I, 47–8.
[3] *Ibid.*, I, 42–4, trans. in *English Historical Documents*, II, 777–8.

approved Henry's nomination in 1173 of clerks in the royal service who had been prominent in the campaign against Becket. Richard of Ilchester, confidant of the king, whom the archbishop had excommunicated at Vézelay, succeeded Henry of Blois, brother of King Stephen, in the immensely wealthy bishopric of Winchester.[1] Geoffrey Ridel, who had taken over from Becket both the chancery and the archdeaconry of Canterbury ('archidiabolus' Becket's friends called him), was promoted to the bishopric of Ely, the revenues of which he had already for several years exploited as royal custodian.[2] The see of Bath received Reginald FitzJocelin, who had been one of Henry's trusted messengers to Rome, but who to Becket was 'that offspring of fornication, that enemy to the peace of the Church, that traitor'.[3] In 1175 John of Oxford was promoted at the king's nomination to the bishopric of Norwich. He had been the royal clerk whom Becket hated most and always referred to as 'that notorious schismatic' for the part he played as the king's envoy to the emperor's council at Würzburg.[4] Despite Becket's poor opinion, they were worthy men who rose to their responsibilities as bishops; but there can be no doubt that their presence on the episcopal bench gave Henry II the voice and vote which he had so signally lacked in 1164.[5] There was no policy, however, of packing the bench. Not all the bishoprics vacant in 1172 were filled by royal clerks: the obscure John of Greenford was appointed to Chichester, and Robert Foliot, sometime clerk of Becket and nephew of the bishop of London, to Hereford. In these cases the election was apparently freely made by the cathedral chapter.[6] These were the less wealthy and less important sees: but to the most important of all, that of Canterbury, a free election was also made. Finding a successor to Thomas Becket was protracted by a wrangle between the monks of Canterbury and the bishops of the province as to their respective share in making an election,

---

[1] For his career see Duggan, 'Richard of Ilchester, royal servant and bishop', and above, ch. 8, pp. 311–13.

[2] Cf., e.g., *Materials*, Epistolae, V, 91–2, 94; VI, 91, 300 n. 3, 558.

[3] *Ibid.*, VII, 181. He was the son of Bishop Jocelin of Salisbury, but may have been born before his father became a priest, see Knowles, *Episcopal Colleagues of Thomas Becket*, 19. He and Richard of Ilchester were two of the chief negotiators with the legates for the terms of the king's absolution.

[4] He heads the list of Becket's excommunications at Vézelay, *Materials*, Epistolae, V, 388.

[5] This was, at least, in accordance with the instructions of the papal legates to the electors to 'choose such men that you know will honour God in all things and make useful provision for the salvation of your souls *and the peace of the realm*', Ralph of Diceto, I, 367.

[6] Cf. Raymonde Foreville, *L'Église et la Royauté en Angleterre*, 380.

and by the refusal of the first candidate they agreed upon, Roger, abbot of Bec, to accept the honour. At length the choice fell upon Richard of Dover, a monk of the cathedral chapter and prior of its dependent cell at Dover.[1] The king, it seems likely, had made it known that Roger of Dover would be acceptable but he had not tried to force a candidate on the electors and not interfered in the election itself, save to beg the monks not to elect anyone who would be an imitator of Becket and suggesting the name of Henry de Beaumont, bishop of Bayeux.[2] They ignored his suggestion but heeded his warning. Richard of Dover was no time-server, and was to be one of the leaders in a remarkable efflorescence of interest in the development of canon law in England; but he had a different order of priorities from Becket – he gave first place to reform of the clergy and believed that cooperation with the State was essential to the Church's well-being.[3]

The third manifestation of the papacy's support for Henry II was its refusal to give comfort to his enemies in the great war of 1173-4. The demands by King Louis and his brothers-in-law, the count of Blois and the archbishop of Sens, for papal vengeance on Henry for the martyrdom of Becket had fallen flat, but it was nevertheless in the guise of the party of righteousness against a tyrant that Louis attempted to organise the rebellion. Something of the sentiments of those who opposed Henry II may be gauged from the Breton chronicle which records that 'Thomas archbishop of Canterbury was slain on the order of the king'.[4] Henry the Younger was attempting to ride both the popular and papal sympathy for Becket when he wrote to the pope promising that as Henry III he would fully respect the rights of the Church, complaining of his father's influence in promoting royal clerks to bishoprics, and claiming that this was the cause of the breach between them.[5] The pope would have none of it.[6]

This complaisance survived clear indications that Henry II fully intended to salvage as much as possible of the ancient customs of the realm. There could have been no clearer sign of this than his treatment

---

[1] On the election to Canterbury see Raymonde Foreville, op. cit., 374-9.

[2] Gervase of Canterbury, I, 240.

[3] For Richard of Dover's place in the development of canonical studies, see Duggan, *Twelfth-Century Decretal Collections*. John of Oxford, admittedly with a partisan purpose but nevertheless with some justice, complained that Becket was not interested in reform, *Materials*, Epistolae, V, 146, cf. *ibid.*, 149-50.

[4] *Recueil des Historiens des Gaules et de la France*, XII, 560.

[5] *Ibid.*, XVI, 645; *Recueil des Actes de Henri II*, I, 587. He alleged that the monks of Winchester had received from his father a writ which read: 'I order you to hold a free election but nevertheless forbid you to elect anyone except Richard my clerk, the archdeacon of Poitiers.'　　　　　　　　[6] Cf. Ralph of Diceto, I, 338-70.

of papal legates. In July 1176 Cardinal Vivian landed in England on his way to discharge a legatine commission in Ireland and Scotland, but 'without the king's licence', as Roger of Howden relates:

> The king sent to him Richard bishop of Winchester and Geoffrey bishop of Ely, to inquire by whose permission he had landed in England and to intimate that unless he was ready to abide by the will of the king he would not be allowed to proceed further. He, however, fearing for himself and sensing danger in the situation, at length accepted their advice that he should conform to the king's will. The king then made him swear on the word of truth that he would do nothing on his legation hostile to himself or his kingdom.[1]

Yet papal indulgence towards Henry's insistence on being accorded his ancestral dignity is easily explained: Henry allowed Cardinal Vivian to proceed with his mission, and more than that–

> . . . the king gave him an escort and letters of protection, and ordered that the abbots and bishops whom he might encounter on his journey should receive him with honour as a cardinal.[2]

The cooperation of the Crown was convenient – and not very costly. The lesson of Cardinal Vivian's experience was learned at Rome, and when in 1178 a papal envoy, Peter of St Agatha, arrived in England on his way to Scotland with summonses to the clergy of Scotland, Ireland and the Western Isles, to attend a general council of the Church, he sought first the king's licence to pass through his realm, 'and he swore, touching the holy gospels, that in the course of his mission he would seek injury neither to the king nor his kingdom'.[3]

The guarantee which Henry sought from these papal legates was clearly modelled on the compromise arranged at Avranches on the prosecution of appeals. The arrangement might, to the purist, have offensive implications; but it worked to the satisfaction of both pope and king, and that, to both king and pope, was enough.

The conviction, bred at Avranches, that the conflicting interests of Church and State could be reconciled peaceably, with a little give and take on each side, worked to resolve other difficulties. Agreement on several points was reached after direct discussions between King Henry and Cardinal Hugh Pierleone in 1176. A memorandum of the agree-

---

[1] Roger of Howden, *Gesta*, I, 118; cf. *Chronica*, II, 98–9.

[2] *Loc. cit.* Similarly the envoy sent to summon the clergy of England toured the country 'cum licentia regis', Ralph of Diceto, I, 429.

[3] Roger of Howden, *Chronica*, II, 167, *Gesta*, I, 210.

ment, sent by the king to the pope, is recorded by the chronicler Ralph of Diceto:

> The king of the English to the lord pope. On account of the reverence which we have and always will have towards the holy Roman Church, and the devotion which we have for it and your fatherhood, and the affection for yourself and your brethren, we have, at the instance of that prudent and wise man, Hugh Pierleone, cardinal of the holy Roman Church, legate of the apostolic see, our friend and kinsman – despite very much which the greater and more prudent men of our realm might resist and protest about – conceded to be held in our kingdom the underwritten articles, namely,
>
> That a clerk shall not personally be drawn before a secular judge for any crime, nor for any offence, except for offences against my forest, and except concerning a lay fief from which a lay service is owed to myself or other secular lord.
>
> I concede also that archbishoprics, bishoprics, and abbeys shall not be held in my hand longer than a year, unless for urgent necessity and clearly for this cause – not invented in order that they might be held longer.
>
> I concede also that slayers of clerks, who knowingly or with premeditation slay them, convicted or confessed before my justiciar, in the presence of the bishop or his official, shall, in addition to the customary punishment of laymen, sustain perpetual disinheritance, he and his, for the inheritance which appertains to them.
>
> I concede also that clerks shall not be obliged to engage in the judicial duel.[1]

The impression of far-reaching concessions to the Church conveyed by the king's reference to the possible objections of his magnates, was not shared by clerical chroniclers, who commented sharply on the cardinal's indulgence towards the Crown.[2] The king's concessions, although real,

---

[1] Ralph of Diceto, I, 410. It is possible that Henry also obtained from Cardinal Hugh Pierleone release from his vow at Avranches to undertake a crusade. Gerald of Wales, VIII, 170, says that Henry's vow was commuted to the foundation of three monasteries. This he accomplished cheaply, Gerald alleges, by reorganising the house at Waltham as a house of canons regular, by refounding the nunnery at Amesbury as a convent of nuns from Fontevrault, and by a small foundation of Carthusians at Witham. There is no corroboration of this in other chronicles; although Roger of Howden, stating that Henry had vowed to build a house of canons regular in honour of St Thomas, 'in remissionem peccatorum suorum', sought leave from Cardinal Hugh to refound the house at Waltham, *Gesta*, I, 134–5; *see* also *ibid.*, 135–6, 165; Gervase of Canterbury, I, 260–1; Ralph of Diceto, I, 395–6, 420.

[2] Gervase of Canterbury, I, 257, delivered himself of a diatribe against the legate. Ralph of Diceto, I, 410, comments scathingly, before reproducing the memorandum,

were indeed seriously qualified and limited. The withdrawal of the Church's protection from clerks accused of forest offences or pleading about secular land gave the king much of the jurisdiction he desired over the clergy. The qualification in the clause on the custody of vacant bishoprics and abbeys virtually nullified it, for the judgement of what constituted 'urgent necessity' was left to the king, whose financial necessities were always urgent: it amounted, in fact, to little more than an expression of good intentions.[1] The concession that the murderers of clerks should be subjected to special penalties, was hardly a concession at all: the Church was surrendering its claim to exclusive jurisdiction in such cases for the sake of greater security for the clergy. Its weakness in this respect had allowed the murderers of Becket to go unpunished. And as for the participation of the clergy in judicial duels, the king would not have minded if such an antiquated form of proof had been abandoned altogether: women were in any case exempt from it, and the royal courts were shortly to offer a more rational alternative. Nevertheless, the king was conceding important points of principle – to the Church, fundamental points of principle: he was abandoning all claim to bring the clergy to secular justice, save when the Church itself allowed it, and he was acknowledging that the Crown's intrinsic or prescriptive right to the custody of vacant bishoprics and abbeys was seriously limited – in principle to the period required for the election, confirmation, and installation of a new bishop or abbot. For the sake of establishing such points of principle the Church could afford to be generous in making concessions on their practical application.

It may be observed that the clause on criminous clerks was narrowly drawn. Nothing was said on the definition of 'a clerk', and the real point at issue in the Constitutions of Clarendon – the question of whether a convicted and degraded clerk might be punished as an ex-clerk in the lay court after trial in the ecclesiastical court – could only be assumed to be covered in the rather vague phrase 'shall not be hailed before a secular judge'.[2] Becket's successor, Archbishop Richard, in a letter of 1176 to the bishops of Winchester, Ely, and Norwich, spoke scathingly of the kind of argument Becket had used: if ecclesiastical jurisdiction cannot provide adequate punishments it should be assisted

---

'the solicitude he should have had for the liberties of the English Church the contents of the following schedule reveals'. Cf. Roger of Howden, *Gesta*, I, 105, *Chronica*, II, 86.

[1] Cf. Margaret Howell, *Regalian Right in Medieval England*, 34–44.

[2] The Latin is: 'clericus non trahatur ante judicem secularem in persona sua'.

by the secular power; there should be no talk of double punishment when what is begun by one is completed by the other: the two powers need each other's help and 'if one supplements the other's insufficiency this is not a double punishment but a combined punishment'.[1] Opinion at Rome, however, was hardening in two respects against Henry II's proposal in the Constitutions of Clarendon. In the first place it could not allow that convicted clerks should, as the king had insisted, always be degraded from their orders – and hence, as laymen, made amenable to the jurisdiction of the secular power: other punishments, such as imprisonment or suspension from office might suffice.[2] Secondly, it was moving towards the view that degradation was itself a terrible punishment, normally sufficient for even the more serious crimes. This was the view taken by Alexander III in a letter to the archbishop of Salerno, c. 1177–8, which subsequently passed into the official *corpus* of canon law.[3] The Church was not to rule out the possibility of 'double punishment' altogether: it might be appropriate in certain cases and was to be recommended in cases of heresy, but the decision on whether to go beyond degradation as a punishment must rest with the ecclesiastical authorities and never with the secular power.[4] English practice fell into line with such opinions and rulings: Henry II abandoned both his insistence on degradation and any attempt to apply an additional punishment to a degraded clerk for the offence for which he had been degraded. To this extent Becket triumphed: thereafter clerks were to enjoy what was known as the *privilegium fori* or 'benefit of clergy.'

Even so, the Crown was able to qualify the privilege. Clerical status had to be proved before the benefit could be enjoyed; the Crown accepted the Church's definition – a changing definition – of clerical status, but proof had to be made in the secular court to the satisfaction of a royal justice.[5] If the accused had been apprehended he would be

---

[1] *Materials*, Epistolae, VII, 563. It should be noted that the archbishop was speaking of punishment of the murderers of the clergy, and not directly of Becket's defence of criminous clerks; but his quotation of Becket's text, 'nec bis in idipsum', reveals his awareness of the implications of his argument.

[2] Automatic degradation is not explicitly stated but is clearly implied in clause 3 of the Constitutions of Clarendon.

[3] Decretales, II, 1, 4; Duggan, 'The Becket dispute and criminous clerks', 23–4. Duggan points out that this ruling, commonly referred to as the decretal *At si clerici*, is more properly described as one of the chapters in the decretal *Licet praeter*.

[4] See, e.g., the discussion of later legislation in Cheney, 'The punishment of felonous clerks', 220–1, and Duggan, *op. cit.*, 24.

[5] On the definition of *clericus*, see Leona Gabel, *Benefit of Clergy in the Later Middle Ages*, 62.

held in prison until the royal justices came to the county, and this might not be for many months or even for a year or two.[1] If the accused fled from justice before proof of his clerical status were made, he could not be assumed to be entitled to the benefit of clergy and he would be condemned to outlawry like any other fugitive.[2] The chattels of an accused clerk were seized into the king's hand and retained even after he had been handed over to his bishop, to be released only if, and when, he had purged himself of the charge.[3] Moreover there is a strong possibility that, although the Crown did not strictly speaking impose a penalty on convicted clerks, they were sometimes forced 'to abjure the realm' – to go into exile. This was certainly the accepted practice in Normandy before the end of the century; there were clear cases of it in England in and after 1202; and there are hints that it may have happened in England earlier.[4] This would bring the treatment of some criminous clerks close to that of notorious malefactors under the Assize of Northampton: those indicted 'of murder or some other base felony' but who survived the ordeal of water were nevertheless required to 'depart from the realm within forty days'.[5] This is a reminder that with the decline of confidence in the ordeal and before the development of the trial jury, a strong presumption of guilt was held to reside in those accused by the jury of presentment. To this extent a clerk who appeared before the royal justices on the indictment of the jury of presentment went through a form of preliminary secular 'trial' even though he subsequently 'proved his clergy' and was handed over to the bishop for formal trial and punishment. A strong presumption of guilt of particularly obnoxious crimes could account for the instances of the banishment of clerks without formal trial or sentence in the royal court. Indeed the treatment of an indicted clerk differed from that of a layman indicted under the procedures of the Assize of Northampton only in these respects, that instead of being sent to the ordeal of water he was sent to the ordeal of

---

[1] Cheney, op. cit., 229.

[2] Pollock and Maitland, History of English Law, I, 447; Cheney, op. cit., 224. In 1180 the village of Wymondham was fined two marks for receiving an outlawed clerk, Pipe Roll 26 Henry II, 83. In 1182 Ralph archdeacon of Cornwall was allowed to commute his outlawry for a fine of £100, Pipe Roll 28 Henry II, 83.

[3] Poole, 'Outlawry as a punishment of criminous clerks', 242. In the thirteenth century an accused clerk who attempted to avoid arrest but was subsequently acquitted did not always secure restitution of his chattels, Cheney, op. cit., 231. It should be said that the above points cannot always be illustrated from the sparse evidence surviving from Henry II's reign, but that the practices described seem to have been established early.

[4] Poole, op. cit., 243–4.

[5] Assize of Northampton (1176), clause 1; Stubbs, Select Charters, 179.

compurgation before the bishop, and that if he failed the test he would, instead of being subjected to mutilation under the Assize, suffer the less sanguinary penalties prescribed by canon law. He might escape the rigours of the secular law but there was no guarantee that he would avoid all retribution.

Other conflicting claims to jurisdiction were similarly resolved by compromise, concession, adjustment, evasion of the spirit if not the letter of canon law, or a combination of several such methods. Despite Becket's opposition, Alexander III raised no objection to the operation of the assize *utrum*, whereby the question as to whether a disputed property was held by a secular or an ecclesiastical form of tenure was settled in the king's court, as a preliminary to determining in which court the plea itself should be heard. The procedure of the assize, as enshrined in clause 9 of the Constitutions of Clarendon, did of course recognise that the king's court should not meddle with pleas relating to undeniably ecclesiastical tenures; but the pope's indulgence did allow the English Crown to impose its own definition of what constituted ecclesiastical property.[1] This, together with the agreement of Cardinal Hugh Pierleone that land held by secular service, should, even if held by clerks, be justiciable before royal justices, removed straightforward property questions from the sphere of contested jurisdiction. Indeed, the pope would not allow his judges to claim jurisdiction over property seized from the grandson of an absent crusader: in a decision which became part of canon law, he ruled that the question of bastardy which arose in the case should be settled by the ecclesiastical judges, but that they should not attempt to adjudicate on the title to land (*de possessionibus*), for this 'pertains to the king'.[2]

The dispute as to jurisdiction over advowsons presented considerably more difficulties.[3] The notion, once common, that the founder of a

---

[1] English custom and canon law were not always in line on this point, cf. Elisabeth Kimball, 'The judicial aspects of frankalmoign tenure', 6–7. On the difficulty of determining whether or not a tenure was in frankalmoign, *see* Poole, *Obligations of Society*, 6–7.

[2] *Regesta Pontificum Romanorum*, no. 13106, Decretales, IV, 17.7, noted by Ralph of Diceto, I, 427–8, and dated 1 October 1178: 'Nos attendentes quod ad regem pertinet, non ad ecclesiam de talibus possessionibus judicare, ne videamur juri et dignitati carissimi in Christo filii nostri Henrici regis Anglorum detrahere, qui sicut accepimus, motus est et turbatus, quod de possessionibus scripsimus, quum ipsarum judicium ad se asserit pertinere, volumus et ... mandamus quatenus regi possessionum judicium relinquatis.' Cf. Morey, *Bartholomew of Exeter*, 68–70.

[3] This section draws substantially upon the researches of Gray, 'The *ius praesentandi* in England from the Constitutions of Clarendon to Bracton', and the summary of principles and practice in Cheney, *From Becket to Langton*, 108–18. There are important

parish church and his successors exercised full rights of lordship over it had been under steady attack by canon lawyers since at least the end of the eleventh century, as the Church sought to control the appointment of clerks to benefices. Gradually the proprietary right was whittled down to the right of patronage – the right of presenting a candidate to the bishop who would admit him to the church if, after examination, he found him to be suitable. Henry II recognised and accepted this change: he did not, in the Constitutions of Clarendon, attempt to revive ancient custom in its entirety, but confined himself to claiming for the royal courts jurisdiction over the residual elements of proprietorship – jurisdiction over the right of presentation (the *advowson*), and over the exercise of that right:

> If a dispute shall arise between laymen, or between clerks and laymen, or between clerks, concerning the advowson of and presentation to churches, let it be treated and concluded in the court of the lord king.[1]

The trouble was that this ran counter to the Church's endeavour to appropriate to itself all jurisdiction over the filling of benefices, as a necessary part of its concern with the cure of souls. Many decretals of Alexander III and decrees of the Lateran Council he held in 1179 were directed to this end. Ready as Pope Alexander was to recognise secular jurisdiction over *possessiones*, he was adamant that the *ius patronatus* had to be part of spiritual jurisdiction:

> a lawsuit over the right of patronage is so conjoined and bound up with spiritual considerations that it can only be decided by ecclesiastical judgement and settled before an ecclesiastical judge.[2]

The English Crown, however, continued to insist that the right of presentation was a piece of property which should fall within the jurisdiction of secular courts. Here were diametrically opposed views upon which compromise was impossible.

The Crown nevertheless tried very hard to find a basis for the reconciliation of these conflicting interests. The bishop's power to approve or reject a presentee was not challenged, and furthermore the royal courts would not accept as valid any attempt to prove seisin of the right of presentation which did not include a demonstration that the

---

comments and examples in Mary Cheney, 'The Compromise of Avranches and the spread of canon law in England', 190–5, and Raymonde Foreville, *L'Église et la Royauté en Angleterre*, 419–22.

[1] Constitutions of Clarendon, clause 1; Stubbs, *Select Charters*, 164.
[2] The decretal *Quanto te*, Decretales, II, 1.3.

bishop had accepted previous nominees of the claimant or his ancestors. The Crown imposed limitations on actions for the recovery of the right: the action on a writ of *darrein presentment* for recovery of seisin was limited to occasions when the church was vacant, and in an action under a writ *de recto* to establish ownership of the advowson the successful claimant could not, if the benefice were filled, displace the existing incumbent but had to wait for the next vacancy before he could exercise the right he had recovered.[1] Moreover, if the dispute was settled by a compromise the royal court prudently submitted the agreement for the approval of the bishop before ratifying the final concord.[2] Clearly the Crown was anxious to avoid a conflict with the ecclesiastical authorities over the canonical rights of incumbents, and was proposing a division of functions – that the royal court should confine itself to the right of presentation, leaving to the bishop all questions concerning the presentee.

Unfortunately, possible agreement on this basis was frustrated both by the increasing precision of papal pronouncements requiring ecclesiastical judges to concern themselves with all aspects of patronage, and by the ingenuity of advocates in elaborating pleas and exceptions to enter on behalf of their clients which obliged the royal court to trespass outside the narrow question of property. To take an example: the most common exception in an action under a writ of *darrein presentment* was the 'exception of plenarty' – the argument that the action ought not to proceed because, contrary to the requirements of the writ, the church was not vacant and the defendant's own presentee was in possession after being canonically admitted by the bishop. The court, in trying to establish whether the exception was valid, had to satisfy itself about the admittedly ecclesiastical aspects of a previous presentation. This was a problem which could have been met by collaboration between the royal and ecclesiastical courts. Such collaboration was, indeed, a normal part of the procedure in disputes over lay property if a question of bastardy or the validity of a marriage arose. These were questions, it was accepted, which only the Church could adjudicate, and the secular court would adjourn the case until it could have a decision of the ecclesiastical court on the point at issue.[3] There was, admittedly, in practice, a certain amount of consultation with the ecclesiastical author-

---

[1] Cf. *Glanvill*, IV, 10, 50.

[2] This was desirable because the compromise often provided for a pension to be paid to the losing party chargeable upon the revenues of the parish. Alexander III forbad the charging of new pensions without the bishop's approval, Decretales, III, 39.8.				[3] *Glanvill*, VII.13–14, 87.

ities on awkward questions which arose in patronage cases, but it could not become an established and recognised part of the procedure while the Church insisted on claiming exclusive jurisdiction. Moreover, the claim meant that the church courts could not refuse to entertain patronage cases which plaintiffs brought before them in defiance of the Crown's claim to jurisdiction; nor could the ecclesiastical judges with propriety refer to the royal courts questions about the right of patronage which might, and frequently did, arise in disputes concerning the incumbency. It could happen that the same dispute was brought before both the ecclesiastical and secular courts, or that the losing party in the royal court would seek to reopen the case in the ecclesiastical court.

This complex problem was met by a drastic exercise of royal authority: the king issued a writ to the bishop prohibiting the hearing in the church court of a plea which trenched upon the right of patronage, 'since suits concerning the advowson of churches belong to my Crown and dignity'.[1] If the ecclesiastical judges ignored it, the king would instruct the sheriff to cite them to appear before royal justices 'to show why they held that plea in the church court against my dignity'.[2] Bishops were liable to heavy fines or even to the sequestration of their fief for contempt of the royal majesty. It is significant that writs of prohibition make their appearance at about the time that Pope Alexander III, in his decretal *Quanto te, c.* 1179, ruled out the possibility of a division of function between royal and ecclesiastical judges in matters concerned with patronage, or of collaboration between the two jurisdictions. But although the issue of writs of prohibition was a blatant interference with the Church's liberty, it did not, in practice, constitute so gross a violation of the Church's right as might be supposed. In the first place the Church's claim to exercise such jurisdiction was not denied: it was simply prohibited from exercising its jurisdiction in a specified case. Secondly the Crown did not enter a writ of prohibition whenever it heard of the ecclesiastical courts entertaining a case which, directly or indirectly, concerned the advowson: it did so only when one of the parties involved in the dispute applied for the writ. If both parties were content to have their dispute settled in the ecclesiastical court the Church enjoyed the jurisdiction without obstruction. There is no evidence that, in the late twelfth century at least, writs of prohibition were common; and the Church had her own sanctions to apply when both parties to the dispute

---

[1] *Ibid.*, IV.13, 52. On writs of prohibition see Flahiff, 'The use of prohibitions by clerics against ecclesiastical courts in England'. Earlier examples than those cited by Flahiff are to be found, possibly in Pipe Roll 23 Henry II, 171, and certainly in Pipe Roll 26 Henry II, 41. [2] *Glanvill*, IV.14, 53.

were clerks. Bishop Hugh of Lincoln, for example, issued in 1186, without royal rebuke, a synodal decree 'that a clerk should not draw another clerk to secular judgement on an ecclesiastical case'.[1] Moreover, even when the Crown did intervene, it was appreciated that the bishop was placed in an awkward position and the powers of coercion were not used vindictively. Bishop Hugh of Durham was put at Henry II's mercy by the imposition of the enormous fine of five hundred marks 'because he held a plea of advowson in the church court', but no serious attempt was made to collect it, and after his death it was pardoned to his successor.[2]

In short, the king, after fifteen years of trying to obtain agreement, imposed his own compromise. The Church's interest in all aspects of patronage cases was recognised and respected, and while its right to adjudicate on every aspect of such cases was sometimes obstructed the right itself was not denied. In imposing this compromise Henry II made one very important concession: although he continued to claim that cases concerning advowson 'belong to my Crown and dignity', he no longer insisted that they *must* be heard in the royal court. To this extent he retreated from the position taken in the Constitutions of Clarendon.

A similar compromise was imposed by the Crown over pleas of debt.[3] In the Constitutions of Clarendon Henry II had insisted that:

Pleas concerning debts which are owed on pledged faith or without the pledge of faith should be in the justice of the king [*in justitia regis*].[4]

Pleas of debt had customarily been largely a matter for the local courts. What precisely is meant by this clause, and what the king intended to secure by it are alike obscure. Royal interest in pleas of debt may, however, be presumed to have derived considerable impetus from the peculiar relations of the Crown and the Jews.[5] Twelfth-century England was not especially intolerant of Jews, but their activity as the principal money-lenders to a society which needed credit but looked askance at

[1] Roger of Howden, *Gesta*, I, 357.

[2] The fine first appears on Pipe Roll 30 Henry II, 37. For the pardon *see* Pipe Roll 10 Richard I, 28.

[3] The law of debt in this period has been inadequately treated by legal historians. Useful general accounts are Pollock and Maitland, *History of English Law*, II, 185–216, and Plucknett, *Concise History of the Common Law*, 592–6. For comments on Glanvill's treatment of the subject *see* Hall's edition, Introduction, xxv–vi and 189–90. Van Caenegem, *Royal Writs in England*, 254–60, deals with the writ of debt and the evidence of the pipe rolls.

[4] Constitutions of Clarendon, clause 15; Stubbs, *Select Charters*, 167.

[5] Cf. Richardson, *The English Jewry under Angevin Kings*.

Christian usury, did not make them popular. The prosperity of the Jews, however, was of prime importance to the Crown: they were its financiers – tiding the king over when his urgent expenditures depleted his treasure – they were a lucrative source of taxation, and when Jewish money-lenders died their bonds fell into the hands of the exchequer, which collected on them. The Crown therefore not only extended to them its special protection, but also had an interest in debt collection on behalf of money-lenders – an interest which the local courts might not have shared with the same enthusiasm. The earliest surviving pipe rolls show several examples of offerings by Jews 'that the king might help them concerning their debts'.[1]

This somewhat primitive concern of the Crown with the recovery of debts was overshadowed in the mid twelfth century by the rapidly burgeoning interest of ecclesiastical lawyers in the nature of contractual obligations and legal process for the enforcement of promises. The pledging of faith as a solemn method of sealing a bargain put a man's soul in peril and thus became a proper concern of the Church; but in addition to this, canon lawyers were excited by the discovery in Roman civil law of a sophisticated and elaborate law of contract. English customary law knew nothing of contract. There was a strong possibility that the obvious superiority of the Church's jurisprudence in this matter as well as its claim to jurisdiction would draw much if not most of litigation over debt into the ecclesiastical courts. Pleas of debt, it should be observed, covered a much wider field than the repayment of borrowed money: they extended, for example, to a variety of commercial transactions in which immediate payment was not possible or convenient, to rents on leases, hiring arrangements, the mortgaging of property, and the obligations entered into before a marriage on the property settlement which would follow the marriage (the medieval 'wedding' was the exchange of 'weds' – the tokens of a solemn civil compact). The appropriation by the ecclesiastical courts of jurisdiction over such a wide area of ordinary transactions and arrangements between laymen was of obvious concern to the secular authority – a concern which, however, was directed more to protecting the local courts from the loss of their customary civil business than to establishing a common law of contract justiciable before royal justices. It is difficult to say what was in the king's mind in 1164, for even after the development of an adequate machinery of royal justice there was a noticeable reluctance on the part of the

---

[1] Van Caenegem, *op. cit.*, 254–5. The appearance of several payments on the pipe roll of 11 Henry II *pro recto debiti sui* suggests that judicial process is by this date (1166) being substituted for bald administrative action.

king's own courts to meddle with private agreements, and the only action which *Glanvill* can offer for the recovery of debt before royal justices was one upon a writ modelled closely and inconveniently upon the writ *praecipe quod reddat* for land. In such an action the ultimate proof was the verdict of a judicial duel. It seems likely then that the rule propounded in the Constitutions was designed simply to defend the customary jurisdiction of the shire courts by blocking the encroachment of the ecclesiastical courts.[1] The Church did not abandon its claim to comprehensive jurisdiction, but neither did the Crown recognise it. A compromise was imposed. The principle propounded in *Glanvill* is not that of the Constitutions of Clarendon that *all* pleas concerning debts should be 'in justitia regis', but that 'pleas concerning the debts *of laymen* belong to the Crown and dignity of the lord king'.[2] The royal courts did not accept that pledge of faith alone could be sufficient to establish an action for debt; and when the pledge of faith had been accompanied by other forms of security, this element was distinguished from the rest and punishment for the *lesio fidei* allowed to the Church courts.[3] Nor did the Crown seek to extinguish the wider jurisdiction of the ecclesiastical courts over pleas of debt, but simply to obstruct it – if a plaintiff sought royal intervention – by a writ of prohibition. Writs of prohibition were, however, refused, if the case concerned a marriage portion or arose out of the execution of a dead man's testament, for such cases were deemed to be the proper, if not the exclusive, concern of the Church.[4]

The writ of prohibition was Henry II's major contribution to the avoidance of open conflict between Church and State in the matter of competing jurisdictions. It produced what Maitland has called a 'ragged and unscientific frontier' between the courts, instead of the clear line which Henry had attempted to lay down in the Constitutions of Clarendon.[5] This marked a retreat, but it was a retreat from his youthful distaste for ambiguity rather than from his basic objectives. Henry had learned to be flexible. The general control of the processes of ecclesiastical government which he had sought in 1164 was not only crude and offensive, it was also unnecessary for the adequate protection of royal interests. Flexibility brought more selective but no less effective methods of royal control – by agreement where agreement was possible,

---

[1] It is noticeable that this clause does not speak as others do of pleas being heard *in curia domini regis* or *in curia regia* but simply that pleas of debt should be *in justitia regis*. What real difference, if any, was intended, is, however, obscure.

[2] *Glanvill*, X.1, 116.   [3] *Ibid.*, X.12, 126.

[4] Cf. *Glanvill*, VII.18, 93, and Flahiff, *op. cit.*

[5] Maitland, *Roman Canon Law in the Church of England*, 57.

and by the writ of prohibition where it was not. This technique of the haphazard veto was an ingenious piece of practical statesmanship: it asserted the authority of the Crown while allowing in practice the operation of parallel jurisdictions. It left the initiative in the hands of the king without forcing the clergy to the humiliation of abandoning established claims. Henry II was not accused of deviousness without cause; but the practice of prohibition, while undoubtedly vexatious to the clergy, stopped just short of being intolerable. Nothing, indeed, could be said to typify more clearly the policy and methods of Henry II than the writ of prohibition.

The later years of Henry II's reign were singularly free of serious disputes between the king and the bishops. The ecclesiastical *causes célèbres* of those days were disputes among the clergy themselves, notably the bitter struggle by the monks of Christ Church cathedral at Canterbury to prevent their archbishop establishing a collegiate church of secular clergy at Hackington, and the continuing controversy between Canterbury and York as to the relationship between them.

Accusations and recriminations have fogged the real issue in the struggle over the collegiate church at Hackington (a struggle later transferred to a similar proposal to establish a collegiate church at Lambeth). The archbishop's intention seems to have been to provide a collegiate organisation, and a regular income from attached revenues, for the clerks of his administration, but the monks regarded it as a threat to their status and dignity, and harboured wild fears that the college would eventually usurp their functions in the election of an archbishop. To a large degree the proposal and the dispute were a consequence of the establishment at some (by no means all) English cathedrals of monastic chapters – a peculiarly English tradition. At cathedrals where this had not happened, at St Pauls in London, for example, the bishop had canonries (with their associated income-producing prebends) in which to install the clerks of his administrative service. Henry was interested in such proposals as that of the archbishop because he too looked for convenient benefices for the increasing number of clerks in the royal service; but although he exerted himself on the archbishop's behalf, cajoling and threatening the monks or alternatively humouring them and posing as a mediator, he allowed them to carry their case to Rome. It was not an issue which worried him unduly.[1]

[1] For the early stages of this controversy, which, in one form or another, persisted long after the death of Henry II, *see Epistolae Cantuarienses*. For some comments on Henry's part in it *see* Mayr-Harting, 'Henry II and the papacy', 45–6.

The controversy between Canterbury and York pursued a familiar course with familiar arguments. It was a nuisance to the king and threatened to disrupt the dignity of council meetings with disputes over precedence, but Henry II was not so anxious as some of his predecessors had been to secure the ascendancy of Canterbury in the interests of the ecclesiastical unity of the kingdom. The office of resident papal legate for England had been secured for Archbishop Richard immediately after his elevation and that sufficed. When Henry did intervene decisively in the quarrel it was to persuade the rivals to agree to a five-year truce.[1]

The absence of serious dispute between the king and the hierarchy might seem surprising in view of the passions generated by the quarrel with Becket, the cult of the martyr, and the not altogether satisfactory compromises over the contentious points of relations between Church and State agreed by the papacy or imposed by the king. In the manœuvring to secure control over advowsons and pleas of debts, for example, in the dislike of the jurisdiction of forest courts over clerks, in the operation of writs of prohibition, there were innumerable occasions for clashes, bickering, or impassioned argument. That bitterness was avoided is attributable largely to the basic desire of all concerned for peace. It was the desire for the peaceful prosecution of ecclesiastical government which most noticeably divided the bishops from Becket – and indeed the pope from him too. The archbishop, frustrated in his longing to have Henry coerced by excommunication and interdict, had attempted to call an unofficial strike by summoning bishops to join him in his exile, but the pope countermanded his orders.[2] It is doubtful whether many of them would have gone, even if the pope had not instructed them to remain in their dioceses, for there was little approval of Becket's methods even among those who approved his views; and bishops whom Becket and his partisans regarded as natural allies were far from consistent in their support. Robert of Meulun, bishop of Hereford, formerly a celebrated teacher of theology at Paris and Becket's revered master, disappointed their hopes by siding with Gilbert Foliot.[3] Bartholomew bishop of Exeter, an expert in canon law and prominent in the expansion and refinement of ecclesiastical jurisdiction, was known to sympathise but kept his distance from the controversy, preserving his integrity by refusing cooperation to the king and his allies among the bishops, but earning the reproach of Becket as a useless friend.[4] Bishop

---

[1] Cf. Mayr-Harting, *op. cit.*, 46–8.

[2] Knowles, *Episcopal Colleagues of Thomas Becket*, e.g., 106, 107.

[3] *Ibid.*, 104–6.   [4] *Ibid.*, 102–4; Morey, *Bartholomew of Exeter*, ch. 3.

Roger of Worcester, Henry's cousin and with more than a dash of aristocratic outspokenness and independence, was the most open sympathiser with the archbishop and visited him in exile, but he kept the friendship of the king, and lost patience with Becket over his refusal to resign even if by so doing he could have won from Henry a guarantee of the liberties of the Church.[1]

In short, there was no one among the bishops who unequivocally and completely identified himself with Archbishop Becket's cause; and in the years which followed his death there was no champion to take on the martyr's mantle. If Henry II had consistently and persistently obstructed the normal processes of ecclesiastical government, the story might have been very different: it was the threat of this in the Constitutions of Clarendon which united the bishops in opposition; but neither before, during, nor after the crisis did Henry II really attempt this or seriously envisage it. Moreover, despite all the fires of controversy which Becket banked so high, it has to be remembered that even Henry's most extravagant demands trespassed upon only the fringes of a wide and expanding jurisdiction of the ecclesiastical courts. They raised important issues of principle and that made them contentious, but there was more than enough untouched by royal claims about which the bishops and their courts could busy themselves. There was not a whisper in the Constitutions about jurisdiction over the internal economy of the clergy's estates and their revenues, over ecclesiastical dues, tithes, mortuaries, oblations, and pensions, over sacrilege and sanctuary, over marriage and marriage-portions, annulments and legitimacy, over testamentary cases and the claims of legatees, over fornication, adultery, incest, usury, or defamation, closely as most of these concerned the interests of layman, to say nothing of the Church's jurisdiction over the life, habits, and status of the clergy, over heresy and the conduct of the Church's services. In asserting royal authority, King Henry stuck closely to those rights which tradition conveyed to the Crown. He certainly made no attempt to interfere even with the Church's handling of questions concerning property which arose in cases over marriage settlements and testamentary provisions. The Church, indeed, gained a greater degree of control over testamentary cases in England than it did on the continent.[2]

---

[1] *Materials*, Epistolae, VI, 317–18, 321–2; Knowles, *op. cit.*, 106–8; for a revealing encounter between King Henry and Bishop Roger *see* above, ch. 5, p. 216.

[2] Pollock and Maitland, *History of English Law*, II, 332–4. It should be observed that jurisdiction over bequests did not convey jurisdiction over land held by feudal tenure since such land could not be bequeathed.

The movement towards more positive ecclesiastical control over the lives and morals of the laity received no obstruction from Henry. The hardening of marriage law, for example, ruled out the simpler forms of civil contract which, without the necessity of the Church's blessing, had still in the earlier twelfth century constituted a valid marriage; but secular courts accepted the Church's rulings on valid marriages even though these affected the descent of landed property.[1] On questions concerning the morals and behaviour of the clergy, Henry II, in common with most men of conventional piety, shared the views of reformers; and when he intervened in such matters – usually in connection with monasteries and convents associated with royal founders – it was to demand rigorous standards of propriety.[2] Moreover, the later years of Henry's reign are a period of unparalleled activity by Englishmen in the collection and organisation of texts bearing upon the law of the Church, and in the submission to Rome of subtle and knotty questions of canon law for authoritative resolution. It has been suggested that such activity was a consequence of Henry's concession over appeals at Rome, but it is much more likely that it represents a stage in the development of canon law and the presence among English bishops of ardent canonists such as Bishop Bartholomew of Exeter, Archbishop Richard of Canterbury, Bishop Roger of Worcester and his successor in the see, Baldwin of Ford.[3]

With so much freedom, it is not surprising that the Church tolerated some trimming of its jurisdiction in certain rather limited respects, and indulged the occasional royal intervention. Even Bartholomew of Exeter and Roger of Worcester allowed Henry to influence their decision, or

[1] For the development of the Church's law on marriage in this period *see* Kemp, Introduction to *Papal Decretals relating to the Diocese of Lincoln*, xxvi–viii; Dauvillier, *Le Mariage dans le Droit Classique de l'Église;* Cheney, *From Becket to Langton*, 57–9, 156. There was one respect in which the royal courts, while recognising the competence of the ecclesiastical courts in questions of marriage and legitimacy, refused to accept its ruling: canon law held that a child born out of wedlock was legitimised if its parents subsequently married, but feudal law recognised as heirs only children born in wedlock, cf. *Glanvill*, VII.15, 88.

[2] e.g., Henry's intervention in the upheavals within the order of Sempringham, Knowles, 'The revolt of the lay brothers of Sempringham'; Mayr-Harting, 'Henry II and the papacy', 41. For the king's efforts for the reform of the nunnery at Amesbury, *see* Roger of Howden, *Gesta*, I, 135, 165, 354.

[3] English canonical activity has been expertly analysed by Duggan, *Twelfth-Century Decretal Collections*. The views advanced by Brooke in *The English Church and the Papacy*, and in 'The effects of Becket's murder on papal authority in England', on the importance of the settlement at Avranches in this, have been questioned by Mary Cheney, 'The Compromise of Avranches and the spread of canon law in England'; *see* also Mayr-Harting, *op. cit.*, 43–4.

at least to have a share in reaching it, in ecclesiastical cases concerning churches or abbeys in which he was personally interested.[1] There were so many cases in which he was not interested when their jurisdiction, and that of Rome, encountered no obstacle. Furthermore, since there were occasions when the clergy needed the help of the Crown, a habit of cooperation was much to their advantage. There were even occasions when the bishops sheltered behind the 'custom of the realm' from the importunity of Rome. Alexander III's summons to the Lateran Council of 1179 was countered by the bishops' insistence, doubtless for reasons of economy, that on such occasions four of their number were traditionally sufficient as representatives of the whole.[2] When in 1184, envoys from Pope Lucius III arrived in England seeking financial aid from the English clergy 'for the defence of the patrimony of St Peter against the Romans', the king sent messengers to the bishops asking what they would have him do. They, meeting together in London under the chairmanship of the justiciar, Ranulf de Glanvill, warned the king 'that it would be a precedent detrimental to the realm if he allowed envoys of the lord pope to come into England making a collection'. Their advice was that the king himself should make such contribution to the pope's need as he pleased and deemed proper; and they added, judiciously, that 'it would be most pleasing to them that the lord king should accept from them, if he would, recompense for the assistance he had rendered to the lord pope'. 'In this advice,' adds the chronicler, the king 'acquiesced'.[3]

Admittedly some measure of the greater harmony between Church and State is attributable to the presence among the hierarchy of men who owed their promotion to the king as a reward for faithful service as *familiares*. Henry had no difficulty in influencing episcopal elections: Alexander III indeed had to rebuke Archbishop Richard for allowing elections to take place in the royal chapel.[4] But it should not be supposed that royal clerks remained pliant tools of the royal will: Chancellor Geoffrey Ridel, like Becket before him, resigned the chancery when he was advanced to the bench, and John of Oxford, Becket's *bête noire* as a royal clerk, received, as bishop of Norwich, a reprimand from King Henry for excommunicating a royal official without his consent.[5] Nor should it be supposed that royal clerks came to dominate the bench: Henry was judicious in exercising his influence and allowed a balance

---

[1] Mayr-Harting, *op. cit.*, 41–3, cf. *Acta of the Bishops of Chichester*, 128.
[2] Roger of Howden, *Chronica*, II, 171.
[3] Roger of Howden, *Gesta*, I, 311.
[4] Decretales, II, 28.25; *Regesta Pontificum Romanorum*, no. 14312.
[5] *Recueil des Actes de Henri II*, Introduction, 94; Gerald of Wales, VII, 70.

to be struck between men of widely differing experience and backgrounds. He liked his bishops to be upright and preferred them to be pious – complaining, it is said, of churchmen 'who embraced the world with both arms'.[1] He boldly confirmed or actively promoted the election of men who might have been expected to cause him trouble: one of these was Hugh of Avalon, the austere, saintly, and outspoken Cistercian monk who became bishop of Lincoln; another was Gerard Pucelle, a former friend of Becket who had not hesitated to plead a case in canon law before the royal court against the king's interests, but who nevertheless became bishop of Coventry; and a third was an eminent canonist trained by Bartholomew of Exeter, who had been archdeacon of Totnes, then abbot of Ford, and in 1180 was made bishop of Worcester – Baldwin of Ford.[2]

King Henry and Bishop Baldwin had a memorable encounter in 1184. When the royal court was en route for Wales in July of that year it sojourned a while at Worcester, and there was brought before it a young knight, Gilbert of Plumpton, for whom, it is said, the justiciar, Ranulf de Glanvill, had conceived a deep personal hatred. Gilbert had wooed and won to wife a maiden whose marriage was in the king's gift and whom Ranulf had coveted for one of his cronies. Gilbert had not merely seduced her, but, so it was alleged, had broken down six doors in her father's house to reach her, and had carried off a hunting horn, a halter, and other things which took his fancy as well as the maiden. Ranulf demanded the death penalty for robbery with violence and Gilbert was condemned to be hanged. Arrangements were made by the justiciar for immediate execution but since the day was a Sunday and the festival of St Mary Magdalen, Bishop Baldwin intervened to urge a postponement, arguing with the hangmen that they should fear God rather than the king, until he persuaded them to take Gilbert back to the castle and delay the execution until the morrow. King Henry had already left Worcester, but he was told the story that night, 'and from that time forth,' says the chronicler, 'he was warmly drawn to the bishop by a greater affection and reverence'. Gilbert, by the king's order, escaped the gallows.[3] Shortly afterwards the lengthy process began of electing a

---

[1] William of Newburgh, I, 281. On episcopal elections see Cheney, *From Becket to Langton*, ch. 2; Raymonde Foreville, *L'Église et la Royauté en Angleterre*, Bk IV, ch. 2.

[2] On Hugh of Lincoln, see above, ch. 5, pp. 212–14. On Gerard Pucelle's advocacy for the abbot of Battle in a case concerning the brother of the justiciar, Richard de Lucy, see *Chronicon Monasterii de Bello*, 176–8. On Baldwin of Ford ('dilectissimus Baldwinus') see Morey, *Bartholomew of Exeter*, 105–7; Duggan, *Twelfth-Century Decretal Collections*, 110ff.

[3] Roger of Howden, *Gesta*, I, 314–16.

successor to Archbishop Richard of Canterbury who had died in April. The monks of Canterbury put forward a succession of nominations and one by one the king vetoed them. There was only one name to which he would give his approval as the next archbishop of Canterbury – that of Baldwin of Ford.[1]

[1] For the Canterbury election of 1184 *see* Gervase of Canterbury, I, 309ff.; Roger of Howden, *Gesta*, I, 317–18, 319–21.

Part IV

THE ANGEVIN COMMONWEALTH

Chapter 15

FEDERAL GOVERNMENT
(c.1178–1183)

When Henry II made his will on 22 February 1182 he was a fortnight short of his forty-ninth birthday. Strictly speaking it was not a *will* but a *testament*: it conveyed no grants of property, but simply specified the bequests to be made from his personal treasure at the time of his death, for the good of his soul.[1] The territorial dispositions had been made three years previously, and were not changed.[2] There is no good reason to believe that Henry was in failing health when he drew up his testament – indeed, Ralph of Diceto remarks that he was at the time sound in both mind and body.[3] What prompted him to do it was probably his imminent crossing from England to Normandy. The Channel was perilous in winter for small boats with simple rigging and an oar over the stern for steering. The hazards of the voyage were brought home by the adverse winds which had delayed his crossing since before Christmas. He was residing, while he waited, at Richard of Ilchester's manor of Waltham in the bishopric of Winchester. The testament was witnessed by his *familiares*, and copies sent for safe-keeping to the royal treasury and the cathedral chapter of Canterbury.[4]

Yet if the occasion was neither very formal nor solemn, and if the cause no more than common prudence before embarking on a dangerous journey, there was nevertheless a singular appropriateness in the date at which Henry II set his affairs in order. He was at the peak of his career. His realms were at peace. The bitterness engendered by the long struggle with Archbishop Becket and by the great war had faded from

---

[1] Above, ch. 3, p. 148; Gervase of Canterbury, I, 297–300; Gerald of Wales, VIII, 191–3; *Foedera*, I, Pt I, 47; *Recueil des Actes de Henri II*, II, 219–21.

[2] *See* above, ch. 3, pp. 109–10.

[3] Ralph of Diceto, II, 10.

[4] Ralph of Diceto, II, 10, says that the 'majores regni' were summoned to hear it read, but the witnesses were exclusively *familiares*: Richard of Ilchester (bishop of Winchester), John of Oxford (bishop of Norwich), Geoffrey Plantagenet (the king's illegitimate son, chancellor, and bishop-elect of Lincoln), Walter de Coutances (archdeacon of Oxford), Geoffrey de Lucy (archdeacon of Derby), Ranulf de Glanvill, Roger FitzReinfred, Hugh of Morwick, Ralph FitzStephen, and William Rufus.

all but the most partisan minds. His great work of judicial reform had culminated in the *grand assize* of 1179. He was financially secure. He had three sons grown to manhood, and a fourth in reserve. Troublesome neighbours had been tamed: the Welsh were quiescent, the problem of Ireland seemed to have been solved, the king of Scots was now his faithful vassal, King Louis of France was dead and his heir was virtually Henry's protégé. His very purpose in crossing the Channel was to use his good offices to reconcile King Philip and the count of Flanders. Ralph of Diceto speaks of the friendly meeting the previous year of King Henry and his heir, King Henry the Younger, with King Philip and King William of Scotland: 'We have read,' he says, 'of four kings falling together in the same battle, but seldom have we heard of four kings coming peacefully together to confer, and in peace departing.'[1] If, like Thomas Becket, Henry II could have chosen his moment to die, he could not have chosen better than to perish on the crossing of the Channel in March 1182. But in fact he was to live for seven years more, and some of the glory was to fade from his achievement.

There are indications that by the later 1170s Henry II took the view that the main task of life, the objectives he had set himself as a young man, had been accomplished, and that he intended thenceforth to withdraw himself gradually from active involvement in the government of the Angevin dominions – a withdrawal not into retirement, but into a new role as *pater familias*, the chairman of a family consortium which by a grand alliance would keep the peace and shape the destinies of Western Europe. The task which he had set himself had been, it seems, the identification, recovery, and exploitation of all those rights which history and the principles of succession, as he conceived them, conveyed to himself and his wife. The corner-stone of the grand alliance of his sons was to be the defence of those rights. He is said to have remarked, when instructing his eldest son to prevent the encroachment of King Louis into Berry in 1177, 'that when he himself alone bore the responsibility of rule no right was let slip, and it would be a dishonour, now that there were several of them to rule the land, that anything should be lost'.[2] Berry lay on the fringes of the duchy of Aquitaine and Henry the Younger showed some reluctance to defend his brother's interests while Richard was preoccupied in Gascony.[3] Mutual assistance was,

---

[1] Ralph of Diceto, II, 7.

[2] Roger of Howden, *Gesta*, I, 132: '... addens ... quod quando ipse solus erat in regimine regni, nihil de jure suo amittebat; et modo dedecus esset, cum sint plures in regenda terra, aliquid inde perdere'.   [3] Cf. *ibid.*, I, 195.

however, to be the secret, in Henry II's intention, of the survival of Angevin rule in the several provinces of the commonwealth he had constructed. Mutual assistance implied some central organisation for the taking of counsel and the deployment of resources; and the framework for this was supplied by the vassalage oaths which the brothers swore. But beyond the ties of blood and dependent vassalage, Henry II does not seem to have wished to go towards integrating his several dominions into a unity. Each of the dominions into which he divided his territories between his sons was to be internally self-governing. This intention is not only expressed in distinct currencies struck for Brittany, Aquitaine, and Ireland, and in the arrangements made for separate administrations; it is also illustrated in the attempt to secure for Brittany an ecclesiastical organisation independent of the archbishop of Tours. An attempt had been made in the ninth century to free Brittany from the jurisdiction claimed by Tours, by creating an archbishopric at Dol with the bishops of Rennes and Nantes as its suffragans; but the creation was denied recognition at Rome until, at the end of the eleventh century, Pope Gregory VII, in the hope of promoting the cause of reform, conferred the *pallium* – the symbol of metropolitan authority – upon a nominee of his own to Dol. In the middle of the twelfth century it seemed unlikely that this recognition would survive a strong challenge mounted by Tours, and the archbishopric would most likely have disappeared hadnot Henry II used his influence at Rome to secure the renewed bestowal of a *pallium*. The existence of the archbishopric of Dol remained precarious and in 1199 disappeared, for the archbishops of Tours, with their patrons the kings of France strongly in support, were persistent in appeals to Rome.[1] The political implications are clear, however, and Henry's support for Breton independence is significant. There was, of course, a similar story in Ireland: Henry had, in all probability, first been urged to intervene in Ireland by Archbishop Theobald in the hope of reasserting the jurisdiction claimed there by Canterbury; but when Henry went to Ireland seventeen years later he did nothing to disrupt the ecclesiastical independence which Ireland had already won for itself.

Henry II was not seeking the integration of the several dominions somewhat fortuitously gathered under his rule. The seeming obscurity of his intention – which has led some historians to assert the contrary – is simply a reflection of the lack of a terminology in which to express it; but his actions clearly show that, to use modern terms, he conceived the future of the Angevin dominions not as an *empire* but as a *federation*. The

[1] Pocquet du Haut-Jussé, 'Les Plantagenêts et la Bretagne', 18–19.

heart of this federation, ruled over by Henry the Younger, was to be a powerful cross-Channel state – itself a mini-federation – consisting of England, Normandy, and greater Anjou. With this all the other elements in the great federation shared borders. Brittany, under Duke Geoffrey, marched with Normandy and the county of Anjou and Touraine. Ireland might, at first sight, seem an exception: it shared with England and Wales not a common frontier but a broad sea. Experience had, however, taught Henry II that this sea was little more divisive than that between England and Normandy. It is true that by 1177 he had come to see the need for Ireland to be politically unified, and proposed its erection into a monarchy under John, administratively independent of the Crown of England. But Henry's assessment of the situation was clearly that Ireland's complete detachment from England would be politically unwise and socially impossible: its major settler families bridged the seas, retaining estates which gave them standing in England, Wales, and Normandy. It was essential then that the ruler of Ireland should not be divorced from the counsels of the Anglo-Norman state; and just as the king of Scotland, who similarly harboured Norman families, had his place in the council of the king of England by reason of his tenure of the earldom of Huntingdon, so too formal links were to be provided for the king of Ireland. In the plans made for John's future, he was to become one of the greatest barons of the Welsh March by being given the English earldom of Gloucester in marriage to its heiress, and a stake in Normandy by being made count of Mortain.[1]

The federal scheme, in outline at least, was first announced at the peace talks with King Louis VII at Montmirail in 1169. It began to take shape immediately after the great war of 1173–4. Henry's withdrawal from direct involvement with the government of Brittany and Aquitaine was gradual. At first he retained half the revenues, appointed advisers and administrators he could trust, and summoned his sons to frequent family conferences. But step by step the reins were slackened, and, by the time Henry II made his will, had been released. Richard, entitled

---

[1] John was betrothed to Isabella of Gloucester in 1176, Ralph of Diceto, I, 415; Roger of Howden, *Gesta*, I, 124–5; *Complete Peerage*, V, 688–9. For Henry II's intention of making John count of Mortain, *see Gesta*, II, 73. It is significant that when Henry II's scheme for the future of his dominions was in the later years of his reign thrown into confusion and doubt, these plans for John were shelved, together with the plan for creating him king of Ireland. He was married to Isabella of Gloucester and created count of Mortain at the beginning of Richard I's reign. Duke Geoffrey of Brittany also had an English barony, for he was earl of Richmond in right of his wife Constance.

'count of Poitou' in 1169, seems to have been recognised as 'duke of Aquitaine' in 1179.[1] Geoffrey was knighted by his father on 15 July 1178 at the age of twenty, and in 1181 his long betrothal to Constance, the heiress of the late Count Conan IV, was concluded by their marriage. Shortly afterwards Geoffrey formally cast off the shackles of his father's control by dismissing Roland of Dinan, whom Henry had appointed to be seneschal of Brittany in 1175, and replacing him by Ralph de Fougères.[2]

The slackening of the reins of control by Henry was justified by his sons' demonstration that they could control the provinces entrusted to them. Geoffrey had the easier task. The greater barons of eastern Brittany – the richer and more populated half – had been tamed by Henry II's assaults on their castles in the years before and during the great war. Moreover, the balance of power between the duke and the other barons had been drastically altered by the annexation to the ducal demesne of the lands of Penthièvre on the death of Count Conan in 1170, and of the lands confiscated from Eudo of Porhoët during the great war.[3] These, when properly organised and disciplined, gave Duke Geoffrey commanding control of central Brittany. The major remaining political problem lay in the north-west, in Finisterre – remote, wild, and in the fierce grip of the viscount of Léon. Viscount Guiomar, it was said, 'feared neither God nor man' – a not unreasonable accusation since he had assassinated a man who was both his uncle and bishop of Léon.[4] He thought it prudent to proffer his submission to Henry II in 1177, but it was nevertheless necessary for Geoffrey to take an army against him. In 1179 Guiomar's resistance was crushed, and he was persuaded to go on crusade and to take his wife with him. His inheritance was dismembered: his eldest son was allowed to hold the major part of it, but Geoffrey retained control of Morlaix.[5] More important, if less dramatic, and scantily chronicled, was the spread of ducal government. There are signs of it in the wresting of control over the appointment of bishops from the local aristocracy, the division of the duchy into eight administrative districts corresponding to English shires, the introduction of judicial process by sworn inquest, and the enforcement of

---

[1] See Boissonnade, 'Les comtes d'Angoulême', 275.

[2] Pocquet du Haut-Jussé, op. cit., 22.

[3] Robert de Torigny, 267; Boussard, Le Gouvernement d'Henri II, 548. The lands confiscated from Eudo comprised Vannes, Ploërmel, Auray, and half of Cornouaille.

[4] Robert de Torigny, 275; Ralph of Diceto, I, 346. The bishopric of Léon was closely controlled by the family of the viscount, Pocquet du Haut-Jussé, op. cit., 17.

[5] Robert de Torigny, 275; Roger of Howden, Gesta, I, 239, Chronica, II, 192; Pocquet du Haut-Jussé, op. cit., 11.

writs by the seneschal.[1] And the most remarkable evidence that Brittany was ready to shake off ancient tradition and conform to the feudal custom of Normandy is provided by the Assize of 1185, made by Duke Geoffrey with the assent of the barons, which established the principle of primogeniture in the succession to fiefs.[2]

Richard's problems were more numerous, more troublesome, and more fundamental. In Aquitaine the groundwork had yet to be laid for the construction of a centralised administration. Henry II's achievement had been to establish his claims to overlordship; but it was an overlordship of vassals who were accustomed to complete control of the internal affairs of their fiefs, and the task of obliging them to respect the intervention of a superior ducal government had as yet barely begun. It is doubtful indeed if ducal officers as yet exercised much influence outside the estates of the ducal demesne.[3] Such government as the province knew was the government of local *seigneurs*, and such political stability as it could be said to enjoy was conferred by a precarious balance between neighbouring lords, and between lords themselves and their vassals. It was a balance of power constantly put to the test and frequently, if temporarily, disrupted. To call it anarchy would be to mistake the nature of feudal warfare, and to fail to recognise that the pecking order established by challenge and response reflected the realities of power and created a crude but viable political structure; but certainly it conferred nothing of the law and order which in England, Normandy, or Anjou had come to be recognised as the prime benefit of a strong central government.

Moreover, Aquitaine had not experienced the sobering effects of the great war to teach it respect for Angevin authority; for although many of its barons had espoused the cause of rebellion, Aquitaine had not become a major theatre of operations in the epic struggle between King Henry and King Louis. Richard himself had, it is true, tried to make it so in the spring of 1174 by raising the rebels of Saintonge and Poitou to attack those loyal to his father, but his efforts at creating a damaging diversion had been overtaken by the collapse of rebellion in England and Normandy. When he realised that King Louis and his

---

[1] Pocquet du Haut-Jussé, *op. cit.*, 15–26. For the judicial activities of the seneschal *see* Boussard, *op. cit.*, 288 n.2.

[2] Text printed in *La Très Ancienne Coutume de Bretagne*, 321–3; cf. Planiol, *L'Assise au Comte Geffroi*.

[3] On the apparent absence of ducal justice in Aquitaine *see*, e.g., Boussard, *op. cit.*, 288 n.3.

elder brother were ready to make peace without him, Richard 'came with tears to prostrate himself at his father's feet and crave his pardon'.[1] Henry seems to have taken this to mean the end of insurrection in Aquitaine, for after the formal reconciliation with his sons, he appointed Richard to be his governor there and instructed him 'that the castles of the counts and barons which had been fortified against him should be restored to the state in which they had been fifteen days before the war began, and that certain of them should be destroyed'.[2] These were the terms upon which peace had been effected between the king and his barons in the rest of the Angevin dominions; but to the rebels of Aquitaine they were unacceptable. They were not ready to acknowledge that the war was over: for them it had as yet barely begun. The peace of Montlouis offered them nothing. Indeed it offered them less than nothing: King Henry had of necessity relaxed his hold on Aquitaine while he fought the crucial battles of the war elsewhere, so the barons there had enjoyed some of the fruits of successful rebellion without having to fight for them, and were now being required to surrender them without having suffered a defeat. The true nature of the disaffection in Aquitaine was revealed in the sequel: the rebellion of Henry's sons had not been a cause the southerners genuinely espoused, it had simply been an opportunity to repudiate, with a welcome impunity, Henry's overlordship, and they were as reluctant to accept its reimposition at the hands of Richard as they had been to accept it from his father.

Richard's governorship of Aquitaine thus began with his having to fight what was, in effect, the last campaign of the great war. The chroniclers' reports of his successes should not be allowed to disguise the very real difficulties he faced. He captured the castle of Arnold of Bouteville at Castillon-sur-Dordogne, but only after a siege of two months, although Arnold was not a prominent baron and could not call upon powerful allies.[3] Indeed, although Richard is said to have brought together 'a great army' for the siege, and to have constructed engines of war on the spot, it may be doubted whether he had adequate resources in men, money, and equipment for the tasks which confronted him. Richard journeyed to England in the spring of 1176 and laid his difficulties before a family conference at Winchester. It was then that the principle of cooperation between the parts of the federation was first applied, for Henry the Younger was instructed by his father to go to his brother's assistance and to defer his proposed pilgrimage to St James of

---

[1] Roger of Howden, *Gesta*, I, 76.
[2] *Ibid.*, 81.   [3] *Ibid*, 101.

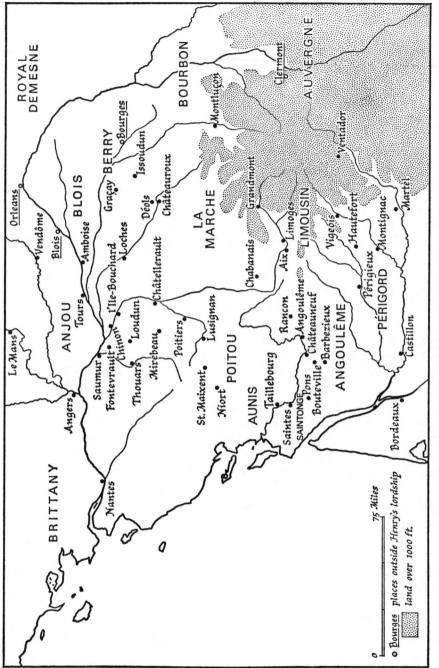

XIII France: Centre–West

Compostella 'until peace had been made in Guyenne'.[1] It also seems likely that considerable sums of money were placed at Richard's disposal, for on his return he was able to recruit mercenaries on a large scale.[2]

During Richard's absence the rebels had taken the initiative. Vulgrin Taillefer, eldest son of the count of Angoulême, led what was reputed to be a large army on an invasion of Poitou. The confidence which King Henry reposed in John aux Bellesmains, bishop of Poitiers – despite his resistance to Henry's ecclesiastical policy – proved to be amply justified, for, in conjunction with Richard's lieutenant, Theobald Chabot, he raised the local defence forces, and repulsed the invaders in pitched battle near Barbezieux.[3] Richard, on his return, completed their discomfiture by pursuing them into the Limousin and routing them in a second battle near Bouteville.[4] With the resources of the Angevin commonwealth behind him, Richard then set about the systematic reduction of rebel strongholds. The castle of the count of Limoges at Aixe fell to him with a garrison of forty knights, and the city of Limoges itself capitulated after a few days' siege. Châteauneuf on the Charente, a castle of the count of Angoulême, fell after a fortnight's siege. Moulineuf was captured in ten days. Then the city of Angoulême itself was invested. Inside were the leaders of rebellion: Count William of Angoulême, Vulgrin his son, Viscount Aimer of Limoges, the viscount of Ventador, and the viscount of Chabanais. Six days of siege were sufficient to convince them that further resistance was useless. Count William surrendered himself, his city, his castles, and his allies into Richard's hands, and gave hostages as a sign of his readiness to seek the mercy of King Henry. Richard sent his baronial captives to his father in England, and at Winchester on 21 September 1176, 'prostrating themselves at the feet of the king the father, they sued for mercy'.[5] This, not the peace of Montlouis, was the true end of the great war.

In the following year, 1177, Richard addressed himself to the same sort of problem which confronted Geoffrey of Brittany in Finisterre: in

---

[1] Roger of Howden, *Gesta*, I, 115. Roger of Howden always refers to northern Aquitaine as 'Poitou', whether or not the county of Poitou itself was involved. The less confusing term 'Guyenne', also used by contemporaries, has been substituted in the quotation above.

[2] Cf. Roger of Howden, *Gesta*, I, 121: '. . . and a great multitude of knights flocked to him on account of the wages which he gave them'.   [3] Ralph of Diceto, I, 407.

[4] Roger of Howden, *Gesta*, I, 120: 'inter Sanctum Megrinum et Butevillam'.

[5] Ralph of Diceto, I, 414; Roger of Howden, *Gesta*, I, 120–1. The terms they received are not specified in the chronicles, but the fact that they are later to be found in possession of their castles, suggests that, as with the other baronial rebels in the great war, they were restored to their property after their renewal of homage to King Henry. ·

the extremity of Aquitaine, in the far south of Gascony, there too were lawless lords who asserted an independence of ducal authority. Rebellion would be too grand a term to put on their insubordination: they had for long been accustomed to do as they pleased simply because they were beyond the reach of effective ducal power. There may, it is true, have been some thought of breaking away from the lordship of Aquitaine, for there are signs that the count of Bigorre – a virtually autonomous *seigneurie* in the central Pyrenees – was trying to establish some sort of hegemony over the march with Spain, or at least a federation of frontier barons.[1] The example of state-making across the border in Navarre and Aragon could have given rise to some thought of the creation of an independent Basque principality in the mountain passes and foothills of the Pyrenees. The allegiance of these regions to Aquitaine, Toulouse, or the kingdom of France itself had always been in some doubt.[2] But it is unlikely that the unification of the marchlands was anything more than a dream of ambitious barons whose power to translate it into reality was minimal: a local overlordship was even less acceptable to the frontiersmen than that of a distant duke of Aquitaine or king of France. The count of Bigorre, for example, formed an alliance with the viscount of Dax and helped him to fortify the city of Dax against Richard, but this interference was resented by the citizens who eventually made him captive, and handed him over to Richard in chains.[3] Richard's problem in 1177 was that of clarifying the allegiance both of robber barons and of those with political pretensions, and of showing who was master. He did not have much difficulty in securing his claims when he went with an army to enforce them. The viscount of Dax and the viscount of Bayonne submitted after brief resistance. The castle of St Peter at the frontier town of Cize was taken in a siege of one day and destroyed. 'And afterwards,' says Roger of Howden, 'he obliged the Basques and Navarrese by force to swear that they would keep the peace; and he put an end to the evil practices they had introduced at Sorde and Lespéron where it was the custom to rob those making pilgrimage to St James of Compostella.'[4]

[1] The history of these regions is uncertain; but for examples of the intervention of the count of Bigorre *see* Roger of Howden, *Gesta*, I, 131, 212–13.

[2] Cf. Boussard, *Le Gouvernement d'Henri II*, 27ff.

[3] Roger of Howden, *Gesta*, I, 212–13; '. . . But Alphonso, king of Aragon, grieving that his friend the count of Bigorre was held in chains, came to Duke Richard and entreating that his friend might be freed from imprisonment, stood surety for him that he would do the will of the duke and of his father the king of England. And moreover the aforesaid count of Bigorre, in return for his release, handed over to the duke Clermont and the castle of Montbron.' This was in 1178.   [4] *Ibid.*, 131–2.

The inheritance of Queen Eleanor seemed to have been restored to peace, but it was an uneasy peace, and the absence of reports of sieges and campaigns from the chronicles for much of 1176 and 1177 should not be taken to indicate that Richard was inactive or that the former rebels had reconciled themselves to the necessity of obedience. Information is too meagre for the situation to be read with any certainty, but the precariousness of peace may be detected in an incident recorded by Robert de Torigny in 1177: on the death of the bishop of Limoges, he writes, 'Richard deprived the viscount of the castle adjacent to the city, and with justification, since he favoured the faction of the count of Angoulême, which was hostile to the duke'.[1] When Richard took his next reported resolute action it was against another ally of Angoulême, Geoffrey de Rancon. He held the fief of Marcillac from the counts of Angoulême, although his principal territorial power and his strongest castles were in the lower valley of the Charente in Saintonge. It was one of these castles, Pons, to which Richard laid siege shortly before Christmas 1177.

There can be little doubt that Richard recognised in Angoulême and its allies a formidable obstacle to the exercise of ducal authority, and that in attempting to take possession of vital castles in the Limousin and Saintonge he was trying to curtail the domination which the coalition exercised over the heart of the duchy. Angoulême ought indeed to have been one of the growth points of 'feudal empires' in France. It commanded major trade routes and the prosperous valley of the Charente. Its economic strength and the widespread network of its lordship – extending beyond the county of Angoulême – should have enabled it to eclipse both Poitou and Anjou in the dominance of west-central France. Its wealth, indeed, helped it to avoid the fate of many lesser lords, crushed by the improvements in military technology, for it could afford to rebuild its fortresses in stone and even to hire mercenaries – it was a force of 'Brabantines' which Vulgrin of Angoulême led against Poitou in 1176.[3] Yet it had fallen behind in the struggle for supremacy, being unable to make the best use of its resources because of crippling family feuds and the insubordination of powerful vassals. In practice it had fallen under the sway of the counts of Poitou, yet had remained unwilling to acknowledge the creation of a duchy of Aquitaine which would eclipse its aspirations to be in the front rank of the French baronage.[4] The submission of the rebels to King Henry in September

[1] Robert de Torigny, 275.   [2] Roger of Howden, *Gesta*, I, 213.

[3] Ralph of Diceto, I, 407; Roger of Howden, *Gesta*, I, 120.

[4] Cf. Boissonade, 'Les Taillefer et les Lusignans'; Boussard, *Le Gouvernement d'Henri II*, 119–24.

1176 had, for the moment, put an end to any speculation about the proper allegiance of Angoulême; yet the acceptance of the overlordship of Richard and his father should not be taken to imply that the count and his friends accepted any diminution of their autonomy within their fiefs – any more than King Henry's homage to the king of France implied any acceptance of Capetian intervention in the affairs of the duchy of Normandy. Angevin government did not readily acknowledge the existence of exclusive lordships under its jurisdiction, but its power to exercise real control over the major baronies of Aquitaine had yet to be made a reality.

It seems probable that, in laying siege to Pons, Richard was not acting without provocation: Ralph of Diceto says that the 'arrogance' of Geoffrey de Rancon had 'frequently exasperated him with many affronts'.[1] It seems likely, indeed, that calculated provocation was part of the strategy of the great barons in the coalition formed by Angoulême: they were testing whether their overlord had the determination, ability, and resources to impose his will upon them, or whether he would be obliged to come to terms with them and solicit their cooperation by conceding to them a wide measure of freedom from interference. A major campaign to enforce their allegiance was one thing; but was he prepared to pit his resources against a succession of strong castles, and perhaps exhaust his revenues, in an attempt to avenge affronts to his dignity and to enforce the acceptance of the day-to-day exercise of ducal authority?

The siege of Pons went badly for Richard. He chose an unusual time to mount a siege – Christmas – perhaps in the hope of taking his enemy unprepared; but after four months the castle was still defiant.[2] At Easter 1178, he left his constables to maintain the siege and himself went hunting easier game in the Angoumois. The castles of Richemont, Genzac, Marcillac, Gourville, and Auville fell in quick succession and were razed to the ground, which must have consoled Richard's pride.[3] But his basic problem still remained: could his barons defy him with impunity from the strongest of their fortresses? At the beginning of May 1178 he seized the nettle firmly, in a manner worthy of his father. Instead of returning to the prolonged siege of Pons, he threw his forces against the most forbidding of all Geoffrey de Rancon's strongholds, the town and fortress of Taillebourg. To Ralph of Diceto this was 'a most desperate enterprise, which none of his predecessors had ventured

---

[1] Ralph of Diceto, I, 431.
[2] Roger of Howden, *Gesta*, I, 213: '. . . sed minime potuit proficere'.
[3] *Loc. cit.*

to attempt; never before had that castle known hostile forces drawn up in assault'.[1] To Robert de Torigny Taillebourg was 'seemingly impregnable, fortified both by artifice and nature'.[2] The castle was perched upon a rock, three sides of which were inaccessible. The township on the fourth side was protected by a triple ditch and a triple wall. It was, according to Ralph of Diceto, exceedingly well stocked with weapons, victuals, and men, 'not the least disturbed' at Richard's approach. Richard set about changing their minds by ravaging his opponent's fief: 'he carried off the wealth of the farms, he cut down the vines, he fired the villages, and having pulled down everything else laid it waste; then at the approaches of the fortress he pitched his tents close to the walls, to the great alarm of the townsmen who had expected nothing of the kind'. The garrison organised a sally to disrupt the siege operations, but Richard was ready for it and his superior generalship turned the tables: after a fierce fight at the gates his men forced their way in at the heels of the retreating defenders, and made themselves masters of the town. Two days later the castle itself surrendered. The walls were levelled to the ground.[3] Geoffrey de Rancon then delivered up Pons, to be followed before the end of May by Vulgrin of Angoulême, who surrendered the city of Angoulême and the crucial castle of Montignac, which controlled the passage of the river Charente.[4] Richard had all their fortifications destroyed, and then journeyed to England to be 'received by his father with the greatest honour'.[5] In July 1179 the aged Count William of Angoulême set off for the Holy Land with his stepson, Viscount Aimar of Limoges, 'and many others'.[6]

The proper management of military forces was no small part of the art of Angevin government. The mastery of powerful, wealthy barons with private armies of vassals depended on it. Generalship – the successful prosecution of campaigns – was a necessary but subordinate part of the art. Chroniclers make much of this aspect, for sieges and battles were 'news', and they tend to give the impression that the ability to lead men in the field was a prerequisite in a medieval ruler. Generalship, however, could be hired. Much of Henry II's success in war probably rested on the experience and advice of the men who served in his household as constable and marshal, and on the skills of mercenary captains. Richard, though certainly much more interested in the business of fighting than his father, probably owed more than his admirers might

---

[1] Ralph of Diceto, I, 431.
[3] Ralph of Diceto, I, 431–2.
[5] Ralph of Diceto, I, 432.

[2] Robert de Torigny, 281–2.
[4] Roger of Howden, *Gesta*, I, 213.
[6] Geoffrey de Vigeois, II, 325.

admit to the advice of professionals such as Theobald Chabot.[1] Generalship, however, was of prime account only when armed conflict was unavoidable. The real art of military management as an aspect of government lay in avoiding the necessity of battle by persuading opponents of the folly of a resort to war and the hazards of disobedience. The recruitment, organisation, and deployment of military strength which went into the maintenance of this deterrent was a matter of administrative decision within the context of a governmental policy. This aspect receives scant attention from the chroniclers and, unfortunately, leaves few traces in the surviving archives, but it cannot on that account be ignored. If the details must remain deficient, it is nevertheless possible to descry, or to make reasonable guesses at, the principal factors involved.

A military dictatorship was out of the question. Great as were the resources of developed Angevin government they could never be sufficient for the maintenance of a military establishment to overawe simultaneously each and every one of its possible opponents. Any attempt to have kept under arms sufficient men for any contingency would have depleted resources to the point of weakening rather than strengthening the government. Efficiency had to be combined with economy. The use of military force had to be selective, and the selection of objectives had to be right. The secret of success lay in the concentration of forces where they could be most useful; and the dangers to avoid lay in the dissipation of effort through faulty deployment, in underestimating the forces required from a false sense of economy, or in overestimating them and wasting precious resources. Unemployed soldiers had still to be fed and paid. One way, indeed, of successfully resisting a powerful ruler was to persuade or oblige him to disperse his forces – widespread conspiracy was the safest tactic of opposition and the most serious problem a ruler could encounter. Henry II's survival in the great war rested on his cool appreciation of the dangers and his economical employment of the forces at his disposal. In the first place he refused to take on too many tasks at once: the temptation to boost loyalist morale by scoring easy victories over weak opponents must have been strong, but it was resisted in favour of trying to break the enemy's main strength. Secondly, Henry displayed a remarkable skill in identifying the appropriate target to attack; and if he could not impose his own choice of target he waited until the enemy selected a target for him by committing themselves to a line of attack. Thirdly he switched his

[1] Chabot, a mercenary captain, is described by Ralph of Diceto, I, 407, as 'princeps militiae Ricardi ducis Aquitanorum'.

forces with astonishing rapidity, achieving not merely surprise but a decisive local superiority in numbers. Henry II may not have been a particularly skilful general, but he was certainly a superb commander-in-chief.

In times other than war, maintenance of the deterrent to insurrection, disobedience, and indiscipline rested on similar skills, for the deterrent was credible only if it were known that the government was prepared to use force and to use it decisively. Sensing the need, calculating the requirement, and anticipating where it would have to be used was the art of military management as a sanction of government. The enemy had to be hit where he was strong and hit hard enough.

It was a difficult art and mistakes were easily made. Richard's campaign against Geoffrey of Rancon in the winter of 1178–9 was very nearly an expensive failure. Indeed, the prolonged resistance of Pons was tantamount to a disaster: the ability to withstand a long siege and to tie up attacking forces indefinitely was part of the defensive strategy castles were meant to serve. It was the attacker who wore himself out, while insubordination flourished elsewhere. Richard's ability to impose instant obedience had been discredited, and the credibility of the deterrent could not be reinforced either by the seizure of less imposing strongholds or even the eventual capture, if it could be effected, of Pons. Richard's problem in the spring of 1179 was that he had to obliterate the memory of his failure at Pons, and he had to do this by showing that Pons was simply a miscalculation, and that he was capable, if need be, of the swift destruction of even more impressive resistance. The assault on Taillebourg may have been, as Ralph of Diceto says, a desperate venture, but only a venture of this nature would serve the purpose. The surest way to recover the initiative was for Richard to perform the seemingly impossible by capturing the impregnable. Desperate it may have been, but it was clearly well calculated and meticulously planned. All the tactics of terror were employed for the demoralisation of the defenders, and the one weak point in an immensely strong defensive system – the necessity of opening the gates to make a sally – exploited with consummate efficiency. The brilliance of the siege as a feat of arms should not, however, be allowed to overshadow the fact that the decision to attack 'impregnable' Taillebourg was a political rather than a straightforward military decision. Richard had displayed the determination to recover from error, the courage to take a hard decision, and the ability to carry through his resolve to success. In short, he had proved himself as a ruler.

*   *   *

Henry, then, when he set his personal affairs in order before crossing the Channel in February 1182, had every reason to feel confident about the future of the Angevin commonwealth. His recognition of Richard as the destined ruler of Aquitaine in the summer of 1179, and the marriage of Geoffrey to Constance of Brittany in 1181, marked the end of the first critical phase in the establishment of the federation: they had served their apprenticeship and proved their capacity. There seemed every reason to expect that Aquitaine and Brittany would now conform to the pattern he himself had established in England, Normandy, and greater Anjou – as orderly political entities, disciplined to accept a considerable measure of central control, their laws reshaped on more rational principles, their administrative structures amplified and systematised to ensure protection of the ruler's interests and to forge links between the community at large and the central government. There were still, in 1182, political problems to be solved. The fringe areas, such as southern Gascony, Berry, and Wales, remained politically untidy, but were sufficiently well under control. The one major element of uncertainty in the future of the federation was Ireland. Since Henry's expedition of 1171–2 it had posed no threat to the security of the rest of the Angevin dominions, but its political instability was distressing and unacceptable. Henry had broken off his work there prematurely to meet the papal legates sent to negotiate a settlement with the Church. He recognised that the arrangements made for Ireland had been unsatisfactory, and that there was no real prospect of stabilising it simply, and cheaply, on the model of Wales. There are no signs, however, that Henry ever seriously contemplated returning to Ireland: the problem there was to be solved, as the problems of Brittany and Aquitaine had been solved, by moving in one of his sons to take direct charge, backed, when necessary, by the full resources of the Angevin commonwealth in experience, men, and money. The project of making John king of Ireland had been adumbrated as early as 1177, but had been deferred because John was then of insufficient age to assume personal responsibility.[1] It is likely that plans were being laid for making it a reality in 1182, and they were put into effect in the spring of 1185, when John was seventeen. By then, it was hoped, the federation would achieve definitive shape. Unfortunately for Henry II his scheme rested on the assumption that his sons would wholeheartedly endorse the federal plan and loyally perform their appointed rôles within it. The assumption was unwarranted, and the first clear signs of the fundamental frailty of Henry's hopes for a family consortium began to

[1] *See* above, ch. 4, pp. 203ff.

emerge as soon as his older sons became capable of imposing their own will on the situation, and that was in 1182. It was over the future of Aquitaine that the divergent aspirations emerged.

After the capture of Taillebourg, Richard's relations with his barons entered a new phase. The evidence for it is less sparse than previously, but still inadequate. It speaks somewhat obscurely of a rumbling discontent and of widespread conspiracy, but at the same time suggests a reluctance to challenge in arms the man who had humbled the pride of the most powerful lords in the land. The reasons for the discontent are not hard to guess: the barons, both great and small, of Aquitaine were having to endure that 'invasion of liberties', that curtailment of accustomed if illegitimate privilege, that circumscription of freedom of action, that critical oversight of their judicial, and perhaps even of their admininistrative activities, which had earlier accompanied the expansion of royal authority in England and of ducal government in Normandy. The administrative records for Aquitaine which might reveal the process are missing; but there are clear indications that something of the sort was happening in the bitter hostility to Richard personally, recorded by the chroniclers. Ralph of Diceto heard that Richard 'oppressed his subjects with burdensome and unwarranted exactions and by an impetuous despotism'.[1] Gervase of Canterbury records that 'the more exalted men of Aquitaine hated their lord, Count Richard, on account of his exceeding cruelty'.[2] Roger of Howden reports that Richard's subjects complained that 'he was evil to all men, to his own men worse, and to himself worst of all; he carried off the wives, daughters, and kinswomen of his freemen by force and made them his concubines; and when he had sated his lust on them he handed them over to his knights for whoring. With these and many other wrongs he afflicted his people.'[3] It would be a mistake to take much malicious gossip reaching England too seriously. It has a close parallel in the unbridled complaints about Henry II in the 1160s and in the venomous diatribes of Ralph Niger.[4] It should be taken rather as a sign that ducal government was becoming effective. Doubtless the gossip represents sentiments genuinely held and powerfully felt, but such sentiments were the bitter, unreasoning outpourings of an incoherent resentment at the unwelcome shift in the balance of power between the ruler and his barons. Unwelcome, that is, to those whose personal interests were damaged, and whose freedom to commit the atrocities they attributed

---

[1] Ralph of Diceto, II, 19.
[2] Gervase of Canterbury, I, 303.
[3] Roger of Howden, *Gesta*, I, 292.   [4] Above, pp. 103, 119, 380.

to Richard was now curtailed. There were doubtless many who approved Richard's rule whose sentiments go unrecorded. It may be significant that Gervase of Canterbury reports that it was 'the men of higher rank' (*sublimiores viri*) who complained; and it is certainly significant that Aquitanian chroniclers record nothing of the alleged atrocities. The best of them, Geoffrey, prior of Vigeois in the Limousin, concluded his chronicle at the year 1185 with the names of the kings who were then ruling in the world he knew, and thought it fitting to append to the list the name of 'Richard, duke of Aquitaine and Gascony, who is ever to the fore in doughty deeds, and whose youth is distinguished by great strenuousness of life'.[1]

On the other hand there are signs that Richard, having demonstrated his military mastery, acted with an impolitic imperiousness and unnecessary harshness. Gerald of Wales, who approved Richard's success in 'subduing that hitherto untamed land' and for bringing to it an 'unaccustomed peace and tranquillity', and who held that the charge of cruelty had been incurred without cause, nevertheless admitted that 'he remained fearless in his determination to make the whole world tremble and fear before him'.[2] That he behaved high-handedly is beyond question: his apparently wanton order to the citizens of Limoges to demolish their walls may possibly have been warranted and a proper exercise of his authority, but his treatment of the Angoulême inheritance was certainly contrary to law as well as unwise.[3] The aged Count William IV of Angoulême died on his way to the Holy Land in the summer of 1179. Less than two years later, on 29 June 1181, his eldest son, Vulgrin III, also died, leaving an only child, a girl, who, says Geoffrey de Vigeois, 'was the cause of great calamity to her country'.[4] Richard claimed the wardship of both the maiden and the fief. Local custom, however, did not admit of such a claim, for Vulgrin had two brothers who could succeed him. The sharing of an inheritance between sons was indeed common practice in Aquitaine, and Vulgrin had associated his brothers, William and Aymer, with him in ruling Angoulême after the death of their father.[5] Nevertheless Richard took

[1] Geoffrey de Vigeois, II, 317.
[2] Gerald of Wales, VIII, 246–50.
[3] For Limoges *see* Geoffrey de Vigeois, II, 326.
[4] *Loc. cit.*; Boissonade, 'Les comtes d'Angoulême', 281.
[5] Bertrand de Born speaks of 'the three counts of Angoulême', cited by Kate Norgate, *Richard the Lionheart*, 38 n.3. Cf. Painter, 'Castellans of the plain of Poitou', *Feudalism and Liberty*, 28: '. . . there is evidence to suggest that the family property was considered the joint possession of the males of each generation'. If there were several brothers, the inheritance did not revert to the children of the eldest until all the

possession of the inheritance as guardian of Vulgrin's daughter and drove out her uncles, who took refuge with their half-brother, Viscount Aymer of Limoges.[1] The motive, of course, is obvious: it was for Richard a tempting opportunity to lay his hands on the most troublesome of the baronies, and to determine its future by marrying the heiress to a man of his choice. In England this would have been a normal exercise of the rights of lordship, but in Aquitaine it involved the imposition of the principle of primogeniture in the face of an established local custom which had all the force of law. Brittany was shortly afterwards, by the *Assize of Count Geoffrey* of 1185, to adopt primogeniture in determining the descent of major fiefs, but Richard did not, as his brother did, take the precaution – indeed the only proper procedure – of securing the assent of his barons to it.[2] Richard's attempt did not prevail: William eventually gained recognition as count of Angoulême, and on his death his brother Aymer succeeded him.[3] Nevertheless Richard's high-handed action in 1181 can only have excited the liveliest apprehension in Aquitaine not merely for the future of local custom, but also for the existing tenure of fiefs. Widespread discontent and active support for the sons of the late Count William IV of Angoulême is understandable.

The discontent was fanned by Bertrand de Born, a man of knightly family from the Limousin, and a troubadour, whose particular claim to fame is as a composer of topical ditties (*sirventes*) of unusual pungency and impertinence. Bertrand was in dispute with his brother about possession of the minor castle of Hautefort, and gives the impression that this private quarrel was the cause of rupture between Richard and the viscount of Limoges, and that the incitements to war conveyed by his *sirventes* were a major influence in the formation of a sworn conspiracy of the barons of Aquitaine against their overlord.[4] Bertrand's importance in his own eyes, and his persistent fame as a troubadour among those who cherish vernacular literature, have beguiled some historians into taking his claims at their face value; but it is extremely doubtful if his name-dropping and assertions of familiarity with the great are anything more than absurd pretensions.[5] It is significant that

---

brothers had died. The prevalance of the custom in Aquitaine is, however, uncertain.

[1] Geoffrey de Vigeois, II, 326.

[2] *See* above, p. 564.

[3] Boissonade, 'Les comtes d'Angoulême', 281. Aymer ruled until 1202, and it was his daughter Isabella whom King John married in 1200.

[4] Stimming, *Bertran von Born;* Clédat, *Du rôle historique de Bertrand de Born.*

[5] Cf. Moore, *The Young King Henry Plantagenet,* 47.

none of the major chroniclers of the time appears even to have heard of Bertrand de Born of Hauteville. Indeed, if his vocal *graffiti* had any influence at all, it seems unlikely that it was as anything more than a minor irritant with no effect on the course of events. Nevertheless Bertrand de Born does have an historical importance as representing the attitudes of a class of men whose collective influence on the situation in Aquitaine should not perhaps be underestimated: those whose fortunes depended on winning favours from the greater lords – or their wives. Troubadours such as Bertrand de Born were the spokesmen, the propagandists, for the interests of *la petite noblesse* – the constables of castles, the holders of minor fiefs, the landless younger sons of knightly families whose only asset was their training in the craft of arms. The conventions of troubadour poetry and the elaboration of a code of *courtoisie* were designed to promote a sense of the solidarity of the nobility, to impose on society distinctions of class instead of distinctions of wealth and power. They sought, and indeed achieved, the integration of the petty fief-holders and the lesser knightly families into a new broader class of nobility than the old aristocracy of power, and distinguished it from the rest of society by supplying it with a common ethic enshrined in a vernacular literature. They sought to persuade the greater barons that those who were both noble and wealthy had a duty to provide for the less well-endowed members of the class – the young, the poor, the unmarried, the unemployed. Beside the retainers of old in the households of the mighty, they set up the new figure of the courtier, who competed with flattery as well as service for rewards in the form of fiefs, castles, heiresses, or at the very least for a share in plunder and ransoms.[1] *L'amour courtois* and hunting were the sports, par excellence, of the courtier, the tournament his proving ground, and war his chief avocation and the best opportunity to improve his condition. 'I would that the great men should always be quarelling among themselves,' wrote Bertrand de Born.[2] He relished the excitement of war: 'I find no such savour in food, or in wine, or in sleep, as in hearing the shout "On! On!" from both sides.' But he frankly admitted, too, its practical advantages. Great barons at war needed the services of valiant knights and would reward them handsomely: 'a rich man is much more noble, generous, and affable in war than in peace'. In time of war, too, a military man had the world at his feet and could

---

[1] Frapper, 'Vues sur les conceptions courtoises dans les littératures d'oc et d'oïl au xiie siècle'; Koehler, 'Observations historiques et sociologiques sur la poésie des troubadours'; Duby, 'La noblesse dans la France médiévale'.

[2] *Poésies Complètes de Bertran de Born*, ed. Thomas, 6.

dispense with the normal rules of behaviour: 'Trumpets, drums, flags, and cannons, standards, and horses black and white – that is what we shall shortly see. And it will be a happy day; for we shall seize the usurer's goods, and no more shall beasts of burden pass along the highways in complete safety; nor shall the burgesses journey without fear, nor the merchant on his way to France; but the man who is full of courage shall be rich.'[1]

Richard's mastery of the great barons, and the prospect of the imposition of Angevin standards of law and order, threatened men such as Bertrand de Born with the disaster of peace. Other such men as Bertrand de Born write of its horrors for 'poor knights': 'the disdainful indifference of the great who would have no more need of them; the importunities of money-lenders; the heavy plough-horse instead of the mettlesome charger; iron spurs instead of gold'.[2] With such influences at work it is not surprising that the task of imposing respect for law and order in Aquitaine seemed never-ending. Yet, in fact, the attempt to set the great barons in arms against Richard in 1182 was not very effective. Richard's work in overawing them had been well done: many were too cautious to join in conspiracy. Bertrand de Born was obliged to admit the failure of his incitements: 'I am making a *sirvente* against the cowardly barons, and you will never again hear me speak of them, for I have broken a thousand spurs in them without being able to make a single one of them run or even trot.'[3] Active conspiracy seems to have been virtually limited to the Limousin and Périgord.[4] Richard struck first, capturing a stronghold of the count of Périgord, in April 1182, and ravaging the Limousin border, without, apparently, encountering any really serious resistance. Nevertheless, for the first time since entrusting Aquitaine to Richard, Henry II personally intervened. He summoned the Taillefer brothers of Angoulême, Viscount Aymer of Limoges, and Count Elias of Périgord to meet him at Grandmont shortly after Whitsuntide.[5] Either he recognised that Richard had acted high-handedly over the Angoulême inheritance, or he at least

---

[1] Bertrand de Born, ed. Appel, nos 40, 10.2, 37, trans. by Manyon in Bloch, *Feudal Society*, 293, 296.

[2] Bloch, *op. cit.*, 298, citing Girart de Rousillon and the *Vita Henrici*.

[3] Bertrand de Born, ed. Raynouard, IV, 147, ed. Stimming, 114, trans. by Appleby, *Henry II*, 277; cf. Kate Norgate, *Richard the Lionheart*, 42.

[4] Kate Norgate, *op. cit.*, 42.

[5] The only English chronicler to mention Henry's intervention in Aquitaine in the spring of 1182, Roger of Howden, *Gesta*, I, 288, says simply, 'Rex Angliae pater ducissae, profectus fuerat in Pictaviam ad debellandum inimicos'. For the revealing details we are dependent upon Geoffrey de Vigeois, II, 330–1. The sequence of events in the years 1182–3 is, however, far from clear.

thought it desirable to investigate the reasons for discontent personally. The conference was apparently inconclusive; Henry went to assist Richard in the siege of castles in the Limousin and summoned his eldest son to join them. By the beginning of July the alliance had collapsed, Viscount Aymer made his submission and promised to render no further help to his half-brothers of Angoulême. Count Elias surrendered Périgieux. Henry II seems to have realised that discontent in Aquitaine could build up into a serious crisis, but at the same time he seems to have believed that negotiation and a show of force by the leaders of the Angevin commonwealth would be sufficient to quell it. The rapid submission of the principal conspirators doubtless confirmed his diagnosis; but he had reckoned without the intervention and devious policies of his eldest son.

Henry the Younger was the only member of the family ever to be accorded unstinted admiration and to achieve a measure of real popularity. He was everyone's ideal of a fairy-tale prince. He was tall and handsome: 'the most handsome prince in all the world, whether Saracen or Christian'.[1] He was gracious, benign, affable, courteous, the soul of liberality and generosity. Unfortunately he was also shallow, vain, careless, empty-headed, incompetent, improvident, and irresponsible. These shortcomings, however, were barely noticed by most contemporaries, and seem to have been overlooked even by some who knew him well, beguiled by his fatal charm.[2] His deficiencies as the future overlord of the Angevin commonwealth remained hidden largely because he did not encounter a serious challenge to his competence. As heir to the direct rule of that part of the Angevin dominions which his father had tamed and organised – England, Normandy, and greater Anjou – there was little for him to do. Little, that is, which engaged his interest or attention. Attempts were made from the time of his coronation in June 1170 to involve him in government and train him in his future duties: he held court in his father's absence, and administrative acts were performed in his name; but he was no more than a cipher. Henry II has been accused of deliberately keeping his son in leading strings and of refusing to allow him any real power or responsibility; but the fact is that Henry the Younger showed neither taste nor desire for responsibility. The real business of being a king escaped his understanding; for him kingship was conceived simply in terms of dignity,

---

[1] *Histoire de Guillaume le Maréschal*, lines 1956–8.

[2] The views and comments of contemporaries are usefully gathered in Moore, *The Young King Henry Plantagenet*.

prestige, and convenient wealth. Administration bored him; he preferred instead to gad about with his friends in search, not so much of adventure, as of entertainment. In the reminiscences of a member of his entourage:

> They sojourned in England
> For almost a year did he pass the time
> With nothing to do but to engage in *pleids*
> Or the hunt or the tourney.
> But to the Young King it was distasteful.
> Such a stay was unpleasing.
> His companions likewise
> Endured a dreadful ennui.
> For to wander would have pleased them more
> Than to stay – to wander they liked.
> For you should know – this is the heart of it –
> A long sojourn dishonours a young man.[1]

The Young King left England in April 1176 and did not return until February 1179 – an absence of nearly three years during a critical phase in the development of English government. His father tried to find useful employment for him in the continental dominions, but Henry the Younger showed as little enthusiasm for the police work of government as for the routine business of administration. At Easter 1176 he was persuaded by his father to go to Richard's assistance in bringing to an end the last instalment of the great war in Aquitaine, but it was midsummer before he brought any help, having dallied in the meantime on a visit to his father-in-law at Paris; and then, having joined briefly in the siege of the lesser castle of Châteauneuf on the Charente, he took himself off again with the main task still undone.[2] In 1179 his father sent him to take possession of the lands of Ralph de Deols, who had recently died, in Berry – a move of considerable political importance; but Henry the Younger was so dilatory and so irresolute in taking action against those who were detaining the inheritance, that his father had to intervene in person and settle the matter with determination and despatch.[3] In 1182 he was summoned to join his father and Richard in quelling the insurrection of Aymer of Limoges and his confederates, but he arrived in time only for the closing scenes.[4] Advisers recommended to him by his father were cast aside. In 1176 he

---

[1] *Histoire de Guillaume le Maréschal*, lines 2391–402.
[2] Roger of Howden, *Gesta*, I, 114–15, 121: 'he would stay with his brother no longer, but following evil counsel departed from him'.
[3] *Ibid.*, I, 132.   [4] Geoffrey de Vigeois, II, 331.

had his vice-chancellor, Adam of Churchdown, publicly beaten and paraded naked through the streets of Poitiers, allegedly for disclosing what was discussed in his household to the king his father.[1] William Marshal, who earned a reputation as a man of probity and honour, and who was to become earl of Pembroke, lord of Leinster, and Protector of the realm of England itself after the death of King John, began his long and distinguished career in the service of the Angevins as tutor in chivalry to the Young King, and leader of his household knights; but enemies accused him of improper advances to Queen Margaret, and Henry the Younger, refusing either to disbelieve the charges or to allow William to prove them false, deprived himself of the one man who could perhaps have dissuaded him from the ultimate foolishness of his behaviour in 1182–3.[2]

Henry the Younger's preferred way of spending his time was at tournaments, and he found a willing mentor and genial host in his cousin Philip of Alsace, count of Flanders – until in 1179 Count Philip discarded him for another young king he hoped both to humour and exploit: Philip of France. Twelfth-century tournaments were convivial, boisterous, but crude affairs, simulating real battle in the general mêlée of knights instead of individual combat as a test of skill – the sport of an idle upper class, and a way of life for bachelor knights offering their services to one team or another, and hoping for rich pickings in the armour and horses of the vanquished or in ransoms for those who were captured. Condemned by the Church as a source of peril both to life and soul, tournaments were discouraged, though doubtless for other reasons, in Henry II's dominions, and his eldest son had to satisfy his craving for excitement, fashionable society, popularity, and the flattery of knights eager for employment, in north-west France – the home both of the tournament and of the developing *cultus* of a military caste glorified as *chivalry*. 'Henry the son of the king of England,' writes Ralph of Diceto, 'leaving the kingdom, passed three years in French contests and lavish expenditure.'[3] The stories told about him were stories of extravagance and display: Robert de Torigny, for example, tells of a great feast he held at Bures at which a hundred and

---

[1] Roger of Howden, *Chronica*, II, 94; *Gesta*, I, 122–3: the Young King would have had Adam executed as a traitor, but the bishop of Poitiers intervened to protest that he was a clerk and should not be subject to lay jurisdiction.

[2] *Histoire de Guillaume le Maréschal*, lines 1939ff., and 5059ff.; Painter, *William Marshal*, 31–49.

[3] Ralph of Diceto, I, 428, cf. Roger of Howden, *Gesta*, I, 207, *Chronica*, II, 166–7; *Histoire de Guillaume le Maréschal*, lines 2443ff.; Moore, *The Young King Henry Plantagenet*.

ten knights all named William were gathered in one room.[1] Henry the Younger, it seems, liked to think of himself as a man of fashion, the leader of 'high society' – a society of men like himself, well-born, gay, pleasure-seeking, and improvident. He was the perpetual 'young man' and his companions were 'les jeunes', a characteristic section of feudal society: those who had not yet become 'men' by settling down and taking on the responsibilities of marriage and lordship which the possession of great estates entailed. They might remain 'youths' for thirty years or more, until they entered upon their inheritance, fit only for the life of a military aristocracy and for self-indulgence.[2]

At twenty-eight Henry the Younger was still the same feckless youth he had been at eighteen, when he allowed himself to be made the figurehead of rebellion against his father. Marriage and coronation had not changed him, but had simply made him wish to play the part that birth and his own inclinations seemed, in his eyes, to have marked out for him – that of patron of chivalry. His reiterated demand to his father was to be allowed some portion of his inheritance, not that he might assume responsibility for it, but that, like the Prodigal Son, he might enjoy it without waiting for his father's death. To be plagued with debts incurred by his own improvidence, and from which he had to be rescued by his father or William Marshal, was galling to the Young King's pride and the frustration of his desire to cut a figure as a leader of courtly society. *Largueza* – largesse, an open-handed generosity – was extolled by the troubadours as the most desirable quality in a noble lord; it was of course the means of survival and advancement for the lesser gentry they represented, and hence was erected into a central feature of the chivalric, courtly ideal which they fashioned.[3] The troubadours tried hard to enmesh the Angevins in their webs of courtly fantasy. Queen Eleanor is portrayed holding court at Poitiers to pronounce judgements on matters of *l'amour courtois*. Such literary conceits may have owed something to the flirtatious, romantic young woman who had at one time graced the court of Paris as the wife of King Louis VII, but owed nothing to the matriarch and hard-headed politician that Eleanor became in later life.[4] It was Henry the Younger

---

[1] Robert de Torigny, 253. On his liberality *see* Gerald of Wales, VIII, 174–5.

[2] Duby, 'Les "Jeunes" dans la société aristocratique'.

[3] For Henry II settling his son's debts *see* Ralph of Diceto, I, 404, and for William Marshal standing as surety with his creditors, *Histoire de Guillaume le Maréschal*, lines 5073–94. For the place of largesse in the literary cult of *courtoisie see* Koehler, 'Observations historiques et sociologiques sur la poésie des troubadours', 29–30.

[4] Cf. Amy Kelly, 'Eleanor of Aquitaine and her courts of love', Chambers, 'Some legends concerning Eleanor of Aquitaine'; Régine Pernoud, *Aliénor d'Aquitaine*.

whom they really influenced, making him the victim of a propaganda which extolled extravagant hospitality, amorous dalliance, martial exploits, and irresponsible war as the proper occupations of nobility.

In the late summer of 1182 Henry the Younger renewed his demand 'that he be given Normandy or some other territory, where he and his wife might dwell, and from which he might be able to support knights in his service'. Henry II refused, and his son took himself off to the court of the king of France.[1] This was precisely the action which a decade previously Louis VII had urged upon the Young King, and it had then heralded the onset of the great war.[2] Henry II was so seriously disturbed that he postponed his intended return from Normandy to England, and plied his son with messengers offering terms. He prudently persisted in refusing to place territories in the unreliable charge of his eldest son, but offered a very generous alternative: he would make him an allowance of a hundred pounds a day in Angevin money, with a further ten pounds a day for the expenses of his wife, and promised that he would for a year support the costs of a hundred knights in his son's entourage. Shortly before Christmas Henry the Younger accepted the offer and returned to his father 'swearing that henceforth he would not depart from his will and counsel, nor demand more from him'.[3]

Henry II's alarm at his eldest son's behaviour probably reflects his awareness of a deepening crisis in relations between members of the family. The chroniclers were not privy to the inner counsels of the royal *curia*, and their record of events is simply the superficial reporting of the public aspects, the incidental consequences, of a debate which eluded them. One sign of the crisis is the prolonged family conclave which took place in the winter of 1182–3. Henry II did not return to England in the autumn of 1182 as he had intended: he did not, in fact, set foot in England again until 10 June 1184, after an absence of two years and three months. The Christmas festivities of 1182 were celebrated at Caen in Normandy, and Henry the Younger, Richard, and Geoffrey were all at court. It was quite usual for Henry II and his sons to meet together at such a time, but they did not as usual disperse immediately afterwards: Henry took his sons with him as the royal court moved to Le Mans, to Angers, and to Mirebeau. When they did break up it was in acrimony and dissension, Richard departing in haste and

---

[1] Roger of Howden, *Gesta*, I, 289.
[2] Above, ch. 3, pp. 117–18.
[3] Roger of Howden, *Gesta*, I, 289, 291.

high dudgeon, 'leaving nothing behind him but altercations and threats'.[1]

The chroniclers' accounts of the causes and course of the dissension are confused, inconsistent, and superficial, but there is sufficient common ground for the essentials of the problem to be pieced together. The occasion for dispute, although not its deeper cause, was Richard's handling of his barons in Aquitaine. Although by 1182 Richard had repeatedly demonstrated that rebellion against his authority was useless, he had failed to establish political control or to ensure the real pacification of his duchy.[2] There were two signs of this which were evident to the chroniclers. One was the open sore of Richard's sequestration of the Angoulême inheritance; the brothers, William and Aymer Taillefer, despite the collapse of the league of their friends formed to defend their right in open rebellion, persisted in a resistance which shows that they had widespread covert support, and which, indeed, was ultimately to be successful. Secondly, Richard signally failed to establish his authority in the county of La Marche, which, having lost its count, ought to have come under his direct rule. In December 1177, Count Adalbert V of La Marche, wishing to end his days in the Holy Land, had sold his rights in the county to Henry II for the paltry sum of six thousand marks and a string of pack animals. The barons of the county had then done 'homage and fealty' to Henry as their liege-lord. Count Adalbert's charter of sale declared that there was 'no one protesting and indeed no one existing who had a right to protest'; but nevertheless Geoffrey of Lusignan, exploiting a distant kinship, claimed that La Marche belonged to him as heir, and, says a local chronicler, Geoffrey prior of Vigeois, 'he secured it'. As a matter of fact the claim was always disputed by Richard, and it was not until 1200 that Hugh Brunus of Lusignan extorted the title of count of La Marche from King John. The situation in La Marche is indeed extremely obscure, but there can be little doubt that the Lusignans had by 1182 so infiltrated the county as to deny to Richard effective control.[3]

[1] *Ibid.*, 292.

[2] It is noticeable that the chroniclers report under 1183 the widespread dislike of Richard and his reputation for high-handedness which has been noted above, p. 575. Cf. Roger of Howden, *Gesta*, I, 292; Ralph of Diceto, II, 19; Gervase of Canterbury, I, 303.

[3] Geoffrey de Vigeois, II, 324. Count Adalbert's charter is given by Roger of Howden, *Gesta*, I, 196–7, *Chronica*, II, 147–8. Cf. Robert de Torigny, 274–5; Ralph of Diceto, I, 425 (under an incorrect date); *Chroniques de S.Martial de Limoges*, 188–9; Richard, *Histoire des Comtes de Poitou*, II, 192–3; Boissonade, 'Les Taillefer et les Lusignans', 49, 52; Painter, 'The lords of Lusignan', 64–6.

These are probably simply two signs – prominent examples – of a general failure by Richard to consolidate the consequences of his military mastery of his vassals. This, apparently so decisive, should have led to a transformation of the situation in Aquitaine, in which the barons, at least the more realistic or sagacious of them, would have tried to retrieve by cooperation with Richard the power they stood to lose by defying him. It could have been expected that, the old-style private war being ruled out, the rivalries of the barons would instead be fought out in Richard's court, with the rivals jockeying for position and favour. Eventually something of this sort did happen: when Richard became king of England and sole ruler of the Angevin dominions his policy in Aquitaine was shaped by a community of interest he established with the Lusignan family; and John, when he succeeded as king and sole ruler, based his control of Aquitaine on a strong link forged with Count Aymer of Angoulême. But in 1182 Richard was isolated. There do not appear to have been any great barons who were ready to cast their lot with ducal government; even those, and they were the majority, who steered clear of conspiracy and insurrection, hesitated to commit themselves in support of Richard. To explain this in terms of the habitual turbulence of the southern barons or their long tradition of independence is barely adequate: self-interest, if nothing more, should have pushed them into recognising the consequences of Richard's manifest superiority. The crucial factor is that there was, as yet, no necessity for accepting Richard's rule, unwelcome and high-handed as it was, as a permanent feature of their lives. If it had to be borne for the time being, with patience or impatience, this was only because of Henry II's disposition of his territories and his policy of not intervening in the way his sons conducted the affairs of their provinces if he could avoid it. There can be little doubt, indeed, that what undermined Richard's government of Aquitaine – and, much more seriously, threatened the structure of Henry II's commonwealth – was the Young King's intimation to the discontented barons of the south that if he were in charge things would be very different. Unmistakable evidence of this is a report by Roger of Howden that in January 1183, when the royal court was at Le Mans,

> . . . Henry, son of our lord the king of England, of his own accord, without any compulsion, touching the Holy Gospels, in the presence of a very large body of clergy and laity, swore that from that day forward all the days of his life he would preserve entire fidelity to King Henry, as his father and lord, and would render him honour and due service always. And since, as he asserted, he did not wish to have preying on his mind any

malice or grudge, by reason of which his father might possibly be later offended, he revealed that he had pledged himself to the barons of Aquitaine against his brother Richard, being induced to do so because his brother had fortified the castle of Clairvaux, which was part of the patrimony promised to himself, contrary to his wishes.[1]

Subsequent events do not suggest that Henry the Younger's professed desire to remove all cause of discord was genuine; rather, it seems likely, Henry II knew enough to tax his eldest son with malign interference in the affairs of Richard's duchy, and that Henry the Younger tried to bluff his way out of it by offering Clairvaux as an excuse. He had some cause for complaint: Clairvaux lay on the limits of the north-eastern corner of Poitou which the counts of Anjou had long controlled. Technically speaking the counts of Anjou held the district as vassals of the counts of Poitou, although homage had probably not been performed for it within living memory.[2] There was a nice point of law involved, and possibly a question of boundary demarcation. But however reasonable the grievance, the Young King's behaviour over it was inexcusable: he should have laid a formal complaint before his father's court.

Whether Henry II, besides accepting his son's oath, really believed in its sincerity is uncertain; but subsequent events suggest that he probably did. Although extremely sensitive to what he took to be betrayal in others, Henry II showed a remarkable capacity for deceiving himself about his sons, and an astonishing indulgence even to their most patent duplicity. Nevertheless he clearly saw, in January 1183, the need for something more than protestations of undying fidelity to restore the tattered fabric of family unity. He tackled the problem in three ways. First he removed the ostensible source of friction by persuading Richard, with some difficulty, to surrender Clairvaux into his own hands. Secondly he acknowledged the need for reconciliation with the discontented barons of Aquitaine, and summoned them to attend a conference at Mirebeau. Thirdly he sought a renewal of the solemn oaths upon which the future of the federation rested. Henry the Younger, Richard, and Geoffrey were required to enter into a compact of perpetual peace: they all swore obedience and eternal fidelity to their father, and they all swore to abide for ever by their father's disposition of territories between them. Then King Henry required the two younger sons to take oaths of homage to his eldest son as heir to

[1] Roger of Howden, *Gesta*, I, 294, *Chronica*, II, 274; cf. Ralph of Diceto, I, 18.
[2] Cf. Kate Norgate, *Richard the Lionheart*, 46 n.1.

the overlordship of the federation. It was at this point that the crisis took a much more serious turn. According to Roger of Howden, Richard at first refused to do homage to his brother, on the ground that they were equals, and then, when he had been persuaded to change his mind and offered to do it, Henry the Younger refused to receive it.[1] In the differing account of Ralph of Diceto, Henry the Younger insisted that Richard's oath of homage should be sworn on the Gospels, and Richard, indignantly refusing, said that it was incongruous that there should be any kind of subjection between children of the same parents, and he argued that if his brother had by right of primogeniture a claim upon the inheritance of the father, so had he an equally legitimate claim upon the inheritance of the mother.[2]

Richard had a case, although, if the reports be correct, he based it on shaky ground, for the laws of succession were uncertain in the twelfth century, and contradictory precedents could readily be cited. Henry II himself had succeeded to the inheritances of both his father and his mother against any claims by his brothers. But Henry II held Aquitaine only by right of marriage, and there had never been any suggestion hitherto that Henry the Younger was to be endowed with any right of lordship over his mother's lands. On the contrary, after Henry II's announcement of his intentions for the dispositions of his territories in 1169, Richard did homage directly to the king of France for Aquitaine, while Henry the Younger did homage to King Louis for Normandy, Anjou, Maine, and Brittany.[3] This most certainly made them of equal standing. If the chroniclers are accurate in reporting that Henry II tried to insist on Richard swearing, not merely an oath of perpetual peace or even of personal fidelity to his brother, but an oath of subjection, then he was trying to change the relationship of Aquitaine not only to the rest of the Angevin federation, but also to the Crown of France. Presumably it was only in this way that he thought he could preserve the shaky union of the Angevin dominions, for the tie between Aquitaine and the rest had always been the weak point in the federal scheme.[4]

[1] Roger of Howden, *Gesta*, I, 292.

[2] Ralph of Diceto, II, 18–19.

[3] Robert de Torigny, 240; Gervase of Canterbury, I, 208; II, 79; Roger of Howden, *Gesta*, I, 7.

[4] Richard, unlike his brothers Geoffrey and John, did not hold lands within Henry the Younger's proposed inheritance for which he might do homage. Brittany was probably regarded as a dependency of Normandy, but in addition to this Geoffrey held the earldom of Richmond in England. Similarly John was to be earl of Gloucester as well as king of Ireland.

After refusing to do homage to his brother, Richard withdrew from the royal court, and, says Roger of Howden, 'returned in haste to his own territory and fortified his castles and towns'.[1]

The sequel to Richard's sudden departure is diversely reported by the chroniclers. In Ralph of Diceto's version, the king 'incandescent from the heat of anger' commanded his son 'to curb Richard's pride'.[2] But according to Roger of Howden, Henry the Younger besought his father to make peace between Richard and the barons of Aquitaine, and Henry II promised that they should have peace as had been proposed the previous summer: 'that reparation should be made for excesses on either side, or, if this was not pleasing to the barons, he would judge them according to the verdict of his court'. The Young King then sought, and gained, his father's permission to go to Aquitaine to bring the barons to terms.[3] Henry the Younger's pose as a peacemaker, however, was a sham: he sent his wife off to Paris where she would be safe, and as soon as he reached Aquitaine he 'secretly accepted security from the counts and barons that they would faithfully serve him as their lord and would not depart from his service'.[4]

A sympathetic understanding, and possibly even a covert alliance, between the Young King and the barons of Aquitaine had probably already existed for several years. In 1176, when he had been sent by his father to help in the pacification of Aquitaine, he had struck up a friendship with those who had supported his cause in the great war. He had been of no real help to Richard, for, as Roger of Howden says, 'after the capture of Châteauneuf he would stay no longer with his brother, but under the influence of perverse counsel, departed from him'.[5] It was for attempting to send a message to Henry II revealing his son's intrigues with the rebels that Adam of Churchdown was flogged and expelled from the Young King's household.[6] It was probably collusion with the discontented barons that made him so dilatory in going to help his father and brother to suppress them in 1182. As he made his way, slowly, to the scene of battle in Périgord, he had received an enthusiastic welcome from the city of Limoges and had presented to the shrine of St Martial there a banner embroidered 'Henricus Rex'.[7] It is not surprising that the southerners should try to ingratiate themselves with Henry the Younger, little as they knew him

[1] Roger of Howden, *Gesta*, I, 292.
[2] Ralph of Diceto, II, 19; cf. Gervase of Canterbury, I, 304.
[3] Roger of Howden, *Gesta*, I, 296.
[4] *Ibid.*, 292, 296.   [5] *Ibid.*, 121–2.
[6] *Ibid.*, 122–3, and above, p. 582.
[7] Geoffrey de Vigeois, II, 331.

personally, for his reputation appealed to each of the main groups of troublemakers: to the troubadours he was the model of those virtues which held out hope of advancement and enrichment for the *petite noblesse*, and to the greater barons his preoccupation with the fun and games of nobility and lack of concern with real government offered an escape from the disciplinary endeavours of Henry II and Richard. If they did not plant in the Young King's mind the notion that he should disregard his father's plans for the division of the Angevin dominions and take over as sole ruler, they may nevertheless be suspected of fostering it enthusiastically. This may indeed be the 'perverse counsel' to which Roger of Howden cryptically refers. Henry the Younger's opposition to his father's scheme of federation is of course implicit in this situation, despite his solemn oaths to observe it, but it is doubtful if he had a set purpose to challenge it; more probably it was simply something he did not like as the diminution of his dignity and prestige. Henry the Younger was not a man to undertake any task which might prove difficult. Perhaps it was he who insisted that Richard should do homage to himself for Aquitaine, as a simple way of establishing his overlordship without having to work hard for it. But with Richard's refusal to do homage, it became necessary to undermine his brother's authority by encouraging the southerners' defiance of it, and at the same time provide some justification for the flattery on which he thrived.

Henry the Younger's desire to succeed his father not simply as chairman of a federation but as direct overlord of all that Henry II held, may have been feeble, but it was not the only threat to the federal scheme. If Henry the Younger wished to unify the federation, there are indications that Richard wished to dismember it, or at least that he was prepared to fight for undivided control of Aquitaine. Quite apart from his refusal of homage to the Young King and his argument that they were equals, it is only on the assumption that Richard was strengthening his border that the curious affair of the castle of Clairvaux can be satisfactorily explained. As Bertrand de Born had sung with deliberate provocation:

> Between Poitiers and l'Ile-Bouchard and Mirebeau and Loudun and Chinon, someone has dared to build a fair castle at Clairvaux, in the midst of the plain. I should not wish the Young King to know about it or see it, for he would not find it to his liking; but I fear, so white is the stone, that he cannot fail to see it from Mathefelon.[1]

[1] Bertrand de Born, ed. Raynouard, IV, 145-7, ed. Stimming, 69.

It might perhaps have been argued that there was a threat to the security of ducal authority in the region, particularly from the numerous sub-fiefs in the dependency of the viscount of Thouars. But Thouars had been subdued ever since the crushing blows which Henry II dealt to the power and prestige of its viscount in 1158.[1] Furthermore, if his sons cooperated with each other in the maintenance of Angevin rule, as Henry II intended, there was no need for Richard to maintain a military presence in north-eastern Poitou, for the region could easily be dominated by the troops of the garrison at Chinon in Henry the Younger's appanage. The arsenal and treasury at Chinon made it indeed one of the key points in Henry II's strategy for the policing of his dominions. But this, presumably, was the very reason why Richard felt it necessary to build himself a castle, and unfortunately selected a site which encroached, as the Young King alleged, on territories pertaining to the county of Anjou.

The fundamental frailty of Henry II's hopes for the future was revealed in February 1183 with the outbreak of open war between members of the family. When Henry the Younger left the royal court for Aquitaine, ostensibly to act as a mediator, his father followed him with only a small escort, evidently believing in his son's good faith; but when Henry II reached Limoges he was greeted by a shower of arrows one of which actually pierced his cloak.[2] Henry the Younger, who was in the city with Count Aymer and other leaders of the discontented, tried to explain the assault as a misunderstanding, and there followed days of farcical attempts at negotiation, with the king greeted by arrows whenever he approached the town, and his negotiators set upon and ill-treated. The delay in the onset of open warfare is probably attributable in part to the king's reluctance, in spite of the evidence, to believe in his eldest son's treachery, and in part to the need of the rebels for time to organise themselves for resistance. The city of Limoges was lacking fortifications since Richard had demolished its walls, and the time gained by pretence of negotiation was used to throw up ramparts of earth, wood, and stone from hastily demolished churches. Moreover, since Henry II had prudently declined to put lands in the charge of his eldest son, the Young King had few forces, apart from his household

---

[1] Continuatio Beccensis, 319–20, and above, ch. 3, pp. 65, 100.

[2] The account which follows is drawn from Roger of Howden, *Gesta*, I, 296ff.; Geoffrey de Vigeois, I, 332–8. It is not easy to reconstruct in detail the confused campaign from the chronicles; but since the details are of little importance, no attempt has been made here to produce a chronological account. For possible reconstructions *see* Kate Norgate, *Richard the Lionheart*, 50–6; Appleby, *Henry II*, 282–90.

knights, with which to assist his allies – whose own insufficiency in resisting Richard had only too frequently been demonstrated. But if Henry the Younger had few resources for waging war, his brother Geoffrey had the revenues of Brittany with which to hire mercenaries. It was the adherence of Geoffrey to his eldest brother which gave the confederates a sporting chance of bringing the ill-prepared Henry II and Richard to their knees, or at least to favourable terms.

Geoffrey's motives are obscure, but it seems likely that he resented his lowly status as duke of Brittany, and aspired to emulate his eldest brother in deeds of chivalry. As soon as he had been knighted by his father in 1178 he had gone off to join the Young King in seeking the meretricious glory of the tournament field.[1] He probably had more native ability than Henry the Younger, although with as little sense of responsibility. No one speaks well of his character, for he was not endowed with the Young King's graces. To Gerald of Wales he appeared as 'overflowing with words, soft as oil, possessed, by his syrupy and persuasive eloquence, of the power of dissolving the seeming indissoluble, able to corrupt two kingdoms with his tongue; of tireless endeavour, a hypocrite in everything, a deceiver and a dissembler'.[2] Roger of Howden sums it all up in one phrase: 'Geoffrey, that son of perdition'.[3] It was probably Geoffrey's scheming which prepared the ground for the Young King's bid for the lordship of Aquitaine: sent by his father to summon the barons to a conference at Mirebeau for the resolution of their discontents, he had instead, according to Roger of Howden, dissuaded them from attending and formed them into a hostile alliance.[4] He went to join the Young King at Limoges, but also arranged for a massive invasion of Poitou by a force of mercenaries from Brittany. At the same time Aymer of Limoges summoned up mercenaries from the wilds of Gascony (brigands it seems likely from the description given by Geoffrey de Vigeois) and more came in from the north-east, sent by King Philip of France to aid his brother-in-law Henry the Younger.

When, at last, Henry II was brought to recognise the full extent of his sons' treachery, it revived in his mind the terrors of 1173, when his lordship seemed to be collapsing around him, and he sent instructions to England for the immediate arrest of all his possible enemies in a new civil war – among them the earls of Leicester and Gloucester.[5] But his fears were misplaced: there was no flicker of insurgency elsewhere.

---

[1] Roger of Howden, *Gesta*, I, 207.   [2] Gerald of Wales, VIII, 177–9.
[3] Roger of Howden, *Gesta*, I, 297; 'filius proditionis Gaufredus'.
[4] *Ibid.*, 295.   [5] *Ibid.*, 294.

Even Aquitaine did not rise in general revolt behind the ringleaders – the rebels of 1182 – but seemed to dissolve into general disorder under the hordes of undisciplined, plundering mercenaries.[1] Richard dealt with them ruthlessly: while his father mounted a siege of Limoges he himself moved swiftly from one part of his duchy to another and had those he captured drowned, butchered, or blinded, knights being made to suffer hugger-mugger with foot soldiers.[2] As Henry II's own better disciplined and properly led mercenaries began to arrive, the position of the rebels became precarious, so much so that Geoffrey advised his brother to patch up his quarrel with William Marshal, for they could ill do without his valour and experience.[3] The Young King slipped out of Limoges – after robbing the townsfolk and plundering the shrine of St Martial to pay his mercenaries – and went to help the Taillefer brothers of Angoulême in trying to create a diversion by attacking some of Richard's more vulnerable castles. When he tried to return to Limoges the citizens – wiser now – stoned him from the walls, crying 'We will not have this man to rule over us'.[4] He moved off haphazardly through southern Aquitaine, picking up reinforcements brought by the count of Toulouse and the duke of Burgundy and robbing shrines as he went to pay for them, but without any clear military purpose. He caught dysentery; it developed into a fever; and at Martel on 11 June he died. Henry II had been told of his son's illness and of his pleas for forgiveness, but fearing another trick he had kept his distance. The news of the Young King's death was brought to him by a monk of Grandmont as, still maintaining the siege of Limoges, he sheltered from the summer's heat in a peasant's cottage.

The rootlessness of the revolt in Aquitaine was then revealed. The Young King's friends faded away; the count of Toulouse and the duke of Burgundy 'made haste to go about their own business'.[5] Geoffrey slipped back to Brittany. On 24 June Viscount Aymer surrendered Limoges. By the end of the month Henry II had left to follow the cortège of his eldest son to burial at Rouen. Geoffrey made his peace at Angers on 3 July.[6] It was all over, save for Richard's punishment of those who had dared to defy him.

[1] Cf. Gervase of Canterbury, I, 304.

[2] Roger of Howden, *Gesta*, I, 293; Geoffrey de Vigeois, II, 332; cf. Kate Norgate, *Richard the Lionheart*, 51–4.

[3] *Histoire de Guillaume le Maréschal*, lines 6525ff. William Marshal cautiously applied to Henry II for a safe-conduct. [4] Geoffrey de Vigeois, II, 336.

[5] *Ibid.*, 338; Roger of Howden, *Gesta*, I, 301.

[6] Roger of Howden, *Gesta*, I, 302–4, *Chronica*, II, 279–80; Robert de Torigny, 305–6.

H—U

Chapter 16

THE END OF THE REIGN
(c. 1183–1189)

Henry the Younger's death put an end to the insurrection he had stirred up, but it did not put an end to the problem his insurrection had highlighted: the lack of support, where it mattered most, for Henry II's scheme for an Angevin federation.

There is a danger, in using the modern term 'federation' to describe Henry II's scheme, of importing into it a quality of constitutional sophistication which it did not possess. In essence it was simply a form of 'family sharing'. The practice of dividing an inheritance between sons, while at the same time preserving some notion of the integrity of the fief, was familiar in many parts of Henry's dominions. The custom in some places was for the eldest to receive the principal castle – the *caput* from which the fief commonly took its name – and to render the sole homage to the overlord, but to receive from his brothers assistance in supplying the service due from the honor. In other places the custom – rather less common – was for the brothers to take turns in holding the lordship of the honor. Even in those territories, such as England, where the sole succession of the eldest male to fiefs held by military service had become, by the later twelfth century, an inflexible rule, the custom of *parage* – as division of an inheritance was termed – still survived in the practice of dividing an inheritance between co-heiresses.[1] Yet the analogy with *parage* cannot be pressed too closely, for Henry's scheme differed in two respects from its normal principles. First, it did not take the form of an equal division between his sons. Second, it did not take the form of a division between all of his sons: when Henry II announced his tripartite division in 1169 he already had four sons. John – born on 24 December 1167 – being excluded from the equation, received the nickname 'Lackland'.[2] It was not until after the unlooked-

---

[1] It should also be remembered that even if primogeniture was established for the succession to lands held by military service in England, the older practice of *parage* might survive for other forms of tenure; it was, for example, common among peasant holdings in East Anglia and Kent, Homans, 'The rural sociology of medieval England'.   [2] William of Newburgh, I, 146.

for acquisition, in 1171, of an additional lordship in Ireland that Henry felt able to provide adequately for his youngest son. Why Henry II should, in considering the succession, have abandoned the principle of primogeniture (a principle which he fostered assiduously in the law of his dominions), while at the same time failing to embrace the principles of *parage*, is a puzzle which needs an explanation. The very fact of John's exclusion in 1169 suggests that there was a clear rationale behind the tripartite division, although what it was is not discussed in any surviving chronicle. It is tempting to suggest that Henry II astutely recognised that the unification of the diverse dominions which had been gathered fortuitously under his rule could never be a practical possibility, and that the tripartite division reflected his appreciation that his dominions fell into three distinct parts, each capable of forming a politically viable entity. But such an argument is not very plausible. It is weakened by the proposed union in Henry the Younger's hands of England, Normandy, and greater Anjou, which as a viable political entity had little to recommend it: later history was to show that even half a century of common Angevin rule was insufficient to prevent such a union readily falling apart. A more plausible explanation of the tripartite division is that Henry argued that England, Normandy, and greater Anjou – his own inheritance – must be passed on to his eldest son *de jure hereditario*, but that the dependency of Brittany, and the separate inheritance of his wife in Aquitaine, could, in their unruliness and distinctive social customs, be a liability to anyone who tried to combine all together – as his own experience showed – and that each was best hived off to someone who could devote his full attention to its peculiar problems. By 1177 Henry had come to realise that Ireland too demanded similar treatment as a peculiar problem, and hence proposed committing it to John. At the same time he seems to have believed that the strength of the Angevin commonwealth rested on the possibility of concentrating the resources of all its parts wherever they were most needed, and hence tried to provide for cooperative endeavour by a scheme of oath-takings which by 1183 had hardened into homage.

Whatever the explanation for the division – and there is room for speculation – there was a strong enough reason behind it for Henry II to remain wedded to it with an obstinacy which tried to override all objections. There were at least three weaknesses in the proposal from the beginning: it assumed the acceptance by his sons of the apportionment, it assumed their cooperation after the removal of his own overlordship, and it assumed their survival to establish dynasties. The events of 1182–3 seriously called into question the first two assumptions, and the death of the Young King without an heir demolished the third assumption.[1]

When his grief over the death of his eldest son had subsided, Henry tried in 1184 to rescue his scheme by abandoning an intention which had not yet been realised, that of making John lord of Ireland. At Michaelmas 1183 he required Richard to hand over Aquitaine to John and to receive his homage for it. The implication is clear, although unexpressed by the chronicler who records the meeting, that Richard, now the oldest surviving son, should step into the shoes of Henry the Younger. Richard begged for two or three days in which to take the advice of his friends; but then, withdrawing from the court without permission, he mounted his horse at nightfall and rode with all speed for Poitou, sending back word to his father that he would never concede that anyone should hold Aquitaine except himself.[2] Throughout the winter of 1183–4 Henry tried to persuade Richard to change his mind, but the reply was always the same: he would never while he lived surrender Aquitaine or even a part of it. In a burst of anger Henry told John to take an army into Aquitaine and fight his brother for it.[3] This – like the impatient, drastic response made to announcements of Becket's obstinacy – was not intended to be taken seriously: John had no army at his command, and his father did not give him one. Instead Henry went about his other pressing business, acting as mediator in the strife between the young King Philip of France and the count of Flanders, and, as soon as he had arranged a truce between them, sailed for England which he had not visited for over two years. But with the father safely out of the way, John formed a league with his brother Geoffrey, and in August 1184 they invaded Poitou with forces from Brittany. Roger of Howden says that they had 'collected a great army', but their attack seems to have been little more than a raid for they merely 'burned towns and carried off booty'. Any hopes that they may have entertained of a rising of the barons of Aquitaine to throw off Richard's yoke were disappointed. Richard retaliated by raiding Brittany. Henry peremptorily ordered all his sons to join him in England, and they remained with him until the end of the year.[4] Most of the chroniclers ignore these family squabbles, and, indeed, were it not for Roger of Howden's assiduous garnering of bits of 'news', whether or not he understood their significance, nothing at all would be known of them.

---

[1] A son was born to Henry the Younger and Margaret in June 1177 and christened William, but he died within three days; some said it was a premature birth, Roger of Howden, *Gesta*, I, 177.

[2] *Ibid.*, 308.   [3] *Ibid.*, 311.   [4] *Ibid.*, 311–12, 319.

The squabbles themselves would indeed be barely worthy of notice, were it not that they reveal Henry's persistent failure to resolve satisfactorily the problem of the succession, a problem which in the end was to overwhelm him.

At the close of a meeting of the great council at Westminster early in December 1184 the king, says Roger of Howden, 'made peace between his sons'; but it is doubtful if this was anything more than a public gesture of reconciliation.[1] Nothing, apparently, was said to clarify uncertainties about the succession; and the discussions, arguments, and concessions which went on behind the attempt to put a decent face on dissension remain dark, although something of their nature may be deduced from the sequel. A concession made by Henry soon stood revealed, for extensive preparations were put in hand for sending John to Ireland in the spring and for setting him up there as king – a clear indication that Henry had set aside his proposal that John should replace Richard in Aquitaine.[2] Richard himself was suffered to return to the province he refused to relinquish shortly after Christmas.[3] Geoffrey, however, was, in the words of Roger of Howden, sent 'into Normandy with the other custodians to hold it in custody'.[4] Behind this totally unexplained and puzzling statement there may be a perfectly innocent intention, but it strongly suggests that Henry was contemplating putting his second son into the place vacated by Henry the Younger. Alternatively it may be supposed that he was threatening his oldest son that this would be the corollary to Richard's refusal to surrender Aquitaine. Geoffrey could not be removed from Brittany because he was married to its heiress, but the union of Brittany with the inheritance of the father would make better sense than the permanent union of Aquitaine with Normandy, Anjou, and England; indeed Brittany was already a dependency of Normandy. That Richard, at least, read some such intention into Geoffrey's appointment as *custos* is revealed by another piece of 'news' recorded only by Roger of Howden: when, he says, Henry returned to Normandy in the following April, 'he gathered a large army to wage war on his son Richard, who had fortified Poitou against him, and had waged war on his brother Geoffrey, against his prohibition'.[5]

Henry's response to this latest and menacing piece of insubordination

[1] *Ibid.*, 320.

[2] Gerald of Wales, V, 359; Roger of Howden, *Gesta*, I, 311, 339, *Chronica*, II, 303.

[3] Roger of Howden, *Gesta*, I, 333–4.

[4] *Ibid.*, 320–1: 'rex . . . misitque Gaufridum filium suum in Normanniam cum caeteris custodibus ad custodiendum eam'.   [5] *Ibid.*, 337.

was to deprive Richard of Aquitaine by a stratagem. He brought over Queen Eleanor from England (where she had been kept in seclusion ever since the great war) and sent word to Richard that, 'he should without delay render up to Queen Eleanor the whole of Aquitaine with its appurtenances, since it was her inheritance, and that if he declined to comply, he should know for certain that his mother the queen would take the field with a large army to lay waste his land'. Richard, adds Howden, 'heeded the wise advice of his friends, and laying aside the weapons of wickedness, returned with all meekness to his father; and the whole of Aquitaine with its castles and fortifications he rendered up to his mother'.[1] But although he had now prised Richard loose from Aquitaine, Henry did not announce any reapportionment of his territories; indeed his policy from 1185 seems to have been to keep his sons uncertain about their future. It was not an easy policy to sustain, and a year later, at a conference with King Philip of France at Gisors, on 10 March 1186, Henry was obliged to behave as if Richard was undoubtedly to succeed him in his own inheritance. The conference ratified an amicable settlement about tenure of the Vexin – the dowry which Margaret of France had brought to Henry II when she married Henry the Younger. In consideration of an annuity to be paid to the widow, Philip agreed to transfer the dowry to her sister Alice, who had been betrothed to Richard as long ago as 1161 and held in Henry's custody ever since. Henry was allowed to retain possession of the Vexin on his oath that Richard and Alice would be married. Philip then swore that he would not henceforth raise the issue of the Vexin 'against the king of England, nor against Richard his son, nor against their heirs'.[2] Henry made no move to have the marriage solemnised, nor to have Richard crowned as joint-king; but the implications of the agreement at Gisors were clear – clear enough, at least to Geoffrey, who saw hopes of acquiring Normandy slipping away. Notorious rumour had it that he tried to bargain privately with King Philip, offering him the homage of Brittany and boasting that he would lay Normandy waste.[3]

Meanwhile John's expedition to Ireland had been a dismal failure: he mismanaged his men and his money, and alienated both the native Irish and the Anglo-Norman settlers. With the money gone and the

[1] Roger of Howden, *Gesta*, I, 337–8. Before leaving the continent for England in April 1186, Henry appointed his own custodians to the surrendered castles, Ralph of Diceto, II, 40.

[2] *Ibid.*, 40; Roger of Howden, *Chronica*, II, 308, *Gesta*, I, 343–4.

[3] Roger of Howden, *Gesta*, I, 350; Gerald of Wales, VIII, 175–6; William of Newburgh, I, 235.

mercenaries deserted, he retreated to England in December 1185.[1] He blamed his failure on the machinations of Hugh de Lacy, lord of Meath, who had been justiciar of Ireland until John's arrival. There is some plausibility in the charge, for Hugh de Lacy probably had ambitions to establish an ascendancy in Ireland which would be submerged if the plan to make John king took effect; but there can be little doubt that the prime cause of John's discomfiture was his own folly. He returned to England still uncrowned. The papacy's approval was needed for the creation of new kingdoms, and Henry's application to Rome had to wait upon the election of a new pope in December 1185. Permission, and a crown of peacock feathers, did not reach England until long after John had returned home.[2] In July 1186, however, Hugh de Lacy was assassinated, and Henry was on the point of sending John over again when news arrived of the death of his son Geoffrey at Paris. He had been fatally wounded while engaging in a tournament.[3] John was hastily recalled from embarkation, and no more was to be heard of his coronation as king of Ireland, for John had now become the sole counter to Richard in Henry's game of keeping his sons in uncertainty about his intentions.[4]

For two years Henry's tactic was successful in obliging Richard to behave as a dutiful son, but it was a dangerous tactic. Mounting rumours and suspicions generated by Henry's well-known partiality for his youngest born were in the end to drive Richard to challenge his father to a fatal showdown. John, at eighteen, appeared to contemporaries as a foppish waster, with a propensity for imitating the less estimable traits of his older brothers, but without the charm of Henry the Younger, the courage of Richard, or the plausibility of Geoffrey.[5] Yet Henry II probably believed, as Gerald of Wales did at the time, that John would outgrow his childish levity, and may have detected in his youngest son a personality much more akin to his own than was revealed by any of his other sons. John, despite his manifest faults, was to show later in life a hard realism, a clear grasp of the complexities of politics and government, and a real interest in the mechanism of administration which fitted him much better for the management of a difficult inheritance

---

[1] Orpen, *Ireland under the Normans*, II, 95–108, and above, ch. 4, p. 204.

[2] Pope Lucius III rejected Henry's request, but Pope Urban III was more amenable to solicitation, cf. Roger of Howden, *Gesta*, I, 339.

[3] Roger of Howden, *Gesta*, I, 350; Gerald of Wales, VIII, 176.

[4] It may be observed, however, that in January 1187 papal legates arrived in England 'ad coronandum Johannem filium suum in regem Hiberniae', Roger of Howden, *Gesta*, II, 4.

[5] Gerald of Wales, VIII, 177–9.

than the cold brutality of Richard, who, as Gerald of Wales says 'cared for no success that was not reached by a path cut by his own sword and stained with the blood of his adversaries'.[1] Certainly Henry II seems to have felt for John an affection which he had displayed only for Henry the Younger among his other sons. There is no sign that there was ever much sympathy between Henry II and Richard – respect perhaps, but even this passed into a barely concealed hostility from the time of Richard's repudiation of the proposal that he should give up Aquitaine. Henry II could tolerate opposition, and treat opponents, when he had mastered them, with remarkable generosity; but he could not bear to be thwarted. Richard was Eleanor's favourite, and when she died in 1204 she was buried beside her son instead of her husband.

It is difficult to estimate the effect of the prolonged estrangement of Henry and Eleanor upon the attitudes of their children, and there is only gossip to suggest that even in her enforced seclusion from affairs of state from the time of the great war, she exercised an influence on her sons and wrought through them a vengeance on the husband who had thrust her from power and the privileges of rank. Though closely watched and travelling only on her husband's command, she was not deprived of all contact with her children, and her confinement was somewhat relaxed after 1184; yet she remained to the end of her husband's life his prisoner and not his companion.[2] Contemporaries liked to moralise on the family troubles of Henry II, portraying his unhappy relations with his wife and sons as the inevitable consequence of the bigamy of Eleanor's marriage to Henry after the scandal of her divorce from King Louis, or because they were related in the fifth degree of consanguinity, or as God's judgement on the man who shamefully ill-used St Thomas of Canterbury.[3] Wedded to such moralisings they say little about the real relationships of Henry with Eleanor and their

[1] Gerald of Wales, VIII, 247.

[2] The notices on the pipe rolls of payments for the queen's expenses suggest that she was kept, usually at Winchester, under the guardianship of Ralph FitzStephen, one of Henry II's most trusted officers of the chamber, for at least twelve years. From 1184 she enjoyed visits from her daughter Matilda, the exiled duchess of Saxony, and at Christmas 1184 she was summoned by Henry to join the court at Windsor, together with her sons Richard and John, Roger of Howden, *Gesta*, I, 313, 333, 334. Gervase of Canterbury, I, 326, says that she was released from captivity in 1185 at the plea of Archbishop Baldwin. This is not supported by other sources (and certainly she was in close confinement at the end of the reign, *ibid.*, 454), but she appears more in public in the later years, and was abroad with Henry from May 1185 to April 1186; *see* the notices in Eyton, *Itinerary of Henry II*.

[3] Cf., e.g., Gerald of Wales, VIII, 298–301; William of Newburgh, I, 281; Adam of Eynsham, II, 184.

children, and nothing about the effects on the family of the breakdown of the marriage. Perhaps Henry the Younger was distressed at the treatment of his mother; perhaps Richard resented it and fought his mother's cause in his stubborn opposition to his father's will; it may be so, but equally it may be not. But whatever the cause, the absence of affection and even of simple loyalty in the sons' relations with the father is patent in events. Some of the poignancy of it is conveyed in a story told by Gerald of Wales. In Winchester castle, he says, there was a gaily painted chamber with one blank space left at the king's command. In his later years the king had the space filled with a design of his own specification:

> there was an eagle painted, and four young ones of the eagle perched upon it, one on each wing and a third upon its back tearing at the parent with talons and beaks, and the fourth, no smaller than the others, sitting upon its neck and awaiting the moment to peck out its parent's eyes. When some of the king's close friends asked him the meaning of the picture, he said, 'The four young ones of the eagle are my four sons, who will not cease persecuting me even unto death. And the youngest, whom I now embrace with such tender affection, will someday afflict me more grievously and perilously than all the others.'[1]

Yet too much should not be made of family disunity and the attempts of Henry's sons to anticipate his death and carve up his territories for themselves. Their squabbles loom large in the story of Henry II's later years because there was little else to tell. The years from 1182 to 1187 were in fact years of comparative peace and tranquillity, with the bickering of his sons little more than a distressing undercurrent in what should have been years of repose for Henry, basking in the honour universally paid to him. Much of the passion which had torn the family asunder in 1173 and plunged them into civil war had abated by the 1180s. Henry, Gervase of Canterbury alleges, had contemplated divorcing Eleanor in 1175, and may have been restrained only by the serious political repercussions it could have caused.[2] But the great love of his life, Rosamund Clifford, with whom he had lived openly since the great war, died about 1176, and although Henry undoubtedly took mistresses after her death there was no one to match her in his affections or threaten to depose Eleanor as his wife.[3] Queen Eleanor began to

[1] Gerald of Wales, VIII, 295–6.
[2] Gervase of Canterbury, I, 256–7; cf. Gerald of Wales, VIII, 232.
[3] Rosamund was interred before the altar in the nunnery of Godstow. In 1191 the tomb was still covered with silken cloths and tended by the nuns in accordance with Henry's benefaction. Bishop Hugh of Lincoln ordered the removal of the body to the

appear again in public from 1184, and after she had been taken over to Normandy in April 1185 to receive the surrender of Aquitaine from Richard, she remained on the continent with her husband until his return to England in April 1186.[1] Her restoration to queenly dignity was precarious, and after Richard's final break with his father it seems that she was once again strictly confined; but the relaxation of her captivity for a few years is evidence that the wound had grown less sore.

The passion generated by the conflict with Becket too had abated, and even the enforcement of the 'customs', which Henry had so craftily salvaged, had become a matter of accepted routine, causing no more than occasional ripples on the smooth surface of the king's relations with his bishops. It must indeed have given Henry some ironical satisfaction that when, in January 1187, he received at London two legates sent by the pope 'to hear and determine ecclesiastical causes', Archbishop Baldwin and his suffragans should have come to him saying that 'nothing but dishonour and detriment could come to the kingdom if the legates were allowed to remain' and suggesting that he should take them with him when he left for Normandy.[2] In just such terms had Archbishop Ralph d'Escures persuaded his grandfather not to allow papal legates into England in 1116.[3]

The great upheavals in law and government were already becoming a matter of history, some of the details of which were uncertain even to royal servants such as Roger of Howden, who served as an itinerant justice in the later years of the reign and gathered texts for incorporation in his chronicles.[4] The last major legislative enactment of the reign was the Assize of the Forest in 1184, and this was little more than a formulation in writing of customs which had long protected the king's rights in the Forest.[5] Its chief importance lay in the fact that it was made

---

cemetery, 'for she was a harlot', Roger of Howden, *Chronica*, III, 167–8. For a possible reference to a mistress of Henry employed in Queen Eleanor's household, *see* Pipe Roll 30 Henry II, 134–5: 'For clothes and hoods and cloaks and for the trimming for two capes of samite and for the clothes of the queen and of Bellebelle, for the king's use, £55 17s, by the king's writ'.

[1] *See* the notices in Eyton, *Itinerary of Henry II*.

[2] Roger of Howden, *Gesta*, II, 4.

[3] *See* above, ch. 11, p. 416.

[4] For Roger of Howden acting as an itinerant justice, *see*, e.g., Pipe Roll 33 Henry II, 88. Roger, though a sober and industrious chronicler, could be guilty of misconception and carelessness, cf., e.g., above, pp. 204 n. 1, 290–1, 295.

[5] A text incorporating elements from differing MS. versions is printed in Stubbs, *Select Charters*, 186–8, and a translation in *English Historical Documents*, II, 418–19. Both the text and the date, as given by Roger of Howden, *Gesta*, I, 323, have been challenged by Richardson and Sayles, *The Governance of Medieval England*, 444–8, *Law and*

'with the advice and assent of the archbishops, bishops, barons, earls, and magnates of England', and thereby converted arbitrary royal will into the certainties of acknowledged law. Forest law did not in consequence lose any of its unpopularity, but in securing assent Henry was perhaps responding to the misgivings of servants such as his treasurer, Richard FitzNigel, who had expressed the view in his *Dialogus de Scaccario* that the custom of the Forest was not true law at all.[1] That Henry could secure at least formal assent to Forest law is a measure of the unchallengeable influence he exercised over the barons in his later years. His sons may have thought to push him aside and take power for themselves, but no one stirred to help them.

Internationally Henry II appeared as the man of peace. From the time that the kings of Castille and Navarre had, in 1177, invited him to act as arbitrator in their boundary dispute, he intervened in affairs outside his own territories only to mediate in others' quarrels. Time and again between 1180 and 1185 he acted as peacemaker between Count Philip of Flanders and King Philip of France, patiently arranging truces and trying to find a basis for compromise in a quarrel which was ever finding fresh grievances or resurrecting old ones to feed upon.[2] He mediated in the famous quarrel between Emperor Frederick Barbarossa and Henry the Lion duke of Saxony, and even for a while secured Duke Henry's recall from exile.[3] The duke, the husband of Henry II's daughter Matilda, spent his exile at the court of his father-in-law; Queen Eleanor was allowed to enjoy the pleasure of her daughter's company, and even Bertrand de Born admitted that the presence of Duchess Matilda added sparkle and gaiety to a court which normally depressed him by its serious and sober attention to business.[4] Henry II was also a marriage-broker: he arranged for the count of Flanders to marry a sister of the king of Portugal, and he found a queen for Scotland, at the request of King William, in a daughter of the viscount of Beaumont.[5] For King William Henry not merely arranged a marriage but provided

---

Legislation, 102, 128–30. The evidence of the pipe rolls, however, strongly suggests that Howden was correct in attributing an Assize of the Forest to 1184. *See* also, Holt, 'The Assizes of Henry II: the texts'.

[1] *See* above, ch. 10, pp. 394–5.

[2] Cf. Roger of Howden, *Gesta*, I, 247, 277, 285–6, 311–12, 334–5.

[3] *Ibid.*, 318–19, 322–3.

[4] Cf. Kate Norgate, *Richard the Lionheart*, 47.

[5] For the marriage of the count of Flanders, *see* Roger of Howden, *Gesta*, I, 310; Ralph of Diceto, II, 28–9, the bride was conveyed from Portugal at Henry II's expense, cf. Pipe Roll 30 Henry II, 80, 86–7, 137. For the marriage of the king of Scots, *see* above, ch. 4, p. 186.

the wedding-feast, and made over his palace at Woodstock for the honeymoon. It was a pleasant gesture to a man who twelve years before had been a dangerous enemy in the great war.

Both Scotland and Wales, despite internal troubles which might have led to friction with Henry II, preserved peace with England. The feuding of Welsh and Normans in south Wales threatened to lead to a more general war in 1184, and Henry was obliged, on his return to England after an absence of more than two years, to gather an army; but Rhys of Deheubarth hastened to meet him at Worcester, did homage and made peace.[1] In Scotland the lords of Galloway tried to involve the king of England in their attempts to preserve their independence of the king of Scots, but Henry, using his authority as overlord, cooperated with William the Lion in bringing them to order.[2]

But the most signal acknowledgement – in the eyes of contemporaries – of Henry II's prestige and influence was the offer to him in 1185 of the throne of Jerusalem. Patriarch Heraclius of Jerusalem journeyed to England and at Reading on 29 January 1185 laid at his feet the banner of the kingdom, the keys to the city of Jerusalem, the keys of the Tower of David, and the keys to the Holy Sepulchre. The imminent peril of the Holy Land was explained: King Baldwin IV was a leper and near to death, his heir-apparent, his nephew, a mere child; the crusading states urgently needed a strong hand and inspiring leadership to save them from the power and daring of Saladin. Henry despatched summonses to all who owed him homage in England, to William king of Scots, to David his brother, to the bishops and abbots, earls and barons, commanding them to set aside all other business and attend him at London on 10 March to discuss so important a matter.[3] The council, meeting at the house of the knights of St John of Jerusalem at Clerkenwell, deliberated for a week. In response to King Henry's request for advice on whether he should take up the offer conveyed by the patriarch, the barons reminded the king of his coronation oath in which was set forth his duty to preserve peace for his people both clergy and lay, to put down crime and wickedness, and to secure justice. And so they said, according to Ralph of Diceto, that 'it seemed better to all of them, and much for the safety of the king's soul, that he should govern his kingdom with due care and protect it from the intrusion of foreigners and from external enemies, than that he should in his own person

[1] Roger of Howden, *Gesta*, I, 314; Gervase of Canterbury, I, 309.

[2] Roger of Howden, *Gesta*, I, 67, 80, 126, 336, 339, 348–9.

[3] *Ibid.*, 335–6, *Chronica*, II, 299–301; Gervase of Canterbury, I, 325; Ralph of Diceto, II, 32–3, Gerald of Wales, VIII, 202–6.

seek the preservation of the easterners'.[1] They suggested instead that he should consult with the king of France about the despatch of a crusade to the Holy Land, and many, indeed, on their own account took the Cross at the hands of the patriarch.[2] Henry conferred with King Philip and they promised to aid the Holy Land in men and in money. The patriarch departed in bitter disappointment: 'Almost all the world,' he is reputed to have said, 'will offer us money, but it is a prince we need; we would prefer a leader even without money, to money without a leader.'[3]

Gerald of Wales relates that in the interval before the council met at Clerkenwell, he himself approached the king one day while he was hunting, and told him how honoured he should feel at the embassy of the patriarch. King Henry replied: 'If the patriarch or anyone else comes to us, it is because they are seeking their own advantage rather than ours.'[4] Gerald, with his customary insensitivity and predisposition to think the worst of the Angevins, assumed from this dismissive remark that Henry had no intention of rendering help to the Holy Land. But this assumption, and suggestions that the deliberation at Clerkenwell was a charade played out for the patriarch's benefit, are alike unwarranted. Roger of Howden reveals that as early as 1176, when the leper king, Baldwin IV, first ascended the throne, Henry II tried to persuade Count Philip of Flanders to defer his proposed pilgrimage to the Holy Land, fearing that he had designs upon the crown of Jerusalem, 'since the king of England then proposed to go to Jerusalem himself, or to send knights and soldiers to defend the king of Jerusalem, his kinsman'.[5] Baldwin was descended from Henry II's grandfather, Count Fulk V of Anjou, by his second marriage to Melisende, heiress of King Baldwin II of Jerusalem. It was in order to facilitate his withdrawal from Anjou that Count Fulk had sought to make peace with King Henry I and had married his son Geoffrey to Matilda of England. After his marriage to Melisende, Fulk himself became king of Jerusalem from 1131–43.[6] He died when Henry was ten years old. It would not have been surprising if Henry II, having achieved the task he set himself of recovering

---

[1] Ralph of Diceto, II, 33–4; Gervase of Canterbury, I, 325; Gerald of Wales, VIII, 208–9.

[2] Roger of Howden, *Gesta*, I, 336–7, *Chronica*, II, 302.

[3] So says Gerald of Wales, VIII, 208, who was doubtless putting words into the patriarch's mouth, but the sentiments are confirmed by Roger of Howden, *Chronica*, II, 304, *Gesta*, I, 338.

[4] Gerald of Wales, VIII, 207.   [5] Roger of Howden, *Gesta*, I, 116.

[6] Cf. Kate Norgate, *England under the Angevin Kings*, I, 245–8; Runciman, *History of the Crusades*, II, 177–8, and 178 n.1.

and securing the inheritance of one of his grandfathers, Henry I, king
of England, should have thought of ending his life in emulation of his
other grandfather, Fulk, king of Jerusalem. But however tempting the
patriarch's offer might be, the timing of it was unfortunate. It was
immediately before the patriarch's arrival that Henry had to summon his
warring sons to England, and arrange a formal reconciliation before the
council, which probably deceived no one. The question of the succession

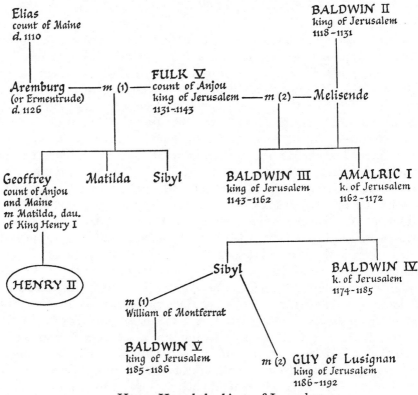

13. Henry II and the kings of Jerusalem

was impaled upon their disloyalty and dissension. In the weeks before
the deliberations of the barons at Clerkenwell, Richard was making war
on Geoffrey.[1] It is understandable that the barons should have feared
that the Angevin inheritance would dissolve into chaos if the strong
hand of the father was removed.

Henry II could not, with propriety, have abdicated in 1185 to take
up the throne of Jerusalem; and it was unthinkable too that he should
allow any of his sons to take up the offer, as the patriarch suggested,

[1] *See* above, p. 597.

while the problem of a satisfactory division of the Angevin dominions remained unresolved.[1] Nevertheless, abdication was one thing, and a crusade quite another, and it was still possible that Henry might lead an expedition to the Holy Land. The moment for it was chosen for him. After the death of Baldwin V, the kingdom of Jerusalem passed under the care of his brother-in-law, Guy of Lusignan, but against bitter hostility from those who despised him as an upstart king-consort. It was a disunited and quarrelsome army which he led to a disastrous defeat at the Horns of Hattin on 3 July 1187. King Guy, and the Holy Cross, fell into the hands of Saladin. In October Jerusalem itself surrendered. Europe stood horrified by the news which swept across it at the close of the year. Richard took the Cross, impetuously, in November; King Henry and King Philip, after more mature deliberation, on 21 January 1188.[2] The king's purpose was entirely serious: one of his *familiares*, Richard Barre, was despatched with letters to the emperor of Germany, the king of Hungary, and the emperor at Constantinople requesting safe passage through their territories and a supply of victuals. The barons of Henry's continental dominions were summoned to a meeting at Le Mans before the end of January, and those of England to a meeting at Geddington, to hear and approve the measures agreed upon by the two kings for promoting the crusade. These fell into two parts; the levying of a tax of the tenth of the value of all moveable property and revenues upon all those who did not themselves take the Cross – a tax soon known as the 'Saladin Tithe' – and secondly a group of miscellaneous ordinances governing the conduct of the crusaders and their privileges, receiving proceeds of the tax and escaping the normal requirements of the law in matters of debt and mortgage. The regulations were detailed and carefully drawn: categories of exemption and the methods of assessment and collection were specified, games of chance were banned, and sumptuary laws imposed, women were forbidden on the crusade save for 'laundresses of good reputation', debts incurred by crusaders were not to bear interest during the duration of the crusade.[3] Enthusiasm for taking the Cross was widespread, but the levying of the Saladin Tithe incurred bitter hostility because of its

[1] John, according to Gerald of Wales, VIII, 208–9, begged on his knees to be allowed to go to the Holy Land; but he was destined at that moment for Ireland.

[2] Roger of Howden, *Gesta*, II, 29–30; Ralph of Diceto, II, 50; William of Newburgh, I, 271–2; Gervase of Canterbury, I, 389, 406; Gerald of Wales, VIII, 239; Rigord, I, 83–4.

[3] Roger of Howden, *Gesta*, II, 30–2; Gervase of Canterbury, I, 409–10; William of Newburgh, I, 273–4.

novelty, its heavy incidence, its merciless assessment, and because many, churchmen in particular, feared it as a precedent for a new form of taxation. King Philip indeed was obliged to suspend its collection in France, and even to apologise for having proposed it.[1] But for Henry's subjects there was no remission – a manifest demonstration of the greater power and authority of the English monarchy.[2] An advance party of English crusaders travelling by sea put out from Dartmouth on 18 May 1189.[3] But Henry II was not to follow them or to see the Holy Land: before he could set out he was overtaken by humiliation and death.

To some contemporaries it seemed incredible that Henry's intention to crusade should have been hindered and deflected by his fellow-crusaders, King Philip and Richard. To some it seemed that Henry was the innocent victim of Philip's ill-will, which picked unnecessary quarrels over minor border problems and cozened Richard into betraying his father by filling him with fears about the succession. To some, Henry brought trouble upon himself by his shabby treatment both of his son and of his overlord in France.[4] The truth is less clear-cut than either of these interpretations.

Since the late 1170s Henry II had been able to impose his will on almost every situation which concerned him. His most dangerous opponents were dead or cowed; he had established a secure domination over his barons; he had manœuvred the Church into accepting a concordat which effectively protected his interests; he had the resources to carry out any of his intentions. Obstacles to his will had all been outflanked, worn down, or pushed into the ground. His sons were troublesome but they could be controlled. His achievement seems to have lulled him into a false sense of security. He ignored warning signs of trouble, brushed aside criticism which earlier would have alerted his defences, and minimised problems which grew into crises. He became obstinate when earlier he would have been flexible or devious. And from 1186 he encountered an obstacle to his will in King Philip II of France – Philip Augustus as his panegyrists were to call him. Philip was a dogged and determined opponent, as wily and slippery as Henry

---

[1] *Recueil des Actes de Philippe Auguste*, no. 252.

[2] Mitchell, *Taxation in Medieval England*, 119–21. For the methods of assessing and collecting the tax, and for the protests, *see* above, ch. 10, pp. 377–8.

[3] They stopped on the way to help the king of Portugal, Ralph of Diceto, I, 65–6.

[4] For widely differing opinions, cf. William of Newburgh, I, 276–7, and Gerald of Wales, VIII, 244, 250–1, 255. Newburgh's account is based on a false assumption of a sudden rupture in 1188 – the difficulties went much further back and much deeper. Gerald's analysis is vitiated by his blind prejudice against Henry II which distorts even the most obvious facts of the situation.

himself, and, which made him dangerous, with enough power to refuse either to be browbeaten or ignored by the king of England.

Philip's opposition was all the more unexpected in that Henry had taken the precaution of cultivating good relations with him. Henry had, of course, an ulterior motive in the protection of his realms from the kind of subversion practised by Louis VII; but it was an honest and open motive, and Henry's dealings with Philip had from the first been touched with magnanimity. From the time of the Treaty of Ivry in 1177 – renewed with Philip in 1180 – he had done nothing to harm the Capetian monarchy. The Young King had been sent to represent him at the coronation of Philip in 1179 and had carried the crown in procession – much to the alarm of Ralph of Diceto, who feared it might prejudice the status of the Angevin kings.[1] In 1183 at Gisors Henry did homage and fealty to Philip 'for all his holdings across the water' in the words of Roger of Howden, who adds, 'for which he had never previously wished to do homage'.[2] In the struggle for control of the young King Philip between his mother's family of Blois and the count of Flanders, Henry had behaved with rectitude and generosity, offering disinterested mediation and help.[3] He had sent his sons to help Philip in a threat of war with Flanders in 1181, and to help him subdue the rebellious count of Sancerre.[4] It is said that in 1181 Philip took the advice of Henry II in preference to that of his friends and his uncles when dealing with rebellious barons; and he demonstrated his respect for Henry's honest intentions by inviting him to arbitrate in his disputes with Flanders in 1184 and 1185.[5] That Henry had achieved his objective in trying to remove the fear and suspicion which had long bedevilled relations with his overlord in France seemed to be demonstrated in the delicate negotiations over the dowry of Henry the Younger's widow. Philip naturally reclaimed the Vexin as Margaret's dowry, but after amicable negotiations, allowed himself to be persuaded to accept a money compensation, in the form of an annuity payable to Margaret instead.[6] In November 1185, when Henry lay sick at Belveir, Philip visited him and stayed three days.[7] Nevertheless, quite suddenly, in the

---

[1] Ralph of Diceto, I, 438–9; cf. Rigord, I, 13, and see above, ch. 5, p. 227.

[2] Roger of Howden, *Gesta*, I, 306, and above, ch. 5, p. 227.

[3] e.g. Ralph of Diceto, II, 8–9; Gerald of Wales, VIII, 188–90.

[4] Ralph of Diceto, II, 9; Gervase of Canterbury, I, 297.

[5] Roger of Howden, *Gesta*, I, 284, 311–12, 334.

[6] *Ibid.*, 304, 305, 306; Ralph of Diceto, II, 40. Margaret quitclaimed her dowry for 2,750 pounds of Angevin money annually, *Catalogue des Actes de Philippe Auguste*, no. 124; *Recueil des Actes de Henri II*, II, 275–7.

[7] Ralph of Diceto, II, 38.

later months of 1186, shortly after the death of Henry's son Geoffrey, these seemingly good relations broke down. King Philip peremptorily demanded that Geoffrey's daughters be placed in his wardship and that Brittany be surrendered into his hand. He further demanded that Richard should be made to withdraw from the county of Toulouse which he was accused of invading. If these demands were not met Philip threatened to invade Normandy. This challenge to Angevin control of two provinces over which Henry had with difficulty established his claims to overlordship was alarming. Henry sent three of his most senior counsellors to Paris – Ranulf Glanvill his justiciar, William de Mandeville, earl of Essex, and Walter of Coutances, archbishop of Rouen – but it was only with greatest difficulty that they were able to persuade Philip to a temporary truce.[1]

Philip was later to display an open and consuming determination to destroy Angevin rule in the kingdom of France, and even in the kingdom of England, and it may readily be supposed that it had been bred in him from infancy, dissimulated during the years when he had need of Angevin support, but breaking out of its disguise in 1186. There is, however, no warrant for such an assumption, and it seems more likely that Philip's hostility to the Angevins was of slow growth, and did not reach the level of implacability until after the Third Crusade. Nevertheless, there are grounds for believing that Philip's apparent accord with Henry II from 1180 to 1186 was something of an illusion, and that any substance there was in it derived not from Henry II's gestures of friendship, but from a sympathetic understanding with his sons, Henry the Younger and Geoffrey. Both of them were dead by 1186, and the underlying fear of Angevin domination at the French court once more revealed itself. It had been easier for the French monarchy to preserve good relations with the Angevins while it could be confidently assumed that within a few years the lands under Henry II's control would pass to his easy-going eldest son, Henry the Younger, the husband of King Philip's sister, Margaret. Indeed the policy of the French court may well have been sustained by the expectation of a close alliance between the families, which could help to solve the problem of making the authority of the monarchy effective in all parts of France. It is not without significance that Philip sent mercenaries to help Henry the Younger in his struggle against Richard and his father in 1183, for it was in the interests of the French king that his brother-in-law should succeed to the whole of Henry II's dominions.[2] The death of the Young

[1] Ralph of Diceto, II, 43–4; Roger of Howden, *Gesta*, I, 353.
[2] Geoffrey de Vigeois, II, 333–4.

King without heirs of his body effectively destroyed the prospects of such an alliance, although hope may briefly have been kept alive by the friendship of Geoffrey. Hence Philip's conspiracy with Geoffrey when he aspired to more than the duchy of Brittany. At Geoffrey's sudden death the young Philip, it is said, was inconsolable, and could only with difficulty be restrained from throwing himself into the open grave with the body of his friend.[1] With the departure of both Henry the Younger and Geoffrey, the one possibility of contriving an alliance between the Capetian and Angevin families lay in the marriage of Richard to Philip's other sister Alice. Hence, it may be presumed, Philip's readiness to indulge Henry II's desire to retain control of the widowed Margaret's dowry on condition that Richard's marriage to Alice was incorporated in the agreement.

It is doubtful if Henry appreciated the importance which the marriage of Richard and Alice assumed after the death of his eldest son: certainly he did nothing either to have them married or to reassure Philip that they soon would be married. Why Richard was not married to Alice is one of the minor mysteries of Henry II's reign. They had been betrothed in 1161 as part of the peace arranged at Fréteval, and Alice had ever since been in Henry's care, although little was heard of her. Rumour said that Richard would not marry her because his father had made her his mistress; but the rumour comes from prejudiced sources and finds no support in French chronicles.[2] It is more probable that Richard simply had no desire to marry her and maintained his reluctance with his customary obstinacy. Henry was unlikely to press the matter while Alice brought nothing of substance, and in 1184 he promoted a scheme for marrying Richard to a German princess. Richard would have none of this either, for about the same time he seems to have formed an attachment to Berengaria of Navarre, whom eventually, after his father's death, he married.[3] Henry had frequently promised the French king that Richard would marry Alice, but without any serious intent, and to him the renewal of the promise in February 1186 was probably no more than a diplomatic formality. Indeed to him the device of regarding the Vexin as the dowry of a Capetian bride was no more than a convenient fiction: in his eyes the 'Norman' Vexin rightfully belonged to him anyway, and the attempt of the French king

---

[1] Gerald of Wales, VIII, 177.

[2] *Ibid.*, 232. The rumour is referred to by William the Breton in his verse history, Philippidos, II, 89, but not in his chronicle.

[3] Roger of Howden, *Gesta*, I, 319, *Chronica*, II, 288; Kate Norgate, *Richard the Lionheart*, 64 and n.4. Richard married Berengaria in 1191.

to treat it as the dowry of Margaret or Alice was fundamentally irrelevant, to be tolerated only because it saved him the trouble of waging war for it. On the other side, however, Philip's increasing conviction of Henry's bad faith over the marriage contributed materially to the breakdown of relations between them: by the spring of 1187, Philip was demanding the return of both Alice and the Vexin.[1] In addition, it is probably not without significance that the deaths of Henry the Younger and Geoffrey coincided with the recovery of influence at the French court of Philip's uncles of the house of Blois, and in particular of Archbishop William of Rheims, who were doubtless still as eager to exploit any grievance against Henry II as they had been to exploit the exile and martyrdom of Thomas Becket.[2] To set the seal on the hardening of Capetian policy against the Angevins, King Philip's wife gave birth in 1187 to a son and heir.

The seriousness, for Henry II, of this shift in attitude at the French court was enhanced by developments in the strength and authority of the French monarchy. The evidence is too scanty for the increase in the resources of the French Crown to be charted with any certainty, but it seems likely that by the time Philip had the main thoroughfares of Paris paved in 1186, the possibility of the city's becoming in a real sense the capital of France was no longer a mere dream.[3] Undoubtedly the gap between the resources of the French and the English kings had narrowed considerably in the years since the great war.[4] Henry's crushing victory had, indeed, turned the attention of the Capetian government from subversion to the consolidation of the royal demesne, and to the expansion of its revenues from land, trade, and royal perquisites. By the time Philip had wrested possession of Vermandois from the count of Flanders (and ironically he did so with Henry's help), and had replaced the *prévôts* of the royal demesne by *baillis* under stricter financial control, he was probably in a position to contemplate exerting his authority against any baron of the realm. That his ability to muster financial resources was still far less than that of Henry II is revealed by his retreat over the Saladin Tithe and by his need in 1180 and 1182 to plunder the Jews

[1] Roger of Howden, *Gesta*, II, 5; Gervase of Canterbury, I, 346; Rigord, I, 77.

[2] Cf. Petit-Dutaillis, *Feudal Monarchy in France and England*, 182, and above, ch. 3, p. 113.

[3] Rigord, I, 53-4, relates that no previous king had dared to undertake the paving of the streets because of the crushing expense; Philip put the work in hand on returning from a victorious expedition into Burgundy.

[4] The conclusion of Pacaut, *Louis VII et son Royaume*, that the Capetians had overhauled the Angevins should be treated with caution; cf. Benton, 'The revenues of Louis VII'.

to raise money; but if his exploitable wealth was less than that of the Angevins, so too were his commitments.[1] Hence the fear engendered by the great war, that in an armed struggle between them Henry was bound to win, had probably greatly diminished, and the French monarchy was becoming ready for another trial of strength with the Angevins.

This readiness should not be attributed simply to hostility, but to the very proper desire of the French Crown to establish its authority over its vassals. The young Philip's struggles with the count of Flanders and the viscount of Sancerre – in which he was aided by the Angevins – were the first signs of a policy which was bound in time to be extended to the Angevins themselves as dukes of Normandy, counts of Anjou, and dukes of Aquitaine. Philip, it is said, imitated Henry II in developing his administration; and he imitated him too in his technique for establishing the authority of the Crown by enforcing rights derived from the principles of feudal lordship, and by developing the royal court as the proper resort for the disputes of his subjects.[2] Hence King Philip's claim to the wardship of Brittany on the death of Geoffrey: it was the corollary to his acceptance from Geoffrey of homage for Brittany in 1186.[3] To Henry the claim was absurd and he ignored it: Geoffrey's homage to Philip was treasonable for the homage was owed to the duke of Normandy.[4] Philip did not gain the wardship of Brittany: in 1187 Henry imposed a guardian by marrying off Geoffrey's widow, Constance, to the young Ranulf de Blundeville, who was both earl of Chester and hereditary viscount of the Avranchin on the borderland of Brittany.[5]

Much more serious, however, as a slight to the dignity of the French Crown than Henry's behaviour over the doubtful allegiance of Brittany, was Richard's feud with the count of Toulouse. The whole vexed question of the relationship of Toulouse to the duchy of Aquitaine was quite properly a matter which the court of the overlord of France might consider; and when, in the summer of 1186, Count Raymond appealed for the help of the king of France, Philip had no real alternative but to

---

[1] Rigord, I, 14–16, cf. Langmuir, ' "Judei nostri" and the beginning of Capetian legislation', 209–10.

[2] Cf. Ralph of Diceto, II, 7–8; Petit-Dutaillis, *op. cit.*, 185ff.

[3] *See* above, p. 598.

[4] The point was in some doubt. Louis VII had, in 1158, during a brief period of harmony, allowed Henry II to claim Brittany as a dependency, but in his capacity as the holder of the vague, honorific, office of seneschal of France (*see* above, ch. 3, pp. 76–8). It is noticeable that in 1186, when accepting Geoffrey's homage, Philip conferred on him the office of seneschal, Gerald of Wales, VIII, 176.

[5] Roger of Howden, *Gesta*, II, 29.

intervene. Just as his father had in the 1150s, he doubtless hoped to extend Capetian influence to the remote south; but even more important than that, he had to entertain the count's appeal if he were to establish the credibility of his court as the forum for disputes of vassals.

The whole problem of Toulouse is unfortunately wrapped in obscurity. Henry II's desire to enforce the claim of Aquitaine to lordship over Toulouse seems to have been satisfied when in 1173 Count Raymond did homage to him at Limoges.[1] But the nature of Count Raymond's homage is not specified in the sources, and it is quite possible that, as in the case of the homage of the leading Welsh princes in 1175, it was a face-saving formula which could be interpreted in different ways and which left the real question of jurisdiction in doubt. Henry could afford to leave it in doubt because, after the ill-success of military campaigns, he had no serious intention of extending his government to either Wales or Toulouse. English chroniclers, it is true, assumed that the county of Toulouse itself was subject to Aquitaine, and always refer to Count Raymond as 'count of St Gilles' – St Gilles being a minor fief from which his family originated; but it is quite likely that the count regarded his acknowledgement of the overlordship of Aquitaine as applying only to certain borderlands which the counts of St Gilles had for long disputed with the counts of Poitiers while they were in process of constructing their respective 'feudal empires'. One of these borderlands was the Cahorsin – the county of Quercy – of which Henry had seized control on his campaign of 1159. Count Raymond probably hoped, as did many others, that it would be possible to recover by friendship with Henry the Younger what had been lost to the determination of Henry the elder; hence his personal assistance to the rebellious Young King in 1183.[2] Whether Count Raymond made a bargain with the Young King is not known, but it seems that during the temporary dislocation of ducal government in Aquitaine he recovered control of castles in Quercy. During the squabbles of Henry's sons this was a problem which received little attention; but in April 1186 King Henry, in the words of Roger of Howden, 'entrusted to his son Richard unlimited funds, bidding him go and subdue his enemies under him; . . . and straightway he collected a great multitude of knights and foot soldiers, with which he invaded the lands of the count of St Gilles and not merely ravaged, but conquered the greater part of them'.[3] Richard, it seems likely, had,

[1] Roger of Howden, *Gesta*, I, 36, *Chronica*, II, 45; Ralph of Diceto, I, 353, *see* above, ch. 3, p. 117.
[2] *See* above, ch. 15, p. 593.
[3] Roger of Howden, *Gesta*, I, 345.

with his usual drastic ruthlessness, deprived Count Raymond not only of his hold on Quercy but also of territories which had never fallen under the direct control of Henry II. The count appealed to King Philip as overlord. Philip's demand in September 1186 that Henry should restrain Richard 'from molesting' Count Raymond was the perfectly proper preliminary to a decision of his court; and his threat that 'Normandy would not be safe from attack' if he failed to comply, was an expression of the perfectly proper, if crude, sanction of an over-lord to harry the land of a disobedient vassal.[1] English chroniclers showed no awareness of the issue of principle involved, but their reports of the high words and threats exchanged indicate that to Philip it was the dignity of the French Crown, and to Henry the untouchability of the Angevin dominions, which were really at stake in the rupture of relations.

The course of the conflict that followed bears a close analogy to a judicial duel. Philip's challenge in September 1186 and its repudiation by Henry were followed by several months of abortive conferences and warlike menaces – just as, in a court case to determine rights, the initial formal challenge and denial were followed by an adjournment before the contest (which was rarely actually fought) during which negotiations were conducted to find a basis for compromise, while the parties paraded their determination and eagerness to fight in an effort to call each other's bluff. So too Philip and Henry paraded their determination. There were skirmishes in the Vexin as border guards encountered each other in warlike array. Henry brought into Normandy mercenaries from the Welsh marches. Philip ordered the arrest of all subjects of the king of England found in his territories; Henry, tit-for-tat, retaliated by arrest-ing all subjects of the French king; but it was a foolish exchange of menaces which hindered trade, and they soon released their prisoners.[2] By May 1187 Philip had decided that it was necessary to take more effective action to demonstrate to the world, and more particularly to his other tenants-in-chief, that he was determined to chastise dis-obedient vassals. He marched into Berry. This was the sensitive march-land where the frontier was indistinct and Capetian rights of lordship met and intermingled with those of the dukes of Aquitaine. He took possession of the castles of Issoudon and Fréteval, the custodians of

---

[1] Ralph of Diceto, II, 43–4. Roger of Howden, *Gesta*, I, 353, seems to have been ignorant of the involvement of Count Raymond and the problem of Tou-louse.

[2] Roger of Howden, *Gesta*, I, 354–6, *Chronica*, II, 315; cf. Pipe Roll 33 Henry II, 40, 63, 131, 215.

which he had already suborned, and laid siege to Châteauroux. Henry brought up massive forces, equally determined to demonstrate the righteousness of his cause. But Philip did not back down and retreat, as Henry might have expected. The fact that fighting did not commence at once is an indication that neither of the kings yet saw the situation as one of open war: it was a test of each other's resolution, a game of bluff and counter-bluff – just the sort of poker-play with which the barons of Aquitaine had sought to test Richard's determination to enforce his rights as overlord. The two armies confronted each other in battle array in the fields before Châteauroux. Again the analogy is with a judicial duel, for this was the counterpart of the confrontation of champions, the pause on the field of combat while mediators made a last effort to compose the dispute. The mediators in this case were the clergy, led by a papal legate Octavian, anxious for the start of the crusade. Both sides tried sly tactics: Henry claimed the privileges of a crusader, and Philip attempted to persuade Richard to desert his father. Mediation failed because neither side could afford to compromise its position: Philip was driven by the exigencies of his stand on the rights of the Crown, and Henry by his refusal to admit that his homage meant that the king of France could dictate to him. There were only two possible sequels to this impasse: to determine the issue by fighting, or to call a truce. They settled for a truce for two years.[1]

Philip, although protesting to his followers his eagerness to fight, was probably glad to accede to the mediators' pleas for a truce because he was not yet sure of winning a war. The Angevins had presented a united front, and their power, when they concentrated their resources, was impressive. The French king was obliged to make a stand in 1187 because his honour was at stake over the Vexin, Brittany, and Toulouse, but he could not yet afford to allow his authority to be put to the test of a trial of strength with Henry II until the odds were stacked more heavily in his favour. His design was to exploit Richard's uneasy relations with his father.

Philip's attempt to suborn Richard at Châteauroux had not entirely succeeded but had revealed the possibility of success. Gervase of Canter-

---

[1] Gervase of Canterbury, I, 369–73; Roger of Howden, *Gesta*, II, 6–7; Ralph of Diceto, II, 49; Rigord, I, 78–9. The account of Gerald of Wales, VIII, 230–2, is garbled. The chroniclers' accounts, though copious, are concerned solely with apparent events; to understand what was really afoot it is necessary to read between the lines. When, for instance, it seemed that Philip might be persuaded by the mediators to consent to allow Henry a crusader's respite from fulfilling his obligations, Henry hastily withdrew his plea – an indication that it was all part of an elaborate game of bluff and counter-bluff.

bury relates that the count of Flanders had been sent into the Angevin camp to sound out Richard:

'Many of us,' he said, 'believe that you are acting extremely foolishly and ill-advisedly in bearing arms against your lord the king of France. Think of the future: why should he be well-disposed towards you, or confirm you in your expectations? Do not despise his youth: he may be young in years, but he has a mature mind, is far-seeing and determined in what he does, ever mindful of wrongs and not forgetting services rendered. Believe those with experience; I too once ranged myself against him, but after wasting much treasure I have come to repent of it. How splendid and useful it would be if you had the grace and favour of your lord.'[1]

Realising the force of the argument, Richard conferred privately with Philip and was instrumental in arranging the truce. And when the armies withdrew from the confrontation Richard went to Paris, where, says Roger of Howden, 'Philip so honoured him that every day they ate from the same dish, and at night the bed did not separate them'. Henry had been alarmed when Richard conferred with Philip at Châteauroux, 'suspecting not peace but perfidy', and was even more dismayed at his visit to Paris, so much so that 'he put off his intention to return to England until he should know the outcome of this sudden friendship'.[2] According to Gerald of Wales, Philip was sowing in Richard's mind the suspicion that his father would disinherit him, and purported to have proof that Henry purposed to marry Alice to John.[3] It certainly seems that Philip succeeded in alarming him, for on leaving Paris Richard ignored his father's request to rejoin him, went instead to the arsenal at Chinon where he supplied himself with money from the treasury, and then set about putting his castles of Poitou in fighting order. Only the most earnest entreaties persuaded him to rejoin Henry's court, relates Roger of Howden, although when he came 'he submitted to his father in all things, and was penitent for having yielded to the evil counsels of those who strove to sow discord between them'.[4]

The news of disasters in the Holy Land and the enthusiasm for the crusade overtook the truce concluded at Châteauroux. It might have been expected to sweep aside all lesser cares, but instead it sharpened the desire of Richard and Philip to settle their unresolved issues with Henry. Richard became insistent on a public declaration of his father's intention about the succession. He was impatient to be off on crusade: he

---

[1] Gervase of Canterbury, I, 370–1.

[2] Roger of Howden, *Gesta*, II, 7; Gervase of Canterbury, I, 371–3.

[3] Gerald of Wales, VIII, 232–3. The details of Gerald's gossip are unworthy of credence.   [4] Roger of Howden, *Gesta*, II, 9.

had taken the Cross without even consulting his father, and begged to be allowed to go on ahead of the main expedition which the mustering of men, transport, and supplies was bound to delay. According to Gerald of Wales, he asked to be allowed to raise money on the security of Poitou, and that 'since he was to undertake a journey which was both long and perilous, and lest anything should be plotted to his disadvantage while he was away, he sought that the king would allow him to receive an acknowledgement of the fealty of the leading men of the kingdom of England, and of the territories beyond the sea which belonged to him by hereditary right, saving in all things the fealty due to his father'. Henry, says Gerald, paid no heed to the request, and insisted that they should go on crusade together.[1]

Richard occupied his impatience in the duchy of Aquitaine, harrying his enemies among the Lusignan family who were alleged to have slain a friend of his. Ralph of Diceto heard and recorded a rumour that Henry secretly assisted the Lusignans in their resistance to Richard, 'who for this cause alienated his mind from his father'.[2] It is possible that Henry, in his devious way, was trying to keep his son busy; but the story may very well be no more than a fabrication – Ralph of Diceto admits that it was gossip (*sicut dicitur*). Gossip and rumour were, however, to play a crucial part in the complete breakdown of confidence between son and father.

Having disposed of the Lusignans and their allies, Richard set about chastising the count of Toulouse for allegedly maltreating Poitevin merchants.[3] The count was almost certainly at fault, and compounded the mischief by seizing two Angevin knights who had been on pilgrimage to St John of Compostella; but Richard, in typically drastic fashion, carried chastisement too far, taking castle after castle and approaching close to the city of Toulouse itself. Count Raymond appealed again for the intervention of his overlord. It was an awkward situation for King Philip. He was reluctant to antagonise Richard and at-

[1] Gerald of Wales, VIII, 244.

[2] Ralph of Diceto, II, 55; reported also by Gerald of Wales, VIII, 245, who says, however, that it was because of Henry's refusal to grant his requests that Richard 'departed from his father in heart as well as body'. For an account of Richard's activities in Aquitaine *see* Roger of Howden, *Gesta*, II, 34.

[3] Ralph of Diceto, II, 55; Roger of Howden, *Gesta*, II, 34; Rigord, I, 90. Gerald of Wales says that Henry stirred up Count Raymond as well as the Lusignans to distract Richard from going to the Holy Land. He does not mention the assassination of Richard's friend or the maltreatment of the merchants. Gerald's account of the last years of Henry II's reign, though heavily drawn upon by many historians, is so blinkered and wildly partisan that it is worthless for the purpose of interpreting events.

tempted first to mediate; and later, when his mediation and been rebuffed, offered that Richard 'should receive his rights and be justly compensated for his wrongs in the court of France'.[1] Cleverly, Philip directed his sternest admonitions at Henry, insisting that Richard should be recalled and amends made to Toulouse, and warning that if not, the truce could no longer be considered binding. Henry at first replied that 'it was not by his counsel or desire that his son had done any of these things, and that he could not justify him'; but then, as he realised that the honour of the Crown of France was again involved, he tried to restrain his son, but in vain. Richard heeded neither commands, entreaties, nor warnings.[2]

In consequence, Philip had no option but to try once more to defend the authority of his court against disobedient vassals, and again, in June 1188, invaded Aquitanian Berry, seizing several castles including Châteauroux. He was careful, however, to confine his harrying to the lands and castles of under-vassals: he avoided besieging castles held by custodians for Henry, presumably in order to avoid making war inevitable.[3] Henry, who was in England making arrangements for the crusade, is reported to have been dismayed, and despatched to Philip a powerful deputation, consisting of the archbishop of Canterbury, the archbishop of Rouen, the bishop of Lincoln, and the earl of Chester, who were, in the words of Gervase of Canterbury, to seek 'any kind of arrangement for the restoration of peace'. Henry followed himself, despite a fierce storm in the Channel, on 11 July, but only to discover from his envoys that Philip was not interested in discussing terms.[4]

Henry's advisers told him, after long deliberations about how to handle the situation, that Philip would respond only to a show of force. So Henry mustered large numbers of troops at Alençon, but kept them in tents in Normandy to avoid the kind of confrontation in which he had, no doubt unexpectedly, found himself involved in 1187.[5] Instead he tried to force Philip to terms by threatening to renounce his fealty, by sending out raiding parties into the marchlands of the Norman border, and by setting Richard to recover what he could in Berry.[6] These tactics discomfited Philip. His challenge had been countered by a threat of serious war and his lands were being ravaged. He had no wish

---

[1] Roger of Howden, *Gesta*, II, 35–6; Gerald of Wales, VIII, 245–6.

[2] Roger of Howden, *Gesta*, II, 36; Rigord, I, 90–1; Gerald of Wales, VIII, 246.

[3] Roger of Howden, *Gesta*, II, 39–40. The connection with Richard's recklessness in Toulouse was clearly appreciated by Ralph of Diceto, II, 55. Rigord, I, 91–2, says that Philip also took border castles in Touraine.

[4] Gervase of Canterbury, I, 432–3.

[5] *Ibid.*, 433–4; Ralph of Diceto, II, 55.   [6] Roger of Howden, *Gesta*, II, 45–7.

to engage Richard instead of Henry, and withdrew himself from Berry, leaving custodians in charge of the castles he had taken. Furthermore, not, apparently, having anticipated a long-drawn-out war of nerves, he had difficulty in keeping his army together: he was obliged to withdraw some of his levies with the approach of the grape harvest, and had to disband some of his mercenaries when he found he could no longer afford to pay them. His barons were no help: they had advised against making war, and refused to bear arms themselves against fellow-Christians while there was a crusade to be mounted.[1]

Outmanœuvred, Philip was obliged to seek terms, while at the same time desperately trying to save face. Henry, however, negotiated resolutely for a really secure peace. He declined the terms that Philip was prepared to offer, which were either a simple exchange of what he had taken in Berry for what Richard had seized from the count of Toulouse, or just to leave the situation as it was. After three days of fruitless discussion at Gisors in August 1188, Philip angrily ordered the destruction of the great elm tree which marked the traditional place of negotiation between the king of France and the duke of Normandy.[2] A further conference at Châtillon on 7 October was equally fruitless. Henry too, however, was now beginning to find himself in difficulties. The cost of maintaining large forces of mercenaries in idleness for months on end was proving onerous, and he released some of his Welsh archers.[3] But even more seriously, Richard was growing restless. At the conference at Châtillon he completely undermined the stand that Henry had taken by offering to submit himself to the judgement of the French court on all the issues between himself and the count of Toulouse 'so that there may be peace between the kings', which, adds Roger of Howden, 'much displeased the king his father'.[4]

The conference was broken off, and so was all semblance of community of interests between father and son. Richard, writes Gervase of Canterbury, 'became reconciled to the king of France because he had heard that his father wished to defraud him of the succession to the kingdom, in that he intended, as rumour had it, to confer the crown of the kingdom upon his younger son John. Disturbed by this, and small wonder, Richard tried to soften the mind of the French king, that in him he might find some solace if his own father should fail him.'[5]

---

[1] Roger of Howden, *Gesta*, II, 45, 49; Gervase of Canterbury, I, 434.

[2] Ralph of Diceto, II, 55; Roger of Howden, *Gesta*, II, 47; William the Breton, Gesta Philippi Augusti, I, 188–9, Philippidos, II, 69.

[3] Roger of Howden, *Gesta*, II, 50.   [4] *Ibid.*, 49.

[5] Gervase of Canterbury, I, 435.

Richard himself arranged another conference at Bonmoulins on 18 November to try to clear up all the uncertainties and points of contention; but the drift of events was demonstrated by his arrival at the place of meeting in the company of the king of France. Tension mounted steadily. As Gervase of Canterbury relates: 'On the first day they were sufficiently restrained and discussed calmly. On the following day they began little by little to bandy words. On the third day, however, they started to quarrel, and so sharply countered threats with threats that the knights standing about were reaching for their swords.' Philip had begun by offering again the terms that had already been offered; but when these were once more refused, he produced a new proposal: he himself would withdraw from Berry yet allow Richard to retain all he had taken in the Toulousain, if Henry would have Richard and Alice married, and require his barons throughout his dominions to swear fealty to Richard as his heir. Henry refused, saying that he would not be blackmailed. Richard then demanded that his father should give him assurance of succession to the kingdom. Henry remained silent. 'Then,' said Richard, 'I can only take as true what previously seemed incredible.' Unbuckling his sword-belt, he knelt before King Philip, and, placing his hands between his, did homage for Normandy and Aquitaine, swearing fealty to him against all men 'save only the fealty which he owed to his father the king', and beseeching Philip as his lord for help lest he be deprived of his right. As the conference broke up in disorder, father and son were observed to walk away in opposite directions, and 'all men marvelled'.[1]

Henry hastily saw to his defences in Anjou and Aquitaine, 'so that he might close his gates to the approach either of the king of France or to Richard'.[2] A truce was arranged by anxious mediators to last over Christmas, with a further meeting to be held on St Hilary's day, 13 January. But Henry fell sick and the meeting was postponed first until Candlemas and then until Easter. Richard meanwhile was plied with invitations, requests, and pleas to return to his father, but he was obdurate; not even the archbishop of Canterbury himself could move him. King Philip treated Henry's sickness as a subterfuge; he declined to extend the truce and carried out raids on the border. Richard helped him.[3]

The meeting arranged for Easter proved fruitless; and all of many

[1] *Ibid.*, I, 435–6, supplemented by Roger of Howden, *Gesta*, II, 50, and Ralph of Diceto, II, 58.
[2] Gervase of Canterbury, I, 436.
[3] *Ibid.*, 438–9, and Roger of Howden, *Gesta*, II, 61.

efforts in the following weeks to find some basis for reconciliation failed. Finally a papal legate, John of Agnani, intervened to try to rescue the crusade, and persuaded the parties to accept arbitration by himself and four archbishops – two from Henry's dominions and two from Philip's. At Whitsuntide in 1189 they met at La Ferté-Bernard in Maine, just over the border from the county of Blois. Philip rehearsed the demands of Richard and himself: his sister Alice should be married to Richard, Richard should be given security for his inheritance, and John should take the Cross and join the crusade. On these conditions he would restore all he had seized of Henry's territories. Richard added that he would not go to Jerusalem unless John went with him.[1] According to Gervase of Canterbury (the best informed source on the negotiations of 1188–9), Henry simply refused to agree, and the parties dispersed to take to arms. Roger of Howden, however, adds another element to the story: Henry, he says, made a counter-offer – he would agree to all the conditions provided Alice married, not Richard, but John. This Philip could not and would not accept, despite the legate's threat to lay France under interdict.[2]

It is not easy to determine whether Henry did intend to disinherit Richard in favour of John. The circumstantial evidence undoubtedly suggests that he did, but it is not conclusive. There is one powerful argument against accepting the rumours: neither in the months following the conference at Bonmoulins and Richard's defection, nor even in the weeks following the conference at La Ferté-Bernard during which Richard made open war on him and hounded him to death, did Henry do anything to secure the succession for John. There can be no escape from the conclusion that much as Henry may have wished to set aside the son he disliked, he could not bring himself to disavow the principles of 'rightful inheritance' for which he had fought from his youth. Henry's behaviour, is, then, explicable only on the assumption that although he privately accepted that Richard must succeed, he was unwilling to recognise him publicly as heir. Roger of Howden comments that Henry II could never put from his mind the injuries which the Young King had done to him as a result of a premature declaration of the succession.[3] But more than this, Henry had adopted the tactic of trying to discipline Richard by keeping him in uncertainty, and had then be-

---

[1] Roger of Howden, *Gesta*, II, 61; Gervase of Canterbury, I, 446–7.

[2] Roger of Howden, *Chronica*, II, 368 (it is not mentioned in the *Gesta*). Gervase of Canterbury probably derived his information from Archbishop Baldwin who, ever since his mission to King Philip in the summer of 1188, had been closely involved in all the negotiations.

[3] Roger of Howden, *Chronica*, II, 355

come caught in the toils of his own deviousness, for King Philip had cunningly exploited the tactic to win Richard's support, and to foster the rumour that the barons of the Angevin dominions might be required to accept John as heir. Henry could not scotch the rumour without both giving Richard the recognition he craved and conceding a victory to Philip as Richard's patron. This dilemma accounts for Henry's refusal to answer Richard at the conference of Bonmoulins, much more plausibly than the construction which Richard put upon it. Henry's alleged proposal at La Ferté-Bernard that Alice should marry John, is explicable as a desperate attempt to turn the tables on King Philip – offering reasonable terms for the settlement of the dispute over the Vexin, which at the same time conveyed an open threat to Richard, and put to the test the bond between him and Philip. It was, indeed, precisely the sort of move that Henry might be expected to have made in the circumstances. Richard's simple-minded inability to see how his fears were being exploited was doubtless the despair of his father as it was the delight of Philip.

Richard, in the crudely naïve way which was his greatest weakness, was determined to force his father to give him the inheritance, and under his compulsion events moved rapidly to an astonishing dénouement. When the conference of La Ferté-Bernard broke up Henry returned to Le Mans, but Philip, disregarding the conventions of parleys, did not withdraw, and instead joined with Richard in a surprise attack upon the castle of La Ferté. They had come armed to the conference and were behind the frontier defences. La Ferté fell and neighbouring castles surrendered. On 12 June 1189 they struck at Le Mans itself and broke into the lower town. The unprepared defenders deliberately fired the suburbs to hold the invaders back, but the wind changed suddenly, sparks blew into the city itself, and soon it was a raging inferno. Henry and his mounted escort retreated hastily but in good order, pausing on a hill a few miles to the north, while the king watched in dismay a pall of smoke rising over his birthplace.[1] Richard left Philip at Le Mans to pursue his father, but was ambushed by a rearguard left to cover the king's flight, and barely escaped with his life.

Henry was ailing, the heat of the summer was oppressive, but the

---

[1] This account of Henry II's last days is drawn from Gerald of Wales, IV, 369–72; VIII, 282–3, 286–7, 294–9; Gervase of Canterbury, II, 447–9; Roger of Howden, *Gesta*, II, 67–71, *Chronica*, II, 363–7; *Histoire de Guillaume le Maréschal*, lines 8377ff. It is impossible to reconcile the inconsistencies of detail in these accounts. Stubbs provides, in his preface to Roger of Howden, *Chronica*, II, lxi–lxii, a convenient summary of the events of the last two weeks of the reign, though he places too much credence in the account of Gerald of Wales.

cavalcade pressed hurriedly on, knights who could not keep up falling by the wayside. It was by such rapid movements as this that Henry had on previous occasions tipped the scales of fortune. By nightfall they

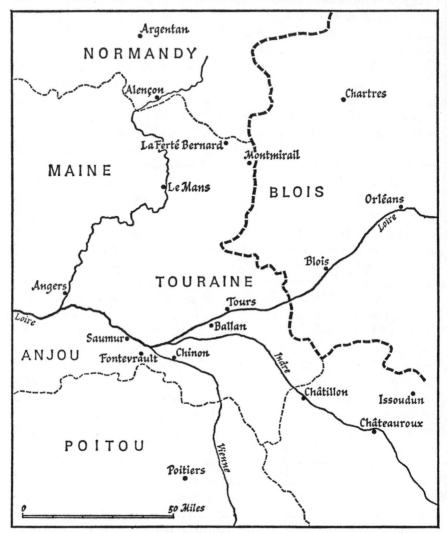

XIV Henry II's last days

were within ten miles of Alençon, the gateway to Normandy. By the morrow he could be behind a line of secure fortresses; within a few days he could have an army behind him for a counter attack, or, if he sought a respite, sail for the safety of England. But Henry did what no one could have expected: he turned back, back towards Anjou. His advisers pleaded with him in vain: he divested himself even of most of his escort, sending it on to Alençon under the command of his chancellor, his bastard son Geoffrey, to alert the garrisons of Normandy. The explanation for this extraordinary decision is not hard to divine: Henry had no stomach for a fight, he was weary unto death, and was going home to die. The roads to the south were infested with Philip's men, and Henry had to pick his way by by-ways and forest lanes, travelling some two hundred miles by circuitous routes to Chinon at the southern extremity of Anjou. There in the great fortress which was a focal point in the government of his dominions, he lay for a fortnight, the sickness which had plagued him for six months and more growing upon him.

King Philip and Richard had rapidly overrun Maine. It is not surprising that castle after castle surrendered to them: men read the signs, and with the prospect that Richard might soon take over, only the strongest sentiments of loyalty could make men fight for Henry. Yet fight some of them did. The city of Tours refused to surrender, although the river Loire was running low in the hot, dry summer, and the defences were vulnerable on the river side. Philip was obliged to bring up siege engines. Messages were sent to Henry by Richard and Philip calling upon him to meet them and make terms. Barons of the French court rode to see him on 2 July offering to mediate. On 3 July Tours fell to Philip's assault. The next day Henry consented to a meeting, and went to Ballan a few miles south-west of Tours. He was so racked with pain that even Philip was moved to pity and proferred a cloak for Henry to sit upon the ground. But Henry said he had come not to sit and talk with Philip but only to hear what was demanded of him. He remained on his horse, his attendants propping him upright. The terms were read to him. He was to place himself wholly at the will of King Philip. He was to do homage to the king of France for all his continental possessions. He was to give up Alice to a guardian named by Richard, who was to marry her on his return from Jerusalem. Richard was to receive the fealty of his father's subjects on both sides of the sea as lawful heir to all his father's lands. King Philip was to be paid an indemnity of twenty thousand marks. Three major castles in greater Anjou or in the Vexin were to be handed over as a pledge of good faith.[1] As the terms were read the still sultry summer's day broke into rolls of thunder. Henry listened, assented, and departed. Too feeble to ride, he was borne back to Chinon in a litter.

[1] Texts of the terms are given by Roger of Howden, *Gesta*, II, 70–1, *Chronica*, II, 365–6.

H—X

As a guarantee of the treaty it was stipulated that Henry should not require the allegiance of those who had gone over to Richard until a month before the start of the crusade. Henry sent for a list of the names. His attendants tried to keep it from him, but he insisted that it should be read aloud. The first name on the list was that of his son John. He would hear no more. The will to live departed from him. He lapsed into a delirium, from which he rallied only infrequently and briefly. In his moments of consciousness he took leave of his friends, asked to be carried before the altar in the chapel of the castle, where, it is said, he spoke some words of confession and received Holy Communion. On Thursday 6 July 1189 he died.

His body, clothed in his finest robes, was borne on the shoulders of those of his barons who had kept faith with him to the end, down from the castle on the great rock of Chinon, and along the bank of the river Vienne to the abbey church of Fontevrault. Richard was not there, for he had discredited all reports that his father was nigh to death. The news that Henry had in fact breathed his last was conveyed to him by a special messenger sent by William Marshal. He arrived at Fontevrault as night was falling and entered the church alone. For a while he was observed to stand silently by the bier. He looked down once at his father's face, and fell to his knees to say a short prayer. Then he rose to his feet, and calling William Marshal to attend him, walked away to take charge of his inheritance.

Henry II was not the only king to have lived too long for the patience of his heirs and his own peace of mind. Although not, at fifty-six, particularly old, even by medieval standards, he seems to have been worn out by a lifetime of arduous travel and the incessant endeavour to impose his will upon the world. From the age of fourteen, and his earliest recorded adventure, he had burned with a restless, consuming energy. Even at the end, when his legs refused any longer to carry him, the fires of his inner will were still undimmed: as he outwardly submitted to the dictation of terms for the ending of the war and gave Richard what purported to be the kiss of peace, he growled in his son's ear, 'May the Lord spare me until I have taken vengeance on you'. When Richard related the incident to the French court, King Philip and all his barons, it is said, were moved to a laughter tempered by a wondering admiration.[1] To Gerald of Wales, King Henry's death was 'ignominious', but it was the ignominy of an ailing lion savaged by jackals.

The drama of Henry II's sudden discomfiture should not be allowed

[1] Gerald of Wales, VIII, 296.

to obscure the fact that Richard and Philip had achieved little beyond the humiliation of a sick man who did not wish for war. Their military success was fortuitous: a combination of their treachery, Henry's refusal to fight, and the understandable hesitations of the barons of Anjou. The anxiety to bring Henry to terms does not suggest that there was any real confidence in sustaining the success. No one indeed seems to have relished the war, save Philip, and it is significant that his barons were the active mediators. The terms, though doubtless bitter to Henry II, were not extravagant. Nothing really changed as a result of Henry's submission, and his death robbed Philip even of the satisfaction of a public ceremony of homage.

The consequence of the war for the succession of Richard was that Henry II, against his better judgement, bequeathed to his son both the whole of his dominions and the impossible task of holding them together. Henry II's political achievement was impressive: his friends gloried in it, foreigners admired it, the French king feared it; but it had serious limitations. There was no natural principle of unity in it, and Henry did not supply one. It says much for his realism that he did not envisage the survival of his 'empire' intact as a political unit, but tried to refashion it as a dynastic federation. But even this was almost certain to be ephemeral, for it ran counter to the political reorientation of France which was to make the court of the Capetians the focus of power within the kingdom. Within a generation the union of England and Normandy was to come to seem, even to many Normans themselves, a curious anachronism. Henry II, one of the last of the medieval cosmopolitans, could not have been expected to perceive this; but he must have seen that the policies he pursued in England and on the continent involved him in a fundamental contradiction. In the process of disciplining his vassals, Henry II prised loose the tentacles of local lordship and undermined the parochialism of local loyalties; but the kind of regional organisation which he tried to substitute for exclusive local lordship on the continent was directly contrary to his disruption of a regional power-structure in England in favour of the authority of the Crown. The kind of authority he tried to establish for himself and his successor as duke of Normandy, count of Anjou, and duke of Aquitaine (and which he defended against the king of France) he sought to deny to men of equivalent rank in England. There was no justification for this in logic or the natural order; his justification was simply precedent and a somewhat selective view of history.

The course of history might have been radically different if Henry II, instead of devoting himself principally to the pursuit and exploitation of the rights of lordship which fell to him fortuitously, had turned his energies to forging the unity of the British Isles. Subsequent history and the growth of national sentiment should not blind us to the real possibility which still existed in the middle of the twelfth century (but for little longer) for the assimilation of the outliers. If political integration had been achieved in the twelfth century, the distinctiveness of the Welsh and even of the Irish might have come to seem regional differences no more divisive than the equally marked regional differences of the Northumbrians or the Cornish. The Normans were a flux which helped to solder together a kingdom of England, and might equally have served to construct a kingdom of Britain. A kingdom of Scotland was, after all, to be formed from elements as diverse as any to be found in England, Wales, or Ireland. As it was, the unifying forces which brought Cumberland, Northumberland and Cornwall within the orbit of government from Westminster, stopped short of the Scottish border, and reached out only fitfully and confusingly to Wales and to Ireland. It may be that Henry II's peculiar talents were not appropriate to such an endeavour, and his decision (a deliberate decision it seems) not to be drawn into it was well judged. The preconditions did not exist on the western fringe of the world for the kind of government at which Henry II excelled – the pattern of lordship, the military techniques required, the social organisation were different. It is a measure of Henry II's discernment of such sociological factors that he learned from his early experiences in Wales that a trackless country sparsely populated and lacking castles, towns, and manors, was no proper sphere for the operation of the kind of military forces and administrative institutions which he best knew how to handle, and that the simplest means for economical control in such regions was to seek an alliance with native rulers who were equipped for it. Nevertheless, Henry II's resourcefulness and his ingenuity might well have found a solution to the problem of integration had he chosen to apply himself to it.

Given the framework within which Henry II chose to operate, his achievement is remarkable. That any man should have tried to rule such wide and diverse dominions by any other means than by allowing local lords a free hand was an astonishing piece of impertinence. With no means of communication swifter than the horse, without the aid of maps and gazetteers, with, at first, only rudimentary means of enforcing his authority, and with no rational body of law or a corps of trained administrators, he set out to establish law and order from the Cheviots to the Massif Central and the Pyrenees. 'He is a great, indeed the greatest of monarchs,' wrote Arnulf bishop of Lisieux to Archbishop Thomas

Becket in March 1165, 'for he has no superior of whom he stands in awe, nor subject who may resist him.'[1] Yet Henry II was then only on the threshold of his major work of reshaping the methods of the past and laying the groundwork for the government of the future. He overcame the old disintegrating force of baronial separatism, and resisted the newer ones of municipal independence and clerical exclusiveness, not in order to destroy – for Henry II was fundamentally conservative – but in order to bring all into balance under royal control. Much of the skill, and wisdom, and ingenuity which went into the work doubtless derived from those who were known as the king's *familiares*; but the will to do it was the will of one man, Henry of Anjou. It was a will which refused to accept that any problem was insoluble. If a frontal assault failed he would find a way in through the back door, or, if necessary, via the sewer. He was an irresistible force demonstrating – and relishing the demonstration – that immovable obstacles could be moved.

Henry II did not seek victories, and seems to have been indifferent both to glory and his own reputation. He was not – whatever his enemies believed – either politically ambitious or interested in power for its own sake. He was acutely conscious, undoubtedly, of his rights and 'dignities': not, however, for the prestige, power, and wealth they conferred on him personally, but rather as a heritage which had to be passed on entire and untarnished to his heirs. Unlike his contemporary Frederick Barbarossa, he had no great vision or grand design; he seems to have set no store by the mystique of monarchy, and did not seek to buttress his regality with symbolic ceremonial or the pretensions of *courtoisie*. He may have been 'the greatest of monarchs' but the court of King Henry II was at its most typical in the way Bishop Hugh of Lincoln found it one day at Woodstock. He had been summoned to answer for his conduct in excommunicating a royal forester. As he approached the royal hunting lodge at Woodstock, the king, who was extremely angry with him, rode off into the forest with his barons, and finding a pleasant spot sat himself on the ground, with the members of the court dispersed in a circle around him. The bishop followed them, but Henry bade everyone ignore his presence. No one rose to greet the bishop or said a word to him, but Bishop Hugh, undaunted, eased an earl out of his place beside the king and sat himself down too. There was a long, brooding silence, broken finally by Henry who, unable to do nothing, called for needle and thread and began to stitch up a leather bandage on an injured finger. Again there was a heavy silence until Bishop Hugh, contemplating the king at his stitching, casually remarked,

[1] Arnulf of Lisieux, *Letters*, no. 42, 73.

'How like your cousins of Falaise you look'. At this the king's anger fled from him, and he burst into a laughter which sent him rolling on the ground. Many were amazed at the bishop's temerity, others puzzled at the point of the remark, until the king, recovering his composure, explained the gibe to them: William the Conqueror was a bastard, and his mother was reputedly the daughter of one of the leather-workers for which the Norman town of Falaise was famous.[1]

It was characteristic of Henry of Anjou that he should rise to anger when his authority was flouted, yet be rocked with laughter when his dignity was gently mocked. St Hugh of Lincoln understood him as few others did. He overflowed the bounds of ordinary men's comprehension. He bewildered them with his contradictory qualities. He baffled them by his disregard of contemporary wisdom. He astonished them by his tireless energy and resilience. He attempted the impossible and achieved the improbable. It seemed hardly credible to contemporaries that he should weather so many storms, and even escape shipwreck on the rocks strewn by Thomas Becket. Yet Henry of Anjou was not superhuman. He had all the frailties and passions of ordinary men – but in larger measure. He was no god-like Achilles, either in valour or in wrath; but in cunning and ingenuity, in fortitude and courage, he stands not far below the subtle-souled Odysseus.

[1] Adam of Eynsham, 115–18.

GLOSSARY
BIBLIOGRAPHY
INDEX

GLOSSARY

ADVOWSON: The patronage of an ecclesiastical office or benefice; the right of presentation to a benefice or living.

AMERCEMENT: A pecuniary punishment or penalty inflicted at the 'mercy' of the king or his justices for misdemeanours, defaults, breach of regulations, and other minor offences. The offender was said to be 'in mercy', he was 'amerced', and paid an 'amercement'. To be distinguished from *damages* (compensation to an injured party) and from *fine* (q.v.).

ASSART: To assart was to make a clearing (known as 'an assart') on virgin land by rooting out trees and rendering the ground suitable for agriculture. To assartain the royal forest without a licence was a grave offence. Land assarted with licence was subject to annual payments to the exchequer.

ASSIZE: A rule, regulation, or law, enforced on the authority of the Crown, though with the assent of the barons, which modified or changed the customary law. By transference the term came to be applied to legal procedures under assize law (e.g., the 'assize' of *novel disseisin*), and eventually to the courts which entertained such actions and the justices who administered them.

BOVATE: A measurement of land. One eighth of a carucate (q.v.); notionally as much land as could be kept under the plough by one ox. Also known as an oxgang or oxgate of land.

CARUCATE (from *caruca*, a plough): A 'plough-land'; a measurement of land, notionally as much land as could be kept under the plough in one year by a plough-team of eight oxen. The amount of land so described varied in different parts of the country between 60 and 120 acres.

DEMESNE: The *Dialogus de Scaccario* defines demesne lands as 'those which are tilled at the cost or by the labour of the owner, and those held from him by villeins'. Such lands were said to be 'in demesne' (*in dominico*). The demesne did not include estates which belonged to the lord but which had been let by him as fiefs to vassals in return for services (such lands being said to be *in servitio*). The *royal demesne* was all land in the realm which had not been put into private hands, and from which the Crown derived rents and other revenues through custodians or 'farmers' (*see* FARM).

DISSEISIN: The act of wrongfully depriving a person of the seisin of lands, rents, or other hereditaments, as where a man not having right of entry on certain lands or tenements enters upon them and ousts him who has the freehold (W. J. Byrne, *Dictionary of English Law*). (*See* SEISIN.)

ESCHEAT: The reversion to a lord of a fief (q.v.) for default of heirs or the outlawry of the holder.

ESSOIN: An excuse tendered by or on behalf of one who is summoned to appear in court to perform suit or answer to an action, by reason of sickness or infirmity, or other allowable cause of absence.

EYRE: A visitation by the king or his justices acting in his name, carried out periodically, usually at intervals of a few years.

FAMILIARIS (pl. FAMILIARES): The *familiaris* was an intimate, a member of the *familia* or household of the king or other great man. The term is used in this book particularly of those close friends, counsellors, aides, and assistants of the king, who owed their standing and authority to their intimacy with the ruler, but who did not hold any formally constituted office or title.

FARM (or FERM, from Saxon *feorme*, food-rent): A fixed sum or rent, usually annual. The *sheriff's farm* was the fixed sum payable annually by the sheriff by way of composition for all the regular royal revenues deriving from the shire, i.e., the sheriff *farmed* the revenues – contracting in advance to pay a fixed amount and deriving his profit from whatever he could collect above this sum. A *custodian*, on the other hand, directly accounted for all the revenues.

FEALTY: An oath of fidelity. Sometimes confounded with *homage* (q.v.) since both were commonly performed together when a vassal received a fief from a lord. An oath of fealty, however, could be performed to one from whom no land was held. Fealty to the Crown overrode all other obligations, even that of homage to a lesser lord.

FIEF (*feodum* or *feudum*): An estate in land (in England normally heritable): held on condition of homage and the performance of services (both customary and specified, including, essentially, military service) to a superior lord, by whom it is granted, and in whom the ownership remains.

FINE (from Latin *finis*, end): (1) In the usage of the twelfth century a *fine* was not necessarily or even usually a monetary penalty. It was, rather, a sum of money which an applicant to the Crown agreed to pay for having some grant, concession, or privilege. The use of the word approaches nearest its modern connotation in payments to escape the consequences of the king's displeasure. *To make fine:* to make one's peace, settle a matter, obtain exemption from punishment.

(2) A 'final agreement'. Blackstone: 'an amicable composition or agreement of a suit, either actual or fictitious, by leave of the king or his justices'. The agreement was embodied in a document known as a *fine* or *final concord*. To avoid confusion the term *final concord* is in this book preferred to the use of the word *fine* in this sense.

FRANCHISE: A privilege or exceptional right (typically, rights of jurisdiction) granted by the sovereign power to a person or body of persons (such as a monastery).

FRANKALMOIGN (or FREE ALMS): The tenure of lands or tenements granted to those who had devoted themselves to the service of God, 'for pure and perpetual alms'. The service rendered by the grantee was the service of prayer, particularly for the souls of the grantor and his kin.

HIDE : An Anglo-Saxon term still used in many parts of the country, and commonly at this period as a measurement of land, roughly equivalent to the carucate (q.v.), but more properly a unit of assessment, e.g., to taxation.

HOMAGE : The ceremony and oath by which a vassal acknowledged himself 'the man' (*homo*) of a lord, and undertook the obligations inherent in fief-holding.

HONOR (from Latin, *honor*): Frequently spelt 'honour', but the form without a 'u' (as in the Latin) is in this book preferred as a technical term for the group of estates from which the greater tenants-in-chief of the Crown derived their prestige and status of honour. A superior lordship upon which inferior lordships were dependent.

HUNDRED : An administrative sub-division of the shire, embracing several vills (q.v.), and having a court to which men of the hundred owed suit at regular intervals.

KNIGHT'S FEE : A fief (q.v.) owing the service of one knight: notionally an estate providing sufficient revenue for the maintenance of one knight, but the size varied widely. In practice, the knight's fee became a unit of assessment to services and taxes, large fiefs being reckoned at multiples, and tiny fiefs at fractions, of the 'knight's fee'.

MARK : A sum of money amounting to two-thirds of a pound sterling, i.e., 13s 4d.

OATH-HELPER (or *compurgator*): One who supports the oath of another. A man who, in court, was required to prove his assertions by 'waging his law' swore a solemn oath to the truth of his declarations, and had to be supported by *oath-helpers* who testified on oath to his truthfulness. Custom, or the court, specified the number of oath-helpers required.

ORDEAL (Old English *ordel*, judgement): A form of proof in a court of law, by which a divine sign of guilt or innocence was invoked. The person who was required to undertake the ordeal (usually the accused but sometimes the accuser) performed some feat such as carrying hot iron or plunging a hand into boiling water, and innocence was demonstrated if the wounds healed cleanly. The ordeal of cold water (described above, p. 283n. 1) was customarily reserved for the unfree, but was the required ordeal for all those prosecuted under the Assize of Clarendon (1166).

PECULIAR : In the law of the Church: a jurisdiction proper to itself, exempt from and not subject to the jurisdiction of the bishop of the diocese.

PIPE ROLL : Properly known as The Great Roll of the Exchequer: the record of the annual audit of the accounts of sheriffs and of other debtors to the Crown.

PLEAS OF THE CROWN : The more serious crimes, breaches of the king's peace, and specially designated offences such as concealment of treasure trove, jurisdiction over which could be exercised by no one except officers of the Crown.

PURPRESTURE: *Glanvill*, IX. 11: 'There is said to be a purpresture when anything is occupied unjustly against the sovereign, as in the royal demesne, or by obstructing the public highway, or by impeding a public water course.'

RELIEF: (*relevium*, from *relevare*, to take up): A payment to a lord by a tenant of full age coming into possession of a fief held of a lord by inheritance.

SCUTAGE: Literally 'shield-money'; a payment in lieu of military service, paid in respect of the knights which a tenant-in-chief owed to the Crown. The personal obligation to serve of the tenant-in-chief himself could not be discharged by *scutage*, but only by *fine* (q.v.).

SEISIN: Feudal possession; the exercise and enjoyment of rights deriving from possession, usually of land, held as a freehold (but not as leasehold or a servile tenure). To be *in seisin* was to be 'seized of' control of such an estate or other freehold rights. *Livery of seisin* (i.e., delivery of seisin by a grantot) was usually by some symbolic act. To be *disseised* was to be ousted from *seisin*. *See* above, pp. 336.

SERGEANTY: A form of feudal tenure on condition of rendering some specified personal service to the lord, but of a more lowly nature than the services performed by those who held by knight-service.

VILL: The smallest administrative unit of the realm, a subdivision of the hundred, corresponding roughly to the administrative 'parish' of later usage. Usually identifiable with a village or township (and sometimes translated as such in the book), but covering the vicinity up to the bounds of neighbouring vills.

VILLEIN: One of the class of serfs – the legally unfree. A peasant occupier or cultivator entirely subject to a lord and bound in service to a manor.

VIRGATE: A measurement of land equivalent to a quarter of a carucate (q.v.) or two bovates. The amount so described varied in different parts of the country, but was commonly about twenty acres. Also known as a yardland.

WAGER OF LAW: To wage one's law was to defend an accusation in court by swearing a formal oath of innocence supported by the oaths of compurgators (*see* OATH-HELPER).

BIBLIOGRAPHY

The following bibliography is intended to serve two purposes: (1) to give details of works cited by short title in the footnotes, and (2) to pay tribute to other works which have been of assistance in the preparation of this book.

To facilitate the identification of works cited in the footnotes, primary and secondary sources are combined in one alphabetical list. Medieval authors are listed under their first name. Works cited by an abbreviated title in the footnotes are listed under the abbreviation (e.g., the *De Necessariis Observantiis Scaccarii Dialogus* is listed under *Dialogus de Scaccario*).

Specialised bibliographies, in which the primary and secondary sources are separately listed, will be found in:

J. Boussard, *Le Gouvernement d'Henri II Plantagenêt* (Paris, 1956).

R. Foreville, *L'Église et la Royauté en Angleterre sous Henri II Plantagenêt* (Paris, 1943).

R. C. Van Caenegem, *Royal Writs in England from the Conquest to Glanvill* (Selden Society, London, 1959).

Useful introductions to the source material of the period for England will be found in *English Historical Documents* (1142–1189), ed. D. C. Douglas and G. W. Greenaway (London, 1953).

ABBOTT, E. A., *St Thomas of Canterbury: his death and miracles*, 2 vols (London, 1898).

The Acta of the Bishops of Chichester, 1075–1207, ed. H. Mayr-Harting (Canterbury and York Society, 1964).

Actus Pontificum Cenomannis in Urbe Degentium, ed. G. Busson and A. Ledru (Le Mans, 1901).

ADAM OF EYNSHAM: *Magna Vita Sancti Hugonis*, ed. Decima L. Douie and H. Farmer, 2 vols (London, 1961–2).

ADAMS, G. B., *Council and Courts in Anglo-Norman England* (New Haven, 1926).

——, *The Origins of the English Constitution* (Yale, 1920).

ADAMS, NORMA, 'The judicial conflict over tithes', *English Historical Review*, lii (1937), 1–22.

——, ' The writ of prohibition of court Christian', *Minnesota Law Review*, xx (1935–6), 272–93.

AILRED OF RIEVAULX: Relatio Venerabilis Aelredi, abbatis Rievallensis, De Standardo, ed. R. Howlett in *Chronicles of the Reigns of Stephen, Henry II and Richard I*, III, 179–99.

ALAN OF TEWKESBURY: Vita Sancti Thomae, Cantuariensis Archiespiscopi et Martyris, auctoribus Joanne Saresberiensi et Alano abbate Tewkesberiensi, ed. J. C. Robertson in *Materials for the History of Thomas Becket*, II, 299–352.

ALLEN, D. F., *A Catalogue of English Coins in the British Museum: The Cross-and-Crosslets Type of Henry II* (London, 1951).

ALLENOU, J., *Histoire féodale de Marais, territoire et église de Dol. Enquête par tourbe ordonée par Henri II roi d'Angleterre* (Paris, 1917).

Ancient Charters, Royal and Private, prior to A.D. 1200, ed. J. H. Round (Pipe Roll Society, 1888).

ANDERSON, A. O., 'Anglo-Scottish relations from Constantine II to William', *Scottish Historical Review*, xlii (1963), 1–20.

——, *Scottish Annals from English Chroniclers, A.D. 600 to 1286* (London, 1908).

——, See *Early Sources of Scottish History*.

ANDERSON, MARJORIE O., 'Lothian and the early Scottish kings', *Scottish Historical Review*, xxxix (1960), 98–112.

Anglo-Saxon Chronicle: *Two of the Saxon Chronicles Parallel*, ed. C. Plummer on the basis of an edition by J. Earle, I (text) (Oxford, 1892).

The Anglo-Saxon Chronicle: a revised translation, by Dorothy Whitelock, with D. C. Douglas and Susie I. Tucker (London, 1961).

Anglo-Scottish Relations, 1174–1328, ed. E. L. G. Stones (London, 1965).

Annales Cambriae, ed. J. Williams ab Ithel (Rolls Series, 1860).

Annales Monasterii Beate Marie Virginis, juxta Dublin, ed. J. T. Gilbert in *Chartularies of St Mary's Abbey, Dublin*, II, 241–86.

Annales Monastici, ed. H. R. Luard, 5 vols (Rolls Series, 1864–9).

Annals of Ireland, 1162–1370, ed. J. T. Gilbert in *Chartularies of St Mary's Abbey, Dublin*, II, 303–98.

Annals of the Four Masters: Annals of the Kingdom of Ireland by the Four Masters, from the earliest period to 1616, ed. J. O'Donovan, 7 vols (Dublin, 1851).

Annals of Margam: Annales de Margan, ed. H. R. Luard in *Annales Monastici*, I, 1–40.

Annals of Osney: Annales Monasterii de Osneia, ed. H. R. Luard in *Annales Monastici*, IV, 1–352.

Annals of Tewkesbury: Annales Monasterii de Theokesberia, ed. H. R. Luard in *Annales Monastici*, I, 43–180.

Annals of Waverley: Annales Monasterii de Waverleia, ed. H. R. Luard in *Annales Monastici*, II, 127–411.

Annals of Winchester: Annales Monasterii de Wintonia, ed. H. R. Luard in *Annales Monastici*, II, 1–125.

Annals of Worcester: Annales Prioratus de Wigornia, ed. H. R. Luard in *Annales Monastici*, IV, 356–564.

Anniversary Essays in Medieval History . . . presented to Charles Homer Haskins, ed. C. H. Taylor (Boston and New York, 1929).

ANONYMOUS OF LAMBETH: Vita Sancti Thomae, Cantuariensis Archiepiscopi et Martyris, auctore Anonymo II, ed. J. C. Robertson in *Materials for the History of Thomas Becket*, IV, 80–144.

ANSELM: *Sancti Anselmi Opera Omnia*, ed. F. S. Schmitt, 5 vols (London, 1946–51).

APPEL, C., *Bertran von Born* (Halle, 1931).

APPELBY, J. T., *Henry II, the Vanquished King* (London, 1962).

——, 'The monastic foundations of Henry II', *Catholic Historical Review*, xlviii (1962), 205–15.

ARCHER, T. A., 'Clifford, Rosamond', in *The Dictionary of National Biography*, IX, 75–6.

ARNULF OF LISIEUX: *The Letters of Arnulf of Lisieux*, ed. F. Barlow (Camden Society, 1939).

AULT, W. O., *Private Jurisdiction in England* (New Haven, 1923).

BALDWIN, J. F., *The King's Council in England during the Middle Ages* (Oxford, 1913).

BALDWIN, J. W., 'The intellectual preparation for the canon of 1215 against ordeals', *Speculum*, xxxvi (1961), 613–36.

BALLARD, A., *British Borough Charters, 1042–1216* (Cambridge, 1913).

——, *The English Borough in the Twelfth Century* (Cambridge, 1914).

BARBER, R., *Henry Plantagenet, a biography* (London, 1964).

BARLOW, F., 'The English, Norman, and French councils called to deal with the papal schism of 1159', *English Historical Review*, li (1936), 264–8.

——, *The Feudal Kingdom of England, 1042–1216* (London, 1955).

——, Introduction to *The Letters of Arnulf of Lisieux* (Camden Society, 1939).

——, 'Roger of Howden', *English Historical Review*, lxv (1950), 352–60.

BARNARD, F. P., *Strongbow's Conquest of Ireland* (London, 1888).

BARNES, PATRICIA M., 'The Anstey Case', in *A Medieval Miscellany for Doris Mary Stenton*, 1–24.

BARRACLOUGH, G., *The Earldom and County Palatine of Chester* (Oxford, 1953), reprinted from *The Transactions of the Historic Society of Lancashire and Cheshire*, ciii (1951).

BARROW, G. W. S., 'The Anglo-Scottish border', *Northern History*, i (1966), 21–42.

——, 'The beginnings of feudalism in Scotland', *Bulletin of the Institute of Historical Research*, xxix (1956), 1–31.

——, *The Border: an Inaugural Lecture* (Durham, 1962).

——, *Feudal Britain: the Completion of the Medieval Kingdoms, 1066–1314* (London, 1956).

——, Introduction to *Regesta Regum Scottorum: the Acts of Malcolm IV, King of Scots, 1153–1165* (Edinburgh, 1960).

——, Introduction to *Regesta Regum Scottorum: The Acts of William I, King of Scots, 1165–1214* (Edinburgh, 1971).

——, 'King David I and the honour of Lancaster', *English Historical Review*, lxx (1955), 85–9.

——, 'The reign of William the Lion, king of Scotland', in *Historical Studies VII*, ed. J. C. Beckett (London, 1969).

——, 'Scottish rulers and the religious orders, 1070–1153', *Transactions of the Royal Historical Society*, 5th series, iii (1953), 77–100.

BARROW, G. W. S., 'A writ of Henry II for Dunfermline Abbey', *Scottish Historical Review*, xxxvi (1957), 138–43.

BAZELEY, MARGARET L., 'The extent of the English Forest in the thirteenth century', *Transactions of the Royal Historical Society*, 4th series, iv (1921), 140–72.

——, 'The Forest of Dean in its relations with the Crown during the twelfth and thirteenth centuries', *Transactions of the Bristol and Gloucester Archaeological Society*, xxxiii (1910), 153–282.

BEECH, G. T., *A Rural Society in Medieval France: The Gâtine of Poitou in the Eleventh and Twelfth Centuries* (Baltimore, 1964).

BEELER, J. A., 'Castles and strategy in Norman and early Angevin England', *Speculum*, xxi (1956), 581–601.

——, 'The composition of Anglo-Norman armies', *Speculum*, xi (1965), 398–414.

——, 'Towards an evaluation of medieval English generalship', *Journal of British Studies*, iii (1963), 1–10.

——, *Warfare in England, 1066–1189* (Ithaca, 1966).

BÉMONT, C., 'La bulle Laudabiliter', *Mélanges d'Histoire du Moyen Âge, offerts à M. Ferdinand Lot*, 41–53.

BENEDICT OF PETERBOROUGH, Passio Sancti Thomae Cantuariensis, auctore Benedicto Petriburgensi abbate, ed. J. C. Robertson in *Materials for the History of Thomas Becket*, II, 1–19.

——, The Chronicle of the Reigns of Henry II and Richard I, known commonly under the name of Benedict of Peterborough. See under ROGER OF HOWDEN, *Gesta*.

BENTON, J. F., 'The revenue of Louis VII', *Speculum*, xlii (1967), 84–91.

BERESFORD, M. W. and ST JOSEPH, J. K. S., *Medieval England: an Aerial Survey* (Cambridge, 1958).

BERNARD, ST, Epistolae: *S. Bernardi, Opera Omnia*, ed. J. Mabillon, Vol. I, Epistolae in *Patriologia Latina*, clxxxii.

BERTRAND DE BORN: *Poésies complètes de Bertran de Born*, ed. A. Thomas (Toulouse, 1888).

  Bertran von Born, ed. A. Stimming (Halle, 1913).

  Bertran von Born, ed. C. Appel (Halle, 1931).

  also edited by F. J. M. Raynouard in *Choix des Poésies Originales des Troubadours*, 6 vols (Paris, 1816–20).

BESNIER, R., *La Coutume de Normandie, Histoire Externe* (Paris, 1935).

BIGELOW, M. M., *History of Procedure in England from the Norman Conquest: The Norman Period, 1066–1204* (London, 1880).

BINCHY, D. A., 'The linguistic and historical value of the Irish law tracts', *Proceedings of the British Academy*, xxix (1943), 195–227.

——, 'Secular institutons', in *Early Irish Society*, ed. M. Dillon, 52–65.

BISHOP, T. A. M., *Scriptores Regis. Facsimiles to identify and illustrate the hands of royal scribes in original charters of Henry I, Stephen, and Henry II* (Oxford, 1961).

BLOCH, M., *Feudal Society*, translated by L. A. Manyon (London, 1961).

——, *Les Rois Thaumaturges. Étude sur la caractère supernaturel attribué à la puissance royale particulièrement en France et Angleterre* (Strasbourg, 1924).

——, Introduction to 'La vie de saint Édouard le Confesseur par Osbert de Clare', *Analecta Bollandia*, xli (1923), 5–131.

BOEHMER, H., *Kirche und Staat in England und in der Normandie in XI und in XII Jahrhundert* (Leipzig, 1899).

BOISSONNADE, P., 'Administrateurs laïques et ecclésiastiques anglo-normands en Poitou à l'epoque d'Henri II Plantagenêt (1152–1189)', *Bulletin de la Société des Antiquaires de l'Ouest*, 3rd series, v (1919), 156–90.

——, 'L' ascension, le déclin et la chute d'un grand état féodal du centre-ouest: les Taillefer et les Lusignans, comtes de la Marche et d'Angoulême et leurs relations avec les Capétiens et les Plantagenêts (1137–1314)', *Bulletins et Mémoires de la Société Archéologiques et Historiques de la Charente* (1935), 1–258.

——, 'Les comtes d'Angoulême – les ligues féodales contre Richard Coeur de Lion et les poésies de Bertran de Born (1176–1194)', *Annales du Midi*, vii (1895), 275–95.

BONGERT, YVONNE, *Recherches sur les Cours Laïques de X au XIII siècles* (Paris, 1949).

The Book of Fees, commonly called Testa de Nevill, Pt 1 (1198–1242), ed. H. C. Maxwell Lyte (London, 1920).

BORENIUS, T., *The Iconography of St Thomas of Canterbury* (Oxford, 1929).

——, *St Thomas of Canterbury in Art* (London, 1932).

BOUSSARD, J., *Le Comté d'Anjou sous Henri Plantagenêt et ses Fils (1151–1204)* (Paris, 1938).

——, 'L' enquête de 1172 sur les fiefs de chevalier en Normandie', *Recueil de Travaux offert à M. Clovis Brunel*, Pt 1, 193–208.

——, *Le Gouvernement d'Henri II Plantagenêt* (Paris, 1956).

——, 'Les influences anglaises dans le développement des grands charges de l'empire de Henri II Plantagenêt', *Annales de Normandie*, v (1955), 215–31.

——, 'Les institutions financières de l'Angleterre au XIIe siècle', *Cahiers de Civilization Médiévale*, i (1958), 475–94.

——, 'Les mercenaires au XIIe siècle: Henri II Plantagenêt et les origines de l'armée de métier', *Bibliothèque de l'École des Chartes*, cvi (1945–6), 189–224.

——, 'Trois actes d'Henri Plantagenêt relatifs à ses possessions francaises', *Bibliothèque de l'École des Chartes*, cxviii (1960), 51–7.

——, 'La vie en Anjou aux Xe et XIIe siècles', *Le Moyen Âge*, 4th series, v (1950), 29–68.

BRACTON, HENRY DE, *see* HENRY DE BRACTON.

BROOKE, C. N. L., 'Gregorian reform in action: clerical marriage in England, 1050–1200', *Cambridge Historical Journal*, xii (1956), 1–21.

——, Introduction to *The Letters of John of Salisbury*, I (London, 1955).

BROOKE, C. N. L. and MOREY, A., 'The Cerne letters of Gilbert Foliot and the legation of Imar of Tusculum', *English Historical Review*, lxiii (1948), 523–7.

BROOKE, Z. N., 'The effect of Becket's murder on papal authority in England', *Cambridge Historical Journal*, ii (1928), 213–28.

——, *The English Church and the Papacy from the Conquest to the Reign of John* (Cambridge, 1931).

——, 'The register of Master David of London and the part he played in the Becket crisis', in *Essays in History presented to Reginald Lane Poole*, 227–45.

BROOKE, Z. N. and BROOKE, C. N. L., 'Henry II, duke of Normandy and Aquitaine', *English Historical Review*, lxi (1946), 81–9.

BROWN, P. A., *The Development of the Legend of Thomas Becket* (Philadelphia, 1930).

BROWN, P. HUME, *History of Scotland*, 3 vols (Cambridge, 1909).

BROWN, R. A., *English Medieval Castles* (London, 1954).

——, 'Framlingham castle and Bigod, 1154–1216', *Proceedings of the Suffolk Institute of Natural History and Archaeology*, xxv (1950), 127–48.

——, 'Royal castle-building in England, 1154–1216', *English Historical Review*, lxx (1955), 353–98.

——, ' "The Treasury" of the later twelfth century', in *Studies presented to Sir Hilary Jenkinson*, 35–49.

Brut y Saesson, ed. O. Jones, E. Williams, and W. O. Pughe, in *The Myvrian Archaeology of Wales* (2nd edn, Denbigh, 1870), 652–84.

Brut y Tywysogion; or the Chronicle of the Princes of Wales, ed. J. Williams ab Ithel (Rolls Series, 1860).

BURLEIGH, J. H. S., *A Church History of Scotland* (London, 1960).

Burton Cartulary: An Abstract of the Contents of the Burton Cartulary, ed. G. Wrottesley, *William Salt Archaeological Society*, v (1884), 1–104.

Calendar of Documents preserved in France, Illustrative of the History of Great Britain and Ireland, I, 918–1206, ed. J. H. Round (London, 1899).

Calendar of Documents relating to Ireland, I, 1171–1251, ed. H. S. Sweetman (London, 1875).

CAM, HELEN, 'The evolution of the medieval English franchise', *Speculum*, xxxii (1957), 427–42, reprinted in *Law Finders and Law Makers*, 22–43.

——, *The Hundred and the Hundred Rolls; an outline of local government in medieval England* (London, 1930).

——, *Law Finders and Law Makers in Medieval England. Collected studies in legal and constitutional history* (London, 1962).

——, 'Studies in the Hundred Rolls: some aspects of thirteenth-century administration', in *Oxford Studies in Social and Legal History*, ed. P. Vinogradoff, VI (Oxford, 1921).

The Canon Law of the Church of England. Being the report of the Archbishops' Commission on Canon Law (London, 1947).

CANTOR, N. F., *Church, Kingship and Lay Investiture in England, 1089–1135* (Princeton, 1958).

Cartae Antiquae Rolls, 1–10, ed. L. Landon (Pipe Roll Society, 1939).

CARTELLIERI, A., *Philipp II August, König von Frankreich*, 4 vols (Leipzig, 1899–1921).

——, *Philipp II August und der Zusammenbruch des Angevinischen Reiches* (Leipzig, 1913).

Cartularium Monasterii de Rameseia, ed. W. H. Hart and P. A. Lyons, 3 vols (Rolls Series, 1884–94).

The Cartulary of Darley Abbey, ed. R. R. Darlington (Derbyshire Archaeological and Natural History Society, 1945).

Catalogue des Actes de Philippe Auguste, ed. L. Delisle (Paris, 1856).

CAZEL, F. A., 'The tax of 1185 in aid of the Holy Land', *Speculum*, xxx (1955), 385–92.

CHARTROU, JOSÈPHE, *L'Anjou de 1109 à 1151* (Paris, 1928).

Chartularies of St Mary's Abbey, Dublin . . . and Annals of Ireland, ed. J. T. Gilbert (Rolls Series, 1884).

The Chartulary or Register of the Abbey of St Werburgh, Chester, ed. J. Tait, 2 parts (Chetham Society, 1920, 1923).

CHAMBERS, F. W., 'Some legends concerning Eleanor of Aquitaine', *Speculum*, xvi (1941), 459–68.

CHENEY, C. R., 'The punishment of felonious clerks', *English Historical Review*, li (1936), 215–36.

——, *From Becket to Langton. English Church Government, 1170–1213* (Manchester, 1956).

CHENEY, MARY, 'The Compromise of Avranches of 1172 and the spread of canon law in England', *English Historical Review*, lvi (1941), 177–97.

CHÉNON, E., *Les Marches Séparantes d'Anjou, Bretagne, et Poitou* (Paris, 1892).

——, 'Les origines et les premiers seigneurs de Montluçon', *Mémoires de la Société des Antiquaires du Centre*, new series, xxviii (1929), 63–97.

CHEW, HELENA M., *The English Ecclesiastical Tenants-in-Chief and Knight Service* (Oxford, 1932).

CHRIMES, S. B., *An Introduction to the Administrative History of Medieval England* (2nd edn, Oxford, 1959).

Chronicle of Holyrood: A Scottish Chronicle known as the Chronicle of Holyrood, ed. M. O. Anderson (Scottish Historical Society, 1938).

Chronicle of Melrose: Chronica de Mailros, ed. J. Stevenson (Bannatyne Club, 1835).

Chronicles of the Reigns of Stephen, Henry II, and Richard I, ed. R. Howlett, 4 vols (Rolls Series, 1884–90).

Chronicon Abbatiae Ramesiensis, ed. W. D. Macray (Rolls Series, 1886).

Chronicon Monasterii de Abingdon, ed. J. Stevenson (Rolls Series, 1858).

Chronicon Monasterii de Bello, ed. J. S. Brewer (Anglia Christiana Society, 1846).

Chroniques des Comtes d'Anjou et des Seigneurs d'Amboise, ed. L. Halphen and R. Poupardin (Paris, 1913).

Chroniques des Églises d'Anjou, ed. P. Marchegay and E. Mabile (Société de l'Histoire de France, 1869).

Chroniques de St Martial de Limoges, ed. H. Duplès-Agier (Société de l'Histoire de France, 1874).

CLANCHY, M. T., 'Magna Carta, clause 34', *English Historical Review*, lxxix (1964), 542–8.

CLAY, C. T., 'The early treasurers of York', *Yorkshire Archaeological Journal*, xxxv (1940–3), 7–34.

——, Introductions to *Early Yorkshire Charters* (q.v.).

——, 'Notes on the early archdeacons in the church of York', *Yorkshire Archaeological Journal*, xxxvi (1944–7), 269–87, 409–34.

——, 'Yorkshire final concords of the reign of Henry II', *Yorkshire Archaeological Journal*, xl (1959–62), 78–89.

CLÉDAT, L., *Du Rôle Historique de Bertrand de Born (1178–1200)* (Paris, 1879).

COLVIN, H. M., general ed., *The History of the King's Works*, I, R. A. Brown, H. M. Colvin and A. J. Taylor (London, 1963).

The Complete Peerage of England, Scotland, Ireland, Great Britain, and the United Kingdom, ed. G.E.C. [G. E. Cockayne]. New edn by V. Gibbs, G. H. White and others, 13 vols (London, 1910–59).

Continuatio Beccensis: [additions made at the Abbey of Bec for the years 1157–60 to a copy of the chronicle of Robert de Torigny], ed. R. Howlett in *Chronicles of the Reigns of Stephen, Henry II, and Richard I*, IV, 317–27.

Corpus Juris Canonici, ed. E. Friedberg, 2 vols (Leipzig, 1879–81).

Corpus Juris Civilis, ed. P. Kreuger and T. Mommsen (Berlin, 1886).

COX, J. C., *The Royal Forests of England* (London, 1905).

CRONNE, H. A., 'The honor of Leicester in Stephen's day', *English Historical Review*, l (1935), 670–80.

——, 'The office of local justiciar under the Norman kings', *University of Birmingham Historical Journal*, vi (1957–8), 18–38.

——, 'Ranulf de Gernons, earl of Chester, 1129–53', *Transactions of the Royal Historical Society*, 4th series, xx (1937), 103–34.

——, *The Reign of Stephen, 1135–54* (London, 1970).

——, 'The royal forest in the reign of Henry I', in *Essays in British and Irish History in honour of J. E. Todd.*

——, 'The Salisbury Oath', *History*, xix (1934), 248–53.

Curia Regis Rolls of the Reigns of Richard I and John, 7 vols (Public Record Office, London, 1922–35).

CURTIS, E., *History of Medieval Ireland* (first pub. 1923, 2nd edn, London, 1938).

DAUVILLIER, J., *Le Mariage dans le Droit Classique de l'Église, depuis le Décret de Gratien (1140) jusqu'à la mort de Clément V (1314)* (Paris, 1933).

DAVID, M., *La Souveraineté et les Limites Juridiques du Pouvoir Monarchiques, du IXe au XVe siècle* (Paris, 1954).

DAVIES, J. CONWAY, Introduction to *Episcopal Acts and Cognate Documents relating to Welsh Dioceses* (Cardiff, 1946).

——, 'The Memoranda Rolls of the Exchequer to 1307', *Studies presented to Sir Hilary Jenkinson*, 97–154.

DAVIS, H. W. C., 'Some documents of the Anarchy', *Essays in History presented to R. L. Poole*, 168–9.

——, 'The chronicle of Battle Abbey', *English Historical Review*, xxix (1914), 426–34.

——, 'England and Rome in the middle ages', *Church Quarterly Review* (1903), reprinted in *H. W. C. Davis: a Memoir and a selection of his historical papers*, ed. J. R. H. Weaver and A. L. Poole (London, 1933), 97–122.

——, 'Henry of Blois and Brian FitzCount', *English Historical Review*, xxv (1910), 297–303.

DAVIS, R. H. C., *King Stephen, 1135–1154* (London, 1967).

——, 'King Stephen and the earl of Chester, revised', *English Historical Review*, lxxv (1960), 654–60.

——, 'The treaty between William earl of Gloucester and Roger earl of Hereford', *A Medieval Miscellany for Doris Mary Stenton*, 139–46.

——, 'What happened in Stephen's reign, 1135–54', *History*, xlix (1964), 1–12.

DE BEER, G., *Genetics and Prehistory* (Cambridge, 1965).

DECK, SUZANNE, 'Le comté d'Eu sous les ducs', *Annales de Normandie*, iv (1954), 99–116.

——, 'Les marchlands de Rouen sous les ducs', *Annales de Normandie*, vi (1956), 245–54.

DELCAMBRE, É., 'Géographie historique du Velay', *Bibliothèque de l'École des Chartes*, xcviii (1937), 17–65.

DELISLE, L., Introduction [a separate volume] to *Recueil des Actes de Henri II* (q.v.).

DEPT, G. G., *Les Influences Anglaise et Française dans le Comté de Flandre au début du XIIIᵉ siècle* (Ghent, 1928).

DEVIC, C. and VAISSÈTE, J., *Histoire Générale de Languedoc avec des notes et des pièces justificatives*, 6 vols (Toulouse, 1872–1905). [Note: sometimes catalogued under 'Vic, C. de'].

Dialogus de Scaccario: De Necessariis Observantiis Scaccarii Dialogus, qui vulgo dicitur Dialogus de Scaccario, ed. C. Johnson (London, 1950).

DION, R., *Les Frontières de la France* (Paris, 1947).

Documents Illustrative of the Social and Economic History of the Danelaw, ed. F. M. Stenton (London, 1920).

DOUBLEDAY, H. A., 'The earl and the third penny of the county pleas', *The Complete Peerage*, IV, 657–64.

DOUGLAS, D. C., *The Social Structure of Medieval East Anglia* (Oxford Studies in Social and Legal History, ed. P. Vinogradoff, IX, Oxford, 1927).

——, *William the Conqueror. The Norman Impact upon England* (London, 1964).

DUBY, G., 'Dans la France du Nord-Ouest au XIIᵉ siècle: les "jeunes" dans la société aristocratique', *Annales*, xix (1964), 835–46.

——, 'Une enquête à poursuivre: la noblesse dans la France médiévale', *Revue Historique*, ccxxvi (1961), 1–22.

——, *Rural Economy and Country Life in the Medieval West*, translated from the French by Cynthia Postan (London, 1968).

DUGDALE, W., *Baronage of England*, 2 vols (London, 1675–6).

——, *Originales Juridicales* (3rd edn, London, 1680).

DUGGAN, C., 'The Becket dispute and the criminous clerks', *Bulletin of the Institute of Historical Research*, xxxv (1962), 1–28.

——, 'Richard of Ilchester, royal servant and bishop', *Transactions of the Royal Historical Society*, 5th series, xvi (1966), 1–21.

——, *Twelfth-Century Decretal Collections and their importance in English History* (London, 1963).

DUNCAN, A. A. M., 'The earliest Scottish charters', *Scottish Historical Review*, xxxvii (1958), 103–35.

DUNNING, P. J., 'The Arroasian order in medieval Ireland', *Irish Historical Studies*, iv (1944–5), 197–315.

EADMER, *Historia Novorum*: *Eadmeri Historia Novorum in Anglia et opuscula duo De Vita Sancti Anselmi et quibusdam miraculis ejus*, ed. M. Rule (Rolls Series, 1884).

——, *Vita Sancti Anselmi*: *Vita Sancti Anselmi: the Life of St Anselm, archbishop of Canterbury*, ed. R. W. Southern (London, 1963).

The Earliest Lincolnshire Assize Rolls, A.D. 1202–1209, ed. Doris M. Stenton (Lincoln Record Society, 1926).

Early Irish Society, ed. M. Dillon (Dublin, 1954).

Early Scottish Charters, prior to A.D. 1153, ed. A. C. Lawrie (Glasgow, 1905).

Early Sources of Scottish History, A.D. 500 to 1286, collected and translated by A. O. Anderson, 2 vols (Edinburgh and London, 1922).

Early Yorkshire Charters, ed. W. Farrer and continued by C. T. Clay, 12 vols (Yorkshire Archaeological Society, 1914–65).

EDWARD GRIM, Vita S. Thomae, Cantuariensis Archiepiscopi et Martyris, ed. J. C. Robertson in *Materials for the Life of Thomas Becket*, II, 353–450.

EDWARDS, J. G., 'The Normans and the Welsh march', *Proceedings of the British Academy*, xlii (1956), 155–77.

EDWARDS, R. DUDLEY, 'Anglo-Norman relations with Connacht, 1169–1224', *Irish Historical Studies*, I (1938–9), 135–53.

English Historical Documents, II (1042–1189), ed. D. C. Douglas and G. W. Greenaway (London, 1953).

Essays in British and Irish History in honour of J. E. Todd, ed. H. A. Cronne, T. W. Moody, and D. B. Quinn (London, 1949).

Essays in History presented to Reginald Lane Poole, ed. H. W. C. Davis (Oxford, 1927).

Essays in Medieval History presented to Thomas Frederick Tout, ed. A. G. Little and F. M. Powicke (Manchester, 1925).

EYTON, R. W., *Court, Household, and Itinerary of Henry II* (London, 1878).

Facsimiles of Early Charters from Northamptonshire Collections, ed. F. M. Stenton (Northamptonshire Record Society, 1930).

FARMER, D. L., 'Some price fluctuations in Angevin England', *Economic History Review*, 2nd series, ix (1956), 34–43.

FARRER, W., *Final Concords of the County of Lancaster* (Manchester, 1899).

——, *The Lancashire Pipe Rolls of 31 Henry I and of the Reigns of Henry II, Richard I, and John; also Early Lancashire Charters of the period from the reign of William Rufus to that of King John* (Liverpool, 1902).

——, *Honors and Knights Fees*, 3 vols (London and Manchester, 1923–5).

FAWTIER, R., 'L'histoire financière de l'Angleterre au moyen âge', *Le Moyen Âge*, 2nd series, xxix (1928), 48–67.

——, *The Capetian Kings of France*, translated by L. Butler and R. J. Adam (London, 1960) from *Les Capétiens et la France* (Paris, 1942).

Feet of Fines of the Reign of Henry II and of the first seven years of the reign of Richard I, 1182–1196 (Pipe Roll Society, 1894).

FEUCHÈRE, P., 'Essai sur l'evolution territoriale des principautés françaises, X–XIIIᵉ siècles', *Le Moyen Âge*, 2nd series, lviii (1952), 85–117.

Feudal Documents from Bury St Edmunds, ed. D. C. Douglas (London, 1932).

Final concords of the County of Lincoln, II, ed. C. W. Foster (Lincoln Record Society, 1920).

FLAHIFF, G. B., 'The use of prohibitions by clerics against ecclesiastical courts in England', *Medieval Studies*, iii (1941), 101–16.

——, 'The writ of prohibition to courts Christian in the thirteenth century', *Medieval Studies*, vi (1944), 261–313; vii (1945), 229–90.

FLICHE, A., 'L'état Toulousain', *Histoire des Institutions Francaises au Moyen Âge*, ed. F. Lot and R. Fawtier, II, 72–99.

FLICHE, A., FOREVILLE, R. and ROUSSET, J., *Du Premier Concile du Lateran à l'Avenément d' Innocent III (1123–1198)*, Pt I (Paris, 1946) (vol. IX of *Histoire de l'Église depuis les origines jusqu'à nos jours*, ed. A. Fliche and V. Martin).

FLORENCE OF WORCESTER: *Florentii Wigorniensis Monachi, Chronicon ex Chronicis*, ed. B. Thorne, 2 vols (London, 1848–9).

FLOWER, C. T., *Introduction to the Curia Regis Rolls, 1199–1230* (Selden Society, 1944).

Foedera: Thomas Rymer, *Foedera, Conventiones, Litterae, et Acta Publica*, ed. A. Clarke and F. Holbrooke, 7 vols (London, 1816–69).

FOREVILLE, RAYMONDE, *L'Église et la Royauté en Angleterre sous Henri II Plantagenêt (1154–1189)* (Paris, 1943).

——, 'Lettres "extravagantes" de Thomas Becket, archevêque de Canterbury', *Mélanges . . . Halphen*, 225–38.

FOSTER, C. W., *Introduction to Final Concords of the County of Lincoln*, II (Lincoln Record Society, 1920).

FOWLER, G. H., 'Henry fitzHenry at Woodstock', *English Historical Review*, xxxxix (1924), 240–1.

—— 'The shire of Bedford and the earldom of Huntingdon', *Bedfordshire Historical Record Society*, ix (1925).

FOX, L., 'The honour and earldom of Leicester: origin and descent, 1066–1399', *English Historical Review*, liv (1939), 385–402.

FRAPPIER, J., 'Vues sur les conceptions courtoises dans les littératures d'oc et d'oïl au XIIᵉ siècle', *Cahiers de Civilisation Médiévale*, ii (1959), 135–56.

FURLEY, J. S., *City Government of Winchester from the records of the XIVth and XVth centuries* (Oxford, 1923).

GABEL, LEONA C., *Benefit of Clergy in England in the Later Middle Ages* (Northampton, Massachusetts, 1928–9).

GALBRAITH, V. H., 'Nationality and language in medieval England', *Transactions of the Royal Historical Society*, xxiii (1941), 113–28.

——, 'A new charter of Henry II to Battle Abbey', *English Historical Review*, lii (1937), 57–73.

——, 'Osbert, dean of Lewes', *English Historical Review*, lxix (1954), 289–301.

GARNIER OF PONT-SAINTE-MAXENCE: Guernes de Pont-Sainte-Maxence, *La Vie de Saint Thomas le Martyr*, ed. E. Walberg (Lund, 1922).

GÉNESTAL, R., *Les Origines du Privilège Clérical* (Paris, 1908).

——, *Le Privilegium Fori en France, du Décret de Gratien à la fin du XIVᵉ siècle* (Paris 1921–4).

GEOFFREY DE VIGEOIS: Chronica Gaufredi Coenobitae Monasterii S. Martialis Lemovicensis ac Prioris Vosciencis coenobii, ed. P. Labbe in *Nova Bibliotheca Manuscriptorum*, II (Paris, 1657), 279–342.

GERALD OF WALES: *Giraldus Cambrensis, Opera*, ed. J. S. Brewer, J. F. Dimock, and G. F. Warner, 8 vols (Rolls Series, 1861–91).

GERVASE OF CANTERBURY: *The Historical Works of Gervase of Canterbury*, ed. W. Stubbs, 2 vols (Rolls Series, 1879–80).

GERVASE OF TILBURY: Otia Imperialia, ed. G. G. Leibnitz in *Scriptores Rerum Brunsvicensiam*, 2 vols (Hanover, 1707–10); Excerpta ex Otiis Imperialibus, ed. J. Stevenson in *Radulphi de Coggeshall Chronicon*, 419–49.

Die Gesetze der Angelsachsen, ed. F. Liebermann, 3 vols (Halle, 1903–16).

Gesta Abbatum Monasterii Sancti Albani: Chronica Monasterii S. Albani: Gesta Abbatum Monasterii Sancti Albani, a Thoma Walsingham, ed. H. T. Riley, I (Rolls Series, 1867).

Gesta Regis Henrici Secundi Benedicti Abbatis: The Chronicle of the Reigns of Henry II and Richard I, A.D. 1169–1192, known commonly under the name of Benedict of Peterborough. See ROGER OF HOWDEN, Gesta.

Gesta Stephani: the Deeds of Stephen, ed. K. R. Potter (London, 1955).

GILBERT FOLIOT, Letters: *The Letters and Charters of Gilbert Foliot*, ed. A. Morey and C. N. L. Brooke (Cambridge, 1967).

Glanvill: Tractatus de Legibus et Consuetudinibus Regni Angliae qui Glanvilla vocatur, ed. G. D. G. Hall (London, 1965).

GLEASON, S. E., *An Ecclesiastical Barony of the Middle Ages: the Bishopric of Bayeux, 1066–1204* (Cambridge, Massachusetts, 1936).

GRAHAM, ROSE, *English Ecclesiastical Studies* (London, 1929).

GRAY, J. W., 'The *Ius Praesentandi* in England from the Constitutions of Clarendon to Bracton', *English Historical Review*, lxvii (1952), 481–509.

GREENE, D., 'Early Irish society', *Early Irish Society*, ed. M. Dillon, 79–82.

GRUNDMAN, H., 'Rotten und Brabanzonen: Soldner-Heere im 12 Jahrhundert', *Deutsches Archiv für Geschichte des Mittelalters*, v (1941–2), 419–92.

GUILHIERMOZ, P., *Essai sur l'Origine de la Noblesse en France au Moyen Âge* (Paris, 1902).

GWYNN, A., 'Archbishop John Cumin', *Repertorium Novum: Dublin Diocesan Historical Record*, i (1956), 285–310.

——, 'The centenary of the Synod of Kells (1152)', *Irish Ecclesiastical Record*, lxxvii (1952), 161–76, 250–64.

——, 'The first bishops of Dublin (1028–1152)', *Repertorium Novum: Dublin Diocesan Historical Record*, i (1955), 1–26.

——, 'The first synod of Cashel (1101)', *Irish Ecclesiastical Record*, lxvi (1945), 81–92; lxvii (1946), 109–22.

——, 'Lanfranc and the Irish church', *Irish Ecclesiastical Record*, lviii (1941), 1–15.

——, 'Medieval Bristol and Dublin', *Irish Historical Studies*, v (1947), 275–86.

——, 'The origins of St Mary's abbey, Dublin', *Journal of the Royal Society of Antiquaries of Ireland*, lxxix (1949), 110–25.

——, 'Papal legates in Ireland during the twelfth century', *Irish Ecclesiastical Record*, lxiii (1944), 361–70.

——, 'Provincial and diocesan decrees of the diocese of Dublin during the Anglo-Norman period', *Archivum Hibernicum*, xi (1944), 31–117.

——, 'St Anselm and the Irish church', *Irish Ecclesiastical Record*, lix (1942), 1–14.

——, 'St Lawrence O'Toole as legate in Ireland', *Analecta Bollandia*, lxviii (1950), 223–40.

HALL, G. D. G., Introduction to *Tractatus de Legibus et Consuetudinibus Regni Angliae qui Glanvilla vocatur* (London, 1965).

HALL, H., *Court Life Under the Plantagenets* (London, 1890).

HALPHEN, L., *A Travers l'Histoire du Moyen Âge* (Paris, 1950).

——, *Le Comté d'Anjou au XIe siècle* (Paris, 1906).

——, 'Les entrevues des rois Louis VII et Henri II durant l'exil de Thomas Becket en France', *Mélanges d'Histoire offerts à M. Charles Bémont* (Paris, 1913), 151–62; reprinted in *A Travers l'Histoire du Moyen Âge*, 256–265.

——, 'La place de la royauté dans le système féodale', *Revue Historique*, clxxii (1933), 249–56; reprinted in *A Travers l'Histoire du Moyen Âge*, 266–74.

HAMILL, F. C., 'Presentment of Englishry and the murder fine', *Speculum*, xii (1937), 285–98.

HAND, G., 'The medieval chapter of St Mary's cathedral, Limerick', *Medieval Studies presented to Aubrey Gwynn*, 74–89.

HARDEGEN, F., *Imperialpolitik König Heinrichs II von England* (Heidelberg, 1905).

HASKINS, C. H., 'Adelard of Bath and Henry Plantagenet', *English Historical Review*, xxviii (1913), 515–6.

——, 'England and Sicily in the twelfth century', *English Historical Review*, xxvi (1911), 433–47, 641–65.

HASKINS, C. H., 'Henry II as a patron of learning', *Essays in Medieval History presented to T. F. Tout*, 71–7.

——, 'The inquest of 1171 in the Avranchin', *English Historical Review*, xxvi (1911), 326–8.

——, *Norman Institutions* (Cambridge, Massachusetts, 1918).

HELTZEL, V. B., *Fair Rosamund: a study of the development of a literary theme* (Evanston, 1947).

HENRY DE BRACTON, *De Legibus et Consuetudinibus Angliae*, ed. T. Twiss, 6 vols (Rolls Series, 1878–83); ed. G. Woodbine, 4 vols (New Haven, 1915–42). Woodbine's edn, revised and trans. by S. E. Thorne (Harvard, 1968, in progress).

HENRY OF HUNTINGDON: *Historia Anglorum*, ed. T. Arnold (Rolls Series, 1870).

HERBERT OF BOSHAM: Vita Sancti Thomae, Archiepiscopi et Martyris, auctore Herberto de Boseham, ed. J. C. Robertson in *Materials for the History of Thomas Becket*, III, 155–534.

HESLIN, ANNE, 'The coronation of the Young King in 1170', *Studies in Church History*, II, ed. G. J. Cuming (London, 1968), 165–78.

HIGOUNET, S. C., 'Une grande chapitre de l'histoire du XIIe siècle: La rivalité des maisons de Toulouse et de Barcelone pour la préponderance méridionale', *Mélanges. . . Halphen*, 313–22.

HILL, J. W. F., *Medieval Lincoln* (Cambridge, 1948).

Histoire de Guillaume la Maréschal, ed. P. Mayer, 3 vols (Société de l' Histoire de France, 1891–1901).

Historiae Dunelmensis Scriptores Tres . . . with an appendix of charters and other documents, ed. J. Raine (Surtees Society, 1839).

Historians of the Church of York and its Archbishops, ed. J. Raine, 3 vols (Rolls Series, 1879–94).

Historical Essays in honour of James Tait, ed. J. G. Edwards, V. H. Galbraith, and E. F. Jacob (Manchester, 1933).

HODGSON, C. E., *Jung Heinrich, König von England, Sohn König Heinrichs II, 1155–83* (Jena, 1906).

HOLDSWORTH, W., *A History of English Law*, I, 7th edn, with an introductory essay and additions by S. B. Chrimes (London, 1956).

HOLLISTER, C. WARREN, *The Military Organization of Norman England* (Oxford, 1965).

——, 'The significance of scutage rates in eleventh- and twelfth-century England', *English Historical Review*, lxxv (1960), 577–88.

HOLT, J. C., 'The assizes of Henry II: the texts', *The Study of Medieval Records*, ed. D. A. Bullough and R. L. Storey (Oxford, 1971), 85–106.

——, *Magna Carta* (Cambridge, 1965).

——, *The Northerners: a study in the reign of King John* (Oxford, 1961).

HOMANS, G. C., 'The rural sociology of medieval England', *Past and Present*, no. 4 (1953), 32–43.

HOVE, A. VAN, *Prolegomena ad Codicem Iuris Canonici* (2nd edn, Malines and Rome, 1945).

HOWELL, MARGARET E., *Regalian Right in Medieval England* (London, 1962).

HOYT, R. S., *The Royal Demesne in English Constitutional History, 1066–1272* (New York, 1950).

——, 'Royal taxation and the growth of the realm in medieval England', *Speculum*, xxv (1950), 36–48.

HUBERT, J., 'Le miracle de Déols et la trêve conclue en 1187 entre les rois de France et d'Angleterre', *Bibliothèque de l'École des Chartes*, xcvi (1935), 285–300.

HUGH THE CHANTOR, *The History of the Church of York, 1066–1127*, ed. C. Johnson (London, 1961).

HUNNISETT, R. F., 'The origins of the office of coroner', *Transactions of the Royal Historical Society*, 5th series, viii (1958), 85–104.

HUNTER-MARSHALL, D. W., 'Two early English occupations in Scotland – their administrative organization', *Scottish Historical Review*, xxv (1928), 20–40.

HURNARD, NAOMI D., 'The Anglo-Norman franchises', *English Historical Review*, lxiv (1949), 289–323, 433–60.

——, 'Did Edward I reverse Henry II's policy upon seisin?', *English Historical Review*, lxix (1954), 529–53.

——, 'The jury of presentment and the Assize of Clarendon', *English Historical Review*, lvi (1941), 374–410.

——, 'Magna Carta, Clause 34', *Studies . . . Presented to F. M. Powicke*, 157–79.

IMBART DE LA TOUR, P., *Les Élections Épiscopales dans l'Église de France du IXᵉ au XIIᵉ siècle* (Paris, 1891).

JAMISON, EVELYN, 'The Sicilian Norman kingdom in the mind of Anglo-Norman contemporaries', *Proceedings of the British Academy*, xxiv (1938), 237–85.

JARRY, E., *Provinces et Pays de France. Essai de géographie historique*, I, Formation de l'unité française (2nd edn, Paris, 1950).

JENKINSON, H., 'Financial records of the reign of King John', *Magna Carta Commemoration Essays*, ed. H. E. Malden (London, 1917), 244–300.

——, 'A money-lender's bonds of the twelfth century', *Essays in History presented to R. L. Poole*, 190–210.

——, 'William Cade, a financier of the twelfth century', *English Historical Review*, xxviii (1913), 209–27.

JEULIN, P., 'Un grand "honneur" anglais. Aperçus sur le "comté" de Richmond en Angleterre', *Annales de Bretagne*, xlii (1935), 265–302.

JOCELYN OF BRAKELOND: *Chronica Jocelini de Brakelonda De Rebus Gestis Samsonis, Abbatis Monasteri Sancti Edmundi*, ed. H. E. Butler (London, 1949).

JOHN OF HEXHAM: Historia Johannis Prioris Hagustaldensis, ed. T. Arnold in *Symeonis Monachi Opera Omnia*, II, 284–332.

JOHN DE MARMOUTIER, Historia Gaufredi ducis Normannorum et comitis

Andegavorum, ed. L. Halphen and R. Poupardin in *Chroniques des comtes d'Anjou et des seigneurs d'Amboise*, 172–231.

JOHN OF SALISBURY, *Historia Pontificalis: Ioannis Saresberiensis Historia Pontificalis: John of Salisbury's Memoirs of the Papal Court*, ed. Marjoric Chibnall (London, 1956).

——, *Letters: The Letters of John of Salisbury*, I, *The early letters (1153–1161)*, ed. W. J. Millor and H. E. Butler, revised by C. N. L. Brooke (London, 1955). [Note: letters of Archbishop Theobald which John of Salisbury penned as the archbishop's secretary, are cited as *The Letters of John of Salisbury*.]

——, *Metalogicon: Iohannis Saresberiensis Episcopi Carnotensis Metalogicon*, ed. C. C. J. Webb (Oxford, 1929).

——, *Policraticus: Ioannis Saresberiensis Episcopi Carnotensis Policratici sive De Nugis Curialium et Vestigiis Philosophorum*, ed. C. C. J. Webb, 2 vols (Oxford, 1909).

——, Vita Thomae: Vita Sancti Thomae Cantuariensis Archiepiscopi et Martyris, auctoribus Joanne Saresberiensis et Alano Tewkesberiensi, ed. J. C. Robertson in *Materials for the History of Thomas Becket*, III, 301–22.

JOHNSON, C., Introduction to *De Necessariis Observantis Scaccarii Dialogus qui vulgo dicitur Dialogus de Scaccario* (London, 1950).

——, Introduction to *Pipe Roll 2 Richard I (1190)*, ed. Doris M. Stenton (Pipe Roll Society, 1925), xiii–xxiii.

——, 'The reconciliation of Henry II with the papacy: a missing document', *English Historical Review*, lii (1937), 466–7.

JOHNSON, C. and CRONNE, H. A., Introduction to *Regesta Regum Anglo-Normannorum, 1066–1154*, II, *Regesta Henrici Primi, 1100–1135* (Oxford, 1956).

JOLLIFFE, J. E. A., *Angevin Kingship* (2nd edn, London, 1963).

——, 'The *camera regis* under Henry II', *English Historical Review*, lxviii (1953), 1–21, 337–62.

——, *The Constitutional History of Medieval England* (3rd edn, London, 1954).

JONES, F. ELMORE, 'Stephen Type VII', *British Numismatic Journal*, xxviii (1957), 537–54.

JORDAN FANTOSME, 'Chronique de la guerre entre les Anglois et les Ecossois en 1173 et 1174', ed. R. Howlett in *Chronicles of the Reigns of Stephen, Henry II, and Richard I*, III, 202–377.

JOÜON DES LONGRAIS, F., *La Conception Anglaise de la Saisine du XIIe au XIVe siècle* (Paris, 1924).

——, 'Le droit criminel anglais au moyen âge, 1066–1485', *Revue Historique de Droit Français et Étranger*, 4th series, xxxiv (1956), 391–435.

——, 'La porté politique des réformes d'Henri II en matière de saisine', *Revue Historique de Droit Français et Étranger*, 4th series, xv (1936), 540–71.

KANTOROWICZ, E. H., *The King's Two Bodies: a study in medieval political theology* (Princeton, 1957).

——, *Laudes Regiae: a study in liturgical acclamations and medieval ruler worship* (Berkeley, California, 1946).

KELLY, AMY, 'Eleanor of Aquitaine and her courts of love', *Speculum*, xii (1937), 3–19.

——, *Eleanor of Aquitaine and the Four Kings* (London, 1952).

KEMP, E. W., *Canonization and Authority in the Western Church* (Oxford, 1948).

——, 'Canon law and its administration in England in the twelfth century', introduction to *Papal Decretals relating to the Diocese of Lincoln in the Twelfth Century*, ed. W. Holzmann and E. W. Kemp (Lincoln Record Society, 1954), xvii–xxviii.

KERN, F., *Kingship and Law in the Middle Ages*. Studies by F. Kern translated with an introduction by S. B. Chrimes (Oxford, 1939).

KIENAST, W., *Die Deutschen Fürsten im Dienste der Westmächte bis zum Tode Philipps des Schönen von Frankreich* (Utrecht, 1924).

——, *Deutschland und Frankreich in der Kaiserzeit, 900–1270* (Leipzig, 1943).

——, *Untertaneneid und Treuvorbehalt in England und Frankreich* (Weimar, 1952).

KIMBALL, ELIZABETH G., *Serjeanty Tenure in Medieval England* (New Haven, 1936).

——, 'The judicial aspects of frankalmoign tenure', *English Historical Review*, xlvii (1932), 1–11.

——, 'Tenure in frankalmoign and secular services', *English Historical Review*, xliii (1928), 341–53.

KNOWLES, D., 'Archbishop Thomas Becket: a character study', *Proceedings of the British Academy*, xxxv (1949), 177–205; reprinted in *The Historian and Character*, 98–128.

——, 'The case of St William of York', *Cambridge Historical Journal*, v (1936), 162–77, 212–14; reprinted in *The Historian and Character*, 76–97.

——, *The Episcopal Colleagues of Archbishop Thomas Becket* (Cambridge, 1951).

——, 'The growth of exemption', *Downside Review*, l (1932), 201–31, 396–436.

——, *The Historian and Character, and other studies* (Cambridge, 1963).

——, *The Monastic Order in England: a history of its development from the times of St Dunstan to the Fourth Lateran Council, 943–1216* (Cambridge, 1949).

——, 'The revolt of the lay brothers of Sempringham', *English Historical Review*, l (1935), 465–87.

KIRBY, D. P., 'Strathclyde and Cumbria: a survey of historical development to 1092', *Transactions of the Cumberland and Westmoreland Antiquarian and Archaeological Society*, new series, lxii (1962), 77–94.

KIRFEL, H. J., *Weltherrschaftsidee und Bündnispolitik. Untersuchungen zur Auswärtigen Politik der Staufer* (Bonn, 1959).

KOEHLER, E., 'Observations historiques et sociologiques sur la poésie des troubadours', *Cahiers de Civilisation Médiévale*, vii (1964), 27–51.

LABANDE, E-R., 'Pour une image véridique d'Aliénor d'Aquitaine', *Bulletin de la Société des Antiquaires de l'Ouest*, 4th series, ii (1952), 175–234.

LA BORDERIE, A. DE, *Histoire de Bretagne*, 6 vols (Rennes and Paris, 1896–1914).

The Lancashire Pipe Rolls of 31 Henry I and of the reigns of Henry II, Richard I and King John . . . also early Lancashire Charters, ed. W. Farrer (Liverpool, 1902).

LANDON, L., 'Gisors and the Norman Vexin', *The Itinerary of King Richard I with studies on certain matters of interest in connection with his reign*, ed. L. Landon (Pipe Roll Society, 1935), 219–34.

——, 'The rate of travel in medieval times', *The Itinerary of Richard I*, ed. L. Landon [as above], 184–91.

LANGMUIR, G. I., ' "Judei nostri" and the beginning of Capetian legislation', *Traditio*, xvi (1960), 302–39.

LAPSLEY, G. T., *The County Palatine of Durham* (New York, 1900).

——, 'The Flemings in eastern England in the reign of Henry II', *English Historical Review*, xxi (1906), 509–13.

——, 'Some castle-officers in the twelfth century', *English Historical Review*, xxxiii (1918), 348–59.

LATOUCHE, R., *The Birth of Western Economy: Economic Aspects of the Dark Ages*, trans. from French by E. M. Wilkinson (London, 1961).

Layettes du Trésor des Chartes, ed. A. F. Teulet (Paris, 1863–1909).

Leges Henrici Primi, printed in *Die Gesetze der Angelsachsen* (q.v.), I, 547–611.

Leges Ville Norht, ed. F. Lee (Northampton, 1951).

LEGG, J. W., *Three Coronation Orders* (London, 1900).

LEJEUNE, RITA, 'Rôle littéraire de la famille d'Aliénor d'Aquitaine', *Cahiers de Civilization Médiévale*, i (1958), 319–337.

LEMARIGNIER, J-F., *Recherches sur l'Hommage en Marche et les Frontières Féodales* (Lille, 1945).

LENNARD, R., *Rural England, 1086–1135: a study of social and agrarian conditions* (Oxford, 1959).

LE PATOUREL, J., 'The Plantagenet Dominions', *History*, l (1965), 289–308.

Letters of John of Salisbury, I, *The early letters (1153–1161)*, ed. W. J. Millor and H. E. Butler, revised by C. N. L. Brooke (London, 1965). [Note: many of the letters in this volume were written by John of Salisbury in his capacity as secretary to Archbishop Theobald, and are in the name of the archbishop. Letters of John of Salisbury himself are cited in the footnotes as John of Salisbury, *Letters*.]

Liber Niger de Scaccario, ed. T. Hearne, 2 vols (2nd edn, London, 1771).

LILLIE, H. W. R., 'St Thomas of Canterbury's opposition to Henry II', *Clergy Review*, viii (1934), 261–83.

LLOYD, J. E., *A History of Wales, from the earliest times to the Edwardian conquest*, 2 vols (3rd edn, London, 1939).

LOT, F., *Fidèles ou Vassaux? Essai sur la nature juridique du lien qui unissait les grands vassaux à la royauté depuis le milieu du IXᵉ jusqu'à la fin du XIIᵉ siècle* (Paris, 1904).

LOT, F. and FAWTIER, R., *Histoire des Institutions Françaises au Moyen Âge*, I, *Institutions seigneuriales;* II, *Institutions royales* (Paris, 1957–8).

LUCHAIRE, A., *Études sur les Actes de Louis VII* (Paris, 1885).

——, *Histoire des Institutions Monarchiques de la France sous les premiers Capétiens (987–1180)*, 2 vols (Paris, 1883).

——, 'Hughes de Clers et le *De Sonescalia Franciae*', in *Mélanges d'Histoire du Moyen Âge*, ed. A. Luchaire, I (Paris 1897), 1–38.

——, 'Le roi Louis VII et le pope Alexandre III', *Comptes rendues de l'Académie des Sciences Morales et Politiques*, cxlvii (1897), 425–60.

——, *Social France at the time of Philip Augustus*, translated by E. B. Krehbiel from *La Societé Françaises au Temps de Philippe-Auguste* (New York, 1912).

LUNT, W. E., 'The text of the ordinance of 1184 concerning an aid for the Holy Land', *English Historical Review*, xxxvii (1922), 235–42.

LYON, B. D., 'The feudal antecedent of the indenture system', *Speculum*, xxix (1954), 503–11.

——, *From Fief to Indenture* (Cambridge, Massachusetts, 1957).

——, 'The money fief under the English kings, 1066–1485', *English Historical Review*, lxvi (1951), 161–93.

MCKISACK, MAY, 'London and the succession to the Crown in the middle ages', *Studies in Medieval History presented to F. M. Powicke*, 86–9.

MACNEILL, E., *Early Irish Laws and Institutions* (Dublin, 1935).

——, 'Military service in medieval Ireland', *Journal of the Cork Historical and Archaeological Society*, xlvi (1941), 6–15.

MADOX, T., *Formulare Anglicanum* (London, 1702).

——, *The History and Antiquities of the Exchequer of England*, 2 vols (2nd edn, London, 1769).

Magni Rotuli Scaccarii Normanniae sub Regibus Angliae, ed. T. Stapleton, 2 vols (London, 1840–4).

MAITLAND, F. W., 'The beatitude of seisin', *Law Quarterly Review*, iv (1888), 24–39, 286–99; reprinted in *Collected Papers*, I, 407–57.

——, *Collected Papers*, ed. H. A. L. Fisher, 3 vols (Cambridge, 1911).

——, *The Forms of Action at Common Law*, ed. A. H. Chaytor and W. J. Whittacker (Cambridge, 1936).

——, 'Glanville, Ranulf de', *Dictionary of National Biography*.

——, 'Henry II and the criminous clerks', *English Historical Review*, vii (1892), 224–34; reprinted in *Roman Canon Law in the Church of England*, 132–47, and in *Collected Papers*, II, 232–50.

——, *Roman Canon Law in the Church of England* (London, 1898).

MANWOOD, J., *A Treatise and Discourse of the Lawes of the Forest* (first pub. 1598, 4th edn 1717).

Materials, Epistolae: Epistolae ad historiam Thomae Cantuariensis Archiepiscopi pertinentes, ed. J. C. Robertson in *Materials for the History of Thomas Becket*, V, VI, VII.

Materials for the History of Thomas Becket, Archbishop of Canterbury, ed. J. C. Robertson, 7 vols (Rolls Series, 1875–85).

MAYR-HARTING, H., 'Hilary, bishop of Chichester (1147–69) and Henry II', *English Historical Review*, lxxviii (1963), 209–24.

——, 'Henry II and the papacy, 1170–1189', *Journal of Ecclesiastical History*, xvi (1965), 39–53.

A Medieval Miscellany for Doris Mary Stenton, ed. Patricia M. Barnes and C. F. Slade (Pipe Roll Society, 1962).

Medieval Studies presented to Aubrey Gwynn, ed. J. A. Watt, J. B. Morrall, and F. X. Martin (Dublin, 1961).

Medieval Studies presented to Rose Graham, ed. Veronica Ruffer and A. J. Taylor (Oxford, 1950).

MEEKINGS, C. A. F., Introduction to *Crown Pleas of the Wiltshire Eyre, 1249* (Wiltshire Archaeological and Natural History Society, Records Branch, 1961).

MEGAW, M. ISABEL, 'The ecclesiastical policy of Stephen, 1135–9: a reinterpretation', *Essays in British and Irish History in Honour of J. E. Todd.*

Mélanges d'Histoire du Moyen Âge dédiés à la memoire de Louis Halphen (Paris, 1951).

Mémoires pour servir de preuves à l'Histoire Ecclésiastique et Civile de Bretagne, ed. P. H. Morice, 3 vols (Paris, 1742–6).

Memoranda Rolls: *The Memoranda Roll for the Michaelmas Term of the First Year of the Reign of King John (1199–1200)*, ed. Doris M. Stenton and others (Pipe Roll Society, 1943).

The Memoranda Roll for the Tenth Year of the Reign of King John (1207–8), ed. R. A. Brown (Pipe Roll Society, 1957).

MILLER, E., *The Abbey and Bishopric of Ely* (Cambridge, 1951).

MITCHELL, S. K., *Taxation in Medieval England*, ed. S. Painter (New Haven, 1951).

Monasticon Anglicanum, ed. W. Dugdale, 3 vols (London 1655–73); new edition by J. Caley, H. Ellis, and B. Bandniel, 8 vols (London, 1817–30).

MOODY, T. W., 'The writings of Edmund Curtis', *Irish Historical Studies*, iii (1940–3), 393–400.

MOORE, O. H., *The Young King Henry Plantagenet, 1155–1183, in history, literature, and tradition* (Columbus, Ohio, 1925).

MOREY, A., *Bartholomew of Exeter, bishop and canonist. A study in the twelfth century* (Cambridge, 1937).

MOREY, A. and BROOKE, C. N. L., *Gilbert Foliot and his Letters* (Cambridge, 1965).

MORGAN, M., 'The organization of the Scottish Church in the twelfth century', *Transactions of the Royal Historical Society*, 4th series, xxix (1947), 135–49.

MORRIS, W., *The Medieval English Sheriff to 1300* (Manchester, 1927).

MORRIS, W. A., *The Early English County Court. An historical study with illustrative documents* (Berkeley, 1926).

——, *The Frankpledge System* (Cambridge, Massachusetts, 1910).

NEILL, S. C. and WEBER, H-R., eds, *The Layman in Christian History* (London, 1963).

NELSON, L. H., *The Normans in South Wales, 1070–1171* (Austin, Texas, 1966).

NEWMAN, W. L., *Le Domaine Royal sous les premiers Capétiens (987–1180)* (Paris, 1937).

NICHOLL, D., *Thurstan, Archbishop of York (1114–1140)* (York, 1964).

NITZE, W. A., 'The exhumation of King Arthur of Glastonbury', *Speculum*, ix (1934), 355–61.

NORGATE, KATE, 'The bull *Laudabiliter*', *English Historical Review*, viii (1893), 18–52.

——, *England under the Angevin Kings*, 2 vols (London, 1887).

——, *Richard the Lionheart* (London, 1924).

ODEGAARD, C. E., 'Legalis homo', *Speculum*, xv (1940), 186–93.

O'DOHERTY, J. F., 'The Anglo-Norman invasion, 1167–71', *Irish Historical Studies*, i (1938–9), 154–7.

——, 'Historical criticism of the Song of Dermot and the Earl', *Irish Historical Studies*, i (1938–9), 294–6.

——, 'Rome and the Anglo-Norman invasion of Ireland', *Irish Ecclesiastical Record*, xlii (1933), 131–45.

——, 'St Laurence O' Toole and the Anglo-Norman invasion', *Irish Ecclesiastical Record*, l (1937), 449–77, 600–25; li (1938), 131–46.

OMAN, C. W. C., *The Coinage of England* (Oxford, 1931).

ORDERIC VITALIS: *Orderici Vitalis Angligenae Coenobi Uticensis Monachi, Historiae Ecclesiasticae*, ed. A. Le Prévost, 5 vols (Société de l'Histoire de France, 1838–55).

ORPEN, G. H., *Ireland under the Normans (1169–1333)*, 4 vols (Oxford, 1911–20).

OTWAY-RUTHVEN, JOCELYN, 'The constitutional position of the great lordships in south Wales', *Transactions of the Royal Historical Society*, 5th series, viii (1958), 1–20.

——, *History of Medieval Ireland* (Dublin, 1968).

——, 'Knight-service in Ireland', *Journal of the Royal Society of Antiquaries of Ireland*, lxxxix (1959), 1–15.

——, 'The medieval county of Kildare', *Irish Historical Studies*, xi (1958–9), 181–99.

——, 'The native Irish and English law in medieval Ireland', *Irish Historical Studies*, vii (1950–1), 1–16.

——, 'The organization of Anglo-Irish agriculture in the middle ages', *Journal of the Royal Society of Antiquaries of Ireland*, lxxxi (1951), 1–13.

PACAUT, M., *Alexandre III. Étude sur la conception du pouvoir pontifical dans sa pensée et dans son oeuvre* (Paris, 1956).

——, 'Les légats d'Alexandre III', *Revue d'Histoire Ecclésiastique*, l (1955), 821–38.

——, *Louis VII et les Élections Episcopales dans le Royaume de France* (Paris, 1957).

——, *Louis VII et son Royaume* (Paris, 1964).

——, *La Théocratie. L'église et le pouvoir au moyen âge* (Paris, 1957).

PAINTER, S., 'Castellans of the plain of Poitou in the eleventh and twelfth centuries', *Speculum*, xxxi (1956), 243–57; reprinted in *Feudalism and Liberty*, 17–40.

PAINTER, S., 'Castle-guard', *American Historical Review*, xl (1935), 450–9; reprinted in *Feudalism and Liberty*, 144–56.

——, 'English castles in the early middle ages: their number, location, and legal position', *Speculum*, x (1935), 321–32; reprinted in *Feudalism and Liberty*, 125–43.

——, 'The family and the feudal system in twelfth-century England', *Speculum*, xxxv (1960), 1–16; reprinted in *Feudalism and Liberty*, 195–219.

——, *Feudalism and Liberty: articles and addresses of Sidney Painter*, ed. F. A. Cazel (Baltimore, 1961).

——, 'The houses of Lusignan and Châtellerault, 1150–1250', *Speculum*, xxx (1955), 374–84; reprinted in *Feudalism and Liberty*, 73–89.

——, 'The lords of Lusignan in the eleventh and twelfth centuries', *Speculum*, xxxii (1957), 27–47; reprinted in *Feudalism and Liberty*, 41–72.

——, *Studies in the History of the English Feudal Barony* (Baltimore, 1943).

——, *William Marshal* (Baltimore, 1933).

PALGRAVE, F., *The Rise and Progress of the English Commonwealth* (London, 1832).

Papal Decretals relating to the Diocese of Lincoln in the Twelfth Century, ed. W. Holtzmann and E. W. Kemp (Lincoln Record Society, 1954).

PAROW, W., *Compotus Vicecomitis* (Berlin, 1906).

Patrologia Latina: Patrologiae Cursus Completus. Series Latina, ed. J. P. Migne, 221 vols (Paris, 1844–55).

PATTERSON, R. B., 'William of Malmesbury's Robert of Gloucester: a revaluation of the *Historia Novella*', *American Historical Review*, lxx (1964–5), 983–97.

The Percy Catulary, ed. M. T. Martin (Surtees Society, 1911).

PERNOUD, RÉGINE, *Aliénor d'Aquitaine* (Paris, 1965).

Peterborough Chronicle: *Chronicon Angliae Petriburgense*, ed. J. A. Giles (London, 1845).

The Peterborough Chronicle, 1070–1154, ed. Cecily Clark (2nd edn, Oxford, 1970).

PETER OF BLOIS: *Petri Blesensis Archidiaconi Opera Omnia*, ed. J. A. Giles, 4 vols (Oxford, 1846–7).

——, Dialogus inter Regem Henricum Secundum et Abbatem Bonevallis, ed. R. B. C. Huygens, *Revue Bénédictine*, lxviii (1958), 97–112.

PETIT-DUTAILLIS, C., *The Feudal Monarchy in France and England from the tenth to the thirteenth century*, trans. E. D. Hunt from *La Monarchie Féodale en France et en Angleterre du Xᵉ au XIIIᵉ siècle* (London, 1936).

——, *Studies and Notes Supplementary to Stubbs' Constitutional History*, I and II, trans. W. E. Rhodes and W. T. Waugh (Manchester, 1911–14).

Pipe Rolls: *Magnus Rotulus Scaccarii de anno 31° Henrici I*, ed. J. Hunter (Record Commission, 1833).

The Great Rolls of the Pipe for the Second, Third, and Fourth Years of the Reign of King Henry the Second, 1155–1158, ed. J. Hunter (Record Commission, 1844). [Note: extracts from the roll of the first year of the reign are to be found in *The Red Book of the Exchequer*, II, 648–58.]

The Great Rolls of the Pipe of the Reign of Henry the Second, 5th to 34th years, 30 vols (Pipe Roll Society, 1884–1925).

Placita Anglo-Normannica: law cases from William I to Richard I preserved in historical records, ed. M. M. Bigelow (Boston, 1879).

PLANIOL, M., *L'Assise au Comte Geffroi. Étude sur les sucessions féodales en Bretagne* (Paris, 1888).

PLÖCHL, W. M., *Geschichte der Kirkenrechts* (Vienna, 1954).

PLUCKNETT, T. F. T., *A Concise History of the Common Law* (5th edn, London, 1956).

——, *Early English Legal Literature* (Cambridge, 1958).

——, *Edward I and the Criminal Law* (Cambridge, 1960).

POCQUET DU HAUT-JUSSÉ, B-A., 'Les Plantagenêts et la Bretagne', *Annales de Bretagne*, liii (1946), 1–27.

POLLOCK, F. and MAITLAND, F. W., *The History of English Law before the time of Edward I*, 2 vols (2nd edn, Cambridge, 1898).

POOLE, A. L., *From Domesday Book to Magna Carta (1087–1216)* (Oxford, 1951).

——, 'Henry Plantagenet's early visits to England', *English Historical Review*, xlvii (1932), 447–52.

——, *Obligations of Society in the Twelfth and Thirteenth Centuries* (Oxford, 1946).

——, 'Outlawry as a punishment for criminous clerks', *Essays in honour of James Tait*, 239–46.

POOLE, R. L., 'The appointment and deprivation of St William of York', *English Historical Review*, xlv (1930), 273–81.

——, 'The dates of Henry II's charters', *English Historical Review*, xxii (1908), 79–83.

——, *The Exchequer in the Twelfth Century* (Oxford, 1912).

——, 'Henry II duke of Normandy', *English Historical Review*, xlii (1927), 569–72.

——, *Illustrations of the History of Medieval Thought and Learning* (London, 1920).

——, *Studies in Chronology and History*, collected and edited by A. L. Poole (Oxford, 1934).

POUZET, P., *L'Anglais Jean dit Bellesmains (1122–1204?), Evêque de Poitiers, puis Archevêque de Lyon* (Lyon, 1927).

POWICKE, F. M., 'The Angevin Administration of Normandy', *English Historical Review*, xxi (1906), 625–49; xxii (1907), 15–42.

——, 'The honour of Mortain in the Norman *Infeudationes Militum* of 1172', *English Historical Review*, xxvi (1911), 89–93.

——, *The Loss of Normandy, 1189–1204. Studies in the history of the Angevin Empire* (2nd edn, Manchester, 1961).

——, 'Maurice of Rievaulx', *English Historical Review*, xxxvi (1921), 17–29.

POWICKE, M., *Military Obligation in Medieval England: a study in liberty and duty* (Oxford, 1962).

PRESTWICH, J. O., 'War and finance in the Anglo-Norman state', *Transactions of the Royal Historical Society*, 5th series, iv (1954), 19–43.

PREVITÉ ORTON, C. W., *The Early History of the House of Savoy (1000–1233)* (Cambridge, 1912).

Quadrilogus: Vita S. Thomae, seu Quadrilogus, ed. J. C. Robertson in *Materials for the History of Thomas Becket*, IV, 266–430.

RAINE, J., *The History and Antiquities of North Durham* (London, 1852).
RALPH NIGER: *Radulphi Nigri Chronica*, ed. R. Anstruther (London, 1851).
RALPH OF COGGESHALL: *Radulphi de Coggeshall Chronicon Anglicanum*, ed. J. Stevenson (Rolls Series, 1875).
RALPH OF DICETO: *Radulfi de Diceto Decani Lundoniensis Opera Historica*. ed. W. Stubbs, 2 vols (Rolls Series, 1876).
RAMSAY, J. H., *The Angevin Empire, or the Three Reigns of Henry II, Richard I, and John (1154–1216)* (London 1903).
——, *Revenues of the Kings of England* (Oxford, 1925).
Receipt Roll of the Exchequer for Michaelmas Term 1185, ed. H. Hall (London, 1899).
Records of the Borough of Nottingham, ed. W. H. Stevenson (London, 1882).
Records of the Templars in England in the Twelfth Century: the inquest of 1185 with illustrative charters and documents, ed. Beatrice A. Lees (London, 1935).
Recueil d'Annales Angevins et Vendômoises, ed. L. Halphen (Paris, 1903).
Recueil de Travaux offert à M. Clovis Brunel (Mémoires et documents publiés par la Société de l'École des Chartes, no. xii), 2 vols (Paris, 1955).
Recueil des Actes de Henri II, roi d'Angleterre et duc de Normandie, concernant les provinces françaises et les affaires de France, ed. L. Delisle and E. Berger, 4 vols (Paris, 1906–27).
Recueil des Actes de Philippe Auguste, roi de France, ed. H-F. Delaborde and others, 3 vols (Paris 1916–66, in progress).
Recueil des Chroniques de Touraine, ed. A. Salmon (Tours, 1854).
Recueil des Historiens des Gaules et de la France; Rerum Gallicarum et Francicarum Scriptores, ed. M. Bouquet and others, 24 vols (Paris, 1738–1904).
Red Book of the Exchequer: Liber Rubeus de Scaccario; The Red Book of the Exchequer, ed. H. Hall, 3 vols (Rolls Series, 1896).
REEDY, W. T., 'The origins of the general eyre in the reign of Henry I', *Speculum*, xli (1966), 688–724.
REES, W., *An Historical Atlas of Wales, from early to modern times* (2nd edn, London, 1959).
Regesta Pontificum Romanorum . . . ad 1198, ed. P. Jaffé, 2nd edn by G. Wattenbach, S. Loewenfeld, F. Kaltenbrunner, and P. Ewald, 2 vols (Leipzig, 1885–8).
Regesta Regum Anglo-Normannorum, 1066–1154, III, *1135–54*, ed. H. A. Cronne and R. H. C. Davis (Oxford, 1968).
Regesta Regum Scottorum, 1153–1424, I, *The Acts of Malcolm IV King of Scots, 1153–1165*, ed. G. W. S. Barrow (Edinburgh, 1960).
The Register of the Abbey of St Benet of Holme, 1020–1210, ed. J. R. West, 2 vols (Norfolk Record Society, 1932).

The Registrum Antiquissimum of the Cathedral Church of Lincoln, ed. C. W. Foster and Kathleen Major, 8 vols (Lincoln Record Society, 1931–58).

RENOUARD, Y., 'Essai sur le rôle de l'empire angevin dans la civilisation', *Revue Historique*, cxcv (1941), 289–304.

——, 'Les voies de communication entre pays de la Méditerranée et pays de l'Atlantique au moyen âge', *Mélanges . . . Halphen*, 587–94.

REVILLE, A., 'Abjuratio regni; histoire d'une institution anglaise', *Revue Historique*, l (1892), 1–42.

RICHARD, A., *Historie des Comtes de Poitou, 778–1204*, 2 vols (Paris, 1903).

RICHARD OF DEVIZES: *Chronicon Richardi Divisensis de tempore Regis Richardi Primi*, ed. J. T. Appleby (London, 1963).

RICHARD OF HEXHAM: Historia Ricardi, Prioris Ecclesiae Haugustaldensis, De Gesta Regis Stephani, ed. R. Howlett in *Chronicles of the Reigns of Stephen, Henry II, and Richard I*, III, 137–78.

RICHARDSON, HELEN (née SUGGET), 'An Anglo-Norman return to the Inquest of Sheriffs', *Bulletin of John Rylands Library*, xxvii (1942–3), 179–81.

——, 'A twelfth-century Anglo-Norman charter', *Bulletin of John Rylands Library*, xxiv (1940), 168–72.

RICHARDSON, H. G., 'Agenda for Irish history: Norman Ireland', *Irish Historical Studies*, iv (1944–5), 254–8.

——, 'The Chamber under Henry II', *English Historical Review*, lxix (1954), 596–611.

——, 'The coronation oath in medieval England: the evolution of the office and the oath', *Traditio*, xvi (1960), 111–202.

——, 'An early fine: its causes and consequences', *Law Quarterly Review*, xlviii (1932), 415–24.

——, *The English Jewry under Angevin Kings* (London, 1960).

——, 'English institutions in medieval Ireland', *Irish Historical Studies*, I (1938–9), 382–92.

——, 'Gervase of Tilbury', *History*, xlvi (1961), 102–114.

——, 'The letters and charters of Eleanor of Aquitaine', *English Historical Review*, lxxiv (1959), 193–213.

——, Introduction to *The Memoranda Roll for the Michaelmas Term of the First Year of the Reign of King John (1199–1200)* (Pipe Roll Society, 1943).

——, 'Richard FitzNeal and the Dialogus de Scaccario', *English Historical Review*, xliii (1928), 161–71, 321–40.

——, 'Some Norman monastic foundations in Ireland', *Medieval Studies presented to Aubrey Gwynn*, 29–43.

RICHARDSON, H. G. and SAYLES, G. O., *The Administration of Ireland* (Dublin, 1963).

——, *The Governance of Medieval England from the Conquest to Magna Carta* (Edinburgh, 1963).

——, Introduction to *Select Cases of Procedure Without Writ under Henry III* (Selden Society, 1941).

——, *Law and Legislation from Aethelbert to Magna Carta* (Edinburgh, 1966).

RIESENBERG, P. N., *Inalienability and Sovereignty in Medieval Political Thought* (New York, 1956).

RIGORD: Gesta Philippi Augusti, ed. H-F. Delaborde in *Oeuvres de Rigord et de Guillaume le Breton, historiens de Philippe-Auguste*, 2 vols (Paris, 1882).

RITCHIE, R. L. G., *The Normans in Scotland* (Edinburgh, 1953).

ROBERT DE TORIGNY: Chronica Roberti de Torigneio, Abbatis Monasterii Sancti Michaelis in Periculo Maris, ed. R. Howlett in *Chronicles of the Reigns of Stephen, Henry II, and Richard I*, IV, 81–315.

ROBERTSON, J. C., *Becket, Archbishop of Canterbury. A biography* (London, 1859).

RODERICK, A. J., 'The feudal relation between the English Crown and the Welsh princes', *History*, xxxvii (1952), 201–12.

——, 'Marriage and politics in Wales, 1066–1282', *Welsh History Review*, iv (1968), 3–20.

ROGER OF HOWDEN: *Chronica Rogeri de Houedene*, ed. W. Stubbs, 4 vols (Rolls Series, 1868–71).

   Gesta Regis Henrici Secundi, ed. W. Stubbs, 2 vols (Rolls Series, 1867). [For the attribution of this work to Roger of Howden *see* Doris M. Stenton, 'Roger of Howden and Benedict', *English Historical Review*, lxviii (1943), 574–82.]

ROGER OF PONTIGNY: Vita Sancti Thomae, Cantuariensis Archiepiscopi et Martyris, ed. J. C. Robertson in *Materials for the History of Thomas Becket*, IV, 1–79. [The attribution to Roger of Pontigny was doubted by the editor who cites this Life under the title of 'Anonymous I'.]

Rolls of the Justices in Eyre for Gloucestershire, Warwickshire, and Shropshire (1221–2), ed. Doris M. Stenton (Selden Society, 1940).

Rolls Series: *Rerum Britannicarum Medii Aevi Scriptores, or Chronicles and Memorials of Great Britain and Ireland during the Middle Ages*, published under the authority of the Master of the Rolls (London, 1858–97).

Rotuli de Dominabus et Pueris et Puellis de Donatione Regis in XII Comitatibus, 31 Henry II, 1185, ed. J. H. Round (Pipe Roll Society, 1913).

ROUND, J. H., 'The alleged debate on Danegeld in 1163', *English Historical Review*, v (1890), 750–3; reprinted in *Feudal England* (1964), 377–80.

——, 'The chronology of Henry II's charters', *Archaeological Journal*, lxiv (1907), 63–79.

——, 'The counts of Boulogne as English lords', *Studies in Peerage and Family History* (London, 1901), 147–80.

——, 'The date of the Grand Assize', *English Historical Review*, xxxi (1916), 268–9.

——, 'The dating of the early pipe rolls', *English Historical Review*, xxxvi (1921), 321–3.

——, 'The earliest fines', *English Historical Review*, xii (1897), 293–302.

——, 'Early Irish trade with Chester and Rouen', *Feudal England* (1964), 353–4.

——, *Feudal England: historical studies on the eleventh and twelfth centuries* (first pub. London, 1895; new edn, London, 1964).

——, 'The first fine', *Feudal England* (1964), 385–91.

——, *Geoffrey de Mandeville* (London, 1892).

——, 'A glimpse of the Young King's court', *Feudal England* (1964), 381–4.

——, 'The honour of Ongar', *Transactions of the Essex Archaeological Society*, new series, vii (1898), 142–52.

——, 'The Inquest of Sheriffs (1170)', *The Commune of London and other studies*, 125–36.

——, 'The introduction of knight service into England', *English Historical Review*, vi (1891), 417–43, 625–45; vii (1892), 11–24; reprinted in *Feudal England* (1964), 182–245.

——, 'The Saladin tithe', *English Historical Review*, xxxi (1916), 447–50.

——, 'Stephen and the Earl of Chester', *English Historical Review*, x (1895), 87–91.

——, Studies in the Red Book of the Exchequer (privately printed, 1898).

Royal Writs in England from the Conquest to Glanvill, ed. R. C. Van Caenegem (Selden Society, 1959).

Sacrorum Conciliorum Nova et Amplissima Collectio, ed. J. D. Mansi, XXI, XXII (Venice, 1776–8).

SALTER, H. E., 'The charters of Henry II at Lincoln cathedral', *English Historical Review*, xxiv (1909), 303–13.

SALTMAN, A., *Theobald Archbishop of Canterbury* (London, 1956).

SALZMANN, L. F., 'Early fines', *English Historical Review*, xxv (1910), 708–10.

SANDERS, I. J., *English Baronies. A study of their origin and descent, 1086–1327* (Oxford, 1960).

——, *Feudal Military Service in England. A study of the constitutional and military powers of the barons in medieval England* (Oxford, 1956).

SAYLES, G. O., Introduction to *Select Cases in the Court of King's Bench*, I (Selden Society, 1936).

SAYRE, F. B., *A Selection of Cases on Criminal Law* (Rochester, N.Y., 1927).

SCAMMEL, G. V., *Hugh du Puiset: a biography of a twelfth-century bishop of Durham* (Cambridge, 1956).

SCAMMEL, JEAN, 'The origins and limitations of the Liberty of Durham', *English Historical Review*, cccxx (1966), 449–73.

SCHOLZ, B. W., 'The canonization of Edward the Confessor', *Speculum*, xxxvi (1961), 56–60.

SCHRAMM, P. E., *A History of the English Coronation*, trans. G. Wickham Legg (Oxford, 1937).

SHAW, I. P., 'The ecclesiastical policy of Henry II on the continent', *Church Quarterly Review* (1951), 137–55.

SIMPSON, W. D., *Exploring Castles* (London, 1957).

SMAIL, R. C., *Crusading Warfare (1097–1193)* (Cambridge, 1956).

SMALLEY, BERYL, 'Capetian France', *France: Government and Society*, ed. J. M. Wallace Hadrill and J. McManners (London, 1957), 61–82.

The Song of Dermot and the Earl, ed. and trans. G. H. Orpen (Oxford, 1892).

SOUTHERN, R. W., 'The Canterbury forgeries', *English Historical Review*, lxxiii (1958), 193–226.
——, *The Making of the Middle Ages* (London, 1953).
——, 'The place of England in the twelfth century renaissance', *History*, xlv (1960), 201–16.
——, 'The place of Henry I in English history', *Proceedings of the British Academy*, xlviii (1962), 127–69.
——, 'Review of *The Episcopal Colleagues of Archbishop Thomas Becket* by D. Knowles', *English Historical Review*, lxvii (1952), 87–90.
——, *St Anselm and His Biographer. A study of monastic life and thought, 1059–c. 1130* (Cambridge, 1962).
STENTON, DORIS M., 'The development of the judiciary, 1100–1215', Appendix 1 to *Pleas before the King or his Justices, 1198–1212*, III (Selden Society, 1967), xlvii–ccxciv.
——, 'England: Henry II', *The Cambridge Medieval History*, ed. J. R. Tanner, C. W. Previté Orton, and Z. N. Brooke, V (Cambridge, 1929), ch. xvii.
——, *English Justice between the Norman Conquest and the Great Charter, 1066–1215* (London, 1965).
——, Introduction to *The Earliest Lincolnshire Assize Rolls* (Lincoln Record Society, 1926).
——, Introduction to *Pleas before the King or his Justices, 1198–1202*, I (Selden Society, 1953).
——, 'Roger of Howden and Benedict', *English Historical Review*, lxviii (1943), 574–82.
——, 'Roger of Salisbury, *regni Angliae procurator*', *English Historical Review*, xxxix (1924), 79–80.
STENTON, F. M., 'Acta Episcoporum', *Cambridge Historical Journal*, iii (1929), 1–14.
——, Introduction to *Documents Illustrative of the Social and Economic History of the Danelaw* (London, 1920).
——, 'An early inquest relating to St Peter's Derby', *English Historical Review*, xxxii (1917), 47–8.
——, *The First Century of English Feudalism, 1066–1166* (2nd edn, Oxford, 1961).
——, *Norman London*, an essay by F. M. Stenton with a translation of William FitzStephen's description by H. E. Butler, and a map of London under Henry II by M. Honeybourne, annotated by E. Jeffries Davis (Historical Association pamphlet, 1934); reprinted in *Social Life in Early England: Historical Association Essays*, ed. G. Barraclough (London, 1960), 179–207.
——, 'The road system in medieval England', *Economic History Review*, vii (1936), 1–21.
STEPHEN OF ROUEN: Stephani Rothomagensis Monachi Beccensis Poema cui Titulus 'Draco Normannicus', ed. R. Howlett in *Chronicles of the Reigns of Stephen, Henry II, and Richard I*, II, 585–781.
STEPHENSON, C., 'The aids of the English boroughs', *English Historical Review*, xxxiv (1919), 457–75.

STRAYER, J. R., 'Knight service in Normandy', *Anniversary Essays . . . presented to C. H. Haskins*, 313–27.

STUBBS, W., *The Constitutional History of England*, I (6th edn, Oxford, 1897).

——, *Historical Introductions to the Rolls Series*, collected and edited by A. Hassall (London, 1902).

——, *Lectures on Early English History*, ed. A. Hassall (London, 1906).

——, *Select Charters, and other Illustrations of English Constitutional History, from the earliest times to the reign of Edward I*, ninth edition revised by H. W. C. Davis (Oxford, 1921).

——, *Seventeen Lectures on the Study of Medieval and Modern History* (Oxford, 1887).

Studies in Medieval History presented to Frederick Maurice Powicke, ed. R. W. Hunt, W. A. Pantin, and R. W. Southern (Oxford, 1948).

Studies presented to Sir Hilary Jenkinson, ed. J. Conway Davies (London, 1957).

SUGER: *Vie de Louis le Gros par Suger, suivie de l'Histoire du Roi Louis VII*, ed. A. Molinier (Paris, 1887).

SYMEON OF DURHAM: *Symeon of Durham: Historical Works*, ed. T. Arnold, 2 vols (Rolls Series, 1882–5).

TAIT, J., ' "Common assizes" in the Pipe Rolls and Dialogus de Scaccario', *English Historical Review*, liii (1938), 669–75.

——, 'Knight-service in Cheshire', *English Historical Review*, lvii (1942), 437–59.

——, *The Medieval English Borough* (Manchester, 1936).

——, 'A new fragment of the Inquest of Sheriffs (1170)', *English Historical Review*, xxxix (1924), 80–3.

TARDIFF, E. J., *Études sur les Sources de l'Ancien Droit Normand et spécialement sur la législation des ducs de Normandie* (Rouen, 1911).

THALAMAS, A., *La Société Seigneuriale Française, 1050–1272* (Paris, 1951).

THOMAS, A., *Poésies Complètes de Bertran de Born* (Toulouse, 1888).

THOMAS AGNELLUS: De Morte et Sepultura Henrici Regis Junioris, ed. J. Stevenson in *Radulphi de Coggeshall Chronicon Anglicanum* (Rolls Series, 1875).

THOMAS OF ELMHAM: *Historia Monasterii S. Augustini Cantuariensis, by Thomas of Elmham*, ed. C. Hardwick (Rolls Series, 1858).

THOMAS, P., *Le Droit de Propriété des Laïques sur les Églises et le Patronage Laïque au Moyen Âge* (Paris, 1906).

Thómas Saga Erkibyskups, ed. E. Magnússon, 2 vols (Rolls Series, 1875–83).

THORNE, S. E., 'The assize *Utrum* and the canon law in England', *Columbia Law Review*, xxxiii (1933), 428–36.

——, 'English feudalism and estates in land', *Cambridge Law Journal*, xvii (1959), 193–209.

——, 'Livery of seisin', *Law Quarterly Review*, lii (1936), 345–64.

Three Rolls of the King's Court in the Reign of Richard I, 1194–5, ed. F. W. Maitland (Pipe Roll Society, 1891).

Transcripts of Charters relating to Gilbertine Houses, ed. F. M. Stenton (Lincoln Record Society, 1922).

La Très Ancienne Coutume de Bretagne, ed. M. Planiol (Rennes, 1896).

TURNER, G. J., Introduction to *Select Pleas of the Forest* (Selden Society, 1901).

——, 'The sheriff's farm', *Transactions of the Royal Historical Society*, 2nd series, xii (1898), 117–49.

ULLMANN, W., *The Growth of Papal Government in the Middle Ages. A study in the ideological relation of clerical to lay power* (London, 1955).

——, 'The pontificate of Adrian IV', *Cambridge Historical Journal*, xi (1953–5), 233–52.

——, *Principles of Government and Politics in the Middle Ages* (London, 1961).

VALIN, R., *Le Duc de Normandie et sa Cour (912–1204). Étude d'histoire juridique* (Paris, 1909).

VAN CAENEGEM, R. C., 'Studies in the early history of the common law', Introduction to *Royal Writs in England from the Conquest to Glanvill* (Selden Society, 1959).

VASILIEV, A. A., 'Manuel Comnenus and Henry Plantagenet', *Byzantinische Zeitschrift* (1929–30), 233–44.

VERBRUGGEN, J. F., *De Krijgskunst in West-Europa in den Middeleeuwen* (Brussels, 1954).

——, 'La tactique militaire des armées de chevaliers', *Revue du Nord*, xxix (1947), 161–80.

Veterum Scriptorum et Monumentorum, historicum, dogmaticorum, moralium, amplissima collectio, ed. E. Martène and U. Durand, 9 vols (Paris, 1724–33).

VIDAL DE LABLACHE, P., *Atlas Historique et Géographique* (Paris, 1951).

VOSS, L. *Heinrich von Blois Bischof von Winchester (1129–1171)* (Berlin, 1932).

WALBERG, E., *La Tradition Hagiographique de Saint Thomas Becket avant la fin du XIIᵉ siècle* (Paris, 1929).

WALKER, D., 'Charters of the earldom of Hereford', *Camden Miscellany XXII* (Camden Society, 1964).

——, 'The "honours" of the earls of Hereford in the twelfth century', *Transactions of the Bristol and Gloucestershire Archaeological Society*, lxxix (1960), 174–211.

——, 'Miles of Gloucester, earl of Hereford', *Transactions of the Bristol and Gloucestershire Archaeological Society*, lxxvii (1958), 66–84.

WALKER, MARGARET S., Introduction to *Feet of Fines for the County of Lincoln 1199–1216* (Pipe Roll Society, 1954).

WALNE, P., 'A "double charter" of the Empress Matilda and Henry duke of Normandy, c. 1152', *English Historical Review*, lxxvi (1961), 649–54.

WALTER MAP, *De Nugis Curialium*, ed. M. R. James (Oxford, 1914).

WARD, P. L., 'The coronation ceremony in medieval England', *Speculum*, xiv (1939), 160–78.

WARREN, W. L., 'The interpretation of twelfth-century Irish history', *Historical Studies VII*, ed. J. C. Beckett (London, 1969), 1–19.

——, 'Royal justice in England in the twelfth century', *History*, lii (1967), 171–5.

WAQUET, H., *Histoire de Bretagne* (3rd edn, Paris, 1958).

WASHINGTON, G., 'The border heritage, 1066–1292', *Transactions of the Cumberland and Westmoreland Antiquarian and Archaeological Society*, new series, lxii (1962), 101–12.

WEST, F. J., 'The Curia Regis in the late twelfth and early thirteenth centuries', *Historical Studies: Australia and New Zealand*, vi (1953–5), 173–85.

——, *The Justiciarship in England, 1066–1232* (Cambridge, 1966).

WHITE, A. B., *Self-Government at the King's Command* (Minneapolis, 1933).

WHITE, G. H., 'The career of Waleran, count of Meulan and earl of Worcester (1104–1166)', *Transactions of the Royal Historical Society*, 4th series, xvii (1934), 19–48.

——, 'The *Constitutio Domus Regis* and the king's sport', *Antiquaries Journal*, xxx (1950), 52–63.

——, 'Financial administration under Henry I', *Transactions of the Royal Historical Society*, 4th series, viii (1925), 56–78.

——, 'The household of the Norman kings', *Transactions of the Royal Historical Society*, 4th series, xxx (1948), 127–56.

——, 'Stephen's earldoms', *Transactions of the Royal Historical Society*, 4th series, xiii (1930), 51–82.

WHITE, H. V., 'The Gregorian ideal and St Bernard of Clairvaux', *Journal of the History of Ideas*, xxi (1960), 321–48.

WHITE, L., *Medieval Technology and Social Change* (Oxford, 1962).

WIGHTMAN, W. E., 'La famile de Lacy et ses terres normandes', *Annales de Normandie*, xi (1961), 267–77.

——, *The Lacy Family in England and Normandy, 1066–1194* (Oxford, 1966).

WILLIAM FITZSTEPHEN: Vita Sancti Thomae Cantuariensis Archiepiscopi et Martyris, auctore Willelmo Filio Stephani, ed. J. C. Robertson in *Materials for the History of Thomas Becket*, III, 1–154.

WILLIAM OF CANTERBURY: Vita, Passio, et Miracula S. Thomae Cantuariensis Archiepiscopi, auctore Willelmo, monacho Cantuariensi, ed. J. C. Robertson in *Materials for the History of Thomas Becket*, I, 1–546.

WILLIAM OF MALMESBURY, De Gestis Regum Anglorum libri quinque, ed. W. Stubbs, 2 vols (Rolls Series, 1887–9).

——, *Historia Novella*, ed. K. R. Potter (London, 1955).

WILLIAM OF NEWBURGH, Historia Rerum Anglicarum, ed. R. Howlett in *Chronicles and Memorials of the Reigns of Stephen, Henry II, and Richard I*, I, 1–408; II, 409–53.

WILLIAM THE BRETON: Gesta Philippi Augusti, ed. H-F. Delaborde in *Oeuvres de Rigord et de Guillaume le Breton, historiens de Philippe-Auguste*, 2 vols (Paris, 1882), I, 168–333; Philippides, *ibid.*, II, 1–385.

WILLIAM THORNE: Chronica de Rebus Gestis Abbatum Sancti Augustini Cantuariae, ed. R. Twysden in *Historiae Anglicanae Scriptores Decem* (London, 1652), II, cols 1757–2202.

WILLIAMS, G., *The Welsh Church from the Conquest to the Reformation* (Cardiff, 1962).

WOLFF, ILSE, *Heinrich II von England als Vassall Ludwigs VII von Frankreich,* (Breslau, 1936).

YOUNG, C. R., *The English Borough and Royal Administration, 1130–1307* (Durham, North Carolina, 1961).

YVER, J., 'Les châteaux forts en Normandie jusqu'au milieux du XIIᵉ siècle: contribution à l'étude du pouvoir ducal', *Bulletin de la Société des Antiquaires de Normandie*, liii (1955–6), 28–115.

——, *Les Contrats dans le Très Ancien Droit Normand (XIᵉ–XIIIᵉ Siècles)* (Domfront, 1926).

——, 'Contribution à l'étude du développement de la compétence ducale en Normandie', *Annales de Normandie*, xiii (1958), 139–83.

INDEX